VILLA AND ZAPATA

France and the Jacobite Rising of 1745
The Jacobite Army in England
The Jacobites
Invasion: From the Armada to Hitler
Charles Edward Stuart
Crime and Punishment in Eighteenth-Century England
Stanley: The Making of an African Explorer
Snow Upon the Desert: The Life of Sir Richard Burton
From the Sierras to the Pampas: Richard Burton's Travels in the Americas,
    1860–69
Stanley: Sorcerer's Apprentice
Hearts of Darkness: The European Exploration of Africa
Fitzroy Maclean
Robert Louis Stevenson
C.G. Jung
Napoleon
1066: The Year of the Three Battles

VILLA AND ZAPATA

A Biography of the Mexican Revolution

Frank McLynn

JONATHAN CAPE
LONDON

Published by Jonathan Cape 2000

2 4 6 8 10 9 7 5 3 1

First published in Great Britain in 2000 by
Jonathan Cape
Random House, 20 Vauxhall Bridge Road,
London SW1V 2SA

Random House Australia (Pty) Limited
20 Alfred Street, Milsons Point, Sydney,
New South Wales 2061, Australia

Random House New Zealand Limited
18 Poland Road, Glenfield,
Auckland 10, New Zealand

Random House (Pty) Limited
Endulini, 5A Jubilee Road, Parktown 2193, South Africa

The Random House Group Limited Reg. No. 954009
www.randomhouse.co.uk

A CIP catalogue record for this book
is available from the British Library

ISBN 0–224–05051–6

Papers used by Random House are natural,
recyclable products made from wood grown in sustainable forests;
the manufacturing processes conform to the environmental
regulations of the country of origin

Typeset by Deltatype Ltd, Birkenhead, Merseyside
Printed and bound in Great Britain by
Biddles Ltd, Guildford and King's Lynn

To José Briseño, Compadre

CONTENTS

Illustrations   ix
Preface   xv
The Mexico of Porfirio Díaz   1
The Rise of Zapata   33
The Rise of Villa   53
The Rise of Madero   72
The Fall of Díaz   88
Madero and Zapata   105
Villa and Madero   127
The Revolt Against Huerta   160
Villa at his Zenith   187
The End of Huerta   213
The Convention of Aguascalientes   244
The Convergence of the Twain   264
Civil War   286
The Punitive Expedition   313
The Twilight of Zapatismo   335
The Decline of Villismo   363
Epilogue   386

Conclusion   399
Sources   407
Index   441

ILLUSTRATIONS

First section

Emiliano Zapata: the dandy as hero
Porfirio Díaz in 1910
Francesco Madero
Francisco Villa
Pascual Orozco
A dynamited troop train
Rebels crossing railway tracks
General Victoriano Huerta
Huerta and Orozco
The Madero family
Francisco Madero
Venustiano Carranza
Álvaro Obregón
Villa in the revolutionary's 'full dress uniform'
Rodolfo Fierro

Second section

Zapatistas in Sanborn's restaurant
The meeting in the Presidential Palace in 1914
American forces occupying Veracruz, 1914
Villa with his enemies, Obregón and General Pershing
Villa in a happy mood
Zapata also in a happy mood (for him)
Félix Díaz
Orozco
Venustiano Carranza
Obregón at the battle of Celaya
The women of the Revolution
The last authentic image of Zapata
Villa putting on a brave face in adversity

Maps

Mexico   *xi*
Northern Mexico   *xii*
Southern Mexico   *xiii*

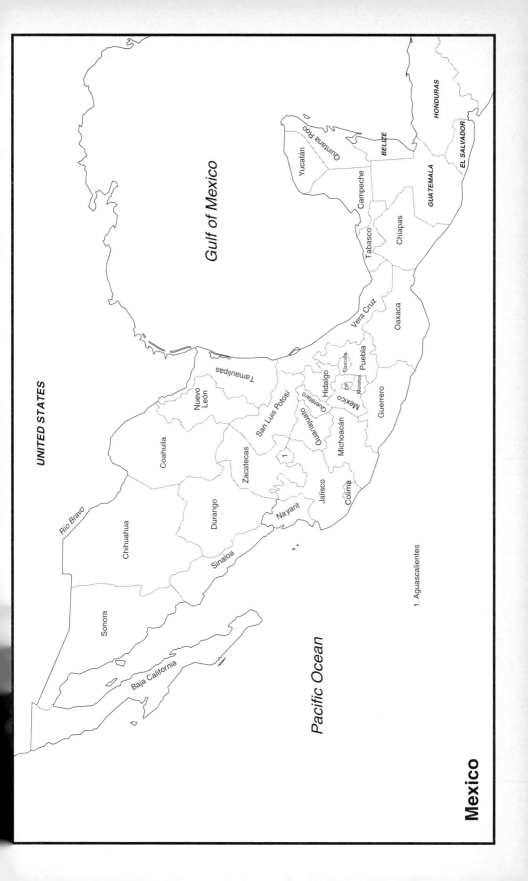

Mexico

Northern Mexico

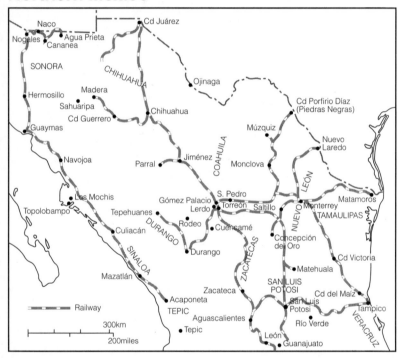

Railway

300km
200miles

Southern Mexico

HIDALGO
• Pachuca

Gulf of Mexico

MEXICO

• Mexico

TLAXCALA

• Jalapa

• Toluca   DF

Amecameca

• Tlaxcala

Veracruz •

Cholula •
• Puebla
• Atlixco

VERACRUZ

• Cuernavaca

Tochimilco   PUEBLA

MORELOS

• Izúcar de Matamoros

Taxco •

Iguala

Ayoxustla
•
• Chiautla

•
Huitzuco

• Hilpancingo

GUERRERO

OAXACA

• Oaxaca

• Acapulco

Pacific Ocean

PREFACE

Three outstanding volumes have acted as my lodestar while writing this book: Alan Knight's two-volume *The Mexican Revolution*; Friedrich Katz's *The Life and Times of Pancho Villa* and John Womack's *Zapata and the Mexican Revolution*. I here and now acknowledge my great debt to these peerless scholars. But in recent years all roads have seemed to lead to Mexico City, for all my interests appeared to point in the same direction, whether it was the war reporting of Jack London, the paintings of Diego Rivera or the movies of Sergio Leone. I hope, if nothing else, that I have communicated my enthusiasm for the incredible story of the years 1910–20, which if written as fiction would be dismissed by prospective publishers as 'over the top'.

Any author writing such a book owes a debt to hundreds of unknown writers of monographs and journal articles and even to long-forgotten newspaper reporters. Among those who inhabit the face-to-face world, I cannot fail to mention the 'three musketeers' at Jonathan Cape – Will Sulkin, Tony Whittome and Jorg Hensgen – whose enthusiasm and support have been crucial. If I mention an even more salient influence, it is only because my wife Pauline, editor, collaborator and *inspiratrice*, is the d'Artagnan of the piece. Others who deserve honorific mention are Professor Alan Knight of St Antony's College, Oxford, who made research materials available to me, Dr Malcolm Chapman, whose keen editorial eye was an asset, and Mr Paul Taylor, master of maps, draughtsmanship and the Internet.

Frank McLynn, Twickenham, March 2000

THE MEXICO OF PORFIRIO DÍAZ

As the year 1910 moved into autumn, even the most reckless gambler would not have bet on the likelihood that the century's first major revolution (and the fourth-ranking in importance in the entire century) was about to break out. The year had so far been a quiet one. The Chinese had abolished slavery, Portugal was about to jettison its monarchy, and South Africa became an independent nation with Dominion Status within the British Empire. Otherwise the year's most significant developments had been in the arts rather than politics. Rodin, Braque, Matisse, Léger and the dying Henri 'Douanier' Rousseau all produced important works, as did Ravel, Stravinsky, Vaughan Williams and Mahler in the world of music. England was enjoying a golden period in literature, with Shaw, Barrie, Wells, Forster and Bennett all active, but the major public event that year was the death of Edward VII at sixty-eight and the succession of his son George V. In accordance with the strict protocol governing royal mourning, it was announced that there would be no official British representation at the forthcoming jamboree in Mexico to which representatives of all the nations of the world had been invited, expenses paid.

Few had heard of the obscure fourth-century Greek saint Porfirio, whose feast day fell on 15 September, but everyone in Mexico knew of *the* Porfirio, who shared the saint's birthday. Porfirio Díaz was the absolute ruler of Mexico and had been for thirty-four years. Now, on the evening of 15 September 1910, he was about to celebrate his eightieth birthday. The occasion was special in more ways than one, for Mexico itself was also celebrating the centenary of its struggle for independence from Spain. The nation basked in a month-long siesta, and huge sums, equivalent to the country's annual spending on education, had been earmarked for fiestas, banquets and dances.

On the illuminated balconies of the National Palace in Mexico City, special diplomatic envoys from the four corners of the world and Díaz's own handpicked guests watched a dazzling firework display before retiring inside to a ten-course meal. The sixty guests were already weary with a day of spectacle, during which Díaz bade fair to be a second Moctezuma, king of the Aztecs; 10,000 people had taken part in an historical pageant representing Mexican history from the Aztecs to Díaz. Even as the envoys from Europe, Japan, Latin America and the United States gourmandised their way through the eight savoury courses served on silver plates and the two dessert courses brought in on plates of solid gold, their ears were bombarded by the multiple counterpoint and polyphony of sixteen bands in Mexico City's main square or Zócalo below. Since all sixteen were playing different tunes, the complex mariachi rhythms and the unbarred passages, accelerandos and ritardandos produced the effect of a Charles Ives symphony scored for a 200-piece orchestra.

How much of the real Mexico City the envoys were seeing is more dubious. Out of a total national population of 15 million the capital city had an officially registered 471,000 in 1910, but large numbers of these people were either working class, unemployed, underemployed or in various stages of disguised unemployment, all clustered in densely packed slums in the north and east of the city, covered in dust or mud (depending on the season), lacking adequate sanitation, surrounded by piles of garbage and the myriad and ubiquitous *pulquerías* or grog-shops. A typical Hogarthian slum scene would feature a series of drunken clients of the *pulquerías* reeling intoxicatedly through streets infested with mangy dogs and half-naked children. Díaz made sure the special emissaries who came to pay him homage saw none of this. Instead, all beggars, ragged-trousered peasants and any who did not obey an unwritten sumptuary code were expelled from the central section of the capital with its paved streets and confined to the outer ghettos. In the streets around the Zócalo Díaz created his own Disneyland *avant la lettre*, with street cleaning and anti-litter campaigns redolent of a later age and a very different sort of society.

The distinguished visitors were encouraged to admire Mexico City's heterogeneous and eclectic architecture, symbolised by the Cathedral which, begun in 1573 and completed in 1813, was like a palimpsest or an archaeological site with many strata. Little remained of the Renaissance city of Cortés and the first Spanish viceroys, and even less of Tenochtitlán, the fabled ancient Aztec capital on this site (except that the three great avenues that led to the Zócalo followed the course of ancient Aztec avenues), for fires, floods, earthquake and the sheer ravages of time had done their worst. The last trace of Tenochtitlán was the network of canals, along which Indians still travelled into the centre in their distinctive boats or *trajineras*, bringing flowers and vegetables to the central market. Although the first automobiles were starting to be seen, Mexico City was scarcely a magnet for the 'horseless carriage' because the roads outside the capital were not paved. Transport for the upper classes was still mainly by horse, and for the lower classes by the tramways that spiralled out from the centre to the suburbs.

Something of the sixteenth century was still there in the form of the grid pattern of the main streets in the centre and the most ancient churches, though most of the architectural showpieces went back no further than the seventeenth century. The baroque churches of the 1600s, the monasteries of the regular clergy (Franciscans, Dominicans, Jesuits, Augustinians) dating from that century and the religious hospitals, to say nothing of twenty convents, still existed, but this pattern was partly overlaid by the neoclassical building boom of the late eighteenth century. The recent vogue for French styles in housing and design irritated some of the locals and put a dent in the predominantly Spanish colonial ambience, and the new National Theatre was widely considered an eyesore. This heap of white marble, thrown up with no sense of style at all, was across the street from the new central post office, itself a Disneyland version of an Italian palazzo of the Renaissance. Ominously, twentieth-century mainstream architecture's chief contribution so far was in the shape of a new prison and a mental hospital.

On and on went the celebrations. Some thought the high point was on 23 September, when 2,000 guests attended a sumptuous ball in the National Palace, where rivers of champagne were drunk. Pampered and spoiled as they were, and cribbed and confined to the elegant centre of the capital, few of Díaz's guests would have had any interest in the history of Mexico City and still less in the social reality of Mexico that underlay the glittering façade with which Díaz tried to dazzle them. Some were impressed with the autocrat's recent technical innovations, his improvement of the water supply and street lighting. Interested visitors were shown the railway terminal and the telephone, telegraph and postal offices, which purported to show how Mexico was a modern country with modern communications. Perhaps a couple of reporters took the time to investigate the new seismology station and the elaborate drainage system, designed at once to solve the capital's horrendous sewage problem as well as the perennial threat of flooding. However, most of the envoys who made reports to their governments concentrated on Díaz himself. Who was he, this white-haired dictator of amazing personal and political longevity, and what was the secret of his lifelong power?

Professional historians notoriously dislike history narrated through biography, and of course no thumbnail sketch can do justice to the complexity of Mexico's social and economic structures in the nineteenth century, but to say that the *political* history of Mexico during its first hundred years can be summed up by the careers of three dominant personalities is not far short of the truth. The first of the three great autocrats was Antonio López de Santa Anna (1797–1876), the self-styled 'Napoleon of the West'. For nearly forty years, from 1821 onwards, Santa Anna straddled Mexico like the colossus he aspired to be. First, in 1823, he overthrew Agustín de Iturbide who, two years earlier, had set himself up as the first 'emperor' of Mexico after expelling the colonial power of Spain. Always the power behind the scenes, Santa Anna turned the first forty years of Mexican history into a kind of *opéra bouffe*, in which he would frequently lose caste and be exiled, only to return and seize power once again. It was said that Santa Anna issued more *pronunciamientos* than any other figure in Hispanic or Latin American history. President of Mexico in 1833, he pursued the reactionary policy that led to the loss of Texas. It was Santa Anna who entered the Lone Star State at the head of a powerful army in 1836, annihilated Davy Crockett, Travis and Bowie at the Alamo, and was defeated by Sam Houston at San Jacinto.

Imprisoned for eight months, Santa Anna returned to Mexico to find his star on the wane, but it rose again after he lost a leg during the defence of Veracruz against a French blockade in 1838 and was hailed as a patriotic hero. Returning in a blaze of glory three years later to the presidential chair, he spent another four years as Mexico's master before being exiled again. In 1846 he was recalled to resume office during the hard-fought war with the United States (1846–8), which ended with utter defeat for Mexico and the loss of California, Arizona and New Mexico; Texas, an independent republic for ten years from 1836–46, joined the United States as a fully–fledged state. Exiled once more, Santa Anna was recalled from Jamaica by a revolution in 1853 and appointed president for life, but two years later was again overthrown and banished to Cuba. During the French occupation of Mexico in the 1860s, he intrigued shamelessly and attempted a comeback at the age of seventy; captured once more and sentenced to death, he retired to New York but was allowed to return for his final years to Mexico, where he died in poverty.

If Santa Anna was a character out of a putschist melodrama, and increasingly regarded as an embarrassment by Mexicans trying to build an honourable heritage they could feel proud of, the second great autocrat in the nation's history provided them with an authentic hero. A Zapotec Indian, Benito Juárez (1806–72) made his mark as a lawyer and then became governor of the southern state of Oaxaca in 1847. By the 1850s

Mexican politics had become dangerously polarised between a Conservative party led by Santa Anna and the Liberal opposition led by Ignacio Comonfort and Juan Álvarez. Juárez was a leading light in the Liberal party and, as a consequence, he was exiled in 1853 when Santa Anna seized power. On Santa Anna's overthrow two years later, Juárez became minister of justice in Álvarez's government. Proposing fundamental changes, he abolished the *fueros* (traditional feudal privileges), seized control of Church lands, tried to nudge Mexico towards liberal capitalism and passed the anticlerical constitution of 1857. Álvarez was soon succeeded by Comonfort, who appointed Juárez president of the Supreme Court, but when Comonfort moved to make himself dictator, Juárez declared his action unconstitutional; according to the articles of the constitution Juárez was now the president.

Taking advantage of Liberal factionalism, the Conservatives raised an armed revolt. The result, once Juárez had dealt with Comonfort and sent him into exile, was a ferocious civil war between Conservatives and Liberals, which lasted from early 1858 to late 1860; all the time Juárez was president *de jure*. Finally the Liberals were triumphant, but there was scarcely to be a breathing space before Mexico was plunged into warfare once more. Great Britain, France and Spain claimed reparations from Juárez for damage and losses sustained by their nationals during the civil war, but Juárez now ruled a bankrupt country and could not even pay the interest on existing foreign debts. When he suspended payment on all foreign debts for two years, the emperor Napoleon III took advantage of the immersion of the United States in its own civil war and launched a quixotic foreign adventure. He tried to impose the Austrian Hapsburg prince Maximilian as emperor of Mexico. Britain and Spain refused to back Bonaparte in this ill-advised intervention and withdrew their claims, but Juárez was left to deal with the military might of France.

This was the context in which Mexico's third great autocrat first came to the fore. Porfirio Díaz, a Mixtec Indian with some Spanish blood in his veins, was born in the town of Oaxaca in 1830, narrowly escaped death from cholera in childhood and trained as a priest before switching to the law. Díaz became a national figure during Juárez's five-year struggle with the French, being wounded twice and imprisoned thrice (each time he escaped). At first the French swept all before them, but they could never subdue the countryside, and the quick victory Napoleon III hoped for soon evaporated. When the United States turned its attention south of the border after Lee surrendered to Grant at Appomattox in April 1865, ending the American Civil War, Bonaparte faced the logistical nightmare of having to supply an army across 5,000 miles of ocean in order to fight what was in 1865 probably the most military nation on earth. The aptly named 'Little Napoleon' took the prudent course and pulled out of Mexico. Refusing to withdraw with his military protectors, Maximilian was captured by Juárez and executed at Querétaro, north of Mexico City, in 1867.

A war hero with a reputation for financial probity, Díaz was never liked by Juárez, but it was from Juárez that Díaz learned the taste for constant presidential re-election. In 1871 the all-conquering president sought a fourth term as chief executive, but was vehemently opposed by both Díaz and the hitherto faithful henchman Miguel Lerdo de Tejada. In the ensuing election, no candidate received a clear majority, showing that Juárez, for all his autocratic tendencies, really did believe in democracy and free elections. The election was thrown into Congress, who nominated Juárez as president. The disgruntled Lerdo had to make do with the consolation prize of presidency of the Supreme Court but Díaz, made of sterner stuff, raised the standard of revolt. This was crushed, and Juárez seemed set for undisputed hegemony. Then, in July 1872, he had a fatal heart attack. Lerdo succeeded as president, but in 1876 made the perennial mistake of all nineteenth-century Mexican presidents and tried to overstay his welcome through re-election. Once again Díaz raised an armed rebellion, fighting under the slogan 'effective suffrage and no re-election'. After initial reverses and when the situation looked hopeless, Díaz was rescued from despair by a new outbreak of liberal factionalism, this time between Lerdo and the new president of the Supreme Court, José Iglesias. Able to deal with his enemies piecemeal, Díaz defeated both in turn and entered Mexico City in triumph in November 1876.

Díaz aimed at absolute power and he had learned enough under Juárez to know how to get it. He had worked out that, provided you conciliate certain key social groups, you can repress the rest. Díaz offered deals to landowners, generals, local elites, foreign capitalists, sections of the middle class and even powerful bandit leaders; the rest he killed or cowed. He was convinced that every man had his price and, when confronted by a recalcitrant politician or general, always tried bribery first; he liked to cite a peasant tag from his childhood, illustrating his base view of human nature: 'This rooster wants corn.' If bribery failed, he turned to murder. This was Díaz's famous *pan o palo* system – bread or the club. He made it clear that he wanted no opposition, either in presidential elections or elsewhere. Two generals, García de la Cadena and Juan Corona, allowed their names to go forward as presidential hopefuls only to be mysteriously murdered. It became known that sudden death awaited all who opposed don Porfirio.

Usually, however, there was no need for extreme measures, for money did the trick; as Díaz, in another of his farmyard saws, put it: 'A dog with a bone in its mouth neither kills nor steals.' Díaz quickly built up a hierarchy of political influence, with himself at the top, then the twenty-seven state governors he appointed, followed by 300 *jefes políticos* (local political bosses) and 1,800 mayors or municipal presidents. Díaz nominated representatives to the toothless Congress in Mexico City, sometimes accompanied by rigged elections, and controlled the Supreme Court by appointing placemen and stooges. He showed particular favouritism towards the men of his native state: out of 227 representatives he nominated in 1886 to comprise the paper tiger masquerading under the name of Congress, sixty-two came from Oaxaca.

There was rigid government control of all aspects of education. The press Díaz dealt with by carrot and stick. The *ley mordaza* or gagging law, which he cunningly put on the statute book during the chaotic 'presidency' of Manuel González (see below) abolished the right to a jury trial for journalists guilty of 'libel' or 'sedition' and such guilt was established by the mere say-so of a single magistrate, inevitably a Díaz stooge. Newspapermen could also be jailed without trial if anyone reported their unpatriotic or seditious 'state of mind' or even their 'intentions' to the police. On the other hand, Díaz paid out generous subsidies to proprietors and editors, provided they reported the news as he wanted it reported. He even maintained the fiction of 'opposition' newspapers so that, at judicious intervals, they could be given the nod to destroy the reputation of anyone in the Army or politics Díaz thought was becoming too powerful. If the generous 'subsidies' did not work, Díaz sent in his gangs of thugs, known as the *bravi*, to smash up presses and newspaper offices or to provoke unwary editors into fatal duels. At the limit Díaz could silence any press critics by sentencing them to noisome tropical penitentiaries from which scarcely anyone returned alive. One intrepid editor, a one time Díaz supporter named Filomeno Mata, actually beat the odds by going to jail no less than thirty-four times during the *Porfiriato*.

Díaz's next task was to perpetuate his rule. At first he trod carefully, mindful of the resonance of the 'no re-election' slogan in the Mexican unconscious. In 1880 he appeared to step aside, allowing Manuel González to become president. However, González was his creature and did his bidding in every respect. The years 1880–4 were notorious for government profligacy and financial incompetence, so that Mexicans in 1884 welcomed Díaz back as a saviour. This was a favourite Díaz ploy. If he spotted a man with ambition, he found a political bed of nails for him, some post as governor where he would lose all reputation and credibility. By 1888 Díaz's grip on Mexico was so tight that he no longer needed the farce of proxies like Manuel González. 'No re-election' was forgotten about, the constitution was amended in 1887 to allow a second successive term, and again in 1890 to allow an infinite series of successive presidencies by the same man; between 1884 and 1904 Díaz had himself re-elected six times (the other 'elections' were in 1888, 1892, 1896 and 1900).

Díaz's regime was a repressive tyranny but he lacked the technology to impose a totalitarian dictatorship or police state. He did not seek to control every aspect of Mexican life and was relaxed about conflicts between local elites or powerful families within a state; his main concern was that no one should emerge who could contest his power at the centre. Díaz's rule was thus an intermittently coercive tyranny, whose chief outward sign was the *rurales*, the quasi-military mounted police force that patrolled the countryside. The *rurales*, uniformed in suede and armed with the latest Mauser rifles, were effectively above the law outside Mexico City and were much feared as a consequence. Their favourite method of dealing with opponents was through the *ley fuga*, or law for dealing with fugitives from justice: this allowed anyone to be shot dead who 'tried to escape'. The Houdini-like propensity of Mexicans was evidently high in the Díaz years, for over 10,000 people died under the *ley fuga*.

It is sometimes suggested that Díaz's 34-year hegemony was an easygoing dictatorship, but the evidence suggests that there were few revolts only because of the terrifying consequences. The rebellion in Veracruz by supporters of the exiled Lerdo in 1879 resulted in execution for innocent parties as well as the genuine rebels. In all regions of Mexico the *jefes políticos* allowed themselves the privileges of *droit du seigneur* in the villages, taking any woman who caught their fancy. In the state of Hidalgo, Indians who had rebelled after their lands were unjustly seized were buried up to their necks in their ancestral lands and trampled to death by the *rurales*, who rode over them at the gallop. Those who opposed Díaz or his officials, or were disliked by them for any reason, were branded 'criminals': the penalty for 'crime' was to be worked to death on chain-gangs or sent to plantations in the extreme south of Mexico, where the broiling sun or tropical diseases would do the executioner's job for him.

The level of violence in Mexico during the so-called *Porfiriato* has also been downplayed by Díaz's apologists. This is because most of them were foreigners, for whom Mexico was indeed a land of peace, safety and security. It was otherwise for most Mexicans, and especially for the indigenous ones. In the 1880s there was a bitter and bloody war with the warrior tribe of Sonora, the Yaquis, predictably on the issue of land stolen from the Indians by Díaz's henchmen. At first the Yaquis were invincible and defeated every army Díaz sent against them; but in the end a remorseless campaign of attrition reduced them to starvation and surrender in 1887. The governor of Sonora interviewed the Yaqui chief, Cajemé, after his capture and found him highly intelligent and well versed in military strategy – not surprisingly, since he had fought with Juárez against the French in the 1860s. However, the governor's sympathy was unavailing: he had his orders from Díaz, so Cajemé went to the firing squad. Fortunes were then made by the governor and his cronies, who sold the Yaqui warriors at 75 pesos (£7) a head for slave labour in the plantations of Yucatán, where most of them died an early death under the tropical sun.

It is difficult to overstate the sufferings of the Yaquis during the dreadful thirty years after 1880. In the 1890s, following another Yaqui rebellion, Díaz offered a bounty of 100 pesos (about £10) for the ears of all dead Yaqui warriors. This prize-money degenerated into a cruel farce as bounty hunters slaughtered unarmed peasants, cut off their ears, and claimed they were Yaqui organs. Other brutalities included the extermination of the entire male population of the town of Navojoa in 1892, and in the same year 200 Yaqui prisoners were taken out in a gunboat into the Pacific Ocean off Guaymas and thrown into the sea to drown or be food for sharks. When the desperate Yaquis rose again in 1898, they were slaughtered in droves at Mazacoba by the federal army, now equipped with the most modern Mauser rifles. In 1908 a boatload of Yaquis, bound for slavery in Yucatán, committed mass suicide.

Díaz always believed in divide-and-rule: in a political clash, support a state governor against the local military leader until the governor had won, then change tack and build up the military leader again as a counterweight so that the governor was not too powerful. Don Porfirio extended this thinking to the indigenous peoples: by transferring the Yaquis to Yucatán he hoped to set the most martial Indians in Mexico at the throats of the second-most bellicose. The so-called War of the Castes – a full-scale rebellion by the Mayas which had flared violently in 1848–51 and was a race war in the true sense, where the Mayas killed whites on sight and vice versa – had never been fully extinguished. However, when the Yaquis died in droves on the plantations of Yucatán, Díaz decided he would have to make a huge military effort to crush the Mayas. In 1900 he sent in the Army on a massive search-and-destroy operation. For two years, under the brutal General Victoriano Huerta, the Army systematically laid waste the Yucatán peninsula, scorching the earth, burning villages, destroying food until at last, as with the Yaquis in Sonora, the final Maya strongholds were reduced through starvation.

Divide-and-rule was just one of the ways in which Díaz's regime presented a dual, ambiguous or ambivalent face. There was no set of official state doctrines or myths, so that the ideology of the regime was a confusing mixture of positivism and Catholic piety. Positivism (roughly, the application of scientific method in all intellectual contexts and the denial of a distinction between fact and value) was a powerful force in Europe, itself representing a reaction to the Romantic movement which had challenged the wisdom of the Enlightenment. During the *Porfiriato*, Díaz's most influential advisers were the so-called *científicos* or Mexican positivists, who believed in capitalism, industrialisation and modern technology; they despised Mexico's colonial past and Indian heritage. Most of the Mexican elite – politicians, bankers, editors, businessmen, generals – subscribed to *científico* ideals: capitalism in preference to the *hacienda* mode of production; the white creole as the racial superior to the *mestizo* or Indian; the foreign entrepreneur with his greater skill to the native Mexican one; and Gradgrindian fact-worship and number-crunching to all talk of spirituality or ancient values.

Positivist bankers and economists, who with Díaz's help quickly became millionaires themselves, formed a powerful ruling clique under the dictator's tutelage. Three *científico* positivists had a particular influence on Díaz. The first was his secretary of the treasury in the 1880s, Manuel Dublán, a believer in sound money and balancing the budget, who cleared up the mess left behind by Manuel González and achieved economic stability through classic deflationary policies. González had promised to pay the debts of 91 million pesos (£9 million approximately) owed to British bondholders since Juárez's repudiation of foreign debt and, though this was widely criticised as a climb-down 'giveaway' to the gringos, Dublán honoured the pledge.

The second great influence was Romero Rubio, formerly Lerdo's political manager, who rapidly switched sides once he realised Díaz was there to stay. Rubio was given the important post of minister of the interior and control of the police and *bravi* and was thus Díaz's enforcer-in-chief. However, Díaz kept back a trump card by conniving at Rubio's acquisition of a string of illegal gambling dens in the capital; if ever it became necessary, Díaz could indict him on grounds of moral turpitude. To cement ties even further, in 1881 the 51-year-old dictator married

Rubio's 18-year-old daughter Carmen; doña Carmelita, as she was usually known, was an important influence on Díaz.

The third *científico* was the most important of all. When Romero Rubio died in 1895, a new leader emerged, José Yves Limantour. Under his aegis Dublán's dream of balancing the budget was finally achieved: in 1894 revenue amounted to 43 million pesos and expenditure to only 41 million. Limantour was in some respects the Bernadotte of Mexican history. Of lowly origins, the illegitimate son of a French adventurer who had panhandled for gold in the 1849 California gold rush, Limantour made a new life in Mexico, where he revealed entrepreneurial talents of a high order, first as a speculator in confiscated Church lands and later as a stockbroker and financier in the twilight world between graft and big business. Limantour, given a free hand by Díaz to manage the economy, swept away such feudal residues as internal tariffs, established state banks, abolished bimetallism and put Mexico on the gold standard. International confidence in the Mexican economy skyrocketed and government bonds began to be sold on the international market.

This emphasis on capitalism, modernisation and scientific ideas, grafted on to the *juarista* programme of liberalism, free trade and anticlericalism should logically have made the Díaz government as strongly anticlerical as the regimes of Carranza and Calles in the twentieth century. However, once again Díaz revealed his peasant caution and his instinct to play both sides against the middle. During his presidency the Catholic hierarchy – or at any rate the conservative sections thereof – enjoyed a halcyon period. He kept the Catholic Church in line by neither repealing nor implementing the anticlerical Laws of the Reform, which Juárez had introduced in the late 1850s; he maintained an official stance of anticlericalism while secretly colluding with the Church, especially his close friend Archbishop Eulogio Gillow of Oaxaca.

This entente with the Church had two main sources. One was his young wife Carmelita. Captivated by Carmelita, Díaz returned from honeymoon outwardly a new man: instead of the coarse, unmannerly Indian peasant of yore, there was a dapper, well-groomed, courtly Porfirio Díaz, fastidious and meticulous in appearance, etiquette and social graces. More importantly, he heeded his wife's devout Catholicism. Romero Rubio, like Bernadotte, had begun life as a Jacobin but, again like the Gascon apostate, had changed his spots once he got his hands on power, becoming a pillar of the establishment and a bastion of the Church. Through the good offices of Carmelita, Díaz held a secret meeting with the head of the Roman Catholic hierarchy in Mexico, Archbishop Labastida y Dávalos. It was agreed that the Laws of the

Reform would not be enforced and that the Church could own property; in return Labastida pledged the Church to submit all ecclesiastical appointments to Díaz for his approval and to encourage parish priests to preach submission to don Porfirio. It was yet another in the long line of Faustian pacts between the Catholic Church and the powers temporal.

The other impetus towards an accommodation came from his youth. Until old age blunted his faculties, Díaz had remarkably good political antennae, and his instinct told him that conflict with the Catholic Church was a mistake. When governor of Oaxaca in 1870 his brother Félix had implemented Juárez's Reform Laws with Jacobin zeal, closing church schools, expelling nuns, banning the teaching of the Catechism, destroying or defacing statues or idols of favourite saints. Particular offence was given to the village of Juchitán when Félix Díaz stole the statue of its patron saint and returned it with its feet cut off. In 1871, when Porfirio Díaz staged his unsuccessful revolt against Juárez, Félix joined him, fled on the failure of the rebellion, and was pursued and captured by the vengeful men of Juchitán. First they cut off the soles of his feet, then his genitals, and finally forced him to walk on shards of glass and burning coals before leaving him to die an agonising death. Díaz learned the lesson: he never asked how many divisions the Pope had and, even when he had supreme power, did not seek to avenge his brother.

Díaz seemed to have attained all his political aims, but his economic ones were more difficult to achieve. He was neither the first nor last dictator to find that the economy will not yield to an autocrat's fiat. The problems he confronted were myriad: how to turn Mexico into a modern capitalist economy, without delivering it wholly into the hands of foreign interests; how to integrate the hacienda and the Indian villages into this system; and, most of all, how to juggle the fissiparous interests of a nation-state with centrifugal and conflicting economies. Roughly speaking he faced the dilemma of the United States before the American Civil War, except that the North had to integrate just one antagonistic economy whereas Díaz had to rationalise several.

Mexico has always been an artificial creation as a nation-state. In twentieth-century Africa the artificiality of nation-states is a legacy of the colonial powers who drew boundaries across tribal lines instead of creating homogeneous units corresponding with tribalism. In Mexico the problem was God-given or geographical. The eighth largest country in the world, with an area of 761,000 square miles, Mexico is a curious mélange of tropics, plateaux and mountains. One quarter of Mexico's area is made up of the various cordilleras of the Sierra Madre. The western Sierra Madre is in geological terms a continuation of the North American

Rockies, while the eastern Sierra Madre runs from Nuevo León in the north-east to the coast. Broad in the north, with a 2,000-mile frontier with the USA, Mexico narrows rapidly towards the isthmus, where the two Sierra ranges merge in a tangle of peaks and valleys – the heartland of the old Aztec empire. In this central plateau, at an average altitude of around 4,000 feet, in one-fifteenth of the country's total area, one-third of the population lived, including most of the whites. Here were located the large cities: in 1910 Mexico City was not far short of a half-million in population, and the second city, Guadalajara, had 120,000 inhabitants.

The southern tropical areas bordering the Pacific and the Gulf of Mexico were overwhelmingly Indian. Here temperatures were excessive, rainfall exiguous and disease – especially malaria and yellow fever – rampant. It takes an effort of imagination to appreciate that the steamy jungles and foetid swamps of the south were in the same country as the lofty peaks of the cold, mountainous country of the Sierra Madre, but whereas about a third of the national area was below 1,600 feet, more than a half was above 3,000 feet, with the altitude of Mexico City itself at 7,350 feet. Above this level towered the great peaks of the Sierra Madre, including the permanently snowcapped Orizaba (18,700 feet), Popocatépetl (17,887 feet) and Ixtaccíhuatl (17,343 feet).

The very different nature of the landscape in the thirty-seven different states meant that Mexico's economy, even at the pre-industrial level, was bewilderingly heterogeneous. In the mountainous and plateau areas mining, especially of gold, silver, lead, copper and zinc was important; in the northern states cattle and other livestock, hides, corn and chickpeas were dominant; and in the tropics coffee, sugar, vanilla, rubber, chicle and henequen – the agave plant native to Yucatán, whose fibre was used to make rope and string – were the principal moneymakers. All these products were grown for export and, additionally, maize, beans and chilli were produced for domestic consumption.

Mexico's agricultural sector was particularly complex, being centred on the two very different institutions of the village and the hacienda. Five million people, mainly Indians, lived in villages which before 1857 had been free and held communal lands; another four and a half million worked on the haciendas. The hacienda, a primitive colonial institution geared to local consumption of foodstuffs rather than production for the market, in theory had a strict hierarchy of owner/master, manager/overseer and peons who did the backbreaking labour. The haciendas were generally inefficient, their working methods had not changed over three centuries, and most of their owners and managers were incompetent. The whole issue of water rights was a legal mess, soil erosion was an endemic problem about which nothing was done, and most of the *hacendados* refused to cultivate more than a small portion of their lands. Hence the paradox that a country where three-quarters of the population lived off the land could not feed itself and had to import food even at the height of Díaz's 'economic miracle'.

However, it is one of the infuriating aspects of Mexican economic history that almost no generalisation about the hacienda can be hazarded. It was unique, one of a kind, *sui generis*. By Díaz's time some *hacendados* had overcome the traditional creole contempt for business and were producing for the market; looked at from that point of view, one could align the haciendas with a capitalist mode of production, but there were other aspects of the system that looked classically feudal: peonage, serfdom, service in kind, the *corvée*, and so on. Any attempt to classify the hacienda in terms of the classic Marxian modes of production leads merely to the how-many-angels-on-the-point-of-a-needle quasi-theological debate of the sort beloved of a certain kind of academic sociologist. The only safe general statement, banal as it is, is that agriculture gradually became more commercialised in the nineteenth century.

In any case, the term hacienda covered so much ground: conditions varied from state to state and from locality to locality. There were haciendas in northern Mexico as well as in the south; some were backward, some progressive; even within the same area different estates would use different types of workers or a mixture of resident labourers, seasonal employees amd sharecroppers; some gave up on peonage altogether and paid wage-labour. It is easier to discuss the hacienda in terms of the lifestyle of the *hacendados*. Many were absentee landlords, living in Mexico City or Paris – for France, despite Louis Napoleon and Maximilian, enjoyed a remarkable cachet during the *Porfiriato*. Louche, hedonistic, decadent and courteous in that unworldly way only the very rich can manage, the *hacendados* and their families have been the subject of many Latin American novels. Devoutly Catholic in ideology, if not in practice and behaviour, they gave their children a European education; more than one social historian has remarked on the penchant for sending boys to the Jesuit school of Stonyhurst in England.

It was difficult for Díaz to prod the lazy, reactionary, reluctant *hacendados* into becoming modern capitalists without losing their support, so the hacienda system always remained an obstacle to his plans. The problem of the Indian villages seemed easier to solve. Indian titles to their lands dated from the Conquest and many had never been formally registered; on paper it seemed a simple matter to use the law to deprive the Indian owners of their patrimony. Juárez, by the *ley Lerdo*, aimed to abolish the traditional lands held in common (the *ejido*) as part of his project for turning Mexico into a nation of property-owners, and this was why the Indians had overwhelmingly fought for Maximilian in the wars of the 1860s. Stripping the Indians of their lands provided a bonanza for speculators, many operating through proxies to preserve the myth of small landholding. Foreign real estate corporations were particularly predatory when it came to buying up or simply stealing land that formerly belonged to Indians; how many legal niceties were observed depended on local power politics, the relative strength of the villages and the *rurales* and the degree of corruption in the courts.

The result of the assaults on Indian land by Díaz and his realtor cronies, both domestic and foreign, was spectacular. More and more Mexican land, whether former Indian *ejido*, confiscated Church land or public lands in the north put up for auction, was concentrated in fewer and fewer hands, especially after 1894, when the legal limits on ownership by any one individual were lifted. Domestic real estate corporations were given one-third of all lands they surveyed, and public lands in this era made up 125 million acres, or a quarter of the national territory. In Baja California four plutocrats owned thirty million acres; in Chihuahua the Terrazas family acquired seventeen million acres; just 3,000 families owned almost half of Mexico, and one-fifth of the country (that is, an area as large as the whole of Japan) was in the hands of seventeen individuals. One result was the rise in the north of *rancheros* as a class, grazing vast herds of cattle on otherwise empty grasslands.

By rewarding his loyal followers with so much land Díaz hoped both to keep them loyal and to encourage their 'improving' tendencies, for, under the influence of the *científicos*, he aimed to provide Mexico with modern industry and infrastructure. The age of Díaz was also the age of the railways. When he came to power in 1876 there were just 400 miles of track, completed in 1873, linking Mexico City with Querétaro and Veracruz. By the 1880s 1,250 miles of track were being laid each year so that by 1910 Mexico had about 12,000 miles of railway. Such was the mania for railway building that the prodigal and extravagant puppet government of Manuel González (1880–4) actually promised to pay American railroad builders 6–9,000 pesos for every kilometre of track completed; the inevitable result was that Mexico had a skewed railway system. One of Limantour's undoubted scoops was his taking the railways into public ownership. Nationalisation of these vital communication arteries reduced Díaz's dependence on the United States at a time when he was becoming seriously concerned about the inroads of the colossus of the North.

The coming of the 'iron horse' was a necessary if not sufficient condition for the Mexican Revolution. By 1910 there were no lines south of Mexico City, but three different railways linked it with the United States border. From Mexico City one line ran west through Guadalajara, Tepic and Mazatlán then up the Pacific coast to Hermosillo and Nogales. The central line ran from the capital up to León and Zacatecas, then threaded its way north via Torreón and Jiménez to Ciudad Juárez, across the border from El Paso in Texas. The eastern railroad snaked up to Nuevo Laredo, across the border from Laredo, Texas, after following a track that took it through San Luis Potosí, Saltillo and Monterrey. All this meant that the great landowners could increase their harvests and take advantage of economies of scale, since they could now produce for a national market, not just a local one.

Hand in hand with the railways went a hard-driven programme of industrialisation. Iron and steel works were constructed in Nuevo León, textile mills in Veracruz, and there was a massive mining boom, especially of lead and copper, stimulated by new technologies for refining precious metals. Most of all there was oil, the black gold of the twentieth century. The first geological discoveries and drillings took place on the coast of the Gulf of Mexico at the turn of the century, making Tampico the new boom town. Oilwells were spudded in and production began in 1901. By 1910 Mexico was one of the world's leading producers and by 1918 was second only to the United States. Such was Díaz's myopia, however, that his 1884 mining code vested the ownership of subsoil rights in the proprietor of the surface land. Those who had acquired public lands at a giveaway price now found they had a second and much more lucrative bite of the cherry when petroleum was found on their territories.

This was the context in which foreign capital, already a leech on the Mexican economy, became a veritable octopus. It is doubtful if Díaz ever did say: 'Poor Mexico, so far from God, so near to the United States' – it sounds too witty for him – but he was aware of the truth contained in the remark. Viewing the Mexico stabilised at gunpoint by Díaz as an investment cornucopia, American capitalists flooded across the border. Among the famous names with substantial holdings south of the Río Grande were Hearst, Guggenheim, McCormick and Doheny; Mexicans became familiar with the corporate identities of Standard Oil, Anaconda, United States Steel, and many others. Soon the Americans owned three-quarters of the mines and more than half the oil fields and they also diversified into sugar, coffee, cotton, rubber, orchilla, maguey and, in the northern provinces of Sonora and Chihuahua, cattle. Out of a total foreign investment of nearly three billion dollars in Mexico by 1910, the American share was 38 per cent, or over one billion dollars, more than the total capital owned by native Mexicans. In 1900 Edward L. Doheny acquired huge swathes of oil-rich Tamaulipas, near Tampico, complete with subsoil rights, for less than a dollar an acre. Once oilwells were installed, Doheny's plant could literally suck Mexican national treasure out of the ground, to the tune of 50,000 barrels a day, all completely tax-free except for an infinitesimal stamp duty.

The Americans were not the only economic predators. The British (who still held 55 per cent of all foreign investment in Latin America as a whole), were well represented with 29 per cent of foreign investment in Mexico, mainly in mines, banks and oilwells. The great English entrepreneur in Mexico was Weetman Pearson, later Lord Cowdray, whose construction firm, Pearson & Son, had built the Blackwall Tunnel in London, the East River tunnel in New York and a number of railway bridges in Mexico. As a personal friend of Díaz, Pearson was able to cash in on the oil bonanza and obtained the rights to the Tuxpan fields in 1909; Díaz thought it a good idea to build up Pearson's oil company, Mexican Eagle, as a counterweight to Doheny and Rockefeller's Standard Oil. Eventually, Lord Cowdray (as he became in 1910) extended his business ambitions into Ecuador, Colombia and Costa Rica, exacerbating pre-existing Anglo-American tensions in Latin America and leading Washington to invoke the Monroe Doctrine.

The Anglo-Saxon nations, though by far the biggest foreign investors, were not the only ones. The French, forgiven for their sins of the 1860s, were allowed to control the textile industry while the widely hated Spanish or *gachupines* dominated the retail trade and the tobacco plantations. All foreign capitalists were secretly resented to greater or lesser degrees – the Spanish sometimes openly – but Díaz rigged his judiciary so that in any dispute involving foreign companies and Mexican nationals, the foreigners would always get a favourable judgement. It was a standing joke that only gringos and bullfighters (another of Díaz's favourite groups) could get justice from a Mexican court. Nor did the foreigners endear themselves to the locals by their lifestyle and obvious contempt for Mexico and Mexicans. Disdaining to acquire Mexican citizenship, the expatriate community lived in splendid and luxurious isolation, repatriating profits and making sure their own nationals rode the privileged managerial gravy-trains. To all complaints about the exploiters in their midst Díaz returned the same answer: the foreigners were needed to make Mexico a modern nation, since the Mexicans themselves lacked the know-how.

By the time of his eightieth birthday in 1910 Díaz was feeling relaxed, not to say complacent, about the achievements of his seemingly perpetual presidency. The revenues of the federal government stood at 110 million, an almost threefold increase in fifteen years, and of the individual states at sixty-four million. Used to running a budgetary surplus every year since 1894, the government had accumulated a total of 136 million in the fiscal black, much of which was held as a cash reserve in the treasury. Mexico's credit was more than just good on the foreign exchanges, and Díaz could argue that thirty-four years of 'stability' had produced this healthy economic situation; in the old days of Santa Anna, Juárez and even Manuel González, it was always deficit, deficit, deficit. It was, after all, a deficit which led Juárez to suspend payment on the national debt, which in turn had brought in Maximilian and the French.

Seeing only the superficial prosperity and being themselves the major beneficiaries of the *Porfiriato*, foreigners had long been used to showering accolades on Díaz, so that his eightieth birthday was simply an occasion for tributes more hyperbolic than usual. Díaz now expected such treatment as his right, for had not the greatest and the best uttered accordingly? Andrew Carnegie's tribute to the 'Moses and Joshua of his people' was well known, Cecil Rhodes thought him a beacon of civilisation, Theodore Roosevelt pronounced him 'bully' and even Tolstoy, whose sympathy for peasants should have alerted him to the plight of the Mexican peon, extolled him as a political genius whose government was unique. Elihu Root, US Secretary of State from 1905–9 and a future Nobel Prize winner, went right over the top in a much-quoted encomium, in which he described Díaz as 'one of the greatest men to be held up for the hero-worship of mankind'. The American journalist James Creelman, who had a famous interview with Díaz in 1908 on the heights of Chapultepec Castle indited the following: 'There is no figure in the whole world who is more romantic and heroic than that soldier-statesman whose adventurous youth outshines the pages of Dumas and whose iron hand has transformed the warlike, ignorant, superstitious and impoverished Mexican masses, after centuries of cruel oppression by the greedy Spaniards, into a strong, progressive, pacifist and prosperous nation that honours its debts.'

Creelman saw only the glittering surface of don Porfirio. Those few who got close to Díaz noted many psychological peculiarities. Like Francisco Franco, the dictator he most resembled, in personality as well as political longevity, Díaz was an intellectual mediocrity of no sophistication and little imagination, who none the less possessed a peasant cunning (Díaz's state of Oaxaca is in this sense a good mirror for Franco's Galicia), a peerless talent for political manipulation and an intuitive sense of men's weak points. Like so many autocrats, he knew the price of everything and the value of nothing. Extremely reserved, he liked to refer to himself, even in private conversation, in the third person and thus to use indirect speech as if reporting the words of another person. This psychological peculiarity of many despots, sometimes excused as the 'Caesarean third person' (after Julius Caesar's usage in his book on the Gallic war) is in fact more indicative of a fragmenting personality in an uneasy relationship with outer reality.

Many people at the time (it was, after all, a 'politically incorrect' era) liked to explain Díaz's personality in terms of his Indian blood; there is an old Mexican saying: 'When the Spaniard wanes, the Indian waxes.' Certainly the closer one got to Díaz, the more one discerned the savage under the veneer of cultivation; some interviewers even claimed that Díaz's white skin seemed to darken the more you looked at it. Many idiomatic expressions, to say nothing of his intonation and pronunciation, revealed his Mixtec origins. He believed that true leadership meant constructing a godlike cult of oneself, for in Indian culture godhead was the one true sign of authority. Díaz was proud of his cult and even more so of the rude health that never seemed to fail him, and which he boasted he would not swap for all the millions of the American robber barons. Even in his seventies he rose at dawn, did exercises and weightlifting in the gym at the military academy, took cold baths and rode tall horses. His athletic bearing was much commented on: well-built, ramrod-straight, broad-shouldered and barrel-chested, he seemed as solid and monolithic as a great oak. However, he lacked the immobility of a tree; instead, his restless energy, his prowling intensity and the swift flashes from his eyes suggested a panther or some other big cat.

Yet underneath the placid surface of Díaz's Mexico the magma of a future volcano was taking shape. Díaz could effectively cow the villagers and the peons with his *rurales*, but his crash programme of modern capitalism and foreign investment was having unintended effects, the most important of which was the rise of an urban working class, not so easily dealt with as the peasantry. The first group to trouble the dictator was the textile workers, mainly clustered around the area between Puebla and Veracruz. Thirty-two thousand strong according to the 1910 census, textile workers made up the biggest group among the urban proletariat properly so-called, and they were the first to be hit by economic recession. Already working under a very paternalistic form of capitalism, with company stores and housing – some scholars indeed have referred to the Mexican textile industry as the 'urban hacienda' – they were further demoralised after 1900 as the industry, facing threats of overproduction, cut back on output, slashed wages and shed workers. In response the textile workers became increasingly unionised; in 1906 there was a general strike in the industry, with 30,000 idle hands. The unions asked Díaz to arbitrate and he did so, marking the first entry of the Mexican state into industrial relations.

Perhaps Díaz realised that the intransigence of the employers rather than the excessive demands of the workers was to blame, for his arbitration award was not as harsh on the workers as expected. However, he soon proved the truth of the old saw that one swallow does not make a summer. In subsequent troubles at the Río Blanco textile plant, he sent in police and the Army; they left more than seventy workers dead, effectively cowing the workforce. Yet there were no calls for revolution. Mexican unions were reformist organisations and the proletariat arrested at the stage Lenin called 'trade union consciousness' where the working class makes simple demands on the existing system instead of trying to destroy it root and branch. Even when real wages declined in the last years of the *Porfiriato*, Mexican workers did not dream of armed struggle.

Unintended consequences were more severe in the mining industry, mainly located in Mexico's northern states, and in 1906 these led to real trouble in the Cananea copper mine. The wages of miners had risen while those of the textile workers had declined and there had been halcyon days until 1906, when the veins started to get played out. Unfortunately, aspirations had been aroused which could not simply be extinguished like turning off a water tap. The Cananea mine had hitherto looked like a textbook triumph for 'rugged individualism'. The American owner was William Greene, one-time gambler, Indian fighter and miner. With bravado, bluff and brio he had carved himself a cattle and mining empire in Sonora. The Cananea mine employed 5,360 Mexicans as miners and 2,300 foreigners, most of them Americans in managerial or administrative positions. The North American ethos itself had spawned a high level of unionisation, and Cananea was, on paper, an 'organic' community, with friendly relations between management and labour, Mexican and gringo.

The snag was that it all depended on a buoyant copper industry. Faced with falling production, management unilaterally changed wage scales and conditions of service. The workers went on strike and demonstrated in the streets of Cananea. Feelings ran high: seeking to persuade the carpenters in the workshop to come out in solidarity with them, the strikers marched on the carpentry shop, where the American manager turned the hoses on them. Matters escalated rapidly: demonstrators rushed the building; armed Americans inside fired on them and killed two men; in retaliation the enraged strikers then burned down the building, killing four Americans in the blaze. As the violence spiralled out of control, the strikers acquired firearms and gunfights took place between management and labour in which there were a further thirteen deaths.

Greene browbeat the governor of Sonora into allowing American irregulars across the border and summoned the Arizona Rangers at Bisbee. The governor was in an impossible position, having to balance this insult to Mexican sovereignty against Díaz's well-known complaisance towards the *yanquis*; he solved his dilemma by the legal fiction of swearing in the Rangers as soldiers of Sonora. A furious shoot-out now developed between armed strikers and a combined force of Arizona Rangers, local police and the *rurales*; even so, the rebellion was quelled only when the veteran Sonoran oligarch Luis Torres arrived with a regiment of federal troops to garrison the town. The upshot was that Greene removed three unpopular foremen but the strike leaders were sentenced to fifteen years in jail (they were released in May 1911, after the Revolution broke out).

Díaz lost much caste through the bloody repression of this outburst. Needless to say both the dictator and the Americans blamed this clear-cut case of spontaneous combustion on unidentified 'outside agitators'. The use of the Arizona Rangers particularly angered Mexicans, but the importance of this incident can be overstated. In no sense did it 'lead to' or trigger the Mexican Revolution. By 1910 copper production was back to the levels of the halcyon days, mainly because of new management and improved technology and efficiency. Greene, suffering liquidity problems in his empire, sold out to another American consortium, and the incoming Colle-Ryan group handled its labour relations tactfully. Although Cananea was built up in revolutionary mythology after 1910 as a precursor of the Revolution, its main significance was to reveal some less palatable possible consequences to Díaz's industrial revolution and to show that the Mexican economy was less solid than the more complacent *científicos* thought. If final proof were needed that industrial relations, even strikes, inhabited a different universe from revolution, one might cite the curious case of Manuel Diéguez. Leader of the miners at Cananea in 1916, ten years later he was the federal military commander in Sonora, in which capacity he acted like the formerly radical John Wilkes towards the Gordon Riots in the London of 1780.

Although worsening economic conditions did not *cause* a revolution in Mexico – they had deteriorated before in the Díaz years without causing an explosion – rising prices and declining real wages in the years 1907–10 meant that if ever Díaz did come under serious threat, fewer and fewer hands would be raised to save him; and after 1907 there could be no doubting that, looked at structurally, instead of in a narrow balance-of-payments way, the Mexican economy was in trouble. A crisis on Wall Street in 1907 had a ripple effect in Mexico, where Limantour restricted credit and followed deflationary policies. Wages failed to keep pace with rising prices, the cost of staples doubled between 1890 and 1910, and the fall in living standards was exacerbated by bad harvests, particularly in 1909 when there was famine in some rural areas, and *campesinos* died of hunger. After 1907, even the relatively privileged miners, who had always done better than industrial workers, were hit by lay-offs and mine closures.

Díaz could hope to ride out a short-term financial and economic crisis, relying on the inevitable upturn in the business cycle, but he never looked like solving Mexico's root problem: the disharmony between the backward hacienda system and his aspirations for a modernised capitalist nation. Superimposing capitalism on the hacienda mode of production simply did not work: after all, even the mighty United States had been torn apart by a civil war in 1861–5, fought to correct the disequilibrium between an industrial north and a plantation economy in the south. Díaz's attempt to impose a capitalist revolution 'from above' was impossible because the power of the landlord and *hacendado* class, its labour-repressive agricultural methods and in particular the institution of a semi-servile peonage all worked to impair the efficiency of the market. Díaz was not a stupid man and he was aware of the problem, but to attempt to extirpate the hacienda in favour of the capitalist mode would mean curtailing the privileges of the very people on whom he relied to stay in power. The political imperatives of the *Porfiriato* pointed in one direction, and the economic ones in exactly the opposite direction.

By 1910 even the political system of repression was beginning to look frayed around the edges. His *jefes políticos* had become complacent and filed reassuring reports to Díaz, containing only what he wanted to hear. His network of spies and agents became impossibly swollen in size, full of corrupt and timeserving drones who regarded 'intelligence' as a sinecure. In Mérida in Yucatán, far from the most rebellious state in the country, the governor employed 700 paid agents in a city with a population of 50,000. Most corrupt and incompetent of all Díaz's agents, however, were the *rurales*. Used to meting out summary justice by shooting prisoners 'while trying to escape' (the *ley fuga*) or beating them black and blue with a bull's penis (the *bastinado*), the *rurales* grew lazy, and the calibre of their recruitment declined. Nepotism was rife, discipline lax, and the officers were usually illiterate oafs who behaved as petty despots. Supposed to sniff out all opposition to don Porfirio, they utterly failed to do so, largely because they were too busy handing worthless sons and nephews into sinecures, padding payrolls, and arranging for kickbacks, sweeteners and payola from protection rackets. The *rurales* were a fitting symbol of a lazy, corrupt and unpopular regime, and the general impression of superannuated senescence was reinforced by the governors of the various states, who in themselves formed a gerontocracy: Querétaro's governor was sixty-eight, Guanajuato's was seventy, Aguascalientes's seventy-two, Puebla's seventy-five, Tlaxcala's seventy-seven and Tabasco's seventy-eight.

If there were signs that Díaz was losing his grip both economically and politically, even clearer evidence was provided by his disastrous new bearing in foreign policy in the first decade of the century. It is axiomatic in Latin America (and especially in Central America and the Caribbean) that only a nation wholly behind its leader can hope to resist the awesome power of the 'colossus of the North'. Yet in the 1900s Díaz seemed deliberately to set out to alienate the United States. Alarmed by the stranglehold American capital seemed to have on Mexico, he made particularly generous grants of public lands to the Pearson company, favouring Lord Cowdray over Standard Oil and the Doheny interests.

That might have been construed as sound national self-interest, but other anti-American attitudes seemed gratuitous. When President Zelaya of Nicaragua was overthrown by a pro-American coup, Díaz gave him sanctuary. In 1907 Washington, worried by the rising power of Japan across the Pacific, asked for a permanent lease of Magdalena Bay in Baja California as a naval base. Díaz dithered, then granted a lease for three years only, on severely restricted conditions. A meeting in 1909 with William Taft, the US president, on the international bridge linking Ciudad Juárez with El Paso, Texas, did not go well either and Díaz compounded the offence he had given over Magdalena Bay by offering an ostentatiously friendly welcome to a party of Japanese marines visiting Mexico. To Washington Díaz now seemed like an ingrate: where previously they had cooperated with him and even deported his political enemies back to Mexico, now they made it clear that Díaz's enemies were free to use American soil as a base for their activities.

All these factors indicated Díaz's weakening political grasp but, even in combination, they were not sufficient to trigger the social earthquake in 1910. Revolution broke out late that year principally because the 80-year-old Díaz could not decide what to do about the succession; in this respect he was Mexico's Elizabeth I. General Bernardo Reyes, governor of Nuevo León and military commander of the north-east, had long considered himself the heir apparent, but the *científicos* favoured Limantour. Díaz played his old game of favouring first one side, then the other. He built up Reyes, making him minister for war, then dismissed him abruptly and seemed to incline towards Limantour. Then, in 1904, he extended the presidential term from four to six years, agreed to establish a vice-presidency, and nominated a nonentity, Ramón Corral, as his vice-president and successor, thus casting down Limantour. Díaz was again playing games, for he knew that the mediocre Corral was dying of cancer and that anyway nobody would want such a man in the presidential office. It was an abiding fear of Díaz's that if he appointed a credible figure – whether Reyes or Limantour or some third party – as his vice-president and successor, he would then fall victim to assassination.

Having eliminated all viable presidential hopefuls, Díaz then over-played his hand. In 1908 he gave a long interview to the US journalist James Creelman, which was largely a self-serving puff for his achieve-ments, real and alleged. When Creelman gently taxed him with repression and severity, Díaz replied that he was much more severe on the rulers of Mexico than the ruled. He admitted that there was no mercy for anyone caught cutting telegraph wires and that anyone so appre-hended had to be executed within hours of being taken, and with no appeal. On the other hand, owners of all haciendas along which the wires ran were themselves liable to the death penalty if the wires were cut, as were all magistrates who did not catch the wire-cutters. Having thus, in his own mind at least, established himself as a figure of Solomonic impartiality, Díaz tried to prove himself a figure of consummate statesmanship: he said that he would like to see the emergence of an opposition party now that he had guided Mexico into an era when it was ready for democracy. To prove his seriousness, he was ready to state here and now that he would not be a candidate in the 1910 presidential election.

The announcement caused a sensation and proved to be the biggest mistake of Díaz's career. Naturally he had no intention of keeping his word and duly had himself re-elected when 1910 came round, but the opposition immediately manifested itself, all the way from the revolution-ary socialism of the exiled Magón brothers to a newly formed Democratic Party, a front for the political ambitions of Bernardo Reyes. The Reyists at first made merely the 'innocuous' demand that their man should succeed Corral as vice-president in 1910, but everyone knew what that meant. In alarm at the growing popularity of the Democratic Party, Díaz banished Reyes to exile in Europe. Reyes, lacking the stomach for rebellion and in any case alarmed that the Democratic Party was acquiring a real life of its own which he could no longer control, went quietly. There now seemed no possible obstacle to Díaz's peaceful re-election in 1910. The Creelman interview, it turned out, was a blind and commentators were left to ponder the reason for Díaz's promise. Was it simply a sop to liberal opinion in the USA, to palliate Díaz's recent anti-Americanism? Had the old man simply lost his political senses? Or was it, as most suspected, a stratagem to lure the unwary from their bolt-holes, so that the dictator could learn exactly who the opposition was and how great its strength?

This was the context in which Díaz was suddenly challenged from the most unexpected quarter. The man who launched the Mexican Revolution was surely the most unlikely revolutionary of all time. Insignificant to look at, only 5 feet 3 inches tall, with a neatly trimmed goatee beard – allegedly grown to mask a chin that was as weak as the rest of his physique – Francisco Madero was a vegetarian and teetotaller, with a nervous tic and a high-pitched voice that would become falsetto at moments of excitement. Widely regarded as a crank because of his enthusiasm for spiritualism and theosophy, Madero had no social or economic programme; his opposition to Díaz was purely political and, had Mexico really been the democracy Díaz mendaciously claimed it was, he would simply have functioned as the leader of a parliamentary opposition. However, as the usual threats from Díaz failed to burn off this new challenger, diplomats and journalists increasingly asked: who is Francisco Madero?

Aged thirty-seven in 1910, Madero was in line to inherit the fortune of the fifth richest family in Mexico. In the northern state of Coahuila, Madero's grandfather Evaristo founded the dynasty through shrewd entrepreneurship and speculation. In his *Compañía Industrial de Parras* he at first specialised in vineyards, cotton and textiles, but soon diversified into *guayule* plantations, silver mines, rubber plantations, cattle, coal, foundries and banks. Evaristo's business empire extended its tentacles into virtually every state in Mexico: his cotton mills alone stretched from Sonora in the extreme north-west to Yucatán in the extreme south-east. The cream of the northern landed elite, the Maderos were, from the 1880s, the wire-pullers who supplied the state governors of Coahuila.

The patriarch Evaristo married twice and both times produced a large family. Francisco, his eldest son by his first wife married an oligarch woman named Mercedes, who bore him a son, also called Francisco, on 30 October 1873. The full name of the child, the eldest of fifteen, was Francisco Ignacio; he was named for St Francis of Assisi and Ignatius Loyola, though more fanciful biographers have suggested that his surname (*madera* is Spanish for wood) carried connotations of the wooden cross of Calvary. At the age of twelve he entered the Jesuit school of San José de Saltillo. He was impressed by the Jesuits' capacity for self-discipline, but the fathers had got him too late (not by the legendary age of seven) so that he always received the religion inculcated into him with a silent question mark. After further schooling in Baltimore, he spent five years in Europe (mainly in Paris), then studied English and agriculture for a year at the University of California, Berkeley, where he dabbled in theosophy and tried to work out a general theory fusing Madame Blavatsky and spiritualism. His critics say that in all his travels, and especially his time in Europe, the only thing that really impressed him was spiritualism. Blind or indifferent to the art and culture of France and Italy, he came back to Mexico obsessed by the dreariest mania of the Victorian age: the belief in a world of spirits 'on the other side'.

In late 1893, aged twenty, he returned to Mexico to begin his real training as a businessman. His first job was to administer one of the family haciendas, San Pedro de las Colonias, and he acquitted himself well. In his youth he was a weedy specimen, often in poor health, but he had worked hard to acquire physical strength and was now an excellent swimmer and dancer. A workaholic and radical 'improver', he was full of bright ideas and new schemes: for a soap factory, for importing new strains of cotton from the USA, for a meteorological observatory, for an ice factory. He made his name as an entrepreneur in cotton and an expert on irrigation; his pamphlet on water rights on the Río Nazas was praised by Díaz himself. A good businessman and manager, he built up his purely personal capital to 500,000 pesos by the turn of the century.

This was not achieved by dire exploitation of his workers, for Madero was a compassionate man who lived in austerity in imitation of Francis of Assisi. The workers on his hacienda of San Pedro lived in clean houses and received high wages and good health care. Apart from feeding sixty homeless children and contributing to numerous charities, Madero, as a believer in homoeopathic medicine, did his own doctor's round, dispensing lime charcoal, *nux vomica* and other nostrums to his peons. In January 1903 he married Sara Pérez, a like-minded woman, and together they created schools, hospitals and soup kitchens, supported even more orphans and funded scholarships. However, the turning point of Madero's life was not his marriage to Sara but two events that occurred a couple of years before.

In 1901 Madero's beloved mother Mercedes died of typhoid. Severely affected by this and probably at an unconscious level guilty that he had 'caused' her death, Madero gave up drink and tobacco and sold his wine cellar. Perhaps not coincidentally, his interest in spiritualism moved up a gear. His first attempts to contact the spirits had scarcely been auspicious: practising automatic writing, he came up with the banal sentence: 'Love God above all things and your neighbour as yourself.' However, in 1901 he also began to receive daily 'visits' from the spirit of his brother Raúl, who had died by accident in a fire at the age of four. 'Raúl' instructed him to practise self-mortification and self-denial, to avoid the material in favour of the spiritual. Some Madero scholars say this, rather than the death of his mother, was the real trigger for the new regime of vegetarianism and explains why he gave up smoking and destroyed his wine cellar.

Until the age of twenty-eight Madero was apolitical. His first glimmerings of political consciousness came when Bernardo Reyes, governor of Nuevo León, used excessive violence when dispersing a political demonstration on April 1903–2. For the first time Madero started questioning the very roots of Díaz's power. Conveniently, 'Raúl' now instructed him that the best way to help his fellow-man was to enter politics. He became a candidate in municipal elections, founded the Club Benito Juárez to get Mexico back to the liberal principles of the Constitution of 1857, and narrowly lost his first electoral contest. He wrote articles for the press, trying to link the world of politics with spiritual values and signing them 'Arjuna', the hero prince of the Hindu epic, the *Mahabharata*. He went on to contest the election for governor in Coahuila in 1905 and was nearly arrested when his rival Miguel Cárdenas won. Cárdenas, returned a third time as state governor, was sufficiently alarmed by Madero's challenge to warn Díaz that the 'crank' Madero showed every sign of becoming a political embarrassment and one, moreover, who, with unlimited funds at his disposal, could develop into a real headache. Cárdenas pointed to the way Madero had financed his own newspaper (*El Demócrata*) as well as a satirical publication (*El Mosco-The Fly*). Alarmed, Díaz consulted Bernardo Reyes and asked him if he should jail Madero. Reyes advised against: the best first step was to persuade Francisco Madero Senior to get his wayward son to simmer down.

Madero did not lose hope after his defeat by Cárdenas but consoled himself with a fervent belief that his hour would come. Seeing himself as an apostle with a mission, and his political work as a fulfilment of the words of a crucified Saviour, he wrote to his brother Evaristo in Paris, asking him to come back and join in the great work. Meanwhile, starting in 1907, he began to have visitations from 'José', a more militant spirit. Biographers of Madero have compared his notebooks, detailing the messages from 'José', to the 'spiritual exercises' of Loyola. The notebooks are suffused with a profound sense of guilt – not just guilt that he is 'failing' Mexico but also that he cannot beget a child on Sara Pérez; there is the suggestion that Madero is being punished and that his wife will become pregnant once Madero fulfils his patriotic mission.

Soon another spirit arrived to reinforce 'José' and ordered him to preach his political message nationwide. Madero wrote prolifically in all opposition newspapers, even buying them up to make his message known. Early in 1907 the spirits ordered him to abstain from sexual intercourse, but then, in October 1907, the spirits gave him the nod that he had 'purified' himself sufficiently and had triumphed over matter; he was now to read Mexican history copiously in preparation for a struggle that would reach its apogee in 1908. To make himself an ever worthier vessel, Madero increased his campaign of austerity, cutting down on sleep, eliminating the siesta, going to bed late and rising early. By now a virtual recluse, teetotal and with no pleasures, he began eating less food and set himself a massive programme of reading in Mexican history. After the Creelman interview he also decided to write a long tract on the 1910 presidential election.

On his thirty-fifth birthday – 30 October 1908 – Madero got a message from 'José': 'You have been chosen by your Heavenly Father to carry out a great mission on earth . . . for this divine cause you will have to sacrifice everything material, everything of this world.' In November a new visitation – this time the spirit of Benito Juárez – told him that the pamphlet he was writing would send Díaz into a panic and that he should use the 'sword of truth' against the president. Against Díaz's shrewdness, use loyalty, 'Juárez' urged; against his falsity, sincerity; against hypocrisy, candour. Madero finished his book, then went into retreat for the biblical forty days and forty nights on a desert ranch he called 'Australia'. He told his father that he had been chosen by Providence for a great task and that his book on the election would be published not later than 25 January 1909.

The first edition in 1909 of Madero's *The Presidential Succession of 1910* sold out immediately. Madero structured his book on a twofold spine of diagnosis and cure. The diagnosis was that absolute power in one man was always bad and had harmful consequences: Madero instanced Czarist Russia and its humiliating defeat by Japan in 1905. He pointed out that Díaz had come to power expressly on the slogan 'No re-election'. While conceding that don Porfirio had made some economic progress, Madero pointed to the debit column: the enslavement of the Yaquis, the repression of the workers at Cananea, the national levels of illiteracy, the toadying to Standard Oil and other US interests, and the entire system of autocratic centralism. When condemning Díaz's 'patriarchal politics' he went into full flight: 'This is the cause of . . . the corruption of the spirit, the disinterest in public life, a disdain for law and the tendency towards deception, towards cynicism, towards fear. In the society that abdicates its freedom and renounces the possibility of governing itself, there is mutilation, a degradation, a debasement that can easily translate into submission before the foreigner . . . We are sleeping under the cool but harmful shade of a poisonous tree . . . we should not deceive ourselves, we are heading for a precipice.'

The cure prescribed by Madero was a simple return to the Constitution of 1857, fair and valid voting, and no re-election. On 2 February 1909 Madero sent a copy to Díaz, calling on him to attain real historical immortality by embracing democracy. In May 1909 he sold much of his property at a loss to raise cash for his political programmes, set up the Anti-Re-election Centre in Mexico City and published a journal, *El Anti-Reeleccionista*, edited by José Vasconcelos and Luis Cabrera. His grandfather Evaristo, founder of the Madero dynasty, remarked cynically: 'It's the struggle of a microbe against an elephant,' but, undeterred, his grandson made a whistlestop tour through Coahuila in September 1909 and was mobbed by enthusiasts.

By this time Díaz's patience was running thin. Just before the first convention of the Anti-Re-election Party, Díaz decided to strike at the Madero family, to show them the danger of letting their cub run wild. First, he tried to take over the Bank of Nuevo León, but was compelled to beat a hasty retreat when it became clear that the public would accept only money issued directly by that bank. After vainly pressurising Evaristo Madero, Díaz decided to go straight to the nuisance and arrest Madero himself, on a trumped-up charge of dealing illegally in rubber. A warrant was issued for Madero's arrest but never served, because of protection extended to the Maderos by their old family friend José Limantour, still Díaz's indispensable minister of economics.

The new party's convention took place in 1910. The day before it opened, Díaz tried to pre-empt Madero by inviting him to an interview. This was, predictably, a dialogue of the deaf in which platitudes and bromides were exchanged. Madero professed to admire Díaz as a man but insisted that his system must give way to democracy. Díaz hinted that the man who took power from him would be accepting a poisoned chalice and asked ironically who Madero had in mind as the next president. When Madero said that it did not much matter as long as he was honest, Díaz commented sardonically that to govern Mexico a man needed to be much more than honest. Madero said he wanted Mexicans to take seriously the idea of free and fair elections and Díaz said, again possibly ironically, that that was a laudable ambition. Each man went away from the meeting with a low opinion of the other. Díaz said he had just met a lunatic to match the genuine madman (Zúñiga y Miranda) who had been put up by students as a presidential candidate in 1896. Madero turned Díaz's farmyard similes back on to him by remarking that don Porfirio was no longer the fighting cock of yore. To his intimates he said that Díaz was in his second childhood, but still retained the cunning of a senile control freak.

In the convention hall next day the strength of Madero's movement was apparent. Madero was nominated as presidential candidate and chose as his running mate the career politician Francisco Vásquez Gómez, formerly physician to the Díaz family and a leading supporter of Bernardo Reyes. It was notable that most of the *reyistas* had moved over to Madero now that their leader had been exiled. Most of the finest intellects in Mexico, including José Vasconcelos, had joined him and the speaker list was studded with names that would become very familiar in the next three years: Roque Estrada, Federico González Garza, Pino Suárez, Félix Palavicini. Convinced by his meeting with Díaz that peaceful change was impossible, Madero began to hint that perhaps only a revolution could shift the dictator and warned that force would be met with force. Following the successful convention, the momentum of the Madero campaign seemed unstoppable and he set out on a nationwide tour. He was acclaimed by a crowd of 30,000 in Puebla City, by 10,000 in the city of Jalapa and by another 20,000 supporters in Orizaba. In Veracruz he announced his manifesto, to include individual rights, municipal liberties and the autonomy of states.

Díaz had meanwhile not been idle. Having exiled Reyes, he dealt with the next hopeful, Limantour, by removing him from his inner circle and failing to consult him about the next batch of 'nominees' to Congress. In the summer of 1910 Limantour angrily departed for Europe, aware that his presidential chances were over; ostensibly he was going to negotiate a new debt agreement with European banks, but it was an open secret that he would not be back this side of the presidential election. Still saddled with Corral, whose cancer had gone into remission, Díaz even tried to sideline him by building up another hopeful, governor Teodoro Dehesa of Veracruz, as the rising star. However, as the crowds flocked around Madero on his triumphant whistlestop tour, even the myopic Díaz realised at last that he had a serious challenge on his hands. When Madero reached Monterrey, he was arrested on charges of plotting armed insurrection and imprisoned in San Luis Potosí.

Díaz now ordered a purge of the new party. After more than 6,000 arrests of the leading lights, the smaller fry went into hiding and Díaz was left free to fix voting turnout figures and intimidate the electorate. Madero remained in jail while Díaz's lavish birthday celebrations went on in September, and it was from his prison cell that same month that he heard the unsurprising news that Díaz had been re-elected president by a record margin, with Corral as the vice-president. With that nice concern for phoney procedure and statistics that characterises so many autocrats, Díaz actually allowed Congress three months (from June to September) to 'scrutinise' the election results and then announced an exact figure for the presidential votes cast for the Anti-Re-election Party: 196 for Madero and 187 to Vásquez Gómez; doubtless this diaphanous travesty was laid on for the benefit of US observers.

In prison Madero considered his options. His was a middle-class movement, with purely political aspirations, with a definite appeal to the literate urban elites and intellectuals for whom the *Porfiriato* was a blot on the national escutcheon. It is futile to look for deep socio-economic currents in Maderismo and even Madero's 'radical' statements were fustian rhetoric. He rumbled a lot about US penetration of Mexico, but his movement was not a backlash against foreign investment; both Madero and his principal lieutenants deeply admired the USA and looked to it for inspiration. That being so, Madero was in a dilemma. To call for an armed uprising would put property at risk, might lead to the kind of slippage towards real social change that had occurred in the French Revolution, and would probably not succeed anyway, either because Díaz's military power was too great or because the USA might intervene to prevent 'chaos'. On the other hand, to do nothing would be to hand Díaz victory on a plate. Reluctantly, Madero concluded that Díaz would have to be opposed by force, and laid plans for a national uprising to begin on 20 November 1910.

Restless and workaholic even when behind bars, Madero deluged his followers with letters, promising them he would not weaken. When Díaz was declared president, he submitted a huge dossier on electoral fraud to Congress, where it was predictably buried. Meanwhile his father intervened with the state governor and posted a substantial bond, allowing Francisco to ride around San Luis Potosí by day, accompanied by guards. Soon the guards became drugged by the boring daily rhythms and grew inattentive. On 4 October Madero jumped bail, simply galloping away from his lazy jailers. He found refuge in a nearby village and from there travelled incognito by train to the border with the USA where he was smuggled across to Laredo. In San Antonio, Texas, in late

October he issued his Plan of San Luis Potosí, which proclaimed the elections of 1910 null and void, declared that he was the real president of Mexico and called on all Mexicans to refuse obedience to Díaz. He proposed himself as provisional president and promised the restitution of lands to villages and Indian communities and an amnesty for political prisoners. Most of all, he called for armed revolution and specified the hour and day when it was supposed to break out: 6 p.m. on 20 November 1910. Whether revolution was now to break out in Mexico depended on the national response to that tocsin call.

THE RISE OF ZAPATA

Among those who watched Madero's challenge to Díaz with keen interest was a 30-year-old village chief from the state of Morelos named Emiliano Zapata. Morelos, one of the smallest states in Mexico, lay fifty miles to the south of Mexico City and had borders with Mexico State, Puebla, Guerrero and the Federal District itself (within which the capital was situated). Zapata's native state was in some ways a microcosm of Mexico, since in a relatively small area it contained both the mountain terrain typical of northern Mexico and the tropical lowlands more usually associated with the plantation states of the extreme south-east.

Zapata was a *mestizo*, of mixed white and Indian parentage. Race was a factor of extreme importance in Mexican society; in 1910 a third of the population was Indian and half *mestizo*. As to the extent of racial prejudice, experts differ. On the one hand, many oligarchs were racist, despised the benighted Indian as a drag on the national chain, and embraced a form of social Darwinism whereby Mexico's future lay in transcending its Indian past; for this reason they looked to England and France for their inspiration and sent their children to school there. On the other hand, the national ethos of Mexico officially took pride in the achievements of the Aztecs and the Mayas, and on a day-to-day basis overt racial prejudice was rare. Everyone knew, though, that whiteness was the supreme ethnic value, and the aim of all aspiring Indians was to be 'whitened'.

Like the Plains tribes of North America, the Mexican Indians never made common cause against their white rulers. This was because differences between tribes were perceived as just as important as between Indians and whites. There were more than 100 indigenous languages and dialects among the tribes, most of which were clustered in central and southern Mexico, where they made up anything from 50 to 75 per cent of the population. There *were* Indians in northern Mexico – the Mayos of Sinaloa, the Tarahumaras of Chihuahua and, especially, the martial and powerful Yaquis of Sonora – but for the most part the tribes were located south of Mexico City: the Tarascos of Michoacán, the Tzeltales,

Tobojales, Chontales, Tzotziles of Chiapas, the Zapotecs, Mijes, Zoques, Huaves and Mixtecs of Oaxaca, the Huastelos and Totonacos of Veracruz, the Mayas of Yucatán, plus an assortment of tribes (Mazahuas, Nahuas, Otomis, Coras and Huicholes) in central Mexico.

Even so, generalisations about southern Mexico are difficult. Oaxaca, Chiapas (both states a mixture of jungle and high valleys) and Yucatán were overwhelmingly Indian, all living on a subsistence economy of corn, beans and squash, but each of the three was in important ways unlike the other two. Oaxaca had two great advantages: it had a higher proportion of *mestizos* in the population, curbing racial tensions, and it had more free village land. In Chiapas, by contrast, the plight of the Indians was such that large numbers of them lived as bandits in the area of the coastal lagoons, sustained by their communities and pursued ineffectually by the *rurales*: they were the classic 'primitive rebels' or 'social criminals' so beloved by sociologically minded historians. Yucatán, situated on a limestone plateau, was different again. Here the disastrous wars of the castes had raised racial tensions to boiling point, and the white city of Mérida sat uneasily as an island in a sea of Maya communities, with the creole communities owning the enormous sisal hemp haciendas. Cut off by jungle and swamp from the rest of Mexico and plagued by malaria and yellow fever, Yucatán was an unhappy land, taking its inspiration from the Caribbean and harbouring vague aspirations towards independence.

Without question the Mexican Indian was socially combustible material, but without leadership from outside there was no possibility of the deprivation and resentment in the villages being converted into revolutionary activity. *Caciquismo* – the absolute dominance of a chief or *cacique* – worked against this, as did the extreme factionalism and parochialism of the villages. There were over 100,000 of these in 1910, often a few miles from each other, but each one had a totally distinctive culture. Regionalism was so intense that there was extreme localism even within a region. In the state of Hidalgo eleven neighbouring *pueblos* were identified, all utterly different in politics, economics and culture. Indians were devoutly Catholic in that syncretic mode that allowed them to fuse their old pagan beliefs with the teachings of the Church, and parish priests usually counselled bowing the head, except perhaps on 12 December, the greatest date in the Church calendar, when the feast of the Virgin of Guadalupe was celebrated.

All other factors worked in the same quietist direction. There is some evidence of a cosmic despair inculcated in the collective Indian unconscious by race memories of the demographic disaster of the sixteenth century. When Cortés and the Conquistadors arrived, Mexico had an estimated population of eleven million but eighty years later this was down to one million, and population levels revived only in the eighteenth century. Lack of knowledge was also lack of power for the Amerindians. The levels of literacy, political awareness and education were abysmal, but this was a feature of Mexico in general. In the 'advanced' north, a mine owner, thinking to educate his workforce, held a mock election for president among the miners while Díaz was having himself re-elected and discovered some surprising results: out of 300 voters, 150 had voted for the long-dead Benito Juárez, 100 for a bullfighter and fifty for the local bandit leader.

Above all else, however, was the issue of land; it was no accident that the great slogan of the Mexican Revolution (equivalent to 'liberty, equality and fraternity' in the French Revolution) was *Tierra y Libertad* – land and liberty. The core problem of the Díaz years was the way the hacienda had encroached on village lands. Most villages had enjoyed their communal lands for centuries through customary right and had not filed documentary title to the territories in Mexico City. The *hacendados* and their lawyers took advantage of this to assert ownership in the village lands and water. By 1910 half of the rural population of Mexico had been reduced to dependency on the hacienda and many villages were hacienda *pueblos*. Even where the villages were not in hacienda territory, their inhabitants were often landless and had to work in the haciendas. The free non-hacienda villages were largely Indian and these were squeezed mercilessly until only a few retained their own ancient lands. Peaceful resistance was all but impossible, since the *hacendados* controlled the state courts and dominated local politics, making local democracy or free elections impossible.

The villagers could in a sense count themselves lucky, for there was an even more exploited group of people: the peons who lived and worked permanently on the hacienda grounds, as opposed to the villagers who worked as day labourers. These peons were ground into the dirt by the nefarious system of debt peonage, common in the south, which made the states of Veracruz, Campeche, Chiapas and Yucatán the closest thing to the notorious serfdom of Russia and eastern Europe. The peon, indentured to the hacienda and unable to leave, toiling all day under the sun, at the mercy of brutal overseers and harsh discipline enforced by whips and riding crops, had perforce to buy all his needs at the company store, where debts were run up either honestly or dishonestly. When these debts were made heritable, so that children inherited their parents' debt, peonage became slavery in all but name. Echoing the cynical transactions in Gogol's *Dead Souls*, owners bought and sold each other's peons and used bounty hunters to track down fugitives, who would then be beaten to death as a bloody warning to the others.

It is difficult to overstate the cynical savagery of debt peonage. Many peons owed up to three years' wages in debt which could never be repaid, especially as their employers cynically fiddled the figures. One company storekeeper was reputed to add the date at the top of the page to each peon's debt. The *hacendados* liked to keep their charges in ignorance, and on many haciendas schoolteachers were expressly forbidden to teach arithmetic to the permanent workers. Since Spaniards often held positions on the hacienda as keepers of the company store, clerks, foremen or managers, the *gachupines* were particularly hated, and Spain was always the main target for xenophobia in Mexico. The threat to all villagers was clear: if they lost their lands to the haciendas or became economically unviable, they would face starvation unless they became permanent employees on the haciendas and thus got sucked into the maw of debt peonage.

Although the state of Morelos did not suffer from the worst excesses of the hacienda system farther south, the mind of Emiliano Zapata cannot be understood without appreciating the role of land in his mentality: both his mystical feeling for the soil of his ancestors, and his negative appreciation of what lay in store for the villagers of his state if they did not resist the big *hacendados*. He was born on 8 August 1879 to Gabriel Zapata and Cleofas Salazar, the second son and ninth of ten children (of whom the two boys and two of the girls survived into adulthood), in the village of Anenecuilco (literally 'the place where the waters swirl'), an ancient settlement that predated the Spanish Conquest. Zapata was the ancient Indian name of the *pueblo*. The Zapatas were an important family in Anenecuilco, with a reputation for political activism going back to 1810: they had fought in the wars of independence and, notably, against the French in the 1860s.

Many legends have attached themselves to Emiliano's birth, but two facts seem well grounded: he was born with a cherry-coloured birthmark, the shape of a small hand; and his birth was attended by an Indian healer woman or *curandera*. Childbirth had a powerful mystical resonance among the people of Morelos, and it is thought that the pre-Conquest Indians of the area had a bizarre religious baby cult. Fathers were present at births, assisting their wives who bore children in the sitting position. Directing the entire operation was the *curandera*, who would massage the pregnant woman's body, sprinkling incense or *copalli*, a gum made from resinous pine wood and chanting magic formulae. When the child was delivered, the *curandera* cut the umbilical cord, tied it and washed the baby, leaving the mother to sleep. Once she had wrapped the child, she handed it to the father in a stylised, ritualistic way that everyone understood. All the other children would have been present at the birth. A successful live birth, in a culture that so prized children, was the occasion for setting off fireworks and rockets and drunken carousal.

Emiliano Zapata was born into a troubled land. The basic social conflict in Morelos was between the villagers (mainly small farmers) and the owners of the great sugar-cane plantations. Sugar haciendas and subsistence villages had coexisted uneasily since the sixteenth century. By 1910 Morelos produced one-third of Mexico's sugar crop and was the third largest sugar-cane producing area in the world (behind Hawaii and Puerto Rico). Seventeen owners of thirty-six huge haciendas owned one-quarter of the state and all the best land. Since Díaz came to power in 1876, there had been an enormous expansion of the haciendas at the expense of the villages and the small farmers. In this conflict the Zapata family had played an important if ambivalent role; despite his reverence for his ancestors' lands, Emiliano must have realised that not all his forebears' political actions bore close investigation.

In the 1870s the family had been *porfirista*, and a José Zapata (not Emiliano's uncle of that name) had been Díaz's political fixer in the state. In 1874 this José Zapata, now the village chief of Anenecuilco, wrote to Díaz, then a war hero but not yet dictator, about the tyranny of the sugar mills and their owners. In 1876, when Díaz was supreme ruler, the new village chief wrote again to don Porfirio, asking for his help and mentioning that the earlier petitioner, José Zapata, was dead. Díaz promised to do all he could, but nothing was done. Tensions continued. In 1878 Manuel Mendoza Cortina, the owner of the hacienda of Cuahuixtla, tried to get his hands on Anenecuilco's water supply; when the villagers learned that one of their elders was secretly helping him, they caught the man and cut off his head. In 1887, when Emiliano was eight, Cortina annexed the eastern end of the village, prompting the villagers to tax themselves to buy guns, but the Zapata family was not prominent in this initiative. At this stage they tended to align themselves with the *hacendados*: the owner of the giant Hospital hacienda had actually been Emiliano's godfather at his baptism.

However, in 1895, when Emiliano was sixteen, there was trouble with the new owner of the Hacienda Hospital – a name that would recur in Zapata's biography. The *hacendado* occupied the villagers' grazing land, killed some of their animals and put up barbed wire fences. Getting no satisfaction through local channels, at the turn of the century they hired a top lawyer, who sent to the National Archives in Mexico City for their title deeds; on receipt the lawyer confirmed that the village's title was inalienable. The young Emiliano Zapata was deeply impressed by this incident and developed something of an obsession about title deeds, which he would come to see as a living symbol of the soil of his beloved Morelos. He also developed a detestation of railways, seeing them as a sign of *hacendado* power.

In the burgeoning conflict in Morelos between villages and the sugar plantations, the *hacendados* were dealt a trump card in 1881 when a branch line of the Veracruz–Mexico City line was extended down to Morelos, giving the planters access to larger markets and allowing them to import heavy machinery to build bigger sugar mills. The role of the railways as an important and exponential, though not exclusive, cause of conflicts between villages and haciendas should never be underrated: during the 1877–84 railway building boom, fifty-five serious armed conflicts were noted by the authorities. Zapata saw that certain phenomena seemed always to go hand in hand: whenever there was rail expansion, the *hacendados* sent armed men to seize village land, to increase their acreage and meet the growing demand for sugar in national and international markets. His xenophobia was fed by the presence of the hated Spaniards in every stage of hacienda expansion, and he felt the force of the ubiquitous slogan: 'Death to the *gachupines*.'

It is easy to see the influences that made Zapata acquire his political consciousness, but details of his early life are otherwise sparse. Naturally, when he became famous all kinds of legends grew up around him, many centering on the verifiable fact that he was born with a birthmark on his chest, but only a handful of early anecdotes are well grounded in fact. It seems that even as a child Zapata was a dandy, with a taste for flashy clothes. His uncle Cristino gave him a pair of trousers decorated with coins. The story was that Cristino had fought with the bandits known as the *plateados* ('men dressed in silver') who ravaged Morelos in the latter part of the nineteenth century and dressed his nephew in this elaborate way so that he would be reminded of his one-time comrades. Not to be outdone, Emiliano's father's other brother gave him a present of a muzzle-loading rifle dating from the same campaign.

Two other formative incidents we owe to Zapata's own recollections. He remembered seeing his father weeping when one of the orchards that had been in the family for generations was appropriated by a powerful hacienda; Emiliano vowed that one day he would regain the stolen land. On another occasion, when people in a neighbouring village resisted the fencing off of their common land by a powerful *hacendado*, the man sent for the *rurales*, who burned the village to the ground. As a boy Emiliano stood with his brother Eufemio and his father, watching the flames lick skywards. Zapata's friends later said you could guarantee to get Emiliano into a rage simply by mentioning this incident, which seemed to make his eyes glow like hot coals as he remembered it.

We know little about Emiliano's childhood and youth except that he went to an elementary school in Anenecuilco, where his education included the basics of book-keeping. However, we do know an extraordinary amount about everyday social life in Morelos in the late nineteenth century, which enables us to reconstruct his milieu. He came from a prosperous 'upper peasant' family, so would have been spared the worst privations, but it was impossible for him to avoid seeing the misery around him. Although debt peonage in Morelos was not at the levels of Chiapas and Yucatán and there were no instances of the *hacendado* demanding *droit du seigneur* over the nubile women on his estate, as happened in some other states, only a humbug would have described the lot of most Morelians as happy.

Mrs Alex Tweedie, a British traveller, described conditions at the San Gabriel hacienda in Morelos in 1901, which was widely regarded as a model plantation in its treatment of its workers. Enclosed by enormous walls, as if it were a gigantic monastery, the hacienda housed nearly 3,000 souls and, with its long corridors, ornate balconies, plethora of rooms, outbuildings, church and company store, seemed like a village in its own right. Without any security of tenure, the peons were allowed to build primitive dwellings with walls of bamboo and roofs of palm-leaf intertwined like thatch. All purchases had to be made at the company stores, everything was done on a ready money basis and employees were paid in cash on a Saturday night – this alone made the San Gabriel notable, for on most haciendas the peons had to take their wages purely in goods from the store. Average wages were 50 cents a week which enabled the peons to eke out a bare subsistence, though some of them were already 400 pesos in debt.

For the independent villagers life was better though still hard. The plough had replaced the *coa* – a narrow, long-handled digging stick – and donkeys did the work of the traditional Indian porter or *taneme*. It was considered a mark of civilisation that white trousers and shirts had replaced loin cloths as the accepted clothing for working in the fields. The more prosperous houses were still usually pre-Hispanic, with adobe walls or walls made of reed grass, thatched roofs and wooden shingles. For a man of Zapata's class diet would extend beyond the traditional Indian corn, beans, squash, cacao, chilli and the occasional turkey – under the influence of the Conquistadors, the Indians, originally vegetarian, had turned carnivore – but even *mestizo* cuisine was primarily Indian in the standard dishes: *pozole* stew, *mole* sauces and cornmeal tortillas.

The Indians had also learned the attractions of alcohol, often with devastating results. Gone were the pre-Conquest days when drinking at times other than religious festivals was a serious crime. Now the men frequented the grog shops, drinking *pulque* or *aguardiente*, and piling up the debt to the company store in the process. When they became ill, the Indians had two choices. If they lived on a hacienda they could consult the company doctor which each *hacendado* was supposed to provide along with a priest on Sundays and holy days of obligation. However, a much more popular option, given that the Indians still believed in magic, animism and folk medicines, was to consult the ancient healers or *curanderos* (*curanderas* if they were female) and take the drugs they prescribed.

The *curanderas* were especially popular, since they were thought to be witches with magic powers. Living embodiments of Jung's 'wise old women', they had the authority of doctors or psychoanalysts, though their folk remedies were more redolent of Thomas Hardy's 'conjurors' than of modern medicine. Like Chaucer's Pardoner, they carried many strange samples in their 'magic bags', mainly bones or organs of animals with which they practised sympathetic magic. Among the elite they had a bad reputation, for though they were the accepted midwives in Morelos, childbirth mortality was high (which some ascribed to their dubious methods) and many of their adult patients died from gangrene or blood-poisoning. In the rapture induced by the hallucinogenic drug peyote, the *curanderas* would prophesy in the Nahuatl tongue. In many ways these women, as herbalists, homoeopathic healers, doctors, midwives, counsellors, fortune tellers, were the eyes and ears of a village, its true intelligence system; they were respected and feared as much as they were cherished and admired.

By the standards of late twentieth-century urban life, everyday existence in Morelos – lived close to nature and the soil, circumscribed by the Catholic Church, with villagers permanently nervous about the encroachments of the haciendas – was dull and tedious when it was not menacing or threatening. In common with other Morelians, the young Emiliano Zapata looked forward to the high spot on the calendar, the village's annual fair, an occasion of social, religious and economic significance. Economically, the fair was a market in more senses than one, for the Morelos villages followed a strict division of labour when it came to producing goods exchanged by barter. Each village had its own specialisation, whether pottery, leather, straw mats, saddles, blankets, clothes; Tepac, for example, specialised in black pottery, Cuautla in leather, and Iguala in silver jewellery. With so many villages and so many fairs, traders in these goods lived an itinerant life, often travelling 100 miles from one fair to another.

Socially, the annual fairs were designed as a gigantic, week-long fiesta, reaching a climax on the Sunday nearest the feast day of the village's patron saint. The atmosphere was carnival, with all that that connotes: exotic costumes (usually a different jester's 'uniform' from each village), elaborate dances, the singing of folk songs or *corridos*, gourmandising, drunkenness, letting off fireworks. The bars and *pulquerías* opened around midday and closed at dawn the next day, when the clientele were either in jail for disorderly conduct or sleeping it off at home. The village plaza would echo to the peculiar yip-yipping, high-pitched scream or *carcajada* of inebriated Indians. While the men were getting drunk, the women and children would amuse themselves on the fairground, complete with acrobats, primitive ferris wheels and freak shows.

Religiously, the celebrations gathered pace on Friday and climaxed on Sunday, when the priest would say Mass in a church so packed that worshippers spilled out on to the plaza. Devout Indians filed past statues of the crucified Christ, then lined up inside the church to kiss the feet of the Saviour on a gigantic wooden crucifix. The bizarre week-long synthesis of God, Mammon and the Flesh would finish, suddenly and mysteriously, on Sunday night. Nobody blew a whistle to end proceedings, but by a kind of pre-established harmony the revellers seemed to know the exact time to drift away and resume their normal lives. By Monday morning back-breaking toil and the everlasting struggle between villages and haciendas would be resumed.

When Emiliano was sixteen, both his parents died, within a year of each other; the head of the family was now his brother Eufemio, five years his senior. Eufemio was always Emiliano's moral and intellectual inferior, and without his famous brother would have disappeared unknown into the mists of history. In 1892, at the age of eighteen, he had revealed his basic conformism by enrolling in a local *porfirista* club. Joseph to Zapata's Napoleon, Eufemio early revealed his deep character as a drunkard, lecher and no-good but Emiliano usually revered him and deferred to him, at any rate in these years. For all his qualities, Emiliano never transcended the limitations of the narrow Morelos village culture, and so never entered a room where Eufemio was without kissing his brother's hand. Of his relations with his two surviving sisters, María de Jesús and María de Luz we know little, but as a typical male chauvinist

Mexican *macho* Emiliano would have expected to command their automatic deference.

Neither of the brothers had ever been paupers: they had always lived in a stone and adobe house, not a hut, and the family owned land. Now, with their inheritance, they went their separate ways. Eufemio became an entrepreneur and salesman in Veracruz state but was notably unsuccessful and, his patrimony spent, crept back to Morelos to shelter under the aegis of his more successful brother. Emiliano meanwhile bought a team of ten mules and used them to carry corn from farms to the towns, then he diversified into hauling bricks and lime for construction work on the Chinameca hacienda – like the Hospital hacienda this was a name that would recur in his career. Zapata was never the anti-capitalist his socialist champions would like him to have been and was proud of his talents as entrepreneur and his versatility as farmer and muledriver. 'One of the happiest days of my life,' he later recalled, 'was when I made around five or six hundred pesos from a crop of watermelons I raised all on my own.'

Unlike Eufemio, whose reflex action was to go where the power was, Emiliano was from a very early age a passionate opponent of the hacienda system and its enclosure of village lands. Youthful rebellion landed him in trouble in his late teens, though at this stage his opposition to the status quo did not go beyond abstract advocacy; none the less, he was compelled to flee Morelos and hide out for a long time on the ranch of a friend of the family in Puebla. When the dust settled, he returned to Anenecuilco and continued his moderately successful business career, working his own lands, sharecropping intermittently from a local hacienda and building up his reputation as teamster and muledriver. Already his renown as a dandy was part of Anenecuilco folk lore: he loved silver ornaments and elaborately caparisoned horses. Normally these traits would have alienated Morelians but they tolerated them in Emiliano.

His political education continued. In the years 1902–5 he learned the art of local politics by observing the dispute between his own village and the *pueblo* of Yautepec on the one hand and the Altihuayan hacienda on the other. Jovito Serrano, the headman of the Yautepec village, organised a delegation that went up to Mexico City to petition Díaz in person, and Zapata was one of the Anenecuilco delegates. We may take leave to doubt the legendary story that Zapata was the prime mover in an angry confrontation with Díaz and that Díaz marked him down as 'one to note'. It was too early for that and, in any case, Díaz had Jovito Serrano deported out of Morelos immediately afterwards for daring to put his case forcefully in person. If Zapata had spoken out on this occasion, he would have suffered the same fate. Nevertheless, he listened, observed and drew the obvious conclusions about Díaz, the so-called 'father of the nation'.

The year 1906 was a turning point for Emiliano. A schoolteacher named Pablo Torres Burgos settled in Anencuilco, eking out a living by running a market stall and selling second-hand books. Zapata made friends with him and began a crash programme of reading the books in Torres Burgos's library and also the current newspapers, especially the anti-Díaz anarchist organ *Regeneración*. Soon yet another mentor appeared in the shape of an even more sophisticated and politically conscious schoolteacher, Otilio Montaño, an admirer of the Russian anarchist Kropotkin. Zapata listened to Montaño's passionately committed firebrand public lectures and was so taken with him that he invited him to be his *compadre*. This was the highest tribute one friend could pay another, for in Mexican culture the fictional kinship tie of *compadrazgo* (literally co-god-parentage) was the supreme male value.

In some ways Zapata received the classical training prescribed by Marx for a revolutionary, for at the very time he was imbibing Kropotkin and anarchism from Torres Burgos and Montaño, the daily political struggle was in itself raising his political consciousness. The struggle between the villages and the sugar planters of Morelos had moved up a gear, for the *hacendados* in the first decade of the twentieth century perceived themselves to be engaged in a life-or-death struggle with two different enemies: other Mexican producers of sugar cane, and the world's producers of sugar beet. The years 1900–10 saw US capitalists, investing heavily in Mexican sugar, instal the latest productivity-enhancing technologies in the states of Sinaloa, Tepic, Puebla, Michoacán, Jalisco and, especially, Veracruz where productivity was 30 per cent up on Morelos levels. An even worse menace was the introduction of sugar beet into the northern state of Sonora at the very time domestic demand for sugar had already reached saturation point. The plantocracy of Morelos lacked the capital to invest in new technologies and decided to squeeze the villages instead, despite widely voiced fears that soil erosion in Morelos might soon exhaust the land itself.

To win this titanic battle the Morelian *hacendados* had to destroy both internal and external competition. The external threat they dealt with by lobbying and politicking in Mexico City. In 1908, Díaz, by doubling the import duty on foreign sugar, removed the menace from foreign sugar beet, so that by 1910 Morelos regained its position as the world's third-ranked supplier of sugar, behind Hawaii and Puerto Rico, but they were still in danger of being overhauled by the new mills in Veracruz and elsewhere. They desperately needed technological retooling: modern milling machines, access to fresh markets via new railways and, above all, more land, water and cheap labour in Morelos. Peaceful coexistence with the villages was no longer possible; in the planters' minds village lands had to be ploughed under and independent farmers extirpated. The *hacendados* began this new phase of the struggle by seizing all unguarded village lands and trying to make Morelos approximate to the pure debt peonage plantation system of south-east Mexico. New haciendas appeared, creating self-contained economic communities, together with all the familiar by-products such as company doctors and company stores. The aim was to strangle the villages, and to make everyone see that the independent *pueblos* were backward, anachronistic obstacles to the economic programmes Díaz wanted; it was the *científico* project in deadly action.

A new ruthlessness was abroad. *Hacendados* fenced off former communal pasture land and, when cattle used to grazing there knocked down the fence to get to a favourite munching spot, the hacienda guards impounded them and released them to the villagers only on payment of a fine. If the villagers took their case to the local courts, the judges, in the palm of the planters, would rule against them; if the villagers continued to insist on their rights, beatings or even murder would be the next step. Increasingly, the Morelos villages found themselves squeezed from two directions. Deprived of economic spin-offs from the sugar plantations (less and less day labour) while having more and more of their lands stolen, many Indian communities died and disappeared, became ghost towns or the Mexican equivalent of Goldsmith's deserted village. More and more villagers, finding their debts mounting, tried to hire themselves out to the plantations as sharecroppers or day labourers. A vicious circle was created: neglecting their own lands, they found their villages effectively taken over and themselves reduced to resident labour on the plantations – the dreaded fate of debt peonage.

The crisis year for Morelos was 1908. Suddenly Díaz faced a local version of his national re-election crisis just when he thought he had settled Morelos for the foreseeable future. His tame governor Manuel Alarcón had held the ring very effectively there for a dozen years, always basically on the side of the planters but clever and machiavellian enough to throw the occasional bone to the villagers. He liked to play the bogus role of conciliator, as in 1906 when the men of Anenecuilco, armed with their title deeds, petitioned him for justice. With much phoney rhetoric about 'my children', Alarcón called an utterly pointless meeting, attended by the villagers and the managers of the Hospital hacienda; eloquent words were spoken but nothing whatever was done about the problems. When the villagers finally saw through Alarcón's mask of impartiality, they went over his head to Díaz. Taking advantage of a visit by don Porfirio to his son-in-law Ignacio de la Torre, who had a hacienda in Morelos, they waylaid the president with their petition. He promised to intercede, but the only action he took was to identify the 'ringleaders' of this act of 'sedition' and have them transported to the labour camps of Quintana Roo.

In December 1908 Alarcón, aged fifty-seven, unexpectedly dropped dead of a heart attack, having just been elected (in August) for the fourth time in a row. The state's elite of planters met Díaz in Mexico City to decide a suitable successor, but were in considerable disarray for Alarcón had been a consummate fixer, a master of apparent compromise, verbal obfuscation and political camouflage, whose skills had defused an explosive situation for a decade. His would be a hard act to follow, and at first the Morelos *hacendados* were stupefied when Díaz suggested his chief of staff Pablo Escandón as Alarcón's successor. A Stonyhurst-educated effete playboy, forever at the centre of minor corruption scandals, Escandón's only connection with Morelos was that his wealthy family owned sugar plantations there. Then the planters had second thoughts. They were desperately short of land, since there were no more public hectares to buy and the villages would not sell their farms, whatever price they were offered. With this sports-playing, woman-chasing nonentity in the governor's chair at Cuernavaca, the planters would be able to manipulate events to their hearts' content; Escandón would surely look the other way while they stole farms, browbeat judges and exerted political leverage and (at the limit) brute force to get their hands on the villagers' lands.

Díaz set his political machine in motion to make sure that Escandón was imposed as governor, but the nomination triggered a huge wave of resistance in the state. The political opposition turned to the Grand Old Man of Morelos politics, a hero of the war against the French, General Francisco Leyva, now in his seventies. Though long since marginalised by Díaz, Leyva commanded the respect of all factions in the state and he immediately agreed that his sons should run in the election to prevent an Escandón walkover. In February 1909 Patricio Leyva, the general's eldest son, put his name forward as opposition candidate.

Díaz and the *jefes políticos* were seriously alarmed at the prospect of a genuinely free contest in Morelos. After the Creelman interview, with new presidential hopefuls setting out their stalls in Mexico City, it seemed plausible for provincial dissidents to cock a snook at Díaz and his system by building links with these would-be national politicians. The Morelos opposition pinned its hopes on a newly formed party headed by Sánchez Alcona, which in turn wanted to back Bernardo Reyes for the presidency in 1910. The result was a bitter struggle between Escandón and Leyva in 1909, a struggle exacerbated by realisation of the national implications.

Rising aspirations by the 'out' groups and increased exasperation at the scandal of Escandón's imposition by the Díaz machine led to a serious riot in the town of Cuautla in February 1909. The *jefe político* there used his powers to browbeat, obstruct and threaten the *leyvistas*, using all the usual dodges such as withdrawing police permission for political meetings and then using thugs to break up any demonstrations that took place. At one of Escandón's ill-attended campaign rallies, *leyvista* heckling escalated to stone-throwing, which provoked the bloody intervention of the *rurales*. The *jefe político* put up posters declaring that any shouting of *leyvista* slogans was *ipso facto* a breach of the peace and ordered mass arrests. The resulting riots, in which fortunately there was no serious bloodshed, scared the Morelos elite and even the *leyvistas*, for they saw the spectre of class war forming.

Repression, intimidation, hostage-taking, police brutality, rigged ballots, improper distribution of voting slips, packing local polling commissions with 'safe' members: these were only some of the ways the *jefes políticos* secured the foregone conclusion of Escandón's victory. Even after all the fiddling, gerrymandering and vote-spoiling, the *leyvistas* still secured one-third of the vote, so there had to be a second wave of figure-massaging before Escandón could be declared the victor with a 'landslide'. On 15 March 1909 the playboy was sworn in as the new governor, but proved to be an almost permanent absentee, away in Mexico City visiting the fleshpots. With no strong hand on the tiller, the local bosses did exactly as they pleased, with consequent anarchy and decay in the state's services and infrastructure.

On the rare occasions when he put in an appearance, Escandón stupidly fired all the experienced Alarcón bureaucrats and gave their jobs to incompetent placemen of his own. Meanwhile he connived at the local bosses' petty, and not so petty, persecution of known *leyvistas*. If these were minor faults, his failures in macropolitics were more serious. Escandón openly, blatantly and bigotedly favoured the planters against the villagers; there was none of Alarcón's obfuscation and camouflage, none of his deals in smoke-filled rooms. The owners of the sugar plantations were now free to declare open season on the villages. The most militant village leader, Genovevo de la O of Santa Maria, later to be one of the great names in the Zapata story, very early decided that prospects of reform from within the Díaz regime were now hopeless and went into hiding, preparatory to emergence as a guerrilla leader.

Escandón's stupid and brutal actions sharpened and aggravated the already vicious social conflict in Morelos. In 1909 more and more villages were deprived of water, their cattle stolen, their lands fenced off, and all appeals to political or judicial authorities were ignored. It was now clear that Escandón aimed to break the *pueblos* as institutions, leaving an almost Marxian division between the plantocracy and a vast body of dispossessed ex-villagers who had only their labour to sell. He introduced a new valuation of the haciendas for tax purposes, grossly undervaluing them and thus allowing tax evasion by the planters to become legal tax avoidance. In June 1909 the administrator of the Hospital hacienda raised the stakes by refusing even to rent the lands it disputed with Anenecuilco to the village. A charitable view of Escandón's folly is provided by the historian John Womack, who remarks that Escandón and the planters seemed to be aiming at the 'perfect plantation' – a Platonic ideal of the hacienda that would eventually convert Morelos into hacienda-only territory, squeezing out everyone else, even shopkeepers and merchants.

This was the context in which, in September 1909, the elderly José Merino resigned as village chief of Anenecuilco and Emiliano Zapata was elected in his place. Zapata was a popular figure in the *pueblo*, known to like brandy but to drink only in moderation and conspicuous both by his dandyism and his huge moustache (later to be a worldwide trademark); he claimed that he grew it so luxuriantly so that it would set him apart from those lesser breeds 'girlish men, bullfighters and priests'. A slightly built man, no more than 5 feet 6 inches tall, Zapata had few strikes against him in village opinion. His vehement opposition to Díaz and Escandón favoured him as did his love of Anenecuilco, which (in the manner of his Indian ancestors) he seemed to imagine as a personal entity. In a macho society what might have been regarded as a blemish by later *bien-pensants* – his compulsive womanising – was regarded in Anenecuilco as a badge of honour.

Zapata had always been known as a ladies' man. He was said to be a master of seduction, in contrast with his brother Eufemio for whom courtship of a woman usually meant intimidation, violence or rape. In 1908 Emiliano had been involved in something of a scandal even by lax Morelos standards when he abducted a Cuautla woman, Inés Alfaro, set up house with her and begat three children – a son Nicolás and two daughters. Inés's mother denounced Zapata to the authorities, who gave him the minor punishment of serving a stint in the 7th Army Battalion. He bribed his way out and was back in Anenecuilco early in 1909 to take part in the *leyvista* campaign against Escandón. Yet even if the Anenecuilco villagers had been disposed to think Zapata had gone too far in his behaviour with Inés Alfaro, they would have turned a blind eye because they so esteemed Zapata's skill and reputation as a horseman.

In contrast to the men of northern Mexico, who had the wide open spaces of Sonora and Chihuahua to ride through, horsemanship of the *charro* variety was not a feat expected of Morelos males, so Zapata's prowess made an exceptional impact. The *charros* or Mexican cowboys were admired by oligarchs and peons alike. The *charro* had to prove himself by riding a wild horse barebacked. An untamed steed, deliberately starved to make it especially savage, without bridle or saddle, would be brought into a bullring. A number of cowboys would ride round and round, making the horse gallop faster and faster. At a pre-ordained sign, usually a pistol shot, the cowboy performing the stunt would then ride up at an angle to the wild animal on his own horse and, timing his movements perfectly, would vault from his own horse on to the back of the angry and agitated wild horse. With nothing, not even a mane to grip on to (since this was always roached first), the rider had to stay on board while the horse went through the entire permutation of pitching, twisting and bucking, using just his knees, legs and innate sense of balance. Usually the demonstration ended when the horse, despairing of unseating its rider, charged the enclosure railings, at which point the wise rider would jump from the horse on to the fence. It was a superb feat of horsemanship and those who saw Zapata demonstrate it swore that they had never seen a better rider in all Mexico.

Zapata carried his superb equestrian skills into bullfighting. One of the tricks was for a horseman to lasso the hind legs of a bull in the arena. When the bull had been tripped a mass of men descended on the stricken animal to put a halter on him. Once the bull was bridled, the horseman was summoned back to ride the bull as if it were a bucking bronco. An even more flamboyant trick was *coleando* or 'tailing' a bull. A young bull was driven out into the ring, and the rider rode up to it, challenging the bull to catch him. As the chase quickened, the rider would lean over, grab the tail of the steer, wrap it round his legs and then ride off at an angle so that the hindquarters of the animal were pulled crosswise. The trick required exceptional strength and dexterity but, if successfully executed, the bull would stumble and roll over on the ground. The rider would then leap from his horse before the bull recovered and throw a loop around its hind legs. Though not as expert in this as in the wild horse riding, Zapata was still rated among Morelos's best at *coleando*.

Such was Zapata's fame as a horseman that his reputation extended beyond the state. His prowess brought him not just the admiration of men and the conquest of women but tangible economic rewards. Some time before 1909 he was invited to be personal trainer and manager at the Mexico City stables of Ignacio de la Torre. De la Torre had a string of thoroughbred Arabian horses and his stables in the capital were magnificent, built like palaces, with feed mangers of marble and floors of tiny cobblestones laid in patterns. Elegant carriages were parked against the walls, their wheels always gleaming with fresh paint, their seats made of tapestry or quilted silk. Like all Morelos planters, an exponent of vulgar and meretricious 'conspicuous consumption', de la Torre shod his horses with silver and had silver tyres on his carriages. Zapata discovered, however, that de la Torre ran his 'town house' – a vast millionaire's mansion, complete with courtyard and extensive grounds – as a miniature hacienda: his peons lived in squalor in noisome hovels hard by the splendid stables and it was obvious that the *patrón* held his horses in much higher regard than his luckless employees. Disgusted, Zapata made polite excuses, left after a month and returned to Morelos. The experience left him with a conviction, never to be extinguished, that the city was a place of corruption and that goodness was to be found only in the countryside.

The role of horsemanship in Zapata's life partly explains his taste for gaudy clothes. The traditional *charro* costume consisted of a huge, broad, peaked felt hat; tight-fitting black cashmere trousers with silver buttons or a kind of silver fin down the outer seam; a white silk or linen shirt and jacket; a tight waistcoat ornamented in silver; and a scarf round the neck. Boots, spurs and a pistol at the belt would complete the ensemble, and in addition he would possess a highly ornamented saddle, a machete and a silver whip, usually made from a bull's penis, dried and twisted into rawhide with a spring in it like whalebone. Later it became the fashion for the *charro*'s jacket also to be embroidered, but this was not the custom in Zapata's time. Dandyism was usually regarded in Morelos as a manifestation of the effete *hacendados*, with their well-known taste for building 'follies', for polo ponies and landscaped gardens, but for a *charro* like Zapata an obvious exception would be made. The people of Anenecuilco were proud of their Emiliano and confident that he would make his mark as village chief.

The first task Zapata set himself was to study all the historical documents relating to the village and its lands. Among the other young men elected to village offices was Francisco Franco, the *pueblo* secretary, and together with Franco Zapata he spent eight days 'brainstorming', stopping only to eat and sleep, absorbing the history and legends of

Anenecuilco almost through his pores. Finding that many of the documents were written in Nahuatl – a tribe related to the Aztecs but by now mightily reduced in numbers and concentrated in just six villages where they made up about 10 per cent of the state's population – Zapata sent Franco to the village of Tetelcingo to hire a priest to decipher the Nahuatl writings; the priest was himself one of the last literate members of this once flourishing tribe. When all the documents, maps, title deeds, charters, legal opinions and notarised translations had been completed, Zapata put the contents in a tin box and buried it, so that his enemies could never destroy the evidence of Anenecuilco's rightful claims. Zapata had an almost fetishistic feeling about this strongbox and its contents. He told a later secretary, Serafín 'Robledo' Robles, that if the box was ever lost he would hang Robles high on a *cazahuate* tree.

Sure of his ground after such exhaustive research, Zapata now felt confident enough to confront the administrators of the Hospital hacienda. After taking the precaution of getting yet another favourable and up-to-date legal opinion, he rode to the hacienda. The manager of the Hospital was unaccommodating and answered Emiliano's petition harshly: 'If the people of Anenecuilco want to sow their seed, let them sow it in a flowerpot, because they will get no land, even on the barren slope of a hill.' Perhaps not coincidentally, Zapata was almost immediately afterwards drafted into the Army. From 11 February to 29 March 1910 he served as a private in the 9th Cavalry Regiment stationed at the state capital of Cuernavaca. Why he was demobilised after such a short time remains a mystery, but we may speculate that money played a part in such a rapid 'mustering out'.

The Hospital hacienda, evidently in collusion with governor Escandón, took advantage of Zapata's absence to put pressure on Anenecuilco, to destroy the village as a community. On his return Emiliano tried one last time for a peaceful settlement of the dispute; he wrote to Escandón for a definitive decision on ownership, knowing that he held all the trump cards in his strongbox. When Escandón failed to reply, he wrote to Díaz himself, who predictably passed the buck back to the governor. The village then decided to beard Escandón in his lair and, finding one of the rare occasions when he was in Cuernavaca, sent a delegation there. Cornered, Escandón continued to stall and asked that he be sent a complete list of all persons harmed by the actions of the Hospital hacienda. Tired of this prevarication, Zapata finally decided he had had enough. He armed eighty men, went to the disputed fields where the hacienda's labourers were working, and ordered them to depart; he added that he had no quarrel with the men personally but they were trespassers.

This was the exploit that first brought Zapata's name to a wider, non-Mexican audience. An Englishwoman named Rosa King, who owned a small hotel in Cuernavaca, wrote about a 'fellow over near Cuautla' who had been stirring the people up. This was the first appearance of the story of Zapata the troublemaker that would finally reach its apogee in the legend of the 'Attila of the South'.

Preoccupied by Madero and the other pressing problems of the year 1910, neither Díaz nor Escandón took military action against Zapata. The Hospital hacienda took no action for several months, then sent in a claim for 'rent' on 'their' land. When Zapata ignored this, the hacienda appealed to the district prefect, who ordered a preliminary hearing. At the tribunal Zapata spoke eloquently for Anenecuilco. He disputed the rightness of the Hospital claim but added that, if the verdict went against him, Anencuilco would anyway be unable to pay because of the recent bad weather and poor harvests. After hearing him and realising the depth of feeling the issue engendered, the prefect decided to postpone a final decision on this hot potato. He made an interim would-be Solomonic judgment that no rent was payable by Anenecuilco in 1910 but that the matter would be reviewed in 1911. Determined to force a resolution before that time, Zapata sent a deputation to Díaz to get the disputed lands restored permanently to Anenecuilco.

By this time Zapata, Anenecuilco and the villages of Morelos were solidly behind Madero in his struggle with Díaz, which reached a climax in the summer of 1910. Madero had a huge ideological significance for Zapata and his followers, for *maderista* propaganda had penetrated the far corners of Mexico, and the Morelos *pueblos* now realised they were not alone in their wish for reform and an end to the *Porfiriato*. By now alarmed at the threat from Madero, who had jumped bail and was in the United States, Díaz decided he could handle the troubles in the north only if he had peace in the south. To widespread amazement Díaz suddenly ordered the owners of the Hospital hacienda to return to Anenecuilco everything they had appropriated in the last forty years and pronounced Zapata's claim to the title proved beyond question. A fuming *jefe político* was forced to ride out to the Hospital hacienda to deliver this unpalatable judgement.

While the enraged *hacendados* met in conclave to decide how they could reverse or sabotage this bombshell announcement from Mexico City, and their trigger-happy guards glared at the jubilant *zapatistas* from behind the new boundaries, Anenecuilco went wild with delight. In December 1910 Zapata in person broke down the stone walls with which the Hospital had enclosed stolen land and carried out a distribution of the lands regained for the village; on his own land he planted a huge field of watermelons. A rodeo was held in Anenecuilco to celebrate this almost incredible triumph, but the euphoric Emiliano neglected his usual precautions in the bullriding and was gored by a steer. Making light of his wound, he joined with gusto in the alcoholic binges in the *pueblo*. Three centuries after the Spanish viceroy Luis de Velasco had made the original land grant to Anenecuilco (on 25 September 1607), the villagers finally got back what was due to them.

The clear-headed Zapata, however, knew this was not necessarily the end of the story. Everything would depend on the success or failure of Madero's rebellion, and Emiliano knew it had to succeed. At the turn of the year he took his first tentative step into the Mexican Revolution by sending his mentor Pablo Torres Burgos as his envoy to Madero in Texas.

The two giant states of northern Mexico, Sonora and Chihuahua could in many ways have been in a different hemisphere from Morelos, instead of being in the same country. They were separated by the Sierra Madre, and it was in Chihuahua, the very largest state – a land of cattle ranges, haciendas, mining camps and isolated towns and cities – on the broad plain between the two arms of the sierra, that much of the fighting in the Mexican Revolution would take place. Most of the north was desert, so that water was a scarce resource and the struggle for control of water supplies was a prime factor in political conflict. Naturally the problem of land was crucial but, unlike Morelos, other issues were also prominent. The northern states had long-standing traditions of federalist opposition to central control from Mexico City, had a culture of anticlericalism and, most importantly, had a common border with the USA. When Díaz consolidated his power in the 1880s he had two powerful henchmen in the north, governor Luis Torres in Sonora and Luís Terrazas in Chihuahua.

Everything here was different from the region south of Mexico City, except that here too there was an Indian problem, albeit of a very different kind. In the years 1876–1910 Sonora was the scene of the most violent resistance to Díaz and his governors by the warlike Yaquis, whose sustained war against the whites and *mestizos* was second in ferocity only to Yucatán's dreadful Wars of the Caste. Warrior for warrior, the Yaquis were probably superior even to the Mayas of Yucatán, and the sanguinary rebellion unleashed by Cajemé, the great Yaqui *cacique*, was still simmering in the 1900s. Cajemé was long dead, the victim of Ramón Corral and the *ley fuga*, but his successor Tetabiate continued the struggle. It was war to the knife, for the Yaqui sacred places and *pueblos* had been redistributed to *mestizo* settlers and colonists from the USA, who grew chickpeas and fruit for the Richardson Company, bound for markets in California.

By 1900 the Yaqui wars had scaled new heights of savagery, with an escalating pattern of atrocities. Federal troops dispatched north by Díaz mowed down women and children with their Mausers and sent the men off to a slow death on the plantations of Yucatán and Quintana Roo. The governor of Sonora cynically justified his actions by referring to Yaqui cruelty: they flayed their victims alive and strung them up with ropes made from their own skin. Díaz was keen to crush the Yaquis and used a variety of excuses for his brutality. His motives were likewise several: racial hatred, the 'improving' ideology of the *científicos* and the overriding issue of credibility – let the Yaquis alone and who knows what fresh challenger to his authority might not arise. Yet for all his efforts, the Yaquis were still undefeated when the Revolution broke out in 1910. By this time the proud Indian nation was riven by faction: there were the so-called *mansos* – corresponding to reservation Indians in the USA – who submitted to superior force and went to work in the fields; and there were the wild Yaquis or *broncos*, who remained at large as guerrillas, raiding and killing, having taken a vow to fight to the death or until the last white man had been killed. When the Revolution finally broke out in November 1910, the *mansos* enlisted under Madero's banner but the *broncos* remained in their strongholds, beholden to no man, still determined to exterminate all whites, be they revolutionaries or *porfiristas*.

Chihuahua, by contrast, had no remaining Indian problem of its own but had not long emerged from another deadly contest of red man against white. From the mid-eighteenth century there was a grave problem with Apache raids, as the desert warriors were pushed farther south by the Comanches, the 'Spartans of the plains'. The colonial authorities of New Spain bought the Apaches off and encouraged them to settle and become agriculturalists. At first independent Mexico followed the same policy, but by the 1830s the Apache problem again became acute, partly as a consequence of Santa Anna's loss of Texas. Despairing of its northern outreaches, the government in Mexico City stopped its subsidies in food and cash at almost the exact moment (as if by a perverse kind of pre-established harmony) the Apaches sensed the military weakness of the Mexicans and went on the warpath. The *hacendados* of Chihuahua fled, and only the armed peasant freeholders and military colonists, who had no choice, stayed and fought.

There followed a savage fifty-year war, with multiple atrocities on both sides. Particularly during the turbulent years of 1830–67 – when Mexico faced in rapid succession the loss of Texas, the war with the United States, the civil war between Liberals and Conservatives and finally the great patriotic war against the French – Chihuahua was virtually an independent state, with no pretence that the writ of the federal government ran there. After the defeat of the French in the late 1860s, the *hacendados* returned. Foremost among them was Luis Terrazas, founder of a powerful dynasty, an able administrator and reformer who used the tax revenues of the state to form and train anti-Apache militias instead of sending the money to Mexico City. In this he had the support of Díaz, who feared that if he did not solve the Apache problem in his northern states, the USA would use the lawlessness as a pretext to annex Sonora and Chihuahua.

The return of the *hacendados* and the determined policies of Terrazas did not happen a moment too soon, for from 1830 to 1880 some of the great names in Apache history were active in northern Mexico. In the 1830s and 1840s Cochise, the famous Chiricahua Apache chief, fought in the Apache band of Pisago Cabezón, taking part in the inconclusive battles and peace conferences with the Mexicans at the Gila River, Arizpe (Sonora) and Janos (Chihuahua). From 1847 onwards much of Sonora was laid waste in incessant Apache raids, many featuring the war chiefs Narbona and Cochise. Another widely feared Apache chief was Mangas Coloradas of the Eastern Chiricahuas, active in northern Mexico from the 1830s; such was Coloradas's hatred of the Mexicans that in 1846 he actually tried to enlist the aid of the US Army in his raids and met General Stephen Kearny for this purpose (admittedly this was during the Americans' 1846–8 war against Mexico).

One of the abiding problems with the Apaches was that they raided on both sides of the US-Mexico border, from Arizona to Texas and from Sonora to Chihuahua. This meant that a general peace, involving tripartite agreement between Americans, Mexicans and the tribes, was difficult to achieve. Mangas Coloradas did sign such a general treaty at Acomas in 1852, but it brought a lull, rather than a cessation, in the eternal cycle of murder, destruction and reprisal. In 1858 Cochise and Mangas Coloradas collaborated in a savage foray into northern Sonora to avenge the deaths of Mangas's sons and then went on to assault the Mexican fort at Fronteras Presidio. Fortunately for Mexico, the attention of both Chiricahua chiefs was taken up in subsequent years by the 'Anglos' north of the Río Grande; Mangas Coloradas suffered a gringo version of the *ley fuga* in 1863 while under arrest by the US Army, and Cochise did not send his men south of the border again until 1872.

It should not be thought that Mexico ever achieved any real respite from Apache raiding, for a peace treaty signed with one tribe in the nation did not bind the others. Other feared war chiefs active in Sonora and Chihuahua in the 1850s were Delgadito and Victorio of the Mimbres Apaches. In the summer of 1855 Victorio and Juh led a small army of their warriors in a giant sweep through Sonora and Chihuahua, returning across the US border with thousands of cattle and captives. Intercepted at Namiquipa, Chihuahua, by a powerful Mexican force, Victorio and Juh defeated them and made good their escape. The Mexicans took their revenge two years later with a 'peace offering' of food and whisky to the Mimbres, which was deliberately poisoned with arsenic; Victorio survived because he was teetotal.

The steady westward expansion of the United States brought Apaches into violent collision with the United States, and the bloody clash bought northern Mexico some breathing space. However, the years 1875–85 saw the worst Apache troubles to date. Victorio and the Mimbres appeared to have been tamed when they were placed on the San Carlos reservation in Arizona in 1877, but the Indian Agency made the mistake of trying to settle them alongside some of their ancient tribal enemies. In 1879 Victorio led his warriors off the reservation on one of the greatest exploits in Indian annals. Crucial to his success was a diversionary raid by Juh, directed from Mexico. Juh by this time had found a new ally in the shape of the Bedonkohe war chief Gerónimo, a man who hated Mexicans with a blind passion after they had massacred his mother, wife and three children at Janos, Chiricahua, in 1850.

Juh and Gerónimo raided San Carlos in August 1879 in a brilliantly executed cavalry manoeuvre that drew off the US Cavalry, allowing their ally Victorio to bolt with hundreds of warriors. At first on US territory, Victorio fought off his American pursuers in a number of skirmishes, then struck across the border into Chiricahua. Disregarding the niceties of international law, US Cavalry Major Albert Morrow followed the Apaches across the border, but in the meantime Juh and Gerónimo had doubled back from Arizona and joined Victorio. Together they turned to face Morrow and, in a grim battle fought by moonlight north-east of Janos, forced him to retreat. Victorio then moved east into the Candelaria mountains in Chihuahua, where he ambushed two companies of *rurales*, killing thirty of them without loss to himself. He then avoided the resulting hue and cry by recrossing the border into New Mexico. At this stage, however, Juh and Gerónimo felt they had had enough, surrendered and settled for a time on the San Carlos reservation.

In 1880 Victorio and his men felt secure in their mountain fastnesses of the Black Range, but the US Cavalry trapped them in a canyon there and heavily defeated them. The Mimbres would probably have been annihilated had not the Americans run short of ammunition at the vital moment, allowing Victorio to slip away into Mexico once more. Yet again they made their base in the Candelaria mountains, but wasted precious time by fruitless attempts to penetrate the heavily patrolled border with

Texas, hoping to raise the Mescalero Apaches of eastern New Mexico in revolt. These abortive ventures alerted the Mexican authorities to their presence. Porfirio Díaz, nagged by Chihuahua governor Luis Terrazas, at last released some regular army units, and, together with a large party of *rurales* he had collected, the governor's cousin, Colonel Joaquín Terrazas, finally felt strong enough for a decisive reckoning with Victorio. After a long and patient campaign, Terrazas laid a successful ambush in the Tres Castillos hills. On 15 October Victorio and his main war band were cornered. This time it was the Apache ammunition that gave out first, but they fought to the last man with lance and bow and arrow. The Apaches lost seventy-eight warriors dead; sixty-eight women and children were taken prisoner. Colonel Terrazas lost just three militiamen dead and ten wounded, earned $17,250 for the scalps of the dead warriors, and was lionised as a frontier hero.

Mexico was particularly proud that its men had succeeded in ending the Mimbres menace where the fabled US Cavalry had failed, but Victorio's death at Tres Castillos by no means ended the Apache menace. The Mimbres war leader Nana, who was commanding one of Victorio's flanking columns and thus escaped annihilation by Terrazas, struck back in 1881 in one of the legendary Apache raids. Beginning in New Mexico, he covered more than 1,000 miles in his devious circling flight back to the Sierra Madre in Chihuahua, during which his handful of warriors, never more than forty and often only fifteen, fought dozens of skirmishes, killed nearly fifty Americans and took more than two hundred stolen horses and mules across the frontier with them.

Since Nana was joined in the Sierra Madre by Gerónimo and Juh, who had once again left the San Carlos reservation, the authorities on both sides of the Río Grande feared a rerun of the Victorio campaign. Díaz therefore instructed Luis Terrazas to cooperate fully with the North Americans and allow their forces to cross into Mexico in pursuit. Washington meanwhile assigned its greatest Indian fighter, General George Crook, to the task of pacifying the Apache. Crook's 1883 expedition into the Sierra Madre was in its own way as remarkable as the exploits of Victorio, Juh and Nana. Taking only one company of cavalry, but using 200 Apache scouts to enable him to locate the enemy quickly, Crook achieved the noteworthy feat of talking Nana and Gerónimo back to the San Carlos reservation; Juh pointedly avoided Crook and could have been a continuing headache but fell off his horse while crossing the Casas Grandes river in Chihuahua in November 1883 and drowned. In 1885 Nana and Gerónimo again jumped the reservation and spent seventeen months raiding from their mountain bases in northern Mexico, but once again it was Crook who coaxed them back to San Carlos in March 1886.

That was the end of the Apache problem in northern Mexico: Gerónimo's final raid, in late 1886, was a purely US-based affair. However, the importance of the Apache factor in the nineteenth-century history of Chihuahua cannot be overemphasised. It formed the people of Chihuahua in a martial culture, made taking up arms to solve problems seem like second nature, and (following Tres Castillos) greatly increased the prestige of the dominant Terrazas family.

Victorio was still spreading terror through northern Mexico when the man who would be known to history and legend as Pancho Villa was born. On 6 June 1878 a son, Doroteo, was born to Agustín Arango, the illegimate son of one Jesús Villa, and a sharecropper on the Rancho de la Loyotada, which was part of one of the largest haciendas in Durango state, owned by the López Negrete family. Both Agustín Arango and his wife Micaela Arambula were indigent peasants from poor families. Agustín died young, leaving Micaela and five children to fend for themselves. Doroteo, the eldest child, never went to school and from an early age had to support his family by toiling on the El Gorgojito ranch, also owned by the López Negrete clan.

According to tradition, and his own account, the young Doroteo Arango became an outlaw at the age of sixteen, after don Agustín López Negrete tried to rape his sister Martina or (in some versions) demanded that she become his concubine. Not long after this he changed his name to Francisco ('Pancho') Villa, on the grounds that his grandfather's name was Villa. Dating this traumatic incident precisely to 22 September 1894, Villa claimed that he shot Negrete in the foot to stop his predatory advances towards his sister, as a result of which Negrete's men were about to execute him, but the *hacendado* forbade it. Fearing that Negrete might have second thoughts or have him arrested, Villa fled into the mountains of Durango.

It is typical of the obscurity that surrounds all aspects of Villa's early life that even those scholars who accept this story cannot agree on its details. Who was Agustín López Negrete? Some say he was the son of the owner of the hacienda, others that he was the administrator. According to another version, the gunshot wound was more serious, Villa tried to flee, was caught, jailed and then given a death sentence under the *ley fuga* for 'trying to escape'. Villa then wounded his jailer with a pestle and made his getaway.

Thereafter Villa claimed to have had all manner of hair-raising adventures: eluding posses, being captured and then escaping, outwitting unskilled *rurales*, outwitting soldiers. Eventually he joined a 'supergroup' of outlaws led by Ignacio Parra and Refugio Alvarado. From being a fugitive, eking out a bare living, he became a left-handed form of entrepreneur: his share of the loot in the first week with Alvarado was 3,000 pesos – ten times what a peon in the fields of Chihuahua would get in a year. Shortly afterwards the gang robbed a wealthy miner of 150,000 pesos, of which Villa's share was 50,000. He claimed to have spent it all within a year, probably on high living, but, by the time he told the story of his early years, he was keen to portray himself as a 'social bandit', so claimed he gave most of it away to his family or on charitable work. Keen to burnish his image as a latter-day Robin Hood, the myth-making Villa later claimed: 'After eight or ten months I had returned to the poor the money the rich had taken from them.'

When his money ran out, for whatever reason, Villa returned to the gang. By this time Parra was the most famous bandit in Durango, the king of the mountains, prestigious enough to have the hitherto most notorious bandit in the state, Heraclio Bernal, serving under him; Bernal and his four brothers had been the scourge of Durango in the 1880s. Just as Villa was to learn from Parra, so Parra had learned from the Bernals, and the most vital lesson he digested was the importance of cultivating good relations with peasant support networks; if you paid your way with hard cash in the villages, the peasants would always protect you against the authorities. Parra added the refinement that a good bandit leader would also have secret friends among the forces of law and order. He befriended, bribed, or intimidated judges and police chiefs so that, if apprehended, he would receive light sentences or even find the authorities turning a blind eye. In these years Villa undoubtedly made the acquaintance of corrupt judges and magistrates who would serve him well in the future.

In 1902 Villa learned just how valuable such contacts were. The first record of him in official Porfirian documents mentions him as one of Parra's band, but shortly afterwards he fell out with him – he alleged it was because Parra had gunned down a harmless old man who would not sell him bread. This was a slice of luck for Villa; almost immediately after he had left the gang, Parra was shot in a gun battle with state police. Clearly in straitened circumstances, Villa was arrested in January 1901 for stealing two mules. He was saved from the inevitable *ley fuga* death sentence for such an offence by the powerful black marketeer Pablo Valenzuela, to whom the Parra gang used to sell stolen cattle. Primed by Valenzuela, on whose payroll he was, the judge in the case dismissed the charge 'for lack of evidence'. Always a man to push his luck, Villa was rearrested four days later for assault and robbery. This time there had to be some punishment, so he was sentenced to a year's service in the Army.

In March 1902 he deserted and, finding Durango too dangerous, fled to Chihuahua, where he made his base of operations thereafter. Some say Villa worked in mines in Arizona for a time and on the railways in Colorado, but Villa later told his secretary Ramón Puente that he was never in the USA: at the time he was supposed to be among the gringos he was actually running a butcher's shop in the city of Hidalgo del Parral. The story of Villa in the USA seems to be a corruption of the verifiable fact that he did work for a short period for two American citizens, named Stilwell and Burkhead, who were particularly impressed by Villa's knowledge of cockfighting. Villa seems to have worked for the Americans as a mule driver, which came in handy later: he was able to cite Stilwell and Burkhead as character witnesses when his bandit past threatened to catch up with him.

The fact of the butcher's shop would seem to be well based. According to one story, Villa suddenly saw the light and realised that a life of banditry would lead only to the gallows. After working as a miner, mason and brickmaker, he had to flee when his true identity was discovered. For a while he rustled cattle and tried to sell them on the Chihuahua meat market, but could not make a go of his butchery business, as the Terrazas, the owners of the slaughterhouses, would not give him access. Refused permission to slaughter his own cattle on their high-technology premises, and unwilling to pay the middleman's commission, Villa gave up the idea of becoming a career butcher. Again he tried mining, again his identity was discovered and again he fled, this time turning to the only sure-fire way he knew of making a living: cattle rustling.

Here again the noose might be thought to be beckoning but Villa escaped the hangman, or the executioner's bullet, mainly it seems for two reasons, one cultural, the other personal. Every state had its mortal and venial sins, a consequence of the extreme localism in mores and folkways already noted. Banditry was frowned on in Chihuahua while being a bagatelle in Durango, but in Chihuahua cattle rustling did not attract anything like the same stigma and opprobrium as banditry. The main reason was that the people of Chihuahua simply did not accept the self-assigned right of the hegemonic Terrazas family to end open range and fence it in. On the personal level, Villa traded with a black marketeer, who was also a small rancher and butcher, and disposed of his stolen stock that way. Using black market contacts and the references from his

American employers, Villa was able to navigate his way through the criminal rapids.

The more research that is done on Villa's early life, the more tangled the conjectural chronology becomes. From other sources we learn that he was employed for a time transporting and protecting huge payrolls (as large as 700,000 pesos) for the US-owned North-western Railroad. Another story is that he was employed for eighteen months as a muleteer by a wealthy Englishman, that he proved to be a tough hombre but honest: in charge of transporting ingots of gold and silver he never lost any and was never robbed. Probably the most we can say with certainty about Villa's life until 1910 is that he alternated bouts of banditry with periods of 'normal' existence. The American scholar Friedrich Katz, who has made the most thorough study of Villa's early life, has identified the core problem: there is no agreed history of the first thirty years in Villa's biography but three different traditions, which Katz labels the black, white and epic legends. The black legend makes out that Villa was a double-dyed psychopath, motivated only by hatred and revenge; the white that he was a simple man wanting a simple life who was catapulted reluctantly into a revolutionary milieu; and the epic that he was no bandit lusting only after loot but a genuine Robin Hood, desirous of righting wrongs, taking from the rich to give to the poor.

As Katz points out, each interpretation is backed by circumstantial evidence. Villa claimed that poverty, corrupt officials and the *ley fuga* turned him and a host of other Mexicans into outlaws and, later, revolutionaries, in short that he was a victim of the 'system'. It was well known that the López Negretes were extremely ruthless men, and it is entirely plausible that the young Villa might have suffered under them. Nor is there anything implausible in Villa's story that he was hounded by the Terrazas and their tame police authorities. On the other hand, if all he wanted was a quiet life, why did he not settle down with the 50,000 pesos he had received from the great Ignacio Parra raid instead of (allegedly) giving it to the poor? Even Villa admitted that his mother taxed him about this.

Moreover, the entire story about saving his sister from rape is suspect in its detail; there is no agreement in the traditional accounts even on the identity of the would-be rapist – was it López Negrete senior, the *hacendado*, his son, the hacienda administrator, a sheriff or simply another peon? Villa's critics use the discrepancies in the various versions of the story to argue that the entire story of his early life, including the raped sister, is a fabrication and that Villa was never more than a simple murderer. What is probable is that the 'white' legend is largely the result of Villa's reflections on his life *after* he had received a political education from the *maderista* agent Abraham González in 1910 and that his own account contains more than its fair share of rationalisation.

The 'black' legend of Villa is equally unconvincing, if only because we know that most of the stories in this dossier emanate from the Herrera family, who were involved in a blood feud with him after 1910. The Herrera version denies things we know to be fact, such as Abraham González's patronage of him, and requires almost every criminal act in northern Mexico in the first decade of the century to be the work of Villa. According to his enemies there was almost no enormity he did not commit, ranging from disembowelling to forcing men to dig their own graves before shooting them. In short, Villa was accused of so many crimes that he would have needed to bilocate to have committed them. In this context one is reminded of the sardonic words of the old Australian folk song about the Ned Kelly gang: 'I think I'll steal a horse myself and blame it on the Kellys.' Substitute 'Villa' for 'the Kellys' and you have the encapsulated form of the Herrera version of history.

Yet in some ways John Reed, the celebrated American left-wing journalist and chief promoter of the 'epic' or Robin Hood interpretation of Villa, does give hostages to fortune in his account of Villa's rise to prominence. Reed claimed that in 1901–9 Villa certainly murdered four people and was involved in ten premeditated crimes, including arson, robbery, rustling and kidnapping. The snag about the John Reed view – Villa as champion of the peasantry and scourge of the Terrazas – is that it requires him to be a person of far more importance in Chihuahua before 1910 than he actually was. Given that the same critique knocks the 'black legend' on the head, we need to ask why Madero's political agents should have been so keen to recruit Villa's services in 1910. Would the Madero agent in Chihuahua, Abraham González, really have been interested in Chihuahua's 'public enemy number one' if Villa had been either the Robin Hood of John Reed's imagination or the Jack the Ripper of the Herreras' frenzied fantasies? Documentary evidence from 1910 clearly shows Villa arrested for minor offences, released and even given his gun back, which would scarcely have happened if he was Chihuahua's 'most wanted' man.

Because Villa was not an intellectual – indeed he was not much more than basically literate by 1910 – it has been assumed that he could not have been a 'real' revolutionary, that he must always have been actuated by the desire for loot. However, Abraham González was very far from a fool, and he must have seen in Villa something more than a gun-toting thug when he took him under his wing in 1910. Old-fashioned writers, even ones as distinguished as John Steinbeck, referred to Villa as 'nothing but' a bandit. The entire academic industry relating to 'social bandits', pioneered by Eric Hobsbawm and others, has made us aware that there is no automatic law of excluded middle operating between 'bandit' and 'revolutionary'. To take the most simple example, Che Guevara in the Bolivian jungle in 1967 was, looked at from one point of view, a bandit; but from another he was very clearly a revolutionary. There were in fact compelling reasons why Villa's early banditry could be seen to have objective socio-economic causes. John Reed was on the right lines when he identified the Terrazas as the problem, but he did not pursue his analysis far enough.

Even before his spectacular success against the Apaches, Luis Terrazas had been looking ahead, planning the next stage in his master plan for the dominance by his family of Chihuahua. He began by using his power as governor to acquire vast estates, either buying up land cheaply or expropriating the haciendas of the pro-French proprietors who had backed the wrong side in the 1860s. Soon it was the turn of the courageous but luckless military colonists, the people who had tamed the land and fought the Apaches. As soon as the Apaches were defeated, now that he no longer needed the free villages and the military colonies to provide manpower for his militias, Terrazas began filching their land and curtailing all their customary rights and privileges, such as hunting and wood gathering. Private acquisition of water supplies, fencing grazing land and the erection of barbed wire fences were just some of Terrazas's methods; taxing farming, the removal of local autonomy, and corrupt *jefes políticos* ruling through graft, corruption and nepotism were further weapons. In addition, the military colonist soon learned that Porfirio Díaz was a more dangerous enemy than Victorio, Juh and Nana had ever been: the colonists' position was further impaired by the coming of the railways and the telegraph, the opening of mines and the flood of foreign investment entering the state.

It mattered not who the ordinary people of Chihuahua were. Whether they were the original settlers from the colonial period, the military colonists from the independence period, traditional Indian villagers, squatters on public land or the genuinely landless occupying common land by prescriptive right, they were all swept into the maw of big capitalism. In the USA, the 1862 Homestead Act had, at least in theory, opened up lands owned by the state to a new class of small landowners. Díaz did not even attempt to go down that road. Instead he sold off huge swathes of public land to giant capitalists, whether the domestic variety like Terrazas or, more controversially, large foreign corporations like

Standard Oil. In the late nineteenth century Chihuahua was a microcosm of Mexico itself. Rising gross national product and foreign investment were matched at the state level, there was a flourishing export trade with Europe and the USA, and the alliance between the national oligarchy and foreign investors provided an arrangement perfectly beneficial to both. Terrazas was even an imitation Díaz: strikes were outlawed, dissidents murdered and the press muzzled.

Such was the dominance of Terrazas that his Banco Minero de Chihuahua was either broker or partner in all foreign investment schemes in the state. His political control was absolute and his power so great that he could even nudge Díaz on occasion. The dictator thought it the better part of valour to ignore Terrazas's support for Lerdo in 1876 and contented himself with wresting formal political control from Terrazas in the years 1884–1903. Nobody doubted, however, that Terrazas was the real power in the state, and that don Porfirio's regime depended for stability on the coexistence between him and Chihuahua's strongman. Only in the 1890s did Terrazas have to fire a warning shot across Díaz's bows. Fearing that Terrazas was becoming too powerful, Díaz nominated one of Terrazas's enemies, Lauro Carrillo, as governor. Terrazas decided to teach Díaz the facts of Chihuahuan life by discrediting Carrillo. He tacitly engineered a rising at Tomóchi which he knew Carrillo would not be able to contain. In the end Díaz would be forced to turn to Terrazas for a solution.

Inter-elite rivalry was thus the deep cause for the Tomóchi affair, which showed Díaz there were limits to his power. Tomóchi was a village in western Chihuahua where, thanks to some adroit behind-the-scenes manipulation by Terrazas, an insignificant revolt snowballed into a major confrontation between veterans of the Apache wars and federal troops sent by Carrillo. The federals were defeated again and again by the doughty Indian fighters, even when the odds were ten to one in their favour, and this demonstration of military incompetence by the Army encouraged resistance elsewhere in Mexico. Díaz's prestige was badly damaged and he was forced to ditch Carrillo. Once Terrazas achieved his aim of ousting the governor, he pulled the plug on the Tomóchi revolt. Starved of arms and money from Terrazas, the Tomóchi rebels could not go on.

Bowing to the inevitable, realising there was no power in Chihuahua except Terrazas, Díaz formally co-opted him in 1903 by appointing him governor of Chihuahua. Constrained by bonds of honour to the villages and military colonists, the machiavellian Terrazas baulked at openly crushing them. He therefore resigned his office, pleading old age, and handed over the reins to his son-in-law Enrique Creel, who had made no promises and commitments to villagers or colonists. Creel turned on these unfortunates ruthlessly. He and his family coveted new land so that they could make a killing from land speculation. The key was the new railways, for the Mexican North-western line, the Kansas Orient and the Pacific Railroad were all laying track through Chihuahua. In 1904–5 Creel passed two laws of special moment: the first replaced elected heads of municipalities with officials appointed by the governor; the second amended Juárez's 1857 legislation so that the state, not the federal government, became the final arbiter in the case of expropriation of village lands. Creel's hatred of the free villages was noteworthy. Apart from the fact that they were an obstacle to his money-making schemes, he seems to have genuinely detested them as a 'fetter' on economic progress in general; in short Creel was a genuine *científico* ideologue.

Creel picked off the least sophisticated Indian villages and non-Spanish speakers first. Expropriations immediately created a new class of landless labourers, whose only recourse was an appeal to Mexico City. Appellants to the capital would then be given the runaround, told to appeal from local authorities to governors and then to state courts in a meaningless vicious circle – meaningless because Creel controlled everything and there was no way to break out of it.

Once Creel was confident of total support from Díaz, he began to move against the hardcore of ancient military colonies. First, he refused to accept any custom-hallowed traditional rights. In the case of agreements legally entered into, he asked to see the title deeds; often there were none, or they had been deliberately destroyed. When copies of the originals were requested from the archives in Mexico City, Díaz's bureaucrats would refuse to accede to the request, or would tell the truth but not the whole truth: for example by saying that no such deed existed in the National Archive, knowing full well it was in the provincial archives.

It is at first sight surprising that Creel's chicanery did not trigger armed rebellion, but conditions were different from those during the Tomóchi revolt of 1891–5. Then there was economic depression, but now there was boom, with rising wages and, at least in the short term, plenty of openings for the dispossessed villagers. More importantly, this time there was no hidden hand of Luis Terrazas manipulating events; the Creel-Terrazas clique was monolithic and there were no divisions in the Chihuahua elite.

However, just as Díaz had eventually decided that Luis Terrazas was too powerful and tried (unsuccessfully) to clip his wings, so he now felt that Creel needed to be taken down a peg. Fearing that the more militant villages could be pushed too far, and he would have another Tomóchi on his hands, Díaz counselled Creel to ease up on his programme of expropriations. Creel contemptuously rejected the advice, arguing that any such concessions would be perceived as weakness. Angered by Creel's attitude, Díaz suddenly declared in correspondence with the governor that his 1905 Land Law was unconstitutional – a direct slap in the face. Creel retaliated by an implicit threat of rebellion, saying that those who would be dispossessed, through having obtained land by the 1905 law, were among the most powerful men in Chihuahua and would surely revolt. Once again, Díaz backed off, leaving the villagers, whose hopes had been raised by his intervention, high and dry. Once Díaz capitulated, Creel moved against the recalcitrant villagers with even greater harshness.

Chihuahua under Creel was a divided society, with a clear line demarcating the haves from the have-nots. The unfortunate villagers who declined were balanced by those who managed to cash in on the land bonanza and its spin-offs: these included artisans, urban shopkeepers, small ranchers, miners and other employees of foreign enterprises. However, ranged alongside the dispossessed villagers were the rural shopkeepers who had depended on them for a living and, more importantly, many local magnates who would have been elected to high office if Creel had not abolished elections and imposed his own nominees. Gradually the tide of dissidence increased, informed not just by nostalgia for the old days of village autonomy but backed up also by anti-American xenophobia and resentment at the privileges granted US nationals over Mexicans.

Anti-Americanism as a phenomenon should not be overstated, but it did make some headway in the final years of the Díaz regime, especially among railwaymen and mineworkers. Chihuahua was fertile ground for the anarcho-syndicalist revolutionary *magonista* party, led from exile in Texas by the Magón brothers who preached spontaneous revolution by the peasantry, which intellectuals would head as a 'vanguard'; the problem was that the peasantry required leaders *before* they would rebel. The *magonistas* also called for all who invested in Mexico to become Mexican citizens, as well as for no re-election for four-year presidents. Their particular target in Chihuahua was the Mormon settlers, protected by Creel, who were hated thrice over: they practised polygamy, were hostile to Catholicism and had bought up expropriated land. The *magonista* movement did not make the impact expected, partly because it was honeycombed by Creel's spies, not to mention Díaz's, and was subject to systematic persecution on both sides of the Río Grande.

Moderate non-violent opposition to the Creel-Terrazas coterie in Chihuahua came mainly from Silvestre Terrazas, one-time secretary to the bishop of Chihuahua and a man destined to play an important part in the life of Pancho Villa. A journalist of great talent and courage, Silvestre Terrazas founded the newspaper *El Correo*. At first he trod carefully, never criticising Díaz directly, but using the anti-capitalist ideas of the Catholic Church in the papal encyclical *Rerum Novarum* to mount a subtle critique of US penetration of the Mexican economy. After 1906, however, *El Correo* had Creel and Luis Terrazas firmly in its sights. Silvestre Terrazas introduced the novel idea that Creel had no right to be governor, for Creel's father was a US citizen and, according to Mexican law, the fathers of all state governors had to be native-born. Soon *El Correo* was the focus for all legal opposition in Chihuahua, whether this meant backing strikes or resisting the expropriation of villages. Silvestre Terrazas became a marked man in the eyes of the regime, and was jailed for long periods in 1907, 1909 and 1910. Díaz dared not have him assassinated, however, for Terrazas had an international reputation.

By 1909 politics in Chihuahua had reached a brittle, pre-revolutionary stage, compounded by the Creel-Terrazas assault on the villages, the general national political crisis involving Madero's challenge to Díaz, and the consequences of the 1908 economic depression, which hit Chihuahua harder than other parts of Mexico. Mines closed down as the world price of silver and copper plummeted; food prices shot up because of bad harvests; and Creel responded to these events by raising taxes (to compensate for falling revenues) on the very people who could least afford them. As the villagers shimmered in anger at Creel's class war – there were no augmented taxes on his *hacendado* cronies or on foreign capitalists – an event happened that, so to speak, put the cap on Chihuahua's general crisis of political legitimacy.

Enrique Creel and his brother Juan owned their own bank, the Banco Minero. Suddenly, in March 1908, it was announced that 300,000 pesos had been stolen from the vaults. Suspects were rounded up and tortured to extract confessions, but Silvestre Terrazas caused a sensation by revealing in *El Correo*, with an unimpeachable list of affidavits and alibis, that all the charges were trumped up; there had been no robbery; the theft was an 'inside job' and Juan Creel had arranged to have his own bank robbed because, it seemed, he had lost 200,000 pesos playing the New York stock exchange and needed to replace the money quickly. Nobody reading Silvestre Terrazas's lucid account could possibly doubt that Juan Creel was the real culprit. His brother at once arrested Silvestre Terrazas and tried to muzzle the press, but the damage to the Creels' credibility was done. Coinciding with Madero's nationwide presidential candidacy, this *cause célèbre* in Chihuahua merely underlined the rottenness of the entire Díaz system.

Such was the political and economic context of the society in which Pancho Villa spent his twenties, erratically tacking in and out of normal life and legal activity. The schizoid nature of his existence can be gauged from two simple facts: in 1909 Villa led a gang of desperadoes on a raid, during which they burned down the town hall and archives of Rosario in the Hidalgo district; yet the following year he bought himself a house in Chihuahua city, as if he were a solid bourgeois.

The zigzag pattern in and out of banditry was even more pronounced in 1910. There is something Zorro-like about the way Villa conducted his parallel military and civilian lives in this year of decision. On the one hand, Villa was building up his reputation as a bandit chief and building up the nucleus of a guerrilla army. Early in 1910 he and his men raided the San Isidro ranch, ransacking the place and killing the owner and his young son. In October he and Tomás Urbina, his most prominent lieutenant robbed the Talamontes ranch in the Jiménez district of Chihuahua. In July 1910 came his most famous pre-revolutionary exploit. One of his comrades, Claro Reza sold him out to the authorities and fingered him as a bandit. Villa retaliated coldly and violently by gunning him down in the streets of Chihuahua City. There are various versions of this event, but John Reed's account may well be the most accurate: Villa was eating ice cream on the Paseo Bolívar (he always had a passion for ice cream) when he saw Reza approach with a girlfriend. He challenged Reza to draw, gunned him down, then nonchalantly strolled away, defying bystanders to do anything about it.

Yet at the same time he was building up contacts among the opposition to Creel and Díaz. He certainly met the editor Silvestre Terrazas in 1910, but perhaps even more important was the encounter with Abraham González, Madero's political agent in Chihuahua. González had every reason to remember his first brush with Villa. It had been arranged by intermediaries that they would meet after dark at the headquarters of the Anti-Re-electionist Party in Chihuahua City; Villa and his comrade Feliciano Domínguez went to the rendezvous with serapes pulled over their faces. González approached his office just as Villa arrived and reached into his back pocket to take out his office keys. In the darkness Villa mistook the movement for a quick draw. To his amazement González found two cocked pistols pointing at his head. Calmly he reassured Villa as to his intentions, and Villa was so taken with González's utter fearlessness that he became an admirer on the spot.

Once inside the office, González gave Villa a brief history lesson and explained the aims of his party. He pointed out that so-called bandits could be seen as political rebels, and that Madero would wipe the slate clean for all his supporters. This was a key event in 'consciousness raising'. Immediately Villa saw how everything fitted into place, how the hardships of his own life made sense in the overall social and political context. He became Abraham González's ardent disciple. Some sceptics have queried why González should have wanted to concern himself with a minor bandit, but it is likely that Silvestre Terrazas had had a preliminary interview with Villa and recommended him highly. Certainly Villa always revered González thereafter and always spoke of him with affection. González also introduced Villa to his chief when Madero came to Chihuahua City. According to one story, Madero interviewed Villa at the Palacio Hotel. Tearfully Villa poured out the story of his life, as if to a priest, and asked Madero's forgiveness for his sins. Madero granted him absolution and told him the Revolution would redeem him. Where cynics say that Villa used the Mexican Revolution to legitimate his own murderous instincts, more sympathetic critics are inclined to see Villa's long commitment to the Revolution as a quest for redemption.

It is certain that after he became involved with Abraham González, the Creel-Terrazas clique identified Villa as a dangerous enemy. Why had they not done so before? Possibly the answer is that before 1910 Villa was not – or at least was not perceived to be – a danger to the elite, and they took the complaisant attitude to banditry that the FBI is said to take towards the Mafia: it's just one set of mobsters killing another. However, three things changed in 1910. First Villa became more confident or more cavalier. He stepped up his rustling activities, selling huge herds under an alias, and he took part in a raid on the hacienda of Talamontes. Next he killed Claro Reza who, unknown to him, was a police informer of long standing (Reza had actually taken *rurales* into the mountains to capture Villa by treachery, but he escaped by mere chance. Villa intercepted correspondence making clear Reza's spy status). Finally, most worrying of all for the Terrazas and Creel, the bandit was becoming politicised by his contacts with Abraham González and Madero.

We can form a very accurate picture of Villa on the eve of his great exploits. Aged thirty-two, 5 feet 10 inches in height, weighing 170 pounds, he was muscular with a strongly protruding lower jaw, badly stained teeth, crinkly black hair and a thick black moustache that made him look like a Hollywood heavy. People commented most of all on his hypnotic brown eyes that held and dominated the listener like a snake with a mouse, or seemed to strike sparks when he was angry. He was a great horseman, who rode straight and stiff-legged, Mexican style and so loved horses that he won the soubriquet 'the Centaur of the North'. He could ride 100 miles over mountain trails in a single 24-hour span. He dressed plainly, with none of the stereotypical Latin love of glamour and the meretricious. As for his prowess as a quick-draw gunfighter, one anecdote is eloquent. Silvestre Terrazas once asked him to hit a tiny branch of wood that was floating on a river 200 yards away. Villa drew his pistol, took deliberate aim and shot the piece of wood into two equal chips.

He was hugely respectful of learning, passionate about education and deeply regretful about his own ignorance; sometimes he would tearfully confess himself out of his depth in intellectual matters. He was the classic case of the man who comes through from obscurity purely because of revolution, in this respect resembling Bernadotte, Hoche, Humbert and Augereau of the Revolutionary and Napoleonic period in France. It is extremely unlikely that the world would ever have heard of Pancho Villa had there not been a Mexican Revolution, for his lowly origins, his lack of education and family ties, his political inexperience and his reputation as a bandit would all have marginalised him. Not even his great energy – a quality he possessed in abundance and more so than any other personality in the Revolution – would have availed him if he had been born in 1858 instead of 1878.

Villa neither smoked nor drank, and used no drugs, but he liked to sing and dance. Emotionally he was not an integrated person, as he had no middle range. Volatile and manic-depressive, he could run the gamut of emotions with astonishing quick-change rapidity, veering from anger to tears or from generosity to cruelty within minutes. Highly intelligent and shrewd except when his judgement was clouded by anger, he was an implacable hater though steadfastly loyal to those he respected. He was a compulsive womaniser who raised the idea of serial monogamy to a new power. He liked to humour his women by going through bogus marriage ceremonies: one of his earliest 'wives' was Petra Espinosa whom he abducted and with whom he lived for a short time in Parral.

Comparisons with Zapata are instructive. Born within a year of each other, both men had been in trouble with the authorities, served time under duress in the Army and acquired intellectual mentors; both were outstanding horsemen, dedicated womanisers and both had singularly useless brothers (Hipólito Villa in this respect being fully the equal of Eufemio Zapata). Both lived in violent times, but the milieu of Chihuahua was 'organically' violent, as that of Morelos was not, largely because of the frontier tradition of the north and the long wars against the Apache. In the short term, Zapata faced far the more difficult task as a revolutionary leader. For Villa, revolts in the northern sierras could mobilise the entire community in pan-regional 'popular front' resistance with trans-class coalitions and no class traitors, in part because rebellion in the north was concerned with local autonomy as well as land. Conflicts in the north were not just peasants and peons against landlords but often the whole locality in arms against the central government.

Because of their martial traditions, the men of Chihuahua and Sonora were more explosive and less long-suffering than the Morelos peasants or Yucatán peons, and their military traditions made them more capable of armed resistance; put simply, for them the transition from protest to guerrilla warfare was much easier. Villa had the military advantage that the armies he raised would all be cavalry armies, formed of sharpshooters who had honed their skills in frontier wars. Additionally, he could escape across the border to the USA, or import arms from North America more easily. Moreover, it was easier to co-opt northern rebels as they sought no major socio-economic changes and still less a classless utopia, but wanted merely freedom from interference from Mexico City and freedom to live undisturbed in a macho, martial culture.

Zapata, however, did have some compensating advantages. For the very same reasons, revolt once initiated in the south was more difficult to suppress or turn off. Since there was no real ideological content in the northern rebellions, and even in what later came to be called Villismo, it was just as easy for the central government to co-opt these movements, or buy off and suborn the leaders with money and lands. It is clear that the issue of land *was* important in Chihuahua, but in terms of the revolutionary slogan *Tierra y Libertad*, perhaps the second was the more important in the north. Villa had none of Zapata's mystical feeling about the soil or about the village as personality. He was more of a political opportunist, proactive where Zapata was reactive. In 1910 he showed this clearly by being first into the revolutionary breach. Three days before Madero's call for a general rising on 20 November expired, Villa and four comrades he had recruited from his cattle-rustling days attacked the hacienda of Chavarría to obtain horses, money and supplies. Meeting resistance, they fought their way into the hacienda, killing the administrator. Villa's life as bandit had ended and his career as a glorious hero of the Revolution had begun.

As Madero's 20 November deadline approached, tensions in Mexico were screwed tight. At the very last moment it even appeared that potential revolutionary energies would be dissipated in anti-Americanism. On 3 November 1910 in Texas, a young Mexican accused of murdering a woman was dragged out of jail by a mob and lynched. Throughout Mexico there was a spontaneous explosion of anti-gringo riots. Genuine revolutionaries used the turmoil to foment dissatisfaction with Díaz, allegedly the protector of the tens of thousands of *yanquis* in Mexico, and the aged dictator had to allow the anti-American inferno to rage unabated, fearful that he himself might be swept away in the whirlwind. Also, he calculated that the turmoil could be contained within the system, for the demonstrators were mostly students or the urban middle classes. Where people depended for their jobs on the gringo, as in Sonora, where the greatest volume of US investment was located, there were no riots.

Yet to thoughtful observers the wave of anti-American disturbances that swept across the country was evidence of a new edginess in the people, of a volatility that had not been there before. However, at first, the *maderistas* were unable to capitalise on it. All their early attempts to engineer risings in the cities came to nothing; many Madero agents were either arrested or gave up in despair. In retrospect, the problem was that the *maderistas* were aiming at a mere palace revolution or political transfer of power, to be carried out by urban middle-class intellectuals. At this stage rural guerrilla warfare was not a perceived option, and the few people who tried to launch revolt in the countryside chose the wrong areas. One of Madero's chief agents, Colmenares Ríos, left Veracruz with copies of the Plan of San Luis and went first to Orizaba, where he found the *maderista* movement in chaos. He then headed south for the hot lowlands of the isthmus, where he knew the terrain, and linked up with seventy disorganised and badly armed guerrillas in the Tabasco plantations. Unable to attract more recruits, the guerrillas wandered around for a time in a daze, constantly harried by federal troops. When desertions reduced the sorry band to no more than a dozen, Colmenares declared the rising at an end and returned in disgust to Veracruz.

First blood in the struggle clearly went to Díaz. In Puebla police went to search the house of an important *maderista*, Aquiles Serdán, a cobbler. Serdán's extended family happened to be in the house at the time, feelings ran high, and armed resistance ensued. In the shoot-out the police chief of Puebla was killed; the police called up reinforcements, sealed off the house, picked off Serdán's most courageous sharpshooters and forced a handful of survivors to surrender. Nobody lifted a finger to help Serdán, who was taken out and shot, even though Puebla had featured as a key area in *maderista* plans. Madero's men in Puebla were cowed, and energetic police action in other states in central Mexico made his supporters go to ground. At Orizaba the federal garrison easily beat off a rebel attack, while elsewhere in central Mexico police dragnets hauled in some prize catches, including eventually Alfredo Robles Domínguez, the man who was supposed to ignite the rebellion for Madero in the south.

Madero received the news of these early setbacks gloomily as he prepared to cross the Río Grande. His own operation scarcely began propitiously. On the morning of Sunday 20 November he rode down to the banks of the river, intending to cross, on the assumption that his uncle Catarino would be waiting for him with 400 well-armed pistoleros from Coahuila. His uncle duly appeared at the rendezvous, but with only ten men. Abandoning his plans for an attack on a northern town, Madero went into hiding for a few days, then, after further vacillation, travelled incognito to New Orleans with his younger brother Raúl (who had been given the same name as the brother who died in 1887). Despite his aimless wanderings (he would later shift his base of operations to Dallas, then back to El Paso), Madero remained absurdly sanguine about the outcome of the Revolution, as his upbeat letters to his wife (addressed under the pseudonym Juana P. de Montiú) from New Orleans show. In one letter he outlined a typical day, in which he had slept well, had a siesta, read in the library, exercised in the YMCA and gone to the opera. He continued his eccentric researches into the *Mahabharata*, still deeply influenced by its teachings about the unreality of death, the illusory world of the senses, the necessity for renunciation, and the overriding importance of duty, even if unrequited.

In Mexico City Díaz was incandescent with rage about 'Yankee collusion' with Madero. Some US opinion-makers were quite happy about this, feeling that Díaz had got his come-uppance for his favouritism towards British capitalists; there was also a strong rumour that President

Taft and the Standard Oil Company were backing Madero. The truth is that Washington had little interest in the Mexican Revolution in the years 1910–11. Taft was quite content with Díaz as a strongman guarantor of stability, and the State Department in no way frowned on him for the anti-American demonstrations of November 1910, blaming them instead on 'agitators'. The USA was likely to swing against Díaz only if their nationals or property were damaged, which had not happened. All stories that Standard Oil bankrolled Madero were mere canards. It is true that Díaz was genuinely angry with Taft but, as a dictator, he failed to understand that American laws did not permit Taft to stop Madero organising political activities and buying guns.

The Revolution had stalled, Madero was stalemated and the USA was uninterested. For a while it seemed that Díaz had prevailed. Then came thunder out of Chihuahua – ironically the very spontaneous revolution the *magonistas* had spoken of, but not in accordance with their blueprint. For all the reasons already mentioned, the people of Chihuahua had had enough of Creel, Terrazas and Díaz; their response to a crisis of political legitimacy was to take up arms and fight, as their forefathers had fought the Apache. It is significant that the first outbreaks of rebellion occurred in the villages in northern Chihuahua particularly associated with the Apache wars: Namiquipa, Bachíniva, Cuchillo, Parano, San Antonio, San Carlos. Soon the entire state was consumed in revolution as an unstoppable chain reaction occurred. From the very beginning the names of three revolutionary leaders were heard everywhere: Castulo Herrera, Pascual Orozco and Pancho Villa.

The number one ranking revolutionary leader in Chihuahua was Pascual Orozco, a tall, rangy, gaunt-looking, 28-year-old with blue eyes and a formidable reputation. Orozco was no middle-class *maderista* but was the barely literate son of a village storekeeper who, in his early life, specialised in leading convoys laden with precious metals through the mountain passes of western Chihuahua. This was dangerous work in bandit country, and Orozco soon gained the reputation of being a sharpshooting mountain man who knew the sierra trails backwards. His background as a muleteer aligns him superficially with Villa and Zapata, but Orozco, already worth 100,000 pesos, was a living oxymoron, a kind of primitive capitalist-cum-revolutionary. Abraham González had tried to recruit him for Madero early in 1910, on the basis that he was known to be 'agin the government', but Orozco's horizons were limited. Uninterested in national politics, he wanted to knock his business rival Joaquín Chávez off his perch. Chávez, a client of the Terrazas, had a freight business that threatened Orozco's interests; appropriately Orozco's first 'revolutionary' act was to loot Chávez's house. However, Orozco was a formidable organiser, who was soon able to unite a number of different bandit groups and lay siege to Ciudad Guerrero.

When the red-letter day of 20 November arrived, Pancho Villa took his gang down into the Chihuahua plains and joined the revolutionary manpower commanded by Castulo Herrera. Next day the combined force occupied the old military colony of San Andrés, only to learn that a federal troop train was already on its way there. Villa took his own men down to the station and opened fire as soon as the troops started disembarking. After the federal commander and several of his men had been killed, the survivors clambered back on board the train and shunted backwards down the line in full retreat. The news of this 'great victory' over the federals was talked up, and within days volunteers were flocking in.

Herrera appointed Villa his second in command, with effective control of 325 men, but already the deficiencies of Herrera as a guerrilla commander were becoming apparent. Primarily a politician, and unable to control or impose his authority on the wild ex-bandits of the sierras, Herrera was forced to connive at his men's indiscipline, their rowdyism and firing guns into the air in the streets of San Andrés. Annoyed at the waste of ammunition, Villa browbeat the rowdies and made them come to heel. In a macho society such dominance was decisive, and effective, if not yet nominal, authority shifted from Herrera to Villa.

Euphoric and overconfident, Villa decided to start at the top by attacking the state capital, Chihuahua City, with just 500 men. He commanded in person a reconnaissance platoon of just forty men, which he divided into four units of ten, probing the city from different directions. Such was the gung-ho attitude of Villa's unit that they did not back off when they saw 700 federals advancing to oppose them. Villa's men dug in and fought; heavily outnumbered, they were forced to retreat within half an hour, but not before Villa had employed one of the tricks that would make him a legend. Along his defensive position, on the top of El Tecolote hill, he ranged dozens of sombreros to make them look like the hats of defenders. Seeing the hill apparently stoutly defended, the federals advanced slowly, wasting their ammunition against the phantom rebels. Villa sent out a runner to bring back the rest of the units and despatched a message to Herrera to come with all speed with the main force. He and his handful of defenders were about to be overwhelmed when the thirty men of the recalled units arrived; thus reinforced, Villa held off the federals for a further hour, expecting any minute that Herrera would come up with a flanking force. Herrera never arrived: he lacked the courage to commit his men to an engagement whose outcome was uncertain.

That was the end of Herrera as rebel commander. Extremely bitter and contemptuous towards him, Villa froze him out. Faced with a choice between following the lacklustre Herrera or the vigorous Villa, the guerrillas plumped for Villa. Any lingering chance that Herrera could reassert his position was destroyed when Tomás Urbina, Villa's friend, deliberately led a breakaway movement from Herrera and headed south on an extended raid through western Durango and the towns on the Chihuahua-Durango border. Encouraged by this, revolutionaries on Durango's other border, with Coahuila, attacked the town of Laguna and briefly occupied it, but the 200 guerrillas did not enjoy their triumph long and were soon flushed out by federals. The federal troops gave the first sign of the grim warfare to come over the next ten years by announcing that they would not be taking any prisoners; they shot their captives out of hand and left their corpses to rot as a warning to others.

Having overthrown Herrera, Villa decided to make common cause with Orozco, who had enjoyed a golden initial campaign. After taking Ciudad Guerrero, Orozco defeated the federals at Pedernales. When the rebels gained another victory at Malpaso, Orozco decided that, with Villa's help, he was ready to fight a pitched battle, and chose the town of Cerro Prieto on the North-western Railroad. This was a bad mistake, for the poor calibre of Orozco's Indian infantry and the immense superiority the federals enjoyed in artillery resulted in a heavy defeat for the rebels. After several hours of ferocious battle, during which at times 2,000 men fought hand-to-hand combat, Villa and Orozco were obliged to break off and flee to the mountains. The lesson was clear. Guerrilla armies could not yet defeat Díaz's forces in set-piece pitched battles.

After their victory at Cerro Prieto, the federals counterattacked, retaking Ciudad Guerrero from Orozco and relieving the pressure on Ojinaga, Chihuahua City and Ciudad Juárez on the border with the USA. Seeing that the rest of the country was not joining the rebels, Díaz felt confident he could crush Chihuahua. To save the expense of sending a large federal army north, he first offered the rebels a four-week truce, hoping that by its expiry the Chihuahuans would see the futility of their insurrection and lay down their arms. Naturally Orozco and Villa wanted to learn Madero's reaction, so they neatly solved an embarrassing problem by sending the feckless Herrera as their envoy to him, but even before an answer came back, Díaz himself wrecked the truce by deciding he could not afford to offer terms to the rebels. Business confidence in his regime had been severely dented by the revolt, and in Europe Limantour, trying to reschedule the external debt, found the terms of foreign banks rising steeper and steeper as the revolt continued. Believing that only a decisive military victory would now restore confidence, Díaz sent an extra 5,000 troops to Chihuahua under his friend General Juan Hernández, a man who had campaigned in the north and knew the terrain.

However, Díaz's political touch was failing, as his next action showed. Faced with persistent rumours that the Terrazas family were playing both sides against the middle in Chihuahua, he tried to force them off the fence by replacing the Creel puppet José María Sánchez as governor with his own nominee. This was a bad mistake, for the Terrazas clan would have had to fight Orozco and Villa anyway. By painting himself into a political corner with uncompromising action against the Terrazas, Díaz had raised the stakes and now had to win an outright victory in Chihuahua. Yet even though it was double-or-quits, Díaz felt he had an unbeatable hand: 5,000 fresh troops plus federal resources already in the state *must* defeat 1,500 rebels. For a few weeks Díaz's confidence seemed well founded: the string of rebel defeats at Cerro Prieto, Ojinaga and Ciudad Guerrero was followed by upbeat reports from his new governor, asserting that Orozco was on the point of surrender.

It was all a chimera. By January 1911 it was becoming increasingly apparent that both political and military factors favoured the rebels in the long run. Politically, both Díaz and the Creel-Terrazas faction could prevail in Chihuahua only if the ruling classes and the beneficiaries of the Creel land laws held firm. However, government officials fled, peons on the estates refused to fight, and the *hacendados* declined to arm them anyway, for fear they would go over to the rebels. The *hacendados* had long known that, ever since the end of the Apache wars, the nexus of rights and duties binding the peons to them had collapsed and that they had made themselves hated by introducing the southern idea of debt peonage. They kept their heads down, deaf to appeals from Díaz and the Terrazases, hoping that if they stayed quiet, the revolutionaries would ignore them. As for other beneficiaries of the Creel-Terrazas regime, goodwill from the 'winners' in expropriated land deals had largely evaporated when Creel brought in his tax laws of 1908, since these appeared to take back with one hand what had been given with the other.

Militarily, the situation was not much better, and here the fabled superiority of the moral over the material came to the fore: the rebels were fighting enthusiastically for core values and ideals, but the federal troops were there simply because they had been sent. Most of the federals were recent recruits, ill-trained and reluctant fighters. Most of the poorly equipped and badly fed battalions had a purely nominal strength, since corrupt Army officials had practised 'payroll padding', or simply pocketed the money earmarked for the soldiers' upkeep. When federal officers became frustrated at being unable to catch a highly mobile guerrilla force and requested more horses and pack animals for hot pursuit of hit-and-run groups, they found themselves snarled up in an Army bureaucracy intent on penny-pinching, querying all supplementary estimates and requiring officers to fill in huge, mindless questionnaires.

Besides, although the federals still had a firm grip on Chihuahua's towns and cities, they could not control the countryside, which was abandoned to the guerrillas. Even 5,000 extra troops could make no impression, since they needed the know-how only local militias could supply – and there were no local militias; the woodcutters, ranchers and hacienda foremen who had previously manned them had almost all joined Villa and Orozco. His advisers pointed out to an aghast Díaz that to control Chihuahua he would need the same population ratio as the British had enjoyed in the Boer War of 1899–1902; ten troops for every rebel. The arithmetic was simple: if rebel strength went up to 3,000, this would entail having 30,000 regulars in Chihuahua – an impossible number, not only because it was the entire strength of the Mexican Army but because the rest of Mexico would explode in revolution if Díaz sent all his troops to one state.

Díaz's advisers wrestled with this conundrum. In theory it should have been possible to increase the size of the Army, but there were no recruits to be had: no one wanted to serve outside the territory of his own state, and nobody wanted to fight for Díaz. To use the *leva* to press-gang men would only compound the likelihood of rebellion elsewhere, and on the few occasions it was tried, either the localities rose in revolt or the population melted away in a mass exodus to the jungle or mountains. Increasingly despondent, General Hernández, the military commander in Chihuahua, advised Díaz to ditch the universally hated Terrazases. He also urged a machiavellian pseudo-political solution, in which Díaz would appear to compromise, then, when the rebels had disarmed, he would enforce draconian repression and mass executions.

Díaz underrated the rebellion in Chihuahua at both the political and military level, seeing it one-dimensionally as just a gang of desperadoes on the rampage, encouraged and whipped up by Madero. He failed to see the long-term advantages accruing to the rebels from the terrain, which were principally threefold: Orozco and Villa could smuggle arms across the US border; they could raid and loot the state's haciendas for horses, money and supplies, making the *hacendados* the unintentional arsenal of the Revolution; and, if too hard-pressed in the plains, they could retreat into the mountains. No longer the master of his brief, Díaz decided to take Hernández's advice. He put in another phantom governor, this time of 'doveish' camouflage, and even released the editor Silvestre Terrazas from jail, hoping to use him as an intermediary.

Pancho Villa meanwhile was turning himself into *the* military hero of the Revolution. While still officially number two in the hierarchy behind Orozco, he was more and more building up a personal power base. After the defeat at Cerro Prieto he detached himself from Orozco and operated on his own, garnering more and more laurels in a whirlwind campaign from January to March 1911. He withdrew to San Andrés and decided to ambush a federal ammunition convoy. Successful in this, he foolishly allowed his men to disperse to their homes, but was then hit by a surprise federal counterattack. He and his bodyguards barricaded themselves in a railway station and held the federals at bay until evening, when they made their escape to the mountains, having lost most of their horses and supplies.

In spite of the freezing weather, Villa's scattered men rallied to him and there was even an influx of new recruits. To equip his army he raided hacienda after hacienda, scooping up 400 horses in one and arms, money and supplies in another. After a successful raid on the mining town of Naila had provided him with all the *matériel* he needed, Villa felt strong enough to attack the large town of Ciudad Camargo. A ferocious firefight took place as the *villistas* stormed it. They were just flushing out the last federal residues when government reinforcements arrived and they in turn were driven out. Believing in constant momentum, Villa barely broke stride but led his men on an attack, again abortive, on the town of Valle de Zaragoza.

Noting some slight signs of demoralisation in his men, Villa decided it was time for another of his great feats of daring. Taking just one comrade, Albino Frías, with him, Villa sauntered into Parral, undisguised in broad daylight – into a city where he was well known. The two men were soon recognised and challenged and had to shoot their way out, Hollywood-style. Separated from Frías in the mêlée, Villa returned to his camp to find it deserted. It turned out that Frías had reached it before him and told the men their leader was certainly dead; but no sooner did they hear of his miraculous survival than they all flocked back, convinced that 'don Pancho' really was Fortune's darling. Riding the crest of the wave, Villa then led his men on a successful assault on a 150-strong force of federals, gathering up further precious supplies of arms and equipment after the federals had cut and run.

Although the national press and the federal army still spoke largely of

Orozco as the fount of opposition, with Villa relegated to a footnote as 'the bandit Villa', he was already making his mark in local lore and *corrido* as a great charismatic leader. His leadership qualities and the magnetic appeal he had for his adherents were a function both of his great personal courage and his exceptional ability to read men. His followers were bowled over by his coolness, audacity and poker-faced acceptance of risk, by his skill as a gunfighter and by the gallery touches such as the 'raid' on Parral with a single comrade. He knew human psychology, kept casualties low, allowed looting, and always paid his men in advance, if necessary by raiding haciendas before giving battle to get the necessary funds. He mixed tough discipline – shooting anyone who broke his rules – with affability, showing up without notice at the campfire of a unit, and asking to share its food. He had the Napoleonic trick of either knowing, or appearing to know, everything about every man in his army, where he came from, whether he was married, how many children he had, and so on. In sum, he achieved the difficult feat of making his men fear, admire and respect him at once.

So far, however, Orozco, operating separately, had kept pace with him in terms of prestige. In a great double-headed feat, he managed to lure a federal troop train into an ambush in the Cañón Mal Paso, while one of his lieutenants sprang a trap in another canyon and massacred 200 troopers. Reporters covering the federal campaign against Orozco said it was the Boer War all over again – ponderous regulars trying to swat fast-riding sharpshooters. Faced with repeated guerrilla ambushes, the federals abandoned all attempt to reconquer the sierras, with the result that Chihuahua City became choked with fleeing *hacendados* and their families. Civilian life became increasingly parlous: mines could not operate because of the government ban on dynamite, food prices were rising, unemployment increasing, and the presence of 7,000 federal troops racked up civilian-military friction. Tensions heightened when thirteen people were killed during a mass jailbreak in Chihuahua City in February 1911.

For Díaz the problem about the success of the revolt in the sierras was that more and more malcontents in the villages of the plain were encouraged to have a go. There were instances of trans-class movements in the *pueblos* – small ranchers, migrant labourers and the villagers themselves combining to throw the federal authorities out. A domino effect was created, whereby the more the rebels succeeded in different locales, the more other disparate groups emerged to take revenge for local grievances; managers of haciendas, administrators of cotton plantations and *jefes políticos* all joined the ranks of death. More and more the federal authorities were being driven out of the smaller towns by concentration of force, to be replaced by revolutionary officials. Some mines reopened, with the owners paying protection money to the new authorities. As a rule of thumb, revolutionary bureaucrats would throw open the jails, release all prisoners and destroy all tax records and official archives.

Until April 1911 Díaz's response to the crisis in the north was still amazingly complacent. He and his minions continued to denounce the rebels as 'bandits', 'desperadoes', or even 'communists', while trying to alternate repression with conciliation. Repression merely alienated the crypto-*maderista* middle class even further, while conciliation was either perceived as too little, too late, or taken as an admission of weakness. The most worrying long-term sign for Díaz was the serious level of desertion in the federal army. The riff-raff of Mexico City could be dragooned into the ranks but, once in the open country of Chihuahua, they immediately deserted or joined the rebels. Finally the chickens seemed to be coming home to roost after thirty-four years of the *Porfiriato*. Even before Madero returned to Mexico to take charge, the rebels controlled a huge swathe of land from the US border down to the states of Nayarit and Zacatecas.

On 14 February 1911 Madero, with just 130 men, crossed into Mexico at a frontier point near El Paso. The action was forced on him, as he had broken anti-neutrality laws in the USA and had to go south of the border to avoid the arrest warrant that had been issued on him. Madero had hoped to enter Mexico via his home state of Coahuila, where he had a vast extended family and a huge network of friends and sympathisers; instead he had been forced into Chihuahua to make common cause with the sierra revolutionaries. From this one circumstance would arise a host of misunderstandings. Madero both appeared to be, and was portrayed by Díaz propaganda as, a far more revolutionary figure than he really was. He had hoped to come to power via a political coup in Mexico City or with support from the Army, and now he found himself dependent on Pascual Orozco and Pancho Villa. The seeds of future disaster were sown: the revolutionaries thought Madero more radical than he was and thus hoped for more from him, only to be disappointed; in Mexico City meanwhile, the Army took his revolutionary rhetoric seriously, hated him for it and would never be loyal to him.

Madero rode across the desert to San Buenaventura, gathering recruits as he went. A grand conference and mustering of revolutionary forces was called, where Madero first realised the political maelstrom he was caught up in. It was the men of Chihuahua who had rescued the *maderista* movement from extinction, and the educated middle-class followers of

Madero, who had failed to ignite urban revolution, were now playing second fiddle to rural warlords, who fought under the Madero banner purely as a flag of convenience and to legitimate local and sometimes personal grievances. The result was doubly unsatisfactory: in his heart Madero had no real sympathy for the revolutionaries of Chihuahua, but he was dependent on them, as he could not control events in the north.

Madero had expected to be received with enthusiasm as president-in-waiting, but found the local revolutionaries cool. He had expected that the *magonista* faction would not take orders from him, but was alarmed to find that he cut no great figure in the eyes of local leaders, especially as he could not supply them with the weapons they needed. Most disappointing of all was the arm's-length treatment from Orozco. His envoys had asked Orozco to converge on Ciudad Juárez and stop federal reinforcements reaching there, but the guerrilla replied that he accepted no authority in Chihuahua save his own, and ignored the request. Orozco was particularly offended by well-authenticated rumours that Madero intended to appoint someone else as military commander in Chihuahua; as far as he was concerned, there could be only one commander-in-chief in the state: himself. Madero thus found the revolutionary opposition to Díaz split three ways: between *maderistas*, *magonistas* and *orozquistas*.

Taking a leaf out of Orozco's book – Orozco had said he would fight on against Díaz, but independently and in his own way – Madero concluded that what he needed was a military victory that would give him the local prestige Orozco and Villa enjoyed. In March he decided to attack Casas Grandes on the North-western Railroad, where he thought his 600 men would face roughly equal numbers; he was unaware that the federals were even then reinforcing the town. As a further refinement, Madero decided to stage the assault at night, to cause maximum confusion. The attack, on 6 March, was a fiasco, though Madero's raw recruits showed great courage. The federals at first pinned the rebels down in ditches outside the town and dealt out terrible slaughter with machine-guns; armed only with Winchester and Springfield rifles from the 1860s, Madero's followers were outclassed. Even so, by dawn they were on the point of victory, when federal reinforcements suddenly arrived. To firepower went the victory as, outgunned and outmanoeuvred, the *maderista* vanguard, dug in within an adobe building, were surrounded and forced to surrender. Any chance that the rest of his raw levies could mount a counterattack was shattered when Madero found himself attacked in the rear. The rebels broke and fled, leaving behind more than 100 casualties (fifty-one dead) and most of their equipment and *matériel*; Madero himself was wounded in the arm and came within an ace of being captured.

The lesson of Casas Grandes was that the federals' monopoly of machine-guns and heavy artillery fire gave them a decisive advantage in open country; it was only through caution, defensive strategy, low morale among the troops and uncertainty about the political future that they failed to follow up: when Madero retreated in confusion to the hacienda of Bustillos, the federals, fearing ambush, did not pursue them.

Díaz hoped that Madero would be discredited by the rout at Casas Grandes but the reverse happened. In the eyes of the revolutionaries, Madero's courage and his very presence counted for more than his defeat, and more recruits, hearing stories of the incredible bravery of the Indian infantry at Casas Grandes, flocked in to Bustillos. There were political gains too. Having rejected Madero earlier, Orozco now acknowledged him as chief of the Revolution, but he still adamantly refused to accept Madero's choice, Giuseppe Garibaldi, grandson of the Italian liberator, as commander-in-chief.

Such was the confused situation when Villa arrived at Bustillos with 700 crack troops. Villa at once set about melding Madero's men with his own veterans and creating a unified, disciplined army; but for his fortunate advent at this juncture, Madero's force might have dwindled away. Madero was shrewd enough to see that Villa was just the man needed: his courage and daring appealed to Chihuahuans, his tight discipline impressed Madero, and everyone thought it unlikely that this man of the masses, from an impoverished background, would ever do deals with the hated oligarchs. Orozco's decision to keep Madero at arm's length now looked like a bad mistake, for it was Villa who had the ear of the would-be president. In gratitude and enthusiasm Madero wrote a letter, printed in the *El Paso Morning Times*, lauding Villa to the skies as a Robin Hood. This was probably the first time a US readership had heard of Pancho Villa.

Madero confided to Villa his worries about the armed *magonistas* who would not obey his orders, and Villa immediately thought of one of his artful tricks. He pretended to leave Bustillos and took his men down to the nearest railway station, inveigling the unarmed and curious *magonistas* to troop down with them and watch the departure. At a given signal, Villa's men jumped off the train, overpowered the onlookers and bore them back in triumph to Madero, having spilled not one drop of blood. Madero was delighted and promoted Villa, first to major, then to colonel, taking care to promote Orozco *pari passu*, always one rank ahead, so as not to alienate him. Díaz's propaganda organs made great play of Madero's promotion of 'bandits', but Madero, though not in so many words, declared Villa to be a 'social bandit' – a man forced into crime and later the armed struggle purely by Díaz's tyranny.

The entente between Madero and Villa has puzzled some historians. The diminutive man getting on so well with the man of iron, the spiritualist with the arch-materialist, the oligarchic intellectual with the semi-literate ruffian – none of this suggests natural synergy. However, Madero was increasingly aware that in Chihuahua he was an isolated figure. Most of those who opposed Díaz and the Terrazas were either *magonistas* or *orozquistas*. The one man with a large following who was prepared to accept his orders was Villa, and in such circumstances Madero was willing to lay on the flattery with a trowel. For his part, Villa, though occasionally exasperated by Madero, especially later, never really recovered from the confession he had made to Madero when Abraham González introduced them in 1910. Being already disposed to idolise Madero, he was further bowled over at Bustillos by the way the little man spoke to him as an equal. Here was a man with an intellect – a quality Villa admired – who used his brain idealistically to help others and with a complete absence of arrogance. For Villa, always in search of intellectual mentors, this was a powerful brew.

By April, revolution had spread to eighteen states in Mexico and new leaders had emerged in every state north of the isthmus. Some of these leaders were bizarrely untypical: in Sinaloa the historian Alan Knight has identified a species of landlord rebel – what he calls Mexico's Jacobites (in contrast to the *maderista* 'Whigs') – whose objective was to restore traditional prerogatives which Díaz had curtailed. Increasingly, an enduring truth about the Mexican Revolution was revealed, that it was always a revolutionary mosaic, made up of disparate, often contradictory, elements. The line between banditry and revolution was especially blurred, with local heroes seizing arms caches and military equipment through sheer bluff. Typically a bandit leader with a handful of men would threaten a hacienda and gain possession of its armoury by pretending to have ten times the apparent number hidden just out of sight; so psychologically wrong-footed were the *hacendados* by true tales of the exploits of such as Villa, Orozco and Tomás Urbina that they would invariably believe the bluff and surrender.

By the beginning of April General Hernández informed Díaz that the situation in Chihuahua was hopeless. So far from being able to reinforce his army there, Díaz had to pull out more and more men to deal with revolts elsewhere in Mexico, especially in Durango, where Orozco's power was increasing daily; the 5,000 fresh troops soon dwindled to

4,000. It was clear to all that by failing to stamp out the initial revolt in Chihuahua, Díaz had unwittingly lit a national brush fire. Hernández knew he could not pursue the rebels even if he beat off their attacks for, if he sent a force in pursuit, the townspeople would rise up and slaughter the skeleton garrison left behind.

In despair, Díaz in April offered land reform and a purge of his most unpopular Cabinet ministers as the price of peace. Jumping the gun, he dismissed all his top-ranking colleagues, replacing them with Limantour (who finally returned to Mexico City on 21 March) and Francisco de la Barra, ex-ambassador in the USA, who was promoted to foreign minister. Díaz by this time knew in detail the terms on which Madero was likely to settle, for on his return from Europe Limantour had stopped in New York, where he and de la Barra negotiated possible peace terms with Madero's father, Francisco, and with Gustavo Madero, the family banker. Díaz learned that the Maderos were financing the Revolution by diverting 375,000 pesos advanced to Gustavo as business broker by a Franco-Spanish railway consortium, so he was under no illusions that the revolutionaries would run out of money. Almost certainly, though, Limantour and de la Barra did not reveal to Díaz how cosy and cordial their talks with the Maderos had been, and still less how they had been willing to sell their master down the river.

All Díaz's Limantour-influenced concessions were in vain. Once again it was too little, too late: the rebels merely read them as weakness. Heartened by Díaz's remaining on the defensive, Madero decided to go for the jugular and attack Ciudad Juárez. A successful assault would allow him to control cross-border traffic of all kinds and could well be the final push needed to topple the *Porfiriato*. As a diversion, he sent forces to attack the town of Agua Prieta in Sonora, across the border from Douglas, Arizona. Agua Prieta had already been the scene of one rebel probe in March, but the April assault was a more serious affair. This was the first time a train played a significant role in a rebel attack. Disembarking troops by train gave the rebels the element of surprise, and in their initial foray they managed to blow up the enemy headquarters. The federals rallied strongly and were counterattacking when US Cavalry intervened from the American side of the border to stop the fighting, on the grounds that bullets were causing damage in Douglas.

Fighting battles on the US doorstep always carried the danger of forcing a major US intervention; as a precaution against the war spilling over the border, President Taft had sent 20,000 troops to police the US–Mexico border. Díaz fumed impotently at this 'national humiliation' and protested that Taft's action was a provocative move against a sovereign state, clearly designed to favour Madero. There was some humbug in the US stance for, while protesting that any damage sustained by American nationals or their property would invite massive retaliation, they did nothing to stop the throng of border sightseers who went in harm's way. Ever since the first Battle of Bull Run in 1861, there had been a peculiar US tradition whereby highborn ladies organised picnics at sites where they could view battles in comfort. On 17 April the sightseers at Douglas enjoyed another mêlée, as 1,500 federals moved in to recapture Agua Prieta. The action was short, sharp and, from the federal point of view, successful.

Agua Prieta, however, was never more than a sideshow. On 7 April 1911 Madero advanced on Ciudad Juárez with two columns of 500 men each, one commanded by Villa, the other by Orozco. Along the way they occupied Casas Grandes without resistance, but at Bauche the federals made a stand and Madero was able to overrun the position only after a bloody battle. Next day Madero invested the 700-strong garrison at Ciudad Juárez on three sides, leaving as the federals' only outlet the exit route to El Paso on the US side of the border. Both sides were confident of victory. Hitherto, all attempts by the rebels to engage the federals head-on had been a disaster, but Madero was now confident he had found the 'equaliser' weapon. The guerrilla leader Ramón Iturbe first showed how regular army firepower could be matched, and fortified towns taken. A dynamite man who had once blasted his way block by block from the outskirts to the centre of the sierra town of Topia, Iturbe advised Madero that the same tactics would work at Juárez. It was in this battle that the (cinematically ubiquitous) use of dynamite as *the* weapon of the Mexican Revolution first came to the fore.

For his part, the federal commander Juan Navarro, who contemptuously refused Madero's surrender demand, was also full of aplomb. Knowing nothing of Madero's secret weapon he felt that his firepower was more than sufficient to see off the raw rebel levies. Moreover, Madero would never dare to press his attack too hard in case stray bullets winged their way across to El Paso and killed or wounded citizens there, thus provoking American intervention. The one worry was that the federals could not play their most obvious card. The textbook tactic was for the federals to advance north from Chihuahua City and catch the rebels in a pincer between themselves and the Juárez garrison, but for fear of a rising in the city the troops in the capital dared not attempt a sortie.

Faced with the siege of Ciudad Juárez, and with his supporters in a panic, Díaz tried a 'peace offensive'. His advisers counselled him to try to detach Madero from the rest of the revolutionists. Since Madero was campaigning for free elections and 'no re-election', Díaz should concede these reformist demands, patch up a truce with Madero, and then crack down hard on the genuinely revolutionary demands being heard elsewhere in Mexico; otherwise the continuing anarchy would lead to total loss of international confidence and the probable armed intervention of the USA. José Limantour, fresh from his tussles with European finance ministers strongly advocated the two-stage strategy of conceding to Madero and then crushing peasant revolutionaries, but General Victoriano Huerta, the hardline spokesman for the Army, argued against, on the grounds that to recognise Madero would be to recognise his forces as a rival to the regular Army. Despite despondent reports from all field commanders, Huerta arrogantly boasted that he could relieve Ciudad Juárez with just 2,000 cavalrymen.

Díaz was aware that similarly ludicrous boasts had been made on the western frontier of the USA in the 1860s and 1870s by colonels Fetterman and Custer, with disastrous results, so he ignored Huerta and listened to Limantour. *Porfirista* envoys were sent north to Juárez to learn Madero's terms. These proved surprisingly mild: he insisted on the principle of no re-election, demanded four governorships and four cabinet posts for his followers but, astonishingly, did not make Díaz's resignation a precondition. Madero, more conservative than his followers, did not want a fight to the death and agreed to a truce, which eventually ran for two weeks from 24 April to 7 May. Not only was he worried about the possibility of US intervention and under pressure from his family and oligarchic friends to cut a deal with Díaz, but he was also concerned that the burgeoning peasant movements of the south would become uncontrollable. Morelos was in flames and everywhere in the south the name of a new peasant leader was being heard: Emiliano Zapata.

Where Villa was impulsive, emotional, pragmatic and volatile, Zapata was deep-thinking, slow to make up his mind but adamantine and inflexible once he had decided on a course of action. Villa dived into the Revolution on Day One, heedless of consequences, but Zapata thought through all the consequences and implications before he committed himself. This was why there was no initial response in Morelos to Madero's call to arms. Gradually, though, as news of rebel successes in Chihuahua came in, Zapata and the Morelos villagers began to flex their muscles, seeing how far they could push Díaz and his minions. Zapata's first revolutionary act was to lead eight villagers in a seizure of land that had long been a bone of contention between Anenecuilco and the haciendas. When the authorities decided to let sleeping dogs lie because of the tense situation in Chihuahua, his reputation was made overnight and his name became known in other villages. By the beginning of 1911 revolutionary electricity in Morelos was on surge power.

The first overt movement into armed guerrilla warfare was made by Genovevo de la O of Santa María village, who led twenty-five men into the mountains north of Cuernavaca, although at this stage they fought with hoes and pikes, for de la O was the only one in the band with a firearm – an antiquated .70 musket.

When the hitherto friendly prefect of Ayala district resigned, Zapata, sensing the power vacuum, came forward as the overall leader of the villages. He built up a defence fund and began to organise and arm a growing number of farmers. In every single one of Morelos's 100 *pueblos* he had the hacienda fences taken down, and by January 1911 he had a sky-high, statewide reputation. The new prefect wisely did not tangle with him, but contented himself with branding Zapata the state's principal *maderista*. As yet, though, with few armed followers at his side, Zapata did not seek an open confrontation with the authorities.

In January 1911 Zapata controlled the central region of Morelos, the most important part both geographically and economically. Luck was on his side, in several senses. Had Díaz not been preoccupied with

Chihuahua, he would undoubtedly have sent an army to crush this incipient peasant movement. His putative rivals as masters of Morelos, the Leyva brothers (Patricio and Eugenio) lost caste by ducking confrontation with Díaz, pleading ill-health. Moreover, Madero's original plans for southern Mexico assigned Morelos a purely peripheral role. His agent, Alfredo Robles Domínguez, aimed to focus rebellion in Guerrero and Puebla, with Morelos a mere sideshow. Had these plans been followed, Zapata might never have emerged as a revolutionary leader.

When Díaz's police swept up the entire southern *maderista* network in its November purge, revolution in the south took a spontaneous form. As already related, Zapata's first action in November 1910 had been to send Torres Burgos to learn more of Madero's intentions. As far as Zapata could understand the Plan of San Luis Potosí, Madero's thinking on land reform was confused: he made vague promises to the Indian *pueblos* but retained the totemic position of Juárez and his 'capitalist' stance of individual ownership. Torres Burgos was away, incommunicado, for three months and in his absence Zapata had tough decisions to make. He knew the planters were arming themselves and growing stronger by the day, which meant he should really strike them first, but what if Madero had some other master-plan in mind? In the end, Zapata reluctantly decided he would await Torres Burgos's return. However, he could not control the hotheads among the village leaders, and was in danger of being upstaged by the Morelians who had already taken to the mountains as guerrillas. There were no less than three groups. Genovevo de la O had been at large since late 1910, and now Gabriel Tepepa of Jojutla made his mark, sacking the town of Tepoztlán in February and gutting the archives and municipal offices. Yet a third band was headed by Bernabé Zabastida, an ex-*leyvista* who had been sentenced to hard labour in Quintana Roo, and now returned, thirsting for revenge against the people who had sent him to that graveyard; finding them fled, he killed two of their relatives and decamped to the hills with a handful of followers.

The relief of Torres Burgos's return in mid-February, and the envoy's favourable reports on Madero, were offset by the 'orders' Madero sent to Morelos: Zapata, it appeared, was to be only the number three ranking *político* in the state, behind the feckless Patricio Leyva and Torres Burgos himself. It soon became clear that Leyva was out of the reckoning, and for the time being Zapata accepted the political suzerainty of Torres Burgos. When governor Escandón started bringing in more *rurales*, Zapata decided the time for military action had come. On 10 March he, Torres Burgos and Rafael Merino discussed the final details of the uprising, using the annual fair at Cuautla as cover. Next day Zapata led a revolt at nearby Villa de Ayala, disarmed the police and harangued the crowd about Madero's Plan of San Luis Potosí, ending his speech with the slogan: 'Down with the haciendas! Long live the *pueblos!*'

On 12 March armed rebels spread out along the Cuautla river – where Zapata earlier in life used to drive his mules – gathering in more volunteers. Making their camp in the hills, they then swept into the neighbouring state of Puebla, garnering more recruits as they went. Though at first Torres Burgos still retained nominal leadership, Zapata was the master strategist. His long-term aim was to take Cuautla, from which he could take the state capital at Cuernavaca and then control the road to Mexico City and all routes to the south. First, however, he had to train his raw recruits and blood them in battle. He took them on guerrilla raids below a line drawn from Jojutla to Yecapixtla, giving them easy targets and building up morale by assaults on outnumbered police forces. He intended to strike at Cuautla as soon as his own forces were strong enough and Cuautla itself weakened by the loss of troops Díaz would surely have to pull out to deal with the revolt in Chihuahua.

Zapata's tatterdemalion army made up in commitment, zeal and revolutionary élan what it lacked in training and equipment. Foreign observers in Morelos, like Rosa King in Cuernavaca, were patronising about the peasants in their white shirts and trousers, their mock-military habit of pulling multicoloured socks over their trouser legs as if going on a hike, their half-starved, spavined horses, and the motley selection of firearms, some of them flintlock muskets dug out of attics or unearthed in pawn shops. Eyebrows were also raised at the number of women soldiers (*soldaderas*) serving in the peasant army, some wearing pretty dresses across which bandoleros were slung. However, Zapata's charisma and the revolutionary willpower of his men counted for more than mere weaponry. They loved his economical oratory – 'We have begged from the outside not one bullet, not one rifle, not one peso; we have taken it all from the enemy' – and most of all, the slogan he invented, which would be appropriated by La Pasionaria in the Spanish Civil War: 'It is better to die on your feet than live on your knees.'

Zapata's slow, methodical approach did not please Torres Burgos, who intemperately linked up with Tepepa and his group, declaring that they were good enough to take on federal troops. Zapata expressed his misgivings, but Torres Burgos overruled him and ordered an immediate attack on Jojutla. Governor Escandón panicked and pulled his troops out of the town on 24 March, leaving only a few snipers to oppose the rebels. A new convert to Zapata's cause, a young Mexico City lawyer named

Octavio Paz Solórzano, saw Zapata in action against one of these sharpshooters. From the town hall someone took a pot-shot at Zapata, an easy target, mounted as he was on his favourite horse – a powerful dark chestnut given to him by the parish priest of Axochiapan – and chomping the trademark cigar he always had in his mouth, even in battle. Enraged, Zapata rode into the town hall in pursuit of his would-be assassin, mounting the staircase to the upper rooms on his charger.

The rebels soon showed how much they were in need of Zapata's steadying hand. Torres Burgos, who had overruled Zapata, was now in turn snubbed by Tepepa, whose men refused to take orders from anyone but their chief. In defiance of Torres Burgos they looted and sacked wholesale in Jojutla, a prime target being businesses belonging to the hated Spaniards. In disgust Torres Burgos threw up his command, but on the way back to Villa de Ayala he and his two sons were caught by federal troops (they were literally caught napping, arrested while taking a siesta) and executed out of hand. Perhaps sobered by this event, Tepepa backed the majority of rebel leaders in forthwith electing Zapata 'Supreme Chief of the Revolutionary Movement of the South'.

Not all the *gachupines* learned the obvious lesson from the sack of Jojutla. A Spaniard named Carriles, hated both for his nationality and for being administrator of the Chinameca hacienda, foolishly challenged Zapata to attack the hacienda, boasting that he had enough men and guns to swat aside this military flea. Incensed by the insult, Zapata sent his own handpicked units against Chinameca. The assault was completely successful and was the first exploit to make Zapata the hero of a *corrido*. The sack of Chinameca also enabled him to provision his army thoroughly. As he moved on through the smaller towns of Morelos, more and more men, attracted by his growing reputation and caught up in the euphoria of regaining lands and anti-Spanish xenophobia, or simply having nothing to lose, swelled his numbers; significantly, the high wage-earners in the foreign-owned enterprises held aloof.

Despite his magniloquent title of Supreme Chief, Zapata did not yet have undisputed sway over all local leaders in Morelos and still less, at this stage, in neighbouring states. His rivals saw clearly enough that, if the revolt in the south was successful – which seemed more likely as weeks went by – whoever had the title of military supremo would almost certainly be the next state governor. Zapata had the inside track, for he alone had received significant financial backing – from Rodolfo Magaña, a middle-class revolutionary, who 'grubstaked' him to the tune of 10,000 pesos – and he also had other advantages: nobody had his long-standing record, his reputation, and no one else was so trusted by villagers.

However, like Villa, he was a charismatic leader dependent on prestige; he was only as good as his last exploit. None the less, nobody was surprised when on 14 April Madero's new agent in Morelos officially designated Zapata as Madero's principal representative in the state.

Díaz tried to stem the revolt in Morelos by co-opting the Leyva family. They were willing accomplices but were paper tigers, their credibility already shot to pieces. All Díaz accomplished was the definitive removal of another set of rivals to Zapata. Even though Emiliano still did not have the absolute allegiance of all southern guerrilla leaders – de la O, for instance, though friendly, wrote to him as 'señor Emiliano' and signed himself 'Don Genovevo' – more and more local chieftains acknowledged his overlordship, each one bringing in a further band of men between 50 and 200 strong. By mid-April Zapata was directing operations with all the aplomb of a veteran commander. He learned the art of breaking down personal allegiances other than to himself by, for example, sending Tepepa to fight on the Puebla/Guerrero border with men not from Tepepa's original band; these he meanwhile melded with the rest of the army.

Zapata's rise in southern Mexico was meteoric. His fame and influence spread like wildfire, into the states of Puebla, Tlaxcala, Mexico, Guerrero, Michoacán. This soon brought him into collision with the influential political power brokers of Guerrero state, the four Figueroa brothers, who were to Guerrero what the Terrazas were to Chihuahua, and who had hitherto looked on Morelos as a traditional political appendage to their hegemony in the south. Zapata was determined that independence for his state meant not just freedom from Díaz but also freedom from the Figueroas. What he required, either from Madero or from the Figueroas themselves, was a formal guarantee of Morelos's autonomy. This meant that he had to have in his possession all the major towns of Morelos by the time Madero started serious negotiations with Díaz. When hostilities outside Ciudad Juárez were suspended in April, Zapata realised he was in a race against time.

On the first day of Madero's truce (22 April 1911) he met Ambrosio Figueroa, patriarch of the dynasty in Puebla, at a conference brokered by Madero's Puebla agent. It was agreed that both Figueroa and Zapata would have the rank of general, and that their forces could operate freely and independently anywhere in Mexico. If there were joint operations in Morelos, Zapata would be supreme commander; if in Guerrero, Figueroa. This was a great propaganda victory for Zapata, but in his heart he doubted the Figueroas would keep their end of the bargain. He knew they had their own reasons for not wanting Jojutla attacked again, for they took protection money from the town, and he suspected that, when it came to it, Ambrosio Figueroa would not allow him to lead the Figueroa men in Morelos. Besides, he learned from his spies that Figueroa intended to stab him in the back by pulling his forces out in the event of any *zapatista* attack on Jojutla, and leaving Zapata to deal with a numerically superior federal force.

Aware of the potential treachery of the Figueroas, Zapata decided not to go for the softer option of Jojutla but to attack the heavily defended town of Cuautla. First he disguised his intentions by attacking and occupying the towns of Chietla and Izúcar de Matamoros. Driven out initially, the federals counterattacked with reinforcements and machine-guns; they managed to retake Izucar but could not dislodge the *zapatistas* from Chietla. Some of Zapata's commanders, notably Felipe Neri, complained bitterly that many peons still would not join them and those that did would often join up just for loot, returning to the haciendas to get their wages on top. Neri threatened to cut off the ears of any such 'moonlighters' he encountered, but Zapata was more tolerant, realising that the peons would join him in droves only when he had broken Díaz's power in Morelos.

Having feinted towards Chietla and Izúcar de Matamoros, and leaving his rearguard to mop up the resistance, in early May he circled round Cuautla, first taking the towns of Yautepec and Jonacatepec and raiding Metepec and Atlixco in Puebla state, all the time levying forced loans, securing provisions, capturing arms and ammunition and generally building up his strength. By mid-May only Cuautla and the capital Cuernavaca were in federal hands. All the time, however, there was the impending threat that in the north Madero would patch up an agreement with Díaz that would leave the true revolutionaries out on a limb. It was vital for Zapata to take Cuautla.

On 13 May he hurled 4,000 men, full of enthusiasm but with no experience in sieges, against 400 crack troops of the elite Fifth Cavalry Regiment of the federal army – the so-called 'Golden Fifth'. The battle for Cuautla secured Zapata's national fame and ensured that he would not be just another forgotten southern commander when peace came. Eyewitnesses spoke of 'six of the most terrible days of battle in the whole Revolution'. Combat was house to house and street by street, with bloody hand-to-hand fighting, bayonet against machete, and men firing at each other from point-blank range through embrasures in walls. On many occasions hastily erected defences of earth and brick suddenly collapsed, leaving startled but murderous warriors staring each other in the face. In every street the objective was the same: capture the high killing ground from which a withering fire could be directed at the other side. When bullets ran out, the enraged combatants used rifle barrels and butts to bash the enemy's brains out. Everywhere there arose the smoke and gore of the charnel house.

No prisoners were taken, no quarter was given, both sides fought like savages. One detachment of federal troops tried to turn a railway carriage into an impregnable pill-box, complete with machine-guns, but the *zapatistas* doused the carriage with petrol, set it alight and reacted with joy or indifference to the agonised screams of the incinerated soldiers. While the battle was raging, 600 federal reinforcements arrived in Cuernavaca under the fire-eating General Huerta, but made no attempt to relieve their suffering comrades in Cuautla, doubtless because Huerta knew the city would rise in his rear if he marched out. Finally, on 19 May, the few battered survivors of the once proud Fifth Regiment pulled out of Cuautla, leaving the smoking ruins of a virtual bombsite in Zapata's hands. His timing could not have been more felicitous, for on 21 May Madero signed the treaty of Ciudad Juárez with Díaz.

It was none other than Díaz who testified that Cuautla was the last nail in his coffin, that he could perhaps have held the line in Chihuahua if Morelos too had not been ablaze. Cuautla made Zapata a national hero and new *corridos* immortalised *zapatista* valour. Felipe Neri, one of Zapata's best captains, a kind of Desaix to his Napoleon, sustained a bizarre injury while capturing the heavily defended Convent of San Diego. A hand grenade flung at the wall of the church bounced back and exploded at his feet, seriously wounding him and leaving him deaf for life. It was said that the damage to his hearing made Neri particularly harsh in his treatment of prisoners; those he did not execute he liked to line up, then clip their ears as a mark of Cain.

While Zapata was achieving in five months one of the fastest ascents to fame in all history, Villa and Orozco were champing at the bit outside Ciudad Juárez, as Madero made concession after concession to Díaz. As the armistice stretched on, with disillusioned guerrillas deserting and Madero appearing to do all in his power to let don Porfirio off the hook, Villa and Orozco finally put their collective foot down. In stormy conferences on 30 April and 1 May they told Madero bluntly that Díaz's resignation was an absolute precondition for any permanent peace. Still Madero dithered: he drew up a 'fourteen-point' ultimatum, then repented of his hard line, then repented of having repented. Finally, he told Díaz he required his resignation and that of vice-president Ramón Corral.

Too late Díaz realised the gravity of his position and began to make serious concessions. The stress of having to conciliate on a national scale began to affect the old dictator: everyone who saw him remarked that he had suddenly aged, seemed weak, inert and feeble-minded, evincing clear signs of declining mental vitality and failing health. Right at the height of the Ciudad Juárez crisis he was suffering from an ulcerated jaw, but still the old peasant cunning was in evidence. He sacked his entire Cabinet and made vague promises about returning land to the dispossessed. On 7 May, the day the truce expired, he issued an ambiguous manifesto, declaring he would resign 'when anarchy no longer threatened'. Aware that the federal garrison at Ciudad Juárez was running low on ammunition and that the rebels had cut the water supply, he tried to bamboozle Madero with scare stories about certain US intervention if he attacked.

Amazingly, Madero took this prevarication seriously and confessed to his intimates that he was full of heart searching, but Orozco and Villa by now had had enough of Madero's vacillation; in their view the only beneficiary from the armistice was Díaz, whom they suspected of secretly rushing reinforcements northwards. Taking matters into their own hands, they launched an attack on Juárez, forcing Madero's hand and telling him that the resumption of hostilities was a spontaneous flare-up which they had been unable to control. Madero tried to stop the fighting and asked the federal commander, General Juan Navarro, to hold his fire. Navarro did so but Orozco and Villa ignored him, Madero and the federal white flags. Ferocious fighting then began. A desperate Madero sent Castulo Herrera to Villa to insist that fighting stop, but Villa contemptuously ignored the man he already regarded as a coward. Orozco and Villa practised all kinds of ingenuities to avoid seeing Madero and having to refuse a direct order from him. When Madero finally ran into his military commander, Orozco told him fighting was by now so far advanced it could not be stopped.

Taking care that no bullets winged across the border to El Paso, Orozco and Villa both attacked Juárez at an angle, Orozco coming in from the north and Villa from the south. Among the combatants was a sizeable contingent of foreign mercenaries and adventurers, particularly experts in machine-guns and dynamite. Names that recur in the copious sources for the battle are the Boer Ben Viljoen, who had fought the British in the South African War of 1899–1902; A. W. Lewis, a Canadian machine-gunner; Lou Carpentier, a French artillery technician; Oscar Creighton from New York, a dynamite man; and Tom Mix, later to be famous as the star of Hollywood westerns of the silent era.

Ciudad Juárez was another gory revolutionary battle, again with savage hand-to-hand combat. The federals had organised a defence in depth, with an outer ring of trenches, and an inner ring of interconnected buildings protected by barricaded streets. However, they had left a gap in their defences, possibly through lack of numbers, on the eastern side. There an irrigation canal ran parallel to a river, and the undefended terrain between them was piled high with silt dredged from the canal, providing excellent cover. The attackers made their way to the suburbs by this route. To avoid the withering fire of the federal machine-guns, the revolutionaries used dynamite bombs, axes and crowbars to crash through adobe walls, making their way methodically from suburbs to city centre without coming under artillery fire.

The attackers fought in relays, 'spelling' each other, retiring to eat and sleep before returning to the fray; thus they were always fresh while the hard-pressed federals were always tired. Carpentier's cannon, in a flukey shot, managed to destroy the federals' water tank, on its second fusillade, just before malfunctioning and playing no further part. By nightfall on 9 May most of the city, apart from the bullring, main church and army barracks, were in rebel hands. Early on the 10th the revolutionaries wheeled up a captured mortar and began systematically pounding the barracks into submission. Federal resistance slackened, and soon the *maderistas* were close enough to lob grenades over the wall. By midday Navarro's situation was desperate: he held on to no more than a few buildings in the centre and was without water. His superior firepower in the form of machine-guns and Mausers was being whittled away hourly by hand-grenade attacks. At 2.30 that afternoon he ran up the white flag for surrender. The federals had lost 180 killed and 250 wounded, against an unknown number, probably higher, of revolutionary casualties.

Navarro's surrender precipitated another clash between Madero and his commanders. For Villa and Orozco, Navarro was already a marked man after his behaviour at Cerro Prieto in December, when he had bayoneted all rebel prisoners to death in defiance both of the Geneva Convention and the Plan of San Luis Potosí; Villa and Orozco had spared the captured federals. Here, surely, was a man to be taken out at once and shot by firing squad, but Madero promised he would spare his life. Always one for saving the life even of a brutal reprobate, Madero did not so much temper justice with mercy as requite injustice with inappropriate compassion. Moreover, he did not want to alienate the Army by executing one of its generals. A true revolutionary would have accepted the logic of the situation and not only dispatched Navarro but told the Army it was finished. By this single action Madero revealed himself clearly as no revolutionary, merely a within-the-regime reformist.

Madero's weakness was too much for Orozco. At 10.30 a.m. on 11 May he stormed into Madero's office, Villa at his side, to demand that Navarro be handed over to a court martial immediately; while he was at it, Madero might consider paying his own troops instead of thinking up ways to mollycoddle the enemy. Orozco was also incensed by another matter, for he had heard that Madero was thinking of appointing one Venustiano Carranza as minister of war after the Revolution, when the position should clearly be Orozco's. When Madero refused all these demands, Orozco drew a pistol and held it to Madero's chest. A Madero aide then drew his gun and trained it on Orozco. Faced with this literal exemplification of the Mexican stand-off, Villa stepped outside and bawled an order for his elite squad to come at the double.

What happened next is confused, but Madero somehow got free of Orozco, rushed outside, jumped on top of a car and started haranguing the troops. According to one version of the story, he pushed rudely past Villa, who spat an obscene oath at him. Madero's eloquence did his work and the soldiers started cheering him. At this point, fearing a shoot-out that would destroy all they had worked for in the past few days, Orozco conceded defeat and shook hands with Madero. Villa's reactions were typical. At first enraged with Madero, five minutes later he was in tears, begging his forgiveness. Allegedly Villa said: 'I have committed a black crime and my heart is between two stones'; the words sound like Villa in maudlin mood. Madero, knowing Villa's volatility, made sure he got Navarro over the border at once and then formally announced that Carranza would be his new secretary of war; but he shrewdly sugared the pill by agreeing to pay Orozco and Villa's troops in full that very day.

In yet another version of the story, it was Villa who drew the gun on Madero, who then declared: 'I am your chief; if you dare to kill me, shoot.' This would explain why Madero was able to break free and escape from the office, for these Napoleon-on-the road-to-Grenoble sentiments would certainly have cut no ice with Orozco. Villa found a displaced outlet for his anger at not being able to execute Navarro by shooting the 60-year-old Díaz official Félix Mestas with his own revolver. Curiously, this entire crisis, straight out of a melodrama, which should logically have united Villa and Orozco against Madero, drove them apart. Madero had revealed that inevitable concomitant of the weak man – stubbornness – but Villa forgave him, partly because he had no political ambitions himself, and partly because of his psychological 'Madero complex'. Orozco, a man of frightening ambition, never forgave Madero's snub and went away brooding on Carranza's elevation.

It may even be that darker plots were afoot that day. One theory, which Villa later came to believe, was that Orozco was secretly in the pay of Díaz. There is some circumstantial evidence to back this, for it is known that Orozco met don Porfirio's agents four times on 10 and 11 May. One version of the day's events on 11 May is that Orozco had concocted an ingenious plan to sweep both Madero and Villa off the playing board. Knowing Villa's volatility and propensity to rages, he had worked him to snapping point over Navarro's pardon. Then, when he and Villa burst into Madero's office, the plan was that Madero would be shot dead, and that Villa would appear as the killer and the ringleader of a plot. Meanwhile he, Orozco, would keep Díaz dangling and play both sides against the middle. In the best-case scenario, Madero would be murdered, Villa executed as an assassin and Díaz forced from office, leaving Orozco as *the* power in the land and the obvious choice as Mexico's next president. Certainly Orozco's subsequent behaviour is consistent with such a thesis.

The fall of Ciudad Juárez, however reluctantly Madero achieved it, was a great fillip for his movement and boosted his credibility enormously. US journalists poured across the border to give him the big build-up, commenting particularly on the efficient way his men policed the city. Madero named Juárez his provisional capital and appointed an interim cabinet, but it still took Díaz another ten days to concede defeat and resign. His intransigence was, if anything, helped by Madero's absurdly anaemic response to his victory. The agreement he drafted insisted on Díaz's departure but left his system virtually intact. All other officials, judges, mayors, police chiefs and bureaucrats remained and, in a key clause, Madero agreed to retain the Army unchanged, with its existing officer corps. He insisted on fourteen *maderista* governorships and the withdrawal of federal troops from northern Mexico, but said nothing about the south, in theory leaving the Army free to turn its guns on Zapata and the revolutionaries of central Mexico.

Finally Díaz saw that his only option was to go into exile; Limantour advised him that further civil war would make US intervention a certainty. The two of them overruled the absurd sabre-rattlers in the Army, such as Huerta, whose Custer-like boasts they knew were ignorant, vainglorious bluster, and on 21 May the treaty of Ciudad Juárez was signed. Díaz agreed to depart for Europe and Francisco León de la Barra took over as provisional president, with a remit to organise autumn elections. The end of the *Porfiriato* represented compromise on both sides, since both the old regime and the liberal middle-class *maderistas* were seriously concerned about the revolutionary genie released from the bottle. The pace of revolution was now like that of a tornado with new leaders and new groupings emerging in every state. If their political composition was turbid, their social message was clear: they wanted real socio-economic change, not just a political transfer of power.

Though deadly enemies, Díaz and Madero shared a mortal terror of the 'anarchy of the masses' and were particularly apprehensive about Zapata, the so-called 'Attila of the South', whose bloody triumph at Cuautla seemed like the harbinger of a new 'War of the Castes', in which the Morelos leader would unite the Maya of Yucatán and the Indians of central Mexico in a campaign of genocide against the white man. From the elite point of view, Madero's challenge to Díaz had been reckless – which was why most of Madero's family were lukewarm about his enterprise. Men like Bernardo Reyes had backed off rather than push Díaz to the limit, because they had thought through the consequences. Once Mexicans saw the fallacy of 'there is no alternative to don Porfirio', aspirations would be aroused that could not be contained, and the end of the road might be a convulsive social revolution. If you did not have to put up with Díaz, you did not have to put up with the *hacendados* either. Madero never grasped that he was merely the Mirabeau in an unstoppable process, and that after him would have to come the Robespierres, the men of Thermidor and the Bonapartes.

Almost all other revolutionary leaders opposed the deal he made with Díaz in the treaty of Ciudad Juárez. They, rightly, saw no need for such generous accommodation, since Madero had the whip hand. By this time it was not just the countryside but also cities like Durango, Chilpancingo and Cuernavaca that were in rebel hands. Even Carranza, no firebrand, warned Madero that he was 'delivering to the reactionaries a dead revolution which will have to be fought over again'. Villa, violently opposed to the Ciudad Juárez treaty, prophesied (or so he later said) that Madero would end up assassinated and pleaded with him to let the Revolution continue until he had strung up all Establishment politicians from the highest tree. He was particularly disillusioned that Madero was not going to purge the Army and that nothing was said about retribution against Creel and the Terrazas. When Madero brushed his misgivings aside, Villa offered his resignation.

Madero was happy to accept it, but offered Villa 25,000 pesos in severance pay. When Villa protested indignantly (and truthfully) that he had not fought for money, Madero insisted that he take 10,000 pesos as a personal favour to him. What Villa really wanted was a grand title that would recognise his heroic role in the struggle, but the macho code of honour and respect left Villa no choice but to agree to the money gift; he promised himself he would now buy the elusive butcher's shop and settle down – but first he had a private score to settle. Giuseppe Garibaldi had been boasting that he and a handful of American volunteers had really taken Ciudad Juárez on their own. Apoplectic with rage, Villa tracked Garibaldi down to the Hotel Sheldon in El Paso, where he found him in company with three US Secret Service men. It transpired that Washington had heard of Villa's threats against Garibaldi and had taken steps to prevent an international incident. Gustavo Madero, who was with Villa, tried to get him out of the hotel without incident, but Villa uttered vociferous threats. The mayor of El Paso ordered Villa out of his bailiwick, and he suffered the humiliation of being run out of town by the Secret Servicemen, who deposited him on the middle of the international bridge and warned him not to come back.

The first stage of the Mexican Revolution was now complete. Militarily, some ominous lessons had been learned, principally that well-garrisoned cities were not invulnerable to attack. Trains, aircraft, the wireless and even barbed wire had not yet made the impact they would later – though the theory of barbed wire in warfare was well understood, after its employment by the Italians when occupying Eritrea in 1885 and, especially, by the British in the Boer War, who used it to link forts in their blockhouse system – but above all the 1910–11 period showed the deadly efficacy of dynamite and machine-guns; perhaps the proximity of the USA was relevant, for the four most important figures in the history of the machine-gun – Richard Gatling, John Moses Browning, Hiram Maxim and Colonel Isaac Newton Lewis – were all Americans.

The basis of the machine-gun was a series of parallel barrels, six in some models, ten in others, which were revolved round a fixed axis by a crank, and usually fed automatically from a drum mounted above the barrels; early models fired up to 100 rounds a minute, later ones up to 1,000. The Gatling gun was first used significantly in battle at Tel-el-Kebir in 1882, when six Gatlings manned by thirty British sailors were said to have accounted for half Arabi Pasha's 12,000 Egyptian dead. However, the Gatling was not a self-firing gun of the type that continued to fire as long as the trigger was pressed. It was Hiram Maxim who introduced a method of gelatinising nitrocellulose, which allowed the burning speed of powder to be accurately controlled. Maxim worked out a method enabling him to use the recoil automatically to eject the first round, pull another round into position, then fire the second round. The recoil from this second round repeated the cycle, which continued as long as the trigger was pressed, the rate of fire being adjustable up to 600 rounds a minute.

Browning used the energy of escaping muzzle gases to operate his weapon, then developed the improved recoil-operated mechanism. Lewis had a gas-operated gun, charged from a flat drum magazine and this became the preferred method of combat in the aerial dogfights of the First World War. Machine-guns had featured prominently in the terrible trench-warfare battles of the Russo-Japanese War of 1904–5 – although they were not mass produced until the First World War – and were thus a treasured item in the armoury of the opposing forces in the Mexican Revolution.

Their impact could well have been decisive but for the 'equalising' weapon of the dynamite bomb, the favourite device of guerrilla revolutionaries. Although Hollywood movies anachronistically show dynamite in use in Juárez's wars with the French, the development of this unique high explosive was a feature of the late 1860s. One of the amazing stories in the history of technology was the discovery that, by adding nitric acid, cotton-wool could become explosive gun-cotton, and that an emollient cosmetic liquid, glycerine, could become nitroglycerine, a heavy, oily-looking liquid which explodes with tremendous violence. It is more destructive than gun-cotton, and can be exploded by a fuse containing fulminating powder, fired from a distance by electricity. Ten times as powerful as gunpowder (gun-cotton six times), it became the favourite blasting agent for miners. It was first used in liquid form as 'blasting oil', but because of the dangers of handling it, it was later mixed with a powdered substance (itself without action and merely a vehicle for containing the nitroglycerine), and this became known as dynamite. The art of detonation became more nuanced: if one wanted to blast an object to smithereens, one used 'high explosive' or dynamite; if one wanted to blast, say, large granite blocks to make building stone, or a coal seam to yield lumps of coal, one used 'low explosive' or gunpowder.

There were many nineteenth-century developments in dynamite, notably the use of chlorate of potassium instead of nitrate as the oxygen-supplying material. The great name in the history of dynamite is Alfred Nobel. Although Sobrero had discovered nitroglycerine in laboratory experiments, several grave accidents in the late 1860s seemed to put a question mark against 'blasting oil'. Nitroglycerine was perceived to be so dangerous that Britain prohibited its import in a liquid state; it had to be pre-processed into dynamite. The breakthrough came when Nobel discovered a detonation method, enabling nitroglycerine to be absorbed by an inert porous material, a silicaceous earth of which one part would absorb three times its weight in nitroglycerine. Later, other substances were used for absorbing the liquid, and in the end there were two types of dynamite: one with inert absorbents and the other with absorbents that were themselves combustible or explosive, such as charcoal, nitrate, chlorate and even gunpowder, gun-cotton and nitro-mixtures. But the first significant use of dynamite in bomb form was in the Mexican Revolution.

If the impact of military technology on the Revolution was palpable, the social significance of the Revolution was less clear-cut. In retrospect it is easy to see Villa and Zapata as the two most important figures. Zapata represented the agrarian peasantry – the villagers, sharecroppers and smallholders who suffered from the greed of *hacendado*, *ranchero* or cacique and who wanted their stolen lands back. Agrarian grievances were overwhelmingly the biggest issue in the Revolution, hardly surprisingly, given that four-fifths of the population lived in the countryside. For every 1,000 peasants, there were 120 artisans, 100 small farmers, forty factory workers, thirty miners, ten ranchers and two *hacendados*.

Zapata's achievement was to give a concrete form to peasant aspirations that had remained dormant and even partly unconscious. This was why his fame had already transcended state boundaries. It was his inspiration that enabled peasant revolutionaries in Oaxaca and Veracruz to break free of the grip of the *hacendados*. In Sinaloa rebels 'legitimated' their rebellion by reference to Zapata's ideas and went into battle crying 'Viva Zapata' – an eloquent testimony to a man they had never clapped eyes on. The local Sinaloa warlords, Manuel Vegas and Juan Banderas, yielded to no one in their admiration for Zapata. Even in distant Chiapas, during a quickly suppressed local revolt, the Indians who fought the *rurales* used 'Viva Zapata' as their warcry. Zapata was the man the oligarchs most hated and feared – a hatred fuelled by the realisation that they were opposed by an intelligent revolutionary who had built up an ongoing movement, which would not collapse overnight like the traditional peasant jacqueries. Those who felt confident they could co-opt Madero liked to contrast the 'respectable' revolution conducted by Madero in the north with the 'brigandage' of Zapatismo in the south.

Zapatismo necessarily implied class-conflict, but the centaurs of the north, like Orozco and Villa, headed more fluid movements, opposed to Díaz because of unemployment, economic hardship, taxation, the *ley fuga*, conscription and press-gangs. Because they fought for local independence against the centralising tendencies of Mexico City, these rebels could transcend class issues, to the point where some sceptics have referred to them as 'non-revolutionary rebels'. One could argue that Villa and Orozco fought, not like Zapata for the issue of land itself, but merely against the particular way it had been divided up by a contingent corrupt clique in the form of Creel and the Terrazas. In the north it was possible for Madero to recruit ex-*villistas* and Orozco men as *rurales*; for obvious reasons, this would have been unthinkable in Morelos.

The groups headed by Zapata and Villa were the cutting edge of the Revolution, but there were other social elements that played a subsidiary role. Although the urban masses played little part in the events of 1910–11, the fear that they might was ever-present in Díaz's mind. Alan Knight has established that, in so far as urban rebels did play a part, the driving force was provided by artisans, a disaffected group under the last years of the *Porfiriato*, as they had lost out to large-scale factory production. In the 1910 census there were 67,000 carpenters, 44,000 shoemakers, 23,000 hat-weavers, 23,000 potters and 18,000 hatters. These artisans were in the vanguard of the city riots that played an important part in the demoralisation of the propertied classes, and helped to erode the traditional principles of hierarchy and deference. As soon as news of the treaty of Ciudad Juárez came in, towns like Celaya, León and San Miguel de Allende were torn by rioting. Prisons were flung open, shops looted, archives and government records destroyed. In general, the older industrial and administrative towns of central Mexico, where the economy was declining and the workers impoverished, were worst hit by rioting. When *maderistas* intervened on the side of the propertied classes and suppressed the riots with vigour, they lost further caste with the workers, appearing simply as old *porfirista* wine in new bottles.

Durango was another state to suffer after the treaty of Ciudad Juárez. Durango City itself, which had been strongly defended by the federals, surrendered peacefully and the handover was smooth, but in Torreón there was widespread looting of the property of Chinese immigrants and 250 Chinese were killed in a vicious pogrom, which featured beheadings, disembowellings, death at the horse's tail and death while naked before drunken firing squads. It was always the Chinese and the Spanish, rarely the Americans, who were the targets for Mexican xenophobia. The Chinese had made the mistake of getting themselves tagged as 'the Jews of Mexico' by going into moneylending, shopkeeping and pawnbroking; as 'class enemies', they were considered fair game by the mob.

There was at one time a notion, plugged by the French *Annales* school of history, that mineworkers were a significant element in the Mexican Revolution. Certainly there were 90,000 miners, dispersed throughout Mexico, especially in the north, where Sonora was noted for its copper, Coahuila for its coal and Durango, Hidalgo and Chihuahua (with 4,000 different mines) for their silver. However, Mexican miners did not form the same kind of coherent group as British coalminers, say, in the same era. Most of them were transient Indians, temporary drifters, migrant villagers, opportunistic part-timers. Being a miner meant little in terms of social or political profile, and there was no question of the formation of a revolutionary core or *foco* like that of the Bolivian tinminers in the 1950s. It is implausible that economic recession in the mines could have radicalised miners and provided a 'watershed of rebellion', if only because the hard core of Mexican miners were highly paid and unrebellious; it was the transients, first to be laid off, who went to join Villa and Orozco in the sierras. The evidence suggests that the miners' only real loyalty was to the foreign owners who paid them well, and not to Díaz nor Madero nor Orozco.

The Mexican Revolution was not yet, and never would be, an all-consuming civil war. Certain social groups played no part at all in the early stages, notably the urban working classes, the resident peons on the great estates in central and northern Mexico and the debt-peonage unfortunates in the tropical south-east. This is hardly surprising, for the Mexican Revolution would never be a nationwide phenomenon. It was never a nation in arms for, even at the apogee in 1915, there were no more than 100,000 men under arms. Fighting was never widespread, but was confined largely to the northern and central areas, especially Chihuahua, Durango, Mexico State and Morelos. This geographical limitation was particularly noticeable in 1910–11. The states of Coahuila, Nuevo León, Tamaulipas and Jalisco were largely quiescent, though these areas had been vociferous in their opposition to Díaz in 1908–10.

The most notable absentee state in 1910–11 was Sonora. Perhaps the main reason was that the struggles of Madero, Villa and Zapata seemed irrelevant here. The anti-Díaz grievances of Sonorans focused on the state's elite with their snouts in the trough, and there was also the feeling that a quick transfer of power in Mexico City to head off more radical grievances was the consummation most devoutly to be wished. Only among the Yaqui Indians was there a profound moral and 'organic' resentment comparable to that of the *zapatistas* in Morelos. The Yaquis, peaceful since 1908, broke out into rebellion again when Madero raised his standard, but purely for reasons of their own; they joined the *maderistas* on the basis that their lands would be restored and their exiled comrades returned from Yucatán and Quintana Roo. Madero reluctantly accepted the Yaquis as allies and by June 1911, there were 1,000 Yaqui warriors in the field. Yet Madero had no intention of acceding to Yaqui aspirations. Convinced, like Lampedusa's prince, that things had to change so that everything could remain the same, Madero was about to disappoint every group in Mexico with the exception of the one he had ostensibly overthrown.

Díaz formally resigned on 25 May 1911 and boarded a train for Veracruz and thence for France (whose troops he had defeated at Puebla nearly fifty years earlier) – but not before his machine-gunners had enjoyed one final massacre of demonstrators in Mexico City's Zócalo on the 24th. Students and workers converged on the Zócalo that evening in a mood of triumphalism, but Díaz had stationed a dozen machine-guns on the roof of the National Palace and several companies of riflemen on the roof of the Cathedral, plus a regiment held in reserve on the south side of the square. Clearly he meant to go out of Mexican history as bloodily as he entered it. Between 9 and 10 p.m. a crowd of 75,000 jammed the Zócalo, and when police charges failed to disperse them, the troops opened up, first the riflemen on the Cathedral, then the machine-guns. The demonstrators seemed disinclined to cut and run, even as their comrades fell around them in dozens. It was fortunate, therefore, that a violent squall of rain sent everyone scurrying for cover before a terrible massacre could occur. Even so, over 200 people lay dead and 1,000 were wounded.

After such brutality, it was a moot question whether Díaz would leave Mexico alive. General Victoriano Huerta took the old dictator down to Veracruz in convoy, with Díaz's train in the centre protected by two troop trains – a necessary precaution, as it turned out, since the convoy was attacked by rebels. At Veracruz Díaz spent five days as the guest of Lord Cowdray's company before boarding the German steamer *Ypiranga* on the 31st. As he embarked, he is alleged to have said: 'Madero has unleashed a tiger; let us see if he can control him.' Sadly, like Díaz's 'so far from God' remark, this quip must be assigned to the ranks of the apocrypha, but it did accurately sum up Madero's dilemma.

On 3 June Madero set out from Coahuila for a four-day 700-mile triumphal progress to the capital. His frenzied reception at every station and halt made him appear not so much a liberator in the tradition of Bolívar, as a deliverer in the Messianic sense. People fought and jostled to touch the 'promised one', as if he possessed the power of healing.

Lionised, cheered and applauded with bells, *vivas* and fireworks all the way down from the border to Mexico City, when he arrived on 7 June to the ecstatic greeting of 100,000 people – one-fifth of the capital's population lined the route for his afternoon entry – Madero was essentially living in a fool's paradise.

At dawn on the day of his arrival Mexico City had been convulsed with one of the greatest earthquakes in national history. Lasting fifteen minutes, it destroyed hundreds of houses, the main railway station, the San Cosmé army barracks, the church of Santo Domingo, and it paralysed gas and electricity supplies. Coinciding with Madero's arrival, the earthquake was interpreted variously, according to political belief, either as God's punishment of the people for ousting Díaz or as his warning that the man soon to arrive was the chosen one. The sober facts were that 207 people died. Already the Mexican Revolution was proving profligate with human life. Within a month, if we include the Chinese ethnically cleansed in Torreón, the demonstrators massacred in the Zócalo, and those killed by the earthquake, nearly 1,000 people who were nowhere near a battlefield had suffered violent deaths.

Amazingly, the horrors of the earthquake were quickly subsumed in the rejoicing when Madero arrived. There were many anecdotes illustrating the godlike status the little man enjoyed for a while. The American journalist John Reed asked a soldier why he wore the Madero colours on his uniform. 'I don't know,' said the man. 'My captain told me he is a great saint.' Another man, found shouting out: '*Viva Madero. Viva democracia*,' was asked what democracy was and replied: 'I don't know, señor. I think that must be the fine lady at Doctor Madero's side.' On 7 June 1911 reason had surrendered to emotion. In retrospect, the earthquake, overwhelmingly read as a good omen – a symbol of the man who shook Díaz – should have been read the other way.

Madero had already made two mistakes that were to prove fatal: he had demobilised the revolutionary armies of the north, demoralising his own supporters and diminishing his own status, while putting himself entirely in the hands of the regular army; and by allowing León de la Barra, Díaz's foreign minister, to remain as interim president until the October presidential elections, he made a rod for his own back. With Díaz supporters still in the majority in Congress and de la Barra as chief executive, Madero needlessly faced four months of 'Porfirismo without Porfirio', during which he was constantly beset by hostile intrigues. De la Barra made little secret of his intention to derail Madero's policies at all points, and his first aim was to drive a wedge between Madero and

Zapata, who had neither been a signatory to, nor consulted over, the notorious treaty of Ciudad Juárez.

If Madero had been a true revolutionary, Zapata could reasonably have expected to become the next governor of Morelos, but it soon became apparent that he could advance under Madero only by abandoning his land-reforming credentials, the core of his identity. Meanwhile, other jealous anti-*zapatistas* were jockeying for position in Morelos. The Figueroas threw down their gauntlet by sending their men to occupy Cuernavaca and Jojutla while Zapata was engaged in the bloody struggle for Cuautla. They then tried to marginalise Zapata by building an alliance with the two-faced Leyva family, who had taken no part in the recent armed struggle. When Patricio Leyva made overtures to Zapata as if to an equal, Zapata wrote back angrily: 'You are no channel of authority for me, for I take orders only from the Provisional President of the Republic, Francisco Madero ... I only tell you that if you do not turn over Cuernavaca to me, I will have you shot.'

Within weeks it became obvious to Zapata that nothing in Morelos was going to change: the planters were not going to be stripped of their power, Zapata himself was expressly ordered by Madero's agent Robles Domínguez to take no action against the haciendas, and on 26 May Madero himself announced that Clause 3 of the Plan of San Luis Potosí, relating to land reform, could not be implemented 'in its entirety'. Zapata correctly read this to mean it would not be implemented at all. He was angry and stupefied to see the entire power structure of Morelos – the very people who had been in arms against him weeks before – confirmed in their privileges and positions. The world seemed turned upside down: it was almost as if it was the *zapatistas* who were the enemies of the Revolution and who deserved punishment. Within days there were reports that the planters had gone back to their old practice of fencing off village land.

Faced with this amazing reversal of fortunes, Zapata seemed to become momentarily paralysed with indecision, as if he was no longer sure of his purchase on reality. He rode down to Cuernavaca and wired Robles Domínguez for Madero's permission to proceed to appoint a temporary governor. There was no reply – hardly surprisingly, for the planters had already nobbled Madero and got their own stooge nominated for the position. Zapata could have used his 4,0000 armed men to impose his will, but did not do so; still strangely supine and dazed, he did not even react when the planters treacherously seized Tepepa and had him shot. Refusing to remain in Cuernavaca while the planters installed their puppet governor, he rode away disconsolately, brooding on Madero's treachery. He still thought of Madero as a man with genuine free will. He had not yet come to the awful realisation that, by so stupidly forfeiting real power, Madero had lost the capacity to deliver land reform even if he had wanted to.

Zapata decided to brace up by revisiting his roots. His first call was on Genovevo de la O, the most outstanding of the independent *zapatista* chiefs, whom he had not yet met. The meeting was a great success, and there was an immediate rapport. Buoyed up by this encounter, Zapata went up to Mexico City on 8 June for his first meeting with Madero. At a conference at the Madero family mansion on Berlin Street, attended by Carranza and two other Madero aides, the president-in-waiting began by imploring Zapata to get on with the Figueroas. Zapata brusquely replied that he had no reason not to get on with them, as his sole interest was land reform, not high political ambition. Madero replied that land reform was a matter for later, once the *zapatista* armies had been disbanded. Zapata asked what guarantees he had that an unreconstructed federal army would obey Madero in Morelos once all the revolutionaries were disarmed.

When Madero gently reproved him for lacking the spirit of reconciliation, Zapata cut through the refined atmosphere of a high bourgeois Mexico City salon with some blunt talking. He stood up slowly, picked up his rifle and went over to Madero. Pointing to the gold chain on his waistcoat, he said: 'Look, señor Madero, if I take advantage of the fact that I'm armed and take away your watch and keep it, and after a while we meet, both armed the same, would you have a right to demand that I give it back?' Madero nodded. 'Well, then,' said Zapata, 'that's exactly the situation in Morelos.' This was particularly uncomfortable talk for Madero; it was the second time in two months he had been menaced by a gun-toting revolutionary, but this was a man unlike Villa and not likely to burst into a flood of tears and beg forgiveness. Madero was concerned enough to offer to visit Morelos, and accepted an invitation from Zapata for 12 June.

The visit turned out to be a fiasco. Once again the Morelos planters, more politically sophisticated than Zapata, hobbled Madero and hijacked his programme to the point where Zapata in disgust refused to attend the welcome banquet for Madero. The latter, a mere shuttlecock being batted about by special interests, did not see how he was being manipulated, but he did note Zapata's absence and interpreted it as intransigence. Zapata's boycott was politically naïve, for Madero went on to see the Figueroas, listened to their apparent reasonableness, and returned to Mexico City convinced that Zapata was a hothead and that his followers were an uncontrollable *canaille* – a conclusion reinforced by sight of the bombed-out ruins at Cuautla.

Zapata meanwhile continued to press Madero by letter for guarantees on land reform and the future of his men. Madero predictably stalled on the agrarian question, but insisted on the immediate disarmament of all save 400, who would serve under Zapata as commander of the federal police; moreover, should the *zapatistas* rise again over their grievances, it would be Zapata's duty to suppress them with main force. Zapata was angry with this order that he should become in effect a political eunuch, with no leverage in Morelos; he read Madero's requirements, correctly, as a demand for unconditional surrender. Yet he was determined to exhaust all peaceful avenues. In mid-June he returned to Cuernavaca and started mustering-out some of his units; he took in 3,500 arms and paid out 47,500 pesos in demobilisation pay.

Having demonstrated good faith, he asked for formal confirmation as commander of the federal police, but the Morelos planters put pressure on Madero to rescind the offer. Even while this matter was in limbo, with Madero dithering as usual, a resolution of sorts was effected when Zapata asked the interim puppet governor, Juan Carreón, for 500 rifles for his police. When Carreón refused, Zapata raided the arsenal and took them anyway. Immediately the howls about a 'modern Attila' went up again from Mexico City's yellow press. A media 'scare campaign' featuring 'hordes' and dreadful atrocities kindled atavistic fears of a new War of the Castes, of pyjama-clad Indians with machetes, high on peyote, seeking out the white man on murder raids. This toxic black magic worked its poisonous spell. Madero, now under pressure from elite opinion to deal decisively with Zapata, summoned him to Mexico City to answer the planters' charges of sedition and treason.

Still Zapata remained conciliatory. At a meeting with Madero in the capital on 20 June he accepted with a heavy heart a new deal, whereby he would no longer be police chief but simply retire into private life with fifty bodyguards. Within a month he had gone from odds-on favourite as Morelos's next govenor to being a nobody, a retired revolutionary.

The planters' euphoria did not last long. They found that it was one thing to get Madero to humiliate Zapata, quite another to get his followers to accept this as the way things were to be. The villagers had tasted the heady brew of freedom from the haciendas and military victory, and this was a genie that could not be put back into the bottle. A spontaneous 'Zapata for governor' movement rose up; when the planters tried to use force against the villages, they found they had a serious problem of banditry on their hands. Seeing their cunningly devised *coup d'état* unravelling before their eyes, the planters panicked. They approached Zapata, offering to back him as governor if he would drop his demands for land reform.

They had seriously misread their man. A normal political boss or bandit chief could have been made over in this way, but not Zapata. He began secretly to rearm his demobilised men, aided surreptitiously by the new minister of the interior, Emilio Vásquez, who had never liked Madero's 'everything as is' treaty with Díaz, and who now tried to subvert the policy by clandestinely allowing arms and ammunition to come into the possession of the *zapatistas*. Tensions rose another notch on 2 July after a bloody slaughter of *zapatistas* by federals in Puebla City, following a dispute over arrest jurisdiction. Zapata's instinct was to march at once to Puebla, but Madero wired him not to intervene. Still stoical, Zapata obeyed, but it was an open question how much longer he could remain quiescent in such an atmosphere of fear and suspicion.

In August, de la Barra, determined to destroy Zapata before his interim term expired, appointed a hardline *porfirista*, Alberto García Granados, as minister of the interior, knowing that he despised Madero and was itching to crush the revolutionaries of Morelos. Echoing the mantra of all hawkish autocrats – 'we do not do deals with terrorists' – the minister ordered Zapata to disband all his units forthwith or he would use the Army against this 'nest of bandits and brigands'. Madero, desperate to avoid war in Morelos, many times invited Zapata to the capital for talks, but Zapata had had enough of Madero's prevarication, and stalled him each time. While publicly supporting Madero and making this clear in writing, he told his followers that Madero was so weak that the *porfiristas* manipulating him would not be above calling a conference of all revolutionary leaders and then massacring them all in one spot.

Under extreme pressure, Zapata eventually sent his brother Eufemio to confer with Madero. It was agreed that there would be elections in Morelos on 13 August, and that the *zapatistas* would then demobilise finally. However, any chance that Zapata might retire into private life was torpedoed by de la Barra, who issued an order for the immediate suppression of the *zapatistas* and sent two forces to apprehend him: federal troops to Cuernavaca and Jonacatepec, and Ambrosio Figueroa's men to Jojutla; for good measure, he added that Zapata and his representatives would be barred from any further talks in Mexico City. As a deliberate slap in the face for Zapata, de la Barra appointed his enemy Ambrosio Figueroa as governor and military commander in Morelos. Madero not only concurred in this but told Figueroa: 'Put

Zapata in his place for us, since we can no longer stand him.' Any thoughts that Zapata could retire to the countryside and be another Cincinnatus were brutally banished by this blatant provocation, and especially by the news that the most hated man in Mexico, General Victoriano Huerta, was commanding the troops on their way to Cuernavaca. Zapata wrote to Madero to ask either for an explanation or an order to halt Huerta; Madero did not reply, and provided neither. Anticipating all-out war, governor Carreón hurriedly postponed the state elections.

Huerta's orders were to compel the immediate demobilisation of all *zapatistas* and shoot any who resisted, but he interpreted this as licence to destroy anything he regarded as a legitimate military target, to impose martial law and to search out and destroy Zapata. However, Huerta was also cutting across the interests of all other parties in Morelos. The planters found they had a Frankenstein's monster on their hands, for he was not interested in them and their land-grabbing schemes. He wanted to impose a regime in the state that would redound to the advantage of his friend Bernardo Reyes, who was running against Madero in the October presidential election. Francisco Figueroa, a shrewder political operator than his brother, saw that the new dispensation would not be in his family's interests and warned Ambrosio that to cooperate with Huerta would be ruinous; he should therefore reject the offer of governorship. Conflict between Huerta and the Figueroas was not long coming: Huerta declared that Carreón was a weakling and must be replaced, but Ambrosio refused. Huerta hit back by suspending the state constitution and imposing martial law, using as the pretext a recent attack on his forces near Cuernavaca by Genovevo de la O's band.

Madero, importuned by the Morelos planters, by the Figueroas and even a loyally protesting Zapata, now intervened to try to restore order to an increasingly chaotic situation. His first task was to sound Zapata's intentions. Zapata told him he would demobilise at once provided martial law was lifted, Huerta's forces did not move beyond Cuernavaca and Raúl Madero was made military commander in Morelos, but he added that further issues would then have to be dealt with: the removal of all Díaz supporters from the state, the supervision of state elections by his own handpicked scrutineers and a guarantee of agrarian reform. Both de la Barra and Huerta refused to pay any attention to these negotiations, de la Barra, who nursed a particular hatred for Zapata, declaring that it was intolerable that Madero should allow a 'bandit' to dictate terms. He got his war minister to wire Huerta with orders to advance from Cuernavaca to Yautepec if Zapata did not disarm that very day. Huerta replied that he

would advance once he had 1,500 infantry, 600 cavalry and 500 75mm shells for his cannon.

Madero was completely hoodwinked by de la Barra. On the morning of 16 August he left Cuernavaca jauntily for the capital to get de la Barra's rubber stamp on the agreement he had negotiated with Zapata, unaware that an hour after his departure Huerta put his men on the march for Yautepec. When he learned the truth, in a letter from his mother, who urged him to come down hard on de la Barra, he was angry and in a mood for confrontation. However, de la Barra himself had meanwhile had second thoughts: it was dangerous for him to be seen openly defying Madero and supporting Huerta, who was known to be backing Bernardo Reyes in the presidential election. Moreover, he had on his desk a protest memorandum from all the municipal authorities of Morelos, stating that Huerta's troops were an infringement of state sovereignty and must be withdrawn. He therefore sent Huerta an order to suspend all military operations. Huerta played dumb and pretended not to understand the wire, so de la Barra was forced to repeat it.

Madero returned to Cuautla for a final round of negotiations with Zapata. Once he was gone, de la Barra rethought his position and sent Huerta an ambiguously worded order to suspend all 'offensive operations' while Madero was in the state; this left Huerta free to engineer a situation where he could open fire 'in self-defence'. After conferring with Zapata, Madero on 25 August sent a stinging cable to de la Barra, demanding respect for villagers' rights: 'They want to be paid attention to and listened to. Just because they make a protest, nobody can try to shut them up with bayonets.' The talks with Zapata had been a success, even though Madero had to endure a lecture about letting the Revolution go off at half cock and not making land reform a priority. At the first meeting at Cuautla railway station, they had greeted each other cordially and Madero had called Zapata his truest and most honest general. When they parted later, Madero made a speech calling Emiliano 'the valiant and most honourable general Zapata', declaring he could see through all the slanders of his enemies.

A euphoric Madero travelled back to the capital. He had met and got on well with all the principal village leaders, they had accepted the idea of his brother Raúl as military governor with enthusiasm, and Zapata had agreed to demobilise without mentioning agrarian reform. All they required in return was the withdrawal of Huerta and his army to Mexico City. Prospects for a permanent peace looked rosy, but in Mexico City de la Barra's intrigues continued unabated. By this time he had got it into his head that Madero was playing him at his own two-faced game: having fathomed the extent of de la Barra's support for Bernardo Reyes, Madero had made a secret deal with Zapata, whereby the demobilisation would be bogus; then, if a defeated Reyes revolted after the election, Zapata would be ready to raise the standard for Madero.

His head full of paranoid imaginings, de la Barra sent another cable to Huerta, telling him to restore order 'in those areas that Zapata did not control'. Huerta resumed his advance on Yautepec. The municipal president of the town came out to meet Huerta with a white flag, but Huerta, pleading 'self-defence' against one man and a flag, fired on him. When he heard of this latest act of sabotage, a stupefied Madero cornered de la Barra in the presidential office, where an angry altercation took place. Shaken by this, and the appearance of *maderista* demonstrations in the city, de la Barra ordered another 48-hour truce in Morelos. This time he proposed a general muster in Cuautla, the *zapatista* demobilisation to be supervised by police units from Veracruz and Hidalgo. For once Huerta, halted outside Yautepec, seemed to be obeying orders; in fact he needed the 48-hour interval to prepare his artillery.

There followed yet another conference between Madero and Zapata, in Cuautla, and *zapatistas* began handing in their arms. However, when the 48-hour truce expired, Huerta advanced and occupied Yautepec. Zapata was in an impossible position: he had to resist this or lose all credibility and see himself supplanted by other revolutionary leaders. Declaring that his aim was 'to reduce Zapata to the last extremity, even hang him or throw him out of the country', Huerta advanced towards Cuautla; his vanguard was reported approaching even as the *zapatistas* in the city were laying down their arms. Zapata read this as treachery by Madero and was inclined to acquiesce when his brother Eufemio suggested they shoot 'that little dwarf Madero'.

Madero was reduced to impotently firing off another missive to Mexico City, insisting that *his* will, not de la Barra's, should be done in Morelos. He left for the capital, promising Zapata that all would be well. On his arrival he found it impossible to locate de la Barra, who avoided him and refused to speak to him on the telephone. This was Madero's chance to denounce de la Barra publicly and expose all his treachery and double-dealing, but the little man merely blustered in private to his associates. Astonishingly, given that his own credibility was on the line, he did not pursue de la Barra but weakly departed for Yucatán on the campaign trail. This was the last straw for Zapata. He concluded, reasonably enough, that Madero had been playing him false all along. He never forgave him and ceased to believe in him at any level.

Any chance of avoiding conflict in Morelos disappeared when

Ambrosio Figueroa occupied Jojutla and executed sixty *zapatistas* there. In response Zapata issued a manifesto on 27 August, explaining to the people of Morelos that the outbreak of hostilities was the result of blatant aggression by the federal government. Prompted by his brother Raúl, Madero vainly attempted mediation, but at a Cabinet meeting on 29 August, de la Barra, heartened by the way Madero had turned tail and fled to Yucatán, ordered 'the active pursuit and arrest of Zapata', who was now an outlaw in all but name. Zapata replied with defiance, telling de la Barra that any blood spilt henceforth would be on his head.

Having occupied Cuautla, Huerta sent a commando squad to try to snatch Zapata at the Chinameca hacienda, but the operation was badly bungled. Ambrosio Figueroa, deeply resentful of Huerta's presence on 'his' territory, had had the same idea and also sent a snatch squad to Chinameca. The Figueroa commander decided to charge in past the hacienda guards, who opened fire. Zapata immediately intuited what was afoot, ran out of the main compound and made his escape through the hacienda grounds via a maze of cane fields at the back. He then put eighty miles between himself and his pursuers in a gruelling 72-hour trek that saw him emerge in a Puebla mountain town a long way south. The enraged Huerta asked de la Barra for plenipotentiary powers to wipe out a 'nest of bandits' and was given them.

It was not just the Figueroas who resented Huerta. The Morelos planters too were gnashing their teeth, since Huerta's repressive strong-arm methods were converting hosts of waverers and non-politicals to Zapatismo and thus making their own position more precarious. Meanwhile Zapata was raising a considerable force on the Puebla/ Guerrero borders. In a new manifesto he called for free elections, denounced the political illegitimacy of the governors of Morelos, Puebla, Guerrero and Oaxaca, demanded the postponement of the autumn presidential elections, plus political amnesty and agrarian reform. De la Barra tried to blunt the impact of this declaration by announcing that he agreed to political amnesty in general, but not for 'rebel criminals' – that is, Zapata.

Huerta then advanced into south-eastern Puebla and Zapata enticed him on, stretching his lines of communication. In October, feinting with a fake retreat into southern Puebla, Zapata launched an attack on Huerta's flank with 300 veterans. Covering vast tracts through little-known trails, the guerrillas then reappeared in eastern Morelos, where discontented villagers flocked to join them, swelling numbers to 1,500. After threatening Cuautla, Zapata's mobile army then moved into Mexico State, gathering up more and more recruits. On 22–23 October *zapatistas* overran villages in the Federal District, just fifteen miles from the Zócalo itself. All Mexico thrilled to the exploit. José María Lozano, most eloquent of Congressmen, put it well: 'Emiliano Zapata is no longer a man, he is a symbol.'

Zapata's sensational mobile raid through four states coincided with Madero's election as president. Anyone but Madero would have insisted on taking power immediately Díaz left, but his exaggerated concern for constitutional niceties meant that he spent five months as a lame duck, refusing to purge the old *porfirista* guard and allowing it to consolidate its power. In this crucial five-month period he lost the support of Zapata and Orozco for ever. Sensing Madero's declining popularity, Bernardo Reyes returned from exile and contested the election, posing as a new Díaz, a strongman who would guarantee order and prosperity. However, once Reyes realised he could not beat Madero, he resigned from the presidential race and settled in Texas to plot revolts. The Americans arrested him and his supporters, but he escaped, slipped across the border, tried to raise a revolt in the desert, failed, and ended up surrendering to the *rurales* on Christmas Day 1911. If anyone but Madero had been president, Reyes would have been executed for treason, but instead he was taken to a military prison in Mexico City, where he lived in some style.

Madero did not have much to beat in the October election. The Magón brothers remained in the USA, pointlessly (if accurately) denouncing Madero as a bourgeois opportunist, but the *magonistas* had no electoral clout; as Madero's supporters pointed out, they were hardly the stuff of which revolutionary heroes were made, and their sole accomplishment in 1910–11 was to capture the town of Mexicali in Baja California, the state which had the distinction of experiencing least violence in the Mexican Revolution. In the end, the main electoral opposition to Madero came from the Catholics, but they could make only slight headway against the little man with the bowler hat. In a free and fair presidential election, probably the first in Mexico's history despite the predictable opposition cries of 'foul' and 'fix', Madero secured 98 per cent of the vote and his running mate, Piño Suárez, got 53 per cent as vice-president.

This thumping electoral mandate did not improve Madero's performance as a politician. Instead of dealing firmly with his many enemies, he published (pseudonymously) a *Spiritualist Manual*, discussing politics purely in terms of high-flown concepts plucked from his beloved *Mahabharata*. His Cabinet was the kind some philosopher, trying to find a Hegelian unity through the fusion of opposites, might have selected, not a credible working group selected by a real politician. Far from believing in the art of the possible, Madero seemed never to hit a realistic mark; he either shrank from reality or tried to vault straight past it. He allowed press freedom, but was rewarded with lampoons and insults. He was criticised for every conceivable fault: for being short, uxorious and lacking gravitas; for deferring to his parents; for being friendly to Zapata; for being a mason, vegetarian and spiritualist; even for his love of dancing and for going up in an aeroplane. The newspapers bit the hand of the man who freed them from Díaz's censorship, but Madero, at least at first, refused to gag them with another *ley mordaza*.

Beyond these superficial expressions of spite and bile, there were authentic criticisms to which Madero was genuinely vulnerable. He alienated the people who had fought for him, while truckling to those who had fought against him, hated him and would never be reconciled to him. His was the classic fate of pleasing nobody and falling between two stools. He did not please the *hacendados*, army officers, bureaucrats and political bosses, and he bitterly disappointed peasants, sharecroppers, *vaqueros*, artisans, proletarians and debt peons. If forced to choose between the propertied and the dispossessed, Madero invariably opted for the former, if only to reassure them that he was 'sound' on private property and wealth. It is said that the one thing that infuriated him more than any other was to find that many revolutionaries had expropriated lands and given the owners IOUs which read: 'Don Pancho Madero will pay it all.'

Madero found it impossible to solve any of the problems bequeathed to him by Díaz. On land reform he was particularly vacuous, for he announced that the state would not expropriate land – rather it would return real estate to the *hacendados* or compensate them – but would look to the market for a solution, when everyone knew the market could not deliver agrarian reform, since Díaz had already carved up all the public lands and given them away for a song. The logical conclusion for the *zapatistas* and others was to work for Madero's downfall – something the Right was already trying to accomplish. On debt peonage Madero was worse than useless. Although its abolition was official government policy, his weak provincial governors could not make their writs run against the entrenched elites of plantation owners. Where these elites point-blank refused to cooperate with even the mildest *maderista* reforms, Madero, lacking the stomach for a fight, simply shrugged his shoulders and looked elsewhere. In any case, land reform always conflicted with social order, and in Madero's book order always came first. This was why he found it easy to impose order in the deep south: in Yucatán, Chiapas, Tabasco and

Oaxaca life returned to normal as in the Díaz days, with the plantation owners firmly in power.

Madero's presidency was in many ways the continuation of the *Porfiriato* by other means. Self-confessedly uninterested in agrarian reform, he failed to make his mark even in the areas where he was interested, such as education and finance. Economic reform was ruled out because the state governments were all in debt through the cost of maintaining garrisons. Forever caught between two fires in every arena he entered, Madero had to navigate between provincial demands for funds and a retrenching, deflationary Congress. Scholars debate the soundness of the Mexican economy in the Madero period, but the president's failure cannot be set down to economic causes. Mostly he lacked the will and élan for taking on any significant opposition. He detested drunkenness and bullfighting, but did not dare to tamper with the pleasures of the masses.

Madero was just as feckless when it came to military problems. He found it utterly impossible to integrate revolutionary and regular Army units and structures, both because recent enmities and hostilities were too strong and because the revolutionaries regarded the old guard as bogus *maderistas*, johnny-come-latelies who had joined Madero only when he was certain to win. Guerrilla leaders particularly objected to being fused in military hierarchies where they were expected to take orders from people who had done no fighting, and young warriors resented the fact that Madero gave most of the plums to the middle-aged. In the end, Madero could not get enough recruits for the Army, and was forced to introduce compulsory military service and press-gangs, Díaz's *leva* in all but name.

Above all, Madero could never extinguish the old culture of reflex violence and casual atrocity he had inherited from Díaz. The *ley fuga* continued to flourish; the Army continued to expose the corpses of rebels 'as a warning'; in Guerrero, Ambrosio Figueroa had a journalist executed simply for writing an article in praise of Zapata; in Puebla, federal troops machine-gunned more than 100 *maderistas* even after Madero had been elected president.

Yet Madero's victory in the election of 1911 did at least mean the end of de la Barra and, in Morelos, of Huerta. Zapata's great October campaign meant he could retire from the fray with honour if peace terms were forthcoming, and at first it seemed they were. Madero issued a public letter in his home state of Coahuila on the eve of the poll, saying that when he was president there would be a pacific settlement of the Morelos rising. Gustavo Madero, who had always realised the value of the *zapatista* movement as a counterweight to the would-be putschists like Bernardo Reyes, again made contact with Zapata, bringing the new president's fraternal greetings. Madero's agent Robles Domínguez went south with an attractive-looking deal that would clear the Figueroas out of Morelos, even their stronghold in Jojutla, and make the state over in its entirety to Zapata.

In this all too brief interregnum in autumn 1911, before misunderstandings once more took over, Zapata was able to devote a few precious weeks to his private life and take the honeymoon that had been so violently interrupted in August, when Huerta burst in upon Morelos. For in August 1911 Zapata had married, this time with full legal panoply. The bride was Josefa Espejo, one of the daughters of a prosperous Ayala livestock dealer who died in 1909. Before the old man died, Zapata seems to have bid for Josefa's hand and been turned down, on the grounds that he had no solid wealth in real estate. With the patriarch dead, and Zapata a general of the Revolution, there was no longer an obstacle. Emiliano's many earlier affairs and even his common-law marriages would not have been considered an impediment to wedlock in Morelos society; the macho code endorsed a 'boys will be boys' attitude to sexuality.

Marriage in Morelos was an institution entered into primarily for the purpose of fixing property, lands and title deeds on heirs; it fixed the roles of the powerful in society, making clear who the leading lights in a community were and who their legitimate children: in a word it was a solemn contract concerned with money, bequests and succession. Despite the Catholic ceremony, the teachings of the Church had little weight: marriage was certainly not about the 'allayment of mutual concupiscence' and it was not even about the procreation of children; still less was it concerned with 'love'. Zapata already had children by at least one woman and would not have remotely imagined that marriage committed him to sexual fidelity; nor would any Mexican woman have expected monogamous constancy. None the less, in a solemn marriage there were certain rituals concerning courtship and engagement that had to be gone through and that were taken seriously.

Before marriage, the girl of good family, who was always a virgin, would meet her future husband only under heavy chaperonage. Their conversation would be a pat, ritualised formulaic affair, in which they would exchange *dichos* – traditional sayings or clichés, which were meant to ward off 'improper' declarations of passion. 'Birds of a feather flock together', 'A monkey in other clothes is still a monkey', 'The eyes are the windows of the soul', 'Beauty is in the eye of the beholder', 'Death is always preferable to dishonour', might be some of the exchanges in the rather less than Attic dialectic. The lover would then have musicians serenade his lady at night, returning in a state of drunkenness at about 5 a.m. to sing *las mañanitas* or the morning song.

Zapata married Josefa in a Catholic church, as would have been expected in Morelos. We know little of her, and photographic evidence of Mexican women of this period is unhelpful, since most snapshots show them looking particularly mournful and dolorous, as if wishing they were a thousand miles away. Perhaps significant of a macho society is the formal wedding photograph showing Zapata sitting while his wife stands. Anecdotal accounts of the Zapata wedding are unhelpful, since they cannot even agree on what Emiliano was wearing: some say he went to the wedding ceremony in a black *charro* outfit, embroidered with silver, others that he was married in the ill-fitting business suit in which he appears on the photograph.

Domestic matters did not detain Zapata long, because a new and unexpected crisis arose in November. Madero, always a hopeless politician, unwontedly tried duplicity only to find his whole tangled web ensnaring himself most of all. He issued a strong statement, designed to appease the hawks in Congress, saying that he would deal uncompromisingly with Zapata. His official letter, handed to Robles Domínguez was harshly worded: 'Let Zapata know that the only thing I can accept is that he immediately surrender unconditionally and that all his soldiers immediately lay down their arms. In this case I will pardon his soldiers for the crime of rebellion and he will be given passports so that he can go and settle temporarily outside the state. Inform him that his rebellious attitude is damaging my government greatly and that I cannot tolerate that it continue under any circumstances, that if he truly wants to serve me, to obey me is the only way he can do it. Let him know that he need fear nothing for his life if he lays down his arms immediately.'

In private he offered Zapata a more favourable deal, which was to be communicated orally by Robles Domínguez, together with an assurance that the sabre-rattling communiqué was purely for public consumption. The plan misfired badly, because the Army commander in Cuernavaca would not let Robles Domínguez proceed into Morelos. Zapata meanwhile read Madero's public text, saw military preparations being made, and drew the obvious conclusion. He wrote back blisteringly to Madero: 'You can begin counting the days, because in a month I will be in Mexico City with 20,000 men and I will have the pleasure of coming to Chapultepec . . . and hanging you from one of the tallest trees in the forest.' Fighting broke out again and Zapata retreated, heading into the mountains of Puebla, once more sweeping up volunteers as he went.

Zapata continued to brood on Madero's treachery. This was the worst crime of all in his book. He said: 'I can pardon those who kill or steal because perhaps they do it out of greed. But I never pardon a traitor.' In late November, at Ayoxustla, a small mountain town in south-eastern Puebla, Zapata issued the manifesto on which he would fight for the next seven years. The famous Plan of Ayala utterly repudiated Madero, spoke of his treachery and tyranny and recognised Pascual Orozco as the legitimate chief executive in Mexico. The motif of treachery was still uppermost in his mind, for the word 'betrayal' (*traición*) occurs five times in the manifesto.

The Plan of Ayala made Zapata out to be a perfect Ishmael: 'I am resolved to struggle against everything and everybody.' The joint work of Zapata and Otilio Montaño, the Plan began from the premise that peaceful change was an illusion. Zapata told his intimates that his ancestors who asked for justice always suffered one of three fates: 'shot while escaping' (the *ley fuga*); being drafted into the military; or banishment to Yucatán or Quintana Roo. One of his sayings had a particular relevance: 'You must never ask, holding a hat in your hand, for justice from the government of tyrants, but only pick up a gun.'

The Plan contained detailed proposals for land reform. First, there should be restitution of lands seized by *hacendados* or caciques; then there should be expropriation of one-third of all large estates, assuming a peaceful transfer of assets; if there was armed resistance by landowners, the remaining two-thirds would be expropriated to pay for war indemnities and widows' pensions. The Plan has been described hyperbolically as 'communism by a man who did not know he was a communist', but in fact it was not even socialism – there was no proposal to expropriate all haciendas as a matter of policy – merely the restoration of lands illegally seized, yoked to a dream of a community of small independent landowners.

In alarm at this 'extremism', Madero sent another mission in December. This one got through, but when the envoys met Zapata on the Morelos/Puebla border all they offered was the absurd 'pledge' that Zapata personally could leave the country in complete safety to go into exile; nothing was said about the problems of Morelos and there was not even an offer of amnesty for his men. This was the apogee of the dialogue of the deaf which always characterised relations between Zapata and Madero. The two men could never agree on anything: for Madero the Revolution had ended when he took power, but for Zapata it would end only when there was true and lasting agrarian reform. Zapata could see only Madero's betrayal, and Madero could see only Zapata's pig-headed obstinacy.

Zapata was convinced that Madero's downfall was only a matter of time; until then he would keep fighting and hope to make a deal with the new government. He formed a junta of *zapatista* chiefs committed to the Plan of Ayala, even though not all the Morelos warlords came under his direct orders; Genovevo de la O still preferred to operate independently. By mid-January there were *zapatista* revolts in the states of Tlaxcala, Puebla, Mexico, Guerrero and Michoacán. In Morelos itself the situation was complicated. Zapata took the south-east as his personal fief, leaving his colleague José Trinidad Ruíz, a member of the junta, to control the north-east and use it as a jumping-off point for raids into Mexico State. The usual pattern presented itself: federal troops controlled the cities and large towns, but the *zapatista* guerrillas, albeit still short of arms and money, ranged free over the countryside.

Mexico City tried to portray Zapatismo as a played-out movement on its last legs, but events in late January 1912 showed how potent a force it still was. A see-saw battle took place in northern Morelos between the federals and Genovevo de la O, with the advantage shifting first one way, then the other. De la O came close to capturing Cuernavaca, then the federals hit back with a vicious counteroffensive on de la O's village of Santa María on 26 January. When this offensive ground to a halt short of its objective, de la O counterattacked, and for a week there was a series of terrible slugging battles, each one lasting at least four hours each day. From Cuernavaca observers could see the black smoke from gutted ruins, the plumes sent up by exploding artillery shells, and could hear the distant clatter and stutter of machine-guns.

Madero once more tried the tack of conciliation, and sent his brother Gustavo south to try to patch things up. Circumstance rather than sentiment lay behind the move, for by this time Pascual Orozco had launched a great rebellion in the north. At first fortune favoured Madero, for Ambrosio Figueroa abruptly resigned as governor of Morelos in January, finally conceding that he could not impose his Guerrero henchmen on the state. As the new governor Madero appointed Francisco Naranjo, a northerner from Nuevo León with a reputation as a political radical; he was a respected figure and a friend of Díaz Soto y Gama, a leftist intellectual who would later be a member of Zapata's 'think tank'. Naranjo said that on his arrival: 'I found that Morelos lacked three things – first ploughs, second books and third equity. And it had more than enough latifundias, taverns and bosses.'

Yet Naranjo's problem was that he was really Madero writ small, faced by the same dilemmas and caught between the same two fires: his plans for land reform foundered on the intransigence of the planters, and his plans for law and order were opposed by the *zapatistas*. De la O rejected Naranjo's radical credentials and issued a public challenge to him by declaring that he would blow up any train that entered Morelos. On 6 February he resumed his attack on Cuernavaca, which had nearly fallen to him the month before, and then the federals escalated the conflict by burning de la O's village, Santa María, to the ground; among those who died in the flames was de la O's daughter. This was the kind of mindless atrocity that set back hopes of reconciliation in Morelos by years. Swooping on the village in great force on 9 February, the federals first doused all the houses and buildings with kerosene and set light to them. They then compounded their vandalism by firing artillery shells into the surrounding woods, turning them into an inferno also. By evening, with glowing embers and a coating of ash everywhere, Santa María looked like a second Pompeii overwhelmed by Vesuvius.

In despair at this atrocity which he had not authorised, Naranjo appealed to Madero, but the president either ignored the import of his message or overruled him by sending to Morelos a tough, fanatical, hardline ex-Indian fighter, General Juvencio Robles, whose unspoken motto was that the only good rebel was a dead one. Robles was such a fanatic that he thought even the Morelos plantation owners were *zapatistas*. 'All Morelos, as I understand it,' he declared, 'is *zapatista*, and there's not a single inhabitant who doesn't believe in the false doctrines of the bandit Emiliano Zapata.' His first action was to have Zapata's sister, mother-in-law and sisters-in-law arrested and brought to Cuernavaca as hostages. His troops began shooting and arresting people at will or at Robles's whim.

Robles had studied the 'pacification' methods used by the British in the Boer War and by the US military in the Philippines – principally 'resettling' villagers in concentration camps. Once entire populations had been herded into the camps, he sent out flying columns into the countryside, killing all they met, on the grounds that all non-rebels should already be in the camps. Robles then burned down the villages, so that guerrillas could not return to get food or use the houses as redoubts. On 15 February federal troops found the village of Nexpa occupied only by women, children and decrepit old men. Amid the ululations and lamentations of these people, they gutted the place, black 'smoke signals' telling the guerrillas they would find no refuge in Nexpa. Other villages burned in the same way included San Rafael, Ticumán, Los Hornos, Villa de Ayala, Coajomulco and Ocotepec. Robles's men brutalised and intimidated all they met, including docile peons resident on the great estates and even hacienda managers.

Robles's career as an incendiarist alarmed even the people he was supposed to be defending. The planters tried to find a middle way, coaxing General Leyva to go to Cuernavaca with an offer of mediation, on the grounds that he had influence with de la O, and petitioning Robles not to burn villages for which they could vouch personally. The burning campaign was totally counterproductive, for it created new recruits for Zapata and made the *zapatistas* feel they had nothing to lose by staying in the field and nothing to gain from negotiating with Madero. Also, they were encouraged by news of the increasing seriousness of the Orozco rising in the north, which forced the president to withdraw troops from Morelos.

In March Zapata coordinated a grand offensive. His agents were active as far afield as Oaxaca, where 3,000 nominally *zapatista* guerrillas were led by Jesús Salgado. An admirer of Zapata and ideologically committed to his programme, though not yet linked to the leader by formal alliance, Salgado found it as impossible to control his followers as Zapata did in Morelos, and the peasant uprising in Oaxaca tended to shade into banditry. However, in the Zapata heartlands, everything ran smoothly. De la O once more probed towards Cuernavaca, and again there were deadly daily battles of attrition with the federals, this time around Huitzilac. While guerrilla bands penned in the federal garrison at Tepoztlán, the *zapatista* chieftain Lorenzo Vásquez laid waste the haciendas of central Morelos. Zapata himself launched a series of devastating raids into southern and western Puebla. Robles was dazed, caught off balance and outmanoeuvred by so many simultaneous attacks, and his spirits sank further at news of Orozco's victory over the federals in Chihuahua on 23 March 1912. By April Robles and his men had been forced to abandon the countryside to the *zapatistas* and were once again cooped up in the major towns. Madero meanwhile cut the ground from under the state's liberals by announcing there would be no land reform in Morelos until the Army had total control of the state.

Zapata's perennial problem was that he could blow up trains, occupy towns and even defeat the federals in battle, but he lacked the strength for a knockout blow. Even so, April 1912 was good for him. On the second of the month he attacked and took Jonacatepec, the day after his men finally cracked the garrison's resistance at Tepoztlán. On 6 April he and the principal chiefs made simultaneous assaults on Tlaquiltenango, Tlaltizapán and Jojutla, managing to take them but not to hold on to them. Zapata's abiding headache was that his ammunition always ran out before the enemy's. Federal reprisals were brutal: when they re-entered Jojutla, they executed fifty *zapatista* 'sympathisers'.

Fighting continued almost continuously throughout the month; there was a particularly sanguinary encounter around Huitzilac, which was blown apart by shelling. In late April de la O closely invested Cuernavaca and set up his artillery for a bombardment. The city authorities contemplated surrender, but the expected attack never came; it was the old story of shortage of ammunition. By early May the *zapatista* offensive had run out of steam, or more properly out of ammunition. Stocks were so low that they had to revert to guerrilla activity, frantically trying to replenish their ordnance by theft, robbery and the black market. Zapata sent an urgent message to Orozco in Chihuahua, asking him to send ammunition via the Pacific coast of Guerrero (the Costa Chica), but Orozco was himself hard pressed because of a US arms embargo and had nothing to spare.

Forced back on to guerrilla tactics, Zapata in late May sent some of his chiefs on an extended raid through northern and eastern Morelos while he himself publicly threatened to advance on Mexico City, in reality shifting into eastern Guerrero. De la O moved into Mexico State; to his great chagrin the trains between Mexico City and Cuernavaca started running to timetable again. Nothing could disguise the *zapatistas'* failure, and in June they were dealt four further blows: many rebels went home to plant the harvest in their villages; black market supplies of ammunition dried up when a renegade Army captain, the principal conduit, was arrested; the *zapatista* intelligence network in Mexico City was penetrated and broken; and in the north the Orozco rebellion started to falter. The one hopeful development was the marginalisation of Robles, as the moderates took power in Morelos following the success of the Naranjo-Leiyva faction in the municipal elections. Having tetchily refused to rein in Robles earlier, Madero was forced to shunt him out of Morelos into a command in Puebla.

The heavy rains in June and July forced a halt in the campaigning, but on 20 July Zapata announced his presence with a vengeance. Making his closest pass to the capital yet, de la O attacked a train at Parres station, on the border between Mexico State and the Federal District. There were over a hundred civilian casualties, and forty troops out of the fifty-three in the escort detail were killed. As Madero called an emergency Cabinet meeting in Mexico City, Zapata himself came close to taking Jojutla and Yautepec. Frustrated with their governor for being 'soft on Zapata', the new deputies in the state legislature at Cuernavaca sacked him and named a figurehead provisional governor, but it was clear to all that the new power in the land was Patricio Leyva, returned from the political dead. Madero recognised the new dispensation in the state by dismissing Robles from all military duties in the south.

The new military commander there was a man destined to play a key role in the Mexican Revolution, General Felipe Ángeles. Ángeles had some sympathy for Zapata and was in a good position to follow a policy of conciliation, now that Leyva and the moderates were his civilian counterparts and co-workers, but his position was made difficult by Zapata's uncompromising response. On 12 August *zapatistas* attacked another train, this time at Ticumán, between Yautepec and Jojutla; this time thirty civilians and thirty-six soldiers in the escort were killed. Madero cabled Ángeles urgently to find a solution with all speed, but left it open whether this was to be by negotiation or military repression. Angeles opted for the olive branch. He had Zapata's in-laws released from jail and offered amnesty, encouraging guerrillas to return to their villages, ranches and haciendas.

Ángeles's new bearing was a remarkable success, and it went to his head. He boasted that all it took was intelligence, that his predecessors had been blinkered morons who could think only in terms of military occupation and repression. Huerta and Robles fumed at the insult and angrily called for Ángeles to be court-martialled, but Madero was pleased with the way things were working out. Morelos seemed to be turning against Zapata, and he and de la O were forced out of the state, Zapata to raid in Puebla, de la O in Mexico State. In vain Zapata tried to get a rolling strategy going, trying to create a snowball effect that would take him into Mexico City; his efforts soon petered out in hard fighting around Tetecala and Jonacatepec. Had the moderates in the Morelos state legislature pressed on with their reform programme, they might have left Zapata and de la O as isolated and marginalised figures with nowhere to go; this was the period of greatest danger for the entire *zapatista* movement.

Whether through overconfidence that the rebels were losing, or through pique that, despite their moderation, Zapata and de la O still remained at large, the moderate deputies of Morelos suddenly changed tack, began complaining that law and order was *the* issue in the state, and asked Madero for tough measures. At the same time the promised reform programme slackened, then fizzled out altogether. The turning point was December 1912 when Patricio Leyva became governor and instantly vetoed the proposed bills on communal property. The shelving of these reforms, on which the villagers had set their hearts, was a terrible shock and seemed like just another in a long line of government betrayals. The people of Morelos turned back to Zapata: he had been right all along and he had never wavered, never truckled.

Zapata swung back into favour, his movement taking heart also from a new, albeit short-lived, rebellion in Veracruz in support of Félix Díaz, which made Madero pull troops out of Morelos. There was a new ruthlessness in Zapata's methods, and it seemed as if he had learned something from General Robles, the Cromwell of Morelos. His novel idea was to make the haciendas pay for the costs of his campaigns; if they refused to pay up, he simply burned down their cane fields. By the end of the year this fate had been meted out to recalcitrant owners at the haciendas of Altihuayan, Chinameca, Tenango, Treinta, Santa Inés, San José and San Gabriel, causing the planters losses estimated at two million pesos. Soon the *hacendados* saw the light and the money began to flow in. The added advantage of the new policy was that Zapata no longer needed to risk alienating the villages by asking them for funds. Moreover, by destroying the cane fields he gained recruits, since the unemployed peons had nowhere else to go but into the *zapatista* army.

The planters were now in an impossible position: if they paid Zapata his 'tax', they could be accused of collaborating with the enemy and arrested for treason; if they did not, Zapata would burn their crops. They begged and pleaded with Ángeles to take decisive action. Forced out of conciliation mode as much by Leyva's new hard line as by the revival of Zapatismo, Ángeles began to burn villages and order executions, though his was never a brutal regime on the same scale as Huerta's or Robles's. His military position was increasingly precarious, to the point where no army group less than 800 strong dared venture out of the cities. By the beginning of 1913 Zapata's fortunes had revived spectacularly. De la O, who had no more than 100 men a few months before, now had 1,000 and the same applied pro rata throughout the *zapatista* movement. One thing was clear. Madero could defeat Zapata if, and only if, that was the only military threat he had to deal with. As the events of 1911–12 elsewhere in Mexico showed, Zapata was in some ways the least of his worries.

After he left Madero's service, Villa went into the meat business, taking on as partners his brothers Hipólito and Antonio. With his 'golden handshake' from Madero, he bought four butchers' shops, all with the latest fridges and freezers from the USA. His property included 200 horses, 200 head of cattle, 115 mules, plus fields of corn and beans; he deposited only 1,700 pesos in the bank. He settled down to life as a prosperous businessman, though his enemies and aficionados of the 'black legend' say that he took part in organised crime. There is no evidence for this. There *is* evidence of a continuing interest in politics, for Villa told Abraham González of his anger when Madero pressurised González not to investigate further the notorious Banco Minero robbery. Most of all, he was angry that his veterans had not been given their furlough money or the land grants promised to them during the Revolution, and he had an intemperate interview with González on the subject. Continuing pressure secured some cash payments from Mexico City but, as Villa wrote to remind Madero, he himself had to support the families of three of his men killed in the Revolution, as the government refused to do so.

For most of 1911, however, Villa was taken up with his private life and love affairs. This was the year he married Luz Corral, a woman he had first met in November 1910. She was a simple girl who lived with her mother in straitened circumstances in the old military colony village of San Andrés. Like all households, the Corrals were asked for a 'voluntary contribution' to the revolutionaries' war chest when they rose against Díaz. In despair Luz's mother went to Villa and explained her crushing poverty. Villa was sympathetic, went to the house to see for himself and agreed that the 'tax' should be a nominal amount of coffee, corn and tobacco. While there he saw Luz and liked what he saw; he came next day and asked Luz to marry him. Between being the wife of a guerrilla leader and eking out a living in crushing poverty it was no contest, so she agreed. Her mother, however, did not take the same benign view of this development but, not daring to oppose Villa openly, suggested that Luz make him a shirt. She knew of her daughter's non-existent calibre as a seamstress and hoped that Villa would become disillusioned when he saw Luz's domestic incompetence. She scarcely knew her man: unlike Zapata, Villa was careless about what he wore and would certainly not have allowed a shirt to come between him and his sexual desire.

The naïve Luz Corral seems at first to have imagined she was marrying Villa on the same basis that Josefa Espejo had married Zapata in Morelos. The ceremony, in a Catholic church, may have bamboozled her, but even then she must surely have had her doubts when Villa, asked by the priest if he wanted to be confessed before the ceremony, replied that it would take too long. There must be doubts about whether Villa was ever married in any full legal sense, and the marriage to Luz Corral had no more validity than Villa's earlier espousal to Petra Espinoza in Parral. Additionally, Villa already had maybe a dozen women all over Mexico to whom he had either promised marriage or with whom he had gone through some kind of ceremony. Villa took the pragmatic line that liaisons with women were all about the satisfaction of carnal appetites, and that if women were stupid enough to want a meaningless ceremony of wedlock, he would not disappoint them. However, Villa was aware that the law formally forbade polygamy so, although he 'married' dozens of women in the presence of priests or civil officials, once the liaison was consummated, he would have his men destroy all relevant marriage records and copies. In Norse mythology the goats slain in Valhalla by the warriors for their feasts were always alive again the next morning. In a similar way, Villa emerged from every honeymoon a bachelor.

Both Zapata and Villa were in effect serial polygamists. This would not have occasioned the shock in turn-of-the-century Mexico which it does in our politically correct age, but then the entire male population of Mexico would have been regarded as 'misogynistic' by the standards of the twenty-first century. Villa believed in ritual courtship, compliments or *piropos*, gallantry and chivalric behaviour. Although he abducted women, he never raped them but waited for them to give their love freely; of course, because of the circumstances in which they found themselves, many of Villa's women acted under duress. Unlike Eufemio Zapata, he was rarely casually brutal to his women. Soledad Seañez, one of the last of his 'wives' and certainly one of the most beautiful, testified that in private life Villa was as volatile as in public, terrible when in a rage, but tender and loving when in a good mood.

Throughout 1911 Villa watched with mounting impatience as everything he had fought for in Chihuahua was thrown away. Victorious in the Revolution, his men returned to their homes in peacetime to find that nothing had changed: the *hacendados* and oligarchs were still in control.

For a year they waited patiently for Madero to keep his promises. Abraham González, the new governor of Chihuahua, genuinely wanted real change but was frustrated at every turn. First he had to endure the long waiting period for handover of power that had so bedevilled Madero; then he was told that Madero had replaced the Chihuahuan Vásquez Gómez as his vice-presidential running mate with Pino Suárez from Yucatán – a blow to state pride; finally, when he was actually in the governor's chair, he found himself intrigued against by the Creel-Terrazas clique, who still retained all their old power, and sabotaged by lack of support from Madero.

González, a large portly man from the middle classes, who looked the embodiment of bourgeois affluence, justified the confidence Villa felt in him. He built up a genuinely trans-class political movement in Chihuahua – the only one in Mexico – but it eventually fell apart because Madero failed to back him. González abolished company stores and *jefes políticos*, reformed taxes and wanted to place a law outlawing debt peonage on the statute book. His progressive taxation system – preventing anyone from owning more than 30,000 acres and distributing the rest to the land-hungry middle classes – brought him into direct collision with the Terrazases. They tried everything to blunt González's reforming zeal: bribery, black propaganda to whip up the Americans on the other side of the Río Grande, intrigues to get Orozco to rebel. González stood firm: he had the trump card over the Terrazas in the form of a permanent threat to reopen the file on the Banco Minero robbery. However, what the Terrazas could not do Madero did, with a series of blundering interventions.

First, still engaged on his Sisyphean project of conciliating the old *porfirista* elite – which would never be reconciled to Madero, no matter what he did – he ordered González not to reopen the Banco Minero case. The Terrazas were delighted: at a stroke Madero had removed González's master weapon. In disgust, González retaliated by releasing the text of Madero's letter about the Banco Minero affair to the press. Madero's next move was either stupidity, machiavellianism or sheer selfishness. He announced that the services of González were indispensable as his minister of the interior and he was to come to Mexico City. Although González continued to be governor while 'on sabbatical', he lost caste in Chihuahua since absentee governors were, by an inevitable association of ideas, *the* mark par excellence of the *Porfiriato*. In González's absence, his feeble deputy allowed himself to be browbeaten and dominated by the Creel-Terrazas clique.

Particularly after González departed to Mexico City, Villa found his position in the state increasingly uncomfortable. Every day he listened to complaints from his veterans and he sympathised: why should they have to return to the *status quo ante* Díaz and then be pursued by the *rurales* simply for taking from the haciendas what was their due anyway, and for the bagatelle of cattle rustling. The problem was that Madero had given Villa no power whatever, so that when he spoke up for his men, he tended to get snarled up in vociferous, and potentially violent, clashes with local authorities, especially in Parral where the military commander, José de Luz Soto, a veteran of the French wars, hated him like poison. A crisis arose when two of Villa's men, accused of banditry, died in a shoot-out while resisting arrest by Soto's troops. Villa and Soto appealed to González, who initially sided with Villa. Soto then evidently appealed to the General Staff and Huerta in the capital, for the next thing was that a highly minatory letter from Soto made González change his mind. Villa then appealed over González's head straight to Madero. The president responded with an emollient but non-committal letter, so an angry Villa went public, voicing his complaints to the press. He attacked Soto, without naming him, as a corrupt old man, ridden with hypocrisy and ambition and condemned those who protected him – an obvious jibe at Madero.

By the end of 1911 northern Mexico was a tinderbox. In the summer Sonora was again consumed by a Yaqui war. Fighting for an agrarian programme very similar to Zapata's, the Yaquis rose up once more and fought a brilliant guerrilla campaign. Defeated once, the Yaquis went on the warpath again when Orozco rose in Chihuahua in 1912, and by 1913 had Sonora in the grip of the most serious Indian rebellion yet. As in Morelos, Madero's initial instincts towards conciliation were subverted by hardline landowners and military commanders, who refused to yield an inch to the Yaquis and fought a war of extermination. Durango was also highly unstable by the end of 1911. Another quasi-*zapatista* group, taking its inspiration from Morelos and operating similarly, even down to the seasonal dispersal for the harvest, opened yet another guerrilla front, and was as difficult to extirpate as its counterparts in the south.

However, it was Pascual Orozco's rising in Chihuahua which lit the fuse that would eventually detonate the Madero presidency. For months the discontented revolutionary veterans had been hoping that Orozco, widely considered a more significant figure in the state than Abraham González, would take the field against Madero. This was also in Zapata's mind when he paid tribute to 'the illustrious General Pascual Orozco' in the Plan of Ayala in November 1911. Gradually in the north a cult developed around Orozco as a Messianic 'expected one'; women gave themselves to him as to a guru; mountains and rivers were named after him, and it was said that there was even a commemorative Orozco spoon minted somewhere. However, Orozco proceeded cautiously; when Bernardo Reyes rebelled and called on him for support, he called in vain.

Orozco's caution disappointed his disciples and at first they turned to other leaders. The first rebels to raise the standard were the followers of Francisco Gómez Vásquez, the man Madero had humiliated by dropping him as his vice-presidential running mate. The *vazquistas* were initially no more than a fleabite, but there was a danger that their example could be contagious. Then, in February 1912, a group of disgruntled *rurales*, about to be mustered out, fired shots in the air and called out '*Viva Zapata*'. Orozco was on notice that if he did not act soon, his mantle as deliverer would pass to others. Throughout Chihuahua there were gun battles, riots and lootings, including the sacking of government offices in Ciudad Juárez. Abraham González hurried north from Mexico City with 300,000 pesos to buy off the malcontents and tried to form an army to restore order in Juárez. The revolt in the north gained in ferocity, but still Orozco did not commit himself. He was determined to be on the winning side; as one of his critics said: 'He is for Pascual Orozco, first, last and always.' Finally he got the nod from the Terrazas: they would bankroll his movement if he removed the 'communistic' González.

Issues and motives in the Orozco rising were confused and complex. The social historians of Mexico tend to take a broad-brush approach, seeing the simultaneous opposition of Orozco and Zapata to Madero as the conflict of urban, middle-class, educated, national, progressive sectors, based on universal suffrage and rational legal authority, ranged against rural, plebeian, illiterate, parochial, nostalgic, backward-looking groups based on traditional and charismatic authority. Even more tempting is to see the Zapata and Orozco movements as the inevitable 'second stage' of all true revolutions, when the bourgeois victors of the first stage (the overthrow of the old regime) confront the lower orders whose aspirations they have unwittingly aroused. Such a neat schema has some validity in the case of Zapata, but is totally inadequate as an explanation of the Orozco rising.

The northern rising of March 1912 was above all the cynical manoeuvring by different personalities and power groups for control of Chihuahua. At the simplest level, it was a three-way fight between conservatives (such as the Terrazas) representing the oligarchy and the old Díaz system, González and Madero representing the middle classes, and the dispossessed looking to Orozco. To defeat Madero and González, the Terrazas first had to make common cause with Orozco; clearly their

intention was to defeat Madero first, then turn on Orozco. The oligarchs, in short, were playing the old game of divide and rule: use Orozco's wretched of the earth against Madero's huddled masses and, through Orozco, control the entire revolt from behind the scenes. The Terrazas and their ilk saw themselves in a 'no lose' situation: whoever won, hundreds of rebellious peasants would have been killed and they would emerge as the *tertius gaudens*.

Orozco's trans-class alliance of Left and Right, with its army of cowboys, smallholders, villagers, Indians, frontiersmen and bandits bankrolled by the oligarchy represented the attempt by the Terrazases to use a 'strongman' to do what they could not do themselves; but what were Orozco's real motives? Both he and Vásquez Gómez denounced Madero for not implementing the Plan of San Luis, but this was mere ideological window dressing. Some say that money was the principal motive with Orozco, that he had expected a pay-off from Madero of 250,000 pesos and a Cabinet post, and had been fobbed off with 100,000 pesos and the nugatory role of military commander in Chihuahua. Certainly Orozco's propaganda organs repeatedly alleged that the Maderos were financially corrupt, drawing particular attention to the 375,000 pesos 'loan' from the Franco-Spanish consortium that Gustavo Madero repaid from an 'emergency' fund, once his brother was in the presidential palace. Orozco, unlike Villa, was interested in money, and the Terrazas were the right people for such a man to deal with.

Had Orozco sold out, or was he in turn manipulating the oligarchy? It is true that he told his supporters in no circumstances to lay a finger on Terrazas territory or property, but then he could hardly bite the hand that fed him. The real answer is that Orozco never sold out, for the simple reason that he never bought in. He was always an ambitious political adventurer, using whatever weapons and whatever social classes came to hand. During the siege of Ciudad Juárez he had had behind-the-scenes meetings with Díaz's agents, and it is likely that he would have supped with whatever devil helped him towards his ultimate ambition: occupying the presidential chair. As a final twist, there are those who maintain that revolutionary leaders among the *orozquistas* had no illusions about Orozco and in turn were using *him*.

When Orozco at last appeared in open rebellion, González faced a dilemma. He badly needed Pancho Villa's help, but if he made him his strong right arm, Villa might desert to Orozco, his old chief. On the other hand, to give Villa no command would be an insult and might drive him into Orozco's arms. González solved the dilemma by appointing Villa colonel in the forces earmarked to suppress Orozco but giving him only

250 men. At the end of February 1912 Villa and his men rode into the mountains of western Chihuahua. Soon their numbers grew to 500 and, because of the tight discipline Villa insisted on, they were very popular wherever they went; in Luz Corral's home town of San Andrés, there was heard for the first time a cry that would soon echo around Mexico: *Viva Villa!*

Villa's support for González and Madero has puzzled some historians, who see his interests more naturally aligning him with Orozco. Alan Knight speaks of a 'naïve personalist ethic' and talks of 'the Orozco-Villa vendetta, a violent subplot in the drama of the northern Revolution'. It is true that Villa had never liked Orozco and resented his cult of personality; moreover, an alliance with him was out of the question now that Creel and the Terrazas were backing him. There was also the pragmatic consideration that if he stayed neutral, he would probably end up hated and despised by both sides and a universal target. But, most of all, despite his misgivings about their political programmes, Villa was still psychologically in thrall to González and Madero because of the understanding way they had treated him in 1910.

González ordered Villa to seize Chihuahua City, but Orozco was too fast for him and got there first. Villa retreated to the Valle de Zaragoza and was on the sidelines until the end of March. At this stage Orozco looked unbeatable. He had a larger army than Zapata in Morelos, had financial backing from the oligarchy, and was well armed and equipped, able to import guns and *matériel* from across the US border. His weakness – and it was to prove fatal – was that he did not enjoy the mass support the *zapatistas* enjoyed. None the less, in these early weeks Orozco was euphoric and confident, and there was already wild talk of a march on Mexico City.

Another blow for Madero was further sabre-rattling by the USA. Taft, in effect, now did to Madero what he had earlier done to Díaz, demoralising the uncommitted in Mexico by ordering another massive mobilisation on the Mexican border; this time he sent no less than 34,000 men to the Río Grande.

At first Orozco was as good as his boasts. A 6,000-strong federal army advanced north from Torreón under the command of Madero's defence secretary, José González Salas. On the afternoon of 23 March, at Rellano – the southern edge of the desolate Bolsón de Mapimí desert region, previously famous as a stronghold for Apache raiders – the federals were surprised by the *orozquistas*. Emilio Campa, a former *maderista* who had joined Orozco, introduced the second great military innovation of the Revolution (the dynamite bomb had been the first) by pioneering the use of the 'loco loco' or *máquina loca*. Packing a locomotive with dynamite, he sent it like a missile straight into the federal vanguard; it killed sixty men outright and caused chaos, confusion and finally panic. The *orozquistas*, fighting under their notorious red flag, which gave them their usual nickname, the *colorados*, then closed in for the kill. In the rout that followed there were many ugly scenes. One federal battalion mutinied and killed its two officers; other mutineers slew the chief of staff. González Salas, seeing the ruin of all his hopes, committed suicide. On paper the defeat was not so bad – total federal casualties were around 300 – but the shattering effect on morale made many think Madero was doomed.

Orozco now controlled all of Chihuahua except the city of Parral, to which Villa fled after the disaster at Rellano. Orozco at once set up his own government in Chihuahua and issued bonds to the value of 1.2 million pesos to finance the campaign. He suppressed the *maderista* newspapers and issued his own scandal-sheets which poured scorn on Madero at every level, from his short stature to his urban manners and the mere fact that he lived in a city. Orozco shared Zapata's view that the countryside was the repository of virtue, and the city of vice. He even allowed the Terrazas to peddle the favourite oligarchic line, which took over the Catholic idea that spiritualism involved contact with the forces of darkness; the oligarchic gloss on this was that a spiritualist proposing land reform 'must be' in contact with the devil.

On 25 March Orozco promulgated his manifesto, which called for the resignation of Madero and Pino Suárez. More radical aspects of the Plan, which drew an endorsement from Zapata in the south, were the call for higher wages for workers, restrictions on child labour, the nationalisation of all railways, the abolition of company stores and the demand for agrarian reform. A few days later Orozco declared grandiloquently that no opposition to him remained in Chihuahua 'save that of the highwayman Francisco Villa, on which point I congratulate myself'. As soon as he took Parral, he intended to march on Mexico City. One obstacle remained: the US arms embargo passed by Congress on 13 March. Although the Hearst press urged President Taft to back the strongman who could fill the void left by Díaz, Taft had no choice but to cut off all arms supplies except to the legally constituted government of Madero; had he not done so, Madero would have been justified in regarding it as a hostile act. The Orozco movement thereafter evinced signs of anti-Americanism; Orozco himself had no intrinsic anti-gringo feelings, but always turned nasty when thwarted.

In Parral, Villa's old nemesis Soto came out for Orozco, but loyalties in the garrison were divided, and not all felt like heeding the dictates of the military commander. When fierce fighting broke out among the soldiers, Villa, who had been hovering nearby, saw his opportunity, slipped into the city with just sixty men and tipped the balance against Soto. Contrary to expectations, Villa did not execute Soto but sent him down to Madero in Mexico City under armed guard. Then he set about the defence of Parral, impressing the businessmen and foreign residents by the iron discipline he exerted over his men. He confiscated all arms and ammunition and obliged the wealthiest citizens to make him a forced loan of 150,000 pesos. He mulcted the leading citizens, knowing very well from his long residence in the city who they were, keeping them under arrest until they paid up, but giving receipts for everything, except to the Banco Minero, whose funds he considered the Terrazas to have stolen anyway.

When Orozco's 2,500-strong army advanced on Parral, Villa had a tough choice to make: should he stand and fight against far superior forces or pull out and revert to guerrilla warfare. He decided to fight. The first clash came on 2 April when 1,000 *orozquistas* with a cannon and two machine-guns tried to establish themselves on the heights outside Parral from which they could pound the city into submission. However, as they manhauled the cannon up the hillside, Villa unveiled his first secret weapon in the shape of US mercenary Tom Fountain, a crackshot in charge of a machine-gun. Fountain's shooting was so accurate that he took out all the mules and men dragging the cannon. Unnerved, the *orozquistas* fled down the hill, abandoning the cannon; this loss shook the morale of the rest of the troops and, after heavy fighting in the outskirts, they withdrew around 6 p.m. as darkness came on.

Villa continued his stubborn resistance for three days with just 300 men. By the afternoon of 4 April, heavily outnumbered, Villa could no longer hold out, so he ordered a retreat under cover of night. A remarkable number of *villistas* managed to escape, though surrounded by 2,500 of the enemy, and their order and discipline contrasted sharply with what was to come. When the *orozquistas* entered Parral after nightfall, they gave themselves over to an orgy of looting and rapine. Never ceasing to fire off their guns, the crazed soldiers first broke into the liquor stores and got roaring drunk. Then they proceeded to sack the other shops and stores, killing all who resisted, entering houses at will, manhandling the occupants, stealing jewellery and other valuables. Having gutted the Banco Minero, the drunken soldiery terrorised middle-class families by racing through their homes with the safety catches off their rifles. When the troops finally withdrew, sated with drink and booty, a second wave of pillage overwhelmed the city as the town mob went on the rampage, looting and raping. Drunken pillagers hurled dynamite bombs at every door that would not yield to an inebriate 'open sesame' command.

Orozco admitted that he had lost control of his troops on the night of 4 April, and news of the sack of Parral did incalculable damage to his cause. Although by and large foreign nationals and property were not touched, he was widely condemned for executing the manager of the slaughterhouse and his brother for being *villistas*. Angry that Parral had been wholeheartedly behind Villa, Orozco was determined to teach it a lesson, but he went too far in ordering the execution of Tom Fountain, the American soldier of fortune, who had been unable to get away with Villa. Holed up in a drugstore for three days, and starving when the owner found him there, Fountain might have expected that his US citizenship would have given Orozco pause. However, he was taken out before a firing squad and executed on the spot, without trial.

Villa's valiant action at Parral had delayed Orozco a vital three days and allowed Madero to reinforce Torreón. The president sent Villa a letter of congratulation, but again showed a shaky grasp of his psychology by offering him money. Convinced that Villa would always be loyal to him, Madero gave him a colonel's rank, but insisted he and his men would have to serve under the regular Army commander. When Villa arrived at Torreón, he found that this was none other than the much-feared 'iron man', Victoriano Huerta. Villa's men begged him not to accept Madero's offer, but Villa had not yet taken the measure of Huerta, the monster he agreed to serve. Huerta seemed to loathe and despise all other human beings, especially those who were not members of the Army or the oligarchy. He particularly hated Abraham González for being middle class, and as for Villa, this uncouth, semi-literate bandit, as Huerta saw him, needed to be taken down a peg or two.

Villa was now at close quarters with the most repulsive figure in the entire Mexican Revolution. Nudging sixty, of uncertain date of birth (perhaps it was even as early as 1845), Huerta was the son of a *mestizo* peasant woman and a Huichol Indian father from Nayarit (some said this was the clue to his mixture of stoicism and cruelty). He entered the Army at fourteen, became the protégé of General Donato Guerra, and under his patronage graduated from the Military Academy. Joining the corps of engineers, he campaigned all over Mexico: in Tepic in 1879; Guerrero in 1893 (where he put down a rebellion under Canuto Neri); in Sonora against the Yaquis in 1900; again in Guerrero in 1901; and finally in the Yucatán where he at last ended the rebellion of the Mayas in the War of the Castes. A believer in the use of force to solve all problems, Huerta was a cruel, bloodthirsty authoritarian, who went in for press-gangs, deportations, firing squads and summary executions. A long-time supporter of Bernardo Reyes, he urged his patron to attempt a coup d'état in 1904. By 1907 Huerta seemed a busted flush, took extended leave to do civilian engineering work in Monterrey, and by 1909 was on an Army pension, which he supplemented by part-time teaching.

It was Díaz, a fellow authoritarian, who brought him back from obscurity in April 1911 by asking him to pacify Guerrero, and it was Huerta who accompanied Díaz to Veracruz after the dictator resigned. De la Barra gave him the assignment against Zapata that made his name a byword for savagery in Morelos, and Huerta never forgave Madero for dismissing him from that command. However, Huerta was always lucky. Five months later one of his cronies, García Peña, became war minister and persuaded a reluctant Madero to give him the command against Orozco. Stocky, bullet-headed and myopic, Huerta was distinctive with his crew-cut hairstyle and dark tinted glasses. Almost never seen without a frown on his face, Huerta was one of those people who seem to be in a permanent near-apoplectic state of exasperation. As a drinker he was legendary for his consumption of brandy; one wag said that his only friends were two Europeans named Martell and Hennessy. Mrs Rosa King, who knew him in Cuernavaca, recounted an incident when Huerta was due to lead his troops against Zapata, but instead spent the whole day in a bar while his men shivered outside in driving rain. Villa confirmed that Huerta would start drinking at seven in the morning and would continue all morning, afternoon and evening, so that he was never wholly sober.

It would not have taken great insight to predict that the meeting of Villa and Huerta was a personality clash waiting to happen. The martinet against the man of caprices, the drunk against the teetotaller, the snob against the humanist, the desiccated calculating machine against the overemotional dynamo, the by-the-book plodder against the inspirational and improvisational leader: such a collision could have but one ending. It did not help that Villa revered Madero while Huerta hated him. The relationship got off to a bad start when a tired and dusty Villa reported to Huerta's headquarters. Huerta and his officers, all in full dress uniform looked the upstart up and down through pince-nez and upturned noses. Villa later remembered: 'Those men looked me up and down as though I were a stray mongrel with a bad smell.'

After establishing his headquarters at Torreón, Huerta planned a slow campaign of attrition. Since morale was low and his troops decimated by typhus, he refused to be hurried and reorganised his army at leisure, working out the logistics of the coming campaign in a ponderous, mathematical way. Although he had been promised a free hand, he was further angered by a constant fusillade of anxious telegrams from Madero – who had been badly shaken by the defeat at Rellano and even imposed press censorship in his panic – and by the intervention of his brothers. Huerta's hatred and contempt for Madero was hardly a secret: when a *maderista* sent him a consignment of Madero lapel buttons, Huerta had them thrown into a rubbish bin.

Yet, as both Zapata and Villa conceded, the man did have some military talent. His dispositions were clever for, dug in around Torreón – which Orozco would have to take in order to advance on Mexico City – he left the enemy only three options, given that the Sierra Madre barred large-scale westward movement: stalemate by remaining in Chihuahua; an eastward march into Coahuila; or a frontal assault on Torreón. Orozco, seeing the danger, went for the Coahuila option, but the poor did not rally to him and the miners and urban middle classes, fearing the radical policies and looting practices of the dreaded *colorados*, declared for Madero. Orozco defeated the so-called rising military star of Coahuila, Pablo González – who would eventually gain the unwelcome reputation of 'the general who never won a victory' – on several occasions, but could never dominate the state.

Beginning to run low on ammunition and badly needing another victory to maintain revolutionary momentum and prevent desertions, Orozco was finally tempted south. On 12 May at Conejos he clashed with Huerta and was badly mauled. The *colorados* fell back, ripping up railway track as they went to slow Huerta's advance, but on 22 May Huerta overhauled them near the scene of Orozco's great victory two months before. In the second battle of Rellano, the *orozquistas* were cut to pieces by Huerta's cavalry; Orozco fled from the scene, leaving behind 600 casualties (including 200 dead) and large numbers of horses and guns. Dogged by Huerta and plagued by desertions, Orozco turned at bay for a last-ditch stand at Bachimba canyon, forty miles from Chihuahua City, and in desperation tried a variation on the *máquina loca* trick that had won him the first battle of Rellano. He drew up his army to invite Huerta to attack, and seven miles south of his position he mined the railway track with 100 pounds of dynamite, hoping to annihilate the federals as they steamed north in troop trains. However, the explosion was a failure, destroying just one coal car, and the disembarking federals soon routed the main *colorado* force.

Huerta entered Chihuahua City on 8 July, restored Abraham

González, and recaptured Ciudad Juárez by mid-August. Leaving his subordinates to mop up, he returned to Mexico City to a hero's welcome. Madero, furious that Huerta either would not or could not give an explanation for a gaping hole in the campaign accounts, was forced to promote him to divisional general, when he ought really to have charged him with peculation.

The Orozco movement was not quite finished yet; although Orozco himself fled across the border to the USA, he still had hopes of directing a viable guerrilla movement, and to this end ordered his men to make the long march to Sonora. Three thousand *colorados* braved the mountain passes of the Sierra Madre and debouched in Sonora, only to find they were no more welcome there than they had been in Coahuila. After some unpleasant skirmishes with the local peasantry, the *orozquistas* gave up and left the state. By autumn 1912 they had been expelled everywhere, but not before a young cavalry commander named Álvaro Obregón had made his mark in action against them.

The *orozquistas* dispersed into guerrilla bands, full of bitterness, spreading stories that their leader had been holding orgies in his private train while his men were dying in battle, and had salted away 500,000 pesos in a bank in El Paso. The great Orozco rising that was to have swept the hero into the presidential palace petered out in acrimony, but for a while it had been touch and go, and Mexico City and Madero himself had trembled. Villa, who played such an important role in thwarting Orozco, learned many lessons from this campaign that would be invaluable the following year, but the real significance of the Orozco rising was the way it placed Madero in thrall to the Army. Faced with the threat in the north, the president had had to secure a 20 million peso loan and double the military payroll. Previously a stern critic of press-gangs, Madero was obliged to connive at Huerta's use of them.

In general the result of the Orozco rebellion was what has been called 'the militarisation of politics and the politicisation of the Army'. Once again, there are those who detect the spirit of Machiavelli abroad. Huerta's fiercest critics say that, even before he defeated Orozco, he was dreaming of ousting Madero and becoming the new Díaz, and that the failure to wage war to the knife against the defeated *orozquistas* was because Huerta thought they might be useful pieces to bring on to the board later. Some anti-Huerta commentators even allege that he was already secretly in communication with the exiled Orozco for this purpose.

This would make sense of a sensational event that occurred in the middle of the campaign against Huerta. The predictable non-meeting of minds between Huerta and Villa soon escalated to something far more serious. From the very first Villa had been irritated by his new position, for he heard Huerta's officers laughing at his title of 'honorary general' behind his back, and deeply resented it. Then, Villa's position as charismatic chieftain, responsible for his people, collided with Huerta's insistence that everyone in his camp, even the irregulars, had to obey strict military discipline. In May Villa's favourite lieutenant, Tomás Urbina, raided the Anglo-American Tlahualilo company and demanded money with menaces. The US ambassador in Mexico, Henry Lane Wilson, who had an irrational hatred of Madero, made a vigorous protest to Huerta, who promised to execute Urbina. Hearing of the threat, Villa and all the irregular commanders said they would pull out of the campaign if Urbina was shot. Huerta backed down, but from that day his loathing of Villa was intense, and he vowed to take his revenge once Orozco was beaten.

Further petty clashes between the two men over horses, with Villa being insubordinate in Huerta's eyes, led to unacceptable tension. Once Orozco had been beaten at Rellano, Villa sent a cable to Huerta on 3 June, announcing that his own force, which he now named the División del Norte, would cease to come under Huerta's orders, with immediate effect. Villa was within his rights: according to the deal he had signed in 1910–11, irregulars needed only campaign while there was a prospect of battle, and here was Orozco thoroughly defeated. Huerta, though, regarded the cable as an express act of desertion and sent Colonel Guillermo Rubio Navarrete to exterminate the *villistas*. Rubio Navarrete was the wrong man for such an act of callous butchery. When he came on the *villistas* unawares and found Villa and his men asleep, he surrounded their camp with troops and returned to Huerta to get the orders confirmed.

Next morning, finding his compound encircled by federals, Villa began to get some vague inkling of what was afoot and decided to take out insurance by sending a cable to Madero. Unfortunately, to send the telegram he had to go to Army headquarters, where he was arrested; Huerta then ordered him executed as a deserter, without court martial. Rubio Navarrete performed his second life-saving action by alerting Emilio and Raúl Madero to what was going on. Raúl Madero cabled his brother in Mexico City, asking for a stay of execution until the whole matter could be investigated. Villa meanwhile was taken out into the yard, where the firing squad was ready. The platoon sergeant in charge of the detail made a cross on the wall with a mattock and asked Villa to stand at the foot of it. Villa kept exclaiming, 'Why, why? Why are they going to shoot me? If I am to die, I must know why.'

At this point Villa broke down, wept pitifully and begged for his life. The fact is undisputed, but the reasons are not. Those hostile to Villa portray this as the clichéd reaction of the coward/bully; Villa said that he was playing for time, knowing that Raúl Madero had cabled Mexico City, trying to stall until the reply came in. Villa was enraged that he had been seen kneeling and grovelling, and later rationalised his guilt and shame to his own satisfaction: 'I could not continue for the tears that choked me. At the time I hardly knew whether I was weeping from mortification or from fear, as my enemies said. I leave it to the world to assess whether my tears in these supreme moments were due to cowardice or despair at seeing I was to be killed without knowing why.' Cynics will draw the obvious conclusion, but in Villa's case tears of frustration are not implausible, given his psychology – frustration at not being told the reasons and at having fallen so stupidly into Huerta's trap.

For the third time Rubio Navarrete intervened to save Villa's life. He halted the firing squad when it was in the very act of presenting arms and took Villa back to headquarters. Stupefied at the reappearance of the man he thought safely dead, Huerta raged at Rubio Navarette and threatened him with execution too. The colonel answered calmly that he had never seen any sign of hostility or armed resistance from Villa such as one would expect from a deserter. Huerta was in a difficult spot, for he could not admit that he already had in his pocket a cable from Madero, forbidding the execution, which he was going to pretend had arrived too late. He therefore sent Villa on to Mexico City, incorporated the *villista* units into his army, and wrote Madero a long screed of self-justification, accusing Villa of theft and rebellion. Huerta's letter was a farrago of lies: he claimed to have 'high regard' for Villa and alleged that Villa had offered him armed resistance.

All of this verbal froth was an elaborate charade, since Huerta had already made plans to dispose of Villa under the old *ley fuga* dodge. Huerta sent orders to the commander of the Torreón garrison, Justiniano Gómez, to intercept Villa's escort and execute him. Gómez, uncertain of his ground, consulted his senior officer, General Gerónimo Treviño, who, doubtless having been sent a copy of Madero's original cable, countermanded Huerta's order. Enraged, Huerta tried another tack and issued the same orders to the garrison commander at San Luis Potosí; he too would not accept the responsibility, contacted Mexico City, and was told to send Villa to the capital, alive and unharmed.

Once in Mexico City, Villa was incarcerated in the Federal District

Penitentiary, where he commenced a seven-month struggle for freedom. At first he pinned his hopes on the restoration of Abraham González, and González cannot be faulted for the strenuous efforts he made on Villa's behalf. In his representations to Madero, González reiterated four points: Villa had remained loyal at a crucial stage in the rebellion, even after Orozco offered him large sums to turn his coat; his three-day defence of Parral had given Huerta the vital breathing-space to form up around Torreón; any confiscations Villa carried out in Parral were fully in accord with revolutionary practice; and Orozco had anyway destroyed Villa's four butchers' shops and arrested Villa's two brothers. However, Madero remained deaf both to González's pleas and Villa's direct appeals. He refused to intervene, grant Villa an audience or answer his letters, except briefly and coldly. Again and again he made it clear to all petitioners that he would not intervene in a matter where the military had jurisdiction.

Madero's attitude is puzzling. He was an ingrate, since Villa's loyalty was the hinge on which the successful outcome (for Madero) of the Orozco rebellion hinged. His harsh attitude towards Villa contrasts startlingly with the misguided mercy he had shown to General Navarro at Ciudad Juárez the year before, which entailed defying the letter of the law. One obvious conclusion would be that he disliked Villa, either because he thought him an unprincipled loose cannon, or because he still harboured a grudge over the gun-toting incident at Ciudad Juárez. A more likely explanation, however, is that he was now so deeply in thrall to the military that he thought it too risky to overrule Huerta again. Besides, he was under enormous pressure from Henry Lane Wilson, the crazed US ambassador. Wilson's insane hatred for Madero extended to, and was exceeded by, his hatred for Villa. He had tried to bully Madero into executing Villa, and was furious that his intended victim had escaped with his life. When the State Department reprimanded Wilson for pursuing a private vendetta over Villa and the Tlahualilo affair, and not acting in concert with the British (who owned the lion's share of the company), Wilson had the impudence to say he had not acted hand in glove with his colleague because the British ambassador was too lazy.

As Villa languished in jail, he became more and more despondent. The news he heard from Chihuahua seemed preposterous and he had to pinch himself to be reminded that he had been on the winning side and Orozco the losing. Huerta, with the aid of Madero's reactionary uncle Rafael Hernández, was pitching hard to have Abraham González removed in favour of a stooge of the Terrazas. After so many unsatisfactory *ad hoc* alliances with unreliable revolutionaries like Orozco, the Creel-Terrazas clique had finally found their solid rock in Huerta. Madero drew the line at ousting the faithful González, but he bypassed his authority by conniving at Huerta's outrageous actions, including the granting of an amnesty to the *orozquistas* so generous that their fortunes were everywhere restored. The height of absurdity was reached when Madero amnestied Luis Terrazas, Orozco's paymaster, who had absented himself in the USA during the actual fighting. The Army, under Huerta's direction, then turned the screws on González, persecuting his followers and making common cause with yesterday's enemies.

It soon became clear to Villa that Huerta would never allow him to walk free, to be the possible focus for another rising in Chihuahua. Despairing of political solutions to his plight, Villa tried a twin-track strategy: concentrating on building a powerful legal defence to the Army's charges while making ever more far-fetched proposals to Madero. He asked to be freed from military jurisdiction; Madero refused. He asked to be sent into exile in Spain; again Madero refused. Finally, he offered to fight Zapata in Morelos; this time Madero did not think the offer worthy of a reply. The confrontation of Villa and Zapata on the battlefield remains one of those intriguing historical might-have-beens, but the suggestion was not intrinsically absurd: after all, Zapata had publicly declared his support for the Orozco rising.

In his legal battle with the Army, Villa had the aid of some good lawyers, provided by the sympathetic Gustavo Madero. It soon became clear that the Army had nothing conclusive to pin on him but would seek to exhaust the possibilities inherent in one charge, before moving on to another, thus dragging proceedings out interminably and keeping Villa in jail. The desertion line of enquiry proved an unrewarding one for the military advocates, and their cause was not helped by Army bureaucracy. The provost-marshal's office deluged Huerta with lengthy question-naires, hoping to find the 'smoking gun' that would convict Villa, but Huerta was too arrogant, lazy or drunk to answer. It is possible that he knew only too well how wafer-thin the case against Villa was, and feared a public airing would damage his own credibility; in the meantime Villa's limbo position suited him very well. Most likely, he was already plotting Madero's downfall and reckoned he could take care of the monkey once he had disposed of the organ-grinder.

The principal weakness of Huerta's initial charge was his assertion that the rules of engagement in 1912 were different from those in 1911, for it was only in terms of the 'new' rules that Villa could be said to have deserted. However, there he faced the difficulty that the new rules had not been promulgated, and it is one of the oldest legal principles that no law can command obedience if it has not been promulgated. Realising that the charges of rebellion or desertion would not stick, as there were no credible witnesses and Huerta's assertions were obvious nonsense, the prosecution lawyers shifted their attention to the more promising area of theft, concentrating on the exactions from businessmen in Parral. Scraping the barrel, they soon had the bank manager of the Banco Minero and all who had been roughed up or threatened during the *villista* occupation trooping up to Mexico City to make their depositions. When the defence made mincemeat of these flimsy claims, the prosecution in desperation began trawling through provincial archives to find some proof that Villa was wanted for other crimes, but once again came up empty-handed.

Villa's lawyers also found a defence that the prosecution knew it could not shake. Basing its case on the fact that Villa was under the orders of the governor of Chihuahua when he occupied Parral, not Huerta's or the Army's, the defence was able to show that the Army had no jurisdiction. Had Huerta made his elevation of Villa to 'honorary general' official, the Army might have been on firmer ground, but once again Huerto had been too lazy or too drunk. Villa's lawyers ran rings round the Army by innocently asking for Villa's back pay as a general. The War Department refused, on the grounds that they had no record of Francisco Villa as a general. The defence pounced: if Villa was not a general, but only a colonel of the Chihuahua state militia, by definition the Army had no jurisdiction.

Since the Army could not make any of its charges stick, and it was increasingly clear that Villa was being detained for purely political reasons, the warden at the Federal Penitentiary gradually eased the conditions of his confinement. Originally held in solitary, Villa won the right to be with other prisoners, where his reputation and money won him friends. He struck up a particular rapport with Juan Banderas, the revolutionary leader from Sinaloa and with two *zapatista* intellectuals, Giraldo Magaña and Abraham Martínez, formerly Zapata's secretary and chief of staff. The two *zapatistas* certainly coached Villa through an understanding of the Plan of Ayala. It is further alleged that Martínez taught Villa to read and write, but this can hardly be so, since Villa had written letters to Madero, albeit with primitive spelling, from the very beginning of his captivity. We may well believe, though, that Magaña and Martínez improved his literacy skills, for we learn that Villa read a history of Mexico, *Don Quixote* and *The Three Musketeers*.

By the beginning of October 1912, Villa's conditions had eased to the point where he was allowed to have a typewriter in his cell and even to have 'conjugal visits'; this time the object of his affections was a girl

Emiliano Zapata: the dandy as hero

Porfirio Díaz in 1910

Francesco Madero,
the spiritualist who started
the revolution

Francisco Villa,
Centaur of the North

Pascual Orozco,
the permanent revolutionary
who fought Díaz, Madero,
Huerta and Villa

The remains of a troop train after dynamite had done its work

The rebels cross the tracks in triumph, having blown up a train

General Victoriano
Huerta: tiger, assassin
and drunkard

The Judas
embrace:
Huerta and
Orozco

The ill-starred Madero family: Gustavo, Raúl and Francisco

The other three principal players in the Villa–Zapata drama: (*clockwise from top left*) Francisco Madero, Venustiano Carranza and Álvaro Obregón

Villa in the revolutionary's 'full dress uniform'

Villa's hired killer and chief executioner, Rodolfo Fierro

named Rosita Palacios whom Villa archly describes as 'a great comfort in those lonely days'. Meanwhile he and Magaña set to work to plan a prison break. Villa bribed the guards for information on the prison layout, the shift system and the number of warders on duty at any one time, and fashioned and perfected a duplicate key by taking a wax impression of the original. However, the escape bid was a fiasco. Villa and Magaña found their would-be exit route barred by guards who should not have been there, according to the information Villa had paid for, and the two men retreated disconsolately to their cells. Magaña lost all confidence in Villa and told him it would be better if he made his next break alone.

By this time Villa had heard that Félix Díaz, the dictator's nephew, had launched an unsuccessful rebellion and that Madero had dismissed Huerta. On 24 October he wrote to Madero to congratulate him on these two events and to request a transfer to the military prison at Santiago Tlatelolco, where Bernardo Reyes and other important political prisoners were lodged. This time Madero replied to Villa in a more friendly way and agreed to the transfer. Three factors seemed to have weighed with Madero. For some time he had been lobbied by a group of conservative lawyers, mysteriously acting for Villa. In reality these were agents of Félix Díaz, who had been hoping to spring Villa from the less security-conscious Tlatelolco jail, so that he could lead a diversionary rising against Madero in Chihuahua. Madero knew nothing of the motivation, but always tended to sit up and take notice when lobbied by representatives of the Right.

In any case, by the end of October Madero felt more confident than at any time in his presidency. He had defeated Orozco, vanquished Félix Díaz and humbled Huerta. Villa no longer seemed a figure of much consequence and Madero no longer had to fear alienating the Army if he released him. Additionally, he was influenced by the many pro-Villa interventions of his brother Gustavo, who still feared Huerta and thought that Villa was valuable as a counterweight. So assiduous was Gustavo Madero that he visited Villa every day or sent his secretary along. By the end of October Madero might even have been disposed to release Villa as a final snub to Huerta, had not his other brother Raúl advised him that the Terrazases would take a dim view of this and might again raise Chihuahua in revolt.

At Tlatelolco Villa was made much of by imprisoned *felicistas* (supporters of Félix Díaz) and by the followers of Bernardo Reyes, but he was now determined to escape and found a willing accomplice in Carlos Juareguí, a magistrate's clerk in the prison administration. A lower middle-class nonentity, underpaid, sex-starved and venal, Juareguí was soon bound to Villa by the lavish gifts of money and clothes – suits, hats, shoes, ties – he received from him. Juareguí so far fell under Villa's spell that he proved an enthusiastic, dependable and even ingenious assistant. When Juareguí outlined a detailed escape plot, the planning seemed so meticulous that Villa at first suspected he was being set up for a *ley fuga* police double-cross. Juareguí's scheme involved sawing through the bars in Villa's cell while a band played *mariachi* music in the yard below, drowning the sound.

On Christmas Day 1912, wearing the city suit, hat, dark glasses and two pistols with which Juareguí had provided him, Villa simply walked out of the prison, strolling across the courtyard with his assistant as if they were two city lawyers, fresh from visiting their clients and absorbed in discussing the minutiae of a case. Villa partly hid his face with a cravat, but there was no need, for the guards were all drunk or engaged in Christmas revelry. They then found the getaway car exactly where Juareguí had said it would be and drove off – somewhat to Villa's chagrin, as he had wanted to make the romantic outlaw's time-honoured escape by horse. Together they drove to the city of Toluca in the next state, and took a train to the Pacific port of Manzanillo, where they took ship for Mazatlán. By this time the hue and cry had been raised all over Mexico. On the ship to Mazatlán Villa came close to being recognised by a former paymaster in the División del Norte, who knew him. Alarmed by this narrow escape, Villa stayed in his cabin, bribed the purser heavily, and left in a specially chartered boat before the customs officials boarded the ship in Mazatlán. Still with Juareguí, he made his way overland from Mazatlán to El Paso in Texas, travelling via Hermosillo and Nogales.

Greeted as a hero by the American press, Villa considered his options. Although now very bitter towards Madero, he wrote him a letter asking that he be given the post of military commander in Chihuahua. When he received no reply, Villa wrote a second, stiffer letter, on 20 January 1913, warning that his patience was running out. He also asked Abraham González to come and discuss his future with him. González judged it politically expedient not to go in person, but sent an aide to El Paso, who reported on Villa's continuing personal commitment. González advised Madero to amnesty Villa and give him an important post in Chihuahua, pointing out that Villa might otherwise throw in his lot with the political Right. In fact reactionary elements were already trying to engineer a permanent rift between Villa and Madero, some urging Villa to raise the standard of revolt while others urged Madero to snub Villa publicly.

González, always a staunch ally of Villa, offered him his old post as honorary general with full salary, but Villa insisted on official clearance from Madero first. Again González warned Madero of the danger that an unamnestied Villa might raise the north in insurrection. Madero, influenced by this and by Villa's letter of 20 January, finally saw the light, amnestied Villa and, to show his good faith, also released Tomás Urbina, in some ways the first cause of all the trouble between Villa and Huerta. The Centaur of the North was about to move south of the border when dramatic news came in that both Madero and González had been assassinated. Villa, it seemed, had got out of jail just in time – a further six weeks and he would certainly have been executed, for the murderer of Madero, it now turned out, was the Mexican monster himself, Victoriano Huerta.

Madero's tightrope act, balancing between Right (in the shape of Reyes, Huerta and Félix Díaz) and Left (Zapata, Orozco, Banderas, Contreras, Navarro), finally collapsed in the autumn of 1912. In some ways, though, it was never much of a balancing act, since he consistently favoured Right over Left. Madero lifted not a finger in favour of land reform and shamelessly connived at the brutal suppression of rural revolts by the Army. He would indulge in hand-wringing over atrocities when the peasants were being bloodily put in their place, but without agrarian reform, repression had to be employed. There was no middle way, and in expressing distaste for the razing and burning of villages Madero was being the typical liberal – willing the ends without willing the means. Given that Madero offered the villages, Indians and peons nothing, how else, other than with the bullet and the bayonet, did he think insurrections in the countryside could be suppressed?

By contrast, Madero let the Right have its head. Most of the old *porfiristas* retained their places and privileges, and Madero seemed disinclined to make the most elementary administrative changes. He turned a blind eye to all the old abuses from the Díaz years. Conniving at private armies, vigilantes and personal retainers by *porfirista* caciques simply meant that the proportion of the population in arms rose steadily. Militarisation would have been augmented by the plethora of rebels, revolutionaries, bandit gangs, city mobs and private armies, even if the Army muster roll had not risen from 20,000 in 1910 to an astonishing 70,000 by 1912. The rise of the Army meant that Madero had continually to truckle to the military, to defer to its pomps and delusions of grandeur, and to endure the brutal whims of men like Huerta. Any revolutionary or indeed any halfway sagacious political leader would have tried to build up the revolutionary forces as a counterweight to the Army, but Madero foolishly thought he need take no precautions as he was the will of the people personified. 'There is nothing to fear while the people applaud me' was just one of his many fatuous utterances.

A true politician would have realised that in fact the people were not with him. In June 1912, elections for the 26th National Congress gave Madero's party a small majority in the Chamber of Deputies, but not in the Senate. Even that result would not have happened had not Madero deprived the Catholic PCN party of seats by barefaced fraud. Madero was already coming under serious electoral threat from the Catholics, even though Catholicism itself – split between a reforming 'new' Church based on the papal encyclical *Rerum Novarum* (and in some ways more progressive than Maderismo) and an 'old' Church of benighted conservatism – was by no means a monolithic force. Fraud and low turnout rates – less than 10 per cent outside Mexico City – seemed to suggest that the Madero programme of 'Free elections and no re-election' was either meaningless or perceived as such.

That the elections were far freer than they had been in Díaz's day, and that in areas untouched by revolutionary violence they were reasonably fair, cut no ice with a cynical and jaundiced electorate. They saw clearly enough, even if Madero did not, that ideology and abstract political concepts were meaningless in Mexico; what mattered were bread-and-butter issues of the economy, especially land reform. 'Liberty' might mean something to an educated lawyer in Mexico City, but to the *campesino* the only meaningful liberty was the economic one he had been deprived of by the *hacendados*, with Madero's imprimatur. The trouble about 'No Re-election' as a slogan was that it was taken as a panacea for a host of problems, economic and social, whereas Madero had meant it narrowly, as a technical question to do with presidential succession. By 1912 the overriding feeling among the masses was that if elections changed anything, the elite would abolish them.

Madero still had his supporters, but they were narrowly based, among the middle class and the urban working class. Theoretical revolutionaries who looked to the proletariat as a vanguard class were always going to be disappointed with him. The urban working classes in general did well out of Madero, who recognised labour unions and the right to strike, and such strikes as occurred were opportunistic, taking advantage of government setbacks on other fronts. With labour unions apolitical, 'economist' in the sense of being concerned only with members' wages and conditions, and opposed to political violence, the working class strongly supported the status quo. The working class in Mexico was probably too weak to be a revolutionary force even if it had wanted to be, but rural revolution also made it obsessed with issues like food shortages, again making it hostile to the rebels.

Given that Madero in Mexico was the obverse of Kerensky in Russia five years later, like him a 'bourgeois' leader but making as many concessions to the Right as Kerensky made to the Left, the question arises: why were the forces of reaction and conservatism not more content with him? It seems, as has been well said, that it was a case of liking the music but loathing the conductor. Partly it was because the inapt tag 'revolutionary' hung about Madero; partly because the macho hunting and shooting oligarchs despised the president's intellectual and aesthetic tastes and predilections, and he despised theirs. They disliked the ideological tone of his liberalism and his vague talk of a 'middle way'. Most of all, however, the Right hated Madero for having displaced Díaz and ended the 'good old days' when they could command automatic deference and obedience from the lower orders. They wanted a strong-man and could not see Madero in the role: he was suspect thrice over, as a northerner, a civilian and a liberal. They could never really forgive him for having been prepared to negotiate with Zapata. Since Madero was within their range, the Army commanders especially displaced on to him the impotent rage they felt towards 'upstarts' like Villa and Zapata.

The devotees of law and order were also frustrated with the constant drip-drip of revolts and risings during the Madero years. Although the autumn saw Madero apparently well entrenched in power after the defeat of Orozco, the *orozquista* guerrilla bands were proving hard to eradicate, and in Morelos Zapata's fortunes had revived. There was also a new rebellion in Durango and Sinaloa that was beginning to make headway. None of these events was significant on its own, but their cumulative effect was beginning to exhaust and demoralise the regime, to encourage right-wing coups, and make Madero vulnerable to the forces of reaction.

Madero's bitterest enemies seized their chance to make political capital. Henry Lane Wilson exhorted Washington to rescue US citizens from the 'chaos' about to engulf the Pacific coast from Durango. The State Department responded, and Taft sent the USS *Buford* to the coast of Sinaloa to pick up the desperate American expatriates, but found only eighteen people. As the London *Times* commented sardonically: 'The only refugees collected so far seem to be people wanting to travel gratis to San Diego.' Meanwhile, drinking in a *cantina* in Ciudad Juárez on 15 September, Victoriano Huerta was heard to boast: 'If I wanted to, I could make an agreement with Pascual Orozco and I would go to Mexico City with 27,000 men and take the presidency away from Madero.' When this was reported to minister of war Ángel García Peña, he stripped Huerta of his command.

That there was little in the way of policy dividing Madero and his right-wing enemies became very clear when Félix Díaz finally rebelled in October 1912. Nephew of the exiled dictator, in his forties, a former brigadier and chief of police in Oaxaca, Díaz was in many ways the unseen evil genius of the Madero years. Díaz was the name to which so many plots and conspiracies forever led back, and all the risings in Veracruz and Oaxaca were instigated by him in one way or another. In October 1912 he finally appeared in the field in his own right: the garrison at Veracruz immediately went over to him and he took the city without significant opposition. The inevitable manifesto he then issued denounced the Madero family but dealt entirely in personalities; there was not a word about society or the economy. As Alan Knight remarks: 'Félix Díaz's *pronunciamiento* – in style, pomposity and even location – was in the old nineteenth-century tradition of Santa Anna.'

Díaz's revolt struck a chord with conservative Army figures, who were impressed by his putative role as strongman. Yet the Army did not declare for him, largely because he remained inactive around Veracruz. Soon he found himself bottled up by a besieging army under General Joaquín Beltrán, who proved immune to bribery or suborning. On 23 October Beltrán ordered his men to advance through the undefended railway yards, and by mid-morning the federals controlled the port, having sustained negligible casualties; Díaz's troops had lost fifty dead and wounded.

Díaz himself was captured and all resistance ceased. Humiliated by this catastrophic defeat, Díaz and his minions set about rationalising their own inadequacies: it was variously 'explained' that the federals had advanced through the marshalling yards carrying a white flag, or that Beltrán accepted a 200,000-peso bribe from Díaz to bring his troops over to the rebels and then double-crossed him. The right-wing elements in Mexico City, who had hoped that Díaz's rising might be the *coup de grâce* for Madero, were furious that the president had suppressed the revolt so easily, in contrast to the abortive attempts to suppress Zapata or the protracted campaign against Orozco. Such right-wingers in a bate missed the point and failed to compare like with like: Zapata and Orozco headed rural movements, but Díaz's was a self-contained urban rebellion, easy for a loyal Army to put down.

A military court found Díaz and twenty-six of his officers guilty of treason, and sentenced him to be shot at dawn on 26 October. Madero now had to decide whether to confirm the death sentence. He decided to let justice take its course: his mercy with Bernardo Reyes had been unavailing, so perhaps he finally had to show he was master in his own house. High society and the press immediately began to clamour for clemency for 'uncle's nephew', but the more the opposition tried to sway him, the more Madero became determined on execution. Then the oligarchy found a novel method of looking after its own. The Supreme Court, packed with stooges from the *Porfiriato*, intervened to declare Díaz not a proper object of military justice, since he had *de facto* resigned his commission the moment he rebelled. Díaz was imprisoned, first in a fortress in Veracruz harbour and later, in January 1913, in the very military prison of Tlatelolco where Villa had been held. In yet another of those preposterous absurdities in which the Mexican Revolution abounded, the democratic system, which Díaz rose against, contrived to save him. Always a stickler for legal niceties, Madero acquiesced, but predictably won no plaudits for clemency from his enemies, while being despised by his allies.

Beset from both Right and Left, and with few friends in the middle, in January 1913 Madero at last received significant backing when Venustiano Carranza called a meeting of northern governors at his estate at Ciénega del Toro. All five governors who attended, from Coahuila, Chihuahua, Sonora, San Luis and Aguascalientes, were disillusioned with Madero, for meddling in state affairs and trying to abolish their state militias; they also thought he had been too soft with the *zapatista* rebels. However, they agreed there was a danger of a coup from the Right and that Madero's position needed shoring up. Unfortunately, the northern governors were too late. Extremist factions had already gained access to Díaz and Reyes in the Tlatelolco prison and were planning the next revolt. The entire credibility of the Right meant that the next rising had to be decisive; to avoid civil war, it also had to be a strike of surgical precision.

To unite the various right-wing factions, a mastermind of machiavellian duplicity and consummate depravity was required. Such an individual now came forward in the shape of Henry Lane Wilson, the US ambassador, a 55-year-old career diplomat, short and stooping, with deep-set eyes and beetling brows; like his friend Huerta, he was also a notorious drunk. Wilson had come to Mexico as ambassador in 1910 after service in Belgium and Chile, the perfect dollar-diplomacy envoy, totally the creature of US business interests. Yet there was more. In the entire history of diplomacy, which has known its share of eccentrics, Wilson must rank as the maddest of the mad. He was obsessed with what he called 'the American colony' – the large numbers of US citizens living in

Mexico – and nurtured an insane hatred for Madero that could only adequately be explained by a psychologist of the abnormal. A more intelligent or energetic president than Howard Taft would have recalled Wilson the moment he wrote one of his mad dispatches – such as the request in March 1912 for a thousand rifles and a million cartridges to be sent to the Embassy in Mexico City, so that he could defend 'the American colony'.

Lane Wilson had taken secret satisfaction from the Orozco rising and the Díaz revolt, but to his angry stupefaction both had failed. He was now in a race against time if he was ever to achieve his heart's desire of overthrowing Madero, for in November 1912 Woodrow Wilson was elected as the 28th president of the United States. Madero had made bitter representations to the State Department about Lane Wilson, and by now even Taft realised that his ambassador in Mexico City was a suitable case for treatment. An honourable man would have dismissed Lane Wilson instantly, but Taft's pride stood in the way; he did not want to admit that his entire policy towards Mexico had rested on the gibberings of a crackpot. He therefore did nothing. In those days, an incoming president did not take office until March, so Woodrow Wilson, desperately anxious to sack his namesake in Mexico City, could also do nothing.

Realising that his days were anyway numbered, Lane Wilson entered with rare gusto into planning Madero's downfall. An elaborate conspiracy was hatched, involving twenty-two Army generals, but at first Huerta refused to commit himself outright. Such a far-flung plot could not be kept secret, and on 4 February 1913 a loyal Army officer passed Gustavo Madero a list of names, including those of generals Aureliano Blanquet and Joaquín Beltrán; against the name of Huerta a question mark had been placed. Gustavo Madero raced up to the presidential palace at Chapultepec to show his brother the list. Incredibly, Madero took the line that this was a hoax: if there was any conspiracy, he argued, Huerta would be at the heart of it and not just mentioned as a 'possible', and as for Blanquet and Beltrán, why, these were the men who had fought for him against, respectively, Orozco and Félix Díaz.

This was Madero's greatest, but not yet his final, act of folly. The conspirators had actually agreed among themselves the division of the spoils, once Madero was overthrown. The generals would release Bernardo Reyes and Félix Díaz from jail, Reyes would take over as provisional president until Díaz could be elected president constitutionally, and a variety of posts would be given to the generals. The true reason a question mark had been placed against Huerta's name was that he was playing hard to get: he had been promised the post of commander-in-chief of the Army, but the devious alcoholic thought he could aim even higher. Originally planned for March, the coup was brought forward at Lane Wilson's urging to 9 February.

At dawn on that Sunday morning General Manuel Mondragón, Porfirio Díaz's one-time Army chief whom Madero had foolishly allowed to return from exile, marched 700 men out of Tacubaya barracks and set out to free Reyes and Díaz. The bloodshed, which was to continue for ten days and give the coup the name of *La Decena Trágica* (Ten Days that Shamed the Nation), began almost immediately. At Santiago Tlatelolco prison the commanding general refused the order to hand over Reyes and was shot dead. The released Reyes was now, according to the plan, to proceed to the National Palace, address the nation, and declare himself the new president. However, when the jaunty and confident Reyes entered the Zócalo, he was met by a fusillade, and the Zócalo quickly became a battlefield in which bystanders and loiterers were caught up in the carnage; among 400 people shot dead in a bare ten minutes was Reyes himself. In confusion Félix Díaz pulled back his stricken troops to the old city arsenal at Ciudadela, one and a half miles away, where he paused to reflect on what had gone wrong.

Alerted in the small hours by the rumbling of artillery being transported from Tacubaya, Gustavo Madero had hurried to the National Palace and rallied the garrison there with a rousing speech. Gustavo had a glass eye and was nicknamed *Ojo Parado* ('still eye'), but everyone agreed he had the heart of a lion. Won over by his oratory, the garrison obeyed the orders of the loyal General Lauro Villar, who arrived shortly to take over. They set up machine-guns on the Palace roof, and it was these that dealt such fearsome destruction when Reyes arrived. The rebel troops – mainly cadets – sent to occupy the National Palace had at first appeared to achieve their objective, and messages were sent to Reyes accordingly. Then Villar had counterattacked and forced them to surrender. Reyes, expecting a walkover, rode straight into a heavily defended fortress, with snipers on the rooftops and machine-guns and mortars at all the gateways.

Madero now hastened down from Chapultepec with a small escort. On Paseo de la Reforma, close to the Alameda park, Huerta met him and offered his services; this 'coincidence' has always seemed more than a little suspicious. Surviving an assassination attempt by a sniper firing from scaffolding on the uncompleted Fine Arts Palace (a bystander was killed instead), Madero rode through the heaps of dead and dying in the Zócalo and entered the National Palace, to find loyalist casualties high and General Villar gravely wounded. Some see Villar's removal from the fray as the freak contingency that altered the entire course of *La Decena Trágica*. In an evil hour, persuaded by war minister García Peña, Madero gave the command of the loyalist troops to Huerta. This was dangerous folly. Huerta pledged loyalty and embraced the president with a kiss of Judas, knowing that the fly had just walked into his spider's web.

Félix Díaz and 1,500 rebels now faced Huerta and the Army across downtown Mexico, and for two days there was a stand-off, with both sides hoping for reinforcements. Madero went to Cuernavaca and returned with Felipe Ángeles and another 1,000 troops. Huerta meanwhile executed one of his fellow-plotters, the obese cavalry commander General Gregorio Ruíz. Huerta hoped thereby to prove his loyalty to Madero beyond question, but there are those who say that iron entered the soul of the Mexican Revolution at that moment. There had been atrocities already, but henceforth treachery, murder and crimes against humanity became the norm rather than the exception.

On 11 February government forces launched a sustained attack on the Ciudadela. A heavy artillery barrage was followed by an infantry assault in which there were 500 casualties, including civilians. For four days there was a brutal slugging war of attrition, in which Madero's troops dislodged the rebels from all their outer bastions, but could not take the 'inner ring' in the Ciudadela itself. Mexico City was convulsed and appalled by the novel spectacle of war, as shells and shrapnel tore through the city centre. Shopping centres were palls of smoke, elegant residential areas echoed to the machine-gun's hasty stutter, and the once distinguished heart of the capital was like a gigantic rubbish tip, a tangle of telegraph wire, sandbags and bizarrely skewed lampposts, with the number of human corpses defying the best efforts of improvised ambulances. After the initial loss of life, civilians kept off the streets, taking advantage of the lulls in fighting to decamp to the safer suburbs, often with mattresses on their backs – whether as crude bullet-proof protection or in the hope of sleeping on a friendly floor is uncertain.

Soon food grew scarce, prices became hyperinflationary, and many urban myths arose about dinners of roasted cat and dog. Public health problems were partly solved by desperate expedients, such as burning bodies out on the plains of Balbena, but this called for extra resources which were soon exhausted. Many corpses were simply doused with petrol and incinerated on the spot, creating a Dantesque spectacle of horror as twitching limbs and noisome foetors made a macabre sensory impact on bystanders. There was further mayhem when a rebel shell blew a hole in the walls of Belem prison. In the ensuing mass breakout, many prisoners were shot dead; some turned aside to loot, others were recaptured and still others joined the rebels; the chaos was compounded by casual looters who took advantage of the confusion to go on the rampage. The wildest rumours spread: that the city mob had risen and was consigning property and persons to the flames, or that the *zapatistas* were in the city and the dreaded Genovevo de la O was threading his way through the suburbs, beheading enemies and collecting scalps.

Henry Lane Wilson watched all this with appalled horror. His machinations with Díaz and the generals had not had the required effect, so it was time to move on to the next stage of his plan and force Huerta off his perch. Wilson began by deluging Washington with totally false reports to the effect that people were going over to Díaz in their hundreds and that he was the only hope for peace and stability. He browbeat his colleagues, the European ministers, into presenting a 'joint remonstrance' to Madero, making exaggerated claims about loss and damage to the property of foreign nationals, and on 12 February, together with the Spanish and German ministers, he sought an interview with Madero; the absurd bird-fancying British minister, Sir Francis Stronge, was quite willing to cede all his authority to the hectoring Wilson, provided he could obtain fresh eggs to feed his pet parrots.

Wilson behaved in the high-handed, intemperate and totally inappropriate (for an envoy) way he always did with Madero, blustering and fuming. Summoning all his patience, Madero allowed him through the lines to treat with Díaz, unaware that Wilson's sole purpose in meeting Díaz was to plan the next stage of the conspiracy. Wilson's next action was an impertinent proposal to 'part the combatants'. When Madero retorted acidly that Wilson was overstepping his proper diplomatic bounds, Wilson threatened armed intervention by the USA and claimed this was President Taft's official policy. An indignant Madero cabled Taft in protest, and the bemused president replied that he did not know what Madero was talking about.

One result of Wilson's intolerable meddling was a wave of anti-American protests; nevertheless, his twisted actions wove their black spell. In alarm at the spectre of the Marines crossing the Río Grande, a delegation of Mexican senators called for Madero's resignation and the appointment of a provisional president who would halt the civil war on the streets of Mexico City. This was what Huerta had been waiting for. The senators' action gave him the fig-leaf of legality he needed for his planned coup. By the end of the first week of the military stalemate, close observers noted something very strange about the siege of the Ciudadela: the blockade was so loosely enforced that Díaz and the rebels were able to slip out and get supplies of food, drink and ammunition; the rebels for their part made no attempt to destroy key federal targets. This was all part of a cynical deal between Huerta and Díaz, secretly brokered by Lane Wilson. Huerta further diminished Madero's power by sending units known to be loyal to Madero on suicide missions, ordering frontal charges on rebel machine-gun nests.

Once again it was the energetic Gustavo Madero who found the evidence of Huerta's duplicity. At 2 a.m. on 17 February he arrested Huerta at gunpoint, took him to the president and laid before him the evidence of the secret dealings with Díaz. Huerta raged, blustered and swore up and down that he was not in any plot; he vowed on his scapular that he was loyal, agreeing that his soul should be consigned to the everlasting fires of Hell if he was lying. He further promised, equivocating in the best traditions of the Delphic oracle, that, if Madero would only trust him, he would finish the rebellion within twenty-four hours. Incredibly, Madero believed him, gave him back his pistol and his freedom and granted the twenty-four hours requested. This was one of the most egregiously self-destructive actions in all history. Whatever possessed Madero to behave in such a way? Mexico's literary icon José Vasconcelos later speculated that on the eve of defeat all 'saints' fall victim to a kind of paralysis, and that unconsciously Madero was acting as the Christian martyr, turning the other cheek and allowing God's will to be done. More secular analysts dissent from the 'imitation of Christ' theme, but agree that the answer must be sought in the realm of psychological pathology rather than power politics.

Within twenty-four hours Huerta did indeed bring the rebellion to an end, but hardly in the sense Madero had understood. Just after noon on 18 February, General Aurelio Blanquet arrived at the National Palace with a squad of men to arrest Madero. The president indignantly refused to be his prisoner, and when Blanquet drew his pistol on the president, Madero's bodyguards opened fire, killing two of Blanquet's men before being themselves shot dead. During the shoot-out Madero escaped from his office but was intercepted on the stairs. Blanquet then proceeded with the arrest. Madero slapped him in the face and called him a traitor. 'Yes, I am a traitor,' Blanquet replied blithely. Meanwhile, some thirty minutes before these events, Lane Wilson effectively proved his collusion by wiring Washington that the Army had now taken control of the situation in Mexico.

The serpentine Huerta had meanwhile invited Gustavo Madero to a meal in a downtown restaurant as a gesture of reconciliation. There are two versions of what happened next. One is that Huerta excused himself at table, made a phone call to confirm the success of the coup, and then disappeared, leaving his men to arrest Gustavo Madero. The second version is more melodramatic: a messenger arrived, handed Huerta a note confirming the arrest and telling him he was needed at the barricades. Huerta pretended he would have to go straight there and needed a revolver, so asked if he could borrow Gustavo Madero's. For once Madero was not on red alert and stupidly handed his weapon over. Exultantly, Huerta pointed it at his heart and told him he was under arrest.

Whatever the exact details of events in the Gambrinus restaurant, it is certain that Gustavo Madero was then taken to the Ciudadela, where Cecilio Ocón, a rabidly right-wing Mexico City businessman who had been in the conspiracy from the very beginning, acted as 'judge' in a kangaroo court. Charged with treason, Gustavo Madero indignantly repudiated the accusation, invoked his privileges as a member of Congress and denied the authority of the rebels to try him. Ocón condemned him to execution, then struck him violently in the face, saying: 'This is how we respect your privileges.' Félix Díaz then led Gustavo Madero away to another part of the Ciudadela, but on the way Gustavo was brutally assaulted by rebel soldiers. Incensed, Gustavo lashed out at his tormentors, whereupon a soldier named Melgarejo pierced his one good eye with a sword, blinding him instantly. This outrage was greeted with savage laughter by the mob, and as Gustavo reeled around, groping, staggering, clutching his socket and pouring blood, the 'chorus' of barbaric soldiers taunted him.

Ocón then arrived to take his prisoner outside to face the firing squad. Gustavo pulled away and Ocón tried to grab him by the lapel of his coat but, blinded as he was, Gustavo was still too strong for him. The seedy businessman then settled the argument by drawing his pistol and pumping more than twenty rounds into the stricken Gustavo Madero, who slumped lifelessly to the floor. This atrocity was too much even for some of the rebel soldiers. One of them, Adolfo Basto, quartermaster-general in the National Palace, made the mistake of swearing vengeance, so Ocón had him taken out in Gustavo's place and executed by the firing squad.

The treacherous Huerta was meanwhile revealing himself a monster of perfidy, reneging on his word, forswearing sacred oaths and even double-crossing his own allies. It had always been understood that, once the coup was successful, supreme power would devolve on Félix Díaz, but Huerta suddenly announced that he intended to be president himself. An enraged Díaz was inclined to resist and civil war could have broken out yet again, had not the depraved Lane Wilson once more intervened. At a specially convened meeting, he bestowed the presidential mantle on Huerta and warned Díaz that if he resisted the 'will of the people', he would be fighting the USA as well as Huerta. It was further agreed that, as Díaz had had his way with Gustavo Madero, Francisco Madero and the vice-president Pino Suárez would be at Huerta's disposition.

Huerta did not want to sully his reputation by murdering a president in office, so first he had to get Madero to resign. After Huerta had once again taken a mighty oath on his scapular that no harm would come to Madero and Pino Suárez, the minister of foreign relations, Pedro Lascurrain, volunteered to get Madero to hand over executive power to him. Madero, knowing nothing as yet of his brother Gustavo's murder, anxious to avoid bloodshed, and confident that he would be dealt with as leniently as he had treated Bernardo Reyes and Félix Díaz, wrote out his resignation, as did Pino Suárez. Lascurrain was next in succession according to the Constitution, and he achieved the dubious distinction of being the shortest-lived president in Mexican history. He 'ruled' for forty-five minutes, then turned the presidency over to Huerta.

Madero had been promised exile, safe passage to Veracruz and then a shipboard voyage to Cuba, but already suspicions were arising that Huerta would not keep his word, especially when it was heard that the train to take them to Veracruz had been 'cancelled'. The only person with the power and influence to save Madero now was Lane Wilson, who probably hated him even more than Huerta did. He had been expressly ordered by the State Department to ensure that Madero left the country safely, but Wilson was on the way out anyway and calculated that Washington had no credible sanctions to use against him. He therefore refused to convene the diplomatic corps to present a united warning to Huerta not to harm his prisoners.

By now fearing the worst, Madero's wife went to see Wilson on the afternoon of 20 February to beg him to intervene. Wilson received her with glacial hauteur and said he could not intervene in the internal affairs of a sovereign nation. He added: 'I will be frank with you, madam. Your husband's downfall is due to the fact that he never wanted to consult with me.' Desperate, Sara Pérez de Madero then asked what was to happen to Pino Suárez. Wilson was then even more boorish: 'Pino Suárez is a very bad man. I cannot give any assurances for his safety. He is to blame for most of your husband's troubles.' Wilson revealed his true colours by toasting the new regime with his fellow-drunk Huerta at a reception at the US embassy the following evening.

Francisco Madero's last day on earth was 21 February 1913. That afternoon Huerta's henchmen cruelly raised the hopes of their wretched captives by installing three camp beds with mattresses in the cell shared by Madero and Pino Suárez in the National Palace, deceiving them into believing they would be in this jail for some time. By now Madero had heard of his brother's death and was depressed and grief-stricken. He was less concerned with his own safety for, as he had written to a friend on the 20th: 'Will they have the stupidity to kill us? You know, they would gain nothing, for we would be greater in death than we are today in life.' He soon had his answer. No sooner had the lights gone out at the usual time of 10 p.m. than a major Francisco Cárdenas arrived with another officer and told the prisoners they were being transferred to the Federal District Penitentiary for their greater security. Unknown to Madero, Cárdenas was a die-hard *porfirista* of fanatical stripe.

After some time packing effects, Cárdenas and his party took the prisoners outside the National Palace to a waiting car and ushered them inside. It was about 11 p.m. The car with Madero and Pino Suárez in it was accompanied by a second car, full of *rurales*. The two vehicles careered along a winding road to the penitentiary, drove past the main entrance and skidded to a halt at the farthest end of the complex of buildings. Cárdenas ordered the prisoners from the car and, as soon as Madero stepped out, executed him with a single shot to the neck from a .38 pistol. Pino Suárez received a more formal death, being put up against the penitentiary wall and shot there. Both cars were then riddled with bullets to aid the transparent fiction that the two men had been killed in crossfire when *maderistas* tried to rescue them.

No clear documentary evidence was found to link Huerta with the assassination, but everyone without exception knew he had ordered it. Huerta's supporters, on the rare occasions they admitted that Madero had been murdered by their side, laid a trail of obfuscation, stressing the complex chain of command that bound Cárdenas to Ocón and Blanquet and through them to Huerta; but only a fool imagined that Cárdenas would have acted as he did without orders or tacit consent from Huerta. The foreign press reacted to Huerta and his official communiqués with horrified disbelief, and almost the first action of Woodrow Wilson, on taking over as president of the United States, was to dismiss his odious namesake in Mexico City. Huerta had his moment of triumph, but he soon realised he had made a grave mistake. Not only had he alienated international opinion, but he had created the Revolution's first martyr, a man in whose name unconquerable legions would now arise to fight Huerta and the Army to the death.

Huerta's regime hardly enjoyed a moment's respite, for even as the war with Zapata continued in the south, there came a potentially yet more formidable challenge from the north; 1913 marked the emergence of Venustiano Carranza, governor of Coahuila, as a national figure. Together with Villa, Zapata and Álvaro Obregón he would make up the 'big four' of the Mexican Revolution. An aristocrat and landowner, the tall, bearded, ruddy-cheeked Carranza, rarely seen without his dark smoked glasses, was in his own way an intransigent autocrat fully the equal of Huerta. Humourless and monumental, this hirsute 6 feet 4 inches giant (who always seemed to those who met him to be fully seven feet tall), was dubbed by John Reed, who also called him 'a vast, inert body, a statue', the Lafayette of the Mexican Revolution. However, Carranza himself always had another model in mind. If Félix Díaz was a latter-day Santa Anna, Carranza aspired to be the second Benito Juárez.

Venustiano Carranza was born on 29 December 1859, the second son and eleventh child of Jesús Carranza Neira, a veteran of the Indian wars and a *juarista* liberal during the War of Reform and the struggle against Maximilian and the French. A muledriver and rancher, Jesús Carranza was the intelligence mastermind behind the *juarista* forces in Coahuila, and in 1866 gave Juárez an interest-free loan to support his crusade. When Juárez emerged triumphant from the French war, Jesús, now a patriarch with fifteen children, obtained a huge grant of land in Coahuila that was the foundation of his personal fortune. Educated at the Fuente Atheneum school in Saltillo and later (1874) at the Escuela Nacional Preparatoria, from an early age the young Venustiano hero-worshipped Juárez. He originally intended to be a doctor but was prevented by poor eyesight, so returned to Coahuila to raise cattle. In 1882 he married Virginia Salinas and begat two daughters; decades later he would remarry and sire four sons.

He entered politics at the age of twenty-eight, being elected in 1887 to the office of municipal president of Cuatro Ciénegas. In 1893 he drew Porfirio Díaz's attention by taking part, together with his brother Emilio, in an armed protest by 300 Coahuilan ranchers at the imposed 're-election' of one of Díaz's governors. Díaz, suspecting that the hidden hand behind the Coahuilan ranchers was Evaristo Madero – grandfather of the future president – turned the problem over to his henchman Bernardo Reyes. With Reyes as intermediary, Carranza met Díaz and explained the issue, namely that the reimposition of an unpopular governor was widely perceived in Coahuila as an affront to local traditions of autonomy. Díaz took the point and sacrificed his puppet governor, explaining to Reyes: 'Let us not risk losing them [the Coahuilans], because sooner or later civil war is bound to break out in that state . . . and we must cultivate the little we have going among them.'

The affair brought Carranza and Reyes together. Under the older man's aegis Carranza again filled the office of municipal president of Cuatro Ciénegas in 1894–8, and Reyes proposed him to Díaz as a national senator in 1904. Although a critic of Díaz and the *científicos*, Carranza showed no interest in supporting Madero's new political party in 1909. What swung him against Díaz was self-interest. Despite the universal desire in the state – by incumbent governor Miguel Cárdenas, by Reyes and by Evaristo Madero – that Carranza should be the new governor of Coahuila, Díaz used his patronage to get his own stooge imposed. At this point Carranza joined Francisco Madero, though there was never any warmth or rapport between the two men. While the armed struggle against Díaz was in its early stages and Madero still in the USA, Madero met Carranza in San Antonio, Texas (January 1911), and made him provisional governor and commander-in-chief in Coahuila, Nuevo León and Tamaulipas. However, when Madero crossed the Río Grande in February 1911, the circumspect Carranza crossed it in the opposite direction and stayed out of the fray in San Antonio, until it was clear that Madero was going to win.

He then reappeared in Mexico, playing the role of anti-Díaz hawk. Madero showed him further favour by appointing Carranza his minister of war, even though his performance to date had been lacklustre, slow and ponderous; some even hinted that Madero was really a Reyes supporter still and was simply waiting to see how events would turn out. Without any military experience, Carranza was still allowed to conduct the negotiations with Díaz at Ciudad Juárez in May 1911, which ended the *Porfiriato*. However, he did warn Madero prophetically that simply to accept Díaz's resignation without dismantling his system was a bad mistake, as it would recognise the legitimacy of the *Porfiriato* and leave Díaz's cronies in place, ready to strike back at the Revolution.

Hoping at first to become Madero's minister of the interior, a disappointed Carranza returned home, acted as provisional governor of Coahuila for two months from June 1911, then resigned to seek the verdict of the electorate. Elected governor, he promoted the idea of 'small is beautiful', encouraging municipal autonomy and democracy from the grassroots up; he managed to improve the state's educational facilities, but ran up against the brick wall of foreign mining interests when he tried to improve labour conditions in the mines. From this contretemps grew the conviction that Coahuila's problems could really be dealt with only at the national level.

Increasing ambition brought him into conflict with Madero, who correctly sensed that Carranza'a approach to politics was patriarchal and paternalistic. Carranza accused Madero of having made all the mistakes he predicted at Ciudad Juárez, and of caring nothing for local autonomy; Madero hit back by describing Carranza as 'vindictive, spiteful and authoritarian . . . a phlegmatic old man who asks one foot for permission to drag the other'. A particular bone of contention during the Orozco rising was the role of Coahuila: Madero wanted the state's forces under federal control, but Carranza held out for local autonomy. What he really wanted was for Madero to pay for his state troops while, he, Carranza, had complete authority over them; this was typical of the man and his way of proceeding. However, he was hit by scandal when it was alleged that he had been 'payroll padding' and billing the federal government for non-existent troops. Carranza went up to Mexico City to fight his corner, but Madero won this battle: General Pablo González was foisted on him as the military commander in Coahuila.

Carranza had some political talent – he built up close relations with the governors of San Luis Potosí, Aguascalientes and Chihuahua – but he was most of all that sad spectacle, the professor in politics. A walking encyclopedia of the history of Mexico, Carranza had never thrown off his youthful obsession with Juárez. José Vasconcelos said of Carranza that 'Juárez was for him all of human greatness, above and beyond universal geniuses.' Carranza knew nothing directly of foreign countries, but had travelled the world in his books. He always preferred Europe to the United States, and within Europe his favourite history was French, with France, seen through a rose-tinted and conservative lens, his model and inspiration in politics and culture.

Carranza thought Madero had made two mistakes: he had truckled to the Right and the Díaz supporters, whereas 'a revolution that makes concessions commits suicide'; and he had not acted decisively enough against Henry Lane Wilson and Washington. Carranza was always anti-American in the sense that he resented the Yankee colossus's frequent interventions south of the border, its economic imperialism and, particularly, the gigantic land-snatch of California, Arizona and New Mexico that had capped Mexico's humiliation in the war of 1846–8. From his reading of Mexican history, Carranza saw Madero's downfall in February 1913 as a 'parallel' with the overthrow of Comonfort in 1858. Clearly what was needed was a new Juárez – and who more suitable than Carranza himself?

In the opening weeks of the Huerta regime he proceeded with extreme caution. One of the great myths of the Mexican Revolution is that the three northern states of Sonora, Chihuahua and Coahuila exploded into spontaneous revolt once Huerta murdered Madero. What really happened was that Huerta's bull-in-a-china-shop antics gave them no choice. Always supremely cautious, always with the instincts of a trimmer, Carranza sent a delegation to Mexico City to assure Huerta of his loyalty (this is a well-documented incident which Carranza's hagiographers have tried to rewrite or edit out of the record). Carranza was prepared to bow the head to the tyrant, but Huerta was determined to impose his own Army cronies as governors in all the states and to give no guarantees whatever on local autonomy. Faced with Huerta's intransigence, Carranza saw no future for himself, so rebelled. It is utterly unconvincing to say, as Carranza's apologists do, that the embassy he sent to Huerta was simply a cynical device to play for time.

Always a stickler for protocol and constitutional niceties – in this at least he resembled Madero – Carranza took care to get a mandate for rebellion from the Coahuila legislature. On 4 March 1913 a group of Army officers chose him as first chief of the 'Constitutionalist' Army, and Huerta's presidency was declared illegal, unconstitutional and piratical – but the Coahuilans took this step with great reluctance. It was the same story in Sonora: the death of Madero and Huerta's inability to compromise forced a reluctant elite into rebellion. Even so, it was not until mid-March, with Huerta's armies advancing to seize the state, that Sonoran leaders threw off the mask.

Carranza issued his manifesto as the Plan of Guadalupe. This had the distinction of being the least ideological of all Mexican *pronunciamientos*: nothing whatever was said about agrarian matters or land reform; the Plan was a purely political call for the overthrow of Huerta, after which, it was implied, everything was up for grabs. Interested only in a political transfer of power, and aware that commitment to land reform would merely stiffen the opposition to him, Carranza managed to produce a document that was ideologically blander even than Madero's anodyne Plan of San Luis Potosí. In some ways Carranza's programme was merely a dotting of the 'i's and crossing of the 't's in Maderismo, but there was a toughness and ruthlessness in Carranza's utterances that was very different from Madero-style discourse. Most importantly, Carranza declared war to the knife: there would be no compromises and no deals, his aim was to extirpate Huerta and all his works, root and branch.

For this reason Carranza set himself up as an alternative government. He issued five million pesos of paper money, and announced measures to deal with taxes, exports and expropriations in the territories his army intended to conquer. Most controversially, he revived Juárez's decree of 25 January 1862, which stated that all enemy prisoners were to be executed as rebels against the properly constituted government. This single action began a cycle of atrocities that by the end of the Revolution had spiralled almost out of control. Partly Carranza's motivation was to ape his beloved Juárez, but in part the decree was an accurate manifestation of an autocratic personality, who believed that any opposition to his will merited death.

It is part of the fascination about Carranza that a one-dimensional, cautious, circumspect martinet should yet have had the imagination to bluff his way into the position, never seriously challenged thereafter, of supreme chief of the Revolution. He did start with certain advantages. At fifty-three he was much older than the other revolutionaries, so that he appeared mature and full of gravitas. His height and bearing were on his side, as was the patriarchal beard which he stroked like the archetypal wise old man. He was also ahead of his time in his awareness of image and public relations, and to this end dressed the part of a 'father of the nation', in northern-style wide-rimmed grey felt hat, twill coat, riding breeches and leather boots. The idea was to promote the image of a man of action but, by eschewing meretricious Army insignia, to distance himself from 'the man on horseback' who already had his avatar in the shape of Huerta.

Carranza aspired to the charisma of Juárez and the power of Díaz and was determined to succeed where Madero had failed. However, he was no Juárez, though he adopted the same granite-like persona and had the same irreducible stubbornness. He also lacked Díaz's finely tuned political instincts, but he had mastered Fabian tactics, knew the virtues of stalling and procrastination, and cultivated a deliberate slowness of manner, allowing him to prevaricate in public. A rustic and patriarchal inflexibility, yoked to plodding body rhythms suggested the cycles of Nature and the inexorable working out of Fate. By sidelining and sidetracking people, he made it impossible for them to have face-to-face confrontations with him. In his own mind he saw himself as a bridge between the nineteenth and twentieth centuries, channelling the violent currents of the Revolution into orderly conduits. He wanted the law to be supreme, whereas a man like Villa wanted the myth of action, Sorel-like.

Above all, then, Carranza was an actor. By sleight of hand he built himself up as the only credible *national* alternative to Huerta. As Alan Knight has remarked: 'Other revolutionary caudillos might excel in military power or popular appeal, but none could press a stronger claim to national leadership.' In short, Carranza gambled, took the long view, and arrogantly behaved as if all other revolutionary leaders had agreed to his title as first chief of the Constitutionalist Army. He expected the Villas, Obregóns, Zapatas and others to fall in with his plans, but in return had nothing to offer them: no money, no resources, just pious platitudes. The gamble paid off. As with so many other leaders in history, Carranza – basically a nonentity, lacking genius, heroism or idealism – was taken by others at his own absurdly elevated self-evaluation.

In the early rounds of the military contest with Huerta, it was the murderer of Madero who won all the points. Carranza at first tried to avoid battle, but was worsted by federals in an encounter at Anhelo. Next he attacked Saltillo, but the federals had constructed their defences well and Carranza's assault was badly planned; after fifty-five hours of costly fighting, he was forced to withdraw. For several months he remained inactive at Monclova, unmolested as the federals slowly moved reinforcements north. At this stage in the revolt, Huerta reckoned Zapata a greater threat than Carranza, possibly because he himself had failed against Zapata and then swept all before him in the campaign in the north against Orozco.

Gradually, however, the slow federal attrition told on Carranza, and he was forced across the state line and on a long circuitous retreat to Sonora. The short route was via the USA but Carranza, the anti-American, was determined that he would never set foot on US soil now that he was the 'real' president of Mexico. The other consideration in his mind was that Juárez had trekked north in 1863 on his 'long march' without leaving Mexican territory, and he wished to emulate the exploit of his hero. To achieve this, Carranza made an absurdly roundabout journey from Piedras Negras to Hermosillo, via Torreón, Durango, southern Chihuahua, the western Sierra Madre and northern Sinaloa. Carranza's flight – for that is what it was – was written up by his propagandists as a stirring feat of high adventure, replete with suitable 'heroic' ingredients: crossing the continental divide on horseback with just 100 men, ascending mountain passes in monsoon-like rains, then descending into the valley for an emotional meeting with the revolutionary leaders of Sinaloa and

Sonora. The fat and short-sighted Carranza, once described as 'mediocrity incarnate' needed an 'exploit' like this to establish his reputation and credibility as a revolutionary leader.

He established his government in Sonora and remained there until March 1914. Why Sonora? At least three reasons seem salient. Most obviously, the revolutionary army there numbered 3,000, as against little more than 1,000 in Coahuila. Sonora was also uniquely placed as a hideout for a rebel leader, since there was no direct rail link between the state and Mexico City. The west coast railway line had a gap at Jalisco, between Tepic and San Marcos, so rapid federal troop movements were not feasible; by contrast, the rebels could smuggle in arms across the border from the USA. Sonora also suited Carranza sociologically and ideologically. Socially stable, politically homogeneous, with high levels of literacy and foreign investment, a burgeoning middle class and a *mestizo* population eagerly embracing capitalism, it was a microcosm of the sort of Mexico Carranza wanted to see after the Revolution, a progressive culture that could overwhelm the old colonial, Indian, Catholic Mexico of the central plateau. Above all, land reform was not an issue. As Álvaro Obregón, Carranza's great ally in Sonora, pointed out: 'We are not *agraristas* here, thank God. We are all doing what we are doing out of patriotism and to avenge the death of señor Madero.'

However, there was no disguising the fact that for most of 1913 Carranza avoided a military showdown with Huerta and remained on the back foot. Although Sonora later came to be regarded as the nursery of Revolutionary politicians – producing as it did Obregón, Adolfo de la Huerta, Benjamin Hill, Salvador Alvarado, Juan Cabral and Plutarco Elías Calles – in the initial stages of the struggle against Huerta, Carranza had to build up slowly. After all, the governor of the state, José María Maytorena, fled to Tucson, Arizona 'for his health' after Madero's murder, so that he would not have to commit himself, and though Carranza had divided up Mexico into seven military zones, there were operations in only three of them in 1913, and in only one to any great point. All the real resistance to Huerta in that year was achieved elsewhere, by rebels who were not *carrancistas*. The cutting edge of the anti-Huerta opposition was in Chihuahua, a state Huerta foolishly thought he had tamed, and the protagonist was once again Pancho Villa.

Maderistas in Chihuahua were desperate for leadership, since Abraham González had by now joined Madero on the list of the murdered. Immediately after disposing of Madero, Huerta ordered González arrested and brought to Mexico City. On the way his train was stopped, and he was taken off and shot; for good measure his lifeless body was then mangled under the train wheels. Huerta gave out that González had been killed while his supporters were trying to rescue him. Coming immediately after the similarly transparent 'explanation' for Madero's death, this was universally taken as an insult to public intelligence; the brutal and drunken Huerta could not even be bothered to think up a plausible story. Loyal Chihuahuans now not only had two martyrs (Madero and González) to mourn but could see no future for themselves. The decision to rebel was forced on them, for otherwise they considered themselves certain to be massacred, either by Huerta's army or by Orozco's *colorados*.

Across the border in Texas, Pancho Villa had been spending a miserable exile. The wife of his El Paso hotelier remembered him as a man of uncertain temper, with a passion for ice cream and peanut brittle, who kept a box of homing pigeons in his hotel room. Suddenly there came news of *La Decena Trágica* and Huerta's coup. Villa was overwhelmed by news of Madero's murder. All his differences with him, all the betrayals by the president when Villa was in jail, all was now forgotten and Madero was henceforth remembered as '*Maderito*' – 'dear little Madero'. Villa now had two scores to settle with Huerta: vengeance for the death of Madero and personal revenge for the attempted firing squad and the seven months in prison.

With some vague thoughts of building an alliance, Villa set out for Tucson to interview the cowardly Maytorena. While he was waiting to talk to him, Villa met a more doughty representative of Sonora, Adolfo de la Huerta, a genuine revolutionary, who implored him to go to Sonora and raise the standard there. When Maytorena finally spoke to Villa and learned of this talk of Sonora, he was alarmed for his own position and gave Villa 1,000 pesos, on the strict understanding that he would return to Chihuahua, not Sonora, to start an insurrection. The naïve Villa, unaware of all the undercurrents, actually felt himself to be in Maytorena's debt. With the money he paid what he owed in El Paso, and bought nine horses and nine rifles. On the night of 6 March 1913 he splashed across the Río Grande with eight comrades (including Juaregui). To start a rebellion they had with them a few pack mules, two pounds of sugar, two of coffee and one of salt, and 500 cartridges each.

At San Andrés Villa made contact with his brothers Antonio and Hipólito, together with *villista* veterans like Maclovio Herrera, Toribio Ortega, Rosalio Hernández and, most importantly, Tomás Urbina. At first they did not fare well. Chihuahua rose in revolt, but only a handful of men joined Villa, and the other guerrilla leaders refused to accept him as supreme commander. For a time the state was racked by spontaneous and fissiparous warlordism. One of the early leaders was an ex-schoolmaster named Manuel Chao, whose first exploit was an attack on the federal garrison in the town of Santa Bárbara. At the height of the battle, the townspeople suddenly turned on the federals, shooting at them from their houses and thus catching them between two fires; the garrison surrendered soon afterwards. Chao tried the same stratagem at Parral, in collusion with leading city burghers, but the plan went awry when federal reinforcements arrived at the crucial moment. Forced to evacuate, Chao's men melted into the countryside, fighting as guerrillas, occupying haciendas and destroying railway tracks. By the beginning of April 1913 other guerrilla groups had arisen, most notably one led by Villa's old compadre Tomás Urbina, who directed raids into southern Chihuahua from his base in Durango.

Villa realised that campaigning this time was going to be tougher and bloodier than in 1911. Then the revolutionaries had been fighting for a mere change of leader, now they were fighting for a change of regime, which meant *guerre à outrance*. In 1911 the Chihuahua oligarchs had not fought for Díaz, and Madero's campaign had been well financed. This time guerrilla bands would be fighting on a shoestring against the combined might of Huerta's army, the Terrazas' militias and Orozco's *colorados*. Grand gestures were out of place, Villa knew, so he began to build up slowly. Leaving Chao and Urbina to their spheres of influence, he made his base in north-western Chihuahua where he had many old contacts among the *maderista* veterans, and where he was close enough to the US border to get fresh supplies of arms.

Villa reasoned that the way to get recruits and turn his campaign into a high-profile affair was by spectacular attacks on Terrazas haciendas and dramatic redistributions of land. Madero had called him a Robin Hood; very well, he would act like one. His first target was the hacienda of El Carmen, notorious locally because its manager practised *droit du seigneur* on nubile peon girls and had his own system of debt peonage. Villa attacked the hacienda, executed the manager and his assistant, threw open the granary and distributed food to the peons, urging them to rebel rather than accept such treatment again. He did the same thing at the haciendas of San Lorenzo and Las Ánimas, winning popularity and recruits.

There was something of an irony in the way Villa, with his harem of 'wives', stood forth as the champion of oppressed women, but this stance paid popularity dividends. At the village of Satevo a young girl came to him and denounced the parish priest for having raped her and fathered a child; the priest then compounded his offence by refusing to acknowledge the child and claiming that Pancho Villa was the father. Villa forced the priest to confess and ordered his execution. The village women then interceded to beg for the life of their *padrecito*. Villa agreed, provided the priest made a full confession of his sins from the pulpit, which the shaken cleric was only too pleased to do. The incident enhanced Villa's reputation as a dispenser of Solomonic justice.

Villa's actions in March and April showed him to be a master at winning hearts and minds. While confiscating and redistributing lands, and providing villagers with extra food, he executed all bandits and *colorados* and made a great show of protecting US property. He sent one local bandit, 'El Mocho', to the firing squad after he shot an American. Indeed his pro-Americanism was so overt that it caused grumblings among the more political of his followers, for whom the 'Yankee octopus' was as much a mortal enemy as Huerta. To assert his authority on this point, Villa drove one *zapatista* guerrilla, named Máximo Castillo, across the border into the USA. Americans responded by selling arms and ammunition to the *villistas*; a daring raid on a silver train had given Villa the wherewithal for a bulk purchase in April. The US arms embargo never worked, partly because Villa used women and children as agents of contraband, but mainly because Americans across the border ignored it: some were sympathetic to Villa, others simply refused to allow Washington to interfere with normal business, and others again took the realistic line that there was simply too much border with Mexico to patrol effectively.

By the end of May Villa had 700 well-armed and highly disciplined troops under his command. Impressed with his achievement, one of the major warlords, Toribio Ortega, agreed to serve as Villa's second-in-command and brought in his 500 guerrillas. Ortega was one of the rare genuinely honourable revolutionaries, a man with a reputation for compassion, integrity and financial honesty. His example was persuasive. Gradually more and more warlords took the same decision, seeing in Villa the only credible defender of Chihuahua against Huerta. Chao and Urbina both lost caste irremediably in June and July, Urbina by a disgracefully handled sack of Durango City when his troops ran amok, and Chao by three successive defeats (at Ciudad Camargo, Mapula and Santa Rosalía) when Orozco led a 1,000-man cavalry dash from Torreón to Chihuahua City in the style of Nathan Forrest in the American Civil War. By August, the three-pronged offensive by the Army, the Terrazas militias and the *colorados* threatened to overwhelm Chihuahua. Urbina lacked the discipline and Chao the military imagination to prevail against such odds. To survive, the revolutionaries had to put all their bets on Pancho Villa.

Still Villa proceeded cautiously, not attempting tasks beyond his strength, but making sure he enhanced morale and discipline by cleverly planned strikes. In June he briefly occupied the town of Casas Grandes and in August he defeated a force of 1,300 *rurales* under Félix Terrazas. Finally, in September, he felt strong enough for a major attack on Huerta. On 26 September the guerrilla leaders of Chihuahua held a 'summit conference' at Jiménez. They decided that the city of Torreón, a nodal point on the Mexican railway system and the funnel through which Huerta sent troops north from Mexico City, should be the target – but who should be generalissimo? Chao and Urbina had claims as well as Villa.

Urbina had effectively ruled himself out by not being able to control his men. The revolutionaries could not afford another Durango-style fiasco, when the city was taken apart by a drunken, plundering, indisciplined *canaille*; the middle classes and the Americans were already edgy enough. Chao had the advantage of being Carranza's choice, but only because the 'First Chief' in Sonora was already jealous of Villa. According to legend, Villa and Chao settled their respective claims when the two men confronted each other in 'high noon' fashion. Villa ordered Chao to stand down, Chao went for his gun but found himself outdrawn by Villa: a blurred reflex to the hip, a lightning draw, and then Chao looked down the barrel of Villa's pistol: thus the legend, at any rate. The sober truth is that Chao was not acceptable to most Chihuahuans. He was an outsider (born in Tampico), an intellectual schoolmaster with no charisma. Villa was the man for the job, and the revolutionaries knew it. Despite some sulks from Tomás Urbina, who thought he should have the position, the warlords unanimously elected Villa as supreme chief of the reorganised Division of the North.

The federals faced the attack with confidence. Having confined them to the major towns, Villa was now doing exactly what they wanted: fighting them on their own terms: 2,000 regular troops plus another 1,000 *colorados* and militiamen, all well-armed and equipped, were dug in, waiting, as they thought, for the *villistas* to commit suicide. They reasoned that although Villa had 6–8,000 men, he had no experience of commanding large numbers; and had not the so-called First Chief Carranza already failed to take Torreón? With another federal army advancing from the north to catch the rebels in a pincer movement, the defenders looked forward to an abortive siege, followed by ambush and massacre of the crestfallen revolutionaries as they trooped north. The one factor the federal commander, General Francisco Murguía, had not taken into account was that most of his men were press-ganged conscripts from

Mexico's 'deep south', fighting in an unfamiliar land against men imbued with revolutionary élan.

Murguía had placed artillery on the hilltops commanding the approaches to Torreón, intending to rip the attacking revolutionaries to pieces. Villa got round that obstacle by sending commando forces by night to take each hill in turn. With the artillery in his hands, he was ready to turn the tables. He sent his vanguard into the suburbs and Murguía foolishly responded by sending a small force of around 500 troops to flush the rebels out. This was at once 'eaten up'. Realising that his van had been defeated and his artillery captured on the heights, Murguía succumbed to panic and decided to decamp. To cover his flight, he sent a subordinate general to retake the hills; this assault seemed at first to be making some headway, but when the commander sent back for reinforcements he discovered to his astonishment that Murguía had already flown the coop. Murguía was later court-martialled and convicted of cowardice.

Villa's victory at Torreón made him incontestably a major figure. The arms and *matériel* he captured there were enough to equip his army for months: he seized 1,000 rifles, 600 grenades, half a million cartridges and six machine-guns, plus a huge, railway-mounted three-inch cannon named El Niño (The Child), which became the mascot of the División del Norte. As he now also possessed forty railway engines and vast amounts of rolling stock, captured at the junction's marshalling yards, Villa also had a mechanised and mobile army. To complete his triumph, the federal force supposedly advancing from the north to catch him in a pincer managed to maul its own infantry with 'friendly fire' and then failed to take the town of Camargo, held by a small number of *villistas*.

Villa was determined that Urbina's infamous sack of Durango would not be repeated in Torreón. Some of his vanguard, entering at night, looted and pillaged, but Villa quickly restored order at daybreak. His men were prepared to take tough discipline from him, as he was an inspired commander with a genius for night fighting, who had just achieved what everyone thought was impossible; there was the added bonus that he was no oligarch but 'one of us', a man of the people. The discipline of the *villistas* amazed and delighted the townspeople and the foreign residents. The US consul in Torreón reported that less than 5 per cent of the expected financial losses expected from looting had actually been sustained. From other Americans there came similar plaudits; at this moment Villa's stock in the USA was sky-high. However, local businessmen were less enthusiastic, as Villa levied forced loans of three million pesos from bankers and other plutocrats in Torreón. The banks tried to bamboozle him by writing cheques drawn on US banks, but Villa's intellectual advisers warned him these would not be honoured in the USA. It took an explicit threat of death to make the bankers disgorge.

The dark side of Villa manifested itself in the execution of prisoners, reinforcing the spiral of brutality that would besmirch the campaigns against Huerta. This had been a rare occurrence in 1911, but that had not been a collision of regimes. Both sides this time were in a grim fight for survival: Huerta's habitual brutality had already been matched by Carranza's 'Juárez' decree that to appear in arms against the 'Constitution' was an express act of treason, punishable by death. Villa did not bat an eyelid over ordering hundreds of men to the firing squad, and liked to carry out his executions openly, in broad daylight, rather than skulkingly at night as most commanders did. However, he reserved to himself the prerogative of mercy. On one occasion Tomás Urbina wanted to execute a group of musicians who had been pressed into service as federal bandsmen, but Villa insisted that there could never be too much music and recruited the men for his own army.

After Torreón Villa no longer needed to operate as a guerrilla but could face Huerta in open battle. For a while Huerta considered that Villa's victory was a fluke, that the Centaur of the North was simply a lucky individual, as his prison break the year before seemed to suggest. Moreover, he counted on factionalism among the rebels to do his work for him; after all, not even Madero had been able to hold his motley alliance of heterogeneous elements together, and it was likely, as soon as the rebels sustained their first defeat, that the entire ramshackle revolutionary coalition would collapse.

Huerta's hopes at first looked like being realised for, flushed with victory, the overconfident Villa next ordered a frontal assault on Chihuahua City. As his more cautious advisers such as Juan Medina warned him, this was a mistake. The federal commander there was no Murguía, the city was well supplied with superior artillery, and most of the defenders were Orozco's *colorados*. After three days of wasteful charges, Villa broke off the attack. He was now in a difficult position, because unless he maintained forward momentum, his own men might start thinking, with Huerta, that Torreón was a fluke. It was vital to bring off another coup. As a commander, Villa always disappointed when he held good cards, but was at his best when cornered with his back to the wall or when written off. This he now proved by bouncing back from the defeat at Chihuahua to an amazing exploit at Ciudad Juárez, when he managed to rerun the story of the Trojan horse.

An attack on Ciudad Juárez was the only meaningful option left to him, but it was a tough nut to crack. Much better defended than in 1911, Juárez always carried the danger that any military operations there would provoke US intervention, especially if anyone on the American side of the border was hit by stray bullets. There was also the roving federal army – the one that had failed to take him in the rear at Torreón – still at large in Chihuahua, no one knew exactly where. An attack on Ciudad Juárez was a huge gamble, but Villa had an ace in the hole he had never possessed before – locomotives and rolling stock he had captured at Torreón. His ingenious mind at once saw a way forward.

While some of his men skirmished on the outskirts of Chihuahua City, as if intending to renew the attack, Villa's main force had intercepted two coal trains at the Terrazas station, emptied the cargo and loaded on his own elite corps. With his cavalry following just out of sight, Villa steamed towards Ciudad Juárez. At each station on the run north Villa took the telegraph operators prisoner and had them ask for instructions from headquarters, putting himself on the line and pretending to be the federal officer in charge of the train. At every halt the story was the same: he was returning north to base as the line south was blocked by 'the bandit Villa'. The repeated 'all clear' was answered by the reiterated 'return to base'. At 2 a.m. on the night of 15/16 November 1913, while most of the federal troops in the city were asleep or in bars, brothels and casinos, Villa and his men steamed into Juárez. Disembarking, they took the federals completely by surprise. The signal was given to the cavalry by rocket flare, and within an hour all strategic points in the city – barracks, arms depot, racetrack, casinos, even the international bridge – were in Villa's hands.

This amazing exploit made Villa world-famous. He won further plaudits by his treatment of the federal commander General Francisco Castro, who was allowed to depart unscathed to the USA. Aware that Castro was the same man who had interceded for his life with Huerta in 1912, Villa had already given strict orders that the enemy general was not to be harmed. However, even after such a victory (a signal triumph in more ways than one), he could not rest on his laurels. Huerta still thought that Villa was just a gambler whose luck would sooner or later run out, so sent a fresh army north to retake Torreón. Orders also went out to the garrison at Chihuahua City to sortie and go over to the offensive; 7,000 men under Orozco went north. Villa now had to decide whether to dig in and defend Ciudad Juárez or move south and strike the enemy before they could strike him.

Villa decided to go south, following the railway line. His reasoning was twofold: he lacked the food, ammunition and other resources to withstand a protracted siege in Ciudad Juárez, and he did not want to give Huerta the chance to play the American card by firing over the border and bringing the Marines pouring across. He decided to make his stand at Tierra Blanca, a railway junction some thirty miles south. He knew this was a gamble. He was slightly inferior in numbers to the enemy, and at least 1,000 of his 5,500 effectives were armed with no more than knives and machetes – and a good many were women and young boys – while the federals had an awesome superiority in artillery; the *villistas* had little more in the way of heavy firepower than two Mondragón 75mm field guns. There was no question of somehow achieving a moral or psychological advantage over Huerta's fighters, as most of them were Orozco's *colorados* who, knowing the certain fate that awaited them if defeated, would fight to the last man.

Fighting began on the night of 23 November, but it was on the morning of 24 November that the dreadful two-day engagement of Tierra Blanca really began. By all the laws of warfare, Orozco and the federals should have won the battle easily. They had superiority in every area, especially artillery and ammunition, while Villa had no reserves, no grand strategy and not even any real tactics; it later transpired that he had not coordinated the movements of his various commanders. The opening barrage from the federals devastated the *villistas*, who lacked the firepower to respond. For a long time Villa was on the brink of defeat, on the defensive, trying to conserve scarce ammunition, his left dangerously exposed to enemy cavalry trying to work round the flank, the right being devastated by machine-gun fire. Their infantry lavishly supplied with Mausers and machine-guns, the federals advanced boldly.

However, the federal commander José Salazar paid the price of overconfidence. He should have lain down a blanket artillery bombardment, then launched an all-out attack, which would surely have carried the day, but he sent his infantry in too soon, and they were caught by a felicitously timed charge by one of Villa's commanders with 300 cavalry. Taken aback, the federals retreated to their initial positions, thus handing the initiative to Villa. For the rest of the day Salazar and Orozco rested on the defensive and at night formed themselves into a tighter inner perimeter.

Before dawn on the 25th Villa ordered a general advance and a flanking movement by the cavalry, while he sent one of his newest aides, Rodolfo Fierro, south behind the enemy to blow up the railway line. The *villista* infantry advance petered out that morning in the face of fusillades from machine-gun nests, but at noon Villa's cavalry appeared on the enemy flanks, forcing them to evacuate their positions and retreat to the troop trains. This was just what Villa had been hoping for. Suddenly there was a tremendous explosion from the enemy rear. Fierro had worked round behind them, and now sent a runaway locomotive crashing into the sidings behind the federals. An old exponent of *máquina loca*, Fierro had packed the engine with dynamite and percussion caps, generating a thunderclap explosion that threw the enemy into panic. As the demoralised federals tried to cut and run, Villa at last brought his artillery into play, adding to the casualties. There ensued terrible scenes of slaughter as white flags were ignored, and hecatombs of *colorados* were butchered where they stood. All those captured, including officers, were executed. That evening Villa threw a huge fiesta to celebrate.

With this victory Villa became undisputed master of the state of Chihuahua. At a cost of 300 casualties (federal losses were at least 1,000) he acquired a further four locomotives, eight field guns, seven machine-guns, horses, rifles and 4,000 rounds of ammunition. He controlled Ciudad Juárez and the border traffic and, in addition, the federal General Mercado hastily abandoned Chihuahua City, heading in panic for the American border, together with Creel and the Terrazas – but not before hanging all political prisoners from poplar trees. The city's oligarchs had begged and pleaded with him to stay, offered him huge sums of money and reminded him of the likely arrival of a relief column, but Mercado had had enough, especially as he could no longer control the *orozquistas*, who had turned to banditry and were intimidating the oligarchs. The terrified Creel-Terrazas-Mercado convoy fled across the desert on foot, in cars and on horseback, strewing the wasteland as they went with discarded baggage, supplies and ammunition. On 1 December Villa entered Chihuahua City, where he received the tumultuous ovation of the crowd from the balcony of the state palace.

Tierra Blanca was a striking triumph of the moral over the material, of élan over technology, morale over *matériel*, but to more thoughtful observers there were some worrying pointers to the future. Villa won the battle through luck rather than talent and committed every mistake in the textbook. He did not direct the battle firmly enough, but left too much initiative in the hands of individual commanders; he weakened his front when sending reinforcements from one sector to another; he had no notion of reserves and threw all his men into the attack; and he had no idea how to handle his artillery or how to minimise the impact of that of the enemy. These faults would be fully exposed in the future, but for the moment they were overlooked as Villa was master of Chihuahua.

Villa's triumphs were viewed by Carranza in Sonora with mounting jealousy and concern. Here was this peasant bumpkin, as Carranza saw him, succeeding in Chihuahua where he had failed, refusing to recognise his overall authority and winning more and more converts. The USA did not even recognise the 'Constitutionalists' as *bona fide* belligerents. It was essential for Carranza to create or discover his own military hero. His favourite general was Pablo González, possibly the most incompetent commander in the entire history of the Revolution. Not only had the lacklustre González made no progress in the north-east against the target cities of Monterrey and Nuevo Laredo, but the leaders of Coahuila refused to accept Carranza's designation of him as commander-in-chief in the north-east. The local leader, Lucio Blanco, so despised González that by October 1913 the two revolutionary factions in Coahuila nearly came to blows and started their own civil war. Blanco, a leftist and therefore hated by Carranza, who loathed all men of the Left, eventually moved out of the state altogether so as not to take orders from González.

Carranza therefore steadily advanced the career of Álvaro Obregón, his one truly able commander, trying to build him up as a counterweight to Villa. The 33-year-old Obregón had had a remarkably chequered career. Born in 1880, the last of eight children, he was brought up in genteel poverty by his mother, Cenobia Salido, and three sisters in the town of Huatabampo. His father, Francisco Obregón, who died when Álvaro was three months old, had been a wealthy Sonora landowner, but most of his estate was confiscated by Juárez in 1867 as a punishment for Francisco's support for Maximilian. The next year a disastrous flood devastated the part of the estate that had been left. The Obregón children turned to pedagogy: Álvaro's brother José and three of his sisters were all schoolteachers.

As a child Álvaro Obregón learned all the chores on a farm and spent much time with Mayo Indians, who had a reputation for reckless courage. He attended the primary school in Huatabampo and was a bookish child, but financial necessity forced him to cut short his education after elementary school. Obregón was one of those remarkable individuals who could turn his hand to anything, and in his early years he revealed himself as a jack-of-all trades with innate talent as an entrepreneur. At the age of thirteen he learned photography and carpentry, began raising tobacco, became an expert mechanic and taught himself to read music before forming a family orchestra which he conducted. His formation was not in the liberal humanities but in the hard school of opportunism and ruthlessness.

By the turn of the century Obregón was chief mechanic at the Tres Hermanos sugar mill owned by his maternal uncles, the Salido brothers, who were prosperous *hacendados* in the Mayo river region. In 1903 he married Refugio Urrea, and became a tenant farmer, alternating this with life as a door-to-door shoe salesman. In 1906 he managed to buy a small farm which he nicknamed 'The Poor Man's Manor', and built up a prosperous chickpea business. In 1907 tragedy struck. He had sired a child every year since his marriage, but that year his wife and two of the four children died. His three sisters took in the two surviving children, leaving the widower Álvaro with time on his hands, which he put to good purpose by inventing a chickpea harvester. Soon he had an assembly line producing these for eager buyers in the Mayo valley.

Rich enough by 1910 to be able to go down to Mexico City for Díaz's centennial celebrations, Obregón had the reputation in Sonora for being something of a genius. His outstanding mechanical ability was matched by great natural intelligence and an obvious creative streak. He also possessed a phenomenal memory: it was said he could remember the order of an entire pack of cards, arranged at random, after seeing the cards just once, and he became a feared poker player, so formidable that people actually asked him not to play. Affable, lighthearted and easygoing, Obregón enjoyed wit and humour and fancied himself as a joker. When he became famous he aspired to be Mexico's Will Rogers as much as her Woodrow Wilson. He liked to exaggerate the poverty of his childhood. One of his sayings was: 'I had so many brothers and sisters that when we ate Gruyère cheese, only the holes were left for me.'

Obregón is one of the few leaders in the Mexican Revolution for whom sufficient evidence of his inner life exists that we can hazard a guess at the demons nudging him. Freudians would doubtless say he was death-driven. Some childhood loss, perhaps the death of his father, gnawed at him. As a child he evinced signs of autism and did not speak a word until he was five. Repressed rage was obviously part of the syndrome for, when a friend of his mother's spoke disparagingly of the mute five-year-old as a monkey, the child suddenly found voice and spat out vociferously: '*Vieja loca*' ('Crazy old woman'). There was another significant event when he was fifteen. He was working on his brother Alejandro's farm some miles from home, and the two of them shared the same room. During the night Álvaro cried out as if in agony and woke his brother. He said he had just had a vivid dream in which their mother died. Next morning a man galloped up to say that their mother *had* died, at the precise time Álvaro had had his dream. Further evidence of something buried in the unconscious – something to do with death – appears in the Poe-like poetry he wrote.

In 1910–11 Obregón did not join the revolt against Díaz. He feared to lose his wealth and was anyway sympathetic to the ageing dictator – a fact with which revolutionary Sonorans often afterwards reproached him. Obregón liked to indulge in breast-beating to head off the criticism of others and had this to say about 1910–11: 'The *maderista* party was split into two sections; one was composed of individuals responsive to the call of duty, who left their homes and severed every tie of family and interest to shoulder a rifle . . . and the other of men who harkened to the promptings of fear, who found no arms, who had children liable to become orphans, and who were bound by a thousand other ties which even duty cannot suppress when the spectre of fear grips the hearts of men. It was to the second of these classes that I unfortunately belonged.'

In 1912 he joined Madero's fight against Pascual Orozco. He recruited 300 men and formed the 4th Irregular Battalion of Sonora, under the command of General Sangines. He proved a born captain, his mind full of decoys, ambushes and chess-playing manoeuvres; some even claim he was the first person to advocate that each soldier should dig his own foxhole instead of using a collective trench. Obregón had now converted fantasies of death into an everyday reality, and his family letters are full of references (unconscious wishes?) to death in battle. Promoted to colonel after defeating the *orozquistas* at San Joaquín, he resigned in December 1912 and returned to his farm. When Huerta assumed the presidency after murdering Madero, he at once offered his services to the government of Sonora.

Obregón set out on a mission to capture Sonora's border towns from Huerta at exactly the moment Villa crossed the Río Grande on his great adventure; capturing the border towns would enable the Sonoran rebels to levy customs duties and smuggle in arms. Together with Juan Cabral, Obregón took Nogales in March and then moved on Naco, defended by General Pedro Ojeda, a man in the Huerta mould, who boasted that he always executed every single prisoner of war he took. When Obregón approached, Ojeda, confident that his defences would hold, boasted: 'I will cut off my head before I will surrender or cross into the United States.' Yet a few days later he made the crossing, his head still intact, having blown up the customs house before he went.

Obregón then quickly took Cananea, Moctezuma and Álamos, leaving (of the major towns) only Guaymas in Huerta's hands. The rebels raised forced loans and used expropriated estates as collateral for other credit lines. The US mining companies and the Southern Pacific Railroad were quite content to pay taxes to the Sonoran rebels, who had no radical programme and presented themselves simply as more efficient managers of a capitalist economy than the *huertistas*. By the summer of 1913 Obregón had emerged as *the* military figure in Sonora, and it was in this capacity that he welcomed the fugitive Carranza into the state. He now commanded an army of 6,000 men, including 2,000 Yaquis; Obregón proved expert at holding the ring between Sonora's capitalists and the Yaquis with their radical agrarian aims.

Huerta entrusted the reconquest of the north-west to General Luis Medina Barrón, another figure of Huerta-like ferocity, who knew the Sonoran terrain intimately. In face of his advance, the rebels withdrew from the siege of Guaymas, and a confident Barrón boasted that he would go on and take Hermosillo. In a three-day battle at Hacienda Santa Rosa, Obregón proved his calibre by severely defeating Barrón, who withdrew after losing half his army. A furious Huerta sacked him and replaced him with the atrocity specialist Ojeda, who had so recently fled across the border. Obregón appeared to retreat, luring Ojeda on, then fell on him at Santa María at the end of June. For a cost of twenty-seven dead and thirty-one wounded, the Sonoran rebels killed 300 and took another 500 prisoner, as well as capturing a huge stock of arms, ammunition and *matériel*. Obregón was already perfecting his technique of manipulating the enemy into fighting on ground of his own choosing – the Wellington touch. Ojeda skulked in Guaymas, secure only with the covering fire of two federal gunboats.

Once he had tightly invested the federals in Guaymas, Obregón refused to waste time on frontal assaults. He had already proved himself a military master, drawing the enemy away from his base, extending his lines of communication, picking him off in skirmishes and generally demoralising him *before* giving battle. He planned his battles with graphs, equations, and geometrical figures. At Santa Rosa in May 1913 he calculated his moves to a nicety while encircling the federals, working out trigonometrically how to cut off the garrison's escape.

Many Sonoran generals, such as Benjamin Hill, who had fought for Madero, resented Obregón's meteoric rise and regarded him as a johnny-come-lately. None the less, when Carranza confirmed him as commander-in-chief of the north-west on 20 September 1913, Hill and the others had no choice but to obey his orders. Carranza's appointment contained its own absurdities, for Obregón was now the military supremo, in theory, not just in Sonora, Sinaloa and Baja California, but also in Chihuahua. There Villa was doing all the fighting, but Carranza did not see fit to consult him about the command or even whether he accepted the authority of the 'Constitutionalists'.

In any case, as the summer wore on, Obregón was increasingly taken up with political problems. He had to pacify the Yaquis and, more importantly, to decide what attitude to take to Carranza. The Yaquis were the simpler task of the two. Obregón, who had been brought up among Indians and knew how to speak to them in their own idiom, which buttons to press and which taboos to avoid, was particularly successful at recruiting Yaquis, who became his crack troops. He was not the only commander to recruit them, but he alone had an instinctive understanding of their psychology and how to motivate them. His duplicity emerges in the solemn promise that he would restore the Yaquis to their lands if they campaigned for him like tigers. Once he was successful, Obregón forgot his promise, and it was bitterly ironical that it was he who in the late 1920s finally destroyed them, both as a culture and a fighting force.

Carranza was a more ticklish problem. It particularly irked Obregón that Carranza had come to Sonora as a virtual refugee, and had arrogantly assumed powers and titles that no one had given him. The 'First Chief' had quasi-presidential powers, entirely self-assigned, and the politicians of Sonora had colluded with him in this fraud for entirely selfish reasons, out of jealousy of the governor Juan Maytorena. It was true that Maytorena had done himself no good and won few new friends by his cowardly flight to the USA, but now he was back, to find that Carranza had usurped most of his functions, and was like a gigantic Constitutionalist cuckoo in the Sonoran nest. Since Maytorena returned to find himself marginalised, and Obregón was angry that Carranza had not nominated him supreme military commander of the Constitutionalists, but only commander in the north-west, equal in billing with incompetents like Pablo González in the north-east, it seemed that Maytorena and Obregón should logically make common cause.

Obregón continued his military success. In November he took the city of Culiacán, demonstrating threefold qualities as a captain: mastery of terrain, deployment of men, and timing and positioning of artillery. He was also learning political skills. During a five-month lull in fighting in Sonora over the winter of 1913–14, he became a master of intrigue, using the time to discredit Felipe Ángeles, his only military and intellectual rival among the *carrancistas*. Ángeles had joined Carranza after some close dicing with death under Huerta. When Angeles came back from Cuernavaca with 1,000 men to support Madero during *La Decena Tràgica*, Huerta was furious, as Angeles nearly ruined his intrigue by his loyalty. As a reward he was arrested and placed in the same cell as Madero and Pino Suárez just before Major Cárdenas came for them. Ángeles was lucky to escape the same fate; perhaps only his Army rank saved him.

Obregón was already becoming a skilled political manipulator. He liked to play to the gallery, affect buffoonery, pretend to be amiable, disorganised and self-effacing. At Culiacán he was wounded in the leg but joked that bullets did not take him very seriously: this one had not aimed straight at him but caused the wound by ricocheting off a rock. Yet in reality this 'just folks' persona concealed a frightening ambition, as such a mask often does. The real Obregón was a man with ice in his soul where Villa had fire. Here was a man who dissembled, dissimulated, was secretive, played his cards close to his chest, was opaque and poker-faced and in general hid his true feelings, deep thoughts and ultimate intentions. Villa was an open book, but Obregón was the most enigmatic character in the entire Revolution.

The year of 1913 saw the rise to national prominence of Villa, Carranza and Obregón. Yet there was a fourth national figure in the field, who had the longest-lived credentials of all, as he had been a revolutionary general since the early days of 1911. For Zapata, with his previous experience of Huerta, the bullet-headed dictator presented a greater challenge than Madero had ever done. When he heard the news of the February coup, Zapata wrote at once to Genovevo de la O to caution him not to accept any offers of talks from the new government: 'Beware . . . and strike the enemy wherever he shows himself.' To make his position crystal clear, Zapata made a formal announcement of his undying hostility to Huerta and Félix Díaz in two separate *pronunciamientos* published on the second and fourth of March 1913.

One effect of Huerta's accession to power was to increase factionalism in Morelos, for the state was now split three ways, between *zapatistas*, *maderistas* and those who decided to make their peace with Huerta. Orozco's example in this regard was potent and many guerrilla chiefs sought accommodation with Huerta, citing Orozco and Zapata's praise for him in the Plan of Ayala; Zapata was particularly cast down when the fourth-ranking member of the *zapatista* junta, Jesús Morales, went over to the enemy. Huerta showed how he meant to proceed in Morelos by reappointing the hated Juvencio Morales as military commander there. The dictator gloatingly told his drinking companion, Lane Wilson: 'The best way to handle these rebels is with an eighteen-cent rope to hang them with.'

Zapata made clear this was to be war to the knife by attacking the train from Mexico City to Cuernavaca and killing seventy-five troops. Huerta responded by declaring martial law and announcing that he was to transport 20,000 Morelos peons to Quintana Roo. Zapata then wrote a blistering letter to Huerta and Orozco accusing them of 'mercenary trafficking . . . to assassinate the Revolution'. Orozco and Huerta made the mistake of sending peace commissioners into Morelos to put out feelers to the rebels. Zapata seized them, gave them a show trial, and executed them, thus making clear there would be no compromise. General Robles was keen to head south to avenge this 'atrocity', but in March-April Huerta was preoccupied with the north and advised Robles to wait until he could supply him with the necessary manpower. A sort of uneasy 'phoney war' hung over Morelos in these months, allowing the planters to harvest produce which Zapata would later tax.

Huerta soon evinced his short way with constitutional niceties. When Robles arrived in Morelos and announced that he intended to be governor as well as military commander, the state assembly informed him this was unconstitutional. However, Huerta simply swept up the assemblymen in mass arrests and imprisoned them in Mexico City. He then warned the planters that he was going to use whatever measures were necessary to destroy Zapata; if the planters were caught in the crossfire, that was simply the regrettable collateral damage of warfare. The effect of the dictator's hard line was to eliminate liberals at a stroke and make people either *zapatista* or *huertista*; the hawkish alcoholic was operating his own law of excluded middle.

Zapata would dearly have liked to put together the kind of military coalition Villa forged in the north, but his perennial problem was that disadvantages of geography and social structure meant that he could rarely field large armies. He was restricted to operating with guerrilla units of no more than fifty men each. Whereas a combined operation, involving the armies of Sonora, Chihuahua and Coahuila, was finally achieved by the revolutionaries in the north in 1914, such a grand slam remained a dream for the *zapatistas*. Zapata did try to ignite the whole of southern Mexico, though with limited success. In Mérida, Yucatán, 180 transported *zapatistas* fought a furious gun battle with the authorities for two hours before being overwhelmed and survivors executed, and elsewhere in Yucatán, as well as in Oaxaca and Veracruz, there were many sporadic *Viva Zapata* risings, but Tabasco and Chiapas, where the plantocracy was strongest, saw little action. In general, Zapata continued to operate along well-worn grooves: in Morelos, Mexico State, the Federal District, Puebla, Guerrero and southern Michoacán.

His staffwork was, however, better than in the past. Much of the credit for this went to his new chief of operations, Manuel Palafox, an ex-engineering student, salesman and accountant. Aged twenty-six, short of stature, rickety-looking and pockmarked, Palafox was a workaholic of boundless energy who turned the *zapatista* movement into a streamlined operation. He knew the politics of the north, and legal procedures, and was thus more than just useful; he it was who acted as chief prosecutor at the kangaroo court that condemned Huerta's envoys to death. The one strike against Palafox – and in a macho society it was a serious one – was that he was a homosexual of promiscuous appetites. Zapata was known for his contempt for gays, well summed up by the remark he made in 1912 to Otilio Montaño, when the co-author of the Plan of Ayala suggested they wear disguise at a time when they were being hard-pressed by the enemy. Zapata indignantly refused either to wear dark glasses or to shave his moustache, saying that he was not 'a fairy, bullfighter or friar'.

The day after Robles's 'election' as governor of Morelos, Zapata showed his contempt by attacking Jonacatepec and taking it after thirty-six hours' bitter fighting. Five hundred federals died or were taken prisoner, yielding 330 Mausers, two machine-guns, caches of ammunition and 310 horses. Zapata spared the commander, Higinio Aguilar, and his officers on condition he did not fight *zapatistas* again. For mixed motives of greed and gratitude Aguilar joined Zapata and proved extremely useful, not just in the training of recruits, but by brokering arms purchases from all the corrupt federal officers he knew. The shockwaves of the fall of Jonacatepec were felt at once in Mexico City, where disruption to the Yautepec quarries meant that work on prestige building projects, like the National Theatre and the London and Mexico Bank, had to be suspended.

On 23 April Zapata launched a full-scale offensive. First he invested Cuautla, then on May Day blew up a train on the Mexico/Morelos border, killing over 100 troops. With his outriders probing towards Cuernavaca, Huerta decided it was time to hit back before the *zapatistas* made common cause with the rebels in the north. Huerta displayed in the south the sort of energy that was conspicuously lacking in the north and many of his own cabinet criticised him for this scale of priorities; Zapata, they argued, was a mere gadfly and not *papabile* but Carranza was, and his movement, with its intelligentsia and inchoate bureaucracy, was the real threat.

Disregarding the advice, Huerta sent his 'scourge of God' into Morelos. Intending to corner Zapata at Cuautla, the federals approached in three separate columns to encircle him, but the *zapatistas* disengaged with ease and melted away into Guerrero and Puebla. On 9 May, reinforced to a strength of 5,000 men, Robles began a reign of terror, razing villages, press-ganging 'volunteers', and performing summary executions. He ordered all villagers to concentrate in the major towns and decreed that anyone who remained in the *pueblos*, which he intended to gut and raze, would be executed as a rebel. Once the terrified villagers congregated in the designated towns, Robles packed off all the able-bodied for service against Villa in the north. By June he had deported over 1,000. Robles and Huerta would have approved the notorious later maxim: 'It was necessary to destroy the village in order to save it.' They intended to create a desert and call it peace.

From Cuautla Robles sent a cable announcing a 'triumph', which seemed to consist of his bombardment of the abandoned *zapatista* headquarters. He claimed (falsely) to have uncovered a huge cache of arms, but did truly find the bodies of the envoys sent from Huerta whom Zapata had executed. The only result of Robles's absurd boast was that Huerta took him at his word and withdrew troops for operations in the north. The fallacy of Robles's policy is well summed up by John Womack: 'He was strong enough only to lay waste, not to secure control.' Many villagers, knowing that their houses would be destroyed, fled into the hills or joined Zapata. Previously neutral towns like Tepoztlán went over to him, and new recruits poured in. Most flamboyant was a battalion of Morelos 'Amazons' – a women's armed group from Puente de Ixtla led by a formidable ex-tortilla maker named La China.

The Morelos planters saw the ruin of all their hopes. They faced the loss of their labour force, either to the rebels or the draft, and meanwhile Robles could still not protect them against Zapata's forced loans. In June Robles transported another 2,000 of the able-bodied, and then another 1,300 in July, leaving women, children and old men in the concentration camps. Within months Huerta's strongman utterly destroyed the state's social fabric. Only immense pressure from the planters led Huerta to agree in late June that they could retain 30 per cent of their labour force; to plug the gaps left by his army's winnowing he promised to bring in 30,000 Japanese immigrants. However, nothing halted the insane devastation by Robles; here, if anywhere, was the true 'Attila of the South'. Along with the burnings and the rapes went the mindless destruction and the barefaced theft. Entire farms of pigs and chickens and ranches of horses and cattle were confiscated, the more edible animals being butchered and eaten on the spot.

In face of this onslaught Zapata retreated, ready to strike back when Robles thought all was quiet. Through the mountains the hardy guerrilla bands roamed, enduring incredible privations, aching with thirst, suffering pneumonia and malaria, rarely eating meat and even then never properly cooked, without so much as a tortilla for days, lacking alcohol, tobacco or medicine, sleeping out in the open, but never giving up. Zapata's concern was not so much for the indomitable morale of his men as it was fear of anarchy and chaos. He had to make sure the disparate rebel groups were coordinated, did not fight each other and, above all, did not alienate villagers by looting. Already the edges of the *zapatista* movement were fraying and tending to shade off into banditry. Gangs of unsocialised boys, aged ten to twelve, followed in the wake of the guerrillas, shooting, killing and looting even more mindlessly than the adults. The irony was that the outer rim of Zapatismo was beginning to decay even as the inner core, formerly a quasi-anarchistic movement of rural revolt, started to take on some of the features of a political party, complete with intellectuals like Palafox, secretaries, organisers, political technicians and troubleshooters.

Inevitably, Zapata's intellectuals began to pay more attention to the ideology of the movement. Since many aspects of the Plan of Ayala were out of date – Orozco, for instance, there mentioned as a revolutionary comrade in arms, was now routinely denounced as a traitor and usurper – a revised Plan was drawn up. Additionally, on 30 May 1913 Zapata announced the establishment of a six-man Revolutionary Junta. He was president of the junta, commander-in-chief and first chief of the Revolution; the other members of the ruling council were Genovevo de la O, Otilio Montaño, Felipe Neri, Amador Salazar and the leader's brother Eufemio, with Palafox acting as secretary. This marked the beginning of an attempt to formalise, by rules and regulations, matters that were formerly done spontaneously or informally, particularly those relating to pay, provisions, loans and land grants. In October 1913 the revolutionary army itself was put on a professional footing, complete with hierarchies, officers, and NCOs. A notable step forward was the decree requiring all guerrillas, in whatever band, to obey the orders of officers from another. Here was Zapata trying to break down the old modalities of caudillismo, kinship and clan mentality in favour of a genuinely revolutionary organisation.

The game of cat and mouse with Robles continued. Robles thought he had scored a great hit by capturing Huautla, a mining settlement, where Zapata had briefly had his headquarters, but Zapata had long since moved on; Robles's ponderous attempts to run his quarry to earth looked like the folly of a madman trying to catch the wind. Zapata even had unlooked-for strokes of luck. Huerta's coup had left the Figueroa brothers out on a limb, uncertain what to do next, but prevented by their pride from joining Zapata. Seemingly lost for answers, they eventually took up arms against Huerta in their own right, but almost immediately, in June 1913, Zapata's old enemy Ambrosio Figueroa was captured by the federals and executed.

In August 1913 Robles began a three-pronged offensive against Zapata, who simply moved from Morelos into Guerrero and Puebla; with the demise of the Figueroas, his influence in these states was greater than ever. Robles and his generals rode into a deserted Cuautla on 19 August to find Zapata gone, and the bodies of Pascual Orozco senior, and two other peace commissioners – foolish men who had not yet learned the lesson of no compromise – still lying where they had been executed. Robles claimed the campaign in Morelos was over, and his stupid boast was at first believed. In fact Zapata was not just at large but stronger than ever. Throughout southern Mexico he sent out his men to raid, wipe out federal outposts and tear up railway track. There were successful, and almost simultaneous, *zapatista* attacks in Morelos, Mexico State, the Federal District, Puebla, Tlaxcala, Guerrero, Michoacán and even Yucatán. Robles's empty boasts were revealed as the nonsense they were: the most he could ever hope for was to occupy the large towns.

By this time Huerta was under severe pressure in northern Mexico and could no longer afford expensive failures like those of Robles. He recalled Robles and replaced him with a moderate, General Adolfo Jiménez, who would still exercise the joint mandate of governor and military commander. Jiménez aimed at no more than keeping Morelos ticking over in stasis while Huerta concentrated on the north. The result was stalemate and a breathing space. Zapata had time for matters of high policy and made two decisions: to move his base of operations from Morelos to northern Guerrero, and to disrupt the elections Huerta had called for October. At a junta meeting in southern Morelos, just before the switch of headquarters, two further matters were decided: that the *zapatista* movement would seek recognition from the USA as legitimate belligerents; and it would actively negotiate for an alliance with Pancho Villa. Slowly but surely, it seemed, the paths of the two greatest revolutionary heroes were converging.

The winter of 1913–14 saw Villa master of the state of Chihuahua and at the acme of his fame and influence. The legend of Pancho Villa effectively dates from this time and his immense popularity can be seen as a compound of the personal charisma of the man, his bravery, astuteness, intelligence and military success, the satisfaction he gave to a culture based on machismo, and the appeal he made to the downtrodden sectors of society. Almost a textbook example of a Latin American personalist caudillo, Villa commanded the keenest loyalty and his magnetism drew in the bravest and best from ranch, mine and village, quickly turning bands of brigands and guerrilla groups into highly skilled light cavalry. Villa's self-belief, braggadocio and revolutionary voluntarism combined with the quality of his men – tough, mobile, motivated and high in morale – to create a legendary bond between leader and led.

Always impatient with abstractions, Villa was a personalist at every level. He encouraged his own legend, especially the unique blend of Robin Hood and Don Juan themes, which lost nothing in the telling. In one story he shot a judge in court, in another it was a colonel in a staff meeting, and in yet another it was an Englishman whom he had gunned down before the astonished gaze of other gringos. Skating over the actuality of 1912, he promoted the story that he had shaken his fist in Huerta's face when the general threatened him with execution. Mexican *campesinos* loved all the tall stories: they liked the fact that he was one of them, that he was locked into a grudge match with the oligarchs and therefore would not desert them. Both for Villa and his followers loyalty was the key concept. He was loyal to other people and expected the same from them; he had an elephantine memory for slights as well as past favours and meted out terrible vengeance on those for whom he bore grudges. He liked to lead from the front, plunging into the ranks if his troops faltered, a familiar stocky figure in khaki and sombrero. To begin with, Villa's every act of daring and bravado was attended with success, but unfortunately these early triumphs eventually led him to believe his own propaganda and think himself truly invincible.

In these years of his hegemony, scores of observers, both Mexican and foreign, observed Villa and tried to take his measure. Some hated him obsessively, others admired him inordinately. His critics liked to dwell on his pigeon toes, his habit of puckering his face when concentrating, his thin, reedy voice and his hyperemotionalism. Villa and tears were close comrades: sometimes they were tears of joy, sometimes excitement, often anger and occasionally frustration. The American journalist John Reed, who knew him well at this time, reported that he wept at the funeral of Abraham González and would become lachrymose if the martyred Maderos, Francisco and Gustavo, were mentioned. At times Villa would dissolve into tears of intellectual frustration or at the realisation of his own mental inadequacy; the man who feared nothing and lived with guns as naturally as other people with their spectacles was sometimes seen to tremble superstitiously when he was in the presence of books.

Both friend and foe noted his remarkable eyes which they usually compared to those of a savage carnivore. José Vasconcelos spoke of 'a wild animal who in place of claws had machine-guns and cannon'. One of Villa's secretaries, Martín Guzmán, said he was like a jaguar: 'His eyes were always restless, mobile as if overcome with terror . . . constantly anxious . . . a wild animal in his lair, but an animal that defends itself, not one that attacks.' Most observers traced this to his early life as a bandit, forever on the run, always alert, always with one ear cocked. This was why he never slept in the same location twice, moved his sleeping place during the night and dozed fitfully when he did sleep. Often, too, when he could not sleep, he would go out on the prowl to see if he could catch any sentries asleep at their posts; if he did, he executed them there and then with his pistol. He never walked any distance, always rode; he was not just a centaur but a kind of man-pistol, for many witnesses said the same thing: it was difficult to know where his piercing gaze ended and the barrel of his gun began, for they seemed to fuse in space.

It is curious how independent observers all seemed to reach for the same similes and metaphors when describing Villa. Almost the only animal he was not compared to was a bull, perhaps because he adored bullfighting and loved to measure himself against the horns of a *toro*. He liked to walk right up to a bull in the arena, slap it, then endure being chased and tossed for half an hour before calling on his comrades to grab the beast and pull it off him. John Reed wrote: 'He is the most natural human being I ever saw, natural in the sense of being nearest to a wild animal. He says almost nothing and seems so quiet as to be almost diffident . . . If he isn't smiling, he's looking gentle. All except his eyes, which are never still and full of energy and brutality. They are as intelligent as hell and as merciless. The movements of his feet are awkward — he always rode a horse — but those of his hands and arms are extraordinarily simple, graceful and direct. They're like a wolf's. He's a terrible man.'

Villa never smoked nor drank, but loved singing and dancing and playing the raconteur and yarn-spinner. Like Zapata, he had no interest in money or material things, but unlike him he was devoid of personal vanity, usually dressing in old suits and a cardigan with a sombrero or pith helmet on his head. His travelling headquarters was a red caboose with chintz curtains, fold-up wooden bunks and pictures of dancing girls tacked on a dirty grey wall. He looked prematurely aged, since the travails of a life on the trail had taken their toll; throughout the Revolution he suffered from the ex-bandit's habitual and chronic complaint: rheumatism. Bored by politicians and awestruck by intellectuals, Villa always preferred the rough company of his *vaqueros*, though he never really trusted anyone. His famous campfire visits, when he used to play Henry V or Napoleon by eavesdropping, then revealing himself to his men and asking to share their food, was only partly a populist gallery touch; he also wanted to be sure he could not be poisoned.

Above all else, Villa was a warrior, proud of his martial prowess. He could barely understand a life lived without fighting. When he asked John Reed about 'the war' in the United States and was told there was none, he was stupefied: 'No war at all? How do you pass the time, then?' Although he liked jokes, he could be prissy and humourless when his own status was involved. Reed once saw him being presented with a gold medal by his artillery corps for personal heroism in the field. Villa shambled forward to receive the medal in apparently humble 'just folks' mode, dressed in an old khaki uniform with several buttons missing, unshaven, wearing no hat, his hair unkempt, but when he saw the medal, he expressed disappointment: 'This is a hell of a little thing to give a man for all that heroism you are talking about.'

To compensate for his uncertain literacy Villa possessed a phenomenal memory and, it seems, to compensate for his lack of education, he made a virtue out of trying to solve all problems by main force. With no time for theory, ideology or rhetoric, and a penchant for knifing through to the heart of a problem, Villa predictably tried to solve financial problems by simply printing more money. His impatience was his Achilles' heel in military terms. He was the Murat of the Revolution, all dash, brio, swagger and élan. He lacked Obregón's grasp of strategy, but had a talent for logistics and commissariat, so that his staff always contained first-rate quartermasters and railway experts. Always a strange mixture of cruelty and compassion, violence and imagination, vengeance and stoicism, as well as of despair and hope, he was nowhere near as bloodthirsty as most other revolutionary leaders. He shot prisoners if they were federal officers or *colorados*, but spared the press-ganged conscripts on condition they would join him; in this he was unlike Carranza who always insisted that international conventions of the Hague and Geneva kind did not apply to 'rebels' in a civil war.

As temporary governor of Chihuahua in 1913–14, and later the effective ruler in the state for two years, Villa did a remarkable job. He very quickly restored law and order, and his code was so draconian that he would execute a soldier for stealing a pair of boots. He provided pensions, free food and cheap meat for his followers and their families. He cut the cost of food and other basics, organised distribution and rationing, punished all abuses by death and set his army to work on infrastructure projects – repairing railways, telephones and telegraph lines, running electrification projects, streetcars, the water supply and even slaughterhouses. He also sent his men south to harvest the cotton crop in Durango, although he never attempted to bring Durango under his sway. Politics in that state was too complex, with loyalties split three ways: there were the official *villistas*, led by Eugenio Aguirre Benavides; there was Tomás Urbina's personal fief; and then there were the powerful Arrieta brothers, loyal acolytes of Carranza.

Villa was always fanatical about education, both starry-eyed about teachers and self-conscious about his own lack of learning. He also had genuine compassion for children and decreed that all the hundreds of street urchins be found homes and schools. With his mania about education and homeless children, he hired teachers from Jalisco, vastly expanded the education budget, raised teachers' salaries hugely, built more than 100 new schools and stipulated that there should be an elementary school for each hacienda. He also set up a military college with places for 5,000 students. Even more than land reform, he saw education as Mexico's panacea. He told John Reed he had three priorities: his troops, children and the poor. His idea of utopia was an armed citizenry all attending school, with Mexico as an immense military academy. He envisaged the entire country divided into military colonies, run in a vaguely socialist style, in which men would work for three days and spend another three days on military training. It was the Swiss model of a nation in arms, ready to counter any invasion. His own modest ambition was to live with his *compañeros* in one of these military colonies, raising corn and cattle and spending his time making saddles and bridles.

Chihuahua in 1913–14, though, was still menaced by Huerta, so Villa had to set aside his dreams of a Mexican Shangri-La. He concentrated instead on economic strength, exporting meat to Cuba, the USA and later to wartime Europe, expropriating the estates and selling the cattle of the oligarchs who had fled, while levying duties on the cattle exports by *rancheros* who had stayed put. Most of the local elite – landlords, managers and businessmen – had gone, but those who remained received harsh treatment, especially the hated Spanish, who were expelled bag and baggage. Villa, however, always took great care to respect the property and persons of other foreigners, not wishing to provoke US intervention. He had particular problems in persuading the foreign-owned mines to resume production, halted because of the war with Huerta. Employing carrot and stick, he made the mine-owners extravagant promises, while threatening expropriation if they did not resume production. Even after Villa, in an extravagant gesture of truckling to the gringo, had outlawed trade unions among mineworkers, the foreign owners largely did not respond and decided to call Villa's bluff.

Two aspects of Villa's economic overlordship deserve special attention: his attitude to the money supply and his alleged socialism. An economic simpleton, Villa saw no reason why he could not simply print the money he needed, and to an extent the American banks in El Paso colluded with this by accepting his currency at eighteen-nineteen cents on the dollar, on Villa's guarantee. Villa's assault on market orthodoxy was more difficult to handle, especially when he gave the poor of Chihuahua fifteen dollars each on Christmas Day 1913, and then fixed the price of staples: beef was to be sold at seven cents a pound, milk at five cents a quart and bread at four cents a loaf. Mexican merchants tried to evade Villa's price-fixing by pricing their goods on a two-tier system, one price quoted against Mexican silver money, the other against Villa's paper money. Villa retaliated by ordering a mandatory sixty days in jail for anyone caught discriminating against his currency. When that measure failed to work, and people continued to hoard silver and 'real' bank bills, Villa declared that all such money not exchanged for his currency at par within a week would cease to be legal tender and its holders treated as counterfeiters. This tough measure panicked the hoarders into disgorging.

A primitive welfare state, food subsidies, controlled low prices, hostility to the market and expropriation of land looked like radicalism in anyone's language, and Reed called Villa's system 'the socialism of a dictator'. In fact, Villismo was very far from socialism. It is true that there were some socialist elements in Villa's thinking, even if he was not fully aware of all the implications, and that Villa's organ *Vida Nueva* often attacked Carranza for saying that private property was inviolable – that depends, was the *villista* response – but Villa was more interested in rewarding his veterans with land grants than redistributing expropriated haciendas to peasants. As for expropriation without compensation, this was done not for ideological reasons but simply because the *hacendados* had evaded taxes for decades by undervaluing their lands for taxable purposes; the total of back taxes owed therefore amounted to more than the current market value of the estates, and the confiscations were therefore sequestrations rather than expropriation.

There were many other reasons why Villa's policies could not be called socialistic. The pastoral economy of the north was utterly unlike the plantation economy of Morelos, and was therefore not amenable to the same kind of land division; for one thing, water shortages made huge economies of scale necessary. In any case, the produce of the great estates provided Villa with his 'sinews of war', so he was unlikely to shoot himself in the foot. His approach was simple: where the old oligarchs had fled, Villa gave their haciendas to his generals or put in boards of supervisors; where they had supported him, he left their lands untouched. Land reform was anyway never the pressing issue in Chihuahua that it was in Morelos. In Chihuahua the central feature of social conflict was villages versus caciques or *jefes políticos*, rather than villages versus haciendas; the struggle was not class against class but regionalism against central government. Alan Knight's judgement seems sound: 'Villa's "socialism" was a figment of the *Brooklyn Eagle*.'

Yet the greatest reason for scepticism about Villa's alleged socialism is that in his two-year hegemony in Chihuahua there was never anything that could be pinned down to an 'ism' – except in the obvious sense that Villismo means all the things actually done by Villa and his supporters. The principal reason was a dual set of 'contradictions' – both between Villa's utopian dreams and the everyday realities of running a state, and between the competing demands of peacetime and wartime economies. To begin with, there was no consensus on land reform, no agreement, for instance, on whether land should be distributed free of charge or sold on the open market to rich peasants. Silvestre Terrazas found his job as commissioner of the expropriated estates a bed of nails, especially since every time he suggested a particular village community should be given back its ancient lands stolen by a hacienda, Villa riposted that he really wanted to give it to his troops as the nucleus of his Shangri-La military colony system.

The demands of the revolutionaries and the needs of war were also in conflict. The simultaneous pursuit of guns and butter could go on only so long as Villa enjoyed the halcyon days when there were vast herds of cattle and bumper harvests of cotton to export. Moreover, democratic elections could not be permitted as long as Villa's veterans were at the front, for in their absence his enemies could easily 'steal' elections. Land reform was also halted during wartime, not just because Villa dithered about what his real intentions were, but because he had a personal repugnance against distributing land to anyone not actively fighting; it seemed unjust to him that cowards, self-seekers and black marketeers could stay at home and buy land while his heroes fought Huerta. Meanwhile, Villa's growing corps of intellectual advisers counselled him that his pet project – three days' agricultural work and three days' military training – was unviable and would lead to the collapse of agriculture and widespread famine. Villa solved this problem by stating that he would allow Silvestre Terrazas to distribute land at discretion, but that the former Creel-Luis Terrazas estates had to be reserved as military colonies for his soldiers.

Once the pent-up demand for the state's cotton and cattle had been satisfied, Chihuahua's economy experienced problems. Forced contributions and the sale of the confiscated estates palliated the worst aspects of dearth and inflation, themselves caused by shortage of revenue from the non-operating mines and the declining numbers of cattle, which had either been slaughtered to feed the armies or exported to the United States. Inflation was exacerbated by the huge amount of money printed by the *villista* mint. Villa's paper peso declined from US fifty cents in January 1914 to US twenty cents in June. Rationing was not really an option, as Villa lacked an efficient bureaucracy to administer it. Frustrated by problems that seemed beyond him, Villa lashed out at the mercantile class, accusing them of hoarding and economic sabotage. He put Silvestre Terrazas in charge of a secret police agency to sniff out these 'enemies of the people'. His police travelled on trains, eavesdropped on conversations, intercepted letters, conducted surveillance operations, and generally took the political pulse, but they found few saboteurs to execute. Crime was, in any case, at a very low level during Villa's two-year suzerainty: either the criminals were caught and executed after a summary trial or they were drafted into the Army.

It will be appreciated that Chihuahua under Villa was very far from being a socialist society. Distributing chunks of Terrazas land to his soldiers was not an instance of Villa's 'socialism' but sheer pragmatic necessity; not even Villa could get men to follow him without rewards. With Villismo's evenhandedness between Army and the dispossessed, its lack of a clear ideology and its eclectic 'middle way' approach to problems, the analogy it most calls to mind is Perón's Argentina. A comparison with Zapata's Morelos makes the point at once. Zapata's land redistribution led to subsistence agriculture, not the marketing of cash crops; Villa, by contrast, enjoying the proximity of the USA, both exported and redistributed the profits away from the peasantry. Villa's bureaucrats were under express orders to prohibit the kind of communal land tenure that was second nature to the Indians of Morelos. In Morelos, under Zapata, the state could be said to be withering away; under Villa in Chihuahua it was stronger than ever, intervening at all points in economic and social life. The one area in which Villa retained revolutionary purity was the low level of corruption in his regime. Except for Villa himself and Urbina, no *villista* chief acquired the sort of wealth Obregón did in Sonora. Villa had no equivalent of the rapacious 'proconsuls' whom Carranza sent out into the four corners of Mexico to try to make the writ of the 'First Chief' run. Where the *carrancista* 'proconsuls' were greedy outsiders who bled dry lands in which they had no personal stake or roots, Villa's chiefs operated at a purely local level, with the whole *villista* nexus really no more than a grand coalition of local revolutionary bands.

The radical element in Villismo may have been overstressed by commentators more impressed by attitudes than socio-economic reality. Although the lot of peon, tenant and sharecropper did improve under Villa, what changed most of all was the mentality of the ordinary man and woman. Now that the world seemed turned upside down, with the rich cowed and the poor enjoying unheard-of privileges, with one of their own as ruler of Chihuahua, the dispossessed and wretched of the earth no longer perceived obedience, deference and rigid hierarchy as laws of nature. One of the first casualties of the new attitudes was the Catholic priesthood. Under Díaz the parish priest was widely perceived as a leech – exacting six pesos for conducting a marriage ceremony and the rest pro rata – and a lecher, who took advantage of the confessional to enjoy *droit du seigneur*: 'the girls here are very passionate,' one priest leeringly told John Reed. However, under Villa in 1913–14, anticlericalism was the order of the day. In Durango priests were beaten up and arrested and churches desecrated, and in Chihuahua clerics were sent to the firing squad. Particular targets were priests who owned village lands or supported local elites of the pre-Villa era; especially hated were Spanish priests and nuns, who were expelled *en masse*. Villa's anticlericalism, though, was always pragmatic rather than ideological; he was no more a Jacobin than he was a socialist.

Accusations of socialism notwithstanding, the middle classes of

Chihuahua were mightily relieved by Villa's moderation and conciliation and the iron discipline he imposed on his men. Villa too offered amnesty to functionaries and bureaucrats who had served under Huerta and Orozco, promising no reprisals. His moderation was also aided by the statesmanlike posture of Silvestre Terrazas, the channel through whom all accusations of 'counter-revolutionary' behaviour were processed. Terrazas received many letters addressed to Villa, containing inflammatory and combustible material that might have provoked the volatile Centaur into ordering massacres; Terrazas largely kept such correspondence from his chief.

The one area where Villa would not compromise to win the good opinion of the national bourgeoisie or foreign observers was in his vendetta against Creel and the Terrazas. Villa sent his men into the British consulate, violating diplomatic immunity, to drag out Luis Terrazas junior, son of the clan patriarch. Villa knew that the Terrazas had not had time to get all their gold out of the Banco Minero and suspected that the younger Luis Terrazas knew where it was hidden. Terrazas was accordingly put to torture until he revealed the hiding place: it turned out that gold bars worth US$600,000 were hidden inside a column in the bank. Villa did not reward Terrazas for this information by releasing him; instead he kept him as a bargaining chip, to prevent the Terrazas blocking the sale of their cattle and other assets in the United States. This ploy was only partly successful, for Luis Terrazas senior seemed prepared to let his son die rather than bow the head to Villa. Until 1915 Washington constantly put pressure on Villa to release the young Terrazas, but he ignored all overtures. Finally, after nearly two years of imprisonment, Terrazas did succeed in escaping, but died soon afterwards, possibly as a result of the pent-up stress of his ordeal.

It should not be thought that Villa spent the winter of 1913–14 purely on economic, administrative and civilian matters. One of the reasons he very soon turned over the formal governorship to Manuel Chao was that he wanted to concentrate on the spring military campaign to overthrow Huerta. Villa's army had by now become so large and so complex that it took great administrative talent to keep it in being as a viable, coherent force. Villa was not yet as far advanced as Zapata in being able to streamline his fissiparous military followers into a centralised force. Like Napoleon, he had subordinate commanders and technicians who owed everything to him, and he had others who had had independent careers before him and who still retained a considerable measure of autonomy. To keep them all loyal, Villa had to have recourse to something like Napoleon's marshalate.

Of the commanders who operated semi-independently, the pre-eminent figure was Tomás Urbina, a charismatic leader with a reputation second only to Villa's. An arrogant, drunken roué of sinister appearance, described as 'a broad, medium-sized man of dark, mahogany complexion, with a sparse black beard that failed to hide the wide, expressionless mouth, gaping nostrils and the tiny animal eyes', Urbina really was what Villa was often accused of being – a bandit masquerading as a revolutionary. Urbina was another man who had turned against Orozco in 1912, ended up in jail, and narrowly escaped execution through Emilio Madero's intercession. Like Villa, he was a native of Durango, and his particular sphere of influence was the Durango/Chihuahua border, but there the resemblance ended. Urbina was nowhere near as intelligent as Villa and, unlike him, had not bothered to conquer his illiteracy. A disloyal, obstinate, vain, avaricious ingrate, obsessed with money, corrupt at every level, unable to control his troops, not just a commander of looters but a looter himself, Urbina bamboozled Villa for many years before the great caudillo finally saw through him.

The fact that he was indistinguishable from his men in mentality or intellect may actually have enhanced his charismatic appeal in the short term. One peasant told John Reed: 'A few years ago he was just a peon like us; and now he is a general and a rich man.' Another told Reed that Urbina had a magic aura: 'He is very brave. The bullets bounce off him like rain off a sombrero.' When Reed interviewed Urbina, the chief frankly told him he had just one interest in the Revolution: to become fabulously rich and to replace the Terrazas as chief *hacendado* in Chihuahua. Initially based at Las Nieves hacienda, where he lorded it like the worst of the corrupt oligarchs of the *Porfiriato*, for two years Urbina got away with murder, literally and metaphorically, because with him Villa had one of his famous blind spots and would not hear a word said against him.

In June 1913 Villa sent Urbina south to try to coordinate the various rebel movements in Durango. After assembling 4,000 men, Urbina decided to launch a night attack on Durango City. Seeing that it was likely to succeed, the foreign consuls tried to broker a negotiated settlement, but the federals fired on a flag of truce and then, unaccountably, pulled out, pleading lack of ammunition. On 19 June Urbina's locusts swept into the city and began two days of mayhem and anarchy. They looted shops, burned archives, emptied the jails and gutted the business quarter; all utilities – gas, electricity and water – were cut off; women were stripped naked and run through the streets; the bones of former archbishops were dug up and the mantle of the Virgin of

Durango given to the wife of one of the rebel commanders. Although many doubt the authenticity of the story that fifty virgins, daughters of the best families in Durango, were gang-raped and then committed suicide, it is unquestionably the case that murder and rape were commonplace during the two-day sack of the city. The carnage was particularly high as the city mob joined in the rapine, seeking out federalists and their families, real or alleged, to slaughter. Two days later the charred city of Durango was a ghost town, having sustained ten million pesos worth of damage.

Urbina's stupidity in allowing this holocaust of pillage, atrocity and sacrilege was egregious. The sack of Durango created a sensation throughout Mexico and, even if the stories of mass rape and murder lost nothing in the telling, the olio of real and fictitious atrocities engendered a climate of fear throughout urban Mexico which actually strengthened Huerta's hand. Urbina ratcheted the Revolution up another notch, adding a Jacobin tinge to the civil war and making it seem likely that the rebels were swinging left with a vengeance. The truth of course was that Urbina simply could not control his army – a disparate, heterogeneous collection of genuine revolutionaries, ex-bandits, ex-miners, cowboys, cottonpickers and simple adventurers. It took him three days to regain control; finally he posted sentries on the streets and ordered all loot to be returned.

Urbina kept all the restored loot for himself and continued on a career of self-advancement through theft that would lead, in 1915, to his announcement that he had retired from public life. At the expropriated hacienda of Canutillo he stashed banknotes and bullion worth half a million pesos, the proceeds of his exploitation of Durango. He bled the state dry by forced loans, ransoms demanded on its leading citizens (including the archbishop), and an exit tax of 500 pesos per head for all wishing to leave the territory. For a month Durango experienced the kind of tyranny and arbitrary exaction unknown since the Conquistadores. His departure north at the end of July was greeted with relief, but he had left behind him a legacy of hatred and bitterness, and decisively swung the Arrieta brothers over into Carranza's camp.

Fortunately for Villa, most of his semi-independent 'marshals' were not of the Urbina stamp. Particularly loyal and dependable was the trio of Toribio Ortega, Calixto Contreras and Orestes Pereyra. Toribio Ortega, whose power base was north-eastern Chihuahua, was accorded Ney-like status by John Reed, who praised him as the 'bravest of the brave' but, given his utter lack of interest in money, perhaps nearer the mark was Robespierre, the 'sea-green incorruptible'. Calixto Contreras began his career rather like Zapata, as spokesman for a village in conflict with a hacienda. He had the reputation of being a good politician but a poor military leader, unable to control his men. Patrick O'Hea – a Wimbledon-based Anglo-Irishman who emigrated to Mexico in 1905, accompanied Villa on his campaigns and is preferred as an observer by some Revolution buffs to John Reed – portrays Contreras as an impotent buffoon, invariably replying to official protests at the behaviour of his men with a weary 'boys will be boys' response.

Orestes Pereyra was a former tinsmith who had taken up arms against Díaz in advance of Madero's November 1910 deadline. A veteran of the 1912 campaign against Orozco, he had also been among the first to rise when Huerta brutally seized power. A daring guerrilla leader, who had made his name by raising the peasants who lived around the Anglo-American owned hacienda of Tlahualilo, Pereyra commanded the most heterogeneous collection of revolutionaries after Urbina – free peasants, miners, temporary workers. Contreras's band was another loose collection, but Ortega had the tightest-knit group of all. The trio of Ortega, Pereyra and Contreras supported Villa in good times and bad and predictably met the fate of almost all leaders in the Mexican Revolution: Ortega died of fever while the other two succumbed to Carranza's firing squads in 1915.

More interesting than the loyalists among the 'marshals' were the intellectual generals. One such was José Isabel Robles, an ex-school-teacher and one-time *orozquista*. This should have damned him in Villa's eyes, but Robles had redeemed himself by breaking with Orozco when the latter backed Huerta. At twenty-three, the youngest general in Villa's army, Robles liked reading Plutarch and Caesar's Commentaries while on campaign. The other notable intellectual general was a real thorn in Villa's side. Máximo Castillo was an anarchist *ranchero* of the far Left, who despised Villa's respect for foreign property and was particularly incensed about the privilege of the Mormon colonies in Chihuahua. Political differences soon compelled Castillo to operate as an independent fighting force, at risk from both Huerta and Villa. *Villista* forces badly mauled the Castillo guerrillas in one ambush, which cost Castillo half his men, but he continued the struggle, sustained by strong local support and his reputation as a genuine Robin Hood.

Castillo once captured Villa's 'wife' Luz Corral, treated her with elaborate courtesy and escorted her to the US border. Villa was so touched by this gesture that for a while he stopped sending his forces after Castillo. It was not through Villa that the Zapata of the north met his downfall. Castillo specialised in robbing trains on which Americans were travelling; he would rob the *yanquis* but not harm them. More cynical operators decided to try the same trick, passing themselves off as Castillo's men, and among them was a notorious low-life bandit leader named Gutiérrez. At a place called Cumbre a group of bandits set fire to a tunnel just before the train entered it, then dynamited both entrance and exit, trapping the locomotive in the darkness and leaving a trainload of people to suffocate to death. Gutiérrez disguised his dark deed by pretending it was the work of Castillo. Even though such an exploit seemed totally out of character, the mud stuck and Castillo's career went into terminal decline. He lost all popular support, his men deserted, and he was forced to flee across the border to the hated United States.

The other category of commanders consisted of those men who owed everything to Villa or who were the equivalent of *ronin* samurai: freelance expert military technicians appointed by him to high rank. By far the most notorious was the 'dark angel' of the *villista* movement, Rodolfo Fierro, a murderous ex-railwayman, psychopathic even by the homicidal standards of the Revolution. Patrick O'Hea wrote about Fierro: 'I only know that this man, with his wandering gaze and his cold hand, is evil itself.' There is something of a mystery about Fierro's status as Villa's 'favourite son', for Villa had not even met the man before 1913. Some speculate that it was Fierro's reckless courage and ruthlessness, and his utter loyalty, that appealed most, and that Villa appreciated the gallery touch. At the close of the battle of Tierra Blanca, a trainload of federals tried to escape capture by shunting away from the battlefield. As the engine gathered steam, Fierro rode after the locomotive, jumped on to the caboose and shot the train drivers dead; the train then slowed to a halt and the federals were captured.

The tall, heavily built, moustachioed Fierro would kill anyone at Villa's nod and was expert at 'anticipating' his wishes. In *The Eagle and the Serpent* Martín Luis Guzmán describes the famous scene when Fierro slaughtered *colorado* prisoners. Released from their compound ten at a time, the prisoners were offered their freedom if they could run 100 yards through a corral and scale a wall before Fierro picked them off. All the more sinister in that he spoke in a soft voice, never blustered or threatened and used mild and inoffensive body language, Fierro prepared for this work of butchery by making sure a relay of fresh pistols was handed to him. In the resulting 'turkey-shoot', he never stopped firing for two hours and killed all but one of 200 prisoners. The survivor escaped over the wall at twilight; Fierro explained that he had felt a cramp in his trigger finger and let his attention wander while he massaged the sore muscle.

Killing meant nothing to Fierro. John Reed wrote: 'During the two weeks I was in Chihuahua, Fierro killed fifteen inoffensive citizens in cold blood. But there was always a curious relationship between him and Villa. He was Villa's best friend; and Villa loved him like a son and always pardoned him.' He once gunned down a complete stranger in Chihuahua City to win a bet as to whether a dying man falls forward or backwards; Fierro said forwards and was proved right. The mercenary Edward O'Reilly testified that Fierro liked to shoot wounded *villistas* too, to save the chore of looking after them. On another occasion Patrick O'Hea, then British consul in Torreón, was stopped in the street by a drunken Fierro who told him he was going to shoot him. Fierro pointed his pistol at the consul and squeezed the trigger but nothing happened; there was a safety catch on the weapon of a kind with which he was unfamiliar. Some of his comrades approached the inebriated gunslinger and explained that if he shot the gringo, there would be international repercussions. Fierro lurched off, after advising O'Hea to smile next time he was staring down a gun barrel.

The only man Fierro deferred to was Villa himself, and with him he behaved as meekly as a lamb. Villa once caught him slapping a soldier in Ciudad Juárez for not wearing his cap at the right angle. Enraged by this, Villa slapped Fierro across the face; the killer, who would have executed any other man in the world for such an outrage, literally took it on the chin. When a train carrying food and water to the combatants at Torreón was thirty-five minutes late, Villa ranted and raged at Fierro, whom he had put in charge of the railways. Fierro stood mutely, his head bowed – but when Villa had gone and the train drew in, Fierro shot the driver dead for having 'caused' his humiliation. For a long time Villa would take no action against Fierro, no matter how appalling the outrages reported to him. Then one day a drunken Fierro gunned down a railwayman who had accidentally brushed against him. At this the other railwaymen demanded action from Villa. To placate these workers, vital to his military success, Villa removed Fierro from his job as railway superintendent and set up a bogus 'investigation'. Silvestre Terrazas was appointed presiding magistrate and began collecting evidence, but the trial judge he appointed refused to serve because of fear of reprisals from Fierro. The so-called 'trial' petered out in obfuscation, as Villa intended; he had only wanted to conciliate the railwaymen and, as soon as the dust settled, reappointed Fierro to yet another position where he had *carte blanche*.

Fierro was deeply implicated in the notorious Benton case, which first made Villa an object of intense interest to the British government.

William Benton was a British citizen and the owner of the Los Remedios hacienda. He had a bad reputation as a bloodsucking employer who had been involved in a protracted land dispute with the village of Santa Maria de Cuevas. In 1910 Benton seized village land, fenced it off, denied villagers access, and then fined them for trespass when they were found on the land. He accused all who opposed him of being cattle rustlers and would call in the *rurales* on the slightest pretext. Benton was also a hothead and reactionary, who habitually let his mouth run away with him. Villa detested him and in 1912, citing Benton's close ties with the Creel-Terrazas clique, expressly exempted him from his policy of not taxing foreigners. Benton refused to pay the tax, so Villa expropriated horses, arms and ammunition in lieu. Since Benton continued vociferous in his support for Huerta and admiration for Díaz, Villa warned him in late 1913 that he would be well advised to depart for the USA.

While clinging to his policy of not expropriating foreign assets, Villa was determined that Benton be forced to disgorge the ill-gotten land he had taken from the village of Santa María de Cuevas. The villagers moved back on to the disputed grazing land and shortly afterwards Benton discovered that some of his cattle were missing. It was never discovered whether those responsible were villagers or Villa's men, but the consequence was that on 17 February 1914 an intemperate Benton stormed into Villa's house in Ciudad Juárez, demanding immediate compensation. What happened next was disputed. Some say that Benton reached into his pocket for a handkerchief to mop his sweating brow, and that the gesture was mistaken by Fierro, who shot him dead. Allegedly Fierro merely smirked and said: 'Just a misunderstanding.' Others, more persuasively, say that Benton offered Villa the insult direct and that Villa shot him down in cold blood. Whatever took place, the upshot was that Benton was dead and Villa had an international incident on his hands.

The British press took up the shooting as a *cause célèbre*; questions were asked in Parliament; the British government requested US intervention and mediation in northern Mexico. Having only just lifted his arms embargo on the anti-Huerta combatants, President Woodrow Wilson immediately came under pressure to reimpose it. The British were adamant that Wilson had to take tough action; it was only at his urging that they had abandoned their earlier endorsement of Huerta, and only then on the strict understanding that Wilson would compel the revolutionaries to respect European persons and properties. The international dimension was immensely complicated both by the US insistence that the Monroe doctrine should prevail in the Americas and also as a result of the 1905 Roosevelt Corollary, which declared that in any dispute between Europe and Latin America, the USA would be the sole agency for enforcing European claims.

Villa had stepped into a hornets' nest and was totally unprepared for the international furore that followed the Benton slaying. At first he told American investigators that Benton had been formally court-martialled and executed after due process. When asked to produce Benton's body to prove cause of death, he refused, thus revealing to the world how blatantly he was lying. Villa's violent and irrational behaviour was a godsend to the Huerta propaganda machine and, by embroiling the rebels with foreign powers, angered Carranza twice over: it impaired his cause and it showed that he had no control over Villa. At first Carranza seemed to have played into Villa's hands by insisting that all foreign envoys deal with him, as First Chief of the Revolution; Villa was only too willing to hand over this hot potato. Later it turned out that by getting himself off the hook and accepting a Faustian pact, Villa had unwittingly, if only implicitly, acknowledged Carranza as his overlord.

In international diplomacy Carranza was in his element. He knew that Villa's story was a phoney, but he saw capital to be made out of taking over the case. At first he stalled, then, when it became clear that the affair would not blow over, he appointed a Mexican Commission of Inquiry, refusing, however, to entertain the idea of an international commission or a body of foreign forensic experts. Predictably, Carranza's commission found that Villa's story was a tissue of lies, but Carranza bluffed his way out by claiming that Benton's thirty-year sojourn in Mexico made him a Mexican citizen, subject to Mexican law; he also muddied the waters by presenting a massive dossier of evidence showing that Benton had been a ruthless and inhumane *hacendado*. Most of all, he refused to accept US mediation and insisted that he, and only he, deal directly with Britain. Carranza's Fabian strategy in the end wore down his opponents, and Carranza himself gained great kudos from the affair. He won a brilliant hand of machiavellian poker, using emotive taboos like the Monroe Doctrine and Roosevelt Corollary for his own advantage. He gambled that the USA would not suspend arms sales – they did not – and he gambled that the British, fearing to fall out with the USA when a European war was imminent, would refuse to deal directly with him.

Rightly or not, Fierro was always associated in people's minds with the Benton affair. The perception gained ground, among domestic educated opinion as well as foreign, that whereas Carranza's 'Constitutional' movement had the credibility to deal with foreign governments, Villa always took the short view (in this case, that Benton was merely a gringo sonofabitch) and always surrounded himself with killers like Fierro or another homicidal 'untouchable' named Manuel Baca Valles, a particular *bête noire* of Luz Corral's. This was the context in which the voluntary adherence to the *villista* movement of Felipe Ángeles was especially valuable, and students of Villa are fond of locating Ángeles as the angel of light situated on Villa's right-hand side, with Fierro as the Satanic angel of death on his left.

Felipe Ángeles, ex-federal general, scholar, thinker, ideologue, mathematician and artillery expert, was certainly a great catch for the *villista* movement. Born in the state of Hidalgo in 1868, he had made several trips to France on military missions and was a man of cosmopolitan sophistication. In France when Madero raised his standard, he came back a *maderista* and was sent to subdue Zapata in Morelos. Despite believing that Madero was the only alternative to chaos, Ángeles found himself becoming more and more sympathetic to Zapata and his movement. Because of his strong *maderista* credentials Huerta had him arrested during the February 1913 coup and would have executed him had he not feared splitting the Army. Instead he used on him the same tactics he used on Villa, keeping him in prison on trumped-up charges while spurious investigations dragged on. However, it so happened that Lane Wilson was an Ángeles supporter, and he was the one man to whom Huerta dared not say no. Accordingly, Ángeles was released and, to save Huerta's face, sent off to France on another military mission.

On his return, Ángeles joined Carranza but failed to hit it off with him and transferred his loyalties to Villa. The revolutionary movement in Chihuahua, and Villa in person, gained significantly because of the tension between the men of 1910 and those of 1913. The 'class of 1913', such as Obregón, felt that the 'old guard' of revolutionaries were trading on past glories, while the men of 1910 felt they had risked their lives only to see the rewards and pay-offs going to a bunch of johnny-come-latelies in Sonora. In these circumstances, those (not a few) personally alienated by Carranza or excluded by the possessive jealousies of the 'class of '13' turned by reflex to Villa, whose *maderista* credentials were impeccable. The class of 1910–11 increasingly put their bets on Villa. José Vasconcelos allegedly remarked: 'We'll win now all right. We've got a man,' to which Alan Knight retorts alliteratively: 'It was the recurrent dream of the impotent revolutionary intellectual: to play Plato to some powerful but pliant popular caudillo.' This may well be an accurate analysis of Ángeles, who probably had ambitions to be president of Mexico, with Villa as the power behind the throne but based in Chihuahua, allowing Ángeles free rein to implement radical reforms in the capital.

Villa admired and revered Ángeles, thinking him the perfect man, a combination of soldier and scholar. He knew of Ángeles's benevolence towards the *zapatistas* and could not get enough of his reminiscences of Madero and Piño Suárez. He admired Ángeles's love of books and music, his passion for justice and his compassion; he even baptised one of Ángeles's sons so that he could truly call Ángeles *compadre*. For Ángeles, Villa was Mexico's best hope. It is interesting that almost all Villa's intellectuals were ex-*maderistas*, more concerned with education and political reforms than with land and labour, basically men who wished to return to the liberalism of Juárez. Ángeles probably saw Villa as a *tabula rasa* on which he could imprint his ideology. The problem was that Villa had no taste for abstract thought; as Reed remarked ironically: 'You had to be a philosopher to explain anything to Villa.' However, Ángeles enjoyed one hidden advantage. Unconsciously Villa was looking for a Madero substitute and tended to gravitate to Ángeles for this reason; but, as a divided self, primed by Fierro, he would sometimes lose patience with him as a mere theoretician.

In addition to these military figures, there were significant civilian figures in the Villa entourage. Probably the most important was Silvestre Terrazas, a supporter from the early days and secretary-general of the state government of Chihuahua from December 1913 to December 1915. His position of pre-eminence at first seemed threatened when Manuel Chao took over as governor, but Chao in turn was soon replaced by Fidel Ávila, an undereducated hacienda foreman, and this allowed Terrazas to regain most of his former influence. Terrazas always presented himself as a civilian who moderated Villa's excesses and civilised him, though he probably knew more about his chief's repression (and condoned it) than he pretended. His motive for joining Villa had always been the love of Chihuahuan autonomy, the *patria chica* patriotism that was such an important part of the Mexican Revolution. He showed little interest in land reform, but liked the fact that Villa had put Chihuahua on the map as, in effect, Mexico's premier state.

The extent to which Silvestre Terrazas did and did not have Villa's ear is illustrated by the partial way the leader allowed him to curb the excesses of the military commanders. In theory Villa was committed to selling all expropriated estates and redistributing the land or using it as the nucleus of military colonies. In practice his chief commanders occupied the most palatial houses of the oligarchy in Chihuahua City and took up permanent residence, often burning or destroying precious libraries of rare books or priceless musical instruments in the process. Silvestre Terrazas appealed to Villa to halt this mindless barbarism, so

Villa operated a tripartite policy, hoping to satisfy all concerned. In the case of his special favourites, he simply turned a blind eye to their depredations; he issued a decree reserving to himself the right to decide what was confiscated and what was not; and he allowed Silvestre Terrazas to operate a special squad of archival police, acting in the name of Villa so as to override all other authority, with power to enter expropriated or occupied houses and carry off to the state archives books, musical instruments, paintings and other artefacts deemed to have educational or artistic value.

The array of important middle-class military/administrative figures was completed by Manuel Chao, Maclovio Herrera and Eugenio Aguirre Benavides. Chao, an ex-schoolteacher turned commander of *rurales*, always resented Villa, for having attained the supreme command in Chihuahua that was 'really' his. Behind the scenes he intrigued with Carranza against Villa's interests. So too did Maclovio Herrera, but Villa admired him more than he did Chao, since he was a man of reckless courage who had won his laurels by the desperate but successful cavalry charge at Tierra Blanca. More loyal to Villa was Eugenio Aguirre Benavides, commander of Villa's Zaragoza brigade. It was his brother who had been Villa's most constant visitor in jail in 1912, and the Benavideses had always been staunch *maderistas* and disliked by Carranza for that reason. Eugenio benefited both from Villa's high regard for Luis and for the extended Aguirre Benavides family in general, who were close friends of Raúl Madero. The inheritor of the Madero mantle, Raúl, worked closely with Eugenio as second in command of the prestigious Zaragoza brigade.

If Silvestre Terrazas was his administrative genius, Villa liked to devolve personal finance and general business dealings either to Lázaro de Garza, a shady businessman to whom he entrusted important arms-buying and diplomatic missions in the USA or to his own brother Hipólito, who controlled the gambling concession in Ciudad Juárez. Since Hipólito was literate, Villa also gave him huge sums for arms purchases in the USA, but Hipólito was as insignificant *vis-à-vis* Pancho Villa as Eufemio Zapata was with his brother. A dandy and pretty boy, fond of fast cars and fast women, the corrupt, money-grubbing hedonistic Hipólito had none of his brother's qualities: without him he would have been a pathetic playboy *manqué*. Utterly venal and morally skewed, Hipólito was not beyond cheating and fleecing his own brother to embezzle money meant to buy arms and *matériel*; worshipping Mammon with monotheistic fervour, Hipólito carried the love of money to insane levels that even transcended the avarice of Tomás Urbina.

Villa's attitude towards his middle-class intellectuals was always ambivalent. He found them useful as the respectable face of Villismo, masking the realities of Fierro and Urbina; as bureaucrats with useful skills; as intermediaries with other factions and especially with the *yanquis*; and as expert drafters of Plans and manifestos. However, he had a visceral dislike of lawyers and bureaucrats and tolerated them merely as a necessary evil. The only educated men who could get under his guard were schoolteachers, as they catered to his perennial obsession with education. It was difficult for intellectuals, even men of the world like Felipe Ángeles, to deal with an unpredictable and impulsive loose cannon like Villa. Fond of making policy on the hoof, Villa would endorse a proposal from Ángeles one day, then next day listen to a completely contrary idea from Fierro or some other brutal favourite. One thing is absolutely certain: Villa was always his own man. The absurd idea, sometimes floated, that Villa was a pawn in the hands of manipulative intellectuals, is laughably inaccurate.

As a warrior, Villa was above all interested in the Army. It was a Napoleonic feat for a former bandit leader to weld thousands of fighting men into a coherent force that would take his orders. Here he was greatly helped by the ex-Army officer and former Abraham González protégé, Juan Medina, who became his chief of staff. Medina was a veteran of Díaz's 1903 campaign against the Yaquis, but grew so disgusted by the treatment of the Indians that he resigned from the Army and became a small businessman in Chihuahua. One of Medina's problems was that he was dealing with such heterogeneous material. Men joined Villa for a multiplicity of reasons: to defend local autonomy; to regain village land; to get land grants; out of revenge for previous bad treatment by *hacendados*; because of unemployment; as an alternative to regular work; or simply to get easy pickings of loot, money, drink and women. There were ex-federal rankers who had joined as an alternative to being shot; ex-*hacendados* like the four Murga brothers who had joined for the same motive (but became convinced *villistas*); and a plethora of mercenaries, adventurers or soldiers of fortune who had made the long journey from the four corners of Mexico on the lure of Villa's name.

Foreign mercenaries, however valuable to historians (since most of them wrote detailed memoirs), were a headache for Villa. There were two main difficulties. If he executed one of them, or even if they were killed in battle, there was an immediate problem with a foreign government. More importantly, there was no means of checking their credentials. Foreigners with no battle experience used the same scam over and over again: enlisting for the initial signing-on fee or as a licence to loot, and then vanishing as soon as there was hard fighting to do. None the less among the iron pyrites there was some pure gold. Three who made a particular impression were Sam Drebben, Horst von der Goltz and Ivar Thord-Gray. Drebben, known as 'the fighting Jew', was a veteran of Latin American warfare, having served with the marines in Cuba in the Spanish-American War of 1898, in Nicaragua, and in South America properly so-called. Ivar Thord-Gray had been a soldier of fortune in India, China and the Boer War. Von der Goltz was a curious case of the 'talking horse' who became a real winner: lacking the military experience he boasted of when joining up, he proved remarkably quick on the uptake and soon became an indispensable part of Villa's artillery corps.

Perhaps the main problem Villa and Juan Medina had to solve was how to ensure the loyalty of army units to the commander-in-chief rather than to individual generals. Since each unit came from a particular locality with a local warlord as leader, it proved especially difficult to professionalise the Army of the North and break down these regional solidarities. Villa dealt with recalcitrant generals in a number of ways. Realising that it was pointless to try to bypass the local leaders and appeal directly to the rank and file, he tried to insinuate the idea that all good things came from him rather than these leaders. All important functions – artillery, horses, the supply of arms and ammunition, the medical corps – were reserved as areas where he had direct day-to-day control. At the limit he had his own commissars and bodyguard of 'immortals' whom he could use against particularly insubordinate commanders.

Villa controlled all arms, ammunition and uniforms as well as the supply lines to the USA; he made sure that these lines operated independently of the Carranza supply network. He also issued his own currency. At the beginning of 1914 this was readily accepted north of the Río Grande, since the Americans were convinced Villa and Carranza would win the struggle against Huerta, in which case Villa's currency would be redeemable at par. Villa also made sure that everyone in the artillery corps was personally loyal to him; no cronies of subordinate generals or warlords were ever recruited. The real problem about the artillery was that Villa was forced to use people whose loyalty might be suspect on other grounds, either because they were foreign mercenaries or ex-federals; before 1914 Juan Medina and Felipe Ángeles were the only members of the federal officer corps serving willingly. However, Villa was lucky, for the mercenaries von der Goltz and Thord-Gray distinguished themselves and became the mainstay of the artillery corps.

Villa also created the equivalent of a Praetorian Guard in the form of the *dorados* – an elite corps personally loyal to him, acting as bodyguards, adjutants or a reserve in battle, like Napoleon's Old Guard. The *dorados* originally consisted of three units of thirty-two men each, but eventually evolved into a 400-strong unit. Villa packed the corps with his relatives – in the (often mistaken) belief that kinship would make them loyal – but was always on the look-out for men of exceptional bravery he could recruit. One famous story of a recruit concerns a man whose horse was shot under him when the *villista* cavalry retreated during a battle. When the federals advanced, killing all prisoners and wounded, this man gutted his horse, hid under the skin and then emerged when the *villista* cavalry advanced again.

Although Villa allowed his subsidiary commanders, especially Urbina, a lot of licence, at the limit he was prepared to act decisively against them for acts of insubordination. Members of the *dorados*, or killers like Fierro and Manuel Banda, whose job it was to shoot men guilty or suspected of cowardice, would be sent as hit men or to arrange a summary execution. The drunken General Domingo Yuriar, who contemptuously refused an order from Villa, found himself hauled before the firing squad before he had even sobered up. Even here, however, there were limits to Villa's power. He wanted to execute Manuel Chao for disobeying an order, but Chao held a commission directly from Carranza; to execute him would have meant risking war with the 'First Chief' while Huerta still remained undefeated. Naturally Carranza, who disliked Villa and was jealous of him, secretly encouraged acts of insubordination by Villa's commanders.

Yet overwhelmingly the main reason Villa could overawe fractious or recalcitrant commanders was his own charisma and prestige. He consciously promoted a cult of personality and a *Viva Villa* mentality in his men. *Villista* propaganda plugged away at the same themes: Villa was a lion, a man who believed in true values and ideals, he was on the side of the poor and could never be bought off by the oligarchs, he was a Robin Hood who would deliver on land reform once the fighting was over. He was also presented as a father to his people, ever solicitous for their welfare, and as proof there was his impressive medical corps. Sixty Mexican and US doctors tended the wounded in a mobile army surgical hospital comprising a special train of forty box cars, fitted out with the very latest equipment; the badly wounded were sent back at night to hospitals in Parral or Chihuahua City.

The propaganda was effective, not least because the new recruits in 1914 were drawn by Villa's own success and personality, not that of Urbina or the lesser generals. The Division of the North was a fighting machine all could take pride in. American observers conceded that the fighting spirit, stoicism and endurance of the *villistas* went beyond anything even the US Marines could match. Villa's cavalry was matchless, partly because the Centaur himself knew so much about horse-breeding and selected only the very best mounts from the best farms in Chihuahua and Coahuila. Most of all there was the mobility of the Division of the North, which outmatched anything either Carranza or Huerta could manage. The *villista* warrior could live off the land, encumbered by nothing more than arms, ammunition, canteen and a single blanket. Villa's use of trains impressed all observers: he took ten days to transport 7,500 men from Torreón to Chihuahua, whereas it took Huerta two months to do the same trip in reverse.

One of the reasons morale was so high was that Villa allowed his men to take wives, mistresses and girlfriends on campaign with them. There had long been a tradition in Mexico of women accompanying armies, and not just because they could cook, forage and nurse. More pragmatically, since most armies consisted of press-ganged recruits, the only way to prevent a near 100 per cent desertion rate was to allow the troops to bring their womenfolk along. The distinguishing feature of the Division of the North, in contrast with earlier armies, was the sheer number of women camp-followers. To the despair of Villa and Medina and their plans for 'professionalisation', females actually seemed to outnumber the males in the revolutionary armies. When trains steamed up to the front bearing *villista* troops, women and children could be seen on the roofs or the cowcatchers. A campfire at night was a babel of women baking tortillas on mesquite twigs, giving birth or conceiving loudly. The general bedlam effect was enhanced by day when a veritable convoy of musicians, whores, hucksters and beggars, to say nothing of journalists, photographers and American film crews accompanied the army.

Women also took up arms and fought as *soldaderas*. Villa strongly disapproved, but there was not much he could do about it. His attitude to women was the traditional 'children, church and kitchen' of time-honoured Mexican machismo. John Reed had a most revealing exchange with Villa on this subject, which began when the reporter asked the general if women would be allowed to vote in a future Mexican government. 'I don't think so,' Villa replied, but when Reed told him they did so in the USA, he shrugged: 'Well, if they do it up there, I don't see why they shouldn't do it down here.' Villa seemed mightily amused by the idea and came back to it: 'Women seem to me things to protect, to love. They have no sternness of mind. They can't consider anything for its right and wrong. They are full of pity and softness. Why, a woman would not give an order to execute a traitor.' When Reed insisted that women could be just as tough as men, Villa asked his current 'wife', described by Reed as 'a cat-like slender young girl', what she would do to the traitors he had just caught. She replied that it was not her place to comment, that Villa knew best, but when he insisted she gave a direct answer, she recommended execution. Villa looked at Reed and chuckled. 'There is something in what you say,' he mused.

Villa's private life continued as polygamous, tangled and chaotic as ever. Although he did not salt away huge sums of money for his own use, unlike his brother Hipólito or Tomás Urbina, he was forced to earmark increasingly large sums to indulge his growing army of 'wives', mistresses, concubines and their children. Given Mexican machismo, Luz Corral, the 'number one wife', would not have expected Villa to be faithful; her own credo was that as long as a husband respected a wife inside the home, what he did outside it was not her business. Even so she was taken aback by the avalanche of other women that forced itself on her attention.

When she returned to Chihuahua from El Paso in 1913, she discovered that Villa had fathered three children by three different women. Luz was quite prepared to take these waifs under her wing and made a particular pet of Agustín, son of a woman called Asunción Villaescusa. Luz also discovered that one of Villa's daughters, Reynalda, was living with his sister Martina and found a berth in her home for her too. Confronted by the new ménage, Villa accepted the situation as if it were the most natural thing in the world. Once he realised how tolerant Luz Corral was, he revealed more and more about his private life. He brought another daughter, Micaela, to live with them after discovering that her mother, Petra Espinosa, had been two-timing him with one of his officers.

As long as Luz was acknowledged as the unchallenged number one wife, she was quite satisfied with Villa's polygyny. However, her broad-minded tolerance snapped when she realised there existed another number one wife of equal status, named Juana Torres, with whom she found Villa shacked up on her return. Gradually the full story came out: how Juana Torres had been a cashier in Torreón when Villa took the city, how he had taken a fancy to her, wooed and won her and set her up in a house in Chihuahua City. Now at last she realised why Villa had kept her in El Paso for weeks after he had taken Chihuahua, all the time pretending that he was building a new house for her.

For several months the two women fought a frenzied battle for Villa's affections while he alternated his domicile between the two houses. Eventually it became clear that only Luz Corral had real feelings of love for the hero. The venal Juana Torres became careless and, working hand in glove with her mother and sister, helped herself to 40,000 pesos from

Villa's private funds. Villa found the money missing and immediately guessed who had taken it, though he lacked proof. He jailed the mother and sister while he sought the evidence that would incriminate Juana. She stupidly wrote her mother and sister an angry screed, pouring scorn on Villa as a barbarian and bandit, an illiterate oaf who was anyway useless as a lover and had taken her by force. Naturally, the letter was brought to Villa, who read it and fell into one of his fearsome rages. Villa's apologists say that he dealt with the incident in an understanding way, allowing Aguirre Benavides to make Juana Torres's case for her and showing understanding of her frailty. His enemies tell a story that sounds truer. Villa summoned Juana and brandished the intercepted letter in front of her face. She turned pale with fear, but her ordeal was not over. Villa made her read the letter aloud slowly, and at each insult spat in her face. Weeping and terrified, la Torres staggered through the letter, after which Villa banished her and her family from Chihuahua for life.

Perhaps Villa learned something from this incident for, until 1915, there was no other rival to Luz Corral as premiere wife. Naturally there was the usual glut of mistresses and one-night stands, with Villa indulging in his usual practice of 'marrying' the unwilling or the virginal. He was not a man who took no for an answer and although he did not ravish women, he deceived them by bogus wedding ceremonies or blackmailed them into giving themselves by threatening their family or kin. Technically Villa was never a rapist, but even if he had been, there would have been no repercussions. When John Reed asked him about rape, he looked at him sardonically and said: 'Tell me, have you ever met a husband, father or brother of any woman that I have violated? Or even a mistress?' Villa was known to be madly jealous about his women and he was jealous even of the men who had been their lovers before he met them. Momentarily infatuated with a young woman in Torreón, he was infuriated to learn that she had been the mistress of Darío Silva, one of the magnificent eight who had crossed the Río Grande with him in March 1913. Being one of the originals availed Silva nothing; Villa humiliated him publicly in front of his brother officers and forced Silva to wait at table on them all.

The reality of Villa was often sordid, but early in 1914 the legend moved on another notch. On 3 January Villa signed with the US Mutual Film Corporation a $25,000 contract for a film on the exploits of the División del Norte. Villa agreed to fight all his future battles by day, to ban all non-Mutual cameramen and, if necessary, to simulate combat. Although Villa went beyond the letter of simulation by re-enacting battles, this was not a contractual requirement. Thousands of feet of documentary film were shot, which was intercut with fictional reels in which the young Raoul Walsh, later to be a notable Hollywood director, played the young Villa in a romantic concoction of falsehood and melodrama. Walsh later recalled that Villa was an indifferent actor who could not get the hang of movies: when asked by the director to ride slowly past the camera, Villa would spur and whip his horse so that he shot past the protesting cameraman at full tilt. However, the film crew did get Villa to postpone his executions from dawn to 7 a.m., so that they could take advantage of the better light. Finally, on 9 May 1914, *The Life of General Villa*, with Pancho playing himself in several scenes, opened at the Lyric Theatre, New York; in a typical Hollywood happy ending Villa became president of Mexico. He was now a worldwide legend. The hard fighting due in 1914 would show whether he was worthy of his iconic status.

THE END OF HUERTA

Although Huerta's path to power had been brutal, if he had been cleverer he could certainly have conciliated all factions of the opposition except Zapata. Most *maderistas* acquiesced in Madero's downfall and embraced the new regime, albeit mainly through fear. The privileged classes thought they had their iron man, their Cromwell, though admittedly the common man saw Huertismo as simply a return to the bad old days of the *Porfiriato*. However, brittle class divisions did not mean Huerta was doomed to fail; he failed through his own stupidity. The events of 1913–14 are a classic of self-destructive behaviour by a man who wanted to rule as an untramelled autocrat and would not compromise with anyone in his bid for personal despotism. This partly explains why Díaz, though feared and despised, was never hated in the visceral way Huerta was. Where Villa lusted after women, where Fierro believed only in murder and Urbina only in money, Huerta pursued the mirage of absolute power. The generous amnesty terms he offered to the rebels – and which many accepted – were a purely cynical temporising measure; Zapata saw that clearly, even if his subordinate commanders did not.

Huerta's greatest single problem was that Woodrow Wilson would not recognise him. Despite the inaccurate portrayals of Wilson's Mexican policy as either narrow-minded Calvinism or crude Dollar Diplomacy, it was actually surprisingly subtle and nuanced. Wilson knew a great deal about Mexican affairs, to the point where he preferred to handle this aspect of foreign policy himself, deliberately marginalising his unstable secretary of state William Jennings Bryan. Wilson's position was quite simple: he would recognise the Huerta regime if Huerta held elections and promoted the values of liberal democracy. If Huerta had played his cards correctly, US recognition would have followed as swiftly as that by Britain and the European powers. However, this was the one demand Huerta would not concede, partly because he would not tolerate true separation of powers, with a curb on his executive action by Congress, partly because he was certain that any genuinely free election would be won by the man he double-crossed after the February 1913 coup: Félix Díaz.

This time around Huerta could not use Lane Wilson to discredit those he disliked. Lane Wilson was a lame duck from the moment his presidential namesake took office. In any case, Woodrow Wilson distrusted the advice he got from professional diplomats, whom he (correctly) perceived to have agendas of their own. He therefore preferred to work through special envoys and secret agents, principally his speechwriter William Hayard Hale and John Lind, the ex-governor of Minnesota; he showed his contempt for the diplomatic corps by not replacing Lane Wilson and leaving a chargé d'affaires in control at the US embassy in Mexico City. Both Hale and Lind advised Wilson that he should work for Huerta's overthrow – advice which chimed with Wilson's own instincts. Lind travelled to Mexico City via Veracruz and proposed recognition on condition that presidential elections were held in which Huerta would not stand. After several unsatisfactory meetings with Huerta and his new foreign minister Federico Gamboa, Lind was informed that Woodrow Wilson's proposals constituted unacceptable interference in the affairs of a sovereign nation. Gamboa then insulted Lind personally by handing him a sarcastic note, which insinuated that Wilson's proposals were predicated on an abysmal ignorance of the Mexican constitution. This was fighting talk, and Lind never forgave it nor forgot it.

At first Wilson ordered a policy of strict neutrality as between Huerta and the northern rebels, but his patience wore thin as Huerta evinced total contempt for all democratic forms and constitutional niceties. He made it clear that he had no time for Cabinet government, despised politicians, and wanted to be a simple caudillo autocrat. He crushed the free press of Madero's time, either by closing newspapers or censoring them. He appointed generals to take control of state governments and insisted that all civilian governors had to double as military commanders. The militarisation of Mexican society became palpable, with both schools and the railways used almost exclusively for the interests of the Army. This militarisation not only alienated Washington but also the old-style *porfiristas* who had originally welcomed Huerta's seizure of power. They saw clearly that Huerta was indeed a second Cromwell, that when faced with a choice between Congress or even the *hacendado* class and the Army, it would be the beloved Army every time.

However, Huerta's true crossing of the Rubicon came when he ordered the murder of senator Belisario Domínguez. On 23 September 1913 Domínguez denounced Huerta in Congress, and had his speech privately printed and circulated when Díaz suppressed it in the official Diary of Debates. Two days later Domínguez was arrested at home by the secret police, and a few days after that his bullet-riddled body was found in a ditch. This precipitated a crisis between Congress and Executive. Congress passed a motion demanding an inquiry to get to the bottom of Domínguez's murder. Huerta sent troops into the legislature and demanded that the resolution be retracted on pain of dissolution of the Senate. When he met with refusal, Huerta made good his threat and imprisoned seventy-four deputies. This further alienated Washington and Wilson's displeasure turned to fury when the new British minister, Sir Lionel Carden, who already had a reputation for being anti-American, provocatively presented his credentials the day after the deputies were arrested.

Huerta ordered a slate of new elections in October. He got his tame Congress by the simple expedient of making it impossible for the voters to elect anyone but *huertistas*. The result was a predictable farce with turnout levels as low as 5 per cent. The presidential election was even more of a pantomime turn: since Huerta was constitutionally precluded from presenting himself as a candidate, he allowed Federico Gamboa to run as the *huertista* candidate, while privately telling the US chargé d'affaires that if Gamboa won he would have him shot. Félix Díaz was the main opposition hopeful (there were two other makeweight candidates), and would have won in any kind of fair contest, but Huerta had thought of a new scam. He had his officials put multiple voting slips into the ballot box with his name on them as a 'write-in' candidate, then barefacedly declared that he could not disappoint the evident wish of the people. The decision was thrown to the tame Congress, which did as ordered and declared the elections 'null and void'; pending fresh elections, set nine months in the future, Huerta was to continue as provisional president. Félix Díaz saw the writing on the wall and fled the capital to sanctuary on a US warship berthed at Veracruz.

After this farce Woodrow Wilson was determined that Huerta be forced out. Maximum leverage was exerted on the British, and the foreign secretary, Sir Edward Grey, sent his private secretary to Washington to assure Wilson that London would fall in with any credible American initiative for bringing peace to Mexico. Wilson demanded the dismissal of Sir Lionel Carden as an earnest of British good faith; Whitehall fell into line and kicked Carden upstairs as ambassador to Brazil in order to save face. On 3 February 1914 Wilson signalled an abrupt shift in his Mexican policy by lifting the embargo on arms supplies to the Constitutionalist rebels. Hitherto Villa and Carranza had relied on clandestine purchases, while arms manufacturers in Britain, Germany, France and Spain grew rich on the lucrative trade with Huerta; Washington had been particularly shocked by a shipment of ten million cartridges to Mexico City from Japan.

Huerta would have had enough trouble on his hands simply with the struggle with the USA, but he also faced domestic problems arising from the increased militarisation of Mexico and a series of economic and financial crises. By spring 1914 Huerta had expanded the Army to a strength of 250,000 (4 per cent of the entire male population), though the number of effectives was far fewer because of payroll padding and other forms of creative accounting. Since there were no volunteers, these numbers were made up by press-ganged conscripts, who made poor soldiers and often deserted once they reached the front. Huerta tried to encourage men to sign up by using crude anti-American propaganda – a favourite motif was that the 'traitor province' Sonora was a 'twentieth-century Texas' and Carranza an American agent – but nobody took his bromides seriously. In despair he tried to enlist private armies recruited by sub-contractors, but this too did not work.

The paradox of Huerta's regime was that the more he expanded the Army and the more he militarised civil administration, the less powerful his fighting forces became. Having seduced many rebels away from the cause of revolution, he found he could neither integrate them into civilian life – turn swords into ploughshares – nor persuade them to play a meaningful role in the campaigns against Villa, Zapata and Carranza. The greatest blow was the defection of the *rurales* who, almost to a man, deserted, rebelled or were eliminated, leaving the burden of normal peace-keeping on the hard-pressed Army. Huerta's appeal to the wealthy classes to help him militarily fell on deaf ears; they preferred the prospect of annexation by the USA to disgorging their own funds to pay for troops. Accordingly, all attempts to form militias or volunteer regiments ended in fiasco. Some foreign companies hired 'white guards' but soon found it was cheaper to bribe the local threat, be it federal or rebel, than to pay for expensive private armies.

There can be no doubt that the Mexican oligarchy revealed itself as singularly gutless and cowardly, concerned only for its own privileges and reluctant to spend a peso to defend them. Some analysts see a catastrophic decline in morale and willpower within a single generation on the part of the wealthy and propertied. Where the nineteenth-century oligarchs were prepared to mount up and go into battle against bandits or Apaches, their etiolated early twentieth-century successors had become pampered suburbanites. Some say the elite was shell-shocked as a result of years of revolution and the overnight disappearance of the old modalities of deference and hierarchy, that the peasants had called their bluff and revealed the elite members as paper tigers. Other say that this 'crisis of legitimacy' concealed another one, peculiar to Huerta. Almost nobody, except a few *huertista* cronies, perceived the regime to be legitimate, and indeed how could anyone pay it more than lip-service? Huerta was bankrupt of ideas and believed only in force as the solution to all problems. Madero had mixed reform and repression, but with Huerta there was only repression. Huerta despised Madero for not having used enough repression, but the real reason for Madero's downfall was not that he had been too tyrannical but that he had not been radical enough. Huerta was like a pilot who tries to correct a spin by sending his plane into an even more severe spin.

In such a context, the perennial financial problems with which Huerta wrestled could be viewed as a mere bagatelle. He faced rising expenditure, mainly on the expanded Army, at a time of falling revenues caused both by falling trade and investment and loss of territory to the rebels. The income from import duties, stamp taxes and foreign loans all declined. While the stagnant economies of the south and south-east continued almost unchanged, the previously more vibrant sectors in the north were faring disastrously. The greatest recession was in mining. Mines closed down because their feeder railways were out of commission and because supplies of dynamite were commandeered for military purposes. In 1914 production of silver was one-third the 1910 level, copper half, gold 50 per cent and lead an incredible 5 per cent. Lumber mills and textile factories had shut down, as cotton could not get through; oil supplies from Tampico hung by a thread that could be severed at any moment; the country's chief dynamite factory at Gómez Palacio was now in rebel hands.

The inevitable knock-on effects of the economic slump were felt on the financial markets. Huerta faced hyperinflation as goods became scarcer, prices rocketed and the peso slipped alarmingly against the dollar. The exchange rate of the peso was two to the US dollar in early 1913; a year later it was three to the dollar. From the summer of 1913 Mexico was off the Gold Standard. With no confidence in a depreciated paper currency, employers found themselves having to pay in scrip. Desperate for funds, Huerta found that non-recognition by the USA made the raising of loans, even in Europe, almost impossible, and even when loans were forthcoming, they were consumed in servicing existing debt. In despair, Huerta finally suspended payment on the National Debt, evoking howls of outrage from bondholders, increasing general economic uncertainty and decreasing the likelihood that foreign investors would sink money into Mexico.

Just as much an economic illiterate in his own way as Villa, Huerta increased domestic taxes across the board, further destroying business confidence. Alongside the hike in existing taxes, he introduced a plethora of new ones and forced businesses to make loans under threat of unspecified dire consequences. Huerta thus effectively destroyed his claim to be the champion of the propertied classes, but even the self-destructive act of kicking away the social props on which his regime rested did not help him. His government continued to have cash-flow problems and to be unable to pay its contractors or civil servants. In the final absurdity, Huerta allowed arrears to accumulate in his soldiers' pay, precipitating a mutiny at Ensenada, Baja California, in January 1914.

Sensing Huerta's inherent weakness, Zapata made careful preparations in early 1914 for a campaign that would sweep him up to the gates of Mexico City. His strategy was aimed at capturing Chilpancingo, the state capital of Guerrero. His intention was that all his other chiefs would attack in their areas and pin the federals down along the Morelos-Guerrero-Puebla border; with four simultaneous attacks, Huerta would not know which was the real offensive and which the feint. While he was thus perplexed, Zapata himself would take Chilpancingo in a lightning strike. Having paralysed the federals with the prestige of such an unexpected victory, he intended to proceed to take Iguala and Acapulco, before swinging all forces in southern and central Mexico round for an all-out assault on Mexico City.

On 12 March 1914 Zapata set up his headquarters at Tixtla, confident of victory since he now had 5,000 seasoned fighters to throw against the 1,400 federal defenders at Chilpancingo. There was no chance of federal reinforcements, since the Jojutla garrison mutinied the very day he arrived in Tixtla, destabilising the entire southern sector. After investing Chilpancingo closely, Zapata circled 26 March on the calendar as the day he would deliver the knock-out blow. However, three days early some of his chiefs jumped the gun and a premature attack delivered the city to the *zapatistas* with surprising ease, partly because rebel prisoners broke out of jail at the very moment the attack was being pressed. General Luis Cartón, the man who had been closely associated with Robles's atrocities, tried to flee to Acapulco but was caught and brought back to Chilpancingo where, after a court martial, Zapata had him executed on 6 April.

Elated by this success, Zapata sent his forces out in all directions. Acapulco, Iguala, Taxco and Buenavista de Cuéllar all rapidly fell to his armies, and Zapata felt confident enough to send reinforcements to revolutionary groups in Michoacán and Mexico State. When the envoys of the Michoacán rebels came to see him, they asked for proofs of his revolutionary sincerity; suspicious of bandits and ambitious politicians posing as revolutionaries, they asked what he was fighting for. Zapata asked José Robles to bring out the box containing the Anenecuilco title deeds. As he pointed to the documents, Zapata said: 'That's what I'm fighting for. Not the titles themselves, but this record of constancy and honesty – that's what I'm fighting for.'

Zapata next moved into Morelos, mopping up the federal garrisons at Jojutla, Cuautla and Jonacatepec, most of whom defected to him with their weapons. Meanwhile he sent de la O to open another front in Mexico State, and his brother Eufemio on the same errand in Puebla. By now he had cleared all federals out of Morelos except for the garrison at Cuernavaca which he was too weak to subdue. He did not lack the numbers but, as always, shortage of ammunition was the headache: 3–4,000 men besieging a city for five days needed at least 200,000 rounds of ammunition, and the *zapatistas* did not have it. Many were the occasions when he envied Villa the proximity of the USA, and his surpluses of cattle and cotton with which to buy cartridges and arms. Meanwhile he was reduced to ineffectual negotiations for a loan, either from the US government or American entrepreneurs. He sent envoys, again in vain, to Wilson to get his belligerent status recognised. Wilson, who was officially neutral as between Huerta, Villa and Carranza (but at this stage clearly favoured Villa), strangely refused to take Zapata seriously. Zapata was wounded by this rebuff and tended to listen to his Morelos veterans, who argued that a national role was anyway irrelevant to their needs and aspirations. It was Palafox who stressed the importance of the American connection, arguing that if he was successful in the field, Zapata would have to play a national role anyway.

Woodrow Wilson did, however, assist Zapata unintentionally, for on 21 April Huerta suddenly had to pull all federal forces out of southern Mexico to face a new threat: Mexico seemed on the brink of all-out war with the United States. John Lind, the polar opposite of Lane Wilson, as maniacally hostile to Huerta as Lane Wilson had been to Madero, had continued to deluge Wilson with schemes, proposals and outright demands for Huerta's overthrow. Terrified that Huerta might actually win the imminent war with the Constitutionalists, Lind eventually tired of lobbying Woodrow Wilson from a distance and returned to Washington in early April 1914 to brief the president in person, during which time Wilson was presented with the pretext he needed for intervention in Mexico.

By now the Constitutionalist armies in the north-east had advanced as far as the oil port of Tampico,where the USA maintained a strong naval presence to protect its investments in the oil fields. On 9 April, possibly because they were jittery about the approach of the rebels, possibly through simple incompetence, the federals arrested a landing party from an American warship. Although the local Mexican commander then apologised fulsomely, the problem was that the arrested crew was from a ship flying the US flag and had been on 'US territory' – the intercepted ship's whaleboat – when they were apprehended. Admiral Henry Mayo, commanding the Fifth Division of the Atlantic Fleet off Tampico, decided to teach the 'greasers' a lesson. He sent an officer in full military uniform to demand a public written apology, the arrest of the culprits and the firing of a 21-gun salute to the US flag. Historians have speculated that Mayo, frustrated by the boredom of cruising on the Mexico station, simply wanted to get into action – any action.

Since the demand was considered steep, the local Mexican commander referred it to Mexico City and, when run to ground in one of his drinking dens, Huerta point-blank refused to comply, Wilson welcomed the pretext to remove Huerta by force; Huerta thought he could harness anti-gringo chauvinism into a national crusade. Attitudes hardened on both sides. The dénouement took place not, as expected, at Tampico but farther down the coast, at Veracruz. On 18 April Wilson issued orders for the interception of the German ship *Ypriranga*, which was bearing arms for Huerta from Europe to Veracruz, and to prevent all further deliveries by seizing the customs house there. When he received the order, Admiral Frank Fletcher, commanding the Fourth Division of the Atlantic Fleet, expecting no resistance, decided to carry out the operation without waiting for Mayo to come down from Tampico. However, General Joaquín Maas, with 1,000 men – mainly cadets from the Veracruz Naval Academy – did resist.

Fighting began on 21 April; at first the Americans, assailed by accurate sniper fire and a battalion of heavily armed convicts released *ad hoc*, made heavy weather of their task. By 22 April 3,500 Marines were ashore, but still facing stiff opposition. The US warships *Chester* and *Prairie* then opened up with their three-inch guns and blasted the defenders out of their bolt-holes. By evening Veracruz was in American hands at a cost of nineteen American dead and forty-seven wounded, as against Mexican casualties of more than 200 dead and 300 wounded. Within days the occupying forces had grown to 6,000: they spent the time mopping up pockets of resistance and winkling out defiant snipers.

Many Americans thought Veracruz was the prelude to a general annexation of Mexico, that the Mexican Revolution would end, like its French counterpart, with the tramp of invading armies. The Hearst press ran its predictable, jingoistic campaign, whipping up prejudice against the lesser breeds south of the Río Grande. However, Wilson, who had won overwhelming support from both houses of Congress for the occupation of Veracruz, was now deluged with letters of protest, not least from the business community, when the possibility of wider involvement in Mexico loomed. Those who urged Wilson not to get sucked into the Mexican maelstrom stressed both the absence of compelling US interests there and resentment that white North America might end up governing and financing another set of 'niggers'. There was no need for such overreaction; Wilson's aims were always limited to getting rid of Huerta. Ironically, the Veracruz action helped him rather than the Constitutional-ists, for Washington once again sealed the border, cutting off arms supplies to the rebels.

Wilson was in any case given pause by the strength of Mexican opposition in Veracruz, the violent anti-gringo riots and the stoning of the American embassy in Mexico City, and Carranza's vociferous denunciation of US intervention. However, although Huerta tried to whip up anti-*yanqui* sentiment, his propaganda campaign was wrecked on the shoals of public apathy. In so far as there was anti-American sentiment in Mexico, it was directed at diplomatic and consular officials, not the representatives of American business or other economic interest; few American residents received so much as a scratch. Rebel commanders refused offers from the federals to unite against the common foe. While Carranza and Zapata were incensed at the American action, Villa was complaisant, both grateful for the diversion and anxious to burnish his image in the USA. The US Marines stayed in Veracruz on a kind of hygiene campaign. They made all prostitutes undergo medical examina-tions and weeded out pimps; they cleaned the streets and the market daily with sea water, set up public urinals, regulated sewage and drainage and implemented a campaign to wipe out the mosquito. It was said that for a short time Veracruz became so clean that the vultures could no longer rely on their usual pickings and flew away elsewhere in seach of carrion and garbage.

Huerta used the occasion of the US occupation of Veracruz to make sustained overtures to Zapata: he proposed an amnesty if the *zapatistas* would accept his authority and fight the American invaders. Zapata told his inner circle that the US occupation made his blood boil, but he would never collaborate with Huerta; if the Americans invaded his *patria chica*, he would fight them on his own. Baulked, Huerta tried to work around Zapata's flank by making the same proposals to his subordinate commanders; Zapata told his chiefs that all such overtures from Huerta must be reported to headquarters, and repeated that the only terms he would accept from Huerta were unconditional surrender.

Frustrated at his inability to play the anti-gringo card, and likewise at all attempts to drive a wedge between the revolutionaries of north and south, Huerta tried to make sure Zapata would have a warm welcome at the gates of Mexico City by promoting a campaign of vicious newspaper propaganda, portraying the *zapatistas* as crazed, peyote-drugged, genocidal war criminals. Huerta's jackal-like organs alleged that Zapata and his men crucified prisoners on telegraph poles and cactus trees, that they staked out victims over ants' nests and smeared them with honey, or sewed them up inside wet hides and left them to suffocate as the hides dried in the sun. A peculiar atrocity, attributed to Zapata himself, was staking out a man on the top of a fast-growing maguey cactus. The idea was that during the night the thorn-tipped stalk of the plant would grow a foot or more, boring inch by inch through the flesh of a victim who died in dreadful agony. Needless to say, all these tales of atrocities are apocryphal. *Zapatistas* shot their prisoners without mercy, as did federals, *villistas* and *carrancistas*, but if anything the *villistas* were the most savage, as they went in for mutilation, gouging out eyes, cutting off ears, tongues and noses, severing genitals. The *huertistas* were equally barbaric, trading atrocity for atrocity, war crime for war crime. None the less, it was Huerta, with his control of Mexico City's media, who won the propaganda war, in the process whipping up foreign residents and observers into a froth of panic and paranoia.

Huerta's attempts to set one group of revolutionaries against another – Zapata versus Carranza, Carranza versus Villa – were far less successful. Zapata was convinced from the earliest days that Carranza, opposed as he was to land reform, was at best another Madero – an idea Felipe Ángeles was peddling for his own purposes to Villa. One of the earliest direct contacts between Villa and Zapata came in the autumn of 1913 when Villa wrote a friendly letter to say that he was fully in favour of land reform in Chihuahua. Zapata replied with a cautious but statesmanlike missive, making a tentative offer of alliance, expressing his confidence in Villa, provided always that he would embrace the Plan of Ayala, but most of all warning him against Carranza. He told Villa that, if and when the two of them captured Mexico City, there would have to be wholesale purges; Madero's mistake in 1911–13 could not be repeated.

Zapata's advice seemed well grounded, for Villa's first personal contact with Carranza left him with a bitter taste in his mouth. On 17 January the two had conferred amicably enough by telegraph, with Villa accommodating and deferential and Carranza, taking this as his God-given right instead of an exaggerated gesture of cordiality, replying patronisingly and condescendingly. Then, in March, Carranza moved his headquarters from Sonora to Ciudad Juárez and the first face-to-face meeting took place. It was not a success. Carranza behaved as if he were a missionary among the Bangala in darkest Africa. He reacted with a fastidious stiffness when Villa gave him the traditional *abrazo* or bear-hug. Villa, laughing and joking, ran up against a brick wall of po-faced stolidity. Resignedly he told his aides that Carranza was 'no Maderito'. In private, to his intimates, he was more forceful: Carranza was a sonofabitch, a *hijo de puta*. Later he reminisced: 'I embraced (him) energetically, but with the first words he spoke my blood turned to ice. I saw that I could not open my heart to him. As far as he was concerned, I was a rival not a friend. He never looked me in the eye and during our entire conversation emphasised our difference in origin . . . He lectured me on things like decrees and laws, which I could not understand. There was nothing in common between that man and me.'

Villa started 1914 with a mopping-up operation to expel the Terrazas and their federal protectors from Ojinaga. For a month General Mercado's army lived a starveling, tatterdemalion existence in the blackened bomb craters and pitholes of Ojinaga's feculent slums, eking out a bare subsistence on a diet of dried meat and corn husks, supplemented by whatever they could buy across the border. On the US side of the frontier Presidio joined the lengthening list of boomtown beneficiaries: El Paso, Douglas, Laredo. When Carranza's protégé Panfilo Natera failed to dislodge the federals with a flying column, Villa moved north with the main army and drove the 5,000-strong enemy on to US territory, where they found a kind of haven at Fort Bliss refugee camp. When Huerta heard of the loss of yet another army, he swore that he would shoot General Mercado if he ever came back from Mexico. However, Mercado was not much more welcome at Fort Bliss; *Collier's Magazine* expressed the cynicism of many in the USA by running a full-page cartoon of the camp with the caption: 'If you're tired of Revoluting, try our rest cure. Uncle Sam foots the bills.'

It was mid-March before Villa opened his long-awaited campaign against Huerta in the south. He moved down with an army of 16,000, all in trains, including a hospital train able to handle 1,400 wounded at any one time. All communication between Chihuahua City and the rest of the world was suspended, and all trains and motorised transport were impounded, so that the federals could not be tipped off. He was supremely confident, having at his side the much-admired Felipe Ángeles, friend of Madero, brilliant intellect, master of ballistics and mechanised warfare, and shrewd reader of human nature. Villa's first target was Torreón, the nodal point of the railway and road network in northern Mexico.

Once he had recaptured Torreón from the rebels, Huerta had tried to make it an impregnable fortress that would dominate all approaches to the capital from the north. The garrison was 10,000 strong – a huge number even for an army in the field – all entrenched behind strong defensive positions. Huerta had good reason for believing its commander General José Velasco when he pronounced it impregnable, and by now Huerta and his generals had convinced themselves, or reconvinced themselves, that Villa had simply been lucky in 1913 and had been up against second-rate commanders.

Villa, however, approached the coming battle with insouciance. His huge anaconda of a mechanised army snaked across the desert and halted at Yermo, on an arid, treeless plain where only cactus grew. Away to the east stretched the desert and to the west the peaks of the Sierra Madre were clearly visible. For three days the mighty Division of the North was stalled at Yermo, uncertain where its great leader was to be found; it turned out Villa had been up all night at the wedding of a compadre and arrived at the front flustered and bleary-eyed. Having ascertained that his twenty-eight cannon were in good working order, he ordered an advance on the federal outpost at Bermejillo, forty-three miles south and twenty-seven miles north of the ultimate target, Torreón.

Villa's cavalry surprised the federals at Bermejillo, a town of adobe houses, driving them out in short order and then killing more than 100 in a five-hour running fight on the road south. Meanwhile Urbina at Mapimi and Benavides at Tlahualilo had also been in sanguinary encounters. Having taken the outer perimeter of Torreón's defences, Villa pressed on, but found it harder and harder to make inroads the more the enemy fought on interior lines. The *villista* attack all but petered out in ferocious fighting at Gómez Palacio, eight miles north of Torreón, and especially around Cerro de Pila, the rocky barren hill that dominated the town. To start with, Villa's pioneer corps and maintenance gangs had to make good miles of destroyed rail track, which prevented the artillery, hospital and supply trains from keeping in close touch with the combatants. Then the *villista* vanguard indulged in its customary idiocy of making a premature charge against prepared positions without waiting for artillery support; predictably, they were mown down in droves.

Had the federals advanced at this point, with panic-stricken *villista* survivors of the frontal assault colliding with their own men as they fled, throwing away valuable rifles and ammunition, they could have scored a great victory. However, they stayed in their trenches, fearing a trap. Villa was at last able to restore order and soon Ángeles reported that the railway line was prepared and his artillery within range. There followed a pile-driving slugging battle of attrition on the outskirts of Gómez Palacio, which Villa claimed was the hardest fight he had ever been in. Clouds of smoke and the stench of burning flesh wafting over from the town soon told Ángeles that his artillery bombardment was having the necessary effect, but this was war to the knife in every sense; casualties were enhanced by the barbarous federal practice of poisoning all fresh water, including that in the irrigation ditches in the fields.

In this battle Villa clearly showed that his earlier successes were no fluke. He made up for the technical superiority of the enemy artillery by carefully staged night attacks; in the nocturnal gloom the edge given the federals by their more accurate gunnery was whittled away by *villista* snipers crawling up to take out the gunners at close range. The federals wasted ammunition by blazing away at shadows in the night when they had no clear targets, while Villa's sharpshooters had a close-packed line of troops to fire at. The losses in these night attacks were ultimately disastrous for federal morale, for they were pounded ceaselessly by artillery during the day then at dusk had to deal with a sinister unseen enemy.

The key to Gómez Palacio was the Cerro de Pila. Having softened up the defenders by a non-stop bombardment all day, on the night of 25 March Villa sent the cream of his troops in assault waves against the hill. The federals fought like dervishes and beat off six bruising attacks, inflicting heavy casualties. Finally, on the seventh wave, they buckled. Terrible scenes of hand-to-hand fighting took place in the darkness as the attackers stabbed through embrasures with bayonets, guessing where the enemy bodies might be located; reached through loopholes to wrench rifle barrels from the hands of amazed federals; or lobbed dynamite bombs into machine-gun nests. However, the saga was not yet over. Incredibly, after such feats of heroism, the triumphant *villistas* were left stranded as their commanders failed to rush in the expected reinforcements. Soon the federals counterattacked from Torreón and after a further two hours of savage carnage, Villa's men fled from the hill, some weeping in frustration that all their valour had been for nothing.

In Mexico City the Huerta press talked up the retaking of the Cerro de Pila as if it were a victory on the scale of Cannae or Austerlitz. They failed to mention the dismal sequel. Next day the *villistas* again bombarded the hill, Ángeles personally sighting the artillery after wheeling it into new positions to compensate for defective shells sent down from Chihuahua City. Then at night Villa ordered in his men again. The expected killing barrage from the defenders did not materialise; the defenders had pulled out from the hill, abandoning it and Gómez Palacio to Villa. It had been a close-run thing. After five days of battle, the *villistas* had finally won because their nerve held better, but it had been touch and go: often, crazed by thirst and lupine with hunger, the *villista* morale had seemed about to go into free-fall. Then the personal magnetism of Villa had worked its magic. He was everywhere, inspiring and exhorting his men, and even on one occasion forcing them to turn back and face Gómez Palacio when they were fleeing in panic.

Having lost nearly 1,000 dead and more than 3,000 wounded, Villa tried to secure a negotiated surrender from General Velasco in Torreón, but Velasco refused. Now the struggle concentrated on the hills around the city. First Villa had to beat off a relieving force of 2,000 federals who approached suddenly from the north-east to his stupefaction; angrily he demanded to know why Carranza's pet Pablo González had not taken the most elementary precautions to prevent this happening. Then the battle for Torreón city began. Villa threw everything at Velasco. Ángeles wheeled up his artillery and blasted away at point-blank range; *villista* dynamiters crawled virtually into the mouth of enemy cannon to deliver their deadly charges; amateur aficionados of nitroglycerine could be seen carrying sticks of dynamite wrapped in cowhide, chomping on huge cigars which they used to light the fuses.

On 30 March Velasco tried to break the circle of Hieronymus Bosch horror by requesting a 48-hour truce, so that he could bury the dead and tend the wounded. Villa consulted Ángeles, who told him that federal morale was at snapping point and the requested truce was a delaying tactic to enable reinforcements to arrive. Villa therefore rejected the offer, even though he was concerned about his own level of casualties. Ángeles's judgement was vindicated. Velasco had lost all his best officers and was secretly in despair that none of his counterattacks had succeeded. Sensing that his opponent was about to cut and run, Villa did not block the exits from the city but left an escape route along the railway to Saltillo. On 1 April, to save face, Velasco endured another blistering bombardment from Ángeles, but next day, taking advantage of a blinding dust-storm that produced nil visibility, he made an orderly withdrawal east. Above the dust Villa saw plumes of smoke: were the enemy simply burning their dead or were they destroying their arms dumps? He soon got his answer. On 3 April his men advanced unopposed over piles of dead and entered the stricken and deserted city.

Torreón was Villa's most signal victory to date. John Reed described him as the greatest captain in Mexican history: 'His method of fighting is astonishingly like Napoleon's . . . Villa is the Revolution. If he died, I am sure that the Constitutionalists would not advance beyond Torreón in a year.' The human cost had been extraordinarily high, not just in combatant casualties (one in five for the *villistas* and even higher levels for the federals). Torreón and its environs were like charnel houses, full of the foetor of corpses and the feculence of decay. The trees were charred and stunted, and no birds sang on their branchless trunks. Every house was a billet for many bullets and every public monument was pockmarked with shell and incendiary damage.

Villa found the inhabitants of Torreón eating rats and searching through horse manure for partially digested grains which they could reprocess as tortillas. He ordered mountains of food and lakes of wine to be brought into the city for a victory fiesta so lavish it was said to have attracted down the whores from US border towns. The only group for which Villa felt no pity were the hated Spaniards. After confiscating all their property and possessions, he rounded up 700 *gachupines* and penned them in the vaults of the Bank of Laguna, where he harangued them. After telling them that they were the despised descendants of Cortés who had robbed and murdered his own people, the Aztecs, Villa said they all deserved execution but, to show his generosity, he would simply expel them from Mexican soil. They were driven out of the city at bayonet point and transported on wagons without food and water to the US border, 500 miles north.

Huerta somehow found a fresh army of 6,000, but this force was rapidly imbued by the defeatism of the men they were sent to reinforce. The federals made their last stand at San Pedro de las Colonias, forty miles north-east of Torreón. With the euphoria of a man on a winning streak, the outnumbered Villa attacked as though he held all the aces. Once again Villa's initial forays were beaten off by the 10,000-strong defenders, and for two days the federals stood at bay behind barricades of cotton bales, but then they self-destructed. A furious altercation had broken out between Velasco and General Joaquín Maas, commanding the reinforcements, about who had the superior command. In a fit of pique

Velasco pulled out on 15 April, leaving Maas to his fate. Maas baulked at facing Villa alone and withdrew also, abandoning most of his troops and the bulk of his arms and equipment. San Pedro was left gutted, and most of the abandoned men simply joined up with Villa, helping to staunch the manpower haemorrhage of the recent campaign.

Although the Division of the North was exhausted and had to rest for a month after its martial labours, the road to Mexico City now lay open. Villa's crushing victories had finished the federals as a credible fighting force in the north. The battles of Torreón and San Pedro had had the effect of destroying a federal army 15,000 strong. The survivors scattered eastwards, many dying of hunger and thirst in the desert, a few limping in to Saltillo. Villa had demonstrated his ability to use artillery, to master logistics and to fight a protracted campaign against a well-entrenched enemy. So far he was easily the most able Constitutionalist general, and he now commanded a 16,000-strong elite force which, by common consent, was easily man-for-man superior to the federals.

Villa's stunning victory at Torreón, followed soon after by the movie of his life, made him an immensely popular figure in the USA. Woodrow Wilson, determined to be rid of Huerta and disillusioned with Carranza after his anti-American outbursts, increasingly saw Villa as the horse to put his money on. Not yet exposed to Villa's dark side, Wilson was somewhat naïvely inclined to see the Centaur of the North as a frontier hero in the mould of Kit Carson or Davy Crockett. He was particularly impressed by two things: Villa seemed to lack personal ambition and said he wanted the reputedly pro-American Felipe Ángeles as president; and he supported the US occupation of Veracruz. Villa saw clearly that the attempt to foment anti-gringo feelings in Mexico was simply a cynical ploy by Huerta, and declared robustly about Veracruz: 'It is Huerta's bull that is being gored.' In a conversation with the American consular agent George Carothers, Villa was even more expansive: he told his American friend that no drunkard could drag him into a war with friends.

If Villa had had presidential ambitions, Wilson's favour could have been decisive. Possibly, too, at this stage, Wilson had not taken the measure of Carranza's anti-Americanism and its depth and virulence. Unconsciously, Carranza sought duels with powerful nations, for his hero Juárez had faced down Britain and France in the 1860s, and defeated France in battle. Carranza particularly brooded on the affront to national sovereignty of the 'manifest destiny' US invasion of 1846–8, and on the crimes of Lane Wilson. As always, Carranza's reading of history was partial, for he never acknowledged the role of presidents Lincoln and Johnson in Juárez's defeat of Maximilian. There was always something pathological in Carranza's dislike of the gringo. He distrusted all North Americans, even the so-called 'good yankees'. He made a point of tweaking Wilson's nose over the Benton case, banged the drum over the Veracruz occupation and pointedly kept Woodrow Wilson's envoy waiting for ten days when he arrived in Sonora in November 1913.

Carranza made his predilections clear by ostentatiously refusing to truckle to the colossus of the north and by taxing US businesses in Mexico. Villa meanwhile, with the proceeds of the expropriated estates under his belt, did not need to raise money in that way. His image in the USA was further burnished by the part-time US consul George Carothers, who sent glowing reports to Wilson, all the more persuasive in that Carothers had previously been violently anti-Villa. Villa, with his shrewdness about human beings, soon discerned Carothers's Achilles' heel, or rather the multiplicity of heels. The 38-year-old grocer, catapulted into unwonted status when Wilson appointed him a special agent in Mexico, was an avatar of all the vices – a crook, womaniser, gambler and blackmailer. It was an easy matter for Villa to make him over: he simply gave him a profusion of easy deals, lucrative contracts, sweeteners and kickbacks, on the understanding that Carothers would report faithfully to Washington. All American firms wanting concessions in Chihuahua had to go through Carothers.

Villa was soon able to add another couple of corrupt gringos to his payroll. In Washington he retained the services of the venal lobbyist Sherbourne G. Hopkins, who would work for anyone as long as the pay was good enough, and was not above working for opposing sides simultaneously and selling each one's secrets to the other. Hopkins, however, preferred working for Carranza so sent his agent Félix Somerfeld to Mexico to be at Villa's side. This was a case of Volpone hiring Mosca, for Somerfeld, who controlled an exclusive concession for importing dynamite into Mexico, was if anything even more venal and two-faced than Hopkins. Dealing with three ultra-cynical men as his American agents did not enhance Villa's opinion of the *yanquis*, and in the end adversely affected his own reputation in the USA. Where Carranza increasingly found credible envoys with gravitas, Villa was represented by a trio of reprobates whose only interest was cash, cash and more cash.

Probably Villa's only really solid and genuine rapport with an American was his relationship with General Hugh Scott, commanding US forces on the Mexican border. Scott liked Villa personally, he had a fondness for non-intellectual noble savages, he thought Villa was the man on horseback Mexico needed and, unusually for an American, had a real respect for the qualities of 'Third Worlders' – a respect gained after forty years of fighting Apaches, Cubans (in 1898) and Filipinos (in 1899–1902). No greater contrast could be imagined than that between the reflective Scott and the absurd William Randolph Hearst, whose jingoistic yellow press had virtually created those wars out of nothing and now fulminated against Villa. For all his talents at public relations, Villa never really got on the right side of the American press; even those newspapers sympathetic to him always seemed to take a patronising tone.

Villa enjoyed a certain cachet in radical intellectual and left-liberal circles in the USA. John Reed was the principal influence in creating this climate of opinion and his lead was followed by other prominent leftists, notably Mary 'Mother' Jones, the famous organiser for the United Mine Workers of America, who had a long-standing interest in how Mexican miners lived. When she was jailed in 1914, Villa wrote to Woodrow Wilson, offering to swap the younger Luis Terrazas for her. Yet the attitude to Villa of the American Left was by no means monolithic. The journalist Lincoln Steffens, who shared John Reed's enthusiasm for the Russian Revolution ('I have seen the future and it works'), dissented with him over Mexico, where he thought the Revolution decidedly did not work. Another jaundiced anti-Villa leftist was John Kenneth Turner, author of *Barbarous Mexico*, though his attitude was in part pique because his protégé Ricardo Flores Magón could not get his brand of revolution off the ground.

Perhaps the biggest surprise was the attitude to the Revolution of the bestselling author and socialist millionaire Jack London, who wrote in *Collier's Weekly* that the peons followed Zapata, Villa and Carranza not because they cared for land and freedom but for loot and bloodletting – 'a particularly delightful event to a people who delight in the bloody spectacles of the bullring'. Soon the former international socialist was well into his stride, delighting American oilmen and the financiers of Wall Street with the new bearing in his political thinking: 'The big brother can police, organise and manage Mexico. The so-called leaders of Mexico cannot. And the lives and happiness of a few million peons, as well as the many millions yet to be born, are at stake. The policeman stops a man from beating his wife. The humane officer stops a man from beating his horse. May not a powerful and self-alleged enlightened nation stop a handful of inefficient and incapable rulers from making a shambles and a desert of a fair land wherein are all the natural resources for a high and happy civilisation?'

Perhaps the one American whose relationship with Villa has attracted most attention is Ambrose Bierce, officially described as having 'disappeared' while attempting to make contact with Villa. He was last seen just before the battle of Ojinaga in January 1914, supposedly fighting for Villa, though in what capacity a 71-year-old writer could have fought for the Revolution is unclear. Scholars debate whether he was simply killed in the battle and buried in a mass grave, or whether he anticipated Benton by crossing Villa and being executed. Certainly his last communication, to a relative, sounds very much like a death wish: 'If you should hear of my being stood up against a Mexican stone wall and shot to rags, please know that I think it is a pretty good way to depart this life. It beats old age, disease or falling down the cellar stairs. To be a gringo in Mexico – ah, that is euthanasia.'

The combination of Villa's spectacular victory at Torreón and his huge popularity in the USA simply accentuated Carranza's rancour and jealousy towards him. While Carranza had been a remote figure in Sonora, coexistence between him and Villa was possible because of their virtual independence from each other. When Carranza shifted his base of operations to Ciudad Juárez in March 1914 the honeymoon came to an end. Carranza moved to Chihuahua in an obvious bid to bring Villa to heel, after all his behind-the-scenes machinations had failed. Lacking a power base in Chihuahua, he first tried building up his protégés Manuel Chao and Maclovio Herrera as counterweights, then, when that ploy failed, he tried to humiliate Villa by putting him under Obregón's command; Villa simply ignored this directive.

Carranza had never liked Villa. A man who bore grudges, brooded on past insults and had an elephantine memory for any occasion on which his self-importance had been slighted, he had never forgiven Villa for joining Orozco and rebelling against Madero when he appointed him (Carranza) minister of war in 1911. Even without this scar on his memory, Carranza could never have got on with Villa. The generation gap was important to a man who felt that superior age should automatically entail deference (even though he himself had never been prepared to defer to Díaz). The clash of personalities was, moreover, of an almost textbook type: on the one hand the cold, aloof, ponderous and circumspect machiavellian; on the other the emotional, impulsive, mercurial audacious and energetic workaholic.

In January 1914, with Villa master of Chihuahua, Carranza once more tried to clip his wings. He had three immediate motives: he needed to get his hands on Chihuahua's revenues; he feared Villa's promised land reforms would antagonise the elite; and most of all he dreaded the example of an independent Villa: other military commanders in other states might get the same notion and leave the First Chief as a mere figurehead. However, all his moves were checkmated. When he ordered Villa to shelve land reform, Villa curtly refused. When he sent his most trusted advisers to try to win over Silvestre Terrazas, he got nowhere. When he sent his 'foreign secretary' Francisco Escudero on a mission to Villa, Escudero botched it by insulting Villa at a banquet; Villa raged at the envoy and told him he would already be dead but that he came as the representative of the First Chief.

At first Carranza hoped for great things when Chao became the governor of Chihuahua in January 1914, but Chao soon found he had no real power, circumscribed as he was both by Silvestre Terrazas and Villa's other intellectual advisers, while unable to make military leaders obey his simplest order. Chao further disappointed Carranza by openly announcing his support for the programme of agrarian reform. Carranza's relocation to Ciudad Juárez was a measure of despair; the only way he could make his writ run in Chihuahua was by being on the spot. It has to be emphasised that it was always Carranza who made all the difficulties, forever Carranza who was proactive and Villa reactive. While the First Chief remained in Sonora, Villa had always acted with great tact and diplomacy and had written to him with respect and warmth, but from March onwards it quickly became apparent that Carranza wanted to control the Division of the North, to supplant Villa and issue orders directly to the subordinate generals, and to monopolise the arms supply line to the USA.

The snapping point came over Manuel Chao. When Villa, on the eve of the battle of Torreón, ordered Chao to join him with his contingent, Chao replied that it was within his prerogative as governor to refuse and did so. Villa stormed up to Ciudad Juárez, arrested Chao and ordered him held for execution. He then worked himself up into one of his fearsome rages and ranted at Chao about sabotage. When he calmed down, the governor managed to convince him he had not sought to betray him. All might now have been resolved peacefully, but Carranza deliberately chose to be as provocative as Woodrow Wilson was being over Tampico at that very moment. Carranza peremptorily ordered Villa to halt the execution and summoned him for a magisterial dressing-down. This was admittedly courageous, for Villa's troops were present in force, and Villa could easily have done to him what Huerta did to Madero; even so, it is noteworthy that Carranza had a roomful of aides with loaded pistols present at the interview.

The upshot was predictable. Villa again lost his temper and ranted and raged at Carranza. The glacial First Chief remained as adamant and unmovable as when he dealt with Washington. Eventually Villa backed down and accepted Carranza's authority and a face-saving banquet was thrown for all three men by Silvestre Terrazas. Curiously, Chao seems to have been deeply impressed by the attitude finally evinced by Villa *before* Carranza made his provocative intervention. The *abrazos* of reconciliation he exchanged with Villa were sincere, and when the final break between Carranza and Villa came, Chao was on the side of the Centaur.

Villa was as good as his word. He sacked a Chihuahua editor for criticising Carranza and allowed himself to be gulled into handing over control of the northern railway network. However, Carranza was not deceived by the formulaic expressions of revolutionary brotherhood. Now more than ever it seemed essential to prevent Villa from being the first to enter Mexico City. There was not just the acquisition of the federal arsenal to consider, but access to the rich provinces of Mexico's south-east and the general credibility involved in being first into the capital. Most of all, Carranza was determined to be the next president, and he foresaw that, in an open contest, the old guard of *porfiristas* and *huertistas* would be capable of making a deal with Villa to have Felipe Ángeles confirmed as president. He therefore sent instructions to Obregón, who for months had been doing an irritating imitation of Fabius Cunctator, to gear up for a race to Mexico City against Villa.

Obregón had spent the winter in meticulous preparation, building up his strength, improving drill and mastering railway logistics. He controlled all of Sonora except for the well-defended port of Guaymas which he was much too cautious to attack, and his sole contact with the enemy was in hit-and-run skirmishes, involving casualties usually in two figures. Obregón's approach to war was intellectual where Villa's was instinctive. He really studied strategy, as Villa never did, devouring volumes on the Boer War and the Russo-Japanese conflict of 1904–5, learning all about barbed wire, blockhouses and trench warfare. His aim was to professionalise the Army of the North-west, but this provoked the same backlash from the old sweats that Villa's similar reforms had engendered. His officers hated Obregón's academic approach to war and clung to all the old, inefficient ways – chasing women when they should have been posting sentries. Such was the indiscipline among his troops that one of Obregón's sergeants, sent on a recruiting mission, promoted himself to general when he had raised 300 men and began issuing 50- and 100-peso notes printed on lavatory paper. Obregón arrested him in the middle of a fiesta and gave him the *ley fuga* treatment.

Obregón had his own reasons for heeding the call from Carranza and beating Villa to Mexico City. Now that Carranza had moved to Chihuahua, he was the number one man in Sonora, and he intended to keep things that way. Yet meanwhile Villa was aiding the ambitions of José Maytorena, who wanted to return to his post as governor after his six-month 'sabbatical' in the USA. Obregón and his faction took the view, rightly, that Maytorena had fled when the going was tough and now wanted to return to scoop the prizes won by others. Carranza strongly backed Obregón in this power struggle with Maytorena, keenly aware that he would need Obregón when the inevitable showdown with Villa came. However, Maytorena was a powerful machine politician, with significant backing among the middle classes and the Yaquis. To counterbalance Carranza's support for Obregón, Maytorena lobbied for the support of Villa. Initially Villa was unenthusiastic, remembering the cowardly way Maytorena had skulked in Arizona, but Felipe Ángeles talked him round. Ángeles and Maytorena were already so hostile to Carranza that they founded a Spanish-language newspaper in El Paso, devoted to attacking the First Chief for ducking land reform.

Obregón considered that the best way to beat Maytorena in Sonora was to make himself a national figure and to be on the winning side when the heirs to Huerta's legacy fought over the spoils. In April 1914 he therefore began proceeding cautiously down the Pacific coast, much assisted by Woodrow Wilson's lifting of the arms embargo two months earlier. The salient feature of his campaign was ingenuity rather than flamboyance. He bypassed the ports of Guaymas and Mazatlán, delegating their reduction to favourite generals. In May he found his advance south threatened on the maritime flank by the federal gunboat *General Guerrero* based at Guaymas. At first Obregón tried cunning, suborning one of the three federal gunboats to defect. When this renegade was sunk by the other two, Obregón sent an agent to the USA to buy a replacement, but the man vanished with the cash and was never seen again. The quick-thinking Obregón instead bought a biplane which attacked the federal gunboats in what some historians have claimed (probably inaccurately) to be the first example of war in the air. Alberto Salinas, a pilot in Obregón's army, attacked the gunboats eleven miles out at sea, diving from an altitude of 3,000 feet, while a second plane bombed Mazatlán.

In response to urgent cables from Carranza, exhorting him to accelerate the advance, Obregón leapfrogged past Mazatlán (this fell in July when the combined US, British and German navies evacuated the federals), having first engaged Huerta's garrison at Acaponeta to the beat of Yaqui war drums. By cutting the Guadalajara-Colima road, he severed the lifeline of the two Pacific ports of Mazatlán and Tepic. At Tepic Obregón once again displayed his preference for stratagem over frontal assault. After raising a gigantic dust-storm, he sent his vanguard ahead to tell the enemy scouts that his 5,000-strong force (in reality only 2,000) was about to descend on the city. The 2,000-strong Tepic garrison at once evacuated, leaving behind a huge cache of arms.

At the beginning of July Obregón sent part of his forces to hook round south of Guadalajara, while with the remainder he routed the federals at Orendain. At last Obregón had a victory worthy to rank with Villa's. Eight thousand federals lay dead on the field, and the survivors left behind them 5,000 rifles, sixteen artillery pieces, eighteen trains and forty locomotives. It was now certain that he would beat Villa in the race for Mexico City.

The biographer of Obregón, however, is more likely to be fascinated by the subject's state of mind than his military brilliance, for the unconscious thrust of his letters was that he had joined the Revolution not for ideological reasons but for the opportunity to exorcise personal demons. Throughout the campaign, Obregón seemed death-driven: deliberately carrying no sidearms, making dangerous river crossings when he could easily have waited a few hours to cross in calmer waters, smiling almost with pleasure when grenades fell a few yards away. His letters to Carranza and others were full of a morbid fascination with death and blood. Of the *huertistas* he said: 'Let us satisfy their taste for blood until they choke on it' and 'A people cannot shed too much blood in defence of their freedoms.' He alarmed Carranza by using the language of vendetta, and particularly by the statement that the prime motive for the Revolution must be revenge for the death of Madero. Carranza thought it self-evident that the prime motive was to park his own bulk in the presidential chair.

Obregón, however, in his boastful and self-serving memoirs never acknowledged the part Carranza had played in allowing him to get to Mexico City before Villa. Sabotage is not too strong a word to describe Carranza's chicanery after Torréon: Villa's next logical southward step was Zacatecas but Carranza diverted him north-east into Coahuila. Villa's great whirlwind campaign, in which he had torn the heart out of the federal army, had unlocked the north, leaving Pablo González to mop up in the north-east. Even a general as mediocre as González should have completed the task without difficulty. To be sure, he moved against Monterrey, which the federals evacuated, then advanced on Tampico, whence in turn the enemy retreated to Puebla; soon Nuevo Laredo and Piedras Negras also fell like ripe plums. The next clear objective for González was Saltillo, but Carranza suddenly ordered Villa's Division of the North to capture it.

Carranza claimed that González was not strong enough to take Saltillo, but it was quite clear that his real aim was to stop Villa's southward advance and to weaken his strength, as he was bound to sustain huge casualties against a federal army 15,000 strong. Villa at first protested that Saltillo was so obviously in González's bailiwick that he should be left to deal with it, but Carranza insisted. Grumblingly acquiescing, Villa did not bother to wait for reinforcements from González, which he suspected would be deliberately delayed, but launched another of his blitzkrieg cavalry attacks, entraining his horsemen, then launching them suddenly at the enemy position at Paredón, north of Saltillo. Catching half the federals detached from the garrison at Saltillo, Villa routed them, killing more than 500, taking 2,500 prisoners and sweeping up 3,000 rifles and ten cannon. The retreating federals spread panic among the garrison at Saltillo and, rather than face Villa again, gutted the city and fled overland to San Luis Potosí.

Villa entered Saltillo in triumph, then turned Coahuila over to Carranza who, as a native of the state, set up his new capital there. Villa then asked for control of the northern railway network to be turned over to him, so that he could strike south at Zacatecas. Alarmed that even after diverting him so blatantly into Coahuila, the dauntless Villa might still win the race for Mexico City, Carranza tried a fresh stalling tactic. He formed a new army, comprising northerners jealous or resentful of Villa, dubbed it the 'Army of the Centre' and gave the command to Panfilo Natera, a former *villista* underling. After implicitly insulting Villa by giving the nonentity Natera the same rank, Carranza ordered the Army of the Centre to break through at Zacatecas.

Natera failed dismally at his initial attempt and Carranza now faced a dilemma. He needed the ever-victorious Division of the North to take Zacatecas, but could not stomach the thought of another Villa victory. He therefore ordered Villa to detach 5,000 of his men and assign them to Natera's command. Villa indignantly refused and sent Silvestre Terrazas to Saltillo to explain to Carranza that he was not prepared to allow his elite troops to be used as cannon-fodder by a military ignoramus like Natera. Terrazas ran up against the predictable Carranza brick wall of impenetrable stolidity and returned to Villa without getting the order rescinded. Villa exploded with rage and spoke of going up to Saltillo and hanging Carranza on the spot. When Felipe Ángeles talked him out of this idea, he contented himself with firing off an angry cable which read: 'Who asked you to stick your nose into my territory?'

By now Villa was beginning to fathom the depths of Carranza's duplicity. He was enraged that, after he, Villa, had made so many concessions against his better judgement, Carranza had given him nothing in return. He conferred with Ángeles and Silvestre Terrazas on how they could best turn the tables on Carranza. They considered stage-managing a demonstration whereby the Army would expressly refuse to take orders from anyone but Villa, but before any such scheme could be implemented, Carranza alienated his generals by high-handed and autocratic behaviour. He replied to Villa's intemperate cable by refusing to make any concessions at all, Villa threw up his command, and Carranza, presumably choking on his weasel words, replied that he accepted the resignation 'with regret'.

Felipe Ángeles called a meeting of senior commanders. All were agreed that if Villa no longer commanded it, the Division of the North would disintegrate and Huerta would be offered an eleventh-hour lifeline. Even as they were discussing the next step, the news came in that Carranza had accepted Villa's resignation. Almost speechless with anger, Ángeles and the generals cabled back, asking Carranza to reconsider. The autocrat in Saltillo refused to do so. The high command then petitioned Villa to lead the Division of the North as an independent command, cutting out Carranza altogether. Villa agreed, and a cable was sent to Carranza to notify him of the new situation.

Still unable quite to accept that the Army would not bend to his will, Carranza, summoned six handpicked generals, choosing the ones most likely to do his bidding. To his consternation, they too refused to break rank with Villa and refused even to go to Saltillo to discuss the matter. All eleven of the generals of the Division of the North co-signed a blistering telegram composed by Felipe Ángeles, who had his own compelling reasons to loathe and detest Carranza. They informed Carranza that, with or without his approval, they were marching south to Zacatecas forthwith, impugned his good faith and declared they could see right through his knavish schemes to sideline Villa. With his absurd sense of self-importance, Carranza could not have enjoyed reading the cable: 'We consider your measure a violation of the laws of politics and war and the duty of patriotism . . . We do not accept your decision . . . We know well that you were looking for the opportunity to stop General Villa . . . because of your ambition to remove from the Revolutionary scene the men who can think without your orders, who do not flatter and praise you.'

Villa had won a complete victory and for once the haughty Carranza had to eat humble pie. The rift between the two was irreparable, but in order to deal the *coup de grâce* to Huerta it was necessary to paper over the cracks. At a hasty meeting at Torreón Villa recognised Carranza as First Chief, and Villa was confirmed as unquestioned commander of all armies comprising the Division of the North; he was given the rail network, adequate supplies of coal and ammunition and virtual military *carte blanche*. It was also agreed that, with the fall of Mexico City, a convention for discussing the political programme of the Revolution, land reform and the date of new elections would be held; this marked a significant concession to the Army as against Carranza's Plan of Guadalupe. Yet, with typical duplicity, Carranza accepted the principle of a convention without committing himself to its make-up or the content of any reforms to be discussed there.

Villa was now free to lead 20,000 men against the railway junction of Zacatecas, the gateway to Mexico City. For this do-or-die battle the federals had selected their position well, cynically prepared to see a beautiful old mining town blown to pieces. On the left and right of the strong central defensive positions, where 12,000 defenders were dug in, were two hills, El Grillo and La Bufa, which any attacker would have to scale as a prelude to assaulting the town; attacking infantry had to labour slowly up the steep incline, where they could be slaughtered like game, as had happened to Natera's men on his abortive attack. The defenders were reasonably confident: this time Villa would have to deal with seasoned *colorados* and other elite units, not raw conscripts. The federal strategy was simply to sit back and absorb the attacks, exhausting Villa as he threw wave after wave of assault troops at the impregnable positions. Originally Huerta had hoped to catch him in a pincer movement, using the armies withdrawn from Coahuila for a flanking attack, but the US occupation of Veracruz had ended that dream.

After conferring with Ángeles, Villa decided on a twin-track strategy: surround and assault the town from all sides, while using the superior artillery of the Division of the North to keep up a non-stop barrage on the two hills, leaving the federal gunners not a single second in which to think; meanwhile his best infantry would be working their way to the top. Ángeles insisted on meticulous contingency planning: there would be a large *villista* garrison stationed at the town of Guadalupe to guard the road to Aguascalientes, in case Orozco tried to reinforce the federals that way. On 22 June Villa appeared before his men, riding a 'spirited horse', exhorting them to make one last push for victory. Then at 10 a.m. the first units went in as his army assailed Zacatecas from all sides.

Ángeles's advice proved first-rate and the *villista* strategy succeeded brilliantly against the hill of El Grillo, where a massive artillery bombardment threw so much dust and debris into the air that it masked the approach of crack units scaling the heights; Villa's commandos took the summit around 1 p.m. On La Bufa resistance was more stubborn, probably because of the presence there of the federal commander General Medina Barrón, but the fall of El Grillo had a knock-on effect on morale. This had been thought impregnable and its capture after just three hours spread panic, especially in Zacatecas itself. From the heights federal soldiers could be seen below, scurrying like ants in a disturbed nest but without the same sense of communal purpose. Knowing their fate if taken, the federals snapped in courage and morale, throwing away their uniforms, guns and cartridge belts. After terrible fighting lasting into the late afternoon, La Bufa also fell.

Medina Barrón ordered his remaining troops to retreat by the Zacatecas-Aguascalientes road, knowing that at Torreón Villa had left his enemy an escape route. However, he had bargained without the new dispositions of Ángeles, and as the defeated rabble staggered along the road they found their way barred by the 7,000 *villistas* at Guadalupe. The result was a massacre, with thousands of men eaten up by the terrible enfilading fire. The most frightful slaughter took place as the panic-stricken federals, together with women and children, often with two officers mounted on a single horse, tried to force their way past Guadalupe. Having left Zacatecas under a hail of bullets, they ran into a firestorm at Guadalupe. Witnesses spoke of the hills between the two towns literally running red with blood, the roads strewn with corpses. Some escaped the gunfire only to plunge lemming-like into crevasses formed by disused mineshafts in the mountains around the town.

Those who elected to stay and fight it out in Zacatecas fared no better. From 1 p.m. until 4 p.m. that day the town was an inferno, a hell on earth, with no quarter given or expected. Some federal officers tried to disguise their status by ripping off their uniforms and decorations, but were detected anyway and consigned to the firing squad. However, the real slaughter began when there came an ear-shattering explosion, as a federal colonel blew up the arsenal, preferring to kill himself and hundreds of *villistas* rather than surrender. As a result of this mindless act of sabotage an entire block of buildings lay in ruins and hundreds of bodies mingled with the rubble: some who survived the blast but were cruelly maimed lay groaning in agony; others sustained no direct damage but died anyway, being entombed in the wreckage. In fury at the loss of their comrades, the *villistas* on the hilltops rained down a fusillade of bullets from the heights. One estimate was that a firestorm of 20,000 rifles opened up simultaneously at about 5 p.m. There was a short lull, then the victorious *villistas* started mass executions of prisoners. Captives were taken to the cemetery and the officers separated from the rankers; those bearing the hated federal commission were then executed by Villa's special killing squads. The sun was already setting and the insensate killing still going on when Ángeles arrived and ordered the guns to be silent.

Zacatecas was the bloodiest battle of the entire campaign against Huerta. Six thousand federals were slain (including 3,000 on the road to Guadalupe), but the real body count was probably higher, for only 3,000 enemy wounded were officially recorded. Of the entire garrison of 12,000 defenders, less than 300 reached Aguascalientes in one piece. In addition more than 1,000 *villistas* had died, 2,000 were wounded and vast numbers of civilians killed, maimed or injured. The death toll would have been higher if Ángeles had not intervened. Some say he had a nephew serving with the federals whom he was trying to save, but more likely he was trying to conserve manpower, since captured federal rankers invariably agreed to serve with the Division of the North. So great was the slaughter and so pervasive the stench and contamination of rotting corpses that typhus broke out and claimed the lives of dozens of the victors. Once again Ángeles thought of the solution: he had all the cadavers soaked in petrol and incinerated.

The combination of US intervention at Veracruz and the catastrophic defeat at Zacatecas finished Huerta. Whether at Cuernavaca, Zacatecas or Tampico, the story was the same: mass desertions followed by federal generals returning to Mexico City, coming like Johnny Cope in the Burns poem with the news of their own defeat. The officer class was desperate and in an impossible position; they had to sink or swim with Huerta, for to avoid execution they should have changed sides at a much earlier stage. Huerta simply made a bad situation worse by ordering a scorched-earth policy, wantonly destroying public buildings and property; the federals in rout were more akin to full-time arsonists than professional soldiers, and the vandalism was particularly marked at Monterrey, Piedras Negras and Nuevo Laredo. Even the *hacendado* class and the rancheros turned against Huerta as the federals continued their mindless depredations on the retreat; by now the so-called rebels seemed to have greater respect for lives and property than the 'guardians of law and order'.

The wealthy, the propertied and the middle classes by now wanted Huerta ousted as soon as possible. They were prepared to look abroad – to Panama, the USA or even the Vatican City – for suitable mediators to broker a negotiated peace. Argentina, Brazil and Chile – the ABC powers of Latin America – offered their services and Huerta reluctantly agreed. He sent delegates to the peace conference near Niagara Falls in New York State, hoping to conclude a quick peace before the Constitutionalists reached Mexico City, but Woodrow Wilson was determined to eject him.

When the ABC powers proposed that there should be an armistice first, then proper negotiations for peace, Wilson refused to accept the deal. He saw clearly enough that this meant commiting the USA to depriving the rebels of the fruits of their victory. In any case, Carranza refused to accept the ABC powers as mediators, so their proposal was stillborn. The best the Niagara conference could do was resolve the Huerta/Wilson dispute over Tampico and Veracruz, scheduling a timetable for the withdrawal of the Marines.

As Huerta now faced an inevitable exit, tensions between Carranza and Villa increased. Immediately after the victory at Zacatecas, the ingrate Carranza embargoed all shipments of coal to the Division of the North. Since Carranza controlled the coal mines of Coahuila, Villa was unable to fuel his trains for the final drive on Mexico City. At the same time, Villa was hit by a shortage of ammunition consequent on the reinstated US arms embargo after Veracruz. Again Villa felt stabbed in the back, especially since he saw Carranza's anti-Americanism as the root cause of trouble with Washington. He was puzzled and hurt by Wilson's attitude. Since he, Pancho Villa, had always been a friend of the Americans and had not even denounced the Veracruz intervention, why was the arms embargo being extended to him? If anything, the gringos were favouring Carranza, for they inexplicably allowed arms to be imported via Carranza-held Tampico while sealing the border with Chihuahua. Villa was not to know that this bizarre policy was all part of a 'divide and rule' tactic by Wilson, concerned that no one faction in Mexico should grow too powerful.

What Wilson really wanted was the disappearance of Huerta followed by an armistice and a communal form of government, possibly a president with limited powers (neither Villa nor Carranza) overseen by a troika of trustees, one of whom would be a conservative figure acceptable to Washington. Carranza, however, wanted none of this: he insisted on unconditional surrender of the federal army to him and him alone. Huerta tried to buy time by offering bait to the *zapatistas*, by this time busily occupying the villages on the sierras outside Mexico City, having isolated and bypassed the garrison at Cuernavaca. Huerta offered generous terms to Zapata to detach him from the Constitutionalist cause, but he did not know his man. Zapata contemptuously refused the offer of an alliance that would have allowed him to enter the capital in triumph.

Carranza continued his machiavellian project of weakening Villa even as he dealt the *coup de grâce* to Huerta. Emissaries from the First Chief and Villa met at Torreón on 5–6 July and dickered over restoration of coal supplies and the recognition of Carranza as the future chief executive. Only one concrete proposal was accepted: that a constitutional convention would meet in Mexico City, once Huerta was ousted, to decide the future course of the Revolution; there would be a civilian as interim president and military leaders could choose one delegate to the convention for every 1,000 soldiers they commanded. The two sides agreed to differ about the political future in Sonora, but drew up detailed blueprints for abolishing the old federal army, curtailing the power of the Catholic Church and giving benefits to industrial workers.

Carranza was simply stalling for time and playing his usual underhand game. He had agreed that emissaries should go to the talks at Torreón, but only on the understanding that they were not official envoys and that he would not be bound by any agreement that did not please him. Much pointless talk could have been saved if Carranza had put all his cards on the table. His aims were what they had always been: he himself, not a convention, to decide the future of Mexico; he and only he to pronounce on land reform, which meant no land reform at all; and an utter refusal to restore coal to the Army of the North.

At last, seeing his position was hopeless, Huerta resigned on 15 July. He then went to his favourite drinking den, swigged a bumper of his favourite brandy and told onlookers: 'This will be my last glass here. I drink to the new president of Mexico.' He then sought refuge on the German battlecruiser *Dresden* which took him to Jamaica; thence he and his family proceeded to exile in Barcelona. The new president was his stooge Francisco Carbajal, who tried to dupe Carranza with a transfer-of-power offer of the kind with which Díaz had gulled Madero. When this offer was predictably rejected, Carbajal put out feelers to Villa, proposing to surrender the federal army to him, provided that the lives of all officers were spared and they were allowed to serve under Felipe Ángeles.

This was a tempting offer, for the Division of the North was temporarily paralysed by Carranza's coal embargo. Villa spent long hours with Ángeles and others trying to decide what to do next. Should they withdraw to Chihuahua and convert it into an impregnable fortress? No, advised Ángeles: that would leave Carranza in possession of the whole of the rest of Mexico and would make him too powerful. More promising was a formal alliance with Zapata or a rapid campaign against Sonora while Obregón was away in the south. In the end, Villa proved incapable of Carranza's machiavellianism. He told his officers that to accept Carbajal's terms would be a betrayal of the Revolution. In any case, to accept the surrender of the federal army, he would have to fight his way past Obregón and into a hostile Mexico City, when he had no clear indication of what Zapata's reaction would be.

Zapata was still more interested in ideological purity than in building alliances. On 19 July he republished the Plan of Ayala, declaring that it was his aim to have it enshrined in the new constitution that would be drawn up after Huerta's fall. He then took the town of Milpa Alta, a suburb of Mexico City, after a ferocious two-day battle. Baulked with Carranza and Villa, Carbajal thought he saw a glimmer of a chance with Zapata. He offered to accept the Plan of Ayala as part of a general deal, but Zapata replied that, with 20,000 men, he was now strong enough to take Mexico City on his own and needed no deals. Carbajal turned to Obregón as his last chance. Fortunately for him, Obregón was a pragmatist who lacked Carranza's unyielding character. He saw a chance to scupper Zapata and took it.

Having secured a deal with Obregón whereby the federal army would defend the capital against the *zapatistas* until he arrived, Carbajal and the rest of the Huerta faction fled the country on 12 August. Promoted to major-general by Carranza, Obregón swept on to Mexico City, arriving at Teoloyucán on 11 August, where he signed the documents ending *huertista* rule. The governor of the Federal District, left as the only authority in the capital, went out to meet Obregón on the outskirts and signed the instruments of unconditional surrender. There was general relief among a war-weary population, well expressed in words spoken earlier by an old peasant to John Reed: 'First it was the *maderistas*, then the *orozquistas* and now the – what did you call them? – the Constitutionalists. I am very old and I have not long to live, but this war – it seems to me that all it accomplishes is to let us go hungry.'

On 16 August Obregón made his triumphal entry. Five thousand men of the vanguard accompanied him, creating a sensation by their mixed appearance. Ex-ranchers and miners trooped in, dressed in felt hats, khaki trousers and brown leather leggings, all with Winchester 30/30 rifles and bandoleros. Alongside them were the Yaquis, still wearing the clothes in which they had enlisted in Sonora – cotton trousers and embroidered shirts, marching boots, ten-gallon hats. Seeing their long hair tied back in ribbons and the fearsome armoury of bows and arrows, blowguns and slings, the burghers of Mexico City suddenly felt a shiver of apprehension. They now wondered if they had made the right bargain, having delivered themselves into the hands of 'barbarians' on the basis that Obregón, 'the new Cortés', was preferable to Zapata, 'the Attila of the South'. They would soon learn that their forebodings were well founded.

Into Mexico City, hard on the heels of Obregón, now came Carranza. Stage-managing his entry into the capital so as to ape Juárez's approach on 11 January 1861 after his final defeat of the Conservatives, on 20 August 1914 Carranza began his journey at Tlalnepantla, seven miles from the National Palace, so that he could traverse as much of the capital as possible and receive the plaudits of a huge crowd. This aspect of image-building worked well: 300,000 people lined the route, as against the 100,000 who had greeted Madero in 1911. However, the honeymoon did not long endure. Carranza made a speech warning Mexico City that it could expect no favours. He immediately confirmed Obregón's decree putting the city under martial law and announced tough measures to deal with crime. Throughout 1914–15 burglary was at epidemic levels in the capital, often the work of the notorious Grey Automobile Gang, who specialised in impersonating police officers to gain access to the houses of the rich with phoney search warrants, making their getaway after the burglaries in distinctive grey cars.

Both Carranza and Obregón felt that the citizens of Mexico City were overprivileged, had been protected from the rigours of war and had not pulled their weight in the Revolution – Obregón was heard to remark that the capital needed a good long dose of military rule to put it in its place, before elections let lily-livered Congressmen back in on the act. However, where Carranza was concerned to teach the lesson that the cosy arrangements Madero had made with the old guard were a thing of the past, Obregón's attitude was harsher and more vindictive. Carranza was not pleased to hear Obregón talk of vengeance as true patriotism, since to him patriotism meant the recognition of necessity – which he construed to mean a sense of the nation's destiny such as had animated Juárez, and which therefore implied his own personal rule. It seemed to him that Obregón was dangerously close to a view of the Revolution as a self-justifying and self-sustaining 'thing in itself' – a waltz of death featuring just four men: Obregón, Carranza, Villa and Zapata.

Obregón was never one to be overimpressed by the posturings of the

First Chief. Three days after arriving in the capital, he went to the French cemetery to pay his respects to Madero. Accompanying him were many of the 'notables' who had looked the other way when Huerta murdered Madero. With his love of the histrionic, Obregón handed his pistol to María Arias – a woman who had denounced Huerta publicly in 1913 – and said: 'I give my pistol to María Arias, the only man to be found in Mexico City at the time of Huerta's coup.' Some historians have found Obregón's hostility to Mexico City puzzling, and have speculated that he punished the capital for his own guilt in not having joined the Revolution with Madero in 1910.

Certainly, his early measures were tough and uncompromising. In the mistaken view that the Catholic Church had supported Huerta – in fact Huerta had attacked it viciously – Obregón imposed a fine of half a million pesos, expelled the Vicar-General and sixty-seven other priests from the city, and delighted in humiliating the Church by subjecting priests to medical examinations, which revealed that many of them were suffering from venereal disease. He then attacked all businessmen who had supported Huerta, even if only tacitly, by levying swingeing taxes on capital, real estate, mortgages, carriages, automobiles and even water, sewers and pavements. Those who traded in staples such as corn, beans, oil, lard, tallow and coal were given forty-eight hours to disgorge 10 per cent of their wealth or face total confiscation. When Obregón imposed special taxes on foreigners, they protested, thinking Carranza would not seek confrontation with their governments, but Obregón went in person with an armed guard to the protest meeting in the Hidalgo theatre and broke it up, browbeating the demonstrators with a display of military might, namely a triple row of soldiers with guns pointing directly at the protestors' hearts. To purge their 'contumacity' Obregón imposed a 'moral tax' – forcing the foreigners to sweep the streets.

While Obregón and Carranza made it clear to Mexico City that the halcyon days were over, they turned to face the overriding political imperative: the coming conflict with Villa. Only war-weariness and wariness about the possible response from Washington prevented an immediate outbreak of hostilities. Besides, Carranza reasoned that public opinion had to be brought along gently, otherwise people would see warfare between two factions not divided by ideology as simply a war for the personal ambitions of Villa and Carranza. There had to be a lot of talk before there could be further bloodshed. In the meantime the prime aim was to prevent an alliance between Villa and Zapata.

So far, in all contacts between the two great popular leaders, Zapata had made most of the running. The first envoy he sent north in autumn

1913 was Gildardo Magaña, who had been with Villa in prison in Mexico City in 1912 and taught him the rudiments of the Plan of Ayala. Making one of those circuitous itineraries that all Mexicans during the Revolution seemed always to make, he travelled to Nuevo León via Veracruz, Havana, New Orleans and Matamoros. In Nuevo León the commanding general was Lucio Blanco, a man of liberal sympathies who had often expressed support for agrarian reform and whose secretary (Francisco Múgica) was Magaña's childhood friend. Magaña finally ran Villa to earth in November at Ciudad Juárez. In the interview Villa showed sympathy for land reform and spoke with pride of his 'leftist' commanders like Calixto Contreras and Orestes Pereyra in Durango. Villa began corresponding with Zapata and from March 1914 *villista* envoys to Morelos were received with particular marks of favour.

Carranza's advisers could see the dangers of a Villa-Zapata alliance, especially if masterminded by Felipe Ángeles, but for a long time the First Chief was deaf to their advice. Although he appreciated the power of Villa, he bracketed Zapata as 'rabble' along with the *orozquistas* or the followers of Emilio Vásquez in 1912. The *carrancistas* were reduced to putting out feelers behind their chief's back. They were over-sanguine, misled by Zapata's apparent reluctance to enter a formal alliance with Villa. They did not understand that Zapata was hyper-cautious, that he required Villa to give him abundant evidence of sincerity before putting his name to a deal. Zapata suspected all other leaders of heading temporary, ramshackle and evanescent movements. 'Revolutions will come and revolutions will go,' he said, 'but I will continue with mine in my own way.' Whereas the pragmatic Villa could accept such an approach, the dogmatic martinet Carranza could not.

As Obregón and Carranza moved in on Mexico City, the flurry of peace approaches to Zapata quickened. One *zapatista* agent even interviewed Carranza before his ride into the capital, suggesting a face-to-face meeting at a venue of Zapata's choice. Lucio Blanco and some other *carrancista* generals pressed hard for an entente with Zapata, and sent their own secret agents to negotiate with him. One of them took a personal gift from Blanco to Zapata of a gold-lined .44 Colt revolver, and another suggested a Zapata-Blanco conference. The stumbling block to any meaningful talks was always Carranza's ambition to be Mexico's chief executive – and Carranza anyway thought that all these overtures to Morelos were a waste of time. When one of Genovevo de la O's envoys interviewed him, Carranza declared petulantly: 'This business of dividing up the land is ridiculous.'

Carranza's dogmatic and inflexible hard line infuriated his advisers.

What could they offer Zapata when the First Chief continued to insist that the *zapatistas* were no more than rustic brigands, a mere rabble; that they were weathercocks who had earlier fought for Madero and Orozco; that if they would not disarm he would do to them what Huerta and Robles had done; and that any land reform must be entirely at *his* say-so? However, the irrestible force that was Carranza met the immovable object that was Zapata, and found a man just as stubborn. Zapata had only two demands, and they were non-negotiable: Carranza had to retire so that there could be genuinely representative interim government and then genuinely free elections; and the new regime must conform to the Plan of Ayala which, among other things, in Article 3 declared Zapata to be the supreme head of the Mexican Revolution and in Article 12 specified the composition of the peacetime junta that would replace him. So here were two granite-like men, both refusing to compromise or even to talk until their initial demands were met in full.

While insisting that he could not give way on the Plan of Ayala, Zapata wrote to Carranza to suggest meeting at Yautepec in Morelos, but he made the offer almost impossible to take up by disowning everything that had been said to Carranza to date by any of his agents. He made his true feelings plain over and over again: in a public speech he warned that 70,000 men with Mausers would oppose any Carranza presidency; at a council of his chiefs, he said that Carranza was no more than a corrupt *cabrón* surrounded by shyster lawyers; in a letter to Villa he warned that Carranza's ambitions and greed were supremely dangerous; and in a missive to Woodrow Wilson he denounced Carranza as simply another in Mexico's long line of machine politicians. In table talk with his intimates he warned that the coming war with Carranza would be protracted; it would take Obregón and other ambitious generals years to realise that Carranza was really a fetter on *their* desires.

Carranza, however, saw the point of trying to neutralise Zapata during the coming war with Villa and used a multiplicity of agents to try to stall him. An agent of the American Red Cross interviewed Zapata on Carranza's behalf on 25 August, but came away discouraged by Zapata's unflattering remarks about the First Chief. Carranza was playing a crafty game, conciliating Woodrow Wilson by pretending to be a peacemaker and appearing to want to use the USA as an intermediary between him and Zapata. He revealed his true posture by consistently refusing to meet Zapata in Yautepec, insisting that any such interview had to take place in Mexico City. From his real agent Juan Sarabia he was receiving reports reinforcing his 'rabble' perception; Sarabia claimed the true number of *zapatista* effectives was no more than 15,000 and that all were poorly armed and trained. As for Zapata personally, he was an uneducated man of staggering political naïveté, sustained only by an overweening pride, while his *éminence grise* Manuel Palafox was a mere nonentity.

The skill of Sarabia as an agent was that, while making damning reports to Carranza, he was also acting as go-between for the phalanx of 'middle of the roaders' that included General Lucio Blanco and the reforming governor of Nuevo León, Antonio Villareal. Zapata was keen to meet these men in Cuernavaca and Sarabia advised Carranza that there would be no harm in such contacts, which he would monitor. Still with one eye on Washington, Carranza pretended to go along with this, but prevented Blanco from going; he allowed Villareal to proceed but forbade him to make any concessions. Villareal and other envoys accordingly travelled down to Cuernavaca. Among the party was Alfredo Serratos, a freelance, self-serving 'troubleshooter', who claimed to each of Carranza and Zapata that he was the other's plenipotentiary. His true role may have been as Villa's agent, charged with making sure Zapata and Carranza never reached an agreement.

Villareal and his fellow envoys were shocked by what they saw in Cuernavaca, where the federal garrison had surrendered to Zapata a month before. Such Rousseau-style direct and open democracy, with illiterate farmers speaking up at genuine decision-making meetings, and all men, whatever their rank or status, wearing white work clothes, appalled their northern sensibilities. Everywhere they found what they took to be a fanatical insistence on the implementation of the letter of the Plan of Ayala. They also unexpectedly encountered real hostility, for Palafox had emerged as a 'no compromise' hardliner; his critics claim that he could see no future in a Mexico dominated by the apparatchiks of the Carranza political machine and acted accordingly.

Villareal and his colleagues got on much better with the rising star in the *zapatista* firmament, Díaz Soto y Gama, a lawyer in his early thirties from a middle-class background in San Luis. Soto y Gama began in student politics, developed a talent for oratory, and moved along the spectrum from liberalism to anarchism, where he took his inspiration from the Russians, especially Kropotkin and Tolstoy. In 1904 a severe decline in his family fortunes led him to withdraw from political activism, and in 1910 he took no part in Madero's revolt, regarding Maderismo as simply old wine in new bottles. He later recanted and wrote a 42-point *maderista* manifesto to the people of San Luis, talking grandiloquently of turning the city into the Chicago of Mexico. He supported Madero against Zapata until April 1912 when he converted to anarcho-syndicalism; he finally joined Zapata in spring 1914 and was one of the urban radicals who gave Zapatismo its ideology and theory.

The middle-of-the-roaders found Soto y Gama a valuable ally, for many of them shared his political sympathies. The anarcho-syndicalist movement, the House of the World Worker, split in 1914 when Huerta outlawed it. Some joined up with Carranza and later helped to form his 'Red Battalions'; others, the real leftists, went south to join Zapata. However, there were always those, like Lucio Blanco, who thought that there was more in common between the left factions, that the real divide was between, on the one hand, the bourgeois and reactionary elements in both the Zapata and Carranza movements and, on the other, the real revolutionaries in both. On this view, the personal struggle between Zapata and Carranza was 'false consciousness'; this was what Soto y Gama meant when he referred to Carranza as a bourgeois irrelevance, and it may well have been the reason Carranza forbade Lucio Blanco to travel to Cuernavaca.

The envoys also ran into a more immediate problem: Zapata himself was nowhere to be found. Acutely suspicious of doing any deals – for he had a morbid fear of betraying his supporters or selling them short – and particularly wary of *anything* from Mexico City, above all envoys from that quarter, Zapata solved his uncertainty about what to do by leaving town. When the envoys asked where the leader was, they were told that he had gone to a town that lay sixty-five miles south and would be back 'soon'. However, Villareal soon convinced himself that the people of Morelos were sick of war and would turn on Zapata if he did not deliver a lasting peace. This insight slightly got lost in a pointless slanging match the envoys had with Palafox, who made it clear he had no interest in anything they had to say; Palafox simply reiterated *ad nauseam* that the Plan of Ayala must be accepted in its entirety, without so much as the change of a comma. At a second meeting Palafox asked the envoys for their credentials and harangued them when they claimed to be unofficial observers.

It became clear that Zapata would always be a disappointment to the leftist 'popular front' ideologues. Subject always to the sacrosanct status of the Plan of Ayala, Zapata was a political pragmatist. It might be thought that his obvious berth was in alliance with Villa, but Zapata feared that Villa might become too powerful, so was treading carefully. If all the generals joined Villa, and Carranza was beaten, the new Army would be too powerful for Zapata to withstand. This consideration, plus the perennial shortage of ammunition, was what made him welcome into his ranks the ex-*huertistas* and *colorados* who fled south from the implacable Obregón, even though in terms of political ideology these new recruits could be considered men of the Right. Fear of Villa, too, initially made him pursue a twin-track approach to both Villa and Carranza. Yet another reason for pragmatism was that Zapata's alliances were always fragile affairs; even now, with the movement seemingly at its apogee, de la O announced that he was not necessarily bound by Palafox's centralised administration and its orders.

Finally Zapata returned and invited the visitors to dinner. During the meal some of Zapata's chieftains accused the *carrancistas* of having fired on their forces; for a moment Sarabia thought Zapata was going to order the envoys' execution. Next day there was a final meeting, at which Zapata lost his temper and screamed at his visitors that if Carranza wanted to talk to him, he *had* to come to Cuernavaca. The more Villareal tried to placate him, the more enraged Zapata became: how, he shrieked, could everything he had fought so hard for over three and a half years be parleyed away in all this nitpicking talk? The envoys offered formally to accept *zapatista* control of all the villages they occupied south of Mexico City and to hand over Xochimilco, controlling the capital's water supply. At first Zapata stormed that he wanted no charity, but Palafox and Serratos persuaded him to accept this gift. Having previously prevented the disgruntled envoys from leaving by not issuing the necessary passes, Zapata finally relented and let them go the next morning. They returned to Carranza with the disappointing news that Zapata insisted the Plan of Ayala be signed and that Carranza resign as chief executive; they expressed themselves baffled as to why Zapata was so intransigent and blamed Palafox.

It is tempting at first blush to agree with the emissaries and conclude that Zapata was either a stupid fanatic or was in thrall to irresponsible advisers, but there was method in his apparent madness. Zapata laid down impossible terms because he did not want an agreement with Carranza, but also did not want him to be able to say that the *zapatistas* would not negotiate. Part of this negative attitude was a particular distaste for Carranza, part was general paranoia about any overture that came from Mexico City, the seat of corruption in the eyes of all genuine Morelos isolationists. Additionally, all Zapata's advisers were pushing for a formal alliance with Villa, some like Soto y Gama so that they could make common cause with the 'popular front' leftists in all three camps, others, like Palafox and Serratos, because they thought an entente with Villa would advance their careers.

In any case, Carranza rejected Zapata's terms on 5 September, declaring in exasperation: 'The intransigence of Citizen-General Zapata and his people will not be overcome either by wisdom or threats.' Zapata had his own version: as he wrote to Lucio Blanco: 'I tell you in all frankness that this Carranza does not inspire much confidence in me. I see in him much ambition and a disposition to fool people.' Some observers see the evident failure to communicate as simply another aspect of the *mésalliance* between the nineteenth-century liberalism of the north and the ancient values of the south, the viceregal and pre-Conquest area.

Since influential *carrancistas* and US agents kept lobbying for a Zapata-Carranza pact, in defiance of all logic and probability, Zapata decided to slam the door shut decisively. On 8 September he ordered his followers to implement Article 8 of the Plan of Ayala, which called for the expropriation of all goods belonging to those who 'directly or indirectly' opposed the Plan. This meant that all property in the countryside would be turned over to the villages and all urban property used to pay war pensions for orphans and widows or to make loans to farmers. Effectively, from September 1914 on, Zapata was set on the course of full-blooded social revolution. So far it had been a case of recovering lands taken by government or landlords which had formerly belonged to the *pueblos*; now it was a matter of expropriating new lands. A new form of communal land ownership, the *ejido* would give peasants joint grazing and cultivation rights and shared ownership. Zapata showed he meant business by setting up agrarian commissions to distribute the new land, leaving Mexico City in no doubt what would happen if the *zapatistas* occupied the capital.

While Zapata and Carranza were locking horns, Obregón was again dicing with death, this time at the hands of Villa. The occasion of conflict was Sonora and the revival of fortunes there of ex-governor Juan Maytorena. The Torreón accords in July had put Sonora on the back burner but, with non-intervention by both Villa and Carranza seemingly guaranteed, Maytorena moved quickly to assert his hegemony. His first step was to expel the Obregón supporters Plutarco Elías Calles and Benjamin Hill; with Maytorena as the favourite of the Yaquis, he was in a position now to dominate the state. This posed a direct threat to Obregón, who determined to reassert his status in his native state. While ordering Hill and Calles to counterattack against Maytorena's Yaquis, he travelled north on 24 August to confer with Villa at Chihuahua City, taking with him an escort of just twenty men and thus, it seemed, walking into the lion's den.

Villa played a duplicitous hand. He welcomed Obregón with a guard of honour, invited him to stay at his home, and had Obregón witness a cable he dashed off to Maytorena, telling him to suspend hostilities against the *obregonistas.* He then secretly returned to the telegraph office to send another cable, telling Maytorena to disregard the previous message, which was for public consumption only; he told Maytorena to make an end of Hill and Calles while he stalled Obregón in Chihuahua. However, he changed his mind almost immediately when Obregón offered him a deal: he would abandon Carranza and make sure he did not become president if Villa in turn would restore his (Obregón's) position in Sonora.

Villa and Obregón then travelled to Sonora for a conference with Maytorena on 29 August. Obregón asked his rival to state his grievances against him and Maytorena asked for time to compose his reply; in reality he was now thoroughly confused as to what Villa's real intentions were. Eventually an accord was patched up whereby Obregón was recognised as overall commander-in-chief in the state, but Maytorena had day-to-day control of all military forces. The accord pleased nobody except Villa and Obregón. Second thoughts revealed to Maytorena that he had just agreed to a set-up where Obregón could legally dismiss him; Hill and Calles meanwhile complained bitterly that they were being sacrificed to Obregón's desire for a deal with Villa. The agreement lasted just twenty-four hours before being repudiated by both sides.

On the clear understanding that Obregón would sacrifice Carranza, Villa agreed to break with Maytorena. On 3 September Villa and Obregón announced that the new interim governor of Sonora would be Juan Cabral. Obregón in turn pledged himself to ensure that Carranza would never be president, to put Hill and Calles under Villa's control, and to agree that local and regional elections be held before national ones, so that an incoming national regime could not simply impose its placemen in the provinces. How serious Obregón was is questionable; for the time being he was prepared to promise anything to thwart Maytorena. In any case, the new agreement was stillborn. Maytorena, Hill and Calles all angrily refused to be bound by it. Carranza too got wind of it and announced that he did not accept the accord. He counterproposed an electoral forum in which all the delegates would be chosen by him.

Finding Maytorena intractable, and unable to deliver on his promises to Villa because of Carranza's intransigence, Obregón did something inexplicable in rational terms. Not only did he return to Chihuahua for more talks with Villa, thus putting himself in the Centaur's power when he was in uncertain mood, but he also tried his hand at backstairs intrigue, trying to discredit Villa with his own commanders. By this time Villa had heard that Benjamin Hill was on the march in Sonora and that Obregón had allowed Carranza to face him down over the latest accord.

Obregón must have sensed that he was in dangerous waters when a suspicious and distant Villa insisted that he stand with him to review a military parade at Chihuahua City on 16 September. The march past was an impressive display of *villista* military might: forty-three cannon, tens of thousands of Mausers, over 5,000 elite troops. Obregón sensed that this was a hint, as he put it, that Villa wanted to 'erase him from the book of the living'.

The private talks began. Almost immediately Villa lost his temper and began ranting at Obregón: 'General Hill thinks I can be played with . . . You're a traitor and I'm going to have you shot right now.' Villa was not usually a foul-mouthed man but this time his rage-driven speech was peppered with obscenities. Obregón replied in kind and both men seemed on the point of drawing their guns. Finally Villa halted his tongue-lashing to give Obregón a stark choice: recall Hill or face the firing squad. Obregón said he would never withdraw Hill under threat. In his autobiography he claimed to have countered the threat of execution as follows: 'As far as I personally am concerned, you will do me a lot of good, since through such a death you will give me a personality I do not have, and the only one to suffer from this will be you.'

With anyone else one would suspect *l'esprit de l'escalier* or a Thucydidean speech, but in Obregón's case it is likely that he did speak along those lines. With his death-driven personality, which on so many occasions bespoke an unconscious wish for extinction, Obregón was probably the one man in Mexico who could not have been browbeaten by the threat of instant execution. At any rate it seems likely that by his sang-froid he gradually established a psychological advantage over Villa, making him query his own motives. Obregón quietly plugged away at the motif that he was quite prepared to be a martyr for the Revolution, but that by killing him Villa would puncture his own legend; he hit Villa in his weak spot by arguing that great warriors never killed heralds, even their enemy's envoys.

Villa paced the room for an hour, then dismissed the firing squad which was waiting outside, but he warned Obregón that this was a reprieve only. Then he conferred with his advisers. Ángeles and Raúl Madero were vehemently opposed to the execution, and Ángeles thought of a sure way to prevent it. He went to see Luz Corral and told her that if Villa executed a guest in her home, he would be breaching the most sacred laws of hospitality. Luz then put this point to Villa, expecting to be told to mind her own business. He said nothing, looked thoughtful, then suddenly lifted the execution sentence. Back with Obregón, he underwent one of his rapid personality changes, breaking down in tears.

'Francisco Villa is no traitor,' he cried, 'Francisco Villa does not kill defenceless men, and certainly not you, my dear good friend, who are now my guest.' As he left the room he noticed his secretary, Soledad Armendáriz de Orduño, trembling with the tension of the recent emotional scenes. He ordered two glasses of orange juice, offered her one and apologised for the stress caused.

Obregón went on to dine with Villa, joked with the company and then danced alongside Villa until 4 a.m. at a División del Norte regimental ball. One of Obregón's aides, thinking he was living in a madhouse, asked his chief what exactly was going on. Obregón replied: 'I really don't know. I was thinking how to obtain a safe conduct from don Venustiano in heaven' – a typically laboured Obregón witticism, referring to the general Mexican belief that St Peter had a long white beard just like don Venustiano Carranza. Yet behind the scenes the storm had still not abated. Revolving second, third and fourth thoughts, Villa agonised about Obregón's fate. Predictably the thugs among his confidantes, especially Fierro and Urbina, were all for the firing squad, but all the thoughtful and cerebral ones, especially Ángeles and Raúl Madero strongly opposed it. In the end, Villa came down on the side of his intellectuals: Fierro, Urbina and their ilk, he reasoned, would have to follow him whatever he did, but there was a risk of a mass flight of the middle-class advisers if he proceeded with the execution.

Obregón boarded the train for Mexico City on 21 September, well satisfied with his achievements. He had scored a psychological victory over Villa, had intrigued with his generals behind his back and could now hope to become president, using the excuse of Villa's intractable opposition to Carranza. By this time Carranza too was beginning to suspect Obregón of vaulting ambition. He ordered all communications suspended between the *villista*-occupied Zacatecas and his own HQ at Aguascalientes – an overt statement that he regarded the talks in Chihuahua City as an irrelevance – and ordered the railway tracks between the two towns torn up. These were actions aimed as much at Obregón as Villa. As soon as he heard of these developments, Villa announced that he no longer recognised Carranza as First Chief and issued a manifesto, bitterly critical of Carranza, outlining step by step the stages by which don Venustiano had sabotaged the negotiations between him and Villa. The manifesto was not intended to win over *carrancistas* and *obregonistas* so much as to aim above their heads at Zapata and opinion in the USA. It embraced the Plan of Ayala on the one hand and denounced Carranza's anticlericalism on the other, with the latter point appealing at once to Woodrow Wilson and the *zapatistas*.

Villa also recalled Obregón's train, on which he was travelling with a number of *villista* generals, and which had almost reached the junction of Torreón. Brought back to Chihuahua City, the mystified Obregón asked General José Isabel Robles, whom he had been converting from Villismo to an *obregonista* view of the world, to support him: he realised Robles could not save him if Villa had ordered him executed, but at least he could stop him being brutalised and humiliated before dying, as Gustavo Madero had been by Huerta's thugs. When Robles interceded for Obregón, a contemptuous Villa ordered him south on an errand. There was no talk of executions; it turned out that he merely wanted to harangue Obregón on Carranza's perfidy. Another fraught dinner took place, and Obregón was again allowed to depart, early on the evening of 23 September.

What Villa did not tell Obregón was that earlier that day he had called another emergency meeting to discuss what to do about him. This time it seemed clear that Villa was inclining to the side of Fierro and Urbina. Ángeles and Raúl Madero replied with an explicit threat to leave the movement. Villa persisted and his instinct, however murderous, was pragmatically correct. He accurately predicted the future: 'Obregón will cause far more bloodshed to our republic than Pascual Orozco; in fact he will cause more harm than Victoriano Huerta.' After much heart-searching, Villa decided to proceed with the execution, though not in Chihuahua. He ordered General Mateo Almanza to stop Obregón's train and kill him, concerting the measure with his colleague General Roque González Garza, who was accompanying Obregón to Mexico City.

However, Villa had chosen two generals who agreed with Ángeles and Raúl Madero and both ignored the orders given them. Almanza, who was supposed to intercept the train, let it steam right past him. Garza, frantically cabled by Villa to stop the train so that Almanza's firing squad could catch up, ordered the engine driver to open up the throttle and steam ahead at top speed. An increasingly furious Villa then cabled a second execution squad to intercept Obregón's train at Gómez Palacio, but this time he gave the orders to the very generals Obregón had talked round in Chihuahua City: Eugenio Benavides and José Isabel Robles. They did indeed go north and intercept the train, but removed Obregón from Garza's charge and took him overland to Carranza-held Aguascalientes. It is difficult to overestimate the psychological boost this narrow escape from death gave Obregón. His tactic of fomenting dissension in the Army of the North had worked; perhaps he could still eliminate both Villa and Carranza. His laconic remark when he arrived in Aguascalientes was typical. Asked what he intended to do, he replied: 'Die killing.'

The breach between Villa and Carranza was now overt, and Villa occupied Durango City in preparation for the coming campaign, but first a period of phoney war ensued. Mexico was sick of war and the necessity for a fresh bout of civil conflict had not been explained to the Mexican people; the propagandists and manipulators would first have to be given their heads and, in particular, the generals on both sides needed convincing that they should risk their necks in a personality clash between Villa and Carranza. The uncertainty about US intentions was also a paramount factor, for Wilson's support would be decisive. Much would depend on which side could occupy the moral high ground and pose as the true 'Constitutionalists'. In this sense, two constitutional conventions, at Mexico City and Aguascalientes, were crucial.

Carranza's Mexico City conference, held on 1–5 October, was the brainchild of a man obsessed with control, yet was a dismal failure since everyone but die-hard *carrancistas* boycotted it. Packed with Carranza's stooges and yes-men, the absurd conference was a farce stage-managed by a classical machine politician. Sycophantic resolutions eulogising the First Chief were adopted unanimously and a spurious 'rejection' of Carranza's tendered resignation was bulldozed through. However, after animated debate, the placemen felt obliged, for fear of the military, to endorse the Torreón proviso that the Aguascalientes meeting should be for the military alone. Even Carranza's military supporters regarded the Mexico City proceedings with contempt; the generals on both sides wanted a peaceful settlement. The military junta, meeting under Obregón's aegis at Zacatecas, made it clear that all decisions taken at Mexico City had no validity unless ratified by the more representative convention due to meet a week later at Aguascalientes. Carranza thundered that he would never step aside as presidential candidate and would not be dictated to by a junta of generals, however powerful.

On 10 October the groundbreaking Aguascalientes Convention opened, attended by fifty-seven generals and ninety-five officers. Independents predominated and there was but a handful of *carrancistas*. The *villistas*, only thirty-nine in number, were notable for the moderation of their attitudes and demands and their complaisance towards the 'payroll padding' swathe of *carrancista* officers who represented nobody but Carranza. When twenty-six *zapatista* delegates were added later, the convention was a genuine cross-section of participants in the Revolution – precisely what so infuriated Carranza. The British Minister, taking his cue from the snobbish First Chief in the capital, uncritically reported that the convention 'appears closely to resemble the parliament of monkeys depicted by Mr Kipling in *The Jungle Book*'.

Four main groupings can be identified at Aguascalientes: the *villistas*, the handful of Carranza men, the independents and, later, the *zapatistas*. In the beginning, the *villistas* were the most important, but they were always an uneasy coalition of disparate and fissiparous elements. Many so-called *villistas* were so only in the sense that their rivals in the various states were pro-Carranza. José Maytorena of Sonora was the classic example. Interested only in feathering his own nest, he returned confiscated estates to their former owners in flat defiance of Villa's official policy, while failing to return their traditional lands to the Yaquis, who were supposed to be his main allies. A similar conservative and reactionary stance was adopted by Felipe Riveros, governor of Sinaloa and by the strongman in Tepic, Rafael Bulna. Despite his reverence for Madero, and his express exclusion of their properties from expropriation orders, Villa could not even count on the support of the extended Madero family, which was split, with some members pro-Carranza.

Villa was not prepared to countenance an alliance with former *huertistas* who put out feelers to him, though, short of good officers himself, he saw the point of admitting those who held federal commissions into his ranks. Far more of these joined Villa than Carranza; scholars speculate that Carranza's army was already so professionalised and homogeneous that it could not stand the strain of integrating ex-federals. The most reactionary officers, who had been identified as such, could not find takers either with Villa or Carranza and had to join right-wing forces in Veracruz, Oaxaca and Chiapas if they wanted to continue a military career.

Villa did, however, build bridges to the Catholic Church, rebuffed as it was by Carranza's strident anticlericalism. Villa's attitude to the Church was always ambivalent: he approved in principle of religion and Catholicism, but hated the reality of priestcraft; the clergy he considered thieves, humbugs and exploiters, battening on a credulous and impoverished faithful. Villa once had a stormy scene with Luz Corral because she built a secret chapel in their house; he had it dismantled but Luz had the last word by saying that she would continue to pray for him even though the chapel was no more.

The striking thing about the *villistas* was their willingness to compromise. They were prepared to divide the country into spheres of influence on an 'as is' basis, whereas Carranza insisted on total national domination; they were prepared to have a *carrancista* as president but not Carranza himself, whereas the opposition insisted it had to be the bearded one in person; *villista* proposals formed the basis for credible compromise, whereas Carranza's demands entailed civil war. Most of all, the *villistas* were genuinely trying to find solutions, while Carranza's men attended only to impress gullible observers from the USA. The *carrancistas* at Aguascalientes were a tawdry lot: greedy and venal bourgeois 'proconsuls' who were even more ruthless in their pursuit of wealth than Urbina or Hipólito Villa. Their propaganda for Carranza was confused and self-contradictory: at one moment he was to be the new strongman, though presumably Mexico had had enough of Huertas by now; at another he was supposed to represent 'civilisation' versus barbarism; then, he was alleged to be the only one who could stand up to Washington.

The insincerity and grasping ambition of Carranza was obvious to everyone at Aguascalientes except his cronies. Villa, by contrast, was totally sincere in his desire neither to be president of Mexico nor to impose anyone else, though he did hope that Felipe Ángeles would 'emerge' once the delegates had time to appreciate his qualities. Villa even offered to resign in favour of Obregón's candidate Eulalio Gutiérrez, provided Carranza did the same; in 'joking but serious' mode he even suggested that both he and Carranza be shot to solve the nation's problems. Needless to say, neither solution commended itself to Carranza. Sensing that opinion in the capital was turning against him, he suddenly decamped to Puebla, which was commanded by his most loyal general. Feeling secure there, Carranza behaved defiantly towards the Convention, claiming that Villa had not resigned his candidacy as president and proposing machiavellian schemes for the simultaneous withdrawal of himself and Villa, all ingeniously structured so that he would retain all the cards and Villa emerge powerless.

The *villista* faction at Aguascalientes was led by Felipe Ángeles and Roque González Garza, the man who had saved Obregón the month before. Ángeles was the key figure, aiming to build an alliance with Zapata; Garza, on the other hand, more and more inclined to Obregón. If anything, the autonomous power of the *villistas* gradually dwindled during the month's deliberations at Aguascalientes while that of the independent grouping grew. The leaders of the independents were Eulalio Gutiérrez, the acting president of the republic and General Lucio Blanco, the brilliant, left-leaning cavalry officer who had been shabbily treated by Carranza. The independent group gradually made more and more inroads on Villa's partisans, attracting away from him the intellectuals who had hoped for high Cabinet position in a Villa administration: José Vasconcelos, Eugenio Aguirre Benavides and José Isabel Robles.

The real star of the Convention was Obregón, the only one of the 'big four' to attend in person. Obregón's oratory, wit and charm and his patent reasonableness made a great hit and convinced many waverers that the future lay with him rather than Villa. Both Zapata and Villa made a bad psychological error in not attending the Convention. The *zapatistas* had originally not been invited, but on 12 October Ángeles proposed that their presence was necessary to make this a truly national gathering. The Convention approved a motion inviting them, and to Ángeles himself was delegated the task of persuading the notoriously unpredictable and crossgrained Zapata to take part. Ángeles hoped that Zapata might respect him because of his social origins and the honourable way he had fought the *zapatistas* in earlier campaigns. He took the precaution of including peasant leaders in his delegation, to point up the contrast with Carranza, who in his September overtures had sent merely generals and bureaucrats to Morelos.

All Ángeles's best hopes were fulfilled when he and his delegation met Zapata in Cuernavaca on 18 October. Zapata greeted Ángeles cordially: 'General, you do not know how glad I am to see you. You were the only one who fought honestly against me and by your acts of justice you succeeded in gaining the goodwill of the people of Morelos and even the sympathy of my men.' He was equally affable with Calixto Contreras: 'I am also happy to see you in Morelos, General, since, as a son of the poor and a fighter for land, you are the revolutionary in the north who inspires the greatest confidence in me.' Even so, he told Ángeles that he could not simply order his delegates to go to Aguascalientes as requested; first he would have to consult the various *zapatista* chiefs. Ángeles urged him to send delegates as a matter or urgency, arguing somewhat speciously that unless the *zapatistas* were seen to be present at Aguascalientes as part of a genuinely national Convention, Woodrow Wilson might finally lose patience and order an invasion.

In reality Zapata was in a bind, pulled this way and that by conflicting impulses. On the one hand, having accepted overlordship of his movement twice before, by Madero and Orozco, with disastrous results, he would never again consent to abdicate as leader. On the other, he wanted an alliance with Villa – indeed his entire diplomacy since November 1913 had been geared to that end – and he could scarcely refuse to take part in the Aguascalientes Convention without snubbing Villa. Moreover, he was in a chicken-and-egg dilemma: he could not recognise the Convention until it accepted the Plan of Ayala, but how could it do so if he did not send delegates north to persuade them, which in turn meant *de facto* recognition of the Convention? He solved the conundrum by legerdemain. The men he sent north would be 'commissioners' who could become official delegates once the Convention endorsed the Plan of Ayala. To leave his options open, he appointed his intellectual advisers rather than the peasant leaders as the commissioners. This action was unanimously backed by the other *zapatista* leaders. As John Womack puts it: 'Afraid, like Zapata, of betraying their people, they turned over the chances of doing so to the intellectuals they had always at heart despised.'

Twenty-six commissioners, led by Paulino Martínez, prepared to make the journey north. However, it very soon became clear that Zapata aimed primarily at a political alliance with Villa and thought the Convention a mere talking shop, for on 26 October the train carrying the *zapatistas* steamed straight through Aguascalientes, and deposited the commissioners at Villa's headquarters at Guadalupe. This action marked the effective beginning of the Villa–Zapata alliance. Paulino Martínez made a speech praising Villa and Zapata as 'the genuine representatives . . . of this Homeric struggle . . . Indians both of them'. Martínez and Ángeles agreed that the alliance strategy at the Convention must be to force Carranza to reveal himself in his true autocratic colours and to promote Villa as Mexico's next president.

If Paulino Martínez was the *zapatista* doyen of quiet diplomacy, when the commissioners finally took their seats at Aguascalientes, it was the firecracker oratory of Soto y Gama that attracted most attention. Aguascalientes was this man's true metier, for in Morelos he was always under the shadow of Palafox. Promoted to 'colonel' in order to meet the requirement that all delegates had to be from the military, and dressing in the white peasant clothes of Morelos as if he had spent a lifetime toiling in the fields, Soto y Gama impressed some as an orator while appearing to others as a charlatan. In his speech to the assembly he began by ripping up the Mexican flag, declaring himself an anarchist who, following Kropotkin, had to destroy all abstractions that oppressed the masses. This act of secular sacrilege had some of the generals in the audience reaching for their revolvers, while others tried to rush the platform.

When order was restored, Soto y Gama treated those who remained and had not walked out in protest to a seminar on Russian anarchism. He seemed to take a delight in alienating all factions present, whether they were followers of Magón, Carranza or Villa. He pointed out that *Tierra y Libertad*, the revolutionary slogan taken over from the *magonistas* also came from Russia: Ricardo Flores Magón had simply stolen it from Alexander Herzen. He created a sensation by an intemperate and splenetic attack on Carranza. He then told the *villista* delegates they could not hope to understand the Indians in the south, before launching into a synthesis of world history, which featured Zapata as a kind of grand fusion of Buddha, Marx and Francis of Assisi. Despite attempts by enraged *carrancistas* to interrupt the speech or rush the platform, Soto y Gama secured a standing ovation for his final words: '*Viva Villa! Viva Zapata!*'

Despite the immediate applause, most delegates on reflection considered that Soto y Gama was a suitable case for instant medical certification. Yet there was method in his madness. His role was to whip up emotion while Ángeles worked behind the scenes to cement a Villa-Zapata alliance. Both Ángeles and Soto y Gama agreed that the core weakness in the *zapatista* movement was that it was a local movement not a national one, and that the best way to make Zapata face his national responsibilities was to put him in a position of power where he had no choice. To an extent the smokescreen tactics worked. Other speakers arose to denounce Soto y Gama as a purely verbal socialist, but got sucked into the intellectual quicksands as the debate became more and more precious and rarefied. In the end, with speakers citing Pliny, Voltaire, Rousseau, Spencer, Darwin and Nietzsche, the spiritual paraffin of academe was overpowering in its odour.

On paper the *zapatistas* scored a great victory at Aguascalientes. After a lot of horse-trading, the Convention agreed to sign up to the Plan of Ayala 'in principle' and accepted Articles 4, 6, 7, 8, 9 and 12 as the basis for any future constitution. This showed how far the Revolution had already travelled in the direction of real socio-economic change. For the first time in Mexican history a sovereign body had committed itself to large-scale agrarian reform; the immense influence of Zapata on the Mexican Revolution was clear for all to see. Zapata responded by recognising the Convention's sovereignty *de facto*, but he made it clear that complete *de jure* recognition would follow only when the body had dealt decisively with Carranza and removed him as First Chief. On 30 October Obregón and Ángeles colluded to pass a resolution in closed session which voted by 112 to 21 to dismiss Carranza.

Doubtless Carranza, who pulled the last of his forces out of Mexico City on 4 November, was alarmed by the size of the vote against him, but through his intransigence he had only himself to blame. He replied to the request for his immediate resignation by stalling. He cabled Aguascalientes to say that before he resigned he needed to see the shape of the interim regime that would draw up the new constitution; also, Villa and Zapata must resign their commands and go into exile. Clearly these were impossible demands made by a man with not the slightest intention of resigning. Carranza claimed that his study of French history had left him with a contempt for the 'assemblyism' of the French Revolution. It had obviously not left him with a similar contempt for Napoleonic autocracy, for his every word, every gesture even, conveyed the message that he, and only he, could channel the Revolution into its correct conduits.

Amazingly, the Convention agreed to the three conditions and again asked for Carranza's resignation. The moderate attitude of the Convention was the result of the emergence of a 'third force' under Obregón and the election as provisional president on 2 November of Eulalio Gutiérrez. Obregón, working hard to prevent the *villistas* and *zapatistas* from steamrollering the Convention, was the agency behind Gutiérrez's election. After getting Ángeles to agree that Villa should resign, so as to cut the ground from under Carranza's feet, Obregón surprisingly lobbied for the election of Gutiérrez, an ex-miner and political nonentity. Obregón had been widely expected to support Juan Cabral of Sonora for the post, but Cabral had alienated Obregón by his commitment to radical land reform and through being too much his own man.

Gutiérrez reiterated the demand for Carranza's resignation. After stalling for four days, Carranza sent another cable from Córdoba in Veracruz state, making it clear he regarded himself as above the law: now he said he would resign only *after* his three demands had been met. Gutiérrez conferred with the best minds at the Convention. José Vasconcelos wrote an opinion that from the viewpoint of constitutional law it was crystal clear that sovereignty resided in the Constitutionalist Army rather than in the person of Carranza, and that Carranza was consequently as plainly a rebel as ever a rebel could be. On 10 November the Convention declared Carranza to be in open rebellion. Gutiérrez appointed Villa 'general in chief' and chief of all operations designed to put down the insurrection.

Unfortunately the trigger-happy Villa compounded his original mistake in not attending the Convention by not waiting until the constitutional law had run its course. Before Gutiérrez declared Carranza a rebel, Villa lost patience with the endless second chances seemingly being offered to the First Chief and sent his troops into Aguascalientes. To save face, Gutiérrez had to pretend that he had invited him, but the final sessions of the Convention took place with 30,000 *villista* soldiers billeted in the town. This ham-fisted action alienated many of the 'third way' delegates who were still attempting an eleventh-hour reconciliation with Carranza. The most important man so alienated was Obregón. Initially close to Ángeles, and deeply critical of Carranza's autocratic behaviour, he found, like many liberals in many eras, that third ways are unviable. He faced a stark choice: Villa or Carranza. After his recent bruising experiences with Villa, it is hardly surprising that he chose Carranza.

Obregón, even more than Ángeles, had dominated the Convention and when he chose to throw in his lot with Carranza, many of those who had been present at Aguascalientes went with him, including even some former *villistas*. Villa's great mistake had been to hold himself aloof and come into town only for the signing of the final protocol, allowing Obregón to reap all the rewards of charismatic leadership. Zapata's error had been even more egregious, for he had neither entered wholeheartedly into the business of the Convention nor boycotted it and thus ended up with the worst of both worlds. Zapata was now ineluctably involved with the national struggle even though he was uninterested in it. As Womack remarks: 'In letting their secretaries involve them with Villa, the Morelos chiefs had thus committed their people to a fight that was not theirs.' Zapata could be in no doubt about the outcome of Aguascalientes and, even if he was, Villa soon put him in the picture. In a sombre letter written on 10 November Villa told him that the men who had defeated Huerta were now doomed to fight each other. The Revolution had already become a genuine civil war.

On the evening of 24 November 1914, as the last *carrancistas* left, the *zapatista* vanguard tentatively entered Mexico City. The *zapatistas* found evidence of the most malign vandalism by Carranza, supposedly the torchbearer of 'civilisation' against barbarism. The mint and all government archives had been plundered; vast numbers of horses, trainloads of paintings and other spoils, huge caches of ammunition and *matériel*, all had been spirited away in railway cars, leaving the Mexican railway system in paralysis; as a *pièce de résistance* Carranza's generals attached the railway track to Veracruz to a locomotive, so that it was progressively ripped up as the engine chugged slowly forward. The irony was that Carranza's vandals then entered a Veracruz recently evacuated by the US Marines which the Americans had left as an object lesson in city management – a town so clean and hygienic that its fabled vultures had had to seek sustenance elsewhere.

Zapata's men came not as conquerors or marauders but as awe-struck sightseers, gaping at the unusual features of the city. They were peaceful, deferential, simple folk, the classic country cousins up for the day in the big city, naïvely carrying banners of the Virgin of Guadalupe and displaying their rustic origins by their coarse white cotton clothes, Franciscan sandals and big straw hats. They wandered the streets like lost children, begging and panhandling for coins from passers-by, knocking on doors and politely asking if they could have some food. A terrified *flâneur* was approached by a group of *zapatistas* wielding machetes who, he was convinced, wanted to kill him. However, they took off their huge sombreros, threaded them circularly through their fingers, and said in humble voices: 'Young master, could you let us have a little money?' The most famous story is that the *zapatistas* opened fire on a clanging fire-engine speeding to an emergency, thinking it a kind of primitive tank, and killed twelve firemen.

To the amazement of Mexico City's bourgeoisie, there were no expropriations, except of houses belonging to Morelos planters. It was not long before the middle classes were pointing to the absence of speeches, proscriptions and confiscations, praising Zapata to the skies and contrasting him with the predatory and aggressive Carranza and Obregón. Where Villa and his chiefs always made straight for the most luxurious houses once they occupied a city, Zapata displayed a Cato-like asceticism by staying in a dingy third-class hotel a block away from the railway depot. He left city administration to his underlings and delegated to his brother Eufemio the task of showing provisional president Eulalio Gutiérrez around the presidential palace.

The man who four years earlier was an obscure village leader in Morelos was now master of Mexico City. To the oft-whispered question by an anxious urban bourgeoisie – 'what does he want?' – there was only one answer: nothing. Zapata always hated the national capital and could hardly wait to return to Morelos, but there was more than caprice or personal predilection involved here. A dislike of cities was imbricated in the entire *zapatista* ideology, for cities represented the power of the state and its full-time officials, the ultimate anathema for all attracted by anarchism. Zapatismo was always revolutionary in its visions and aspirations, but it was never so in the Leninist sense of aiming to capture the apparatus of the state and imposing a national ideology.

Few political movements have been more misunderstood than the one headed by Emiliano Zapata. Anarchism is a useful shorthand tag, as long as one appreciates that Zapata merely wanted the euthanasia of all bosses, owners and overseers. In no sense was he actuated by full-blooded anarchistic theory like that of Bakunin, which was anyway an urban theory reflecting the concerns of city dwellers. The peasants of Morelos, with their white pyjamas and banners of the revered Virgin of Guadalupe, were light-years away from the atheistic Russian anarchists. Bakunin was noted for puritanism and asceticism, but Zapatismo was characterised by a free and easy hedonism of the traditional Mexican kind, where drinking, cock-fighting, playing cards and making love to women were the staples of existence. Even in his later years Zapata himself liked to chew the fat with his men in the plaza, chomping his trademark cigar and sipping brandy while he discussed horses, game-cocks, the weather, farm prices and other peasant concerns.

There was a soupçon of Bakunin only in Zapata's hostility to the state, his dislike of the railway (which was politically inspired rather than Luddite) and his cult of simplicity. The uniform of white pyjamas became almost *de rigueur* in Morelos, even for government officials; in villages anyone wearing trousers, a shirt or boots risked being derided as a *catrín*, a dandy. It was said with justification that in Morelos the grand 'coming out' ball had given way to the bullfight, the frock coat and top hat to the baggy white drawers and sarapes. There was perhaps some similarity to Russian rural anarchism, too, in Zapata's dream of a peasant utopia of free villages, with 'small is beautiful' units (families, clans, villages) enjoying self-government and autarky, bonded together in a loose, voluntary association. The Mexican Revolution progressively worked in Zapata's favour in this regard, as it replaced loyalty to landlord and *jefe político* with commitment to village, cacique and local community. The role of political thought in Zapatismo can be overstated. Although Zapata listened respectfully whenever his intellectuals spoke about the finer points of anarchism, in his own mind he was satisfied that all his true political aspirations were already contained in the Plan of Ayala.

One might remark, parenthetically, that once again we note the paradox that intellectuals played a greater role with Villa than with Zapata, even though Zapatismo was, by common consent, the more revolutionary movement. Many factors can be adduced to explain this: Villa's greater bedazzlement by academic learning; the simplicity, economy and coherence of Zapatismo; and, most of all, the fact that Zapata appealed only to anarchists and Christian mystics. Intellectuals of the democratic-liberal kind opted for Villa, as the heir of Madero and a proven campaigner against political corruption. Most of these intellectual liberals vehemently denied Carranza's claim to be Juárez's spiritual heir and insisted that that honour go to Villa instead, as the embodiment of the spirit of Madero; they insisted, rightly, that in the main only cynics and pragmatists opted for Carranza. Villa liked to play up to this version of himself by learning great chunks of Juárez's 1857 Constitution and reciting it to his intellectuals. Fearing the social convulsion that would follow from real reforms in the area of land and labour, the *villista* intellectuals were concerned mainly with political and educational, rather than socio-economic, change and viewed the Centaur as a *tabula rasa* on which they could make their own impressions. Villa always liked to indulge this illusion. Zapata, by contrast, always kept his intellectuals firmly in their place, allowing them occasional furloughs, as at the Aguascalientes Convention.

The core of Zapata's own beliefs was his mystical feeling for the land, 'the mother who nourishes us and cares for us', in the words of St Francis of Assisi in the *Canticle of Beings*. The ideology of Zapata, then, envisaging a free association of landowning villages, was fundamentally nostalgic, backward-looking and defensive. This does not mean it was non-revolutionary; as more than one commentator has pointed out, the Golden Age of the revolutionary can be located in the past as well as the future. This communalist vision of a society free from bosses, caudillos and the subordination of the civilian to the military, was communalistic but emphatically not communist. How far Zapata was from communism or socialism can be gauged from a conversation he held with Soto y Gama which was reported as follows:

SOTO Y GAMA: Emiliano, what do you think of communism?
ZAPATA: Explain it to me.
SOTO Y GAMA: For example, all the people of a village farm put their lands together and then they distribute the harvest equally.
ZAPATA: Who makes the distribution?
SOTO Y GAMA: A representative, or a council elected by the community.
ZAPATA: Well, look, as far as I'm concerned, if any 'somebody' . . . would try to distribute the fruits of my labour in that way . . . I would fill him full of bullets.

As he took stock of the situation in his dingy downtown hotel, Zapata saw four main problems confronting him. He was unable to export his revolution to Mexico's 'deep south'; even in Zapata-controlled areas, he faced the headache of endemic banditry; his own programme seemed out of kilter with the other main currents in the Revolution; and, above all, he could not see the enduring basis on which he could construct an alliance with Villa. There was the further worry that Zapatismo always threatened to leave its founder behind by evolving a different character in different localities. Although Zapata could take pride in land distribution effected in his name in no less than nine states, and although there was a massive transfer of power and resources to peasants and away from landlords and caciques, the Revolution went its own way even in nominally *zapatista* states. In Guerrero, for instance, refusal to pay rents had always been a more important factor than the struggle of village and hacienda, while in Hidalgo and Puebla peasants virtually abolished the sugar-cane industry by invading hacienda land and growing staples like corn and beans there instead of sugar.

In the 'deep south' of Oaxaca, Chiapas, Yucatán and Quintana Roo, the Revolution had so far had little impact, with harvests of coffee and henequen largely unaffected. The hacienda owners in these areas had learned nothing from the events of 1910–14 and all the old abuses – beatings, *droit du seigneur*, debt peonage – continued as before. Indeed, as the new ideas from the north drifted down into south-eastern Mexico, they produced a ferocious backlash from the *hacendados*. Whereas the power of the landlords had been blunted or destroyed in Chihuahua, Durango, Morelos, San Luis and Tlaxcala, because the military power of the revolutionaries there was irresistible, in Yucatán and the south opposition to the old order was weak and sporadic. Zapata could not spare the resources to export rebellion there, even if he had been prepared to conduct military operations outside his *patria chica*, which he was not. Consequently the south-east became a battleground between *hacendados* and the 'proconsuls' Carranza had sent there to make his writ run. The landlords were able to exploit the devout religiosity of the peasants against the anticlerical *carrancistas* in this struggle, but it was abundantly clear that all hope of spontaneous and effective *zapatista* revolt was in vain.

A more serious problem for Zapata was banditry. The hallmark of the Revolution, as in all revolutions, was confusion. In the chaos, ruthless and clear-sighted individuals had a unique opportunity to grab for themselves and to settle all manner of local disputes and personal vendettas under the umbrella of 'the revolution'. *Tierra y libertad* was a slogan used to 'legitimate' any number of family quarrels, blood feuds, sectarian disputes and even the murder of rivals in love or business. The Juchiteco revolt in Oaxaca, ostensibly part of the Revolution, was in fact an ancient conflict, and the locals took advantage of the revolutionary situation to revive it. Furthermore, lacking leaders of the calibre of Zapata, agrarian reform movements in states far from the epicentre at Morelos tended to lapse into jacquerie or banditry. Non-political jacqueries were a particular feature of west-central Mexico, which had remained deaf to the initial call to arms from Madero in 1910.

Outright banditry was a particularly prevalent offshoot of the Revolution. Scholars debate the peculiar socio-economic circumstances in which bandits are apt to arise and whether their 'revolt' can be said to have social content. If in any given state the hacienda was too powerful as an institution for organised political opposition, the enemies of the hacienda tended to appear in the guise of bandits. On the other hand, many bandit chiefs cooperated with whichever side, revolutionary or reactionary, would pay them the most. Was the declared social content to the bandits' revolt mere verbal window-dressing to justify loot, or was it genuinely based? 'Social banditry', like the terrorism/freedom fighting antinomy, is a peculiarly thorny question. A man lacking the ability or objective possibilities of launching a guerrilla movement in support of agrarian reform, as Zapata did in Morelos, could well have no outlet for social protest other than banditry. There is no doubt that hard and fast distinctions are impossible, for a chief of brigands operating legitimately as a 'social bandit' in state X could be said to be an illegitimate terrorist when extending his operations into state Y; so much depends on the context. One generalisation that holds good in the Mexican Revolution is that mining areas were largely free from banditry.

Unfortunately for Zapata, bandits inspired purely by loot and the desire to rape and kill with impunity fastened on the identical victims targeted by the *zapatistas* – principally haciendas and trains – and justified their bloodthirsty marauding as Zapatismo. Genovevo de la O's assaults on trains were widely copied, though for the genuine bandit the troops on the train were not the target. To capture a train established a brigand leader in peasant mythology, and such men were careless of the consequences. The most famous such case was the seizure of locomotive No. 789 near Aguascalientes. The bandit leader simply opened the throttle and sent the train pounding away through northern Jalisco. Luckily there was no other traffic on the line and the empty loco finally ran out of steam thirty miles away, near Encarnación.

Zapata was unfortunate also in that his heartlands were traditional hotbeds of banditry. Puebla, Guerrero and Michoacán were all states with a fearsome reputation for brigandage. These were all areas characterised by sparse population, poor communications, few villages and absentee landlords, where the population was concentrated in towns and the people comprised a rural proletariat rather than a peasantry proper. By 1918 in Michoacán Zapata's influence had largely been eclipsed by local bandits with bloodthirsty reputations. Even in Morelos during the years after 1915, banditry was an acute problem and bandit chiefs arose to dispute the hegemony of the *zapatistas*. Already, in late 1914, Zapata saw the danger. His own movement was broad-based and coherent, but he had noticed how even a state like Durango threatened to dissolve into warlordism when the strong hand of Villa was removed. The *villista* presence there simply overlaid a pre-existing pattern of conflict between Tomás Urbina, Orestes Pereyra and Calixto Contreras who controlled the cotton country and the Arrieta brothers who dominated the mountains.

Yet another issue for Zapata to ponder was the Janus face of the Revolution and how this affected his own programme. There had always been a dualism in the Revolution, with a collectivist ideology running in tandem with a capitalist one. This was because the hacienda was both a means of oppressing the peasantry and depriving them of traditional rights *and* a fetter on capitalism. In 1910, therefore, the hacienda had come under attack from two directions simultaneously: from peasants (mainly, though not exclusively, in the south) demanding land reform, and from northern entrepreneurs keen to use more advanced technologies. Zapata himself was neither pro-capitalist nor anti-capitalist. He was quite prepared to be an entrepreneur himself, but he insisted on the primacy of the political over the economic: he would not allow the principle of profit maximisation to override the principle of independence and autarky for the villages.

This illustrates the wider point that it is impossible to portray people like Villa and Zapata as 'anti-capitalist', just as Mexican landowners cannot be pinned down as being either 'feudal' or 'capitalist'; some were one, some the other, some were neither. A similar inadequacy attends the usual typology of the 'big four' of the Mexican Revolution: Carranza bourgeois, Obregón petit-bourgeois, Zapata peasant revolutionary, Villa social bandit. As Alan Knight has pointed out, it is fruitless to analyse the Mexican Revolution in Marxist terms, for much of it was the work of 'secondary' classes (peasantry, petite-bourgeoisie) who were in no sense the surrogates of the bourgeoisie or the proletariat. The great social change that occurred in the years 1876–1920 is not necessarily a pat and formulaic transition from an alleged 'feudalism' to an alleged 'capitalism'. This is why many scholars play safe and simply refer to Mexico as in 'permanent transition' throughout the twentieth century.

The great class struggle in the Mexican Revolution was that of peasant against landlord. It was Zapata's political genius to understand that the differences between these classes were irreconcilable in a way that the famous Marxist conflict of workers and capitalists was not. Zapata also realised that the Obregóns and Carranzas represented a new type of commercial capitalism which was yet another threat to the ancient modalities of peasant communities, and the Revolution had entered a new phase, to determine which of these values should prevail. This explains much of Zapata's so-called obstinacy and what has been described as his 'dour, suspicious, protective' attitude. For all that, Zapata was not blind to the virtue of producing economic goods to make a surplus. He condemned the attitude of the *zapatistas* in neighbouring states who destroyed their sugar industry to produce subsistence crops. Although living standards in those states (Puebla, Guerrero) improved in the short term, there was no surplus from which the poor and needy could be sustained, or armies of self-defence armed and equipped. For this reason he built four new sugar mills in Morelos and tried to nudge his followers towards a market-oriented economy, instead of subsistence crops of corn and beans.

It is important to be clear that Zapata had no reverence for entrepreneurship as such; its importance in his mind always depended on how far it could bolster and sustain his peasant utopia. In any conflict between ancient rights and customs and new technologies, no matter how efficient, Zapata always came down on the side of tradition. He once hauled over the coals a young university-trained agronomist who had been recruited to Morelos to work on land-partitioning. Zapata rebuked him thus: 'The villagers say that this stone wall is the boundary. You're going to draw the line along it for me. You engineers often care a lot about straight lines but the boundary is going to be this stone wall, even if you have to work for six months measuring all the ins and outs.'

Yet the most immediately pressing of Zapata's problems concerned the proposed alliance with Villa. Zapata was well aware that in many ways the two great revolutionary leaders were poles and worlds apart. He never wavered in his commitment to agrarian reform and local self-government, and the only political compromise he would ever make was to ally himself with anyone hostile to a common enemy. This incorruptibility was what enabled him to survive nine years of constant fighting and ever-present danger. Villa was always more of a political pragmatist, both by temperament and because the social structure of the north demanded it. The Zapata movement was coherent, focused on a strong core, dedicated to a relatively straightforward form of class warfare; the Villa movement was a trans-class coalition, embracing military colonists, agricultural workers, miners, railwaymen, industrial workers, the middle class and even some reformed *hacendados*. Villismo was heterogeneous, eclectic and fissiparous: it did not have one single goal, but several, often mutually contradictory.

The chief reason for the uncertain political profile of Villismo was the dominance in the movement of the *rancheros*. The ranchers were politically ambiguous and ambivalent, sometimes functioning as a brake on the Revolution, sometimes as an accelerator. In states where the *hacendados* dominated, the *rancheros* were their natural enemy; in states where the hacienda was insignificant as an institution, the ranchers tended to fill the hegemonic gap and to be as reactionary as the *hacendados* elsewhere. There was always a tendency with the northern caudillos to turn on the revolutionaries who had fought for them, to tax them or press-gang them. Like Villa himself in his early life, the *rancheros* played the role of the *gabelloti* in the Sicilian Mafia, quite prepared to ally themselves with oppressor or oppressed as occasion demanded. Usually their profile was as counter-revolutionary figures. Good examples were in Guanajuato, Michoacán and Jalisco, where they were conservative, Catholic figures, uninterested in revolution.

This should have meant that the Villa movement could accommodate easily to any regime in Mexico City, but the concern for local autonomy – which too often simply meant warlordism – had the result that *villistas* were just as incompatible with Mexico City technocrats as the *zapatistas*. The Figueroa brothers, who challenged Zapata in Morelos and Puebla in 1912, were classic examples of *villistas avant la lettre*, unable to coexist either with Zapata, Madero or Félix Díaz. This made *villistas* naturally suspect to Zapata. He realised that Villa's land reforms were the product of expediency not conviction or, as Alan Knight puts it: 'In Morelos *agrarismo* dictated the character of the civil war, in the north the civil war dictated the character of *agrarismo*.' In the north the existing economic system had to be kept in being to finance the war; in Morelos Zapata first undertook the distribution of lands and then looked around for finance for the peasant armies to defend it.

Above all, Villismo and Zapatismo represented a conflict of different values. Entrepreneurship was a desirable goal in itself in the north: that is why land reform there delivered most of the land into the hands of smallholders and *rancheros*, rather than to the communal villages or *ejidos* of Morelos. In the north there was always more concern with power and resources for the leaders, rather than with peasant or communal interests. Always there was the clash of the southern programme of communal ownership and the northern policy of confiscating great estates to give them to independent smallholders; but at least Villa did not want to return the land to the original owners, as Carranza did. Villa headed a movement that was primarily concerned with *political* revolt and the transfer of national power; Zapata headed a movement that was primarily social, concerned purely with land ownership in Morelos. Zapata and his followers revelled in parochialism. They even developed their own canting slang to hold outsiders at a distance: a 'buddy' was a *vale* (literally 'a voucher'); 'fun' (*el gusto*) meant trick riding and roping steers; *quebrar* ('to bust') meant 'to shoot'; *pobre* (poor) was pronounced *probe*, *somos* (we are) as *semos*, *fue* (it was) as *hue*, and so on.

The differences extended to points of lifestyle. Zapata was a genuine man of the people, but the northern caudillos lived in some splendour, aping the lives of the *hacendados* they had overthrown. To confiscate an estate and then live on it like a lord, surrounded by flunkeys and retainers, was the abiding ambition of the northern caudillos. Orozco diversified into mining, transport and retailing, while Urbina retired to a luxurious palace in Durango. Whereas in Chihuahua *villista* roughnecks occupied the confiscated haciendas and later, in Mexico City, camped in the mansions of the rich, in Morelos it was the young technocrats and agronomists who occupied the deserted 'big houses' of the vanished planters.

All this helps to explain the deep suspicion entertained by Zapata for Villa and the *villistas*, the enforced allies with whom he was now to share the occupation of Mexico City. Arriving in the capital on 26 November, Zapata refused to attend ceremonies in his honour at the National Palace or to give interviews to reporters. Hearing that Villa had occupied the northern suburbs without consulting him, Zapata decamped a few days later, doing another of his famous vanishing acts and reappearing in Morelos. So alarmed was Villa that he sent a special delegation (consisting of Carothers, Serratos and Juan Bandera) to Cuernavaca to assure Zapata of his good wishes. The envoys delivered a personal letter, in which Villa guaranteed his ally his personal safety, stressed that Carranza would rejoice if there was no Villa–Zapata accord, and offered to meet Zapata on 4 December at the floating gardens of Xochimilco just outside Mexico City. Zapata accepted.

To guide him through the tricky negotiations with Zapata, Villa predictably turned to Felipe Ángeles, whose advice was blunt: in no circumstances allow Zapata to operate independently against Carranza. 'Zapata is a revolutionary, but knows nothing of war,' Ángeles said. 'His "army" doesn't deserve the name. He doesn't have a single general of any talent. If he asks to take control of operations in the south, don't let him. This is the time to chase Carranza to Veracruz . . . If you give Carranza time to regroup, who knows what will happen.'

As his principal adviser for the meeting Zapata chose Paulino Martínez, not a particularly happy choice, as Villa hated him. Zapata had hoped to build bridges to the peasant leaders in the Villa movement, such as Calixto Contreras, but by late 1914 most of the important ones were dead: Toribio Ortega died of typhus and Porfirio Talamantes was killed at the battle of Tierra Blanca. Apart from Contreras, the main peasant leader remaining with Villa was the intellectual González Garza. As mediators Villa and Zapata agreed on two men. The first was General Benigno Serrato who, much later in Mexican history, would be governor of Michoacán and struggle for political supremacy there with future president Lázaro Cárdenas. The second was Juan Banderas, the Sinaloan who had been with Villa in jail in 1912 and then joined Zapata; he had already been acting as broker between *villistas* and *zapatistas* at the Aguascalientes conference.

On 4 December at Xochimilco the two great figures of the Mexican Revolution finally met for the first and almost only time. If we conflate the meeting on 4 December with another two days later – the only occasions on which the two men encountered each other – we are justified in regarding this as one of those great meetings of history where complementary protagonists met just once, putting the Xochimilco affair in the same category as the encounter of Nelson and Wellington in 1805 or that between Hitler and Franco at Hendaye in 1940. However, perhaps the most salient comparison is between the Villa–Zapata conclave and that of Simón Bolívar and José de San Martín at Guayaquil in 1824. In both cases it was the liberator of the south who was discomfited and the liberator of the north who held centre stage thereafter.

Decked with flowers and bunting as if for a fiesta, the high school at Xochimilco was the unlikely venue for the meeting. There was a mariachi band and a choir of children singing *corridos*. Zapata arrived first with his aides, his sister María de Jesús and her infant son, his cousin Amador Salazar and a formidable bodyguard. Asleep in a pair of white cotton trousers was Zapata's son. Also present was an American observer, León Cánova, representing the US State Department. Promptly at noon Villa arrived with his escort. It fell to Otilio Montaño to introduce the two men, who then pushed their way into a packed schoolhouse and went upstairs to an improvised conference room. The principals sat down at a large oval table, where they were jostled by about sixty enthusiasts who crowded around them, and where Cánova observed them minutely and attempted a verbatim transcript of their conversation.

Cánova first of all noted the obvious physical differences between the two men. Villa weighed 180 pounds, had a florid complexion 'like a German', and was much taller than Zapata who, at 130 pounds was short, dark and thin-faced. In their contrasting garb, the two looked like men from very different spheres. Villa wore a pith helmet, a heavy brown sweater, khaki trousers, leggings and heavy riding boots. Zapata, ever the dandy, had donned a lavender shirt, a short black coat and two neckerchiefs, a large blue silk one with a green border and another in a multi-coloured floral pattern. He also wore black, tight-fitting *charro* trousers with silver buttons down the outside seam of each leg and two old-fashioned flat gold rings on his left hand. Topping off the outfit was a huge sombrero, useful for shading the sun outside but absurdly dysfunctional here. The snobbish Cánova remarked that Zapata's sister's entire outfit, clothes, jewellery and all, could have been purchased in the USA for five dollars.

Observers made much of the signs, symbols and subtexts of the unwritten sumptuary code at Xochimilco. Villa's men looked like soldiers, with khaki uniforms supplied from the USA, standard issue firearms and rank tabs clearly displayed. Zapata's men looked exactly like the southern Mexican peasants they were, dressed in white cotton shirts, rustic sandals and a heterogeneous assortment of weaponry. Villa was making the point with his ubiquitous khaki that he commanded a professional army that was the arbiter of Mexico's destiny. Zapata, dressed as though he were about to cut a dash at a country fair, was underlining the notion that the civilian ethos should always take precedence over the military. The sartorial differences formed a kind of objective correlative of the ideological differences discussed above.

Cánova, who wrote up his account of the meeting for the State Department, reported that the atmosphere was initially frosty and that it took half an hour for the ice to thaw: 'It was interesting and amusing to watch Villa and Zapata trying to get acquainted with each other. For half an hour they sat in an embarrassed silence, occasionally broken by some insignificant remark, like two country sweethearts.' Zapata seemed to study Villa for a long time without saying anything. Then Villa achieved a breakthrough by making a disparaging remark about Carranza. 'I always said so,' Zapata agreed. 'I always told them Carranza was a sonofabitch.' For an hour the two of them tried to outdo each other with anti-Carranza stories. Finally Zapata called for cognac and insisted that the teetotal Villa join him in a toast to their partnership. According to Cánova, Villa took a gulp and 'nearly strangled. His face contorted and tears sprang to his eyes while he huskily called for water.' Having purged the taste with water, he offered the rest of his glass to his revolutionary colleague. Zapata, who was enjoying himself and may have pre-planned Villa's alcoholic discomfiture, insisted that the big man drain the glass.

Feeling more at ease with each other, the two men gradually found common ground. Both stated vehemently that they had no personal political ambitions and just wanted a free hand in their own spheres of influence. Zapata's stance was a moral one: he was contemptuous of all full-time politicans. As he told Villa, 'These *cabrones* [referring to politicians] . . . as soon as they see an opportunity, they want to turn it to their advantage and they move in to brown-nose the most powerful man around. That's why I've busted all those *cabrones*. I can't stand them . . . they're all a pack of bastards.' Villa's position was that he lacked the education and background to be president. His explanation to Zapata was a virtual carbon copy of the words he had used to John Reed: 'I am a fighter, not a statesman. I am not educated enough to be president. I only learned to read and write properly two years ago. How could I, who never went to school, hope to be able to talk to foreign ambassadors and the cultivated gentlemen of Congress. It would be bad for Mexico if an uneducated man were to be president.' The two agreed, however, that the next president would have to be under their control. 'We'll just appoint the ones who aren't going to make trouble,' Villa said. Zapata replied: 'I'll advise all our friends to be very careful. If not, they will feel the blows of the machete.'

At mention of the machete there was general laughter. 'Well,' Zapata continued, 'I think we won't be taken in. We've only loosened the rope on them, looking out for them, over here, over there, to keep after them while they're grazing.' Zapata continued with a tirade against big cities that had Villa nodding in agreement: 'The men who have worked and walked the hardest are the last to get any good from these sidewalks. Just nothing but sidewalks. And I'm speaking for myself. When I walk on a sidewalk I feel like I'm going to fall.'

Later the talk turned to agrarian reform. Villa accepted the Plan of Ayala in principle, but was vague about the how, when and where of land distribution. Much of his talk was generalised emotive stuff: 'All large estates are in the hands of the rich, and the poor have to work from morn till night. I am convinced that in the future life will be different, and if things do not change, we shall not give up the Mausers that we hold in our hands.' And again: 'Well, we should give the people the bits of land they want. Once they've been distributed, there will be some who'll try to take them back again.'

These anodyne expressions contrasted with Zapata's impassioned statements. Speaking of the Morelos peasants, he said: 'They feel so much love for the land. They still don't believe it when they're told: "This land is yours." They think it's a dream. But after they've seen other people drawing crops from these lands they too will say: "I'm going to ask for my land and I'm going to sow there." More than anything, this is the love the people feel for the land. Generally everybody gets their living from it.' At this point General Benigno Serrato interjected: 'It seems impossible to them that it has really happened. They do not believe it. They say: "Maybe tomorrow they will take it away." ' Villa tried to reassure the men of the south: 'You'll see. The people will be in command and they'll soon see who their real friends are.' Zapata agreed that the peasants had a very shrewd idea of their friends and enemies: 'The people know these others want to take their lands away. They know that they and only they can defend it. But they would die before they'd give up the land.'

After these public discussions Villa and Zapata withdrew to a private room for a secret conference, accompanied by just a handful of trusted advisers. For this session Palafox was at Zapata's side. They agreed that any future government must give them a free hand in their respective bailiwicks, and they in turn would leave the government a free hand in foreign policy and in the states where they had no vital interests. For the immediate future the two agreed not to impede each other's pursuit of personal enemies and to agree a list of proscribed persons. Villa expressed his concern that Zapata seemed willing to recruit anyone, ex-*porfiristas*, ex-*huertistas* and, most woundingly, ex-*orozquistas*, to his ranks. Zapata replied that not all *villistas* seemed committed enthusiasts for the Revolution.

At this secret meeting land reform was scarcely mentioned. The two leaders concentrated on the coming campaign against Carranza, and Villa promised to let Zapata have the artillery and equipment he needed for his operations. Remembering Ángeles's advice, Villa tried to get Zapata's agreement that he, Villa, should be supreme commander of the allied forces, but Zapata brusquely dismissed the suggestion. 'I don't go north,' he said, 'and you don't go south. That way we respect each other.' 'But, General,' Villa protested, 'keep in mind that these people are very strong.' Zapata said he would deal with Carranza and could guarantee it. Villa shrugged. 'Well, if you can guarantee it,' he said lamely. Thus did he carry out Ángeles's advice.

The sessions on 4 December ended with dinner and speeches; everyone seemed to think the meeting had been a great success. Two days later 35,000 khaki-clad veterans of the Division of the North, wearing stetsons, entered Mexico City to be greeted by 20,000 men of Zapata's army, dressed in loose white cotton and broad sombreros. The two leaders rode side by side, both superb horsemen with different riding styles. At one point in the procession Villa's military cap fell off. Without slowing his horse's pace, Zapata swung down his mount's side, scooped up the cap and returned it to a grinning Villa. Together the two armies paraded through the streets of the capital to the enthusiastic cheering of vast crowds. At the Zócalo the entire army was reviewed by Eulalio Gutiérrez, but Villa and Zapata themselves treated Gutiérrez with contempt and swept past him into the presidential palace. There, as a joke, Villa sat in the presidential chair, then motioned to Zapata to take his turn. Humour was never Zapata's strong point, and his response was po-faced: 'I didn't fight for that. I fought to get the lands back. I don't care about politics. We should burn that chair to end all ambitions.' However, Villa did persuade his comrade to pose for a photograph with him. The famous image shows a euphoric Villa alongside a surly Zapata. As Enrique Krauze remarks, Zapata is on edge, 'always wary of a bullet, perhaps springing out of the camera instead of the flash of a bulb'.

The photograph of Villa in the presidential chair, flashed around the world, convinced foreign observers that Villa was the new ruler of Mexico. However, he was so far from possessing the necessary administrative ability that he did not even plan further follow-up talks with Zapata. Villa and Zapata never met again. Zapata could not wait to shake the dust of Mexico City from him, but Villa stayed on in the capital, touring the fleshpots and chasing women. Having achieved supreme power, both seemed bemused by what to do with it. Because neither wanted the presidency, their meeting to discuss the consequences of victory can be seen in hindsight as setting the seal on their eventual defeat. They wanted to find people who would be loyal to the Revolution, so that they could retire to their provinces, but if they themselves were not prepared to play a national role, who could such people be?

Villa said he was not interested in who would be in a future Cabinet; his only mission was to fight, fight and fight again. The word *pelear* (to fight) was used by Villa no less than nine times in the verbatim transcript of the Xochimilco meeting and seems to reveal a 'permanent revolution' mentality, with everything forever in a state of flux. He made the telling admission that he would submit to a president and Cabinet provided they did not bother him; Zapata felt the same way. This was the *reductio ad absurdum* of the *patria chica* mentality, for no credible chief executive would be content to rule nominally from Mexico City, with large swathes of the country in a state of *de facto* independence.

Why was Villa so reluctant to assume supreme power himself? Maybe it was lack of self-esteem, stemming from his uneducated ignorance, as he said. More likely, he realised only too well that Zapata would not tolerate him in the presidential chair, that he would then have war with the *zapatistas* on his hands before he had finished off Carranza and Obregón. Since no politician, and certainly not Eulalio Gutiérrez, could be entrusted with the Revolution, as Villa saw it, his only option was to fight on until the issue with Carranza was resolved, by which time there might have been a 'second coming' and a new Madero might have emerged.

Even if Villa had decided to bite the bullet and instal himself as president, the resulting presidency would have been centrifugal, with a weak Mexico City depending on strong caudillos at the periphery. Villa would have ruled like Tiberius, with Chihuahua as his Capri, possibly with Ángeles as the real power in the capital. The result would have been highly unsatisfactory, with Villa and his caudillos as dogs in the manger, unwilling to rule but unwilling to give up their power and privileges so that someone else could rule. But at least Villa would have confronted the problems of power. Zapata could plead his ideology of village anarchism as the reason for his refusal to assume power at the centre, but in Villa's case it was laziness, lack of willpower and the taking of the line of least resistance. By his renunciation Villa ensured that however many battles he won, Carranza and Obregón were bound to win in the long run. As Octavio Paz wrote of the opportunity missed by Villa and Zapata in December 1914: 'He who refuses power, through a fatal process of reversion will be destroyed by power. The episode of Zapata's visit to the National Palace illustrates the nature of the peasant movement and its later fate.'

Where Villa's weakness was that he had a truly professional army and could campaign anywhere yet had no national plans nor even interests outside his own region, Zapata's weakness was almost the opposite: the Plan of Ayala had national implications yet his army was too weak and amateurish to campaign nationwide. Zapata's armies never became professionalised like Villa's, and in this respect the contrast between the brown khaki uniforms of the *villistas* and the white pyjamas of the *zapatistas* was truly symbolic. Zapata's armies were geographically isolated and peasant-based, reluctant to campaign outside the *patria chica*, and Zapata was unable to generate the surplus that would enable him to professionalise them, for his warlords preferred to grow subsistence crops rather than sugar cane for profit. By contrast, Villa's armies had many salient advantages: the social composition was not dependent on peasants tied to the agricultural cycle but rested on an elite group of mobile horsemen recruited from a variety of backgrounds; the proximity of the USA meant they were much better armed and equipped; there was a martial tradition of fighting Apaches and Americans in the north that had no equivalent in Morelos; and, most obviously, the terrain in the north was more suitable for the disposition of large armies.

The multifarious 'contradictions' between the *zapatista* and *villista* movements – contradictions that appeared at every level – to say nothing of the wary distrust of the two leaders, meant that the Zapata-Villa alliance was stillborn. Zapata was not encouraged by what he learned from his spies and from Villa's actual military cooperation. On 9 December one of his secret agents filed a report that Villa and Ángeles were simply stringing him along until they achieved their own aims, at which point they intended eliminating Zapata. That might have been speculation, but it was hard fact that Zapata had to send repeated requests to Villa before he could get the promised artillery support. Even then, the *zapatistas* had to manhaul cannon through the pass between the volcanoes of Popocatépetl and Ixtacchuatl because Villa provided no trains to transport the artillery. Villa meanwhile was increasingly irritated at Zapata's complaisant attitude towards former foes. In Mexico City the *zapatistas* had been universally popular and cooperated effectively with the *porfirista* old guard, in contrast to the chaos that began to manifest itself once the *villistas* entered the city. The continuing presence of so many *orozquistas* under Zapata's banner continued to rankle with Villa.

For a while Zapata, at least, kept the faith. With the aid of the big guns from Villa, he was able to occupy Puebla City on 15 December; after one look at the cannon being wheeled into position, the defenders did not even stay to try conclusions. On 16 December, testing the waters, Zapata wrote warily to Villa to say there was abundant evidence that their joint enemies were trying to drive a wedge between them.

Zapata finally became disillusioned when Villa murdered his aide Paulino Martínez and instituted a reign of terror in Mexico City. On 13 December *villista* officers gunned down Martínez, who had long been Villa's *bête noire*, both because he had joined Orozco in 1912 and because he continually denigrated Madero in his articles for the press. It has to be conceded that Martínez was verbally audacious, exactly the kind of man who made bad enemies with his tongue. At the Aguascalientes conference Obregón had asked sarcastically how it was that Zapata, supposedly commanding 60,000 men, had been unable to take Mexico City, when he himself took it with just 23,000 after a march of 2,500 miles. Martínez riposted that Obregón entered the capital so easily only because he had made a secret deal with the federals – something Zapata would never do.

Zapata grieved at the loss of Martínez and was angry with Villa for his treachery, but it seems there was misunderstanding on both sides. At the secret conference at Xochimilco, they had agreed to compromise on eliminating egregious personal enemies, but Zapata always understood there would be executions following purge trials; Villa, however, preferred to eliminate his enemies by hit squads or individual killers like Fierro. Accordingly, Zapata executed an old enemy, Guillermo García Aragón, who had fought with Zapata against Díaz but had refused to join him in the revolt against Madero. Zapata never forgave this 'treachery' and bore a deep grudge. In open contempt of acting president Eulalio Gutiérrez, who had appointed García Aragón governor of the National Palace, Zapata seized the 'traitor', tried him before a kangaroo court and consigned him to the firing squad. Since Zapata had mentioned this man in his secret conclave with Villa, and Villa had mentioned his own animus towards Paulino Martínez, Villa took the view that his elimination of Martínez was a tit-for-tat execution of the kind tacitly agreed at Xochimilco. Zapata did not see the matter at all in the same light.

Villa's murder of Martínez was simply the harbinger of a reign of terror in Mexico City in which *zapatistas* were frequently targets. For their first few days in the capital Villa's men behaved well, but they soon degenerated. Part of the problem was that the middle-class *villistas* – especially Felipe Ángeles – who had kept their less refined brethren in line, were away in the north, so there was no steadying hand. Faced by the temptations of Mexico City, the *villista* soldiery largely regressed to their earlier mode of banditry. They took their example from the top, not just from the lecherous Centaur himself, but from the *villista* high-ups, who all seemed simultaneously on their worst behaviour: Tomás Urbina distinguished himself by trying to rape the wife of the manager of an oil company; Juan Banderas shot a general dead and then trashed the Hotel Cosmos, doing 1,500 pesos worth of damage to the windows and furniture. Banderas was a notable hoodlum: two months later, in Tepepan, he picked a fight with a *zapatista* heavy, which degenerated into farce when his opponent brought an 8omm field gun to the duel.

An orgy of ravishing and murder swept through Mexico City. All told, there were more than 200 murders by *villistas* in a month and thousands of cases of rape. A host of private scores and vendettas was settled under the guise of weeding out *porfiristas* and *huertistas*, and among those killed in the nightly gunfights were *zapatistas*. The difference between Villa's men and Zapata's was clear for all to see: the *zapatistas* were ruthless in using execution for *raison d'état*, but Villa's thugs killed for private vengeance and then dishonestly claimed their victims were enemies of the people; when they started killing *zapatistas*, the transparency of the plea was palpable. The behaviour of Villa's troops blew the cover off the dark face of Villismo, showing the deep levels of banditry in the movement. The middle classes, foreigners and the Catholic Church were massively alienated. Villa's intellectuals had argued for socialism and land distribution, but what they got when Villa was ensconced in the capital was chaos.

In this maelstrom of anarchy and mayhem it almost goes without saying that one of the worst offenders was the egregious Fierro. When a young man named David Berlanga, already a prominent Conventionist, dared to criticise the behaviour of *villistas* and impugned the leader himself, Villa sent his one-man factory of death in pursuit. Fierro engineered a confrontation in Sylvain's, one of Mexico City's finest restaurants. Choosing a time when Berlanga was dining there, Fierro took in a gang of his roughnecks and, after a deliberately noisy repast, refused to pay the bill. Berlanga fell into the trap and upbraided the rioters. Fierro told him he had thereby signed his own death warrant and took him outside at gunpoint. The young man was so fearless that even as Fierro drew a bead on him he smoked a cigar with such a steady hand that the ash did not fall until after he was shot. Villa dismissed the murder as a matter of no consequence, attempting to placate public opinion by rounding up street urchins and dispatching them north to his special schools in Chihuahua.

However, the middle classes were not interested in Villa's would-be status as an educational benefactor, nor in his histrionics when he shed tears at Madero's grave and renamed the Calle de Plateos after the dead hero. The sycophantic *corridos*, especially the famous 'La Cucaracha' with its toadying verses – 'With the beard of Carranza I will make a scarf to be worn on the sombrero of his father Pancho Villa' – moved them not at all. They wanted swift action on the atrocities, now. José Vasconcelos went to see Villa to protest, but was turned away with the excuse that the general was sleeping; Villa's guards then taunted him, to add insult to injury. Vasconcelos then fell foul of Villa's powerful enforcer Juan Banderas, known as *El Agachado* (the hunchback). Threatened with death, Vasconcelos appealed to Villa who simply advised him to leave the capital on the first train; for Villa one intellectual more or less scarcely mattered, especially if it meant antagonising the powerful Banderas.

The Madero ceremony was another occasion when Villa publicly insulted Eulalio Gutiérrez. Villa had Madero's body dug up and then publicly reburied with full ceremony, and ordered all the capital's shops and businesses closed for the day, without even consulting Gutiérrez. Everything Villa did inculcated the message that Gutiérrez's presidential status was meaningless. The worst affront was when Gutiérrez asked Villa to stop Tomás Urbina extorting money from the rich by kidnapping: Urbina was well known to torture wealthy oligarchs to death until they revealed the whereabouts of their money. To Villa this was part of the normal course of events. He had done the same himself many times before, and chafed at having to extort money secretly now, to avoid an open breach with Gutiérrez.

Eulalio Gutiérrez now started detaching himself from Villa, with the aim of founding a new party and staunching the haemorrhage whereby hundreds of disenchanted former *villistas* deserted the cause and went over to Carranza. He openly protested at *villista* excesses and atrocities, and proclaimed a 'third way' for the many disgusted by both Villa and Carranza. Alerted by his spies that Gutiérrez was starting to put out feelers to Carranza, Villa descended on the provisional president's house and a notable confrontation ensued. Villa informed Gutiérrez he would be shot if he resigned, and informed him that all train services out of Mexico City had been suspended. Gutiérrez remained calm and protested that both Villa and Zapata were making him a laughing stock by so openly snubbing his authority. He even dared to bring up the subject of Berlanga's murder. Villa raged at him angrily: 'I ordered Berlanga killed because he was a lapdog who was always yapping at me. I got tired of so much noise and finally took care of him.'

Despite his threats, Villa hesitated to execute Gutiérrez. Apart from having no concrete proof of treachery, he feared the impact on international opinion and the loss of his reputation in the USA. He decided to patch up a compromise: Gutiérrez would be allowed to issue orders to Villa's troops, provided he did not try to flee from the capital. However, intercepted post soon revealed Gutiérrez as a master intriguer, not only negotiating with Carranza but scheming with Obregón to double-cross Carranza. Villa issued orders for Gutiérrez's immediate execution, but unfortunately for him, he chose to give the order to the very man who had already refused an order to execute Obregón: none other than José Isabel Robles, the *villista* general currently serving as Gutiérrez's minister of war. Robles tipped off Gutiérrez, who made immediate plans to leave Mexico City. After assembling a cadre of 10,000 loyal troops, Gutiérrez fought his way out of the capital, taking Villa by surprise.

Once at large, Gutiérrez issued a manifesto, vehemently excoriating both Villa and Zapata for their reign of terror, their inability to discipline their officers and men, their printing of worthless paper money, and for their incoherent foreign policy. Villa's response was to order Gutiérrez shot on sight, and to declare that all adherents of the 'third way' would be executed. Many leading Conventionists were rounded up, but others were forewarned and made their escape – taking with them several thousand troops and the contents of the National Treasury – leaving behind city walls flyposted with anti-Villa slogans. Gutiérrez fled to San Luis Potosí. Villa sent his men in pursuit but Gutiérrez had chosen a 'hot' state, for San Luis was currently being terrorised by Urbina in the authentic Villa style.

Gutiérrez's first step was to try to persuade the Madero family to join him; this would be a great propaganda coup and destroy Villa's claim to be the inheritor of the mantle of Maderito. Raúl Madero was tempted, but stayed loyal to Villa on the advice of his brother Emilio. Gutiérrez's ally General Eugenio Aguirre Benavides made similar overtures to Ángeles, who rejected them contemptuously. Finally, Benavides, with no great opinion of Urbina's military skills, tried to defeat him in battle. He was routed after most of his troops deserted him, then captured by the *carrancistas* and executed as a rebel. The 'third way' was now in terminal disarray. Another of its leading figures, Lucio Blanco, fled to the USA; later, in 1922, he was killed in action during a revolt against Obregón. Gutiérrez himself fled to Nuevo León, realised his position was hopeless, renounced the phantom presidency and went over to Carranza. Henceforth Villa regarded all Conventionists as enemies and ordered them shot on sight. The Convention was finished as an executive body, although as a legislature it lingered on in Mexico City as a spectral entity, still absurdly regarding itself as a sovereign institution.

Zapata watched all these events with a mixture of alarm, anger and cynicism. Every day he was deluged with complaints from Palafox and Díaz Soto y Gama in Mexico City over their treatment by the *villistas* and their clashes with the arrogant González Garza, Villa's official deputy and liaison officer for jobs, funds and railways. Zapata took this seriously, for his own spies reported the existence of a clique in Villa's inner circles intent on assassinating all the *zapatista* advisers, especially Palafox and Soto y Gama. By the end of the year Zapata accepted the inevitable, recalled his advisers and went into retirement at Tlaltizapán in Morelos. His troops went back with him, delighted that they would not have to campaign outside their homelands.

The US diplomat Cánova, who had reported the Villa-Zapata meeting so exhaustively, wrote to Washington on 30 December: 'The break between (Villa) and Zapata is not remote and when it comes señor Palafox will be one of the first Villa will attend to.' Zapata had already lost interest in Villa's coming trial of strength with Carranza and Obregón. He pulled his veterans out of Puebla, leaving behind the ex-*orozquistas* and ex-*huertistas*, who soon degenerated into a lawless rabble, refusing to take orders from Palafox or anyone else at Zapata's headquarters. The *carrancistas* noted the rift and seized their opportunity: on 4–5 January 1915, after heavy fighting, Obregón crashed into Puebla with his army. Zapata seemed as unconcerned as if the action was taking place on the moon. As far as he was concerned, the clash between Villa and Carranza was no longer his concern. The so-called 'war of the winners' would have to be fought without him.

The utter inability of Villa and Zapata to cooperate was one of the great tragedies of the Mexican Revolution and was the principal reason for their ultimate defeat. Perhaps synergy between two such dissimilar personalities and programmes was never really feasible. In one area alone did Villa and Zapata show themselves brothers under the skin: their womanising. Little is known of Zapata's marriage to Josefa Espejo, except that she bore him two children, Felipe and María Asunción, both of whom died in infancy. However, Zapata could console himself with Nicolás – born to an unknown woman in 1906 – the boy who slept through the Xochimilco conference, and three other children with other women, born in 1913–14: Eugenio, María Elena and Ana María. Zapata sometimes aped Villa and went through spurious forms of 'marriage' with his mistresses. This was the case with the early paramour Juana Mola Méndez and the Suárez girls, Catalina and Pepita, whom he and his brother Eufemio were said to have 'married' in a double ceremony. His more spirited gringa mistress Margaret Benton, who used the pseudonym Maggie Murphy, was a genuine adventuress who spurned such absurd niceties. In Tlaltizapán in the 1914–15 period he kept at least one mistress, María Escobar, having dallied briefly with another, Josefa Ortega, in Mexico City.

Meanwhile in Mexico City Villa was enjoying one of his periodic outbursts of satyriasis. Among a host of new girls he slept with was the up-and-coming actress María Conesa, but his most notorious escapade concerned a female cashier in a store owned by a Frenchwoman, where Villa was shopping. The pretty cashier caught his eye and he made heavy sexual advances to her; he said he hoped when he returned next day she would not insult him by rejecting him. When the terrified cashier asked the owner of the store what to do, she advised her to stay home next day. Villa arrived for his expected conquest and flew into a rage when he found that the bird had flown the coop. Unfortunately, out of the corner of his eye he caught the Frenchwoman laughing at him behind his back. Finding his machismo impugned and his 'honour' compromised, he took her hostage. The French consul intervened with a vehement protest, and soon the entire affair had escalated into a Benton-like international incident, which did Villa's global reputation irreparable harm.

Villa was seldom more self-destructive than in December 1914. While his men raped and murdered and he womanised, Carranza and Obregón were making careful preparations to destroy him.

All the campaigns so far in the Mexican Revolution had involved rebel armies ranged against the power of the state, with the federal government in Mexico City seemingly having the drop hand, only to throw away its advantages through military incompetence. In January 1915 there was no federal government and, with the demise of the Convention, no obvious 'rebels'. The war that broke out that month was a straight fight to the death between Villa and Carranza, with Obregón and Zapata at first in secondary roles; but where Zapata increasingly became a marginal figure in national politics, Obregón's importance increased monthly. For a brief moment at Aguascalientes he had allowed himself to hope that both Villa and Carranza might resign, but the two of them had never had any intention of handing the laurels of victory to Obregón. Carranza's resignation was always an unreal hypothesis; he was an egotist with massive self-belief, and would never have withdrawn, believing as he did that he was the only man who could 'save' Mexico.

Obregón began the war with deep feelings of foreboding. He saw clearly enough that if Villa advanced from Mexico City to Veracruz without delay, Carranza could scarcely survive. He had opted for Carranza reluctantly, since he had no realistic alternative. The middle-class ethos of the *carrancistas* appealed to him more than the *serrano* mentality of Villa or the peasant ideology of Zapata. His immediate ambition was to be restored as the premier figure in Sonora and to displace the hated Maytorena, and this ambition dictated an alliance with Carranza. Nor had he forgiven nor forgotten the brutal death threats from Villa a few months before. Finally, and most compellingly, his principal commanders would not have followed him if he had opted for Villa.

Even as they forged an alliance, Obregón and Carranza eyed each other with suspicion. Obregón intended to use the Army against Carranza if they were successful against Villa, but in turn was outflanked by his own ambitious generals – Benjamin Hill, Plutarco Elías Calles and Pablo González – who did not fight to elevate Obregón to supreme power.

They saw more scope for their ambitions with Carranza as president. Carranza was aware of all these currents and the many backstairs intrigues. A skilful politician, he was able to outscheme Obregón and keep him firmly in his place as a subordinate. He gambled, correctly, that whatever happened Obregón would never throw in his lot with Villa.

Obregón's first great military coup was his seizure of Puebla from the *orozquistas* Zapata had left behind there. Everyone expected that Villa would now emerge from Mexico City and direct his army towards Veracruz for a final showdown, but to general stupefaction he ordered his army to march north to Torreón. Ángeles begged Villa to reconsider and not throw away the chance of an early knockout. Villa, deaf to his pleas, insisted on pulling out of Mexico City. With both Villa and Zapata away from the capital, Obregón saw his chance. He moved in to fill the power vacuum and, to the disgust of the burghers of Mexico City, who remembered his earlier hostility, he remained there from January to March.

Ángeles's arguments were so cogent that they would have impressed almost anyone but Villa. From early December he had cautioned against a long sojourn in the fleshpots of Mexico City and, in virtually daily cables, had urged a rapid campaign against Veracruz. He made three main points. First, Veracruz was close enough to Zapata's heartland for the *zapatistas* to take part. Secondly, Pablo González's army of the north-east was a shambles, Obregón had not yet whipped his forces into shape, and Carranza was almost defenceless. Thirdly, if Villa settled in for a protracted campaign, Carranza's greater long-term resources would begin to tell, while Villa would be forced to court the hostility of the USA by expropriating foreign property simply to pay for his army. It was true that Emilio Madero in Torreón had urgently requested Villa to return there, but this should be disregarded. As Ángeles said, incontrovertibly: 'For us the most important thing is to attack Carranza, who is the head of everything. One has always to attack the head.'

Why, then, did Villa throw away his trump card and not advance on Veracruz? Quite apart from failing to achieve a quick victory, Villa's actions in putting his Division of the North on the march meant that his army wore itself out by three months of campaigning while Carranza made careful preparations and built up his strength in Veracruz. Many explanations have been offered. Those most critical of Villa say that he lacked imagination: that he was always ill at ease fighting outside Chihuahua and Durango and did not want to fight in the tropical lowlands of Veracruz, so far from his homeland, where the local population was hostile and he could not recruit more fighting men.

Another critical view is that Villa was always narrowly obsessed with the supply lines from Coahuila for his trains. More generous critics say that Villa feared that an attack on Veracruz would be construed by Zapata as an infringement of the agreement on spheres of influence made at Xochimilco. Others say that Villa was willing to attack Veracruz once he got the all-clear from Zapata, but that he never received it. Yet another school of opinion believes Villa wanted Zapata decisively defeated by Carranza and Obregón, preferably in a pyrrhic victory, which would weaken all the combatants, so that he could emerge as *tertius gaudens.*

Zapata's motives for inactivity have been variously analysed. One view is that he thought he could defeat Carranza on his own (ironically, Villa argued this exact case with Ángeles) but that when this proved impossible, he could not call on Villa for help as Villa had already gone north to Torreón. Another is that he was angry with Villa for not supplying him with arms and reinforcements as promised at Xochimilco. A subtler interpretation is that Zapata, knowing of Villa's animus towards the *orozquistas*, thought the Centaur might divert to settle old scores with the *colorado* garrison at Puebla, thus ruining allied strategy and letting Carranza off the hook. One thing we can say with certainty: Zapata's inactivity was a colossal blunder. Villa later complained bitterly that Zapata had let him down badly in the south, that he had expected him at the very least to impede rail communications between Carranza in Veracruz and Obregón in Mexico City. Villa's complaint was well founded, but what it really amounted to was that he had not really taken the measure of Zapata's *patria chica* mentality. As long as whoever was in power in Mexico City did not bother him, Zapata was interested only in achieving peasant utopia in his beloved Morelos.

Villa's decision to march north meant that Mexico was plunged into nearly a year of bloody civil war. As in all civil wars, there is great interest in what the combatants were fighting for and what groups they represented. Did either side have a clear-cut ideological profile or social programme? Or was the entire 1915 war a giant mosaic made up of very different individual power struggles? Some see Carranza versus Villa as the Directory versus the *sans-culottes*, the middle classes against the peasantry; others see it as the forces of modernity against the forces of backward-looking reaction, with Carranza as the true radical; others again view the entire struggle as merely an aggregate of individual caudillos and leaders struggling against each other and attaching meaningless and adventitious labels to their self-seeking conflicts.

The old idea that Carranza versus Villa represented landowners, the petit-bourgeoisie, the military, professional politicians, apparatchiks and bureaucrats versus frontier horsemen, pioneers, cowboys, the dispossessed, the young and the unattached bachelor will not really wash. There were many educated men and even intellectuals in the Villa movement, of whom Ángeles and Silvestre Terrazas were the most notable. In any case, this was a civil war in which it was far from clear what each side was fighting for, hence the large number of trimmers, fence-sitters, don't-knows and people who genuinely could not decide which faction had right on its side. The most ingenious interpetation of the civil war sees it as a northern power struggle projected onto a national stage, with Sonora and Coahuila, representing Carranza and Obregón, ranged against Chihuahua and Durango, representing Villa. Seen thus, it merely becomes one culture and locality in conflict with another locality and culture.

Certainly there was no ideological coherence among the combatants. Local warlords joined in on either side dependent on who their local rivals supported. Typical of a *serrano* group that for reasons of culture, ideology and interest should have supported Villa but joined the other side was the faction led by the Arrieta brothers in Durango, who commanded 5,000 troops. The Arrietas had long been locked in combat in Durango with Tomás Urbina; since Urbina was Villa's man, the Arrietas signed up with Carranza. There were scores of other chieftains whose culture and interests should have aligned them with Villa but who joined Carranza because of some ancient feud or personal vendetta with a *villista* chief. In the south-east the plantocracy, who strenuously opposed land reform, joined Villa who advocated it, and were against Carranza who was on their side on this issue, simply because the salient power struggle in Yucatán, Chiapas and Oaxaca was between the local *hacendados* and the 'proconsuls' Carranza had sent south to entrench his regime there and to abolish debt peonage. Another group that briefly allied itself with Villa was Manuel Peláez and his private army in Tampico. Peláez was an old-fashioned *condottiere* who commanded a force paid for by the US oil companies and was particularly despised by Carranza as a tool of the Yankees. Peláez received his rake-off for making sure all genuine revolutionaries were kept out of oil-producing areas, but he had no more real sympathy for Villa than the Arrieta brothers or the *hacendados* of the south-east.

Only three issues clearly divided Villa and Carranza: the role of central government, land reform and attitudes to the USA. Carranza was for strong central government and had a ruthless vision of what he wanted; to achieve it he aimed at a near-monopoly of economic power, control of all provincial administrations and an iron grip on the military, which he hoped to achieve by playing off the generals against each other. Proactive in his centralising drive, he contrasted strongly with Villa, who wanted to be left alone operating as a quasi-autonomous state with full power in Chihuahua and Durango. This tendency towards parochialism was always one of Villa's weaknesses.

Villa was only partly committed to land reform. He did not have Zapata's vision of a peasant society based on communalism, but he wanted to use the proceeds of confiscated estates towards his own utopia of military colonies. If he won the civil war, there would be many more confiscations and many more estates would be distributed among his troops. However, on agrarian reform overall he was very cautious, to the disappointment of peasant leaders in the north like Calixto Contreras. Carranza was the only leading figure who wanted to put the brake on all land confiscations and return estates to their original owners. This was why, looked at from a purely economic but not political viewpoint, the conflict between him and the plantation owners of the south-east was so bizarre.

Most striking at this stage were the different attitudes of Villa and Carranza to the United States. Carranza had always been anti-American, and his favourite current project was the nationalisation of the Tampico oil fields. At this stage of his career Villa was notably pro-American. He took Woodrow Wilson's moral posturings seriously and for a time looked on him as a kind of American Madero. Villa's glowing estimate of Wilson derived ultimately from his friend General Hugh Scott, from whose character he wrongly inferred the character of Wilson. Villa was also nudged towards sympathy for the gringo by Felipe Ángeles, and by George Carothers and his two agents in the USA, Felix Somerfeld and Lázaro de la Garza, both of whom had personal financial motives for promoting the Villa-Wilson entente.

At the beginning of 1915 Villa was thought sure to win the coming war. Both the British and the Americans were certain that by the end of the year Carranza would be no more. To American observers Villa seemed to have achieved the impossible: he was popular both with the rich and powerful, who looked to him as a future Cromwell, and with the dispossessed, who saw him as their champion. As Alan Knight remarks: 'Some Americans . . . were capable of seeing Villa as, simultaneously, both the "man on horseback" and the champion of democracy, as Napoleon and Lincoln rolled into one.' Because of Carranza's anticlericalism, Villa was also perceived as the saviour of the Church. No better guardian of liberal, pluralistic democratic principles could be imagined in American eyes than this pragmatic, eclectic and tolerant heir of the mantle of Madero; Carranza, by contrast, with his obvious dictatorial tendencies and never a word about elections, seemed simply a throwback to Porfirio Díaz.

Certainly those who thought Villa would win seemed on solid ground, for his advantages were several. One single victory by Villa would suffice to see off Carranza, but even if Villa was beaten the first time, he would need to be defeated repeatedly before he could be destroyed. He controlled most of Mexico and had unbroken lines of communication, where Carranza's forces were confined to enclaves, between which communication was by sea. In the states which should have been his power bases, Sonora and Coahuila, Carranza controlled only a small area. In the south-east, where the *carrancistas* were more firmly in the saddle, they were regarded as alien intruders and were vulnerable to local uprisings. It was widely known and believed that the USA favoured Villa, and the Centaur was unbeaten and seemingly invincible as a warrior, with a string of victories to his credit. Neither Obregón nor Pablo González could boast anything as impressive as Torreón and Zacatecas. Finally, and importantly, Carranza lacked Villa's personal appeal and magnetism, had no charismatic hold over his followers, and for the common touch relied on Obregón, whose primary loyalty was to himself.

However, this analysis overlooked the many areas where Villa and his movement were decidedly weak. At a personal level Villa was losing his touch, was careless of his image, showing increasing signs of autocratic behaviour, failing to consult his intellectuals and advisers, making policy on the wing and alienating the middle classes by the lawless behaviour of his troops during their occupation of Mexico City. It was true that Villa and Zapata were crowd-pullers and Carranza was not – there were no laudatory *corridos*, no *Cucarachas* about the bearded one – but charismatic machismo carried its own price tag. Villa attracted far more personal envy, spite and jealousy than Carranza; hundreds of local caudillos and bandit chiefs wanted to be Villa; no warlord wanted to be Carranza.

Villa's parochialism was also a drawback. The situation in the south-east made it a ripe fruit ready for his plucking, but he was uninterested and did nothing. It is also a remarkable fact that the Division of the North seemed to lose form when campaigning outside Durango and Chihuahua, and in this respect the contrast with Obregón's long-marching (over 8,000 kilometres) army could hardly be clearer. As many historians have pointed out, all Villa's great victories were 'home wins' and his 'team' proved unable to win away. The Division of the North was an improvement over Zapata's army in that it was able and willing to cover a wider sweep of the ground, and it was more professionalised than the *zapatistas*, but at the same time it was outmatched by Obregón's forces, which were even more professional and capable of fighting anywhere.

Carranza, too, proved more talented at drawing new recruits to his standard. It was Obregón's brainwave to build an alliance with the urban working class, promising them improved conditions in the future in return for support now; to this end he organised his famous 'Red Brigade' in the slums of Mexico City. Obregón liked to humilate the rich and the clergy and to truckle to the proletariat. While fleecing the Church and big business of millions, he produced this typical piece of demagoguery for his working-class followers: 'If my children had no bread, I would go out and look for it with a dagger in my hand until I had found it.'

Yet Obregón was able to recruit the proletariat without antagonising the middle classes. A particular pathway of opportunity, taken by the *carrancistas* yet neglected by Villa, was provided by the new middle-class diaspora. The Revolution blasted many of the bourgeoisie out of their comfortable eyries into contact with the lower classes and even with Indians. They were forced to diversify from land into commerce and industry and even into the armed forces, where Alan Knight compares them to 'the samurai of Meiji Japan or Pirenne's medieval *déracinés*'. Alongside this development, heralding a breakdown of the old conquista-dor contempt for manual work and commerce, was another parallel one – an effect of the first – as a glut of domestic servants was released on to the market with the impoverishment of their masters. The eagle eyes of Obregón and Carranza spotted the new situation, but Villa did not.

Villa also progressively lost the propaganda war. The Carranza organs successfully portrayed Villa as a bandit who was the puppet of reactionaries; why else would the bandit have changed his name from Doroteo Arango except to conceal his history of brigandage? Ángeles was targeted as an agent of Huerta, hired by the ex-dictator to subvert the Revolution. Carranza's ideological offensive contained promises to return villagers' land to them, a pledge to abolish debt peonage, and lavish inducements to urban workers. Villa's propaganda was never as effective. His principal organ *Vida Nueva* tried to build a personality cult of Villa and plugged away at the insane personal ambition of Carranza, but by early 1915 both themes were old hat.

Perhaps the single most damaging thing for Villa in the war of words was that Carranza's propaganda was radical and his practice conservative, but with Villa it was the other way round. The one way for Villa to cut the Gordian knot and underline clear ideological differences between himself and Carranza was to play up the issue of agrarian reform, but his statements on this were as vague as Carranza's. Each side said the other's agrarian policies would cause anarchy and chaos, but said nothing in detail either about what those enemy policies were or indeed what their own were. All attempts made by radical *villistas* to undercut Carranza on land reform were stymied by the opposition of the conservatives in the movement, principally Ángeles and Maytorena. *Villista* mouthpieces faithfully echoed the leader's line that land could be redistributed only *after* a military victory, for otherwise the soldiers, absent from their homelands, would lose out; it was also important not to alienate the United States over the land question until victory had been achieved. Besides, revenues would shrink if peasants began practising subsistence agriculture on confiscated land instead of cash crops for the market.

In general *villista* propaganda fell into every trap laid for it by the *carrancistas*. *Villistas* went on record as opposing workers' rights to strike or form trade unions and denying Indians' right to suffrage on the grounds that most of them were illiterate. Carranza was giving considerable hostages to fortune by taking on the USA and the Catholic Church at the same time, but Villa failed to capitalise on *carrancista* anticlericalism. Instead, by persecuting Spanish priests, he alienated the Church, which increasingly adopted a 'plague on both your houses' posture. Increasingly, too, intellectuals became disillusioned with Villa and switched their allegiance to Carranza. Only a man with no political nous would have acted as Villa did to José Vasconcelos and others in his circle. Ángeles was used to having his superior insights set aside because of Villa's whims, but Ángeles was exceptional, and few other intellectuals were prepared to give Villa the benefit of so many doubts.

Even the objective circumstances that seemed to favour Villa turned out to be illusory. The benefits expected from his popularity in the United States did not materialise, partly, though not wholly, because of the outbreak of war in Europe. Villa still had access to the US market in arms and munitions, but found he was having to pay far more than the 1914 price because of competition from buyers representing the belligerent powers in Europe. In January 1915 1,000 rounds of ammunition cost US sixty-seven dollars, as against US forty dollars in January 1914. The problem was compounded by the venality of Villa's purchasing agents. When the corrupt Félix Somerfeld displayed open contempt by supplying poor-calibre weaponry for top-dollar prices, Villa fired him, but found that his other agents, his brother Hipólito and Lazaro de la Garza, were just as money-grubbing. In addition, Villa was being cheated by his agent de la Garza, who signed a contract with the

Western Cartridge Company for fifteen million cartridges. Having sent the first 700,000 to Villa, de la Garza then 'gazumped' him twice, first with the *carrancistas* and then with an agent for the French.

At the same time Villa was suffering from a shortage of exportable cotton and cattle, and US traders proved increasingly reluctant to accept his inflated paper currency. Irritated, Villa concluded that his entente with the USA was one-way traffic: he had to respect their property and interests in Mexico while reaping no special benefits from his friendliness, except to be rudely informed that he, like anyone else, was subject to the disciplines of the market place. Even though Woodrow Wilson favoured Villa, the only concrete thing he had done recently – pulling the Marines out of Veracruz – had actually benefited Carranza. More and more Villa became aware of a gap between pro-Villa rhetoric from the Americans and pro-Carranza actions.

Gradually Villa's enthusiasm for the United States dwindled as he reflected dolefully that Wilson had let him down once too often. On the surface, though, he was still conciliatory. When Wilson's envoys suggested leasing the oil port of Tampico and taking over Baja California, Villa wrote to Zapata to ask him what he thought. Zapata replied that Villa should feel free to come to whatever arrangement he thought fit – again the Zapata apathy about anything not directly concerned with the *patria chica*. It became clear that the Americans, who disliked Carranza's anti-gringo jingoism, wanted to inveigle Villa into endorsing a 'safe' (i.e. pro-American) Mexican president. Villa became more and more disillusioned. He was disgusted by the shady manoeuvrings and underhand business deals brokered (or attempted) by Wilson's ubiquitous special agent Léon Cánova, and he came to feel that all Washington really wanted was to make Mexico its colony. Where once he had believed in Wilson, he now saw him as a forked-tongue humbug.

Villa's perception was valid and the situation has puzzled historians. There were even occasions during 1915 when Washington was embargoing arms to Villa but not to Carranza. The villain of this particular piece seems to have been Wilson's special representative in Mexico, John Lind, who favoured Carranza, but Wilson cannot be absolved from responsibility. Essentially he decided to cut and run from Veracruz leaving it as a prize to whichever army was in the hinterland, which turned out to be Carranza's. More generally, Wilson was cynically pursuing a policy of divide and rule in Mexico. Preoccupied by the Far East and the war in Europe, he wanted no trouble on his doorstep, especially as Mexico was fertile ground for German agents.

Long-term, too, it seemed as though Carranza held the important cards. He controlled most of Mexico's export ports, especially those in the Gulf. The two key points were the ports that featured in the 1914 crisis with the USA: Tampico and Veracruz. To Veracruz went the coffee of Chiapas and the henequen of Yucatán and to Tampico was pumped Mexico's black gold: oil. The world scarcities resulting from the First World War sent the international price of oil and henequen through the roof, so that Carranza generated three times the revenue from his truncated slice of Mexico than Villa did from his green pastures. The price of oil and sisal hemp kept pace with the accelerating cost of arms, but the price of cattle and cotton plummeted. Since the former were Carranza's products, and the latter Villa's, the consequences were obvious. This financial and economic preponderance by Carranza would make itself felt in the months to come.

For all that, the *villista* military campaign got off to a good start, with Ángeles achieving striking success in the north-east. Planning carefully, executing meticulously, never disfiguring his triumphs with gratuitous bloodshed, he outclassed Carranza's generals Antonio Villareal and Maclovio Herrera, who opposed him in Pablo González's old haunts. Feinting brilliantly, Ángeles sent Emilio Madero on a march to Saltillo, while he himself took nineteen trainloads of troops to Estación Marte in the opposite direction. When the enemy massed to meet him there, he left 800 troops to fight a holding action while doubling back to Saltillo, which he took without a shot, having captured the important town of General Cepeda on the way.

Ángeles then proceeded to threaten Monterrey, Mexico's third city and a key industrial centre. The *carrancistas* made their stand just outside, at Ramos Arizpe and there, on 8 January 1915, a notable but farcical battle took place in thick fog. In the ensuing comedy of errors Raúl Madero was twice captured and released by the enemy, who did not recognise him; the *villistas* meanwhile supplied their foes with ammunition in the thick mist and the *carrancista* artillerymen bombarded their own headquarters. During an interval in the fog Maclovio Herrera had a high-noon shoot-out with a former comrade and killed him. However, the end result was total victory for Ángeles. Carranza's army fled, leaving behind 3,000 prisoners, fourteen locomotives, nineteen wagons, 2,000 cartridges and 11,000 artillery shells. Ángeles did not execute his prisoners, but released them after taking their word of honour that they would not fight again; needless to say, many of them, including most of the officers, broke their word.

Ángeles proved hugely popular in Monterrey, for the *carrancistas* had made themselves unpopular by gutting the railway line. His moderate policies – no large-scale confiscations, no anticlericalism, guarantees of human rights – won him many friends, but Villa undid the good work when he arrived two weeks later by exacting a forced loan of one million pesos. Pleased that he could now supply his trains from the coal fields of Coahuila, Villa was indifferent to the plight of Monterrey, whose people suffered death by famine; severe food shortages were caused by the *carrancista* control of the hinterland. Once again Ángeles urged him to stop chasing shadows in the form of Gutiérrez and concerning himself with sideshows in Sonora, about which Villa continued to fret. Ángeles warned Villa that he was pursuing monkeys while the organ-grinder went free. 'Those *jefes* are like hats strung from a hatband that is Venustiano Carranza.'

Villa hardly needed to come in person to Monterrey, but his presence was needed in Guadalajara. Calixto Contreras and Fierro lost an initial engagement with the enemy there, and Fierro indulged his fury in typical fashion. Passing one of his wounded troops groaning in agony, Fierro bawled at the man, 'What's the matter with you?' 'I'm in pain, General,' the wounded man replied. 'I'll soon fix that,' said Fierro, who drew his pistol and shot him dead. The repulse proved the *villista* armies were far from invincible, and Villa, feeling his credibility was at stake, stormed down to Guadalajara and won the battle of Sayula with one of his famous cavalry charges. It was to be his last victory on a pitched battlefield.

When he occupied Guadalajara, Villa was infuriated to find that Calixto Contreras and Fierro had been extraordinarily incompetent in getting themselves routed, for the *carrancistas* had thoroughly alienated the locals. There had been corrupt deals in wheat, oppression of the working class, anticlericalism and persecution of the clergy, plus looting and indiscipline by the troops. When Villa entered Guadalajara, he was hailed as a liberator; new recruits flocked to him and he held a formal military triumph. The mood soon turned sour when Villa exacted a forced loan of one million pesos and began alarming the rich with talk of land reform. He particularly offended the *hacendados* in the state by closing the loophole whereby the landowners nominally 'sold' their properties to foreigners to avoid taxes. Villa at once outlawed such deals under pain of death and turned the tables on those *hacendados* who had made a low declaration of the value of their properties to avoid tax: he announced that all compensation would be at the declared (low) price.

Having dominated in the war of movement in Jalisco and Michoacán, and achieved such success in the north-east that only the border towns of Agua Prieta, Matamoros and Nuevo Laredo remained in Carranza's hands, Villa decided that his next objective was the oil port of Tampico.

He sent 15,000 men under Chao and Urbina to assault a heavily outnumbered enemy, but after two months the *villistas* were as far from success as ever; Chao and Urbina simply launched mindless frontal attacks against heavily defended positions, where the attackers were eaten up by machine-gun fire.

Obregón was worried, however, that Tampico might fall and with it would go half of Carranza's financial powerhouse; the only way to prevent this was to attack Villa. Carranza meanwhile urged Obregón to pull out of Mexico City, retreat to the south and tempt Villa to fight there – potentially disastrous advice, as Obregón would then have fallen foul of Zapata. Diregarding the First Chief, Obregón moved out of Mexico City at the end of March, but headed north and based himself at Querétaro, tempting Villa to come and fight him in the Bajío. The *zapatistas* then moved back into Mexico City. All now depended on whether Villa would take the bait and attack Obregón on grounds of the latter's choosing.

Obregón was as much a student of human nature as of the art of war. On the one hand he had read Clausewitz, which meant he did not mind abandoning Mexico City to Zapata as long as he could thereby compass the destruction of the enemy armies. On the other, he knew Villa's psychology and thought he could outwit him. It seemed to him that Villa's strategy was seriously defective in two areas. He had dispersed his superior strength in too many arenas simultaneously – Villa in the Bajío, Ángeles in the north-east, Contreras and Fierro in the west, Urbina in Tamaulipas and San Luis Potosí – and had thus offended against the principle of concentration of force. On the other hand, if Villa fought in the Bajío, he would be 1,000 miles from his primary supply base. Tactically, Villa relied overmuch on the cavalry charge, and close study of events in the trenches of France had convinced Obregón that even the most massive cavalry attack could be broken up by defenders with machine-guns, heavily dug in behind barbed wire.

On 4 April Obregón moved up from Querétaro, where the emperor Maximilian had been executed forty-eight years before, to the town of Celaya. The countryside was flat, striated by canals and ditches dug for irrigation, and Celaya lay in a plain by a river. Here Obregón dug in, with 6,000 cavalry, 5,000 infantry, eighty-six machine-guns and thirteen field pieces. Ángeles at once spotted Obregón's game and warned Villa on no account to engage him at Celaya; instead he should retreat, encouraging Obregón to advance, thus lengthening his lines of communication until Villa could cut them. The arrogant Villa contemptuously rejected this good advice. He later explained that he feared morale would dip if he retreated, that Obregón would pick up more recruits on the advance, and the reputation of the *villistas* would suffer. As he saw it, his prestige required a battle at the earliest possible moment.

The one weakness in Obregón's strategy was that he had to be supplied by rail from Veracruz. If Zapata were to move against Veracruz and sever this supply line, Obregón would face a serious shortage of ammunition. However, Obregón's spies in Mexico City reported that Zapata was no longer collaborating with Villa, that he had no intention of moving against Veracruz and perhaps even lacked the ability to do so. On 5 April Obregón's political aide Fortunato Maycotte assured him that all railway tracks had been repaired and the supply line from Veracruz was open and unimpeded. Obregón was optimistic. He knew his man and knew that Villa would not be able to resist the chance of an early offensive.

The battle of Celaya began at dawn on 6 April. Obregón started operations by sending an advance guard of 15,000 to occupy the hacienda of El Guaje, to cut the railway line to Celaya and reduce Villa's mobility. Obregón's first action was a blunder, for he thought the bulk of Villa's forces were at Irapuato when they were in fact already at El Guaje. The consequence was that Obregón's vanguard ran into a hailstorm of bullets and came close to annihilation. Hearing of the débâcle, Obregón boarded a troop train and rode up to El Guaje, trying to deflect attention from the vanguard with a hastily improvised probe. As he covered the retreat of the beleaguered advance guard, it occurred to Obregón that he might be able to coax a euphoric Villa into pressing his advantage and pursuing him back to Celaya.

Villa took the bait. As troop train and vanguard withdrew in confusion and rout that was half real and half simulated, Villa thought he could take advantage of the chaos and land a knockout blow. He ordered a massive cavalry charge, which ran straight into the machine-guns and barbed wire of Obregón's prepared positions. Casualties were enormous, and a wiser man would have pulled back and reconsidered. However, Villa the gambler was playing double-or-quits and launched attack after attack by his unsupported horsemen – the classic mistake made by Ney at Waterloo. He did not even identify a weak point in Obregón's front and try to punch a hole there, but simply ordered wave after wave of his *vaqueros* to charge across a broad front. Such was the sustained pressure that at one point Obregón's defences did seem likely to buckle and he fired off a typically hyperbolic cable to Carranza: 'I will consider it my good fortune if death should surprise me as I strike a blow in the face of its fatal onslaught.'

The attacks petered out at nightfall but resumed at dawn the next day with even greater ferocity. Having ordered ten massive cavalry charges on the 6th, Villa surpassed himself on the 7th by sending in no less than thirty charges from dawn till noon, many of these attacks impeded both by flooded fields and piles of dead horses. Once again Obregón's line came close to cracking. The legend is that Obregón ordered his 11-year-old bugler to call retreat, just when the *villistas* had taken a salient; Villa's men then obediently abandoned the points they had just taken with such bloodshed. By the afternoon of 7 April the Division of the North was exhausted, and at this very moment the ammunition for their Mauser rifles ran out. Obregón then called up his cavalry, unused hitherto, to deliver the *coup de grâce*. Villa had nothing to oppose them with, as he had foolishly kept no reserves to cover a possible retreat. Caught in a pincer movement, the *villistas* fell back in disorganised rout to Irapuato, leaving 2,000 dead in the dykes and polders of Celaya.

The bankruptcy of Villa's generalship was clear for all to see: he had not reconnoitred the field of battle, had kept back no reserves and had committed the most elementary mistake in the book by charging defensive positions with unsupported cavalry. As Obregón gloatingly put it in a cable to Carranza: 'Fortunately Villa directed the battle personally.' Villa himself blamed the defeat on lack of ammunition, but a more telling factor might have been the significant desertions from his ranks to Obregón on the second day of the battle. Obregón had scored a great victory but, because both sides in the Mexican Revolution habitually lied and claimed victory even after near-annihilation, and because Villa's reputation was so high, Obregón's claim to have defeated Villa was widely disbelieved both in Mexico and abroad. Needless to say, both sides claimed they had been heavily outnumbered, but were probably roughly equal at 11–12,000 apiece.

It was obvious now that Villa should finally have taken Ángeles's advice and retreated north, there to secure his supply lines, re-equip himself with ammunition and unite with the troops recalled from other fronts. However, he obstinately refused to accept that Obregón was the better general. At first he tried to lure Obregón out of Celaya by quixotically suggesting a pitched battle on a plain outside Celaya, but Obregón, holding all the cards, treated the idea with the contempt it deserved. By now there was chaos in the *villista* chain of command, with orders sent not received or disregarded, promised reinforcements not arriving and, above all, dissension between the professional army officers, who could see the sense of Ángeles's prescription, and the gung-ho *vaqueros* of the *villista* old guard, who had learned nothing from the first battle of Celaya and attributed the defeat of the cavalry charges to a fluke. On 13 April Villa attacked Celaya again. This time he had 20,000 men to hurl at the enemy defences, but Obregón's numbers had risen too, to about 15,000, among whom were several crack regiments sent by Carranza as reinforcements. More ominously, his defences were even more formidable this time, with far more barbed wire and machine-guns at his disposal. Once again he kept a reserve of 6,000 cavalry hidden in a nearby forest. To have any chance of making a dent in these defences, Villa needed to employ Napoleonic tactics, probe for the weak spot and then throw everything he had at it, in a classic demonstration of concentration of force. Instead, he simply did what he had done at the first battle of Celaya and sent in wave after wave of suicidal cavalry charges.

The *villistas* did everything they could in terms of valour, willpower and grit; taking terrible punishment, they pressed attack after attack. So ferocious was the onslaught that by 14 April they seemed to be making inroads. Suffering heavy casualties, Villa's men rolled back Obregón's Red Battalion (recruited from the proletarians of Mexico City) on their left and came close to encircling the enemy. Obregón sent another of his melodramatic cables to Carranza: 'We have no reserves of ammunition and we have only sufficient bullets to fight a few more hours. We will undertake every effort to save the situation.' Eventually, the *carrancistas* held the line against crazed, courageous and suicidal attacks. Two things especially helped them. The *villista* artillery was of poor calibre in every sense, and tended to rain its shrapnel on the town of Celaya instead of Obregón's trenches; and on the evening of the 14th heavy rain and mud brought Villa's advancing infantry to a standstill.

Timing his move to perfection, Obregón waited until dawn on 15 April before unleashing his cavalry, which he had kept in reserve far behind the lines, some five miles east of Celaya. Obregón's horsemen swooped down on demoralised *villistas*, exhausted after forty-eight hours non-stop fighting. This time defeat turned to utter rout. In their panic the men of the Division of the North left behind thousands of dead, wounded and captured, plus large numbers of horses, field guns and small arms. A count by Obregón's jubilant men turned up 3,000 *villista* dead, untold wounded, 6,000 prisoners, 1,000 horses, 5,000 rifles and 32 cannon. Obregón spoiled his great victory by a signal act of treachery. Terrified *villista* officers had put on privates' uniforms to avoid detection, so Obregón announced that there would be amnesty for all enemy officers; they should have no fears about declaring themselves. One hundred and twenty men were taken in by his weasel words, declared themselves, and were at once consigned to the firing squad.

Obregón, psychological oddity that he was, seemed to get no particular pleasure from his victories but only from his jousts with death. In many of his lugubrious verses he explains that he cannot enjoy the beauties of nature because of thoughts of death. Two of his poems are indicative:

> I have run after victory and I won her.
> But when I found myself beside her I felt despair.
> The glows of her insignia illuminated everything,
> The ashes of the dead, the suffering of the living.

And:

> But Man, the fool, does not even notice
> How near to him is the eye of the rifle of death.

It was amazing that Villa still felt able to fight on after such a defeat, and even more so that his men were still prepared to follow him; this speaks volumes both for his charismatic appeal and his boundless self-confidence. Ángeles, who had been in hospital in the north after a fall from his horse, now joined him and once again urged him to retreat north, if not to Chihuahua then at least as far as Torreón. Villa, who seemed to have learned nothing from his two crushing defeats and still attributed them to bad luck, announced that he intended to make a stand at Trinidad, outside León. Ángeles warned that Villa was in danger of being outflanked and asked him at least to promise not to use cavalry attacks, but to stand on the defensive. Once again Villa rejected his best general's advice.

Villa withdrew north in good order, using his cavalry as a screen between him and Obregón's advance guard, and summoned reinforcements and fresh supplies of ammunition. At the end of April Obregón's troop trains moved north-west into a broad desert valley flanked by sierras, at the other end of which was León and Villa's army. Within four miles of León, Obregón's vanguard was surprised by 6,000 *villista* horsemen and fled in confusion back to the main force. Obregón decided to form a solid square around the railway station at Trinidad – actually an uneven rectangle ten to fifteen miles long, a kind of mélange of Wellington's lines of Torres Vedras and the trenches of the western front in Europe. The scene was set for the climactic battle of Trinidad, a patchwork affair of pitched battles, skirmishes and probes in which the advantage tilted one way and then the other and which claimed 5,000 lives. A 38-day battle, which began on 29 April and ended only on 5 June, Trinidad has variously been described as Villa's Waterloo or his 1812 campaign.

This time Villa did not at first launch waves of unsupported cavalry, but dug in along a twelve-mile front from León to Trinidad. The two sides faced each other across a no-man's land, making the early stages of Trinidad a bizarre parody of the dreadful battles of the western front. At first both sides skirmished and probed, with Obregón hoping that Villa would order another frontal assault, but Villa refused to oblige. Obregón began to fret. He was concerned that his supplies of ammunition would run out if this war of attrition continued, or that his lifeline to Veracruz would be cut. He was particularly worried, for there were signs that Zapata was beginning to bestir himself and attack along his flanks. However, Zapata never did the one thing that would have turned the war for Villa. He never attacked Veracruz. Zapata's few attacks on Obregón's flank were actually a gesture of desperation: he feared that Villa would be decisively defeated and that Obregón and Carranza would then turn their wrath on him.

Even without Zapata's help, Villa should have been able to defeat Obregón, for the Sonoran had made one of his few bad mistakes by occupying a static position in the middle of a desert. A general of ordinary talent could have surrounded Obregón's extended square, cut it off from Veracruz and starved it out. Villa neither did this nor did he heed Ángeles's advice, which was for the *villistas* to retreat to Aguascalientes, forcing Obregón to pursue until his communications were stretched taut, at which point it would be an easy matter to sever the supply line. However, after nearly a month of probe and counter-probe Villa was impatient. He told Ángeles that his credibility depended on hanging on to León, that he must therefore attack: 'I came into the world to attack, even if my attacks don't always achieve victory and, if by attacking today, I get beaten, by attacking tomorrow I shall win.'

Villa accordingly ordered 35,000 men on an all-out frontal assault. The inevitable cavalry charge rolled back Obregón's right wing, but the *villistas* took heavy losses, including a dreadful incident when 300 of their men were shot dead in five minutes by cohorts of Obregón's sharp-shooters. Both sides were being continually reinforced during the battle, Villa from León and Obregón from Veracruz. Obregón had to use all his powers of persuasion to prevent his commanders from breaking out from the trenches and going over to the offensive. 'Keep the shape, don't lose the shape,' became a constant refrain as Obregón inspected his rectangle. Finally on 22 May, after four massive *villista* frontal attacks had been beaten off and a surprise cavalry raid on Obregón's rear had also been contained, Villa sounded the retreat. For a week there was further probing and skirmishing. Then the arrival of yet another munitions train from Veracruz allowed the *carrancistas* to re-arm and reload ready for a counteroffensive. Obregón finally bowed to the entreaties of his commanders. He promised them he would attack on 5 June.

Obregón was dubious of the wisdom of going over on to the offensive, but at the last moment Villa got him off the hook. On 2 June Villa attacked, spurred on to a last effort because his men were becoming demoralised at the continuing trench warfare which was new to them. Again ignoring Ángeles's advice, Villa used his reserves to assail Obregón in the rear. The *villista* reserves took the town of Silao and gutted it, but they failed to capture the key strategic centre of Santa Ana hacienda, the pivotal point of Obregón's planned offensive. A terrible slugging battle developed around the hacienda, with the *villistas* taking huge casualties, failing to make inroads and progressively becoming demoralised.

It was now that Obregón's fantasies of death nearly became reality. Anxious for an overview of the battlefield, he ascended the bell-tower of the hacienda. The tower immediately came under fire, and one of the shells tore off Obregón's right arm. Blood poured from the wound and he was convinced it was mortal. He took out his pistol to give himself the *coup de grâce*, cocked it and pulled the trigger. There was a click, then nothing. It turned out that his aide-de-camp had cleaned the gun the day before, had removed the bullets from the chamber and neglected to replace them. Obregón's men bound up the bleeding stump and rushed the general to hospital at Trinidad, where the surgeons were able to staunch the haemorrhage and save his life.

With or without Obregón, his army was sure to win on 3 June 1915. His deputy and second cousin, Benjamin Hill, carried out his plan to the letter. After beating off the attack at Santa Ana, Hill launched his counterattack at dawn on 5 June. Obregón's cavalry reserve routed the *villistas* on both right and left wings, leaving the road to León open, and his army swept in, reoccupying Silao and taking Guanauato, together with 300,000 cartridges, 3,000 rifles, six field guns and twenty machine-guns. Casualties in the 38-day battle included more than 10,000 *villista* dead, wounded and missing as against no more than 2,000 of Obregón's forces. Villa was badly beaten but not yet finished. He retreated towards Aguascalientes, meanwhile ordering Fierro to raid behind enemy lines and paralyse rail traffic.

Fierro proved an inspired guerrilla commander. Just for a day or two it seemed that he might pull Villa's chestnuts out of the fire, for Obregón had to detach regiments from his pursuing army to deal with this new threat. Fierro actually recaptured León by sending a forged cable to the garrison commander, ordering him to abandon the city. He then collaborated with the *zapatistas* to take Pachuca and brutally severed the communication line with Veracruz, showing how incompetent Villa had been hitherto. Had Villa sent Fierro on this mission in April, he would almost certainly have won the Celaya campaign. Long-term, however, the Fierro raid backfired. Fierro himself was caught and defeated shortly after severing the Veracruz lifeline, and meanwhile the threat to Obregón's ammunition and supplies galvanised him to make a rapid assault on Aguascalientes.

Villa's only chance now was to pursue a Fabian strategy, avoiding battle while he waited for the Fierro diversion to produce results, or at the very least digging in at Aguascalientes. Instead, despite plummeting morale in his ranks, Villa got it into his head that Obregón was already dangerously overstretched, and on 8 July he attacked outside Aguascalientes. When Obregón formed square, Villa stupidly assaulted him head-on, dissipating his resources in more unwinnable charges. Obregón stayed on the defensive until 10 July, then counterattacked. He was completely successful and broke through on both flanks. Once again defeat became a rout, again tons of *matériel* and hundreds of men were lost, and the *villistas* were so panic-stricken that Obregón's men were able to dine off hot stew left simmering in pans by the fleeing enemy. Carranza had won the civil war and Obregón was now the important man in Mexico. The tattered remnants of the once proud División del Norte fled north to Torreón and Chihuahua.

Why did Villa lose so massively in 1915 when everyone thought he was sure to prevail? His personal and military inadequacies were never so clearly on display. He made a number of obvious strategic blunders: fighting on several fronts at once; failing to attack Veracruz; failing to employ Fabian tactics and lure Obregón into the deserts of the north. These were compounded with tactical errors: failing to reconnoitre the terrain at Celaya; foolishly attacking across a wide front; not taking into account the impact of machine-guns and barbed wire. He never interrupted communications with Veracruz and never kept a reserve. A man of parochial vision and limited reading, he had not learned any lessons from the battlefields of the First World War, as Obregón had, and was too arrogant to listen to the advice of those who had absorbed the principles. Above all, he mindlessly ignored the best military mind in his army, Felipe Ángeles, and then disingenuously claimed he had lost the battles of Celaya and Trinidad only because he had listened to him.

Obregón cautiously advanced north, always conscious of his supply lines, mentally clocking up the miles he had advanced in his computer-like way. By the end of 1915 he had notched up the famous 7.227

Zapatistas enjoy the unusual luxury of a meal in Sanborn's restaurant,
Mexico City, December 1914

The meeting in the Presidential Palace, Mexico City, December 1914. On both occasions Zapata looks suspiciously at the camera, as if it contains a hidden weapon

The American forces occupying Veracruz, 1914

Dramatic irony: Villa with his two most implacable enemies,
Álvaro Obregón (*left*) and General John 'Blackjack' Pershing (*right*),
in happier times before the storm

Villa in happy mood

Zapata also in happy mood
(for him)

Félix Díaz: a thorn in the side of all Mexico's leaders for an entire decade

Orozco, not long before death at the hands of the Texas Rangers

'The bearded one':
Venustiano Carranza, president,
autocrat and control freak

At the battle of Celaya
the one-armed Obregón was king

The women of the Revolution: *soldaderas* ready for action

The last authentic
image of Zapata

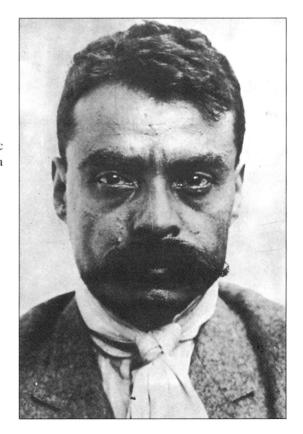

Villa putting on a brave face in adversity

kilometres marching that formed so large a part of the Obregón legend – eighty-five against Orozco, 3,498 against Huerta and 3,644 against Zapata and Villa. He was well aware that he was in effect the new Santa Anna, Juárez or Díaz of Mexico, that Carranza could rule only with his say-so or acquiescence. At thirty-seven he was the same age as Díaz when the liberals finally defeated Maximilian in 1867 and, as with Díaz towards Juárez, Obregón felt that the credit for the victory over Villa was his, not Carranza's. However, he still feared that he had only scotched the *villista* snake not killed it.

In fact Villa was more badly hurt than Obregón realised. He abandoned the siege of Tampico and pulled his men out of Saltillo, Monterrey and Monclova. The four foundations of Villa's power had crumbled: his reputation for invincibility; his largesse towards the have-nots; his promise of future land reform; and the perception that the United States was on his side. A reverse multiplier effect now occurred as Villa's morale and currency collapsed together. Before his defeat Villa had printed far more money than the objective state of his economy warranted, but people were pleased to accept it, thinking he would be victorious in the civil war and would then pledge the resources of the Mexican state to redeem the debt. Now it transpired that the currency was worthless. The *villista* peso plummeted from a value of US thirty cents to US one and a half cents in just two months. Now everybody demanded gold or hard currency. When merchants in Chihuahua refused to accept Villa's money, or raised their prices to compensate, Villa imprisoned them and confiscated their property. However, the result was that the shopkeeping class voluntarily took itself out of business. Severe food shortages resulted as merchants of all types refused to stock goods or sell anything.

The Chihuahua to which Villa returned was a land of chaos. Agricultural production had fallen, because of the war, at the same time as vast numbers of troops, together with their women and children, required to be fed, but the more production declined the greater was the percentage of it used to buy arms. It became commonplace for famished people to watch sheep and cattle being transported to the United States to raise revenue for arms deals while they starved. Villa pleaded overriding necessity. He was now so desperate for money that he was forced to go after previously friendly landowners, foreign capitalists and, most ominously of all, Americans. A forced loan of US$300,000 from American mine-owners was rescinded only after extreme pressure from General Hugh Scott. Business and, especially, foreign interests naturally lost faith in Villa.

Alongside financial and economic chaos was social dislocation. The División del Norte of late summer 1915 was not the 'ever victorious army' of a year before, but a force stuffed full of bandwagon jumpers and ne'er-do-wells who had climbed aboard what they thought was a gravy train and now were engaged in a mad scramble to get off again. Many units deserted to Carranza and those that remained were more interested in looting than fighting. To keep any army in being at all, Villa had increasing recourse to his *dorados* whom he used as political commissars and death squads. Roaming *villista* bands, some still militarily formidable, looted and plundered without let or hindrance now that there was no longer any political imperative against banditry. Naturally the middle classes were intolerant of these attempts to 'live off the land', seeing them merely as the old-style unreconstructed brigandage.

Villa's last-ditch strategy involved an attempted defence of Chihuahua, turning it into a fortress by destroying all rail communication with the outside world, followed by a fallback to Sonora, where he intended to link up with Maytorena and his Yaquis; this would pose Carranza and Obregón a major problem, as there were no railways in Sonora. Since the state had been spared the ravages of war, Villa reckoned that he would feed his troops there easily, while Woodrow Wilson would scarcely make an enemy of Villa by recognising Carranza when there was so much vulnerable American investment there. So pleased was Villa with the idea of Sonora as his fallback position that he soon began entering the realms of fantasy. He wrote bullishly to Zapata that after a short rest in Sonora he would come south again, occupying Sinaloa, Tepic, Michoacán and Jalisco, ready to rendezvous with Zapata just outside Mexico City for a second triumphal entry into the capital.

That was the public façade of Villa in more senses than one: optimistic, euphoric and face-saving. The private Villa was cross-grained, neurotic and irascible, full of fantasies about betrayal. The Maderos were the first to give up on him. After vainly calling on Villa to abandon a hopeless fight, Raúl Madero fled across the border into the USA, taking his brother Emilio with him, but not before warning Maytorena in Sonora to keep out of Villa's way if he should head in that direction. Ángeles too thought the Sonoran redoubt plan a chimera and urged Villa to face facts. Villa was so angry with his favourite intellectual for this advice that for a while observers feared for Ángeles's life, but by September he too was across the border with the Maderos and the other middle-class intellectuals: Juan Medina, José Isabel Robles and the Pérez Rul brothers, respectively private secretary and treasurer to Villa. Some said they were merely in the United States to lobby Wilson, but it was noticeable that none of them came back.

Maytorena scarcely needed the warning from Madero. He had experience of the dyspeptic Villa of old and the last thing he wanted was to see the Centaur in Sonora; he knew only too well what his life and that of the other oligarchs would be worth. When Villa's vanguard entered Sonora in September, Maytorena too fled to the United States, as did Rafael Buelna, leader of the *villistas* in Tepic. Anything was better than a paranoid Villa in full flight. Villa hardly knew Buelna and Maytorena, so accounted their defection no great loss, but he was devastated when his old comrade Rosalío Hernández, one of the inner circle and a veteran of Paredón, Torreón and Zacatecas went over to Carranza. The last straw was the defection of Urbina. His old favourite had already lost caste by his lacklustre performance. Imitating his master by making continued mindless charges during April and May, Urbina had finally been badly defeated at El Ébano on the outskirts of Tampico, when the defenders routed the *villistas*, sustaining one casualty for every seven *villistas*. Villa could forgive military failure, but not insolence and affronts to his honour. Urbina finally moved into forbidden territory. For Villa this was a bridge too far, and he determined on revenge.

The venal and money-loving Urbina was what Villa was often accused of being: a super-bandit. At his hacienda at Las Nieves he had accumulated a huge fortune from robbery, confiscation, extortion and kidnapping. He owned 300,000 sheep, vast herds of horses and mules, fifty-four gold bars and masses of jewellery hidden in the hacienda grounds. Villa had hitherto ignored all complaints about Urbina, even when it was reported that Urbina was looting instead of fighting Carranza, but the break point came when Villa decided to execute Urbina's second-in-command Borboa for murder. Urbina not only refused to give him up but replied insolently to Villa. Predictably, Villa responded by sending a death squad under Fierro, who had begged for the 'privilege' of executing Urbina. There followed a fierce gun battle at the hacienda as 800 *villistas* overwhelmed Urbina's men. At the end of the shoot-out Villa found a wounded Urbina unsteadily pointing a gun at him, disarmed him, and talked privately with him for a long time. The frustrated Fierro saw Villa apparently on the point of pardoning Urbina. Villa made to leave and ordered Fierro to bring Urbina along to headquarters. Fierro took Villa aside and whispered in his ear, reminding him of his promise that Fierro could 'have' Urbina. Villa agreed this was the only solution. On the way back to Parral Fierro stopped the train, took Urbina off and executed him in his usual cold-blooded manner.

Urbina's execution was very popular with the other *villista* leaders, who had always resented Villa's partiality for him. However, Urbina's gold turned out to be a curse every bit as potent as that of the loot in Chaucer's *Pardoner's Tale* or Traven's treasure of the Sierra Madre. Villa delegated the task of finding the gold bars to an officer named Ramírez, saying he would split the treasure trove fifty-fifty with him. Ramírez used great skill in locating the ingots – sunk in various wells – but then reflected that Villa would probably kill him so as not to have to share the loot. He deserted to the *carrancistas*, taking the gold with him, offering them a fifty-fifty share in return for amnesty. The *carrancistas* agreed, then double-crossed Ramírez, leaving him with nothing.

Cast down by all the defections, Villa set out for Sonora. Instead of the 50,000-strong ebullient División del Norte that had won Torreón and Zacatecas, he was now reduced to 12,000 demoralised troops, short of money, ammunition and food; many remained in the army only for fear of what Villa would do to their families if they deserted. They also had to ride or walk through the steep mountain passes linking Chihuahua and Sonora – there were no railways – and the trek through the Sierra Madre turned into a veritable *via dolorosa*. Manhauling wagons through icy defiles, with little water *en route* and no haciendas on the line of march where they could revictual, the men suffered abominably, and were additionally deprived by Villa's orders that all women had to stay behind in Chihuahua.

The one event to lighten the men's hearts was the death of Fierro, the butcher. While negotiating the treacherous sierras, on 14 October 1915, Fierro came to Casas Grandes Lagoon. It seems he was wearing a waistcoat stuffed with gold coins. When his men seemed reluctant to enter the muddy waters, Fierro spurred his horse forward. To his horror he soon found himself in quicksands and called to his men to fetch a rope and pull him out. Fierro was universally hated, so some of his men prolonged his agony by appearing to help but deliberately casting the lassos short. Soon they abandoned even the pretence of helping him, though Fierro screamed in terror and promised his entire crock of gold to the man who would save him. Nobody lifted a finger and all eyes were filled with delight as the detested murderer slowly sank under the man-eating sands.

It had been a bad year for murderous heavies: first Urbina killed, now Fierro. Then came more dramatic news featuring the Grim Reaper. In the spring of 1915, as Villa confronted Obregón, the exiled dictator Huerta had thought he saw a chance for restoration and sailed from exile in Spain to the United States. He proceeded from New York to El Paso to plan a new rising with Pascual Orozco, hoping to energise a counter-revolutionary nucleus around the hordes of exiled generals, landlords, politicians and other disgruntled Mexican émigrés, possibly with assistance from Germany. However, the German factor was also on the minds of US federal agents, who swooped when Orozco met Huerta in New Mexico. Orozco escaped and remained at large for two months before being tracked down and shot dead by Texas Rangers. Huerta was imprisoned for five months in Fort Bliss, morose, drunk and ill. He died in January 1916 after undergoing two surgical operations. The official cause of death was the combined effect of jaundice, cirrhosis and gallstones, but there were persistent rumours that the Americans had poisoned him. He was buried alongside Orozco in Concordia cemetery.

Villa arrived in Sonora to yet another débâcle. Carranza and Obregón, guessing his intentions, had sent two armies to invade Sonora, one seaborne, the other via Sinaloa. The Sonorans, dejected by Maytorena's flight to the USA, put up no resistance. The upshot was that after all his exertions in the mountains, Villa found Carranza in possession of the capital, Hermosillo, and the chief port, Guaymas. Bitterly disappointed, he felt he had no choice, for reasons of credibility, but to proceed with his plan of attacking the 13,000-strong *carrancista* garrison at Agua Prieta. The plan was always a forlorn hope, for in the meantime Woodrow Wilson had recognised Carranza as the legitimate ruler of Mexico and allowed him to reinforce Agua Prieta by sending troops from Coahuila to Sonora across US territory. Thus it was that veterans of Celaya arrived at Agua Prieta via Arizona, eager for another crack at the man they had humiliated in April.

Knowing nothing of these reinforcements, Villa closed in for the assault on Agua Prieta. On 1 November he gave an interview to an American reporter, full of bombast and braggadocio, which Martín Guzmán, Villa's secretary and biographer reported as follows:

REPORTER: General Villa, will you attack Agua Prieta?
VILLA: Yes, and the United States if necessary.
REPORTER: When?
VILLA: I'll decide that.
REPORTER: How many cannon do you have?
VILLA: Count them when they're roaring.

It was unfortunate for Villa that Calles, one of Obregón's best generals, was commanding at Agua Prieta. Like his mentor a master of planning, detail and terrain, Calles had constructed a labyrinthine defence of ditches, fences, trenches, barbed wire, mines and machine-gun nests. Villa tried to nullify this by one of his famous night-time attacks, but Calles was ready for this and turned on a battery of searchlights. In the intersecting beams the *villistas* were easy prey. After just three hours bloody fighting, 223 lay dead around the trenches. Villa, never able to acknowledge that he had been beaten in a fair fight, was adamant that the searchlights were beamed on the battlefield from the American side of the border, and his hatred for Woodrow Wilson grew. Calles wrote laconically to Obregón: 'The chief of the attacking forces did not carry out his pompous promises of the evening before.'

Villa somehow got to hear of Calles's contemptuous remarks about him. Days later, in an act of transmogrified revenge, he slaughtered all sixty males in the small town of San Pedro de la Cuevas, allegedly because many of them had the patronymic Calles. There may be more to the incident than that. *Villista* sources say that the villagers fired on Villa's men, mistaking them for bandits, and that Villa ordered the massacre in retaliation. He would hear nothing of 'mistakes'; there had been too many of them and they all, conveniently, favoured Carranza. He spared a few males on the intercession of the parish priest, on the express condition that the priest did not nag him again. The foolish cleric pushed his luck; Villa pulled out his pistol, shot him dead, and then ordered the reprieved ones executed. Seven men were said to have survived by lying under dead bodies and feigning death.

Yet, however many reverses he sustained, Villa simply would not give up. Hearing that 2,000 Yaquis previously loyal to Maytorena were ready to join him, he decided to attack Hermosillo. Leaving 6,000 men to cover him against a surprise sortie from Agua Prieta, he struck south-west and attacked the Sonoran capital, incredibly still using the discredited method of frontal cavalry charges. Since Hermosillo was heavily defended with trenches and machine-gun nests, it was no surprise that he was once again beaten off with heavy losses. The *carrancistas* then cut the ground from under Villa by a mass kidnapping of the Yaquis' families; the Yaquis gave in, deserted Villa and came to terms with Carranza to save their loved ones. Then came news that the second army he had left behind to prevent a sneak attack from Agua Prieta had been soundly beaten twice, at El Fuerte and Jaguara. There was now nothing for it but that Villa return in defeat and disgrace to Chihuahua.

The return crossing of the Sierra Madre was even more terrible than the outward journey. Men fell into crevasses and ravines, abandoned the artillery in snowdrifts and deserted in thousands. Villa limped back into Chihuahua City on 17 December; this time there was no rapturous welcome for him, just an escort of ten of his *dorados*. Down to just 2,000 men by now, he continued to live in a fantasy world and summoned his commanders to discuss another great campaign against Obregón. To his stupefaction, one by one his generals spoke out against him, denouncing his ideas as dangerous illusions and, in effect, going on strike. Almost speechless with anger, Villa made an emotional appeal to them and offered to resign as their chief. To his horror, his commanders ignored the histrionics and seemed quite happy with exactly that outcome. Finally convinced of the seriousness of the situation by private conversation, Villa announced that all who wanted to leave him might do so; he would meanwhile arrange for the peaceful surrender of Chihuahua City and Ciudad Juárez.

Villa spent his last days in Chihuahua City executing all those of his followers whom he suspected of wanting to seek sanctuary in the United States. He nearly executed Silvestre Terrazas on suspicion of putting out feelers to Carranza, but Silvestre was conspicuously loyal and was able to prove it to Villa. Paranoia was now a dominant aspect of Villa's psychology. He was convinced that he had lost to Obregón only because he had been betrayed, and harboured fantasies of treachery, fuelled by the many cases where he had actually been forsaken. Before executing Mateo Almanza, a *villista* who had defected to Eulalio Gutiérrez early in 1915, Villa told him the firing squad was too good for him, so he would suffer death by hanging instead. Possibly the 'we wuz robbed' fantasy was the only way Villa could keep his purchase on reality; he could rationalise his catastrophic failure in 1915 on the basis that all his setbacks were because someone had let him down or betrayed him.

The last days of December 1915 also saw the last days of the once mighty División del Norte. At a conference at the Hacienda de Bustillos Villa made a final attempt to persuade his generals to stay with him and fight. All but four of the twenty-seven present shortly afterwards made their peace with Carranza. Obregón entered into negotiations with these generals for the peaceful surrender of Ciudad Juárez, offering to amnesty all *villistas* except Villa himself, his brother Hipólito and thirteen top-ranking *villista* bureaucrats. No less than forty generals, 5,046 officers and 11,128 soldiers took advantage of Obregón's offer of amnesty and mustering-out pay. Many of these, including Panfilo Natera, promptly joined Carranza's army and fought their ex-comrades.

Chihuahua was now a wasteland, thronged with the wounded, the desperate and the starving. There were signs of a Hobbesian war of all against all, with kidnapping, murder and rape all at epidemic levels. Many ex-*villistas* decided they could no longer trust Villa and his whims, and retreated to mountain fastnesses to eke out a precarious living as individual bandits or guerrillas. They might have opted for Carranza, but too many local *carrancista* commanders used the pretext of amnesty to invite *villistas* to parleys and then slaughtered them. So it was that Calixto Contreras, once Zapata's white hope among the *villistas*, became the local caudillo in Cuencamé; Tiburcio Cuevas set up as a warlord dominating the area between Durango and Mazatlán; and Miguel Canales became the new bandit chief of Durango. Sometimes these men turned the tables on the treacherous *carrancistas* by offering to surrender and then massacring the enemy when they arrived at the rendezvous to accept the surrender.

The Centaur himself and his handful of retainers headed for the mountains of Chihuahua, intending to wage guerrilla warfare until the inevitable happened and Obregón and Carranza started to fight each other. Some biographers of Villa think he did so with relief, content to be back in the hills with his most loyal followers, no longer burdened with matters of state and high politics. Unlike most defeated Latin American caudillos, Villa did not go abroad into exile with a vast personal fortune siphoned off over the years, but took to the sierras with just 200 hardcore *dorados*. His meteoric rise and fall was a textbook case of anomie and would have convulsed many a tough-minded individual; truly he was a man of iron. In three years he had gone from guerrilla fighter to the pinnacle of power and back again. Nobody could have guessed that he was about to launch an endeavour that would make him front-page news across the world.

Whatever his qualities as visionary and leader, Zapata was no politician. It almost passes belief that while Villa was engaged in his titanic struggle with Obregón and Carranza, Zapata should have spent his time turning Morelos into a laboratory for land reform, as if he lived in some Shangri-La cut off from the rest of the world. Naturally the temptation was great to do something about what John Womack has called 'the utopia of a free association of rural clans', but Zapata's political myopia was egregious. Not only did he take next to no interest in Villa's campaigns, but he could scarcely be bothered with events in Mexico City, right on his doorstep. To some extent Zapata acted out of pique because the Convention was still the official sovereign body. Even though Gutiérrez broke out of the capital with 10,000 men, he had left behind the *villista* Roque González de la Garza as his provisional representative – he was endorsed as provisional president by the rump of the Convention on New Year's Day 1915. Since de la Garza loathed Palafox and Soto y Gama and was permanently locked in combat with them, Zapata self-destructively took the line that Mexico City was primarily the Convention's business.

For twelve months, from August 1914 to August 1915, Mexico City went through its darkest hours. First it had been subjected to Obregón's draconian sanctions, then, after a blessed interlude when the innocuous *zapatistas* roamed the streets, there had been Villa's reign of terror. Then, from 28 January 1915 to 11 March, the capital was once again in Obregón's hands. Obregón proceeded to strip the city of everything valuable that could be carried away to help his war effort. He instituted another savage persecution of the Catholic Church and mulcted its priests and bishops – there was always something crazed and unbalanced about Obregón's anticlericalism, even though the Church had given substantial hostages to fortune by its craven attitude to Díaz before 1910. The worst aspects of the six-week Obregón occupation of the capital were famine and water shortages, caused by the *zapatista* blockade. When the *zapatistas* blew up the pumping station at Xochimilco, water was rationed to one hour's supply per day. Sewage and sanitation problems became acute, and cholera threatened. The struggle for daily existence was exacerbated by the constant change of occupying forces, all of whom ruled their predecessors' currency illegal; there was thus no continuing and reliable means of exchange.

So terrible was life in Mexico City during the second Obregón incumbency that when he pulled out on 11 March, to move north to Querétaro for the reckoning with Villa, the incoming *zapatistas* were greeted as deliverers. Church bells were rung as though for liberators, and at first life improved, for the *zapatistas* restored a full water supply and lifted the blockade so that food could reach the capital. However, this time Zapata's men did not come as naïve country bumpkins. They had learned the ways of the city and were less accommodating. More brusque now in their demands for food and money, they began to ape the *villistas* in mindless looting. Churches, private mansions, gentlemen's clubs, libraries, museums and art galleries were stripped of their precious artefacts, not for resale on the market, but simply out of vandalism. Lovers of horses, the *zapatistas* made a clean sweep through the stables and studs of the city. Soon the citizens of the capital were complaining that Zapata's men were no better than Obregón's or the *villistas*. In his eyrie in Morelos Zapata seemed unconcerned at the unsavoury deeds being committed in his name. He called a halt only when a trigger-happy soldier shot dead an American citizen who had resisted a demand for money with menaces. To assuage Woodrow Wilson Zapata had to purge his troops and pay compensation for the murder.

Largely, though, his mind was elsewhere. At his headquarters in an old rice mill in the village of Tlaltizapán he presided over the new experiment with local democracy and communal ownership. There he dispensed justice Solomonically, deciding on land disputes, making small loans to farmers, even arbitrating between men and women in sexual matters. In the evenings he liked to chew the fat with his cronies, sipping brandy, chomping on his ever-present cigar, discussing the finer points of weather, women, horses and gamecocks. During the day he conferred with Palafox about how best to further his social revolution. Palafox frequently commuted to Mexico City after 11 March, since he was officially secretary of agriculture in the Convention Cabinet. Acknowledged as the brains behind the detail of land reform in Morelos, he was already attracting hostility, from hedonists who detested his workaholism, from macho *zapatistas* who despised him for being homosexual and, above all, from the Americans, who, alarmed by his determination to divide up *all* haciendas, even US-owned ones, regarded him as a dangerous radical. The real power nexus in Morelos was tripartite, running between Zapata as supreme chief of the Revolution, Palafox as secretary of agriculture and Genovevo de la O, the new governor of Morelos.

Zapata worked on two main principles. One was always to support village leaders against professionals. Even when expert surveyors and university-trained agronomists said that the ancient village boundaries made no sense, Zapata always insisted that village opinion was to prevail. The other principle was that the civilian must always take precedence over the military. Inevitably, in the course of a four-year military struggle, the original village leaders had lost their place to quasi-professional soldiers but, now that Morelos finally had peace – it was to be the only interlude in the entire period 1910–19 – it was time for the village elders to reassert their authority.

Palafox himself would have liked full-blooded socialism to supplant Zapata's quaint old-fashioned communalism. He it was who set up a National Bank for Rural Loans and used graduates from the National School of Agriculture to implement land reform. Working through the Convention and using national funds, he assigned ninety-five such graduates to agrarian commissions, which were to distribute lands in Guerrero, Puebla, Mexico State, the Federal District and Morelos. The greatest emphasis was on Morelos, where no less than forty-one of these graduates were employed, based on Cuernavaca. The graduate commissioners examined land titles, settled boundary disputes and marked clearly the limits of each village's land. Once it was settled what the extent of a village's land was, the village could decide either to keep it as common land with user rights, or divide it up and give individual title to smallholders; Zapata's line was that only local custom was to be allowed to decide this outcome. No one could sell or rent any of these lands, thus preventing the possibility of collusion between speculators and corrupt villagers.

All land coming into the public domain through confiscation was allocated by Palafox. Private ownership of non-owner-occupied property was outlawed, and all forms of real estate designed for profit instead of use could be expropriated. Palafox's near-socialism meant that the return to Morelos of even moderate liberal planters was impossible. His expropriation of the sugar mills and distilleries particularly angered de la Garza, the president of the Convention, who resented the pretensions of the *zapatistas* to equal partnership with the *villistas* and thought they had no right to be putting such emphasis on land reform when they were not pulling their weight in the military struggle. Zapata informed de la Garza, through Palafox and Soto y Gama, that Villa's campaigns were the means and land reform the ends; had he perhaps lost sight of that? Besides, he could not open a second front in the south if Villa did not send him the arms and ammunition promised at the Xochimilco conference.

Zapata showed scant interest in the frenzied in-fighting in Mexico City between de la Garza and Palafox during May and June – which on one occasion saw the two of them almost come to blows. As long as events in the capital did not seriously impinge on Morelos, he was basically insouciant about what happened there. More of a worry for him was his inability to generate an economic surplus. Despite his exhortations to produce exports for the market, the villagers of Morelos, left to their own devices, took the line of least resistance and grew merely subsistence crops. However, he felt moderately content with the social progress of his revolution. The army was decentralised and turned into self-defence units operating on a cell-like structure, each based on an individual village and ready to melt into the countryside if a too-powerful enemy attacked.

Zapata was blasted out of his utopian reverie on 11 July when, following Obregón's final victory at Trinidad, Pablo González occupied Mexico City, forcing the Convention to retire to Toluca. Although González pulled out a week later to protect Obregón's lines of communications, and the *zapatistas* briefly returned, it was clear that, with Villa's defeat, González had the whip hand and could return to the capital whenever he chose. At last Zapata roused himself and sent 6,000 men on a flank attack on the *carrancistas* north-east of Mexico City on 30 July. However, on 2 August, with the threat from Fierro's cavalry raiders no more, and Villa in headlong retreat north, González re-entered the capital, and this time he came to stay. Zapata still remained amazingly complacent, apparently pinning his hopes on an Inter-American Conference in Washington that he somehow thought would lead to Carranza's downfall. He also seems to have harboured Villa's illusion that Obregón and his general would immediately turn and rend Carranza, perhaps even signing up with the Convention. As Zapata saw it, to order an immediate mobilisation was to jump the gun.

Too late he realised the danger he was in and attacked along a wide front in September, pushing into Mexico State and the Federal District. However, although he took many towns, and even the power plant at Necaxa which supplied Mexico City's electricity, he could not hang on to his gains. Hard-pressed by the *carrancistas, zapatista* chiefs in Puebla and Mexico State started accepting amnesties from Carranza. With Villa in full flight, the Convention finally accepted that it had outlived its usefulness and wound itself up on 10 October. In Cuernavaca Palafox pointlessly transferred its 'sovereignty' to Zapata himself as the one and only legitimate Chief of the Revolution. On 19 October Woodrow Wilson showed just what that was worth by recognising Carranza's government and embargoing all arms sales to his enemies.

Even into the autumn of 1915 Zapata continued amazingly complacent. He thought Carranza would be as short-lived a phenomenon as Huerta, and continued to raid over a wide area from Oaxaca to Hidalgo. He now had a plethora of unit leaders, some of them women, who commanded bands from thirty to 200 strong, capable of fighting a war of mobility and even a cavalry blitzkrieg against Carranza. However, even while the *zapatistas* were scoring flamboyant victories in the southern sector of the war zone, Carranza's forces steadily tightened their grip on Morelos. In November 1915, aware that Zapata was suffering grievously from shortages of ammunition because of the recent US embargo, Carranza announced a 'definitive' campaign to end Zapata's hegemony in southern Mexico. Gradually the great social experiment ground to a halt as one by one the agrarian commissioners threw up their posts.

Paranoia and suspicion were suffusing the *zapatista* movement now, just as they were with the *villistas* in the north. Brother looked suspiciously on brother; Genovevo de la O told Zapata that telegraph operators were betraying all their secrets to Carranza. More and more chiefs, especially in Mexico State and the Federal District, accepted amnesty from Carranza, prising the gateway to Morelos open still wider. In December 1915 Zapata tried a four-pronged counteroffensive, using four armies of 2–3,000 each. Morelos, southern and central Puebla, southern Mexico State and the Federal District were the arenas for ferocious fighting, as bloody raids were countered with determined *carrancista* incursions into the heartland of Morelos. Once again Genovevo de la O proved to be Zapata's best general. Carranza's troops made a surprise thrust from Acapulco and at first swept all before them, taking Chilpancingo and Iguala and bursting into Morelos. De la O drove them back after a brilliant counteroffensive into Guerrero that took him down to the gates of Acapulco by the end of December.

As 1916 opened, Carranza bent all his energies to destroying Zapata for good. He tried to steal his clothes by offering Morelos land reform; he purged his army of all ex-federals who had acted as Zapata's fifth column; he added a further 20,000 troops to his Army of Morelos, making it 30,000 strong; and he even brought in air squadrons to flush the *zapatistas* from their hideouts in the mountains. Zapata replied with a fiery and uncompromising manifesto, hoping to rally Morelos, but many *zapatista* chiefs wanted to bargain so as to avoid devastation on the scale achieved by Robles and Huerta. Treachery, betrayal and double-dealing were everywhere in the air, poisoning the atmosphere of the would-be social utopia.

Outstandingly treacherous was the *zapatista* chieftain Francisco Pacheco. In March Zapata authorised him to put out feelers to Pablo González, whom Zapata wished either to suborn or assassinate, but Pacheco double-crossed Zapata and laid his own plans with González. Genovevo de la O detected Pacheco in his treachery and alerted Zapata, who at first refused to believe him. Soon there was no possibility for denial, since Pacheco without warning or authorisation abandoned Huitzilac to González, allowing him within striking distance of Cuernavaca. Although de la O saved the crumbling front temporarily, the gravity of the situation was clear. Pacheco actually had the impudence to complain to Zapata about de la O's supposed treachery before he finally revealed his hand openly by capturing Jojutla for González. In his moment of triumph he was captured by de la O's guards and summarily executed.

Events now moved rapidly against Zapata. On the eve of a gigantic spring offensive by the *carrancistas*, he lost one of his most important commanders when Amador Salazar was shot dead by a sniper. Then came the inferno. González encircled Morelos with his huge army of 30,000 men and took Cuernavaca on 2 May; Zapata only just made good his escape. Within days González's sheer weight of numbers told and he had taken all the major towns in Morelos except Jojutla and Tlaltizapán. On 6 May he felt confident enough to telegraph Carranza that he had completed his mission. González taught the lesson that he intended to be another Robles or Huerta. He executed 225 prisoners at Jiutepec on 8 May and sent back 1,300 refugees, who had sought sanctuary in Guerrero, to Mexico City, there to be entrained for forced labour in the Yucatán. The last gasp of the extinguished utopia came in mid-June 1916 when González took Zapata's headquarters at Tlaltizapán. He looted and sacked the town and executed a further 286 people, including 112 women and forty-two children. Beaten and despondent, the remaining *zapatistas* took to the hills. Both Zapata and Villa, who little more than a year earlier lorded it in Mexico City, were now fugitive guerrillas in the mountains.

By autumn 1915 Woodrow Wilson had reluctantly decided he had no choice but to recognise Carranza's government in Mexico. The labyrinthine twists and turns of Wilson's Mexican policy and the myriad nuances provided by the plethora of lobbyists and special interests cannot be followed here, but as late as August – when the Washington Conference of ministers from Latin American countries (Argentina,

Brazil, Chile, Bolivia, Uruguay, Guatemala) convened under the aegis of US secretary of state Robert Lansing – Wilson still hoped he could secure the emergence of a third candidate, neither Carranza nor Villa, as the next president of Mexico. This was the conference on which Zapata set so much store. By that time, however, Carranza had Mexico City in his possession and Villa and Zapata were on the back foot. Carranza remained obdurate and intransigent towards Washington, but gained the backing of US business, labour unions and influential journalists like Lincoln Steffens. After vainly trying to wring special concessions from Carranza, Wilson grudgingly recognised the state of play and extended *de facto* recognition; *de jure* did not follow until March 1917. All important countries followed the American lead: Britain, France, Germany, Russia, Japan, Italy, Spain and most of Latin America.

Wilson had no illusions about Carranza's anti-Americanism, but recognition now seemed the merest common sense. After all Carranza (or rather his general Obregón) had defeated Villa, and he had given explicit promises in private about safeguarding US property. (In public he adamantly refused to make any concessions.) For his part Wilson wanted to concentrate his energies on the critical situation in Europe and he was particularly concerned about the penetration of Mexico by German spies and agents.

Villa regarded Wilson's recognition of Carranza as the blackest ingratitude. He issued a violently worded manifesto, declaring that Wilson's recognition of Carranza was a *quid pro quo* for massive concessions by Carranza, which were tantamount to turning Mexico into an American colony. The bitterness virtually drips from every sardonic cadence: 'I emphatically declare that there is much I have to thank Mr Wilson for, because he relieves me from the obligation of giving guarantees to foreigners and especially to those who had at one time been free citizens and are today vassals of an evangelical professor of philosophy . . . I take no responsibility for future events.'

After the defeat at Agua Prieta, which Villa blamed on searchlights beamed from the US side of the border, his rage, despair and paranoia knew no bounds. Two American doctors foolishly crossed the border to attend to the *villista* wounded. In return for this errand of mercy Villa threatened to have them shot in retaliation for Wilson's treachery and ingratitude, and lectured the doctors on his previously favourable attitude to Americans. Announcing that he intended to attack the border town of Douglas, Arizona, he raged: 'From this moment on, I will devote my life to the killing of every gringo I can get my hands on and to the destruction of all gringo property.'

At the last moment Villa pardoned the doctors and did not make good his threat to attack Douglas, but the anger did not go away. Having lost to Obregón and Carranza, Villa displaced his rage on to the *yanquis*, concentrating on the fact that they had embargoed arms and allowed Carranza's troops to be transported across US territory to thwart him at Agua Prieta. Villa seems genuinely to have believed his own propaganda to the effect that US recognition of Carranza was all part of a sinister plot whereby Carranza had agreed to cede Mexico's railways and oil fields to the gringos. Villa also cynically calculated that playing the anti-American card might revive his prestige and his moribund political movement. For the first time in the Revolution there was genuine anti-American xenophobia and the *yanquis* now joined the Spanish and the Chinese in the demonology of the movement.

The force of Villa's rage against the United States in early 1916 has led some sober commentators to conclude that he was suffering from temporary insanity. It is certain that a letter he wrote to Zapata on 8 January was more than curious. Villa began by outlining the master conspiracy whereby Carranza and Wilson intended to dismember Mexico; the chicanery by which he had been defeated at Agua Prieta was all part of this. He then conceded that Zapata had been right to be so angry when Wilson sent the Marines into Veracruz in 1914. And why did he withdraw them just as Carranza was about to arrive there, almost as though by pre-established harmony? He then asked Zapata to bring his armies north so that together they could defeat the gringos. Why should Villa imagine Zapata would consent to operate in the north, when he had always made it clear he was interested only in the *patria chica* of Morelos? Why would Zapata automatically share his mania about Wilson? How did he expect Zapata to solve the logistics of a 2,000-mile trek through Carranza-held territory for a quixotic attack on the Americans? None of it is rational, but it does indicate Villa's maniacal desire to go for the *yanqui* jugular.

Villa soon showed he meant business. On 19 January 1916 seventy *villistas* under Pablo López stopped a train travelling between Chihuahua City and the US-owned Cusihuiriáchic mine at the Santa Ysabel river. On board were eighteen mining engineers. López ordered them off the train then left them to the mercy of his Mauser-toting cut-throats. Within minutes seventeen lay dead, riddled with bullets; only one survived, through feigning death. When the news filtered over the border there was outrage, and Wilson came under extreme pressure to send military units into Mexico. Villa claimed publicly that the commanding officer had exceeded orders, and López himself said that he had intended only to rob the Americans, but that when they ran away his men lost their heads and opened fire on them. Clearly, López was lying, but did he order the massacre on his own initiative or on Villa's orders? Villa disclaimed responsibility and to 'prove' it executed two of his officers and displayed their bodies publicly in Ciudad Juárez. The problem was that the dead man displayed in Juárez who had allegedly ordered the killing was José Rodríguez; the real culprit, Pablo López, was one of Villa's new favourites, so he was shielded. Despite Villa's protestations about 'exceeding orders', the probability is that López had indeed received the nod from Villa and was acting under a general mandate from him to attack Americans.

The day before the Santa Ysabel massacre, Villa assembled his 200 *dorados* and told them their next target was Presidio, the US border town next to Ojinaga. However, the men were unhappy and the march to Ojinaga turned into a fiasco, with massive desertions. On 30 January Villa bowed to the inevitable and aborted the mission. To prevent further desertion, next day he stopped a train and allowed his men to plunder at will; the spate of desertions suddenly dried up. The débâcle over Ojinaga convinced Villa that if he was to attack US targets, he could no longer confide in his men. He decided to draft men for special, unspecified missions and to this end sent his aide Candelario Cervantes to his home town of Namiquipa to press-gang all former *villista* troops. Having dragooned his quota, Villa refrained from telling them where they were going, but simply threatened to shoot their families if they deserted.

Having trained and prepared his motley force, Villa set out on 24 February for an unknown destination. In his expeditionary force were two regiments, one formed of Chihuahua veterans, the other a mixed outfit containing men from Durango, Sonora (including some Yaquis) and the farther reaches of Mexico. For two weeks the force marched towards the US border through remote regions, moving mainly at night, so that they did not run into *carrancista* patrols. The few Mexican civilians they met were taken prisoner so that they could not give the alarm, but any Americans encountered were roughly handled. Villa executed three American cowboys who simply had the bad luck to have known him from his earlier days; he also captured a woman named Maude Wright, but kept her with them until after the attack. Finally, on 8 March, Villa learned that he was just four miles from his target: Columbus, New Mexico, an undistinguished town of a few hundred inhabitants living in wooden shacks.

Why did Villa attack Columbus? Four very different motives have been suggested, in ascending order of probability. It has been asserted that the raid was an act of purely personal revenge, because Villa bore a grudge against an arms dealer in Columbus called Sam Ravel. It seems that Ravel took money as an advance against delivering a consignment of arms and then welched on the deal. In favour of the story is the fact that during the raid on Columbus the *villistas* wrecked Ravel's property before retiring; against it is the awkward fact that Villa's original target was Presidio, that he chose Columbus only as a *pis aller* after the fiasco of mass desertion on the march to Ojinaga.

A more ingenious idea is that Villa was a pawn in unseen hands. The usual candidates offered for consideration are US business interests or the Germans. The business lobby scenario implies extreme machiavellian-ism: that US capitalists would consent to see Columbus shot up and lives lost simply to provoke Woodrow Wilson into ordering an occupation of Sonora and Chihuahua, where their capital assets were. Though not necessarily impossible on that score, the theory founders on Villa's extreme and insensate anti-Americanism: it is simply implausible that in his then state of mind he would have colluded with any gringo, no matter what the motive. The Germans are more promising as conspirators. The motive would be to inveigle the USA into Mexico and make it impossible for her to intervene in the war in Europe on the Allied side; also to impair arms sales to Britain and France, as weapons and munitions would be needed by the US expeditionary force in Mexico. It is true that Germany was in favour in general terms of getting Villa to attack the USA and supported him after Columbus, but there is no evidence or proof that they set up or fomented the attack. Moreover, it was likely that the State Department could read such transparent intentions and therefore refrain from intervention, thus ruining the entire plot.

The third option is that Villa acted alone. It is possible that he acted on pure impulse and entirely spontaneously – that the raid on Columbus was simply his personal satisfaction for the insult offered by Wilson's recognition of Carranza – but more plausibly, he probably intended to provoke US intervention and discredit Carranza. So far Villa alone had inveighed massively against the *yanquis*: if they invaded, he would be proved right and his propaganda claim that Wilson and Carranza were in secret partnership triumphantly vindicated. Fourthly, it is possible that he really did believe that the USA intended to annex Mexico in due course, and thought it better to ignite the war over that issue in the here and now rather than the future.

On paper Columbus seemed a pushover for the *villistas*. Apparently there were horses, machine-guns, and Springfield rifles there, banks full of money, stores full of food, and just fifty soldiers to defend it all. However, when Villa himself did a reconnaissance of the town, he found that his spies had seriously misled him. There were not fifty troops in the garrison there, but 600. He returned, dubious about the enterprise, but this time it was his commanders who persuaded Villa. Candelario Cervantes pointed out that if they withdrew without attacking after coming so far, the men would desert in droves. Villa shrugged, and gave the order to attack during the night of 8–9 March. He addressed his 400 fighters and told them that the assault was revenge for Agua Prieta. To fire them up, he mentioned the many cases in the lower Río Grande valley in recent weeks when *chicanos* were lynched by the gringos, and the notorious true incident in El Paso where twenty Mexicans were doused with kerosene and burned alive. Allegedly he said: 'The United States wants to swallow Mexico; let's see if it doesn't get stuck in their throats.'

Villa then divided his forces, detailing one section to strike into the southern part of the town and attack the garrison at Camp Furlong, while the other boiled into central Columbus, there to rob the bank, kill Sam Ravel and gut his properties; Villa himself remained on the Mexican side of the border with a small reserve. The attack went in at 4.45 a.m. The garrison was taken completely by surprise, even though there had been repeated warnings that Villa might attempt an adventure like this. Neither General John J. 'Blackjack' Pershing, commanding all US troops on the Mexican border, nor garrison commander Herbert J. Slocum, had taken the warnings seriously. Not only was the garrison not put on alert but officers were routinely allowed to go home to their wives. In so far as Slocum did believe Villa was coming to Columbus, he appeared to think that he was coming alone to seek asylum and to explain that the Santa Ysabel massacre was nothing to do with him.

Although Camp Furlong was caught unawares, the two officers on duty managed to rally their men, helped by a colossal blunder by the *villistas*. Underestimating physical spaces in the garrison, they assumed that the stables were dormitories for the enlisted men. Raking the 'sleeping quarters' with rifle fire, they killed horses rather than soldiers. Once the American defenders opened up with machine-gun fire, the *villistas* beat a hasty retreat, but not before there had been some sanguinary hand-to-hand encounters, especially in the mess-hall. When the *villistas* broke into the kitchens, the cooks assailed them with axes, knives and boiling water; one Mexican died after being clubbed with a baseball bat.

In central Columbus meanwhile there was panic when the raiders arrived firing wildly and shouting: '*Viva Villa! Viva Mexico!*' They smashed their way into Sam Ravel's Commercial Hotel and killed four guests, one of whom foolishly opened fire on the marauders, but they could not find Ravel – not surprisingly, as he had gone to El Paso to see his dentist. His brother Louis managed to bury himself under a pile of hides, but the *villistas* found another brother, Arthur, aged fifteen, and threatened him with death if he did not reveal the combination to Ravel's safe. The youth was genuinely ignorant of it, so the raiders took him across the road to the Commercial Hotel. Later, as they emerged from the hotel, the boy's captors were gunned down by American snipers. The boy ran off into the night, unharmed.

Soon American troops in two separate detachments were converging on central Columbus, one unit with machine-guns, the other consisting of the best sharpshooters. In the pre-dawn darkness it was difficult to counterattack or distinguish raiders from civilians. However, the *villistas* made the mistake of torching the Central Hotel, which had the effect of floodlighting the fighting; the American troops were then able to open up on clear targets. At 7.30 the bugle sounded the retreat and the *villistas* withdrew in good order. US troops crossed the border in pursuit but ran into heavy resistance from Villa's reserves and returned to Columbus. Seventeen Americans, mostly civilians, had been killed in the skirmish and over 100 *villistas*. In the short run the raid was a failure, for Villa came away with no guns, stores or money from the bank. However, the long-term repercussions of this first foreign invasion of US territory since 1812 would give him a new lease of life.

The raid on Columbus caused a sensation in the United States. Woodrow Wilson was up for election in the autumn and an angry Congress and enraged public opinion forced him to act. Wilson himself was reluctant to intervene in Mexico, as he thought this was to play both Villa's and Germany's game, but after discussions with his Cabinet, who unanimously urged military action, he grudgingly accepted that he would have to do something. A number of points were made by the secretary of state and others. There was the obvious argument that unless something was done, Villa would be tempted, and almost invited, to raid US territory again. The administration's credibility in Latin America and Europe was also on the line; a particular fear expressed was that inaction would encourage Germany to step up its submarine campaign in the Atlantic. Most compelling of all arguments, though, was that a feeble response would hand the Republicans the 1916 presidential election on a plate.

Wilson still needed to be sure he would not be dragged into a full-scale war with Mexico, which would prevent his intervening in the war in

Europe. He contacted Carranza, explaining his dilemma, and assuring him that any expedition sent south of the border was not a prelude to a wider attempt at US annexation. Carranza was prepared to accept a small expeditionary force sent south with the limited aim of searching out and destroying Villa – he even helpfully cited the precedent of US–Mexican collaboration against the Apaches in the 1880s – provided he received from Wilson a pledge that Mexican sovereignty and the dignity of the Mexican people would be respected. Wilson gave the necessary assurances. On 10 March he ordered General Pershing to take 5,000 men into Mexico, there to find and extirpate Villa and his band.

On 15 March Pershing crossed the Río Grande with three brigades. His was the classic mission impossible. To catch Villa he had to fight a war of counterinsurgency, and this meant burning villages, taking reprisals, shooting prisoners. Sooner or later this was bound to involve collision with Carranza's armies, especially since Carranza made it clear he would not cooperate actively with what came to be known as the 'Punitive Expedition'. In Washington experts gloomily predicted that war with Carranza was inevitable. War plans were drawn up which envisaged the naval blockade of all Mexican ports and the military occupation of Sonora, Chihuahua, Coahuila, Nuevo León and Tamaulipas; for this huge task no less than 250,000 troops were earmarked in contingency planning. Wilson also had a war chest of millions of dollars with which he planned to recruit a quisling army to fight Carranza; from this fifth column he hoped a future Mexican president, friendly to the USA, would emerge.

Supplying the Pershing expedition was a logistical nightmare. Two hundred trucks were commandeered to drive supplies from Columbus south along an ever lengthening supply line. American pioneers were set to constructing a road into the heart of Chihuahua, for the so-called roads were so bad that the lorries could almost never get out of first gear. For the troops themselves the worst hardship was the desert weather, where men fried and baked at noonday temperatures of ninety degrees plus. Exhausted, dehydrated, with lungs choked with dust during the day, the troops then had to endure Arctic conditions at night, when the water in their canteens would freeze solid. So gruelling was the march that Pershing had to allow a ten-minute halt for every hour of trekking. Cavalrymen threw away their old-fashioned regulation sabres in disgust, expressing the wish that they could have been water-bottles.

By the end of March Pershing was deep into western Chihuahua, already 350 miles from the border. Carranza continued to take a tough line in public, adamant that he would not allow the expedition to be resupplied by rail, but privately conniving at the sleight of hand whereby fresh supplies were sent from the USA, not to the expedition as such but to named individuals in it. Yet though Pershing was well supplied, he could make little headway against a sullen or hostile population. The *carrancista* governor of Chihuahua, Ignacio Enríquez, exhorted the people to support the Americans, but they conspicuously did not do so. In difficult and unfamiliar terrain Pershing was at the mercy of local goodwill and know-how, but the villagers were uncooperative, refusing to sell anything to the invaders or even give the most elementary directions. Guides hired at great expense invariably led Pershing away from Villa, and the locals continually fed the Americans disinformation. Pershing began the long series of epistolary complaints to Washington that would consume most of his energies in 1916.

None the less, even with the active and passive support of Chihuahua, Villa's position was perilous. By the end of March Pershing commanded 7,000 troops and an air squadron of eight planes, and he was assisted in his sweep by Carranza's commanders. As the *villistas* retreated into the sierras, morale in the ranks was low; nothing seemed to have been achieved and they could not even stop to tend their wounded. The inevitable bitter recriminations broke out between Villa's lieutenants, with Cervantes and Nicolás Fernández each blaming the other for the débâcle. Yet Villa, by his sheer force of personality, charisma and the fear he inspired, kept his band together. At each *pueblo* they passed, Villa would harangue the villagers, calling on them to resist the *yanquis*, since Mexico and the United States were now at war. There was a particularly warm response at the village of Galeana, where the locals took Villa's wounded off his hands and cared for them, so that his progress would not be impeded by non-effectives. The only worry was that there were few recruits to his banner and he was forced to press new 'volunteers'.

There were signs that Villa was beginning to win hearts and minds with his anti-gringo propaganda. On 16 March the *villistas* encountered a large force of *carrancista* troops who could probably have finished them off, but the regulars rode on as if blindfolded. In the village of Matachic there was a revolt by the garrison who demanded to be allowed to join Villa and defend Mexico's sacred soil against the *yanquis*. There were many tales of Carranza's troops sheltering, hiding and even feeding the *villistas* to save them from hot pursuit by Pershing. Carranza was angry at all such stories of collaboration and sent several reiterated 'search and destroy' orders to his commanders. On 17 March there was the first skirmish between Villa and federal forces. Ten days later Villa hit back hard, taking Ciudad Guerrero and attacking the villages of Minaca and

San Ysidro in the old Orozco heartlands. The federal commander at San Ysidro beat off the *villistas*, then became overconfident and tried to retake Guerrero. This gave Villa a significant victory, in which he took eighty prisoners and hundreds of weapons.

In the thick of battle, however, Villa had taken a bad wound in the right knee. In great pain he was unable to ride and had to be carried on a litter. Realising how vulnerable he was, he decided to hole up in a mountain eyrie until he recovered, dispersing his men meanwhile into small detachments throughout Chihuahua. The journey to the mountain hideout was a nightmare. Since he had to be stretchered joltingly up mountain passes, and there was no doctor on hand, no medication and no painkillers, every step was an agony, to the point where Villa often wept with sheer pain, became delirious and lapsed in and out of consciousness. He made an interim stop at the ranch of one of his commanders halfway up the Sierra de Santa Ana, but was aware that he would be found if he tarried there too long.

Accompanied by just two men, both of them his first cousins, he was slung on the back of a mule and taken high up the sierra to the Cozmocate cave. The cousins then raised him on ropes to the narrow, slit-like entrance. Here, like those other heroes on the run, Robert the Bruce, Bonnie Prince Charlie and Lord Byron, he lived like a hermit in a cavern, holed up for seven weeks. Each day his comrades brought water and limited food (mainly rice and sugar) to the concealed cave entrance which was masked by leaves and branches. One day from his crow's nest Villa was able to see Pershing's columns ride by in the valley below. For two months he knew nothing of what was happening in the outside world. Recovery from his wound was slow, as no doctor attended him, and the only nursing he received was a crude dressing. The knee set badly and ever afterwards his right leg was shorter than his left, so that he had to walk with a specially made shoe.

Once he was ready to resume command, Villa tried to muster his men to a general rendezvous, but found that most of the detachments had been wiped out and most of his best officers lost. He accounted Candelario Cervantes the greatest loss. When Villa parted from him, Cervantes commanded a powerful detachment, but soon casualties and desertions had reduced his numbers to thirty. Cervantes then tried to find more recruits in his home town of Namiquipa, but found the villagers there grown sleek and fat on Yankee dollars, collaborating with Pershing and selling out the *villistas* and their secrets. Nothing daunted, Cervantes attacked one of Pershing's cavalry troops with his handful of followers and was killed in the fighting. Another *villista* detachment, led by Julio Acosta, was badly mauled by the Americans at Ojos Azules; though Acosta himself got away, he left behind forty-three *villistas* dead and scores of wounded.

In two months the casualty roll of Villa's officers had been alarmingly high. Manuel Baca, another killer in the Fierro class, was butchered by enraged villagers. Pablo López, the villain of the Santa Ysabel massacre, had been left behind wounded at Columbus. He somehow survived seventy-two hours without food and water before surrendering to the *carrancistas*. They took him to Chihuahua City and staged an exemplary execution. Before dying López poured out a fund of priceless information about Villa to an Irish reporter. His words of defiance are worth quoting for the light they shed on Villa's magnetic hold over his followers:

> I am only a poor ignorant peon, Señor. My only education was gained in leading the oxen and following the plough. However, when the good Francisco Madero rose in arms against our despotic masters, I gladly answered his call. We all knew Pancho Villa – and who did not? His exploits are recounted nightly at every fireside. He was the object of worship of all who were ground under the heel of the oppressor. When the call came, I was one of the first to join him and have been his faithful follower and adoring slave ever since . . . I would much prefer to die for my country in battle, but if it is decided to kill me, I will die as Pancho Villa would wish me to – with my head erect and my eyes unbandaged. History will not be able to record that Pablo López flinched on the brink of eternity.

Lopéz made good his boast. He smiled on the way to the firing squad, smoked a last cigar and, when asked for his final wishes, requested all Americans present to be cleared away. He refused to have his eyes bandaged and insisted on giving the firing squad the order to fire. López's bravery made a deep impression, created a martyr and was instrumental in turning Chihuahuans against Carranza, whom they now increasingly perceived through Villa's eyes as a Yankee running dog. It was significant that not even the US$50,000 dollars reward offered for the taking of Villa, dead or alive, could induce any traitors to lead the Americans to the cave of Cozmocate.

With the destruction of many of the *villista* bands, by the end of April Wilson came under pressure to withdraw the Punitive Expedition – ironically by the selfsame Cabinet that had originally talked a reluctant president into sending it. Wilson's secretaries of state argued, now Villa was militarily neutralised, that it was undignified for a sovereign state to pursue a solitary bandit across the territory of another sovereign state.

Tensions with Germany were rising, and it was clear that if the US wanted to go beyond the destruction of the *villista* bands to the imposition of a friendly administration in Mexico City, they would have to settle in for a conflict lasting years, involving all-out war with Carranza.

However, Wilson obstinately – and misguidedly – refused to pull the Punitive Expedition out. His reasoning was that withdrawal now would hand all the laurels to Carranza and immensely strengthen his position, when he had made no satisfactory concessions to Washington. US business interests were pressing for Pershing to remain in Mexico as a bargaining counter until Carranza gave them the economic and financial guarantees they wanted. Wilson, arguing that if Villa was not found he might stage further raids on US territory, suggested a treaty to Carranza, whereby he would withdraw Pershing in exchange for a clause allowing the USA to re-enter Mexico at any future date without any further need to consult Mexico City.

At this point alarm bells started to ring in Carranza's brain, as he realised the Americans intended to settle in for a long stay. He was also concerned at the growing public perception that he was the *yanquis*' poodle while Villa was the true national hero. From the beginning of May his attitude to the Punitive Expedition changed. He announced that Pershing would no longer be able to use the Mexican railways to resupply his forces, even under the old wink-and-nod arrangements. He also replaced Obregón, who had developed a rapport with General Hugh Scott, with the known anti-American Luis Cabrera as his chief negotiator with Washington. Cabrera demanded immediate US withdrawal with an implicit threat of war. Carranza meanwhile let his newspapers off the leash. At first he had encouraged them not to report the expedition, but by April he could no longer restrain them, especially as so many local warlords in Chihuahua were deeply unhappy with the policy of collaboration.

Pershing meanwhile was reporting anti-Americanism rising on a daily basis. When his troops entered Parral on 12 April, they were met by an angry stone-throwing mob, shouting defiance and screaming: '*Viva Villa!*' In the fighting that followed two Americans and dozens of Mexicans were killed. Pershing clamoured for the political restrictions on his campaign to be lifted, so that he could take whatever measures he saw fit. Wilson refused and ordered him to withdraw to northern Chihuahua, thus effectively ruling out the possibility that Villa could be caught. Walking the tightrope, Carranza merely issued a mild rebuke to the

Americans for their 'excesses' at Parral, but said the incident proved Pershing should now return to the United States.

A four-way conflict now developed. While Carranza and Wilson were officially united in their desire to extirpate Villa, Carranza badly wanted Pershing to withdraw, and Wilson just as badly wanted Carranza to authorise joint operations by his troops and Mexican federal forces. Pershing, chafing at his situation, was already hostile to both Carranza and Wilson, wanting only the *carte blanche* that would enable him to go after Villa in his own way. In his dispatches to Washington he was firm yet tactful, but in private he fulminated at the absurdity of the task laid upon him; how could one wage war according to a handbook of etiquette? His officers were even more outspoken. Lieutenant George Patton, later to be the fire-eating general of the Second World War, had so far had a 'good war'. When he shot dead the *villista* commander Julio Cárdenas in a skirmish, Patton recorded: 'I feel about it just as I did when I got my first swordfish. Surprised at my luck.' However, in the scatological obscenities he expended on Woodrow Wilson he excelled himself. Among his more printable opinions of the president was the following: 'He has not the soul of a louse nor the mind of a worm. Or the backbone of a jellyfish.'

In May Villa cocked a snook at the Americans by ordering a second cross-border raid, at Glenn Springs, Texas, which provoked another crossing of the frontier by US troops. This time Carranza reacted fiercely and replaced diplomacy and conciliation with a peremptory note. He told Washington that any further incursion of American troops would be vigorously resisted and he reiterated his demand that Pershing be withdrawn immediately. Pershing was informed that unless he began retracing his steps to the Río Grande, he could expect to be resisted by federal troops. General Jacinto Treviño, the *carrancista* commander, warned Pershing formally that he would be allowed to move his troops in just one direction – north – and that Treviño would attack any columns moving in other directions. There were huge anti-gringo demonstrations in Mexico City, Saltillo and Chihuahua City. War fever mounted: it was confidently expected on all sides that Wilson would again seize Veracruz, leaving Carranza no option but to attack Pershing with all his might, and perhaps even join Villa in a crusade against the *yanquis*.

Villa was particularly enraged by Wilson's statement in June 1916, when he called for an end to the civil war in Mexico and exhorted all Mexicans to unite behind Carranza as the only credible authority. This might be thought pleasing to Carranza, but he was just as appalled as Villa by the US president's blundering and impertinent intervention. As Carranza put it: 'History furnished no example in any age or country of a civil war terminating by the union of the contending parties. One or the other must triumph.' By late June 1916 the slightest spark could have ignited a general conflict, but, amazingly, no war came, even when a firebrand rather than a spark was thrown.

On 21 June there was a major clash between Pershing's men and *carrancista* troops. In defiance of Carranza, Pershing sent Captain Charles Boyd with a force of about 100 men on an eastward sweep. At Carrizal, fifty miles south of Ciudad Juárez, the headstrong Boyd, by all accounts another Patton, took his men into the town in defiance of an order to the contrary by the Mexican garrison commander. The Mexicans opened up with machine-guns, killed twelve and wounded twenty-three; but so accurate was American gunnery that even from their entrenched positions they inflicted thirty-three casualties. Among the dead were the impetuous Boyd and the Mexican commander. The Americans retreated, leaving several prisoners behind.

Here, surely, was the long awaited *casus belli*. Yet war did not break out, mainly because neither Wilson nor Carranza wanted it. Carranza, while quite prepared to play the anti-American card for domestic consumption, did not want a full-scale war that would undo all he had won in 1915, and probably replace him on the presidential chair in the National Palace. Carranza's prime aim was to get Pershing off his territory. He was losing caste with the Mexican public through his inability to make Pershing budge, and the real beneficiary of this contretemps was Villa, who gained support as the anti-American backlash picked up momentum.

Wilson, for his part, did not want to play Germany's game and get sucked into a protracted conflict in Mexico. He resisted all Pershing's pleas, entreaties and angry notes asking to be let off the leash. Whenever Pershing mentioned his favourite projects of occupying the whole of Chihuahua or, at the very least, the urban centres of Ciudad Juárez and Chihuahua City, Wilson replied with a very firm veto. He was even chary about Pershing's project of forming quisling militias in northern Chihuahua, fearful that this would trigger further confrontation like that at Carrizal.

Pershing did manage to get under Villa's skin in one respect, however. He captured the town of Namiquipa, from which so many of the Columbus raiders had come, and secured the cooperation of the villagers, whether by threats or bribery is not clear. Villa never forgot this 'treachery', which to him seemed all the more bizarre as the gringos had recently treated other Namiquipans with great cruelty. Pershing captured a score of those who had taken part in the Columbus raid and sent them back for trial in the United States. Taken to Luna County, New Mexico, and given the merest semblance of a trial before a kangaroo court and a hanging judge, the six 'ringleaders' experienced frontier lynch-law justice at its toughest ('we'll give them a fair trial and then we'll hang them'). Once the six had been hanged, American 'peace officers' turned on the others, who had been sentenced to eighty years' imprisonment. In Silver City sadistic prison guards starved and abused the Namiquipans, to the point where two of them died. The others were put to a regime of hard labour and pardoned only in 1921, when passions over the Columbus raid finally cooled.

Carranza meanwhile made soothing noises, muzzled his jingoistic press, promised to return all American prisoners of war and proposed mediation by the Latin American countries. However, eventual withdrawal of the Pershing expedition took time and was not accomplished until early 1917. Negotiations, which took place in Connecticut, repeatedly stalled over Wilson's desire to control events in Mexico and to secure guarantees and concessions in return for pulling Pershing out. Wilson was clearly being disingenuous, given the original reasons for sending the Punitive Expedition, but he found the obdurate Carranza a stone in his shoe and decided to be just as obstinate in turn. Also, it was a temperamental fault with Wilson, as he demonstrated at Versailles in 1919, that he found others wilfully blind to truths he accepted as self-evident.

Carranza doggedly insisted he would not agree to a joint US–Mexico Commission, to act as a forum for a general review of relations between the two countries, and was adamant that it be limited to the sole question of Pershing's withdrawal. He calculated that American public opinion, already tired of the wild-goose chase, would not allow Wilson to go to war over unclear objectives in Mexico, and that this drift in opinion would strengthen as the months went on. So, Carranza played for time. By the end of 1916 it was clear that Washington could secure no *quid pro quo* for withdrawal of Pershing, and finally Wilson accepted the inevitable. At the end of January 1917 the moribund Punitive Expedition broke camp, and on 5 February the last American soldier left Mexican soil. Carranza had won a great diplomatic victory. His triumph over Wilson in the duel of wills was the one event in his career that went some way to justifying his narcissistic view of himself as Mexico's saviour.

However, the embittered Americans refused to give up in their quest for Villa. Baulked on the campaign trail and the battlefield, they turned to espionage and dirty tricks. The US intelligence community got in on the act and, in an uncanny pre-echo of the CIA's vendetta against Castro of

Cuba in the early 1960s, hired assassins and hitmen to dispose of the elusive Villa. Some Japanese-Americans, posing as Tokyo-based agents, managed to worm their way into his confidence and actually poisoned his coffee, but Villa survived. He had been on his guard against poisoning for some time and always got one of his men to drink the first half of any beverage prepared for him. When all the assassination attempts failed, the US authorities tried to bury the evidence of their endeavours in closed archives.

It is generally considered that the Punitive Expedition was one of the United States's great humiliations. It became orthodoxy on the American Left that the Columbus affair had been a conspiracy involving US business interests, with Villa a conscious or unconscious partner. Germany concluded that it need not fear a US declaration of war, since the US Army was ineffective – it could not even capture a single Mexican bandit. Berlin therefore ordered unrestricted U-boat warfare – which was precisely the factor that brought the United States into the First World War. Wilson took his revenge by embargoing food, arms and (later) even gold and credit to Carranza – measures which seriously impeded the First Chief in his bid to wipe out Villa and Zapata. However, some revisionist historians have argued that the long-term consequences of the Punitive Expedition were beneficial, in that the mobilisation as a result of the tension with Mexico helped train GIs and convinced public opinion of the need for military spending.

The most famous consequence of all was the affair of the Zimmermann telegram. In February 1917 the German foreign secretary Arthur Zimmermann sent a cable in code to his ambassador in Mexico City, informing him of the beginning of unrestricted submarine warfare. In order to keep the United States preoccupied and neutral, Zimmermann proposed to offer Mexico an alliance: if Carranza attacked the United States, triggering a full-scale war in the western hemisphere, Germany would support Mexico both financially and militarily and would help her to reconquer the territories lost to the Americans after the war of 1846–8 – Texas, Arizona and New Mexico. Zimmermann ended his message by proposing a tripartite alliance between Germany, Mexico and Japan. The British broke the German code and contrived to pass on the telegram to Washington in such a way as to suggest that it had been leaked in Mexico City. When it was made public, Zimmermann did not even bother to deny that he was the author. Publication caused a sensation and meant that Woodrow Wilson did not even have to prepare US public opinion for his declaration of war on Germany.

If Carranza and Wilson had both gained in their different ways from the Punitive Expedition, the real beneficiary was Villa. The presence of Pershing and the American troops in Mexico seemed to prove the truth of everything Villa had ever said about the gringos, and Carranza further alienated Chihuahua by his military dispositions in the state. The army he sent to combat Villa and, if necessary, Pershing, was a severe strain on Chihuahua's resources. The commander, Jacinto Treviño, was a martinet who secured the dismissal of Enríquez as governor and his replacement by a more biddable figurehead. Encouraged by the apparent nod from Carranza, Treviño then manoeuvred to get rid of the *carrancista* machine politician Luis Herrera. This time Carranza put his foot down, for Herrera was a loyal placeman.

However, Carranza foolishly let Treviño have the run of Chihuahua, and Treviño soon alienated Chihuahuans by the thousand. Venal, autocratic, complaisant towards banditry, Treviño made himself a bogeyman of the middle class by refusing to allow his soldiers to be charged in shops, restaurants and bars. If anyone objected, they were taken out and shot. The lazy Treviño delegated much power to his lieutenants, who surpassed him in extortion, adding mayhem and murder to their list of crimes. The most spectacular scandal occurred when it was discovered that Treviño was profiteering by exporting food from Chihuahua City even while the townspeople were starving.

Villa gained great kudos in the first half of 1916 for having thumbed his nose at Pershing, for the myth-making stories of his concealment in the cave, and for having apparently been proved right about Carranza. Resentment towards the American invaders was compounded by hatred of Treviño and the exactions and depredations of his hyenas. The villagers forgot their earlier disenchantment with Villa, who was now remembered through a golden nimbus. The time was right for a revival of the *villista* movement, and in the second half of 1916 Villa came roaring back to life as a guerrilla leader, almost as though his career had not missed a beat and there had never been a Punitive Expedition.

THE TWILIGHT OF ZAPATISMO

Expelled from their Eden, the *zapatistas* at first could only watch helplessly as the serpent destroyed paradise. Pablo González was the latest, and most terrible, of the scourges of Morelos. Ambitious, bloodthirsty, brooding on ancient wrongs, González was another of those men propelled from obscurity into the limelight by the Revolution, a kind of Bernadotte of Mexico. Orphaned at six, a peddlar at fourteen, failed immigrant to the USA, quondam merchant and small-time politician in Coahuila, González was above all an opportunist who believed only in González. First a *maderista*, then a fence-sitter, and finally a *carrancista*, González enjoyed the dubious reputation of being the only general never to have won a battle. He aped Huerta's smoked glasses and was generally despised as a prize *stupidus*, with ambition far outrunning his abilities. Most of all, he was Carranza's creature, an overpromoted nonentity, deliberately built up by Carranza as a counterweight to Obregón, who was beyond his control. An unscrupulous sycophant with an eye to the main chance, González was prepared to try anything, do anything, go anywhere in order to climb to the top of the greasy pole.

His first step in Morelos was to obliterate all traces of the Convention and to destroy Palafox's agrarian reforms. He used the methods of Huerta and Robles, burning, looting, executing by the score and deporting by the hundred, but he added a new refinement of his own: the deliberate destruction of food and property to impoverish and starve out the people who had sustained Zapata over six years. If ever there was a true Attila of the South, it was González. Everything was swept into the maw of this all-consuming Moloch: sugar, subsistence crops, cattle, mills, farm machinery, military *matériel*, boxcars, cannon, ammunition, coal, sulphur, gunpowder, dynamite, nitroglycerine, sulphur, copper, hides, printing presses. González and his henchmen made a fortune selling off food and surplus goods to Mexico City middlemen and he justified his vandalism as depriving Zapata of the sinews even of guerrilla war.

From his new headquarters at Tochimilco at the foot of the Popocatépetl volcano, Zapata prepared to strike back. He now operated with detached units of a maximum size of 200 apiece, easier to feed and harder to trace. In July 1916 he made his presence felt. He wiped out two federal garrisons at Santa Catarina and Tepoztlán, raided the Federal District and then fought a seven-hour running battle with González's troops at Tlayacapan, as well as making two different assaults in force on the garrison at Tlaltizapan. González's claim that he had pacified Morelos was revealed as a hollow boast.

Zapata directed a complex cell-like structure of command with at least seven major bands in the field, in the four corners of Morelos, on the border of Morelos and Mexico State, in Guerrero and the Federal District. Altogether he had 5,000 men on active operations at any one time, with another 3,000 held in reserve. Before going over to the offensive, he had to be sure of morale and support, for it was evident that not all Zapata's old chieftains wanted to fight. In a proclamation in August he denounced these fainthearts as time-serving cowards and egotists, interested only in feathering their own nests. Among those singled out for denunciation was Lorenzo Vásquez, formerly a most trusted aide but since then one of those, like Montaño and Pacheco, who favoured doing a deal with Carranza. Zapata announced that Vásquez had been discharged for 'notorious cowardice' and warned that he would visit the same penalty on all who came to terms with the enemy.

In October Zapata felt secure enough to mount an offensive. To blunt González's policy of destruction and deportation, he felt that the best tactic was to target politically sensitive objectives, whose seizure would impair the credibility of the Carranza regime. Accordingly, on 4 October, after a ferocious battle, he seized the pumping station at Xochimilco, which supplied Mexico City with all its water. A week later he sacked the suburb of San Ángel, just eight miles from the Zócalo, and destroyed the streetcar station. Zapata's new policy was to avoid attacking garrisons but to pick on targets – railways, factories, mills – whose destruction would impress foreign consuls and diplomats; cynically he had come to see that foreigners were always more impressed by the annihilation of property than the killing of human beings.

There followed a wave of raids across a broad swathe of territory, all aimed at sensitive plant, installations and buildings – in Oaxaca, Guerrero, Michoacán, Puebla, Tlaxcala, Mexico State and southern Hidalgo. The scale of the operations took Carranza aback. Not only had he wrongly concluded that Zapata was finished, but he had noted that in the great rising in Oaxaca in 1914–15 the tiger of Morelos had played no part; yet now a more sophisticated political consciousness seemed in evidence. Zapata made a point of sending his raiders two or three times a week into the Federal District to keep the citizens in the capital in a permanent state of nervousness, and by a system of political commissars, he took great care that none of his guerrillas alienated the villages and that there were no feuds within or between the *pueblos*.

Pablo González reacted with all the wounded fury of a mendacious moron whose lies have been detected by the boss. He announced that if even one villager was found to have aided Zapata, the entire village would be destroyed and all the males put to death. Anyone straying out of village bounds or caught travelling without a pass was shot on sight. He stepped up the rate of deportation and of looting, with more and more portable property removed to Mexico City by his minions. Then, with his casualties running at the rate of 100 a week, he finally lost patience and resumed mass executions. At Tlaltizapán, chosen for its symbolism in the *zapatista* movement, he consigned 180 men, women and children to the firing squad.

This savagery merely prompted an escalation of the violence. On 7 November, near Joco station in the Federal District, the *zapatistas* blew up a crowded train on the Mexico City-Cuernavaca line. Four hundred passengers and troops died in the carnage. The embarrassment was particularly acute for González, as he happened to be in the capital, conferring with Carranza, when the news came in. His only thought was for more repression. When he returned to Cuernavaca on 11 November, he announced draconian extensions to his pass laws: henceforth anyone found near a railway without official authorisation, with or without a highway pass, would be executed on the spot, as would anyone dishonestly vouching for another so as to get a safe-conduct pass, or anyone who gave his safe-conduct pass to another. González also gave his troops a virtual licence to kill, by issuing a new decree that anyone even suspected of being a *zapatista* would be executed without trial. Zapata's response was to blow up another train, not far from the first one; deaths were well over 300.

As Zapata had hoped, US envoys reported to Washington that Carranza's grip on the country was uncertain, that Mexico was sliding towards anarchy. In desperation González ordered a 500-yard section of no-man's land to be cleared on either side of the railway track from the capital to Cuernavaca. He ranted and raged to Carranza that Zapata would not fight fair, complained that Obregón was sabotaging him in the background, and asked for even more troops. Carranza bluntly told him that if he could not manage with 30,000, a few thousand more would make no difference. Besides, there were no more to be had. Three large armies were already deployed elsewhere, one to deal with Villa, one to conduct surveillance on Pershing, and another to deal with a fresh rebellion in Oaxaca under Félix Díaz. The last straw was when González's troops in Morelos started succumbing in their hundreds to disease: first malaria and dysentery, later typhoid. By December 1916, 7,000 of the 30,000 were dead, or were in military hospitals where many more expired since medical supplies did not reach them; quinine and morphine sent for their relief were seized by black marketeers in league with corrupt officers in the commissariat, and the febrifuge drugs were then sold on the black market in Mexico City. Throughout Morelos sick and dying soldiers could be seen lying in huts and boxcars and even supine in the streets.

Realising that the time had come for a final push, Zapata showed his contempt for González by returning to his old headquarters at Tlaltizapán, from where he launched simultaneous attacks on ten cities and towns: Cuernavaca, Puebla, Yautepec, Jojutla, Jonacatepec, Axochiapan, Paso del Mundo, Izúcar de Matamoros, Chietla and Atlixco. The demoralised federals buckled beneath these coordinated attacks. On the first day of the offensive alone, the *zapatistas* killed or captured 500 of the enemy and González ordered a general withdrawal. On New Year's Day 1917 the *zapatistas* triumphantly re-entered the major towns of Morelos.

Zapata was disgusted by what he saw when he went down to Cuernavaca. The city was a combination of ghost town and bombsite, with just three families in concealed residence; the rest had either fled or been deported. Levels of vandalism by González's men were unspeakable: most of the houses had their front doors ripped off, the sanitation system had been deliberately wrecked so that the feculent streets were like open sewers, churches had been despoiled and images and statues of the saints defaced and desecrated.

In the victorious euphoria of the moment, some *zapatista* leaders lost their heads and talked wildly of pressing on to Mexico City; others imagined themselves back in 1914 and talked in all seriousness of the importance of getting to the capital before Villa. However, Zapata knew that it was one thing for González to cut and run in Morelos, quite another to think Carranza would do likewise in the capital. For a while there would be stalemate, allowing Zapata to resume the task of agrarian reform, but in the end, as Zapata knew, there would be another reckoning.

Carranza was unable to deal effectively with Zapata in 1916–17 as he had a host of other problems occupying his attention, diplomatic, military, social and economic. After six years of virtually non-stop warfare, Mexico was in chaos. Crops were unharvested, cattle had been exported to buy arms, mines and factories closed. In the cities banks failed, capitalists hoarded their assets, black markets flourished. Everywhere there were shortages of food, water, coal and other basics. Agriculture was in crisis as subsistence crops failed and there was no money with which to import grain. Peasants were reduced to eating bran mixed with sawdust or even earth. Deprived of their cattle, they overcame a great Mexican cultural taboo and killed and ate horses. Famine stalked the land, and in its wake came disease and pestilence. The countryside was a wasteland of bent and twisted railway tracks, gutted buildings, burned bridges, dynamited factories, carcasses of dead horses or makeshift mass graves for the human fallen. Even in the parched deserts an endless *vista* of devastation could be descried, particularly with the detritus and abandoned vehicles of the Pershing expedition. In the cities and towns indigence and destitution were widespread, and hundreds of cripples, limbless men, mutilated veterans and gravely wounded walking hospital cases thronged the streets.

The once proud Mexican railways were a mockery of the very idea of infrastructure. All of the great political factions had their particular specialisation in train wrecking. Carranza liked to rip up track, Villa to use *máquinas locas* as improvised missiles, and Zapata to blow up trains – a technique that T. E. Lawrence would start to use in Arabia later in 1917. On the northern plains, alongside the bones of cattle and the charnel-house of human corpses, were dynamited and derailed locomotives and rolling stock – more than 50,000 tons of steel and scrap iron awaiting salvage. The line from Saltillo to Mexico City was in an especially bad state of repair, with rusty spikes, bent nails and decayed sleepers. The Veracruz line had been reduced to just twenty-seven locomotives with roofless cars and the woodwork rotting away in the rolling stock. For lack of coal and oil, all trains ran slowly with frequent stops, because they had to consume wood; a 100-mile rail trip in the interior could take as long as the scheduled railway run from Mexico City to New York, even assuming the hazards of bandits and derailments were avoided. Although the deficiencies in the railway system harmed all aspects of the export and import economies, it was the impact on food supplies that was most keenly felt. For much of 1916–19 Mexico was a hungry land.

Perhaps the worst aspect of the general chaos was financial. All sides in the Revolution had simply printed money and forced people to accept it; the result was a plethora of banknotes and hyperinflation to rival the later astounding phenomenon in Germany in 1923. By the end of 1916 Mexico was switching to barter, while Carranza seized the bullion holdings of the major banks and decreed that only gold, silver and the US dollar would be acceptable as media of exchange. In 1917 he introduced a new metallic currency, fixed all wages and prices in terms of gold and silver, and made the US dollar the only paper currency that was legal tender. The wonder is that there was not even more unrest in the cities during the Carranza years, but he was able to buy off urban malcontents as a result of the huge surge in commodity prices consequent on the First World War. The US price of silver doubled in 1915–18, that of copper rose by two-thirds while the price of henequen actually tripled.

It is a backhanded tribute to Carranza to say that, even when faced with chaos on this scale, he did not put his political programme on hold, heave to and wait for the storm to abate, but pressed ahead as if he presided over a booming peacetime economy. A centralising control freak, he proved much tougher than Díaz, far more able than Huerta and infinitely more skilled as a politician than Madero. He eliminated the *huertista* old guard, rigidly controlled all newspapers, purged the civil service and diplomatic corps, took personal control of the railways, forced loans and taxes on all areas deemed hostile, persecuted Spaniards, and used execution as a reflex action. Carranza regarded anyone who would not come to heel as an enemy to be hunted down without pity. Whereas Juárez had decreed a general amnesty in 1867, his so-called follower was implacable, merciless and bloodthirsty.

Carranza was determined to make his writ run in every corner of Mexico. Where Villa, if successful, would have been content with a loose federalism and a strong assertion of states' rights, Carranza wanted rigid, bureaucratic control from the centre. He pursued a ruthless policy of purging all opposition, whether ex-*porfiristas*, ex-*huertistas*, ex-*villistas*, ex-*zapatistas* and even ex-*maderistas*, in favour of a narrow clique of northern apparatchiks, and was particularly efficient in weeding out potentially disaffected officers in the Army. Intransigence and hostility to compromise became badges of honour and loyalty tests in the eyes of the Carranza political machine.

It was a rich irony that a movement that began life in favour of local autonomy ended by imposing more rigid centralising policies than Díaz or Huerta ever had. Even minor officials were hounded with questionnaires and investigations into their past. Carranza's political machine was Stalinism *avant la lettre*, with spies and informers everywhere. Naturally, those with their hands on the levers of power used accusations of 'disloyalty' to settle private disputes and ordered seizures of land, not for redistribution, but to punish rivals as well as recalcitrants.

Carranza believed in replacing even minor officials in distant places with loyal placemen, but in southern Mexico an additional motivation was at work. Just as Zapata despised the city as the fount of corruption, Carranza despised the south as the home of decadence and hoped to redeem it. He had the same sort of contempt for southern regions as the northern abolitionists had for the ante-bellum South in 1860, or the northern European members of the EU have for their Mediterranean brethren today. In all cases, the suspicion is of a corrupt, brutal, criminal, hedonistic *dolce far niente* mentality. Hence Carranza's classic 'carpetbagging' in the 'deep south' of Tabasco, Oaxaca, Chiapas and Yucatán, when he sent his 'proconsuls' to secure those territories for him in 1914–15, before Villa was defeated. It has also been speculated that Carranza viewed the south as perfect territory for an 'eagle's nest' last-stand redoubt in case Villa was victorious, which was why he had urged a southern strategy on Obregón.

Carranza differed from Villa in that he wanted real control of an area, not just token fealty, obeisance and loyalty from local caudillos and warlords. This was why he laid so much emphasis on the character and personality of his warlords, of whom three predominated: Francisco Múgica, Jesús Agustín Castro and Salvador Alvarado, governors respectively of Tabasco, Oaxaca and Chiapas and Yucatán. However, Carranza's centralising tendencies usually generated a three-way conflict in the remoter states: between the *carrancistas* and the old class of *hacendados* who wanted to run things the old way and resented being ordered by Mexico City to abolish debt peonage; and *within* the Carranza movement between the local *carrancista* apparatchiks and lukewarm supporters and the new favourites sent down as governors and proconsuls – a classic struggle of 'ins' and 'outs' or Court and Country.

Carranza was not a man of great political vision like Zapata or even Villa, but as a politician he possessed strengths they did not have. He was a technocrat, who could work happily in the impersonal area of bureaucracy, political machines, national newspapers and international diplomacy; Zapata and Villa were always limited by the horizons of the village, the hacienda, the state and the *patria chica*. Only Obregón had the imagination to comprehend both. The charge that Carranza was the quintessential bourgeois is substantially correct. Age had not withered or softened this ruddy-faced old man with his long beard and blue-tinted glasses, and he still represented the values of what one historian has called 'clean linen, breakfast trays . . . and ice buckets for wine'.

Yet the middle classes as such did not benefit much in the short term from Carranza. His project was to mobilise the masses to modernise

Mexico and create a more stable state than Díaz's, where the 'contradictions' between modernisation and the haciendas had been ironed out. To
do this he had to employ revolutionary rhetoric if not practice. The effect
of this, as of the previous terrible six years, was to make the middle
classes keep their heads down. Having seen the emotions that could be
aroused by any manifestation of inequality, they no longer paraded in
public in fine clothes but tried to camouflage themselves by merging into
a grey *déclassé* background. Many had fled abroad, principally to the
United States, and would not return while Carranza's precarious state-
building experiment was going on. It was significant that while the US
Marines were in Veracruz, that was the city to which large numbers of
the middle classes gravitated. Most had concluded that whoever headed
the Revolution, whether Villa or Carranza, it was not for them.

Carranza was a workaholic desiccated calculating machine, who made
few friends at either the personal or social level. Hugely unpopular, he
was the living embodiment of Weber's rational-legal leadership, as against
the charismatic spark of Villa and Zapata. People observed him in silence,
without any enthusiasm and never with genuine applause; any cheers
heard at his speeches were the stage-managed efforts of the rent-a-mobs
hired by his supporters. 'Frosty', 'cold', 'icy', 'tepid', 'lukewarm', were
simply the politer terms to describe him as he vainly travelled the country
trying to build a cult of his personality. Kissing babies and pressing the
flesh was not for Carranza; he tended to react to human contact with
glacial hauteur mixed with petulance. Teetotal, a non-smoker, with no
breath of sexual scandal surrounding him, Carranza featured in the
revolutionary *corridos* (notably in *La Cucaracha*) purely as a figure of fun
and a butt for Villa.

Carranza's unpleasant personality was not just the invention of his
enemies, of *zapatista* and *villista* propaganda, but an objective fact noted
by almost all who met or interviewed him. Two judgements from
sympathisers, one of them a close supporter, are eloquent: 'He resembled
an English nonconformist mayor more than a president of revolutionary
Mexico' and 'General Carranza is not what might be termed an easy,
approachable man, or one who might inspire any considerable devotion or
personal loyalty.' Those who met him, from the Spanish writer Blasco
Ibáñez to the American reporter John Reed, went away unimpressed.
Conversation with him was always hard going: he had no small talk, no
gallery touch, no gift with people. His patriarchal beard was a particular
object of irritation. 'Bewhiskered old goat,' people whispered in corners,
and the famous beard was celebrated in hundreds of jokes and songs,
most of them obscene.

Yet one needs to give him grudging admiration for his indomitable willpower. Full of unctuous rectitude, he took on powerful enemy after powerful enemy: socialists, land reformers, US capitalists, the Catholic Church, and a host of rebels and insurgents, and he took them all on simultaneously. The Church had done well under Díaz and even under Madero, but received a rude awakening when Huerta came to power. In his anticlericalism Carranza was the continuation of Huerta by other means. His antipathy towards Catholicism was unfair, in that the Church was by no means monolithic. There certainly were reactionary bishops who deserved the lash from Carranza, but there were also revolutionary clerics whose social thinking was more advanced than Carranza's. The Church, after all, had had no difficulty adapting to the social programmes of Villa and Zapata.

However, Carranza and Obregón both saw Catholicism as fundamentally a reactionary force: it always tried to swim along with whoever held power, it had huge resources and rich lands which it guarded jealously and, most of all, it influenced hearts and minds. As such it was a fetter on a modern dynamic society with a burgeoning economy and needed to be cut down to size – long-term through the education of the masses, short-term through persecution. This latter took violent and vociferous forms. *Carrancistas* drank out of chalices, wore priestly vestments as motley, built fires in confessionals, shot up relics and sacred images, converted churches into barracks and carried out mock executions on the statues of saints. In Mexico State they banned sermons, christenings, confessions, masses and even the kissing of priests' rings.

Carranza did not prevent these anticlerical outbursts as they formed a valuable part of his apparatus of centralised control. In his case a personal puritanism and fastidiousness made him look askance at a Church which connived at hedonism, fiestas, drinking, gambling, bullfights and even the sins of the flesh – in Carranza's mind all signs of backwardness and vice. His mouthpieces accused the Church of revelling in the squalor of the peasantry, to the point where it opposed elementary hygiene and washing with soap. Carranza was well aware of the absurdity of some of these charges, but he wanted the Church firmly under his heel, so that it could not emerge as an ideological rival to his version of the Revolution or mobilise its supporters to form a powerful political party. However, he was no anticlerical zealot, for he knew that virulent anti-Catholicism could be dangerous; when such people genuinely came to power in the 1920s, they triggered the bloody Cristero rebellion.

Even as he repressed one powerful institution, he dealt still more firmly with a far more formidable enemy: foreign capitalism championed by the USA. There had been no hostility to foreign investment as such under Madero, simply an insistence that the companies and corporations pay taxes at the proper level, instead of enjoying the bonanza profits of the Díaz years. However, Carranza saw the penetration of the Mexican economy by foreign capitalists as a deep affront to Mexican sovereignty and, even when hard-pressed in Veracruz in late 1914, made clear his determination to reform the basis on which foreign and oil companies operated in Mexico. In March 1915, when Villa was still expected to win the civil war, he raised taxes on foreign mining interests. When Washington protested vigorously, Carranza riposted by granting exemptions for small companies but not the US giants, and continued to resist all pressure from secretary of state Lansing. In August 1915 he passed a new law, making it illegal for foreign companies to defend their interests by diplomatic means – any defence had to be conducted through the Mexican courts – but although Carranza was anti-American, he was no fool. He may have flirted with Germany, but he did not risk Mexican neutrality by overprovoking the Americans, and he resisted all German machinations, especially in the matter of the Zimmermann telegram.

On land reform Carranza was always ambivalent. He accepted a measure of it opportunistically, with absolutely no scintilla of ideological conviction. His proclamation of 11 June 1915 virtually froze matters on an 'as is' basis with its statement that no land would be confiscated 'which had been acquired legitimately from individuals or governments and which did not constitute a special privilege or monopoly'. His National Agrarian Council took a year to get under way and when it finally started work (8 March 1916), proceeded at a snail's pace. Then on 19 September 1916 Carranza suspended all land grants made by the Council. By 1917 the Council had restored lost land to just three villages in the whole of Mexico. It was small wonder that Zapata called Carranza 'a sonofabitch'.

While contemptuous of the peasantry, Carranza did listen to Obregón and build bridges to the urban working class. The *Casa del Obrero Mundial* (The House of the World Worker – Mexico's equivalent of the TUC) signed an agreement with Obregón and Carranza at the beginning of the civil war. In return for preferential treatment, the *Casa* promised to fight the 'forces of reaction' (i.e. Villa and Zapata) and established six 'Red Battalions' manned by artisans – carpenters, bricklayers, stonecutters, tailors, typesetters, etc. However, as soon as Villa was defeated and the Battalions had outlived their usefulness, Carranza hit back harshly at workers who had the temerity to strike against his government. His real double-cross of the workers came in August 1916. When the call for a general strike went up, Carranza revived a law of 25 January 1862, under which strikers could be condemned to death, and on 2 August Carranza's police shut down the *Casa*. The First Chief justified his cynical brutality by inane rhetoric to the effect that the striking workers had denied 'the sacred recognition of the fatherland'.

Obregón and the radicals were not happy with Carranza's reactionary stance on labour relations and planned to outwit him at the Constitutional Conference called in Querétaro. With his histrionic sense of the past, Carranza set out for the historic conference at 8 a.m. on 18 November 1916, riding all day on horseback from the capital to Querétaro, where Juárez had executed Maximilian. Carranza confidently expected to be able to build continuity with Juárez's 1857 Constitution, but the young Turks in his movement had other ideas.

Part of what Carranza wanted he got. The Constitution, finally promulgated in early 1917, increased the power of the presidency, abolished the office of vice-president and weakened the legislature. Here was irony indeed. The Revolution had not just devoured its own children but had created a new chief executive with powers greater than Díaz had enjoyed. A seismic national convulsion to oust a dictatorship ended by entrenching an even more authoritarian figure at the head of an even more authoritarian system. This was exactly what Carranza wanted. He did not believe in the pluralism of parties, voters and political participation. He defined democracy as the paternalistic state, with himself as the embodiment of both state and democracy or, as he put it: 'Democracy . . . cannot be anything other than the government of noble, profound and severe Reason' (with himself as Reason of course).

However, the radicals had their pound of flesh. They and Carranza could agree on Article 27 of the Constitution, as this gave Carranza what he needed in his battle with the US oil and mining companies. Article 27 declared that private property was not an absolute right but one that could be revoked, as the ultimate owner of land, water and subsoil rights was the nation. It was laid down that in any conflict over subsoil rights (clearly the oil companies were envisaged), foreign owners would not be allowed to appeal to their governments but would have to abide by the decision of the Mexican courts. Yet on Article 123 Carranza was clearly outflanked by his radicals. Paradoxically (in view of the prevailing anticlericalism) influenced by Leo XIII's encyclical *Rerum Novarum*, this article stipulated an eight-hour working day, abolition of child labour, protection for working women and adolescents, holidays, reasonable wages payable in cash, profit-sharing, arbitration and compensation in case of dismissal.

On religion too the radicals at first had their way. In Articles 3 and 130 the Church was refused recognition as a legal entity, priests had to be publicly registered, religious education and all rituals outside churches were prohibited, and the churches themselves were made the property of the state. Carranza had a short way with this. As chief executive he simply refused to implement the articles against religion. He proposed entirely new and conciliatory Articles 3 and 130, and when Congress rejected these, got snarled up in a constitutional crisis on the matter. Carranza took the line that the radical reforms passed against his will at Querétaro were mistaken and that he had the God-given right to ignore, veto or sabotage them.

Yet overwhelmingly Carranza's main problems were military, in two senses, internal and external. Carranza tried to make the military subordinate to his civilian bureaucracy while ultimately relying on the Army to enforce his will – a difficult juggling act. Moreover, because opposition to his centralism was so intense, Carranza had to make sure the Army was reliable. The most obvious means was bribery, and Carranza paid the military so well that the manpower and establishment budget for the Army was ten times the figure under Díaz. However, because of corruption – the favourite scam was padded payrolls – the tax burden on citizens was out of all proportion to the security the military provided. Carranza knew what was happening, but was prepared to connive at the graft of his generals provided they did not challenge him.

To prevent their making common cause with rebels in their own localities, troops from the north were sent to serve in the south, while southern levies were sent to control the north. This created other problems. Northerners could not deal with the humid climate of the steamy jungles of the south nor the southerners with the cold of the north. Such a high degree of mobilisation into alien areas spread disease, and because of homesickness, the troops tended to rebel or desert. Aggravating the situation was the frequent non-payment of soldiers, as the generals had pocketed their wages. The scale of military and government corruption reached the point where the word *carrancear* was coined to describe official embezzlement and defalcation. Carranza's bureaucrats and generals were described as being *con uñas listas* (with fingernails at the ready) and there were many plays on words such as *sociedad* and *suciedad* ('society' and 'filth').

It was with these corrupt and lacklustre officers and men that Carranza hoped to wage war to the knife against a series of determined, deadly and ideologically committed enemies. There were Villa and Zapata, and for a while there was Pershing, but this nowhere near exhausted the list of enemies. There was the formidable private army of Manuel Peláez, which hired out at US$15,000 a month and was used by the US-owned Mexican Petroleum at Tampico and by El Águila, the British oil giant operating at Poza Rica and Papantla. There was endemic banditry – especially in west-central Mexico and Tampico and San Luis – and in the Laguna area guerrilla leaders like Calixto Contreras were active, indirectly helping Villa by their depredations. At various times the towns of Yerbaus, Pedriceña, Rodeo, San Juan del Río and Cuencamé all fell to the guerrillas.

In Sonora there were continuing problems with the Yaquis. In December 1915 Obregón tried in person to broker a deal with the Yaqui chiefs, but refused their demand for absolute dominion over their ancestral lands. While the so-called *manso* (tame) Yaquis surrendered, their *bronco* brethren fought on. In another ferocious Yaqui war, large numbers of troops drove the Indians into the mountains, from which they raided and spread terror through Sonora state. In spring 1916 they took the defended town of Merichichi, but were unable to make further headway because of shortage of ammunition. After a short period of peace, war broke out again in the summer of 1917. Calles, trying to build a political career for himself in the shadow of Obregón, threatened dire retribution, but the Yaquis, so good at guerrilla warfare, made monkeys of the federal troops, to the point where one American reporter later compared the Yaqui conflict to the Rif war in Morocco.

Most of all, there was Félix Díaz's revolt in Oaxaca. Beginning in 1916, this soon overtook the threat from Villa and Zapata as the most dangerous of all the challenges to Carranza's regime. Díaz, the dictator's nephew, was the Revolution's permanent gadfly. Under his uncle he had been a career soldier and Inspector-General of Police, and in 1911 he had briefly acted as governor of Oaxaca before throwing up the office in pique. In 1912 he first made his mark as a putschist when he headed an abortive rebellion in Veracruz. Imprisoned by Madero when he should have been executed, he collaborated in Reyes's failed coup in February 1913 but after *La Decena Trágica* thought he had the presidency in his pocket. Huerta double-crossed him and drove him into exile, first in Havana, then New York and New Orleans. On Díaz's return to Texas Huerta gave him another chance, but Díaz refused to collaborate because of Huerta's links with Germany.

Díaz was always lucky, as his amazing adventures in early 1916 proved. He set out to raise rebellion against Carranza and sailed south from Galveston, but his ship was caught in a ferocious storm in the Gulf; Díaz and his henchmen were shipwrecked and all their papers lost. This proved fortunate when they managed to swim ashore just south of the

Mexican border, for they escaped identification when they were stopped by the local police. After a tortuous journey via Mexico City, Díaz finally reached his destination, Oaxaca, in the summer of 1916. Here he raised an army of 3,000 men, but alienated the locals by forced contributions. As a result they collaborated with government troops against Díaz and, after several bad maulings from the federals, he decided to switch his base of operations to Chiapas. After a terrible trek through the steamy jungles of the south-east, he emerged in Chiapas with just 100 of his original 3,000.

The year Díaz really came into his own was 1917. This time he found a way to coexist harmoniously with the local rebels and gradually to make them over to his cause. He began raiding over a wide area: Tabasco, Oaxaca, Veracruz. His aim was to do in the south what Carranza had done in the north in 1913–14: head a disparate and heterogeneous coalition of rebels. His manifesto, the Plan of Tierra Colorada, dated 1 February 1916, had cunningly asserted that legitimacy and constitutional legality lapsed in Mexico in October 1913, when Huerta dissolved Congress; Díaz could hardly have cited February 1913 as the date for the end of legitimacy, for it was his machinations that had triggered Madero's downfall. Cunning, too, was the programme of liberal conservatism in the manifesto with which Díaz tried to hook all the 'out' groups: priests, Catholics, Spaniards, ex-federals, ex-Army officers, etc. With an eye to possible support from the Allies, he bitterly denounced Carranza's allegedly pro-German sympathies. The appeal of Díaz was to all those disaffected conservative and reactionary groups who were repelled by the radicalism of Villa and Zapata.

Since 1917 was the year of Mexico's allegedly 'socialist' constitution, of the Russian Revolution and of the American entry into the First World War, it was not surprising that a brew consisting of strong pro-Allied sentiment and right-wing social nostrums made a strong appeal. A major breakthrough was Díaz's alliance with Manuel Peláez, which meant that the oil companies paid taxes, officially under protest, to the rebels. In general, property owners were happy to pay levies to Díaz in return for the sort of protection against genuine bandits that Carranza could never provide. The United States viewed the spread of the *felicista* (after Félix Díaz) revolt with particular satisfaction. Angry with Carranza for his plans to tax US oil interests and the subsoil declaration in the 1917 Constitution, and worried about the threat of German sabotage to the pipelines about which Carranza was maddeningly complacent, Washington covertly backed Díaz and Peláez, shipped arms to them and even laid contingency plans to occupy the oil fields if Carranza managed to defeat Díaz and Peláez. Fortunately, perhaps, these schemes remained on the back burner. Washington never actually intervened on the side of Díaz and Peláez and gradually came to terms with Carranza.

The *felicistas* proved as hard to defeat as Villa and Zapata. Even though Peláez did not have the advantage of mobility – he had to defend Tampico – Carranza's forces still could not dislodge him. Although Carranza's propaganda organs lambasted Díaz and his followers as 'counter-revolutionaries', the mud would not stick, perhaps because people were so disgusted by the endemic corruption of the Carranza system that they were not prepared to buy that particular bill of goods from him. Some say that Díaz was lucky in that the Indians of the south supported him, when their objective interests seemed to lie with the *carrancistas* who had promised to abolish debt peonage. However, localism and adherence to the *patria chica* by the Indians need not have been 'false consciousness'. Conflict in the south was always village against village not, as in Morelos, *campesinos* against *hacendados*. Choosing the deep south as the headquarters for his trans-class conservative coalition was a shrewd move on Díaz's part.

The *felicista* movement was at root composed of disaffected conservatives, the last hope of those who had prospered under Porfirio Díaz, but it was also an eclectic mix of all kinds of political adventurers with different power bases in different localities. Some of Díaz's supporters were indistinguishable from bandits, while others identified banditry as Mexico's single biggest curse. It appealed to all who resented Carranza's centralism, all who wanted a loose federal structure and all who thought Carranza and his clique were corrupt land-grabbing opportunists. Most of all, it drew on southern resentment of the north and its dominance in the Revolution and on southern hatred of Carranza's proconsuls. For the same reason, its principal weakness was it had no appeal in the north and could therefore never achieve the critical 'take off' point as a genuinely national movement.

The *felicista* movement was a great help to both Villa and Zapata in the years 1917–20, as it drew off Carranza's forces to deal with a threat considered much more serious. At their most powerful, the *felicistas* could field more than 20,000 men – up to 15,000 in Veracruz, 2,000 in Chiapas, 2,000 in Tabasco, plus a large force in Puebla. Carranza made as little headway against Díaz as Pablo González had made against Zapata in 1916, and for the same reasons: the poor calibre of federal troops, the mistaken use of terror and repression, and the pervasive corruption of the regime, which saw federal generals selling ammunition to the rebels. The result was a stand-off, for Díaz's movement was weakened both by his inability to appeal to the north and by increasing factionalism, with Peláez only nominally under Díaz's control.

Félix Díaz's rebellion posed particular problems for Zapata, for in many ways the *felicistas* were in competition with him – in the case of Puebla, literally for the same space. Although ideologically *felicismo* was not a rival – its leaders were propertied, its concerns local and provincial rather than agrarian, its interest in land reform purely pragmatic – it was an important fact of life in the south. Some *zapatista* leaders secretly blamed Zapata for not having devoted more attention to Oaxaca earlier, thus providing an opportune gap which Díaz filled. Some also actively lobbied for an informal military alliance with Díaz as the best way to defeat Carranza. Zapata would have none of it. Until the very end of his career, he remained impatient and disdainful of all 'popular front' approaches to politics and remained the sea-green incorruptible in his commitment to land reform – but the unlikelihood that Félix Díaz would sign up to Zapata's Plan of Ayala was plain for all to see.

In early 1917 Zapata was again obsessed with getting back to the interrupted work of agrarian reform and local democracy. By now, after seven years of war, the hacienda had ceased to exist as an institution in Morelos. Its labour force had been conscripted, deported or had simply bolted; its buildings had been gutted, its mills and machinery dismantled and removed; its plantations had become a jungle of weeds. More worryingly, the organic community of the village was almost extinguished, agriculture had been neglected and starvation loomed. To boost the morale of demoralised *pueblos*, Zapata reluctantly set up a centralised administration, in the hope of getting the villages back on their feet. His agents acted like political commissars, whose aim was to raise local élan and encourage the democratic ethos. Education was as much a mania with Zapata as with Villa, and he made huge efforts to benefit the population by introducing schools of all kinds.

On the military front, Zapata abandoned his forward policy of attacks on Mexico City – in any case more dangerous now that Pershing had pulled out and Carranza could redeploy one of his armies – in favour of retrenchment, and tried to throw a ring of steel around Morelos, arranging his armies in a square at the four corners of the state, ready to repel all incursions. However, there were three ominous developments which, seen in retrospect, heralded the first signs of decline for *zapatismo*. The first was that Zapata's principle of self-help backfired on him. The policy of arming villages to fight González boomeranged when these self-defence units began resisting Zapata's own foraging parties. The defiance of the *pueblos* rose as Zapata's commanders grew more cynical. By increasingly putting the food supply for their troops above the maintenance of good relations with the villagers, such men jeopardised the careful structure of interlocking rights and duties Zapata had built up.

Allied to this was the problem of banditry. The destruction of Morelos, the years of hard fighting and the multitudinous atrocities had cracked the carapace of civilisation and made it difficult for *zapatismo* to continue as a pristine, coherent force. More and more *zapatista* commanders operated like bandits, and more and more genuine bandits operated under the banner of Zapata, to the point where all distinctions between revolutionary guerrillas, so-called 'social bandits' and old-style brigands became meaningless. In extreme cases Zapata had to take military action against armed criminal bands within Morelos.

The most serious and threatening problem, however, was the crumbling resolve and disaffection of his chieftains, who seemed to be losing their stomach for the struggle. Since Carranza had proved not to be an evanescent phenomenon but a permanent fixture, did that mean that the *zapatistas* were now committed to permanent, eternal warfare? Ought they not either to try to cut a deal with Carranza or at least form an alliance with Félix Díaz? Since Zapata set his face against either proposal and stalled, hoping Micawber-like that something would turn up, it is not surprising that the patience of his generals snapped. First to defect was Domingo Arenas, his commander in Puebla. Arenas's loss meant that Zapata had to abandon his next military project: the capture of Puebla City. Zapata went to extraordinary lengths to try to coax Arenas back into the fold, even promising an alliance in Puebla with the *felicistas*, but Arenas was deaf to all blandishments; he had a good offer of amnesty from Carranza and was now convinced the future lay with the bearded one.

The next round of defections was even more serious. Early in May 1917, in the town of Buenavista de Cuéllar, Otilio Montaño and Lorenzo Vásquez announced they were forming a breakaway movement from Zapata. To Zapata this was double-dyed treachery even more serious than Domingo Arenas's, for Montaño was one of his earliest compadres, the man who had given him Kropotkin to read, studied all the Anenecuilco land deeds and co-authored the Plan of Ayala. Zapata attacked the town of Buenavista on 5 May and hanged Vásquez without any further ceremony. Over Montaño he hesitated, especially when his old comrade argued eloquently that Zapatismo had gone off the rails because of the malign influence of Palafox and Soto y Gama. That pair in turn accused Montaño of conspiring to compass Zapata's death and produced some damning circumstantial evidence.

Zapata was reluctant to proceed with the court martial against his old friend, but Palafox insisted that revolutionary justice must take its course. Zapata therefore did another of his disappearing acts and left Tlaltizapán until the trial was over. The evidence against Montaño was heard in camera and by all accounts never moved beyond the circumstantial. Montaño vigorously denied all the charges and counteraccused Soto y Gama and Palafox of having betrayed the Revolution. Montaño was predictably found guilty. In a final act of vindictiveness, Palafox denied him the last rites and even the customary favour of being able to face the firing squad. He died on 18 May with arms outstretched, declaiming his innocence. Palafox had hung a sign about his neck that read: 'So die all traitors to the fatherland.'

A curse now seemed to hover over the *zapatista* movement. Zapata, like Villa, entered a paranoid phase where he saw conspiracy and betrayal everywhere. While Soto y Gama was ordered to compose a proclamation that traitors and all their families and children would be eliminated, Zapata kept repeating his credo: 'I can pardon those who kill and steal but I never pardon a traitor.' Despite this, disaffection and factionalism continued. Antonio Barona killed Felipe Neri for trying to disarm some of his men, and then went on to liquidate the *zapatista* leaders Francisco Estrada and Antonio Silva. Finally Barona crossed a man even more formidable and ferocious than himself: Genovevo de la O dragged him to his death at the horse's tail, riding at a gallop through the streets of Cuernavaca.

Signs that the movement was in grave, possibly terminal, confusion could be detected with the rise of Valentín Reyes, who bade fair to become Zapata's Fierro, killing large numbers of people personally – thirty in one batch alone in March 1917. Other *zapatista* leaders had taken to tearing down sugar mills to start themselves on a career of racketeering, selling the scrap metal on the black market. The unkindest cut was the behaviour of Eufemio Zapata. Always a useless, brutal, foul-mouthed alcoholic and lecher, Eufemio was involved in more and more bar-room brawls and alienated more and more people. He had the peculiarity of becoming enraged when anybody was drunk while he was sober. Demanding an apology from a colleague for some trivial slight, he roared at him: 'You'll soon have to find out what my machete knows.' He even began to make insulting remarks about his brother. In mid-June 1917 he finally went too far. He lost his temper with the father of his second-in-command Sidronio Camacho for being drunk and beat him savagely with a stick until the old man lost consciousness, berating him with each stroke of the rod. Camacho came after Eufemio, gunned him down in the street, and then dragged the dying man on to an anthill of fierce, stinging soldier ants before decamping. He fled to Carranza, who granted him amnesty.

Eufemio's many enemies whispered behind their hands that God's vengeance was just, that finally the *zapatistas* had managed to kill someone who deserved shooting. Zapata, however, was inconsolable: his paranoid suspicions increased and he spent more and more time in isolation; gone were the heady days of chewing the fat in the plaza. Always taciturn, he now became dark, irascible, neurasthenic, subject to mood swings and violent outbursts, feared by his men for his unpredictability. He sought consolation with his mistresses, especially the new favourite María Flores, and continued to beget children on women other than his wife: a son Diego was born in 1916, a daughter María Luisa in 1918 and another son Mateo in the same year.

The more Zapata reflected, the more he thought that Otilio Montaño had been right after all, that Palafox and Soto y Gama had brought more harm than good to the movement. From autumn 1917 they were out of favour, their influence seriously in decline. No longer would Zapata praise Palafox at the expense of the others, as in his saying: 'Martínez and Soto and Serrato made the smoke, but Palafox cooked the meat.' The new favourite, principal adviser and eventual successor to his mantle was Gildardo Magaña – aged twenty-six, a native of Michoacán, a natural mediator and reconciler – but Magaña's first task for Zapata almost ended in disaster. In August 1917 Domingo Arenas sent a message that he now repented of his decision to seek amnesty with Carranza and wished to return to the fray and secure Puebla for Zapata. Whether suspecting treachery or determined to kill a man he had repeatedly denounced as a traitor, Zapata sent Magaña to meet Arenas with a company of armed men. What happened next is disputed. Some say an altercation between Magaña and Arenas escalated spontaneously, others that Magaña, primed by Zapata, provoked Arenas outrageously. The upshot was that both sides started shooting and Arenas fell, mortally wounded.

Magaña advised Zapata that, with the movement in a cul-de-sac, he should try to find allies among Carranza's putative comrades who secretly loathed him. Zapata argued that outside contacts never produced results: on the one hand, a whole bevy of agents in Cuba and the USA had achieved nothing, and on the other, every time he made a move towards an external alliance, some important *zapatistas* ended up defecting. However, Magaña patiently plugged away, and in the end Zapata agreed they should reopen the channel to Villa, making him the first building block in a coalition. Zapata also seemed more amenable to the idea of making contacts with Félix Díaz. (The fact that Díaz had been involved in Madero's downfall and death would have made it impossible for Villa to work with Díaz, but Zapata was not troubled by this consideration, since he had never had any high opinion of Madero.) However, the most interesting of Magaña's suggestions was that they should approach Obregón, who had recently criticised Carranza.

Obregón's career since his great military triumph in 1915 had been patchy. He remained in Carranza's Cabinet as minister of war until 1917, working to produce a thoroughly professional Army, but at the constitutional conference at Querétaro he had backed the young radicals while superficially remaining scrupulously loyal to Carranza. As soon as the new constitution was formalised, he resigned as minister of war, married María Tapa, his second wife, and withdrew, Cincinnatus-like, to grow chickpeas on his hacienda at Quinta Chilla. He had not abandoned his ambition, however. As he joked later: 'I have such good eyesight that from Huatabampo I managed to see the presidential chair.'

The idea of an entente between Obregón and Zapata remains one of those fascinating historical might-have-beens. They were the only two of the great quartet in the Mexican Revolution who never met and never had personal baggage to bring into their relations with each other. Whereas Carranza and Zapata on the one hand, and Obregón and Villa on the other, were consumed by personal hatred and dislike, Obregón and Zapata were *terra incognita* for each other. Some say the alliance of Zapata and Obregón was just as implausible as an alliance between the classes they represented: the peasantry and the petite-bourgeoisie. Others say class is not the important factor, that a gulf of culture, tradition, *mentalité* and even religion divided the two men.

The possibility of an understanding between them does seem remote. Obregón emphasised national concerns, Zapata local ones; Obregón was a man of the city, at home with organised labour, Zapata despised the city and thought the proletariat an irrelevance; Obregón was Weber's 'rational-legal' man, dedicated to the bureaucratic, the apersonal and the meritocratic, Zapata the charismatic leader linked to the traditions of personalism and caudillismo; in short, Obregón represented the nationalist, urban, literate, secular, bureaucratic, achievement-oriented ethos while Zapata was the champion of the rural, the parochial, the illiterate, the pastoral and the agricultural. At the simplest level, Zapata was a Catholic and Obregón an anticlerical and the latter was a northerner while the former was a man of the south. Obregón was interested in business, economic diversification and producing a cash crop for export, while Zapata headed an agrarian movement of nostalgia, resisting economic change. So how could the two ever have found common ground?

Zapata's search for allies was overtaken by events when, in November 1917, Carranza again sent Pablo González and the Army south to 'pacify' Morelos. González, making use of the invaluable local knowledge of Sidronio Camacho, who had fled to Carranza after killing Eufemio Zapata, quickly took Cuautla, Jonacatepec and Zacualpán. Facing a serious threat to his position, Zapata was rescued when a major revolt broke out in Coahuila under Lucio Blanco, sending ripples all the way down to Veracruz and triggering an army mutiny there. At last it seemed a national resistance to Carranza was forming, if only Blanco could link up and make common cause with Félix Díaz. In euphoria Zapata wrote to his allies in Hidalgo and Tlaxcala to encourage them to link up with Blanco, but it was yet another false dawn. The revolts in both Veracruz and Coahuila fizzled out.

Magaña did not despair, patiently explaining to Zapata that the gulf separating Obregón and Benjamin Hill on the one side from Carranza and Pablo González on the other was so wide that in the end a split would have to come. In February 1918 Magaña actually proposed making overtures to Carranza; the deal would be that Zapata recognised Carranza as president, and in return Morelos would be granted virtual autonomy. This was something like the proposal Zapata had made to Domingo Arenas when he first broke away, but a deal he was prepared to do with a minnow he would not do with the leviathan himself. For his part, Carranza treated all such proposals with lofty contempt. One of Carranza's best attested remarks was: 'I never was a revolutionary, nor am I, nor will I ever be.' He did not reject Magaña's overtures; he simply ignored them.

Zapata meanwhile became alarmed after an interview with the American tycoon, theosophist and amateur archaeologist William E. Gates, who argued that the USA was certain to intervene in Mexico once the war in Europe ended. Zapata foresaw two dangers: either that Washington would back Carranza to the hilt to crush all dissidents, or that Carranza would fall and in the ensuing chaos the Americans would annex Mexico. He therefore abruptly changed tack. In his 1918 manifestoes he stopped mentioning the Plan of Ayala and started emphasising the common cause of national unity. All Zapata's 1918 utterances were popular front in spirit; the old intransigence had gone and with it the tunnel-vision concentration on agrarian reform. As John Womack puts it: 'In his head Zapata had finally learned that the defence of the villages of Morelos was not equivalent to the defence of the nation, that in great crises the local cause was subsidiary. But in his heart it seemed that the two struggles had been one to the end.'

By the summer of 1918 Zapata's popular front mania had reached its apogee. Overtures, feelers and letters went out to almost every conceivable opponent of Carranza: to Villa, to the Americans, to Obregón (who did not respond), to Félix Díaz and to Manuel Peláez. Peláez did reply – both he and Zapata agreed to be deputy serving under the other as supremo – but still nothing happened. When four more *felicista* risings broke out in April 1918, in Tamaulipas, Tlaxcala, Guerrero and Puebla – three of them former *zapatista* areas – Zapata sent a roving envoy to confer with Díaz's men in each theatre. Ironically, Magaña, who had always been for alliances of whatever kidney, now warned Zapata against an alliance with Díaz, arguing that his organisation would very likely be absorbed by the *felicistas* like a sponge and transformed into an essentially reactionary movement.

Magaña was right to be cautious. The reason Morelos had been so long without another visitation from Pablo González was that Carranza was obsessed with the threat from Díaz. By 1918 the *felicistas* had an impressive national network of supporters, not just in Veracruz, Oaxaca and Chiapas, but also in San Luis Potosí, Nuevo León and Tamaulipas, to say nothing of Peláez in Tampico. The worrying thing for Zapata was that Díaz and his allies had supplanted him almost completely in Puebla, Guerrero and Michoacán. In Michoacán indeed, where villages were rare and haciendas and ranches predominated, professional banditry had now completely replaced politically motivated guerrilla warfare. Arising in response to systematic abuses by Carranza's troops and civil authorities, rather in the manner of the endemic banditry in Germany at the end of the Thirty Years War, brigandage swept across Michoacán in three great plagues. In the Balsas region and Tierra Caliente was Jesús Cintora; in the central cities was Michoacán's Al Capone, José Altamirano; and worst of all, in the countryside, there was the scourge of Michoacán, Inés Chávez García.

Apart from Félix Díaz himself and Villa, Carranza rated Chávez García the most serious threat to the credibility of his regime, by this time far ahead of Zapata. Informally linked in alliance to the *felicistas*, Chávez García was the most dreadful monster thrown up in the entire Revolution, a man who made Fierro seem pedestrian. A legendary horseman who could sleep at will in the saddle, he had no home base or the protection of sympathetic locals, but relied on sheer speed to evade capture. Where Villa's thugs clipped ears, Chávez liked to slit throats in person with knives or machetes. In the town of San José he killed twenty men to the sound of music, sadistically granting each victim a last request before he twisted the knife. Another great pleasure was to watch his men gang-rape women and force virgins to take part in 'daisy-chain' orgies. The terror of Michoacán and the most feared man in Mexico, Chávez García contemptuously brushed aside all attempts by the federals to catch him. He succeeded for a time precisely because *zapatismo* had abandoned the struggle in Michoacán, and when he died, it was from the 1918 flu pandemic, not in battle or at the hands of a firing squad.

In Morelos, 1918 was notable for the demise of Palafox. For over a year Zapata had been moving away from him under Magaña's influence. In retrospect he now saw the 1914 alliance with Villa – of which Palafox was the architect – as his greatest mistake. Palafox behaved more and more arrogantly even as his influence declined. He told all who would listen that he, not Montaño, was the true author of the Plan of Ayala. He insulted Zapata's actual and potential allies and continued with the hardline intransigence. However, what finally brought him down in the macho society of Morelos was a homosexual scandal, and Zapata used this excuse to dismiss him. By this time Zapata was so angry with Palafox that he actually wanted to consign him to the firing squad. Magaña advised him against this, saying the execution of Palafox would make him a martyr and pose serious questions of credibility against *zapatismo* as a whole. Palafox fled to Carranza, spreading scurrilous rumours about his former boss. Palafox said that Zapata's fundamental fault was that he was lazy and was far too interested in 'good horses, fighting cocks, flashy women, card games and intoxicating liquors'. He listed the twenty-two women Zapata had had affairs with in the years 1911–18; another disillusioned and mendacious Zapata admirer, H. H. Dunn, later notched the figure up to twenty-six.

Mexico from 1917 on was a country in the grip of famine, pestilence and disease – yet another reason Carranza was not strong enough to attempt a final settling of accounts with Zapata. Dearth and hunger brought the inevitable hoarding, speculating, graft and profiteering in its wake, carried out both by private entrepreneurs and officialdom. With food short, street-cleaning and sanitation non-existent outside the big cities, and squalor everywhere, it was not surprising that deadly diseases laid hold of the population. First to strike was typhus, the time-honoured killer that lurks in the wake of wars and dearth. It claimed 1,000 fatalities a week in 1916–17, and in the south further killers joined in: smallpox, yellow fever and malaria. Nature completed the devastation in Zapata's heartlands that Pablo González had begun.

Then in the winter of 1918 a new enemy appeared in Morelos: the

Spanish flu that would carry off forty million people worldwide. Its effect in Mexico was devastating: whereas in England the mortality was four in every thousand, south of the Río Grande it was twenty to the thousand. Total mortality in Mexico from the pandemic was 300,000, almost the only benefit being that the virus disposed of Chávez García. In Morelos the flu bit particularly deep as it impacted on a populace weakened by dislocation, nomadism, starvation, fatigue, impure water and a particularly severe winter. People dropped like stricken flies and died much faster than they could be buried. By December 1918 the once thriving city of Cuautla was a ghost town. Morelos lost a quarter of its population, both from the deadly virus and from the exodus of Morelians into neighbouring Guerrero, reputed to be flu-free. Zapata therefore suffered severe manpower losses in his army at the very time, by sheer unfortunate coincidence, that all his key agents and gunrunners were rounded up in Mexico City.

Zapata's letters in the winter of 1918 betray a great and overdetermined anxiety. He worried about his manpower losses, grieved for the plight of Morelos, fretted about his inability to find allies, and most of all harped on his major preoccupation: that the United States would finally invade Mexico now that the war in Europe was over. Zapata even wrote to Felipe Ángeles, asking him to use his presumed influence with Marshal Foch, so that France would restrain the USA. He also wondered if the Allied powers would intervene to prevent chaos in Mexico as they had done against the Bolsheviks in Russia. In a very short while Zapata had gone from a parochial outlook to a national one and then an international one. Here was the man who once said he cared about nothing but the land deeds of Morelos villages playing the international statesman and writing for help to the European powers.

What Zapata feared finally came about. Waiting until the rainy season was over, Pablo González came crashing back into Morelos again, this time with 11,000 troops. Facing greatly weakened resistance, he quickly captured Cuautla, Jonacatepec, Yautepec, Jojutla, Tlaltizapán, Tetecala and Cuernavaca. González installed garrisons in all the major towns, imposed his own administration in the villages and began bringing in labourers from other parts of Mexico on a passage-paid scheme. From mid-December Zapata, de la O, Mendoza and all the important chiefs were once again on the run. The military commander of Puebla, General Cesareo Castro, one of Carranza's favourites, offered amnesty to Magaña and all moderate *zapatista* leaders, hoping to lure them away from Zapata and leave him isolated. Despite the huge temptations and pressures on them, the chieftains stayed true to each other – not just to de la O and Mendoza but all the 'second level' leaders.

Despite his jeopardy, Zapata always refused to bow the knee to Carranza. In new manifestoes he excoriated him as the Kaiser's running dog, a supporter of imperialism and an enemy of democracy, hoping thereby to interest the European powers. Meanwhile he saw hope in the minatory notes Washington now began sending Carranza over the mining and oil company laws. He also continued to lobby apparent supporters of the regime who were not in Carranza's inner circle, trying to prise them loose from him. Accepting that he was in some eyes an obstacle to national unity, Zapata offered to step aside as Supreme Chief of the Revolution in favour of Francisco Vásquez Gómez, whom Magaña had indicated as the preferred choice of the moderate enemies of Carranza, like Ángeles and Villareal. Zapata then made Vásquez Gómez the focus for his hopes for a popular front, even writing to Villa and Peláez to urge them to rally round this new leader.

Zapata was still one step ahead of Pablo González, who in February 1919 sent his troops on a wild-goose chase, supposedly on Zapata's tail, from Jojutla through Jonacatepec to Tochimilco. However, the Pablo González who ruled from Cuernavaca in 1919 was a very different animal from the scourge of three years earlier. He now had his sights set on the 1920 presidential election, where he fancied himself a dark-horse candidate, and did not want to blow his chances by making any mistakes in Morelos. In early 1919 there were few armed clashes between *zapatistas* and the Army, just a few isolated skirmishes. Where once he had looted and destroyed, González now tried to bolster his reputation by trying to get Morelos on the move economically. Politically, though, he still faced stalemate, as he was unable to capture a single *zapatista* chieftain, some of whom were so contemptuous of his garrisons and so sure of protection from the locals that they openly sauntered through the larger towns.

Suddenly Carranza sent word to González to make an end to Zapata by whatever means, fair or foul, that he could contrive. Publicly Carranza announced that Zapata was 'beyond amnesty'. What provoked this latest outburst was news from his spies that Zapata and Peláez were on the brink of concluding an alliance, which would in turn open the window for Zapata onto the entire *felicista* revolt. Peláez meanwhile published open letters violently contemptuous of 'the whiskered one', and sent his brother Octavio to Mexico City to confer with pro-Obregón elements. Carranza was also enraged that he was coming under heavy pressure from Washington even as the propaganda efforts of William Gates and his inspirational journalism were making Zapata a hero to American readers. Carranza hinted to González that the demise of Zapata might just be the ticket that secured him the presidential nomination in 1920.

By sheer chance González found a way to achieve by treachery what he could never achieve by armed force. It all began with a genuine row between González and his ace cavalry commander, Colonel Jesús Guajardo of the 50th Regiment. González had ordered Guajardo to pursue Zapata night and day in the mountains around Cuautla, but then caught him drinking in a bar in the town when he should have been on duty. Despite Guajardo's fine record, González jailed him and threatened to have him court-martialled. Hearing of this, Zapata thought he saw a way to destroy González's position in Morelos. On 21 March 1919 he had a note smuggled into Guajardo's cell, asking him to join him with the entire 50th Regiment. González intercepted the letter, waved it in front of Guajardo as proof of his 'treachery' and gave him two choices: cooperate in a plot or be shot for treason. Guajardo agreed to cooperate. González double-checked with Carranza that an assassination plot would be acceptable as a means of getting rid of Zapata, then implemented his stratagem.

At González's direction, Guajardo wrote a note to Zapata, saying he was prepared to come over to him and bring his cavalrymen. To test his sincerity, Zapata asked him to shoot Victoriano Bárcenas and his fifty ex-*zapatista* renegades who were now under the protection of Carranza. Guajardo arranged to meet Zapata at Jonacatepec on 9 April, did so, presented him with a handsome chestnut horse called Ace of Diamonds, and 'proved' his sincerity by executing the fifty men. Zapata then asked Guajardo to come on to Pastor station, a halt on the railway line south of Jonacatepec. At 4.30 p.m. on 9 April Guajardo and 600 of his men mustered at Pastor. Zapata greeted him effusively, giving him the bearhug *abrazo* and the present of a sorrel horse named Golden Age. Taking thirty men each, they proceeded to Tepalcingo. Further conversation took place, but the suspicious Zapata was still not entirely without misgivings. The two men agreed to meet again next morning at the Chinameca hacienda. Guajardo spent the night there while Zapata camped in the hills.

Early on Thursday 10 April Zapata and his escort rode slowly down the hills towards the hacienda – familiar territory as it was one of the first places he had taken in early 1911, so familiar that he claimed to know every blade of grass there. There were various shops outside the hacienda, and Zapata and Guajardo conferred there, within earshot of their escorts. Soon word came in that the enemy was approaching. Zapata organised patrols and went on one reconnaissance himself. By the time this alarum had died down, it was 1.30 p.m. So far only one *zapatista* had ventured inside the hacienda walls: Zapata's ADC Miguel Palacios, who was discussing the handover by Guajardo of 12,000 rounds of ammunition.

Guajardo then invited Zapata inside the walls for dinner. Zapata was wary but finally, tired and hungry, he accepted and, taking a bodyguard of just ten men, at around 2.10 p.m. he mounted a sorrel horse and rode through the gates. Guajardo's guard of honour stood ready, as if to pay the visitor a compliment. A bugler sounded the honour call three times as the men presented arms. As the last note sounded and Zapata reached the threshold of the hacienda building, the guards opened fire at point-blank range. Zapata fell dead immediately; Palacios and two of the escort were also killed in the hail of bullets. The rest of the *zapatistas* fled in consternation.

Guajardo's men pulled the body inside the hacienda, loaded it on a mule, and set out for Cuautla. González was notified at 7.30 p.m., but suspected a trick. At 9 p.m. Guajardo's men arrived in the dark with the body. A flashlight played on Zapata's face showed that this was indeed the tiger of Morelos. González wrote in triumph to Carranza, who rewarded Guajardo with the rank of brigadier-general. However, although González organised public viewings of the bullet-strewn corpse, and even had it filmed by a professional crew before it was buried, the people of Morelos stubbornly refused to accept that Zapata was dead. There were various stories: that Zapata had sent a double to the meeting (he was even named as Jesús Delgado), that the body was not Zapata's since the corpse did not possess the unique Zapata distinguishing marks – a mole on his right cheek, a birthmark on his chest, and a missing little finger. Finally and inevitably, Zapata was seen by eyewitnesses riding his sorrel in the Guerrero mountains to the south. The most outlandish story was that Zapata could not have been killed at Chinameca as he shipped out for 'Arabia' on 9 April at Acapulco.

There may be truth in the most persistent legend: that Zapata had foreseen his own death and that on the eve of his assassination a *curandera* came to him and prophesied that if he went to the meeting next day he would be killed. Completely authentic is Zapata's table-talk in which he told his comrades he did not fear death, for great movements grow stronger from martyrdom. He spoke of men who were greater in death than in life, mentioning Benito Juárez, and claimed that the greatest men in history were always murdered – this time he cited Abraham Lincoln and Jesus Christ. Zapata was a shrewd judge. In Morelos he became an icon almost on a level with the Virgin of Guadalupe. His imperishable legend lives on, and even today is the source of inspiration of the Indians of Chiapas as they fight oppression. *Viva Zapata!*

THE DECLINE OF VILLISMO

When Villa retired to his cave badly wounded and many of the *villista* detachments were defeated and dispersed in the spring of 1916, everyone thought the Centaur's days were numbered. In June, however, Villa reappeared and called a general rendezvous of all *villista* bands. Many responded to his call, for the cotton crop was now harvested and they could go on the warpath again with a clear conscience. Villa's reappearance contributed to his legend. Disproving the countless rumours of his death, the great leader none the less initially scarcely made a striking impression. Now sporting a full black beard, he walked on crutches and, even when he discarded them, always limped; he could not wear a shoe on one foot as the leg was swollen from knee to toes. It was very painful for him to ride a horse, so for long journeys henceforth he tried to travel by car.

Since he was still being sought by Pershing and by a large *carrancista* army, Villa's situation was supremely perilous on paper. However, in the duel with Carranza he enjoyed several advantages that were not immediately apparent. In the first place, Carranza played into his hands by his disastrous policies in the state of Chihuahua, oscillating between letting his corrupt cronies run the state on a spoils system and treating it like occupied territory, under the heel of generals appointed from Mexico City. Whichever tack he followed, it was loathed by the people of Chihuahua. The only mistake Carranza did not make was to bring back the Creel-Terrazas faction, but his own supremo, Ignacio Enríquez, was, if anything, worse than the old guard. Neither Carranza nor Enríquez had any idea how to integrate the amnestied Villa veterans into the state economy; the only offer made to them was to join the federal army, which they all loathed as the ancient enemy. Just as Louis XVIII made the Hundred Days possible by failing to find work for Napoleon's veterans, the clueless Enríquez virtually ensured a recrudescence of *villismo*. When Villa reappeared, many of his veterans concluded that life in the saddle with him was preferable to languishing in indigent unemployment.

Villa enjoyed another advantage. Because of Woodrow Wilson's periodic arms embargoes and the competition from European arms dealers, Carranza was short of ammunition by 1916. Villa, on the other hand, had hidden huge caches of arms and ammunition in secret locations throughout Chihuahua. He also had a dedicated corps of young officers, who had gone with him and the *dorados* into the mountains in late 1915. Although some of these (Pablo López, Candelario Cervantes) had fallen in the series of setbacks in early 1916, the others (Martín López, Nicolás Fernández, Baudelio Uribe) remained. Mini-Fierros in outlook and sensibility, they soon became a byword for terror. Villa was more humane than Carranza, in that he executed only the officers among captured troops, letting the rankers go free, on a promise that they would not fight against him again. Of course many did so, if only because they were press-ganged by the *carrancistas*. Uribe devised a novel method to stop this happening: he clipped the ears of all prisoners so that they would be instantly recognisable, and warned them that if they were caught again, it would mean instant death.

In 1916, too, Villa enjoyed all his old popularity with the people of Chihuahua. Where the *carrancistas* allowed their troops free rein to sack and pillage, Villa and his men paid for the food they bought from the peasants. The harvests in 1916 were good, food was plentiful, and Villa could pay in gold and silver, so his popularity soared. His declaration that he was fighting to save Mexico from the gringo struck a sympathetic chord, as did his redistribution of land and his looting of stores which he then made over, Robin-Hood style, to the peasants. Villa's use of terror and looting was carefully selective: he liked to target American-owned property or towns that had some connection with the *yanquis*. By his blood-curdling threats he hoped to sap the morale of Americans in Chihuahua, making them close mines and send their women home for safety.

The second half of 1916 saw Villa raiding up and down Chihuahua, seemingly without let or hindrance. In July 1,000 of his men took the heavily garrisoned town of Jiménez; at his approach the terrified and demoralised federal troops simply fled. The town was then systematically looted, and Baudelio Uribe pioneered his earclipping technique on the few *carrancistas* who had been foolish enough to remain. Momentarily, Villa grew overconfident and forgot that he was engaged in a game of cat-and-mouse. Moving swiftly down to Durango, he was defeated at Villa Hidalgo, but saved face by winning a couple of skirmishes. As autumn approached, he felt it was time for a major demonstration of Carranza's impotence in Chihuahua.

Accordingly, on 15 September he launched a major attack on

Chihuahua City, aiming to set free the political prisoners in the jail. A large number of *orozquistas* were lodged there and their leader, Orozco's former deputy José Inés Salazar, was under sentence of death, along with many of his men. Gone were the days when Villa loathed *orozquistas* for their betrayal of Madero; now he needed allies wherever he could find them and operated on the basis that 'my enemy's enemy is my friend'. The odds were heavily stacked against Villa, for he had just 2,000 to pitch against the 9,000 troops of the garrison. He counted on the element of surprise, planning his attack to coincide with the Independence Day celebrations. Ignacio Enríquez's tame governor Jacinto Treviño had been advised of Villa's approach but, like Pershing at Columbus, ignored the warning and allowed most of his troops to take part in the national holiday festivities.

Villa struck at midnight. Diversionary units attacked the palace and barracks while the main force stormed the penitentiary. Taken completely by surprise, Treviño panicked and fled. The *villistas* killed all the prison guards and freed Salazar, who was brought in triumph to Villa; a bearhug sealed their compact. In high euphoria Villa started retreating north with the main force, the *orozquistas* and some prize items of plunder, but in an unpardonable mistake, forgot to tell the diversionary units to break off their engagement. Since the *carrancistas* were still firing wildly at anything that moved, the *villistas* thought the main battle was still raging. Too late they realised their error, and then had to fight their way out of the city, losing three-quarters of their number while doing so.

Despite this, Villa had scored a great coup and his supporters made the most of it. People began to ask how it was possible for Villa to have pulled off this feat when there were 9,000 federal troops in Chihuahua City and Pershing still had 10,000 men prowling through the northern reaches of the state. The federals were so demoralised that they had no stomach for a pursuit when Villa withdrew into Santa Clara canyon. Then came news of a defeat of government troops from Coahuila by the *villista* Calixto Contreras in the Laguna area. Villa's fortunes were truly revived. The unemployed and disaffected began to flock to him, so that the period September–December 1916 was a halcyon time.

Villa's next target was the town of San Andrés; this was a debt he owed the *dorados*, many of whom came from there. Its *carrancista* commander unfortunately considered himself something of a military genius. When he heard that Villa was approaching with 400 men, he divided his forces, remaining in the town with his sixty best troops and sending his deputy ostentatiously out into the desert with another 300 soldiers, to make it look as though they were fleeing for their lives. When Villa attacked, the 300 were supposed to wheel round and take him in the rear.

Unhappily for the commander, his deputy panicked when the firing started and led his men into the wilderness instead of falling on the *villista* rear; forty died of starvation and thirst in the trackless and waterless wastes. The luckless commander held out in San Andrés for six hours until, heavily outnumbered, he was forced to surrender. Villa executed him and the defenders without mercy. This was retaliation for the execution of the *villistas* taken as they tried to fight their way out of Chihuahua City. Additionally, Carranza had issued a new martial law decree that anyone caught in arms had to suffer the death penalty without possibility of reprieve. Villa capped his success by obtaining the military code book and telegraphing for reinforcements. Another twenty-five federals arrived, to be led out to the firing squad.

After San Andrés, Villa had the mining town of Cusihuiriáchic in his sights, and tried to secure a bloodless victory by cabling ahead to say he was on his way. The *carrancista* troops panicked and evacuated the town but, just as they were leaving, a dust cloud announced the coming of a large company of armed men. A bloody shoot-out ensued, and it was only when heavy casualties had been taken on both sides that it was realised the newcomers were not *villistas* but federal reinforcements. Cursing their ill fortune, the survivors then turned round to face the real *villistas* who finally put in an appearance. The troops were quickly overwhelmed; all who were not killed in the shooting were executed on the spot.

Villa was on a roll now, for he proceeded to take the town of San Isidro and then, a few days later, defeated another large force of federals at Santa Isabel. Flushed by his string of victories, and overconfident, Villa neglected to post guards and was nearly surprised by a second *carrancista* force. The federals succeeded in capturing the *villista* forces, forcing them to flee on foot, but, crossing the Santa Isabel battlefield, they became demoralised by the sight of so many corpses and failed to press home their initial advantage. Far from falling on the disorganised *villistas*, they progressively lost their nerve, fearing ambush and flank attack. Villa was able to recapture his horses and, next day, counterattacked, defeating the federals with great slaughter.

After the non-stop roster of victories, more and more federals deserted the ranks to join up with Villa, and all the old legends of his invincibility resurfaced. As Carranza's grip on Chihuahua looked increasingly shaky, Villa assumed the psychological offensive and issued a manifesto, as if he was again a credible national leader. Once again the target was the gringos: Villa announced that in future Americans would not be able to own property or pursue any form of economic life in Mexico. To safeguard the fatherland against the Yankee octopus, he announced that there would be universal national service and that all draft-dodgers would be executed. Outraged by Villa's overweening insolence, Carranza assembled a large force to flush out Villa once and for all. This army was to be commanded by Fortunato Maycotte, one of Obregón's most talented aides and an architect of the victory at Celaya. Accompanying Maycotte to the north would be Villa's old enemies from Durango, the Arrieta brothers.

Obregón advised Maycotte that he was accepting a poisoned chalice, since he did not have enough ammunition to mount a credible search-and-destroy operation against Villa on his homeground in Chihuahua. Maycotte and the Arrietas spurned the advice and advanced on La Enramada. Suddenly they were attacked by a contingent led by 'earcutter' Baudelio Uribe. After a few minutes' fighting, the *villistas* appeared to break and run. Thinking this was the main force, the federals charged in pursuit but were soon 'eaten up' by devastating fire from Villa's main force in strong defensive positions. Obregón was angry with Maycotte, incensed that the federals had fallen for the tactic of feigned retreat over and over again. Villa's defeat of Maycotte convinced many that Carranza could never impose himself in Chihuahua. The useless governor Treviño sent his wife and looted fortune of US$150,000 to El Paso and refused to obey orders to take the offensive against Villa.

Between September and December 1916 Villa was victorious in twenty-two armed encounters, in all of which he captured further arms and ammunition. By now, as in the autumn of 1913, he controlled all Chihuahua outside the big cities. His lightning raids resulted in the temporary capture of Santa Rosalía and Jiménez. On 16 November he made his first entry into Parral, and occupied the city again in December. Parral and Jiménez changed hands so many times in 1916 that the citizens hardly knew where they were from week to week.

In his raids on the larger towns Villa liked to target the property of Americans, Spaniards and Chinese and was insouciant when his men killed Chinese and Syrian merchants, but, ominously, he was beginning to alienate the peasantry and the middle classes now that there were no longer any oligarchs' estates to confiscate. The bourgoisie objected to the forced loans, and the peasantry to the forced military service, especially as those pressed in the 'crusade' against the gringos seemed always to end up fighting the *carrancistas* instead.

However, as long as Villa continued to pay his men a silver peso a day, he could always find takers, especially among those who had had property looted by the *carrancistas* and thirsted for revenge. As his confidence increased, he began to dream of reviving the División del Norte and ascending from guerrilla leader to the position he held in 1915 as leader of a regular army. During the second occupation of Parral he actually had new uniforms made for his men. All this caused increased irritation and consternation in Mexico City. Obregón singled out the nepotistic payroll-padder Treviño for particular censure, saying he had no understanding of guerrilla warfare. In reply Treviño blustered, trying to shift the blame for the débâcle in Chihuahua on to Pershing and then on to Obregón himself, pointing out that it was he who had organised the disastrous Maycotte/Arrietas expedition.

On 23 November Villa made his second assault on Chihuahua City. This time his attack was not designed as a mere raid but an attempt to take the entire city, capture Trevino and destroy Carranza's credibility in Chihuahua once and for all. Villa's difficulty was that a relief column was on its way to Trevino and there was a risk that his assaulting force could be caught between the fire of the defenders and the relievers. He therefore tore up all railway track to the south of the city to hold up the advance of the reinforcements, then put his own troops on trains and steamed towards Chihuahua City. There followed four days of grim fighting. Villa's initial cavalry charges were broken up by machine-gun emplacements on the hill of Santa Rosa, overlooking the city, and on 24 November Treviño headed a counterattack that looked like being successful until Villa counterattacked strongly with his *dorados*. Even so Treviño thought he had won and arranged a 'victory dinner' for the 28th.

In the small hours of the morning of 27 November the *villistas* stormed Santa Rosa hill. The attack was led by a wounded Martín López, who rose from his sickbed to be there. Once Santa Rosa fell, trainloads of panic-stricken federals pulled out. Treviño made his getaway without informing any but his inner circle, with the result that many officers found themselves left to deal with Villa after the escape routes had been closed. Some chose to commit suicide rather than be led out to the firing squad, but the remaining defenders, after stout resistance, surrendered on a personal assurance from Villa that their lives would be spared.

The fall of Chihuahua City created a sensation, and mutual recriminations and bickering predictably broke out among the *carrancistas*. Treviño again tried to lay the blame on others, saying that the relief column did not arrive on time. Obregón publicly accused Treviño of cowardice, but astute observers thought Obregón's real target was Pablo González, whose protégé Treviño was. However, Treviño lost the propaganda battle as well as the battle of Chihuahua City. More objective and dispassionate observers pointed out that, whatever Obregón's *parti pris*, Treviño was certainly guilty of corruption, lies and incompetence, even if a bracket was put round the charge of cowardice.

After taking the state capital, Villa truckled to the mob by letting them pillage wholesale. He did not feel strong enough to hold on to the city but loaded tons of stores, arms and ammunition on to his troop-trains. Then he turned to face the relieving force headed by Francisco Murguía, who was destined to be Villa's federal shadow over the next three years. Known as 'the hangman' because of his relish for public executions, Murguía was a cruel and vicious character, utterly corrupt and venal, who specialised in hoarding food for speculation while people starved around him. To deal with the 10,000-strong relief column, Villa sent out 3,000 men under the command of the *orozquista* leader he had earlier rescued from jail, José Inés Salazar. To give Salazar the post of honour seemed unwontedly generous for Villa; students of his methods have concluded that this was typical Villa machiavellism, seeming to confer prestige on a commander who was bound to lose in a 'mission impossible'. Salazar's cavalry charge predictably did not break Murguía's formation, but the *villistas* retired in good order, having taken light casualties, and bought the time necessary for Villa to make an efficient evacuation.

Villa's next target was Torreón, a city full of memories of his glory days. As a prelude he sent Baudelio Uribe to extinguish the garrison at Camargo – a task easily accomplished – but Camargo was destined to deal a mortal blow to the legend of Villa. As he rode into the town, a woman tearfully implored him not to kill her husband, the *carrancista* paymaster. Intending to do her a favour, Villa made enquiries and discovered that the man was already dead. The woman then unaccountably flew into a rage, accused Villa of killing her husband and defied him to murder her as well. In a white heat of fury, Villa pulled out his pistol and shot her dead. This roused the blood lust of his followers, who asked permission to kill all the other 'bitches' who had given their favours to *carrancistas*. Still trembling with anger, Villa agreed; the upshot was that ninety women went before the firing squad. This atrocity received a very wide currency and effectively killed off popular support for Villa.

There was a new brutality evident in Villa from this moment on. He slugged it out with Murguía, matching him brutal action for brutal action, atrocity for atrocity. As in the rest of Mexico, violence begat violence and six years of non-stop warfare had extinguished most traces of humanity and provided a kind of socialisation in barbarism. It can be argued that the true villain was Carranza, who started the cycle by decreeing that all prisoners were to be killed, but in part it seems that

Villa's increasing viciousness was born of frustration and disappointed idealism: he had done so much for people, and his only return was betrayal and gross ingratitude. Villa seemed to feel about the people of Chihuahua almost as if one of his mistresses had been unfaithful to him.

Enough weapons and ammunition had been captured at Camargo to make Villa confident of being able to take Torreón, whose garrison numbered only 2,000. The federal commander sent out desperate pleas for reinforcement to Murguía, but he refused, saying that wiping out Villa's base of operations in the mountains of western Chihuahua must be his priority. Even when given a direct order by Obregón, Murguía still refused to reinforce Torreón. Obregón tried to scrape together a force to send to Torreón's aid, but in vain – by now there were so many risings and rebellions all over Mexico that there were no troops to spare. As a result Villa found it easy, almost to the point of walkover, to storm Torreón on 22 December 1916; the federal commander committed suicide rather than fall into his hands.

Torreón gave Villa more artillery, more troop-trains, more supplies and more press-ganged volunteers. He raised forced loans and instituted a pogrom against the Chinese merchants. Capricious as ever, he requited a throng of onlookers who came to applaud him at the Hotel Francia by arresting them all and then handpicking the most able-bodied as 'volunteers'. The leading Carranza supporter Luis Herrera had been killed in the battle for Torreón, so Villa had his body publicly strung up for two days, with a paper peso in one hand and a portrait of Carranza in the other. His arbitrary actions particularly enraged the consular officials at Torreón, but then Villa had never been a favourite of diplomats, who knew how to deal with Carranza and even Huerta but were out of their depth with the Centaur. One who hated him more than most, Patrick O'Hea, said: 'His career is that of a dog in rabies, a mad mullah, a Malay running amok.'

Overrating his skill and resources, Villa was now confident he could defeat Murguía. However, the Villa who faced Murguía in battle was the same Villa who had failed to think his strategy through and prepare properly at Celaya and León. He rejected Baudelio Uribe's plan for a night attack on the enemy rear with 1000 men and quixotically sent out Nicolás Fernández on another mission with 2,000 men while he blithely confronted Murguía head on. The result was a severe defeat. The usual unsupported cavalry charge was repulsed, and a *villista* rout followed when it turned out that Villa had kept no reserve.

Retreating to Parral, where he stayed no more than twenty-four hours, Villa undid some of the damage caused by the Camargo atrocity when he invited the people of the city to a bonanza of loot. Unable to take with him vast quantities of goods and *matériel* he had loaded in railway cars, Villa invited the citizens to help themselves; in the free-for-all that followed the railway cars were stripped bare in a couple of hours. Villa's largesse seemed misplaced, however, when news came in that the *carrancistas* had seized most of the supplies Villa had cached after the taking of Chihuahua City. Temporarily disconcerted in Chihuahua, Villa divided his force in two, and ordered the two sections to rendezvous at Zacatecas in Durango state, where he hoped to build a unified command with the *villista* rebels already fighting there under Contreras and others.

It was March 1917 before Villa felt ready to face Murguía again in Chihuahua. This time it was Murguía who was overconfident and once again he fell for the stratagem of the feigned retreat. Since Villa had lost the last encounter by an unsupported cavalry charge and no reserve, Murguía treated the battle as a rerun of his earlier success, unaware that Villa had posted men in the hills. When Murguía moved forward to complete the expected rout, he found himself encircled. Attacked from all sides, he took 2,500 casualties and was exceptionally lucky to escape from the field himself. Villa took 600 prisoners and had them all executed. In a macabre and grisly act of butchery, the *dorados* dispatched them in groups of five, shooting a particularly powerful bullet through all five heads at once to save ammunition.

Fortune now once more turned against Villa in the see-saw battle with Murguía. Rafael Mendoza, a major in the *dorados*, was captured by the federals and about to be executed when he offered them a deal they could not refuse. Mendoza was one of the few trusted aides who knew where Villa's arms dumps were hidden, and he led Murguía to a gigantic cache at Chevarría, containing tens of thousands of rifles and several million cartridges. When this catastrophic loss was reported to Villa, he was so devastated that he burst into tears. Reeling from the setback, he decided that the only way to recoup was another attack on Chihuahua City. He built huge bonfires to make Murguía think the attack would come from the south, then took his forces round to the north to attack from there, but Murguía did not take the bait. After a fierce battle, Villa's ammunition gave out. Murguía took all 200 *villistas* prisoner and hanged them in rows on the Avenida Colón in Chihuahua City, much as Crassus had hanged the Spartacists on the Appian way after the slaves' revolt.

Still brooding on Mendoza's treachery, Villa decided to wreak vengeance on all who had betrayed the secret of his arms dumps and directed his steps towards Namiquipa, whose people had betrayed a cache to Pershing. When all the males in the villages fled into the mountains at his approach, he rounded up all the nubile women and let his troops gang-rape them. This was short-sighted folly, for it simply alienated villagers previously sympathetic to him, and was scored with the Camargo atrocity in the tally of war crimes and crimes against humanity charged to his account. Villa soon learned how stupid he had been to indulge his feelings of rage. Whereas previously villagers had alerted him to Murguía's approach, in disgust at the Namiquipa outrage they ceased to help him. One immediate result was that a federal attack on his headquarters at Babicora came as a complete surprise; after surrounding the hacienda, Murguía killed hundreds and Villa and 400 survivors were hard put to break out after the most desperate hand-to-hand fighting.

As he licked his wounds, Villa's gloom was increased by the treachery of one of his *dorado* colonels. On a promise of pardon and payment from Murguía, he plotted to assassinate Villa, but the unusual presence of men on rooftops was noticed, and Villa sent officers ahead who were fired on. For three days Villa sulked in his camp like Achilles, full of paranoid fantasies, uncertain whom he could trust and who was loyal. A further blow came when he bestirred himself and marched to the US border at Ojinaga, where he was expecting another cache of arms from his agent in Presidio, Texas, across the river. There he was told that the arms dealers were too frightened of the wrath of their fellow-countrymen to sell arms to Villa, even at inflated prices.

At this point the *villista* movement started seriously imploding. By his atrocities Villa had lost the hearts and minds of the peasantry and by now, with the betrayal of so many of his arms dumps, he was seriously short of arms and ammunition. Even formerly pro-Villa *pueblos* came to terms with Carranza once they realised Villa could no longer protect them. *Villista* propaganda no longer worked, for the idea that Carranza had sold Mexico to the gringos was refuted both by the withdrawal of the Punitive Expedition and Carranza's support for Germany, which eloquently proved there was no secret treaty between him and Wilson. All hopes of a resurrection of the Division of the North were now seen as the chimeras they were. Forced back once more on to guerrilla warfare and operating with just a few hundred men, Villa divided his strength into small units, which made hit-and-run raids on towns and garrisons; the idea was supposed to be that once the harvest was gathered in, the various units could recombine, but the snag was that Villa could exert no control over what actions the units took in his name. Nor could he explain why he went on fighting, if indeed he knew himself. It was difficult to articulate ideas and policies, for not a single intellectual remained with the *villistas*.

To save himself from becoming marginalised, Villa toyed with more and more outlandish schemes. When a war of words broke out in the Chihuahua press between Murguía and Treviño, each accusing the other of cowardice, Villa tried to cut the Gordian knot by writing to a Spanish-speaking newspaper in the United States (with syndication rights in Chihuahua) challenging Murguía to a duel. When this offer was predictably met with silence, Villa became obsessed with a hare-brained scheme to go to Mexico City, kidnap Carranza, and take him down to Zapata in Morelos for a 'people's trial' there. Incredibly, unaware or insouciant of the obstacles, Villa actually pressed ahead with this idea and took a unit of handpicked men south with him.

Once south of Chihuahua, Villa got his first inkling of what he had taken on. This part of Mexico was an armed camp and every village bristled with militias, aggressive and challenging to strangers. To cover his tracks, Villa had to execute every single person he met. In Durango he fell in with twenty-seven armed villagers out on a posse in pursuit of bandits. True to his principles, he killed them all, but then found himself hounded by the Furies from a collective league of villages, determined to avenge their colleagues. In alarm Villa retreated to Aguascalientes, only to lose his way. With the nerves of his men near to cracking point, Villa was forced to call his great adventure off and return north to Chihuahua. He divided his force and threaded his way back perilously into the state, using all the byways and mountain passes. However, so low was morale in the unit he did not lead personally that there was a mutiny and the commander was murdered. When Villa caught up with the ringleaders and hanged them, the rest of the unit fled to Murguía.

The failure of his quixotic Mexico City operation plunged Villa into profound gloom and for a time he contemplated giving up the struggle. He offered terms for surrender to Murguía, who turned them down, as Villa, like Zapata, had been declared 'beyond amnesty' by Carranza. Villa was now in a box canyon of his own making: Carranza would never pardon him, and if he fled to the USA he would be put on trial and executed for the attack on Columbus. Even if he tried going into exile in Europe, like Díaz and Huerta, he would be extradited either by the Allies, eager to do favours for Woodrow Wilson, or the Central Powers, who were friendly to Carranza. He was lucky that the *carrancistas*, by their stupidity in driving recruits into his arms – by describing anyone who resisted their depredations as a *villista* – still kept his movement alive.

Villa could still count on the hard core of a few dozen comrades, bound to him by indissoluble ties of kinship or *compadrazgo*, but by the end of 1917 there were just too many unfavourable factors working against him.

The impression of the atrocities and gang-rapes lived on in folk memory. The withdrawal of the Punitive Expedition cut the ground from under his feet and made his struggle against Carranza seem either meaningless or the personal pique of a man defeated by an abler politician. Without the prompting of his intellectuals, Villa did not know how to pitch an appeal to the masses and, left to himself, completely forgot about land reform. The rise of village militias or *defensas sociales* groups worked against him, for these armed bands saw themselves as the seeds of a new Chihuahua and fought against both Villa and Carranza.

Increasingly Villa was being marginalised as these militia groups became the focus for struggle within the Carranza regime. Ignacio Enríquez, now civilian governor of Chihuahua, tried to build up these militias as a counterweight to Murguía and the Army. Carranza sat on the fence as his two cronies slugged it out. He could probably have finished Villa for good by giving greater power to the *defensas sociales*, but to do so he would have had to abandon central control via the Army. In the end the conflict reached the point where Murguía tried to assassinate Enríquez, and Carranza was forced finally to take sides. He chose Enríquez, sent him back as commander of all militias and paramilitaries, and reassigned Murguía to Tamaulipas.

The emphasis on armed militias finally started to pay off. Everywhere Villa went he was confronted by them. He issued another manifesto, declaring that he was fighting for Chihuahua's autonomy against Carranza's despotism and threatening the militias with harsh reprisals, but no one paid him any attention. By the end of 1917 Villa even gave up harassing the Americans and allowed US companies to return, provided they paid him taxes. This they were happy to do, so the *villista* movement continued to limp along, still able to pay villagers for supplies with silver pesos. He was just able to survive on popular resentment against Carranza, for in 1918 the First Chief turned hard right and restored their haciendas to the Terrazas family. This was a cynical piece of calculation on Carranza's part: he wanted the elite in Chihuahua united and the confiscated estates, now totally plundered and no longer worked, were a dead weight, generating no income.

For a lot of 1918 Villa was so weary and exhausted that he could not even be bothered to make capital out of this signal 'betrayal' by Carranza. It was a doldrum period in his life: he mainly skulked in the sierras with his faithful *dorados*, raiding occasionally for food but attempting no major enterprises. However, he was jolted out of his apathy at the end of the year by a quite unexpected event: Felipe Ángeles returned from the United States and sought him out. Ángeles had lived in honest poverty at

El Paso, occasionally wandering around other parts of the USA, including New York. Throughout the years 1916–18 he shared Villa's obsession with a US invasion of Mexico and, though no longer part of the struggle, continued to admire Villa, Zapata and de la O from afar. Ángeles's greatest tragedy may have been that, brilliant captain and versatile intellect though he was, he was no politician. He was the one man capable of uniting all factions in the Revolution if Carranza could have been got rid off, but was self-confessedly clueless about how to achieve that desirable consummation. His closest friend was Maytorena, but in the end he became disillusioned with his defeatism and the way he converted the 'art of the possible' into impossibilism, so that the present moment never could be the right time to take action. As Ángeles gloomily noted: 'The Sancho Panzas have never done anything great; whenever anything of real importance is to be done, one needs madmen like Madero or Don Quixote.'

While Ángeles was wondering whether he should cross into Mexico to offer himself as an alternative to Carranza, Villa wrote to him in the most friendly terms. This decided Angeles, who was convinced that, with the end of the war in Europe, the United States would very soon send its armies into Mexico. He crossed the Río Grande in December 1918, and shortly afterwards there was a joyous reunion with Villa. As they talked, however, Villa realised they were still far apart in their thinking. Ángeles seemed to have no idea how firmly entrenched Carranza was, and how ubiquitous his troops. How could Ángeles realistically hope for a government of national reconciliation? Ironically, though Ángeles had come back to talk peace, his presence spurred Villa on to make war and he decided to attack Parral. As though by magic, Ángeles's mere presence seemed to have turned Villa's fortunes. Down to just 500 men by the end of 1918, new recruits boosted the numbers to 2,000 a few months later. It seemed that Ángeles's presence really did mean something to people sick of Carranza.

The *villista* army of 1919 was an entirely volunteer force; Villa had stopped pressing men when he found it so unpopular and unproductive. His supply situation was healthy, for his war chest had grown from the taxes levied on foreign-owned companies and the long lay-off from active campaigning. The arms and ammunition situation, too, was better, for corruption under Carranza had reached the point where there was a thriving black market in weapons filched from Carranza's arms factories. Now Ángeles provided Villa with the political and propaganda arm he needed. Ángeles toured the villages of Chihuahua, making speeches in which he stressed religious toleration and respect for foreigners and their property. Cynics said only the women and old men heard the oratory, for all the young males fled to the mountains whenever they heard Villa was approaching.

The most important change in *villista* policy wrought by Ángeles was a new attitude to prisoners. Ángeles impressed on Villa that he could make a breakthrough if he stopped executing his captives. Villa made two points in his defence: that he had responded in kind only when Carranza started the entire vicious circle; and that if he did not kill them, the prisoners simply rejoined the federals, with or without clipped ears. Ángeles urged him to try, and Villa promised to implement the new policy at Parral. The attack on Parral in March 1919 was bitterly resisted both by the federal garrison and the militia. Villa managed to rout the regular troops – the militiamen accused the troops of deserting them – and the fighters of the *defensas sociales* withdrew to the hill of Cerro de la Cruz and fought on sturdily until at last being compelled to surrender. True to his word to Ángeles, Villa let all eighty-eight surviving militiamen go free, except for the three leaders whom he executed. He had a particular reason for killing José de Luz Herrera and his two sons, for they were part of the Herrera family that had betrayed him; Maclovio and Luis Herrera (killed at Torreón) were the most notorious ex-*villista* turncoats to join Carranza.

Villa also handed over to Ángeles the federal troops he had taken prisoner; Ángeles harangued them and let them go. Ángeles's policy turned out to be a wise one. Once it got around that Villa did not execute prisoners, and word-of-mouth made it wholly credible, garrisons were prepared to surrender to Villa and hand over their arms and ammunition after the most token resistance. Warming to the theme, Villa also stopped executing recalcitrant gringos and instead had Ángeles lecture them. There was a famous incident along these lines at the Santa Eulalia mine in April 1919, when Villa himself joined in the finger-wagging. The new policy paid dividends. No longer under automatic death sentence from Villa, the militiamen began refusing to fight for Carranza, citing their 'betrayal' by the Army at Parral.

Ángeles's next initiative was much less to Villa's liking: he urged him to switch from guerrilla warfare to regular campaigning. Villa protested that he neither had the manpower nor the resources; how could he pit 3,000 men against the 17,000 Carranza had stationed in Chihuahua? Patiently Ángeles explained his thinking: the *carrancista* commanders were at daggers drawn, all of them corrupt payroll padders; the men were mainly press-ganged Indians, half-starved, ill-equipped and suffering from a shortage of horses; and the militias were refusing to cooperate with them. Villa agreed to give regular campaigning a try, but had reached the end of his concessions to Ángeles. Soon there was a vociferous disagreement over politics and Villa shocked Ángeles by his animadversions. Madero, he said, was 'dumb' to have signed the treaty of Ciudad Juárez with Díaz, and even more so for not having Félix Díaz shot after the attempted coup at Veracruz. Feelings ran high and the upshot was a genuine shouting match between Villa and Ángeles. On-lookers thought Villa was sure to order his friend executed, but Villa eventually calmed down and told Ángeles: 'You are the first man who has not died after contradicting me.'

Villa's next venture certainly satisfied Ángeles's prescription that effective action had to be quixotic. Since Chihuahua City was too strong to capture, Villa opted for an attack on Ciudad Juárez. Partly he wished to see whether Ángeles's thinking on regular warfare was correct, partly he wanted to replenish his food and stores, but most of all he wanted to sound the intentions of the *yanquis*. During the row over Madero, Villa had accused Ángeles of going soft on the Americans and being 'gringoised'. Ángeles said the Americans were just waiting for an excuse to cross the border, but Villa maintained they had burned their fingers too badly over the Pershing expedition and were a paper tiger. The attack on Juárez was partly mounted to test which of them was right.

On 15 June 1919 Villa's favourite commander Martín López launched the attack at such an angle that no stray bullets would wing their way over to the American side of the border at El Paso. The assault went well. Equipped with US-made wire cutters, the *villistas* made short work of the barbed wire defences and within a couple of hours had taken the city. López then foolishly allowed his troops to disperse, oblivious to the fact that most of the federals had withdrawn in good order to nearby Fort Hidalgo. A party of *carrancistas* happened to return to retrieve their standard and found the scattered *villistas*. Casually opening fire on such easy targets, they all unknowingly panicked the *villistas*, who thought themselves the victims of a surprise attack. Their panic was contagious, and soon the entire army was streaming out of the city. Unaware that his men were pulling out, Villa rode into town to dine at a favourite restaurant and came within an ace of being captured by the federals. Angrily he ordered his men to regroup and retake the town. They succeeded, driving the federals back to Fort Hidalgo once more, but this time the *carrancistas* had an extra shot in their locker in more senses than one. They deliberately fired across the border into El Paso, provoking the Americans to intervene. The Villa-Ángeles argument was settled decisively when American troops crossed the border in strength and Villa was forced to abandon his hard-won gains.

Ángeles was plunged into the blackest gloom by this outcome. Now that he saw the extent of American hatred of Villa, he realised that Washington would never agree to recognise the government of national reconciliation he proposed to set up. Moreover, all his propaganda in the villages had stressed that the *yanquis* were on the point of intervening against Carranza on Villa's side, and now the reverse had happened. The American intervention at Juárez also undid all his patient work with Villa. Raging at this latest 'betrayal', Villa told Ángeles that the doveish approach had failed and from now on it would be war to the knife; gringos would be killed as and when encountered. In despair, Ángeles abandoned all his dreams and told Villa he intended to return to the USA.

The two men parted as friends. Villa warned of the danger of capture by the *carrancistas* and provided a small escort, but for some reason Ángeles did not immediately cross the border and instead wandered aimlessly around northern Mexico for motives that remain obscure. Did he fear that if he returned to the USA he would be charged with violating neutrality laws? Perhaps he aspired to leadership of the *zapatistas* now that Zapata was dead? The most likely explanation is that after leaving Villa he had second thoughts and could not bear to admit to himself that he had failed, but his actions were so self-destructive that, were we dealing with Obregón, we would be tempted to posit a simple wish for extinction.

One of the *villistas* betrayed Ángeles's hiding place and he surrendered to *carrancistas* after receiving an express promise that he would not be shot. In Mexico City Carranza faced a dilemma. If he followed his own inclinations and had Ángeles executed, this would be a public relations disaster, for he was already anathema to the international community after his treacherous slaying of Zapata. On the other hand, his prisoner was in many ways his most dangerous opponent. His moral and intellectual superior, Ángeles was the one man who could unite all the factions in Mexico to unseat him. He could not allow such a man to live. Whichever he opted for, a summary execution or a protracted trial, Carranza would reap the whirlwind. Always supremely cunning, he thought of a third way that would avoid the dilemma.

Ángeles was court-martialled in the Theatre of Heroes in Chihuahua City, even though he was not subject to military law as he was not a member of the federal army and in front of judges who were all his bitter enemies. Carranza aimed at a quick show trial that would not permit the delays of the normal criminal courts. Ángeles made a brilliant speech in his own defence, praising Zapata, socialism and Villa, stressing redemption and love over hate. He argued that Villa, for all his excesses, was good at heart and that Carranza was to blame for the continuing turmoil in Chihuahua because he had not offered credible terms on which Villa could lay down his arms.

The speech impressed everyone and won over most of those who had been uncertain what their attitude was. Carranza realised that the longer the trial dragged on, the more support Ángeles would get, so decreed that the court must publish its findings within two days. The prosecution rushed through its case and the judges in the kangaroo court, Carranza puppets to a man, sentenced Ángeles to death for 'rebellion'. Carranza refused to commute the sentence and denied Ángeles the right of appeal, even though this was expressly allowed by Article 107 of the 1917 Constitution. Despite protest meetings, petitions and pressure from the USA, Carranza carried out the sentence. Five thousand people defied Carranza by attending Ángeles's funeral, often quoting his dying words that the blood of martyrs fertilises a great cause.

Villa retaliated by attacking the garrison of Santa Rosalía and wiping it out to the last man. He then moved south and attacked Durango, but sustained a reverse as bad as the one at Ciudad Juárez. To prevent his being attacked from behind, he told his men to tear up the railway track leading to Durango City. For reasons unclear they disobeyed orders, and when Villa launched his attack, he was predictably taken in the rear, suffering disastrous defeat and the loss in battle of his favourite commander Martín López. The defeats at Ciudad Juárez and Durango and the execution of Ángeles had a cumulative effect, and once more an epidemic of desertion and demoralisation ran through Villa's army. Nor could he could look for anything from the peasantry. The people of Chihuahua were so alienated from him that he was reduced to taking old men hostage in every *pueblo* he entered, so that the villagers could not denounce him to the authorities; the old men would be released in the next village, a new set of hostages taken, and so on.

Villa was riding his luck and might well have been finished off at this point, but was suddenly rescued by dramatic events in Mexico City. In 1919 Carranza repeated Díaz's mistake and tried to perpetuate his rule. Obregón had retired from national politics, so as not to be breathing down Carranza's neck, but only on the clear tacit understanding that he would be Mexico's next president. At his ranch in Sonora he counted the days, but began to overeat, possibly in reaction to the problems of being one-armed but more likely through simple boredom. He put on weight, he looked bloated, his hair turned grey; at forty he looked like an old man. Concerned about his health, he became a hypochondriac and made frequent visits to US hospitals.

Obregón proved as good a capitalist as he was a general. His acreage increased from 180 to 3,500 hectares; he formed a chickpea collective in Sonora and Sinaloa to cartelise the product; he diversified into cattle and mining, exporting leather and meat and forming an import-export agency. In 1918 the price of chickpeas doubled and he made US$50,000 in that year alone; by the beginning of 1919 he had 1,500 men on his payroll. Obregón was very popular and he carefully cultivated a down-home 'just folks' image. He dressed like a tramp, exaggerated the poverty of his origins and tried to be a Mexican Abe Lincoln, with many references in his speeches to his indigent early years and the overriding worth of the common man. Obregón was immensely self-regarding but he concealed it well by his lack of solemnity, his playing the fool and above all by his jokes.

He shared with Lincoln the genuine characteristic of being the pessimist who believes the only way you can reach people is through humour. He had an immense repertoire of jokes, was a great raconteur and a talented mimic, and had the priceless gift of being able to improvise, ad lib, and cap other people's jokes; the only gap in his humorous armoury was an inability to appreciate irony. His prodigious memory and ability to learn poems and songs by heart enabled him to catch out many a poseur and phoney. It has been suggested that in Mexican culture jokes are the obverse side of death, a sign that the joker thinks life meaningless. This would square with Obregón's death-driven psychological profile. One close oberver of him said: 'Towards life Obregón was capable of anything except taking it seriously.'

In June 1919, after serving his time in the political wilderness, Obregón announced his candidacy for the presidency. Carranza should have bowed to the inevitable and given Obregón's bid his blessing, but he disliked him personally and viewed him as a representative of the military arm Carranza wanted firmly under the control of civilian bureaucrats. He therefore cast around for ways to stop him. A subtle politician, Obregón blocked Carranza's obvious stratagem by coming to terms with Pablo González, making it impossible for the president to play off the two generals against each other. However, Carranza continued to plug away at his mantra that only a civilian should succeed him, citing Juárez's attack on 'the odious banner of militarism'. Having alienated Obregón, Carranza aped Díaz by opting for a nonentity as his successor: Ignacio Bonillas, the Mexican ambassador in Washington.

This was grist to Obregón's humorous mill. At the time there was a popular song about a wandering shepherdess suffering from amnesia, who knew nothing – where she was born, who her parents were – except that her name was Flor de Te. Obregón's supporters popularised a mock slogan that ridiculed Bonillas pitilessly: *Viva Bonillas! Viva Flor de Te!* In November 1919 Obregón began his whistlestop tour and was equally scathing. He told his audiences that he had overcome rain, wind, Orozco, Huerta, Villa and Zapata and was not going to allow a little thing like Carranza to stand in his way. To cheers and klaxons he announced: 'Before the bearded old man can rig the election, I will rise against him.'

Soon Obregón had built a powerful coalition, uniting the military, the huge middle-class opposition to Carranza, and the working class whom Obregón had always favoured and whom Carranza had betrayed. Campaigning as the military genius of the Mexican Revolution, cultivating a populist, cracker-barrel philosophy style, Obregón drew to him the teeming masses of the disaffected – disgruntled politicians and office seekers, guerrillas, Army officers and intellectuals like Vasconcelos. Faced with this tourbillon of opposition, Carranza's famous political instincts, usually so sharp, deserted him. He knew he was battling great odds, despised as he was by the United States, by the ordinary people of Mexico for his corrupt regime, and by the generals and the young radicals for his autocracy. However, he refused to back down. First he had Congress strip Obregón of his military rank, but this absurd act of victimisation simply increased Obregón's popularity. Then he accused him of engineering a military plot and ordered his arrest. Obregón escaped by train to Guerrero, where the military chief was Fortunato Maycotte, his deputy at Celaya. Always one for playacting, when he met Maycotte Obregón snapped to attention, saluted and said: 'I am your prisoner.' 'No,' replied Maycotte, 'you are my commander.'

When Carranza ordered Calles to use troops to end the *obregonista* defiance in Sonora, Obregón raised the standard of outright rebellion. On 20 April 1920 he announced that Carranza was in breach of the Constitution and called for a rising to unite behind provisional president Adolfo de la Huerta. Three days later he issued the Plan of Agua Prieta, which laid out his dreams for a new Mexico. In May, sensing the tide rising against him, Carranza left Mexico City for Veracruz, hoping to repeat his 1915 success. On his last night in Mexico City he read a biography of Belisarius, taking comfort from the story of a man who gave thirty years of brilliant service to the emperor Justinian in Constantinople but ended up blinded in prison. But Belisarius had never been a wrecker. By contrast, when Carranza left the capital, he filled sixty railway carriages with his hangers-on, arms and ammunition, government files and the entire national treasury in the form of gold bars. Accompanying him were Villa's old adversary Murguía, the absurd Bonillas, and a handful of generals and ministers. The so-called 'Golden Train' carrying the president just got clear of the capital before Pablo González and his hordes swept in.

Carranza's nomadic government started to break down immediately after leaving Mexico City. He had been encouraged by the extravagant declarations of support from Guadalupe Sánchez, a general who had devastated the isthmus, Sherman-like, in 1917 in pursuit of the *felicistas*. However, Sánchez immediately double-crossed him, went over to Obregón like most of the generals, and attacked the presidential train. A heavy skirmish at Villa de Guadalupe alarmed the *carrancistas* by the evidence it gave of the depth and persistence of *obregonista* support. Now every station on the line to Veracruz was a potential death-trap and every mile travelled became a white-knuckle affair. On 14 May there was a bloody shoot-out at Aljibes station with more rebels led by Guadalupe Sánchez. In the presidential car Carranza watched the gun battle in a detached and Olympian way, observing the chaos and panic as if he were a Martian. His loyal general Francisco Urquizo pleaded with him to escape, but Carranza sat impassive and poker-faced. Finally, when Murguía added his voice, he got off the train and mounted a fresh horse (his own had been killed in the skirmish two days earlier).

As the battle continued to rage, news came in that the line to Veracruz had been severed. The presidential convoy now looked like a shipwreck, but loyalists were willing to stand and fight, covering the escape of Carranza and his escort. Still calm, unruffled and stony-faced, Carranza with Murguía, generals Barragán and Mariel, and about 100 troops, plunged into the wilderness. After six days of gruelling marching, on 20 May the depleted caravan crossed a river into territory controlled by Rodolfo Herrero, an ex-rebel who had accepted amnesty from Carranza. Herrero greeted his unexpected guests and acted obsequiously towards Carranza, taking him to safe quarters in the remote village of Tlaxcalantongo, where they were supposed to wait for news from General Mariel, who went north to reconnoitre.

The village was no more than a collection of huts. Carranza shared one of them with his private secretary and three other men, and bedded down with a saddle and horse blanket like a *vaquero*. Shortly after midnight on 21 May Herrero came to say that he was called away on an emergency: his brother had been wounded in a nearby village. Carranza was usually a man of ready sleep but this night he tossed and turned and was still awake at 3 a.m. when a message arrived from Mariel to say that the way ahead next day was clear. 'Gentlemen,' said Carranza, 'we can now rest.' He had scarcely lapsed into a light doze when, above the pelting of rain, gunfire could be heard.

Crawling on their bellies like snakes along the muddy ground, Herrero's sharpshooters reached the other side of the hut where Carranza was sleeping. Through the wall his snores could be heard. The snipers opened fire. Carranza cried out that his leg was broken and there were yells of 'Death to Carranza!' and 'Come out, you old bearded goat.' Then, according to one version, the sharpshooters entered the hut and finished him off. Some say, however, that once he realised his leg was broken, he turned his gun on himself. In this version, Carranza put on his glasses, picked up his Colt .45 revolver, steadied it between thumb and index finger, pointed the muzzle at his chest and fired two shots. Witnesses said the death rattle came before Herrero's men burst in. Carranza's body was embalmed, taken to Mexico City and buried in Dolores cemetery. Few mourned him except a gaggle of keening women accompanying the catafalque, chanting, 'Our Father is dead.'

With Carranza no more, Villa had a unique opportunity to secure peace with honour. He began negotiations with all who would consent to correspond with him, sending out shoals of letters to the victors. The early responses were unpromising. Calles replied that the best course for Villa was to go into internal exile in Sonora; Villa correctly read this as the spider inviting the fly to enter his parlour. Obregón made no reply, but increased the bounty on Villa's head to 100,000 pesos. Ignacio Enríquez seemed diplomacy itself and agreed to meet, but Villa suspected a trap. He set up dummies around a brilliantly lit campfire and waited with his men in the shadows for Enríquez to arrive. When men came charging murderously into the camp with fixed bayonets, they were cut to ribbons by Villa's sharpshooters.

Gradually Villa concentrated most of his hopes for amnesty on provisional president de la Huerta. Along with Maytorena, de la Huerta had been one of the men who encouraged Villa to make his famous entry into Mexico with just eight men in April 1913. He had no old scores to settle with Villa and could see ways in which the Centaur could be useful to him in his own future ambitions. Accordingly he sent his envoy, General Eugenio Martínez, north for talks. On 2 July Martínez met Villa at the hacienda of Encinillas. Villa laid out his terms: he wanted a hacienda for himself and his men, which would be a kind of embryonic military colony; he would be made the commander of 500 *rurales*; there would be free and fair elections in Chihuahua; and the deed of amnesty and future contract would be signed by Obregón, Calles and Benjamin Hill.

These terms were conveyed to de la Huerta who made a counter-proposal: Villa was to retire absolutely from public life to Canutillo hacienda with a bodyguard of fifty armed men. This seemed promising, especially when de la Huerta mentioned that Hill and Calles were prepared to sign up to this. The sticking point was Obregón, who refused to sign anything. Obregón put extreme pressure on de la Huerta, warning him in a minatory way of the 'possible violent repercussions' from Mexico's generals and the outrage to be expected from the USA. De la Huerta took the broad hint and suspended all negotiations. His envoy Martínez, an honourable man, warned Villa of what was afoot, and advised that his life was in danger.

Villa decided he would have to show Obregón there was a high price to be paid for not doing a deal with him. He moved his base of operations to Coahuila, threatening to devastate the economic life of this rich and prosperous state, teeming with natural resources. The danger was that Obregón's image in the United States would be ruined, and Americans would withdraw their investments because of the Mexican government's failure to guarantee order. Before Villa could implement this strategy, however, he had to cross the terrible 700-mile desert, the Bolsón de Mapimí, which lay between the states of Chihuahua and Coahuila, and the trek across the waterless wastes proved even more of a nightmare than the most purblind pessimist could have imagined: many died of thirst and others went mad from lack of water. Coahuila came like the promised land. Emerging from the wilderness, the *villistas* quickly took the town of Sabinas and Villa wired de la Huerta that he was still ready to do a deal; if not the consequences were on his own head.

Villa's samurai-like long march to Coahuila took Obregón by surprise. Anxiously he conferred with de la Huerta. It was clear that the government was about to suffer huge economic losses and to be embarrassed in its relations with the USA; at the limit Washington might finally tire of the unpredictability of Mexico and send a quarter of a million troops across the border. De la Huerta decided the only way through the impasse was to isolate Obregón on this issue. He got Hill and Calles to agree to an improved deal for Villa: Canutillo hacienda and the bodyguards as before, and additionally 800 demobilised *villistas* to be given pay and land. Obregón was almost apoplectic with rage when he read the deal. De la Huerta tipped Villa off on the best way to play his cards. Having previously said he would sign only if Obregón put in his countersignature, Villa signed anyway. This put Obregón on the spot. If he refused to sign, he would be branded a warmonger and perhaps would even be the cause of US intervention, which would probably trigger his own downfall. Still smarting at the humiliation, Obregón refused to sign, but told de la Huerta he would not oppose the deal.

On 29 July Villa sent Obregón a friendly and even deferential letter, asking for his friendship and citing their mutual contacts with Raúl Madero. It took Obregón two months to compose a grudging reply, in which he confirmed that when he took over the presidency in December, Villa would enjoy the same terms granted by de la Huerta. On all sides could be heard a collective sigh of relief. Villa flung his arms round Martínez, hugged him and said: 'You can say that the war is over; that now honest men and bandits walk together.' Even Washington, tired of the never-ending strife south of the border, agreed to draw a line under the Columbus incident. Almost the only unregenerate and implacable public enemy left for Villa was Winston Churchill in England, who continued to fulminate about the Benton affair.

Villa and his last 759 men laid down their arms, and were given the promised mustering-out pay and lands. For Villa the march back from Sabinas to Tlahualilo was more like a Roman triumph than the prelude to retirement. In Tlahualilo he was greeted by Raúl Madero and observed at close quarters by his old enemy Patrick O'Hea, who described him rather spitefully as having put on weight. Villa told Madero he had four ambitions now: to stay on good terms with the government, develop his hacienda, live on good terms with his women and safeguard himself from assassination. The death of Carranza and the surrender of Villa effectively ended the Mexican Revolution. Carranza and Zapata had been struck down by assassins, but Villa and Obregón, protagonist and antagonist in that mighty conflict, seemed to have survived.

EPILOGUE

In retirement in his hacienda at Canutillo Villa tried to achieve the afore-mentioned four ambitions: to stay on good terms with Obregón and the government, to turn Canutillo into a showpiece military colony, to sort out his tangled private life, and to protect himself against assassination by one of his numerous enemies, especially Calles, Ignacio Enríquez and Obregón himself. The fourth was the easiest aim to achieve. Apart from his fifty heavily armed bodyguards, Villa could count on his other employees and the many ex-*dorados* settled on neighbouring estates. Additionally, Villa turned Canutillo into an impregnable fortress, limited the number of visitors to the estate and posted a trusted officer at the nearest railway station to report on every arrival and departure.

Villa ran his estate on military lines; within its gates he was the only law. Canutillo consisted of 163,000 acres, 4,400 of which were rich, irrigated land. Before the Revolution the hacienda could boast 24,000 sheep, 4,000 goats, 4,000 horses and 3,000 head of cattle, but in the ten years of the Revolution most of the animals had disappeared: sold, stolen or requisitioned. Villa's first task was to build up these herds and to lease out the remaining lands to sharecroppers. He was an improving landlord, who installed telephone lines, a post office, telegraph bureau, flour mill and even a school for 200 pupils, but Canutillo was never an egalitarian utopia, if only because most of its peons and workers had been bequeathed from the old paternalistic era. Villa's own men – the nucleus with which he had hoped to found the new military colony – were settled on two adjoining estates.

Villa's most tricky task was to retain good relations with Obregón, whose massive victory in the presidential election of September 1920 signalled the end of the Mexican Revolution. Unlike Carranza, whose Achilles' heel was his mania for control, Obregón was a natural politician and fixer, a deal-maker who, by co-optation, cajolery and bribery restored the country to a peace it had not known since 1910. His basic approach was to freeze the status quo, leaving a patchwork picture, a political mosaic: in some states the old elites were still in charge, while in others village communes and agrarian reformers were dominant. He offered all rebels attractive amnesty terms, which they accepted; much of this stabilisation had been achieved in the interim period when de la Huerta was provisional president. Félix Díaz went into exile in the USA, and the *felicistas* laid down their arms. Pablo González was arrested for sedition in Nuevo León, tried for treason, found guilty and sentenced to be shot; to appease American opinion de la Huerta pardoned him, and González joined the other anti-Obregón exiles in the USA. The one comfort for Zapata's heirs was that Jesús Guajardo was taken out and shot by the Nuevo León authorities, without the complication of a trial.

Obregón's greatest triumph of pacific transformation came in Morelos, where the *zapatistas* were co-opted, partly by Obregón's grudging acceptance of the agrarian programme, partly by his winning them over with places and positions. Gildardo Magaña, expressly designated by Zapata as his successor, had long since proved his pro-Obregón credentials by intriguing with him behind Carranza's back in 1918–19. He took advantage of the upheaval and turmoil of 1920 to conclude a very favourable deal with Obregón and soon the *zapatistas* were no longer revolutionaries but an integral part of the *obregonista* system. So great was the swing to the Right in some cases that Zapata's nephew allied himself to a coterie of reactionary generals and tried to eject the possessors of *ejidos* (communal land) in Anenecuilco and get it for himself. Zapata's son, who had famously slept through the meeting with Villa at Xochimilco, became a landowner, got himself elected mayor of Cuautla, sold out to the old elites and ended up a client of the Morelos plantocracy.

Obregón was always a capitalist who believed that the true business of the Revolution was business. He disliked landowners not for ideological reasons but because they were incompetent as entrepreneurs. So keen was he on improving capitalism that he watered down the 1917 Constitution's provisions on subsoil rights, granting the US oil and mining companies far greater privileges than they had had under Carranza, and winning himself a dubious reputation for 'selling out' and truckling to the *yanquis*. He announced that Article 27 of the Constitution would not apply to mineral rights acquired by foreigners before 1917 and, through his treasury secretary de la Huerta, negotiated a deal with Washington whereby the taxes levied on US oil companies would be earmarked to pay foreign (mainly US) bondholders, after nine years in default. With Wall Street now on his side, Washington was nudged into a reluctant recognition of the Obregón government in 1923.

During the four years of his presidency Obregón gained the reputation of being both ruthless and as slippery as an eel. At one moment he would appear anti-American and at another almost obsequious towards Washington; in one state he would distribute land to the peasants, in another he would repress them with a heavy hand; in one city he would support the workers against the bosses, and in another use troops to break strikes. Always a dedicated anticlerical, he continued to persecute the Catholic Church and, partly to try to break its grip on hearts and minds, devoted great resources to education. He brought back the exiled José Vasconcelos as rector of the National University, and encouraged 100 flowers to bloom: it was during the Obregón presidency that the great geniuses of the Mexican realist movement in painting – Rivera, Orozco and Siqueiros – first made their mark. However, towards opposition, no matter how inchoate, Obregón was ruthless. Benjamin Hill started forming an opposition party at the end of 1920 and, in his capacity as minister of war, prepared to prosecute Rodolfo Herrero for the murder of Carranza. This did not please Obregón; on 14 December Hill mysteriously died, allegedly after food-poisoning at a banquet.

Villa was well aware that Obregón was a man you crossed at your peril and was effusively affable, and even sycophantic, in the letters and cables he sent him. In 1922 Villa's old enemy Murguía raised the standard of revolt against Obregón and crossed the Río Grande from the USA with thirty men, hoping to do what Villa had done in 1913. He failed hopelessly and sought refuge at Canutillo. Villa knew where he was and could easily have killed or betrayed him but, perhaps in a rare mood of empathy, did not do so. Murguía was betrayed by someone else without Villa's knowledge or consent, tried and executed. Obregón, who imagined Villa had delivered up this enemy, started to warm to him and began writing cordial letters to Canutillo; he made a point of answering in person every missive that came from an increasingly sophisticated Villa, who now read voraciously and liked to display the results of his autodidacticism. Such was their eventual entente that Obregón bought Canutillo outright and presented Villa with the deeds; between 1921 and 1923 he also paid him an additional sum of US$100,000 for 'improvements' or as 'compensation'.

As he got older, Villa more and more revealed himself as a man of the Right. There was a widespread perception, both in Mexico and the USA, that Villa was now simply another big *hacendado*, that he was not interested in agrarian reform but only in distributing land to *his* soldiers. All the evidence suggests that this perception was correct. Detesting Bolshevism, with which minister of the interior Calles was known to be in sympathy, by 1922 political conservatives more and more identified Villa as 'their' man. His own utterances allowed little doubt in the matter: 'The leaders of Bolshevism . . . in Mexico and outside it advocate an equality of classes that cannot be attained. Equality does not exist and cannot exist. It is a lie that we can all be equal . . . For me society is a big stair with some people at its lower end, some people in the middle, some rising and some very high . . . it is a stair clearly determined by nature. One cannot proceed against nature. What would happen to the world if all of us were generals or capitalists, or all of us were poor? There must be people of all kinds. The world, my friend, is like a big store where there are owners, employees, consumers, and manufacturers . . . I would never fight for the equality of the social classes.'

Nevertheless there were sometimes flashes of the old, more radical, Villa. In 1922 he wrote to Obregón asking him to back the peasants of the agricultural colony of Bosque de Aldama against Ignacio Enríquez, the state governor of Chihuahua. Enríquez, whose loathing of Villa was so over-the-top that Obregón discounted his ritual denunciations of his *bête noire,* was in league with the Terrazas family and attempted to put into operation a scam whereby an American proxy would reacquire the confiscated lands for them, thus avoiding all taxes on the expropriated territories.

In March Villa wrote to Obregón, exposing the scandal and expressing his strong opposition to the bogus surrogate sale, and alleging that it was part of a conspiracy by his three greatest enemies: the Terrazas, Enríquez and the gringos. Obregón decreed the distribution of the Terrazas lands and halted the sale to the American proxy. Faced with an outcry about 'Bolshevism' in the American press, Obregón agreed to compensation: the American proxy, A. J. McQuatters received one million dollars while the Terrazas got US$13 million. The affair seemed to have ended well, but in fact it denoted a major failure of communication between Obregón and Villa. Obregón construed Villa's letter as an implied threat that he would rebel if the sale went ahead; Villa, unaware that Obregón was also under intense pressure from his right-hand man Calles not to approve the sale, misread Obregón's 'capitulation', overrated his own influence and became arrogant and overconfident.

Yet for his first two years in Canutillo Villa was less concerned with matters of high politics and more with his tangled private life. Probably of most concern to him was his brother Hipólito who, if not quite the headache Eufemio Zapata had been to Emiliano, was certainly a sibling he could well have done without. For most of the guerrilla war period of 1916–20 Villa saw nothing of Hipólito. In 1916–17 he was based in Havana, ostensibly as Villa's agent, but in reality an impotent spendthrift under constant surveillance by US secret agents. Some scholars speculate that Villa simply tried to keep his brother out of harm's way, but if that was the intention, it failed. Hipólito was arrested, imprisoned and held for extradition to the USA on charges of blowing up railway tracks on US territory.

From his prison cell Hipólito whinged to Villa that he was only in this mess because he had been about his brother's business. His head was full of chimerical schemes for opening a second front in Yucatán and allying *villista* forces with the reactionary *hacendados* who were struggling with Carranza's proconsuls for mastery of the state. Villa ignored all the quixotry but managed to get Hipólito out of jail through the good offices of his friend George Holmes, who then took Hipólito back to his Texas ranch. There he was soon spotted by American agents, who again put him under tight surveillance. Lacking proof of his involvement in Columbus – or anywhere else for that matter – they could not arrest him, but tailed, pestered and harassed him; they even managed to hold him in jail for a short while on a charge of having entered Florida under a false name. Shortly before the deal with Obregón, Hipólito returned to fight beside his brother and was thus given an honoured place in the hierarchy at Canutillo.

Any problem Villa had with his brother was a bagatelle alongside the twisted skein of his relationships with a host of women, some designated as 'wives', others more blatantly mistresses and concubines. When he took to the sierras in late 1915, Villa sent Luz Corral and his official family away to safety. Then he promoted a woman named Soledad Seañez as 'first wife' and she was queen of the harem until 1917. Shortly afterwards Villa began the most passionate relationship of his life, with a pretty young middle-class Chihuahuan girl named Austreberta Rentería. She was initially noticed, then kidnapped, by 'earcutter' Bandelio Uribe, who knew Villa's taste in women and guessed the *patrón* would be delighted with her. Uribe proved a good judge. Villa was smitten with *coup de foudre* and, when a terrified Austreberta would not submit to his far from subtle overtures, simply raped her. He then went through another of his bogus marriage ceremonies in front of a tame judge and kept her a prisoner in a safe house in Ciudad Juárez.

When the *villistas* evacuated Juárez. Austreberta's father fled with her to sanctuary in the USA, abandoning his bourgeois life in Chihuahua to do menial work in America – anything so long as the ogre could no longer lay hands on his daughter. However, at some point Austreberta decided that she was, after all, in love with Villa and slipped away from her father's protection to rejoin the Centaur. By this time Villa was at

Canutillo, with Luz Corral and Soledad Seañez in an uneasy ménage. The unexpected arrival of Austreberta put a new wheel on Villa's polygamous wagon. He solved the impossibility of entertaining a female troika by humiliating Luz Corral and sending her away in disgrace. Not even permitted to show her face on the neighbouring haciendas, Luz survived for a while on handouts from Hipólito.

Austreberta proved amenable to the bizarre crèche-like kindergarten Villa had assembled at Canutillo. Always passionately fond of children, Villa had at last achieved his ambition of collecting his various offspring and siting them all on a single hacienda. At Canutillo were three sons (Agustín, Octavio and Samuel) and four daughters (Micaela, Celia, Sara and Juana María), all allegedly born to different women. Additionally Austreberta bore him a further two sons, Francisco and Hipólito (the latter born after Villa's death). Although Austreberta was the undisputed queen of Canutillo, and addressed with great tenderness by Villa as 'Betita', eyewitnesses always said she looked like an unhappy woman. Perhaps she was made miserable by the continued presence of the other 'wife' Soledad Seañez and Villa's chief mistress, Manuela Casas, but she toed Villa's line. His rules were clear: he would not tolerate rows between women in his presence, and the females in his harem were expected not to ask questions or otherwise make trouble.

Villa could command his women, but from his brother and his sister Martina he received the usual familiar contempt meted out by all siblings. On one occasion there was a huge family row with Villa on one side and Hipólito and Martina on the other. Villa accused Hipólito of meddling in business that did not concern him. Perhaps this was because Hipólito had helped Luz Corral and had advised her to write to Obregón; more likely it was simply the fall-out from one of Hipólito's shady financial deals. Villa feared that Hipólito was meddling in politics in a way that might end by bringing Obregón's wrath down on Canutillo, on the assumption that Hipólito acted on Villa's orders. In 1922 Villa actually wrote to Obregón, asking him not to make any more loans or entrust any more funds to the useless Hipólito. Presumably by this time nothing about the happenings at Canutillo surprised Obregón. Luz Corral also wrote to him, reminding him of the favour she had done him in 1914 when Villa had wanted to execute him. After mulling over her request for financial aid for a couple of months, Obregón paid her a pension.

Obregón soon had more worrying things to concern him than Luz Corral's request for handouts. There would be a new president in 1924 and Obregón was already concerned about the succession. The main contenders, Calles and de la Huerta, represented the interests of Left and

Right respectively. Obregón favoured Calles and allegedly said, when he, Calles and de la Huerta were driving together in Chapultepec Park in Mexico City, that since de la Huerta was a talented musician, Calles should have the succession. 'You and I, Plutarco,' he said in his well-known mock-buffoonish manner, 'cannot leave politics because we would die of hunger; on the other hand Adolfo knows how to sing and give classes in voice and music.'

Obregón wrote to Villa, asking him to give a press interview in which he would explain that he had no desire to re-enter politics. Villa, however, thumbed his nose at Obregón by giving the interview and saying he would do one of two things: either declare himself a presidential candidate or throw his support to de la Huerta. In typical vainglorious mode Villa could not resist telling the reporters that he was still capable of raising 40,000 armed men in forty minutes. Obregón read the interview as a threat that if he tried to impose Calles by manipulated elections, Villa would rise in rebellion. Even de la Huerta was alarmed by Villa's bluster; he met the Centaur on a train between Jiménez and Torreón and urged him to back Calles. Villa took de la Huerta's attitude for weakness, became disillusioned with him and looked elsewhere for a presidential candidate, eventually opting for Raúl Madero. Public opinion polls showed Calles very unpopular, miles behind de la Huerta and Madero and only marginally ahead of Villa himself. Angered by the turn of events, Obregón and Calles turned violently against Villa and now perceived him as the greatest threat to their plans.

For some time Villa had been plagued by assassination bids by Jesús Herrera, the sole surviving male of the Herrera clan. Under stress from Herrera's continual murder attempts, and often in pain from the old wound in his leg, Villa the lifelong teetotaller took to the bottle and became insanely jealous of the women in his harem. In May 1923 he sent a long letter to the newspaper *El Universal*, denouncing Herrera's sustained attempts to murder him, and followed up with letters to Obregón and Calles, urging them to do something about him. Obregón ordered Herrera to desist on pain of execution. The reason was simple: he had had enough of Villa and was now putting together his own assassination plot.

Even for the president of Mexico, this was not an easy thing to compass. Villa never slept in the same place and rarely even rose in the morning from the same bed he had gone to sleep in. He never allowed anyone to walk or stand behind him, and had his fifty *dorados* keyed to a pitch of eternal vigilance. A handpicked team of assassins went to Parral, but had to wait three months for a chance to strike. This eventually came because Villa grew overconfident and momentarily lowered his guard. He was invited to be godfather at a christening at the village of Río Florido and decided to make the trip, knowing that he could combine it with a visit to Parral to see his mistress Manuela Casas, who by this time had been removed from Canutillo because of the friction she caused. In an evil hour Villa heeded the foolish advice of his secretary, Miguel Trillo, and did not take his fifty-strong bodyguard with him, but simply a couple of armed retainers. Trillo, playing the wise steward, advised Villa that they could save on the considerable outlay for fifty men and fifty horses if just a small group travelled by car.

The would-be assassins had rented a house on the outskirts of Parral, at the intersection of Benito Juárez and Gabrino Barreda streets, where all traffic to and from Canutillo had to pass. On 10 July Villa set out for the christening, ignoring a premonition by Austreberta Rentería, who told him that if he left that day she would never see him again. The gunmen planned to intercept him on the way into Parral, but their plan miscarried for, just as Villa's car drove past, hundreds of children came out of a school at the end of lessons; to open fire in such circumstances and kill innocent children might have detonated a scandal big enough to finish Obregón and Calles.

After the christening Villa returned to Parral and spent some days with Manuela Casas. At 8 a.m. on 20 July he and his men left their hotel to drive back to Canutillo. Villa had no sense of danger: his three secret agents in Parral had given him the all-clear and the garrison commander, Félix Lara, had always been effusively friendly. Villa was unaware that Lara and his troops had been sent out of town on a trumped-up military manoeuvre. The old Villa, though, would surely have smelt a rat, for the town seemed oddly deserted and there were no police on duty; his famous intuition should have told him something was wrong, but perhaps drink, complacency or the ravages of time had desensitised his antennae.

Villa took the wheel for the drive back to Canutillo. The car was a large Dodge saloon, but six men were packed into it; apart from Villa himself, there was his chauffeur, Trillo the secretary, his personal assistant Rafael Medrano and two bodyguards, Ramón Contreras and Claro Hurtado. When the car reached the junction of Benito Juárez and Gabrino Barreda, an old man selling candy at a stall called out '*Viva Villa!*' This was the prearranged signal for the men at the windows of the rented house to open fire. As he turned the corner, Villa ran into a massive fusillade and was killed instantly as nine bullets slammed into him. Also slain were Trillo and the chauffeur. The Dodge careered out of control and hit a tree. The wounded Rafael Medrano managed to crawl under the car and feign death while one of the gunmen ran over to pump more bullets into Villa's lifeless head. Ramón Contreras, though injured, managed to shoot one of the assailants dead before making his escape. Claro Hurtado was less fortunate. He tried to escape by a bridge down to the river bank, found his way blocked, and was then gunned down when he turned back.

The killers made a leisurely escape on horseback. They had pumped over forty shots into Villa's car, using dum-dum bullets. Villa was found doubled up, his right hand still reaching for his gun. At the post-mortem his skull was found to be full of bullet-holes, while his heart had been turned to mush by the internal explosion of the dum–dum bullets. He was buried next day, taken to his resting-place in a carriage drawn by two black horses, accompanied by a military guard of honour, a band and thousands of mourners. Félix Lara, who came galloping back into town once he heard the shooting, filed a report to Obregón, saying he could not pursue the killers because of lack of horses. Obregón, who knew that Lara was in on the plot, minuted that he had never heard such an absurd excuse, but took no action against him.

For several days there was tension in the Parral area. Obregón ordered federal troops to occupy Canutillo to prevent a *villista* uprising, but they were opposed by the *dorados* and a nail-biting three-day stand-off ended only when Hipólito arrived at the hacienda on 23 July. He at once cabled Obregón, assured him of his loyalty and promised he would put everything in order. After ten days of dithering, while he tried to gauge public reaction to the assassination, Obregón rescinded the order to the Army to occupy Canutillo, and the crisis passed.

It was obvious to all that Villa had died as the result of a well-hatched conspiracy. The suspicious circumstances were multiple: the entire garrison of Parral had been sent out of town 'coincidentally'; there was no pursuit of the killers for forty-five minutes, and throughout they had acted in a self-assured manner, showing no urgency about leaving the scene of the crime; the telegraph line to Canutillo had been cut, so that it took six hours for the news of Villa's death to reach Hipólito and the *dorados* in the hacienda. The Mexican Chamber of Deputies tried to conduct an investigation into the killing, but were hampered at all points by local military and civilian officials. Since all these people were under the control of the federal government, and hence of Obregón, when no action was taken against them for egregious incompetence, the man in the street soon put two and two together.

There can be no serious doubt that Obregón planned Villa's assassination. Some said Calles had contrived the whole thing, unknown to Obregón, but this never rang true in psychological, political or even logistical terms. A deputy of the Durango state legislature, Jesús Salas Barrazas, claimed he had organised the killing with no help from the federal government, ostensibly letting Obregón off the hook, but Obregón immediately redirected the finger of suspicion back on himself by absurdly claiming he had no authority to arrest Salas Barrazas, as he was a Durango senator. Even more absurdly, Obregón then changed his mind, arrested him and saw him sentenced to twenty years in prison; three months later governor Enríquez of Chihuahua pardoned him. No one else was ever arrested or accused in connection with the murder.

In fact Barrazas was a very small cog in the wheel of conspiracy. The real author was Melitón Lozoya, administrator of the Canutillo hacienda before it was given to Villa. Lozoya had embezzled huge amounts of money from the estate, and Villa had warned him that he must either make good the losses or take the consequence. Concluding that the only way out of this impasse was to murder him, Lozoya recruited eight men with strong grievances against Villa, rented the house in Parral and set up the ambush. Obregón got wind of the plot and helped to oil the wheels. Through Calles he paid Félix Lara 50,000 pesos to make sure the conspiracy succeeded. Lara not only took all his troops out of town 'on manoeuvres' but actually stiffened Lozoya's murder squad by lending him his best sharpshooters.

A mountain of evidence, both documentary and memoir, implicates Obregón in the plot. Adolfo de la Huerta said that the pressure to kill Villa came initially from Calles and secretary of war Joaquín Amaro. At first Obregón was reluctant, arguing that Villa had kept the agreement he made in 1923, but once talked into it by Calles, he became the prime mover, using a string of secondary plotters – Jesús Herrera, Salas Barrazas and Jesús Agustín Castro – to camouflage his role. Obregón gave Calles the nod on the express condition that the conspiracy must never be traced back to him or his government. Jesús Agustín Castro, governor of Durango and a noted Villa-hater, was a key element in the plot, and there is documentary evidence of the conspiracy in a letter from Salas Barrazas to Castro on 7 July 1923. Salas Barrazas agreed to be the 'fall guy' for Villa's murder, and this was confirmed in letters by Castro and Amaro.

The conspiracy began to unravel with Salas Barrazas. He was under the clear understanding that his position as a Durango deputy gave him immunity from arrest, but Castro refused to abide by this, fearing that suspicion would then fall on him. Salas Barrazas panicked when arrested and wrote to Amaro for help; Amaro had him transferred to Chihuahua, where Ignacio Enríquez pardoned him. The Obregón archive, when opened, showed the president granting extraordinary favours to both

Lozoya and Salas Barrazas. The judicious conclusion is that Obregón's government was not just implicated in Villa's murder but actually organised it. The motive was the 1924 presidential election. Calles and Obregón feared that, if necessary, Villa would back de la Huerta with an armed uprising. If de la Huerta became president, Villa would probably be his strong right arm as governor of Durango, and the two would have taken a tough line against US oil companies. There were also whispers that the price of Washington's recognition of the Obregón government was a final resolution of the 'Villa question'.

If Obregón was the main political beneficiary of Villa's death, Hipólito Villa scooped the financial rewards. He inherited Canutillo, appropriated all the revenues and gave Villa's women nothing. Soledad Seañez and Manuela Casas were the obvious losers in the 'fight of the harem', for their legal claims could not match those of Luz Corral and Austreberta Rentería. Austreberta, left penniless, appealed to Obregón, but he replied with meaningless bromides; he was not about to take any action against Hipólito that might trigger a *villista* revolt. Austreberta, refusing to take no for an answer, wrote to Obregón again, but he replied that he had no jurisdiction and referred her to the law courts. When Hipólito later fell foul of the federal government and Austreberta thought her hour had come, Obregón again rebuffed her; his favourite among the Villa women was Luz Corral, who had interceded on his behalf in 1914 when Villa wanted to kill him.

Although Obregón had eliminated Villa to ensure the presidential succession for Calles, his own incumbency still ended in bloodshed. De la Huerta refused to allow Calles to succeed merely on Obregón's patronage and entered the presidential race. Seeing him likely to win in a fair contest, Obregón intervened with intimidation and disruption against the de la Huerta camp. On 4 December 1923 de la Huerta took the familiar route to Veracruz and declared himself in rebellion against Obregón, citing the president's 'odious and intolerable violence against the sovereignty of the Mexican people'. The Army split fairly evenly, with about 25,000 troops going over to de la Huerta and 30,000 staying loyal to Obregón. The rebellion lasted until spring 1924, but Obregón gained a decisive victory at Ocotlán. In victory he was as merciless as ever and executed scores of his former comrades, including Maycotte, who joined the long line of anti-Obregón rebels who faced the firing squad – notably José Isabel Robles in 1917 and Lucio Blanco in 1922. Obregón was an ingrate: it mattered not a jot to him if he owed his life to another man; execution for rebellion was his inflexible rule. De la Huerta fled to the

United States where he made a living as a music teacher, thus fulfilling Obregón's grim prophecy in Chapultepec Park.

Calles succeeded to the presidency, but the years 1924–8 were dark and barbarous. Although the Revolution had officially ended, there was no end to the savagery and the blood-letting. With the nod from Obregón, who had officially retired to pursue his interests as a businessman, Calles began the final campaign against the Yaquis, using all the resources of modern technology, including air power, to finish them off as a military threat. Even as Calles crushed the tribe to whom he had once promised lands and freedom, he had another serious revolt on his hands. The violent anticlericalism of Obregón and Calles had finally provoked a bloody backlash. In the western states of Jalisco, Colima and Michoacán, and eventually in thirteen of Mexico's provinces, Catholic rebels known as *Cristeros* fought a determined guerrilla war that claimed more than 70,000 lives.

Meanwhile Obregón decided he wanted to be president again. Congress opened the legal door for a second presidential term, and in 1927 he went on the campaign trail. In this bid he was backed by the Army, but bitterly opposed by public opinion and Mexico's intellectuals. One of José Vasconcelos's friends expressed the general view: 'Calles is not the problem. It is Obregón. You cannot imagine the ambition there is in that man! Don Porfirio was a joke in comparison.'

Obregón found himself opposed by two candidates, General Arnulfo Gómez and an old compadre, Francisco Serrano. Obregón made it clear he was determined to overwhelm his rivals by fair means or foul, and his megalomania became so overt that many sage observers thought he had toppled over the mental precipice into madness. When Gómez and Serrano combined to stymie his blatant intimidation and corruption by plotting to arrest him along with Calles, they were betrayed by their military colleagues to Obregón, who sent them to the firing squad without mercy and then purged their followers. Some historians claim the bloodbath in the late 1920s was even worse than during 1910–20, as during the Revolution people fought, at least ostensibly, for causes and ideals, not simply naked personal ambition. Obregón descended into the darkness of tyranny and took Mexico down with him. During 1926–30 agricultural production declined by 38 per cent, 200,000 people migrated from the countryside to the cities, and a further 450,000 emigrated to the USA. Significantly, Jesús Garza Galán, the man who had stopped Obregón committing suicide in 1915, himself committed suicide in despair.

Obregón now became the target for assassination attempts. The first bid was made by a Catholic engineer who threw a bomb at his car in November 1927. Another group of would-be assassins were caught and executed in Orizaba; pessimists said that Mexico would be one big firing squad if Obregón ever got back to the presidential palace. One of the most determined plotters against him was a woman known as Madre Conchita, who devised a series of attempted killings worthy of a thriller writer, culminating in a bid to inject him with deadly venom from a hypodermic while he was dancing with a nubile young woman. Obregón knew of many of these plots but was contemptuous, doubting whether anyone would accept a suicide mission for, as he said: 'I will live until someone trades his life for mine.'

Finally, on 17 July 1928, a killer got through the massive security blanket. Obregón was attending a banquet in his honour at La Bombita restaurant in San Ángel, just outside Mexico City. A 26-year-old Catholic fanatic named José de León Toral, linked to the *Cristeros*, tailed Obregón to La Bombita and got past the guards at the door by pretending to be an artist commissioned to paint the leader's portrait. Toral sketched an impressive likeness of Obregón, then took it to the top table where he was sitting and showed it to him. Obregón liked the sketch and agreed to allow Toral to refine the details. As a man played the tune *Limoncito*, shots suddenly rang out: Toral had pumped five bullets into Obregón's face. He died immediately, two years short of his fiftieth birthday. Toral was executed a few days later. So passed the last of the great leaders of the Mexican Revolution.

CONCLUSION

The Mexican Revolution was a ten-year Iliad, in which Villa, Zapata, Obregón, Carranza and the others played the roles in fact which were played in myth by Agamemnon, Achilles, Hector and Aeneas. The loss of life was frightful as the ever-widening spirals of bloodshed sucked in more and more people. Historians estimate the death toll at anything between a low of 350,000 and a high of 1,000,000, but this excludes the victims of the 1918 flu epidemic, which adds another 300,000 to the list of fatalities. Civilisation's thin veneer was never thinner than in the Mexican Revolution, and the moral is surely that even in advanced societies we skate all the time on the thinnest of ice. A seemingly trivial political crisis can open up the ravening maw of an underworld of chaos.

Apart from the aggregate of fatalities, what strikes the student of the Revolution most forcibly is how few of its major protagonists died in their beds. All the leading figures were assassinated or died violent and sometimes mysterious deaths: not just Villa, Zapata, Carranza, Obregón, Madero and Huerta but most of the second-rank figures too – Orozco, Ángeles, Urbina, Hill, Fierro, Chávez García, Martínez, Montaño, Eufemio Zapata, Lucio Blanco and scores of others. The only two truly important personalities to survive to old age were Plutarco Calles and Genovevo de la O.

Revolutions are supposed to change things, so the obvious question is: what did the Mexican Revolution change? The cynic will say: very little. Capitalism took a firmer hold, older elites were displaced by newer ones, a handful of men achieved fame and fortune, but the lot of the mass of people was scarcely improved. According to the cynical view, the Revolution simply showed sophisticated elites how to co-opt rivals and enemies into a one-party state, a mesh of corruption called the *Partido Revolucionario Nacional*, which, by its nods to voting and democracy, escaped the liberal censure directed at one-party states elsewhere. Demands for change could then be countered with an obvious riposte: it is chimerical to ask for revolution because Mexico has already had one.

To narrow the focus on the Mexican Revolution, comparative analysis is useful. All true revolutions, as opposed to mere transfers of power between elites (the 'American Revolution', say) must at some stage threaten the status quo in a seismic way and portend root and branch change. Usually what happens is that there is a political first stage, which is then utilised by genuine revolutionaries who wish to push on to an entirely new form of society. Either the second stage is achieved or, more usually, counter-revolutionaries intervene, destroy the true revolutionaries and pull society back to the first stage. The successful 'dual revolution' can be observed in China (with the Kuomintang as the first stage and Mao's communists as the second), in Russia (with Kerensky as the first stage and Lenin and the Bolsheviks as the second) and in Cuba, where Castro himself went beyond the overthrow of Batista within two years to an embrace of full-blooded Marxist-Leninism. The unsuccessful attempts to take society in the direction of wholesale change can be observed in the case of the English Revolution of the seventeenth century, when Cromwell, victorious over Charles I, slammed on the brakes and turned on the Levellers and the Diggers; in the French Revolution, when the men of Thermidor arrested Robespierre's radical revolution in 1794; and in France in 1871 when the men of the Third Republic bloodily repressed the Paris Commune.

Because even the possibility of radical change requires the virtual destruction of the existing state apparatus, almost invariably the trigger for revolution is the weakening of the state in external warfare and the creation of an interim situation where for once radicals and conservatives compete on roughly equal terms. It was the defeat of Charles I that enabled the Diggers and Levellers to challenge Cromwell and the Army; it was defeat by Japan that triggered the abortive 1905 rising in Russia and defeat by Germany which ushered in the successful revolution of 1917; it was French defeat in the Franco-Prussian War that made possible the rise of the Paris Commune; it was defeat by Japan that finished the Kuomintang and handed the revolutionary baton to Mao and the communists. Even the French Revolution of 1789 was triggered by the consequences of warfare, for it was the dissipation of French treasure in the American War of Independence that eventually led Louis XVI to summon the Estates-General.

Students of Latin American history have long been aware that Cuba is an exception to the 'revolution through warfare' rule. Even more surprising is that fact that in Mexico both our general propositions fall down. It was not warfare but a seemingly trivial political issue over the presidential election which detonated the Revolution in 1910; and in Mexico there was no 'dual revolution'. Mexico after 1910 did not evince a pattern of purely political transfer of power followed by a bid for socio-economic transformation by genuine revolutionaries. In so far as the second element was present, in *zapatismo*, it was there from the very beginning: Zapata's radical prescriptions for society proceeded *pari passu* with Madero's reformism. The sceptics have seized on this idiosyncratic nature of the Mexican Revolution to query whether it was ever a revolution in the true sense. Was it not after all merely a struggle of one caudillo against another, a sustained dance of death involving Madero, Huerta, Villa, Zapata, Carranza and Obregón? The last four in particular were the killer sharks of the Revolution, and in their wake swam the remora fish, the Fierros, Benjamin Hills, de la Huertas and Lucio Blancos.

It is possible to discern three main strands in the Mexican Revolution. First, there were the improving *hacendados* and progressive capitalists spearheading the rise of an emerging industrial bourgeoisie: in this category we may place Madero, Carranza and Obregón. Ranged against them were the reactionary elements, who saw no reason to replace the hacienda as the premier economic institution in Mexico; here we may locate Díaz, Huerta and duplicitous figures like Maytorena. Secondly, there was the entire village movement of free peasants in communal *pueblos* demanding the return of their ancestral lands; clearly the key figure here is Zapata. Thirdly, there is the least clear-cut category of all, where an alliance of cowboys, miners and other marginal peoples of the northern states aimed at the overthrow of *jefes políticos, científicos* and *hacendados*. Because political conflict in the north so often resulted in plunder, looting and destruction, this face of the Revolution has often been dismissed as mere banditry; its profile is formless and its adherents legion but its name is *villismo*.

Without any doubt it was the Madero strand, especially in the form of the *obregonistas* and *carrancistas*, that emerged triumphant from the Revolution, while Villa and Zapata won at best partial victories. The larger categories will not do: the Revolution was not a transition from feudalism to capitalism or even from the 'comprador bourgeoisie' to a 'national bourgeoisie'. To a large extent the Revolution was a conflict *within* an existing bourgeoisie, between 'ins' and 'outs'. Much argument has centred on the hacienda and whether this is the key to the whole matter, with the *hacendados* as a 'fetter' on the development of Mexico as a modern capitalist state. Some say the hacienda could have evolved peacefully, that the events of 1910–11 bear no large-scale meaning but were purely political and contingent. Others say that the Porfiriato had to be overthrown before progress could be made; whether you identify the problem as the hacienda as institution or simply the person of Díaz as caudillo, a modern economy was impossible while this political and economic system continued in being.

It is sometimes said that a golden opportunity was missed in 1910–20, and that the real ideals of the Revolution were betrayed by Carranza and Obregón, but, even with Zapata, socialist ideals were never on the agenda. The Constitution of 1917 – especially articles 27 and 123 – is often cited as the beginning of a leftward path not taken, but in many ways these articles were a purely adventitious result of last-minute compromises in smoke-filled rooms. The constitutional conference at Querétaro did not witness even the limited ideological conflict in evidence during the framing of the US constitution at Philadelphia in 1787, and Alan Knight is right to suggest that Mexico acquired its own Magna Carta in a fit of absence of mind. If we put a bracket around Zapata's village utopia and Villa's military colonies, it becomes very clear that modern capitalism was always the aim of the influential figures in the Revolution. Obregón's achievement is sometimes said to have been that he accomplished in Mexico what Chiang and the Kuomintang failed to accomplish in China. Obregón mobilised the masses to promote a modern state and a modern economy, destroying, co-opting or placating all dissident elements in such a way that no door to communism opened up on the Left; and because he had to carry the masses with him, he could not swing hard Right into fascism.

So, apart from making Mexico safe for capitalism, did the Revolution change anything? Except in the south-east, it is safe to say that the Revolution broke up the old political monopolies and replaced a brittle gerontocracy with a new elite of thrusting and ambitious younger men. Much as in Napoleonic France, there were many residues of the past – with kinship, *compadrazgo* and corruption still prominent features of the political landscape. As with Napoleon, again, there was a wider circle of co-optation, more meritocracy, more careers open to talents and thus a faster circulation of elites. Sociologically, there was real change. Most of the old landowning aristocracy never returned to their pre-1910 positions of power and influence. Most of them did not lose their lives, as their counterparts did in the French and Russian revolutions, but they lost their estates and their families were permanently weakened. Creel, Terrazas and the other big landowners took no part in the Revolution and were thus able to die in their beds. Most of them fled to the USA where they lived comfortably on the cash and portable property they had taken across the border; in this respect their fate was unlike that of the White Russians, who ended up in France as waiters and taxi drivers. There were similarities, though, with the émigrés after the French Revolution in that many of the oligarchs were proscribed and under sentence of death if they returned to Mexico.

However, proscriptions were never as savagely implemented as in the French and Russian revolutions. Many oligarchs were able to make deals with Carranza and Obregón to get their lands back; Maytorena in Sonora, officially a *villista*, blatantly handed back confiscated estates to their former owners. Special pleading on grounds of kinship or *compadrazgo* also saved many aristocrats. Villa himself protected the Zuloaga family in Chihuahua against expropriation because of their kinship ties with his beloved 'Maderito'. The venal George Carothers made several fortunes by brokering other 'special circumstance' deals involving many unworthy beneficiaries from the old *hacendado* class.

What changed most in 1910–20 were popular attitudes. The Revolution opened the eyes of the downtrodden to a world of possibilities they could not have imagined before. The first casualty was deference, and the first signs of increasing civic consciousness came as people tended to dress in the same clothes, with oligarchs deflecting envy by wearing simple outfits, while the peasantry traded up to reflect their new, self-assigned, status. No longer was there sartorial inequality between the classes as if in obedience to some unwritten sumptuary law. Once the old customs, folkways, mores and morality became a casualty of the Revolution, sexual morality in particular became freer, and losses in battle made women more eager to compete for the remaining males. Promiscuity, prostitution and venereal disease were rampant in the years of the Revolution, and the revolution of rising aspirations also found expression, as it invariably does in all societies, in higher levels of crime. Geographical mobility destroyed the old willingness to endure the unendurable. The Mexican people were on the move in these years – not just the tramp, tramp of the armies (notably Obregón's 7,200-kilometre trek), but the flock of fleeing refugees. Apart from losses in battle and from disease, Mexico had to endure a population drain through a voluntary human exodus: between 1910 and 1919, 170,000 Mexicans entered the USA legally and at least another 80,000 illegally.

The paradox is that while Carranza, Obregón and what they represented were the victors in the Revolution, its heart and soul, its profound resonances and its archetypal significance all derive from Villa and Zapata. Mythical icons both, the subject of innumerable *corridos* and motion pictures, the two of them live on in folk memory as Obregón and Carranza do not. These latter are the Butcher Cumberland of the Revolution, victorious but forgotten by almost everyone but professional historians; Villa and Zapata are the Bonnie Prince Charlie, forever haloed in a golden nimbus. In a real sense Villa and Zapata were the Revolution. Villa was no mere landlord but the kind of independent warrior who thrives when the structure of the state is weak or non-existent. One thinks of such parallels as Pugachev in eighteenth-century Russia, Tippu Tip in nineteenth-century central Africa and Salvatore Giuliano in twentieth-century Sicily. Although the oft-made comparisons with Joan of Arc and Jesus Christ are hyperbolic, Zapata, with his mystical relation to the land, his fanatical incorruptibility and his martyrdom, aligns with those rare warrior saints in history like John Brown and Che Guevara.

The two men were natural allies, although they approached the problems of Mexico from very different perspectives. The man of the south, Zapata, operated in a social milieu of plantations, sugar mills and *ejidos*, while Villa, the man of the north, lived in a world where cattle, slaughterhouses and ranches were the salient economic factors, and proximity to the USA the overriding political one. This divergence, and the fact that each was interested only in the *patria chica*, meant that when their great opportunity to become masters of Mexico came in December 1914, they muffed it. The failure was due to lack of genuinely national ideas, but it was not helped by the very different personalities of the two men. Zapata was cerebral, reflective and humourless; Villa was impulsive, visceral and buffoonish. There were no manic-depressive scenes of weeping followed by laughter in Zapata's biography.

None the less, the gulf separating the two should not be overstated, for their similarities were as striking as their differences. Roughly the same age, both were great horsemen, both suffered grievously from unsatisfactory brothers, both took a polygamous attitude to women, and both fell to assassins' bullets as the result of conspiracy. Both leaned on a core of intellectual advisers and, in adversity, both were liable to fall into paranoid fantasies of betrayal. Each had a 'shadow' in the form of a hated figure in the bureaucratic-military mainstream: Zapata detested Carranza, while Villa's *bête noire* and eventual nemesis was Obregón. In the short-term, Villa was the more important, as he won a string of victories and fought half a dozen pitched battles. Long-term, Zapata took the palm, as his agrarian reforms struck deep roots in the Mexican collective unconscious and he became a role model for all other Latin American peasant revolutionaries.

More than almost any other historical figures, Villa and Zapata had careers that were coextensive with the great events they lived through; they scarcely seemed to have lived at all except in and through the Revolution. Even more than other great men, both are psychologically opaque. The excessive womanising might give a clue to the unconscious in a society less macho than Mexico, but most attempts to fuse their philandering with other significant clues – Zapata's view of the land as a person with a soul, Villa's teetotalism – founder for lack of cogent evidence, even of the indirect kind. Villa's mood swings seem to betray a deeply disturbed personality, one in which great compassion and tenderness could coexist with the utmost cruelty and ruthlessness. The phasic nature of his outbursts indicates not so much a Jekyll-and-Hyde personality as a lack of integration, with no central core of identity strong enough to control the peripheral elements. Zapata could be cruel and ruthless, but only for *raison d'état*. Unless betrayed by a trusted associate – for him the ultimate nightmare – he always mastered emotion with reason. Villa was called the Centaur because he seemed half man and half horse, but perhaps the Revolution's true centaur was the revolutionary amalgam formed by the fusion of Villa and Zapata. They were great men, and their biography is also the biography of the Mexican Revolution.

SOURCES

Abbreviations:
HAHR = Hispanic American Historical Review
JLAS = Journal of Latin American Studies
Place of publication is London unless otherwise stated.

THE MEXICO OF PORFIRIO DÍAZ

Carleton Beals, *Porfirio Díaz: Dictator of Mexico* (Philadelphia 1932) is still the standard biography in English but there is a veritable cascade of works by Mexican historians: Francisco Bulnes, *El Verdadero Díaz y la Revolución* (Mexico City 1992); Ángel Taracena, *Porfirio Díaz* (Mexico City 1983); José López Portillo y Rojas, *Elevación y caída de Porfirio Díaz* (Mexico City 1927); Ralph Roeder, *Hacia el México moderno: Porfirio Díaz*, 2 vols (Mexico City 1985); Jorge Fernando Iturribarria, *Porfirio Díaz ante la historia* (Mexico City 1967). Work by Daniel Cosío Villegas is fundamental: *El Porfiriato: Vida política interior* (Mexico City 1985) and *El Porfiriato: Vida económica* (Mexico City 1985). Two useful collections are edited by Gene Z. Hanrahan, *Documents on the Mexican Revolution, Vol 1: The Madero Revolution* (1976); *Vol 2: The Madero Revolution to the Overthrow of Díaz* (1976).

For Santa Anna see Enrique González Pedrero, *País de un solo hombre: El México de Santa Anna* (Mexico City 1993); W. H. Calcott, *Santa Anna: The story of an Enigma Who Once Was Mexico* (1992); Frank C. Hanighen, *Santa Anna: The Napoleon of the West* (1934); Rafael Muñoz, *Santa Anna: el dictador resplandeciente* (Mexico City 1976); José Fuentes Mares, *Santa Anna el hombre* (Mexico City 1982); Agustín Yáñez, *Santa Anna: espectro de una sociedad* (Mexico City 1982). For Juárez, the Reforma and the struggle with the French see Charles Allen Smart, *Viva Juárez* (1964); Jasper Ridley, *Maximilian and Juárez* (1993); Richard N. Sinkin, *The Mexican Reform, 1855–1876: A Study in Liberal Nation-Building* (Austin 1979); Charles R. Berry, *The Reform in*

Oaxaca, 1856–1876: A Microhistory of the Liberal Revolution (Lincoln 1981).

For more detail on the social and economic history of the Porfiriato there is: Francisco Xavier Guerra, *México: del antiguo régimen a la Revolución* (Mexico City 1988); Justo Sierra, *Obras completas*, 15 vols (Mexico City 1991); Lucas Alemán, *Historia de México*, 5 vols (Mexico City 1985); Karl Schmitt, 'The Díaz Conciliation Policy on State and Local Levels, 1876–1911', *HAHR* 40 (1960), pp. 182–204; F. González Roa, *El problema ferrocarrilero* (Mexico City 1919); John H. Coatsworth, *El impacto económico de los ferrocarriles en el Porfiriato*, 2 vols (Mexico City 1976); Marvin D. Bernstein, *The Mexican Mining Industry 1880–1950: A Study of the Interaction of Politics, Economics and Technology* (Albany 1965); Charles W. Hamilton, *Early Days: Oil Tales of Mexico* (Houston 1966); William D. Raat, *El positivismo durante el Porfiriato 1876–1910* (Mexico City 1975); William D. Raat, 'Los intelectuales, el positivismo y la cuestión indígena', *Historia Mexicana* 20 (1971); David M. Fletcher, *Rails, Mines and Progress: Seven American Pioneers in Mexico, 1867–1911* (Ithaca 1958); Alfred Tischendorf, *Great Britain and Mexico in the Era of Porfirio Díaz* (Durham 1961).

Travellers' tales and eyewitness reports by foreigners add a dimension to Mexico's troubled history. Particularly valuable for the Porfiriato are the following: Frederick Starr, *The Indian Mexico: A Narrative of Travel and Labour* (Chicago 1908); Hans Gadow, *Through Southern Mexico, Being an Account of the Travels of a Naturalist* (1908); C. Arnold and F. J. T. Frost, *The American Egypt: A Record of Travel in Yucatán* (New York 1909); Henry Harper, *A Journey in South-Eastern Mexico* (New York 1910); Hudson Strode, *Timeless Mexico* (New York 1944); Leone B. Moats, *Thunder in their Veins* (1933); John Kenneth Turner, *Barbarous Mexico* (Chicago 1910); George Creel, *The People Next Door* (New York 1926); Donald Brand, *Mexico: Land of Sunshine and Shadow* (New York 1966); Graham Hutton, *Mexican Images* (1963); H. Hamilton Fyfe, *The Real Mexico* (1914); Edward Bell, *The Political Shame of Mexico* (New York 1914); Lesley Byrd Simpson, *Many Mexicos* (Berkeley 1952) and no less than three volumes by Mrs Alec Tweedie, *Mexico As I Saw It* (1902); *Porfirio Díaz* (1902); *Mexico from Díaz to the Kaiser* (1917).

The Indian and the peasant are so inextricably mixed in Mexican history that ethnological, historical and sociological studies cannot really be considered as categories apart. Race and culture come into sharper focus in: Manning Nash, ed., *Handbook of Middle American Indians* (Austin 1967); Nelson Reed, *The Caste War of Yucatán* (Stanford 1964);

Alfonso Fabila, *Las tribus Yaquis de Sonora: su cultura y anhelada autodeterminación* (Mexico City 1940); Evelyn Hu-Dehart, 'Development of Rural Rebellion: Pacification of the Yaquis in the Late Porfiriato', *HAHR* 54 (1974), pp. 72–93; T. G. Powell, 'Mexican Intellectuals and the Indian Question, 1876–1911', *HAHR* 48 (1968), pp. 19–36; George M. McBride, *The Land Systems of Mexico* (New York 1923); Leticia Reina, *Las rebeliones campesinas en Mexico 1819–1906* (Mexico City 1980); Donald F. Stevens, 'Agrarian Policy and Instability in Porfirian Mexico', *Americas* 39 (1982), pp. 153–66; Lucio Mendeta y Nuñez, *El problema agraria de Mexico* (Mexico City 1966); Friedrich Katz, 'Labour Conditions on Haciendas in Porfirian Mexico: Some Trends and Tendencies', *HAHR* 54 (1974); Henry A. Landsberger, ed., *Latin American Peasant Movements* (Cornell 1969); D. A. Brading, *Caudillo and Peasant in the Mexican Revolution* (Cambridge 1980); Friedrich Katz, *La servidumbre agrario en México en la época Porfiriana* (Mexico City 1980); Moisés de la Peña, *El pueblo y su tierra: Mito y realidad de la reforma agraria en México* (Mexico City 1964); Paul Friedrich, *Agrarian Revolt in a Mexican Village* (Englewood Cliffs 1970); Moisés González Navarro, 'El trabajo forzoso en México, 1821–1917', *Historia Méxicana* 27 (1978), pp. 588–615; F. González Roa, *El aspecto agrario de la revolución Mexicana* (Mexico City 1919).

Although land reform, the hacienda and the Indian were the principal problems facing Díaz, they were far from the only ones. For the other players in the drama and the other conflicts he had to resolve see: Robert E. Quirk, *The Mexican Revolution and the Catholic Church 1910–29* (Bloomington 1973); Paul J. Vanderwood, *Disorder and Progress: Bandits, Police and Mexican Development* (1981); Juan Felipe Leal, 'El estado y el bloque en poder en México: 1867–1914', *Historia Mexicana* 23 (1974), pp. 716–21; Paul J. Vanderwood, 'Los rurales: producto de una necesidad social,' *Historia Mexicana* 22 (1972), pp. 34–51; Berta Ulloa, 'Las relaciones mexicano-norteamericanas, 1910–11', *Historia Mexicana* 15 (1966), pp. 25–46; W. Schiff, 'German Military Penetration into Mexico During the Late Díaz Period', *HAHR* 39 (1959), pp. 568–79; Frank Tannenbaum, *Peace by Revolution: Mexico after 1910* (1966); Berta Ulloa, *La Revolución intervenida: relaciones diplomáticas entre México y Estados Unidos, 1910–1914* (Mexico City 1971); Karl M. Schmitt, *Mexico and the United States, 1821–1973: Conflict and Co-existence* (New York 1974). On the disputed question of the importance of industrial workers see Elsa Cecilia Frost, ed., *El trabajo y los trabajadores en la historia de México* (Mexico City 1979) and Alan Knight, 'The Working Class and the Mexican Revolution c.1900–1920', *JLAS* 16 (1984), pp. 51–79.

On this subject the would-be seminal article is F. X. Guerra, 'La révolution mexicaine: d'abord une révolution minière?' *Annales E.S.C.* 36 (1981), pp. 784–814, answered by Alan Knight in 'La révolution mexicaine: révolution minière ou révolution serrano?' *Annales E.S.C.* 38 (1983), pp. 449–59.

The standard biography of Madero in English is Stanley R. Ross, *Franciso I. Madero: Apostle of Mexican Democracy* (New York 1955). There are many studies in Spanish, notably Alfonso Taracena, *Madero: vida del hombre y del político* (Mexico City 1937); Gabriel Ferrer de Mendiolea, *Vida de Francisco Madero* (Mexico City 1945); Pedro Lamicq, *Madero* (Mexico City 1958). The *Archivo de Don Francisco Madero* has been published in two volumes (Mexico City 1985). See also María de los Ángeles Suárez del Solar, *Antología de Madero* (Mexico City 1987). Madero's complex psychology is analysed further in José C. Valadés, *Imaginación y realidad de Francisco I. Madero*, 2 vols (Mexico City 1960); Enrique Krauze, *Francisco Madero: Místico de la libertad* (Mexico City 1987) and José N. Rosales, *Madero y el espiritismo* (Mexico City 1973). Background material on the wider Madero family is provided in Carlos B. Madero, *Relación de la familia Madero* (Parral, Coahuila 1973) and the supremely valuable work by José Vasconcelos, *Don Evaristo Madero: Biografía de un patricio* (Mexico City 1958). A biography of Madero can be constructed from the multi-volume production by Gene Z. Hanrahan, *Documents on the Mexican Revolution, Vol. 1: The Madero Revolution* (1976); *Vol. 2: The Madero Revolution to the Overthrow of Díaz* (1976); and *Vol. 4: The Murder of Madero* (1981).

Madero's political movement is put under the microscope in Charles C. Cumberland, *Mexican Revolution: Genesis under Madero* (Austin 1952); Moisés Ocoa Campos, *La revolución mexicana: sus causas políticas*, 2 vols (Mexico City 1968); Hans Werner Tobler, *La revolución mexicana: transformación social y cambio político 1876–1940* (Mexico City 1994); Alfonso Taracena, *La verdadera revolución mexicana 1900–1911* (Mexico City 1991); Ramon Prida, *De la dictadura a la anarquía* (Mexico City 1958); Jean Meyer, *La révolution mexicaine: 1910–1940* (Paris 1973); José C. Valadés, *Historia general de la Revolución Mexicana*, 9 vols (Mexico City 1985); Jorge Vera Estañol, *Historia de la Revolución Mexicana: orígenes y resultados* (Mexico City 1967); Friedrich Katz and Lloyd Jane-Dale, eds., *Porfirio Díaz frente al descontento regional* (Mexico City 1986). See also Francisco Vasquez Gómez, *Memorias políticas 1901–1913* (Mexico City 1982); Jerry W. Knudson, 'When did Francisco Madero Decide on Revolution?' *Americas* 30 (1974), pp. 529–34; Leone B. Moats, *Thunder in their Veins* (1933). The Creelman interview is recapitulated in James Creelman, *Díaz: Master of Mexico* (New York 1911).

Other works with a direct bearing on Madero's situation in 1909–1910 are as follows: Juan Felipe Leal, *La burguesía y el estado Mexicano* (Mexico City 1972); Juan Sánchez Azcona, *Apuntes para la historia de la revolución mexicana* (Mexico City 1961); G. N. Santos, *Memorias* (Mexico City 1984); Alfonso Taracena, *Madero, víctima del imperialismo yanqui* (Mexico City 1973); Pindaro Uriostegui Miranda, *Testimonios del proceso revolucionario de México* (Mexico City 1970); Miguel Sánchez Lamego, *Historia militar de la revolución en la época maderista* (Mexico City 1983); Pedro Antonio Santos, *Memorias* (San Luis Potosí 1990); Luis L. León, *Crónica del poder: En los recuerdos de un político en el México revolucionario* (Mexico City 1987); Gonzalo G. Rivero, *Hacia la verdad: Episodios de la revolución* (Mexico City 1911); Anita Brenner, *The Wind that Swept Mexico: The History of the Mexican Revolution* (Austin 1971); Eric Jauffret, *Révolution et sacrifice au Mexique* (Paris 1986).

Madero's attitude too the land question appears in Robert Holden, *Mexico and the Survey of Public Lands: The Management of Modernization, 1876–1911* (De Kalb, Illinois 1994) and William K. Meyers, *Forge of Progress, Crucible of Revolt: Origins of the Mexican Revolution in the Comarca Lagunera, 1880–1911* (Albuquerque 1994). For Madero's appeal to the ordinary man and to women see William H. Beezley, 'In Search of Everyday Mexicans in the Revolution', *Revista Interamericana de Bibliografia* 33 (1983), pp. 366–82; Begoña Hernández y Lazo et al., eds., *Las mujeres en la revolución mexicana, 1884–1920: Biografias de mujeres revolucionarias* (Mexico City 1992).

THE RISE OF ZAPATA

The fundamental, and unsurpassed, study of Zapata is John Womack, *Zapata and the Mexican Revolution* (1969). This is qualified in some minor aspects by Samuel Brunk, *Emiliano Zapata: Revolution and Betrayal in Mexico* (Albuquerque 1995). But all the Zapata biographies usually yield a nugget or two, either in the form of a striking fact or an interpretive slant. See, additionally, Peter E. Newell, *Zapata of Mexico* (1979); Roger Parkinson, *Zapata: A Biography* (1980); John Steinbeck, *Viva Zapata* (1991); Roberto Blanco Moreno, *Zapata* (1975); Jesús Sotelo Inclán, *Raíz y razón de Zapata* (Mexico City 1970); Alicia López de Rodríguez, *Emiliano Zapata: biografia* (Cuernavaca 1982); Porfirio Palacios, *Emiliano Zapata: datos biogràfico-históricos* (Mexico City 1960); Baltasar Dromundo, *Vida de Emiliano Zapata* (Mexico City 1961);

Germán Lizt Arzubide, *Zapata* (Mexico City 1973); Anita Aguilar and Rosalind Rosoff, *Emiliano Zapata: hombre de tierra* (Mexico City 1986); Laura Espejez, Alicia Olivera and Salvador Rueda, eds., *Emiliano Zapata: Antología* (Mexico City 1988); Enrique Krauze, *El amor a la tierra: Emiliano Zapata* (Mexico City 1987).

The context in which the *zapatista* movement arose is examined in a number of works: John Tutino, *From Insurrection to Revolution in Mexico: Social Bases of Agrarian Violence 1750–1940* (Princeton 1986); Gildardo Magaña and Carlos Pérez Guerrero, *Emiliano Zapata y el agrarismo en Mexico*, 5 vols (Mexico City 1952); Arturo Warman, *'We Come to Object': The Peasants of Morelos and the National State* (Baltimore 1980); Robert A. White, 'Mexico, the Zapata Movement and the Revolution', in Henry A. Landsberger, ed., *Latin American Peasant Movements* (Ithaca, N.Y. 1969); Antonio Díaz Soto y Gama, *La revolución agraria del sur y Emiliano Zapata su caudillo* (Mexico City 1976); Donald F. Stevens, 'Agrarian Policy and Instability in Porfirian Mexico', *Americas* 39 (1982), pp. 153–66; R. Waterbury, 'Non-revolutionary Peasants: Oaxaca Compared to Morelos in the Mexican Revolution', *Comparative Studies in Society and History* 17 (1975); Moisés González Navarro, 'El trabajo forzoso en México, 1821–1917', *Historia Mexicana* 27 (1978), pp. 588–615; Fernando Horcasitas, *De Porfirio Díaz a Zapata* (Mexico City 1974); Adolfo Gilly, *La revolución interrumpida, México 1910–1920: una guerra campesina por la tierra y el poder* (Mexico City 1971); Marte R. Gómez, *Las comisiones agrarias del sur* (Mexico City 1971).

The social and cultural milieu of Zapata's village is examined in Alicia Hernández Chávez, *Anenecuilco: memoria y vida de un pueblo* (Mexico City 1991); Arturo Benavides, *Ya venimos a contradecir: los campesinos de Morelos y el estado nacional* (Mexico City 1976); Cheryl English Martin, *Rural Society in Colonial Morelos* (Albuquerque 1985); Guillermo de la Peña, *A Legacy of Promises: Agriculture, Politics and Ritual in the Morelos Highlands of Mexico* (Austin 1981) and Juan Salazar Pérez, *Cuadernos Morelenses* (Morelos 1982). Geographical problems appear in Domingo Díaz, *Bosque jo-geográfico de Morelos* (Morelos 1967). Some pointers to the situation in Anenecuilco can be gleaned from Robert Redfield, *Tepoztlán: A Mexican Village. A Study of Folk Life* (Chicago 1973). The vice-regal land grants are the subject of Alicia Hernández Chavez, *Haciendas y pueblos en el estado de Morelos 1535–1810* (Mexico City 1973). The role of Catholicism is dealt with in John M. Ingham, *Mary, Michael and Lucifer: Folk Catholicism in Central Mexico* (Austin 1986). The *corrido* is examined in Vicente T. Mendozo, *El corrido de la revolución mexicana* (Mexico City 1990) and Armano de Maria y Campos, *La revolución mexicana a través de los corridos populares*, 2 vols (Mexico City 1962). The early influences on Zapata and his collaborators are traced in Juan Salazar Pérez, *Otilio Montaño* (Cuernavaca 1982) and Valentín López González, *Los compañeros de Zapata* (Morelos 1980). A valuable eye-witness account is Rosa King, *Tempest over Mexico* (Boston 1935).

THE RISE OF VILLA

For Chihuahua in the nineteenth century see Francisco R. Almada, *Resumen de la historia de Chihuahua* (Mexico City 1955); O. L. Jones, *Nueva Vizcaya: Heartland of the Spanish Frontier* (Albuquerque 1988); Fernando Jordan, *Crónica de un país bárbaro* (Chihuahua 1975); F. C. & R. Lister, *Chihuahua: Storehouse of Storms* (Albuquerque 1966); Barry Carr, 'Las peculiaridades del Norte Mexicano, 1880–1927: ensayo de interpretación', *Historia Mexicana* 22 (1973), pp. 320–46; R. Saudels, 'Antecedentes de la revolución en Chihuahua', *Historia Mexicana* 24 (1975); Daniel Nugent, *Spent Cartridges of Revolution: An Anthropological History of Namiquipa* (Chicago 1993); Ana María Alonso, *Thread of Blood: Colonialism, Revolution and Gender on Mexico's Northern Frontier* (Tucson 1995).

For the Apache wars see Patricia N. Limerick, *The Legacy of Conquest: The Unbroken Past of the American West* (New York 1987); Max L. Moorehead, *The Apache Frontier* (Norman, Oklahoma 1968); Edward H. Spicer, *Cycles of Conquest: The Impact of Spain, Mexico and the United States on the Indians of the South-West, 1533–1960* (Tucson 1962); Dan L. Thrapp, *Victorio and the Mimbres Apaches* (Norman, Oklahoma 1974); Angie Debo, *Geronimo: The Man, His Time, His Place* (Norman, Oklahoma 1976); Dan L. Thrapp, *The Conquest of Apacheria* (Norman, Oklahoma 1967); John C. Cremony, *Life Among the Apaches 1850–1968* (Glorieta, New Mexico 1969); William B. Griffen, *Apaches at War and Peace: The Janos Presidio, 1750–1858* (Albuquerque 1988). The Mormons are studied in F. Lamond Tullis, *Mormons in Mexico: The Dynamics of Faith and Culture* (Logan, Utah 1987) and Karl E. Young, *Ordeal in Mexico: Tales of Danger and Hardship Collected from Mormon Colonists* (Salt Lake City 1986).

The domination of the Creel-Terrazas clique has drawn the fire of many historians, and the following titles are indicative: Francisco R. Almada, *Gobernadores del estado de Chihuahua* (Chihuahua 1981) and *Juárez y Terrazas: Aclaraciones históricas* (n.d.); Harold Sims, 'Espejo de caciques: los Terrazas de Chihuahua', *Historia Mexicana* 18 (1968), pp. 379–99; Mark Wasserman, *Capitalists, Caciques and Revolution: The*

Native Elite and Foreign Enterprise in Chihuahua, Mexico, 1854–1911 (Chapel Hill, North Carolina 1984). Some unconvincing attempts have been made to rehabilitate the Terrazas, as in José Fuentes Mares, *Y México se refugió en el desierto: Luis Terrazas, su historia y destino* (Mexico City 1954) and Lulu Creel de Muller, *El conquistador del desierto* (Mexico City 1982). For the events at Tomochi consult Rubén Osorio Zúñiga, *Tomochi en llamas* (Mexico City 1995); Lillian Illades Aguilar, *La rebelión de Tomochic* (Mexico City 1993); Paul J. Vanderwood, ' "None But the Justice of God": Tomochic, 1891–1892', in Jaime E. Rodríguez, *Patterns of Contention in Mexican History* (Wilmington, Delaware 1992), pp. 227–41; Heriberto Frías, *Tomochic* (Mexico City 1983); Francisco Almada, *La rebelión de Tomochic en Chihuahua* (Chihuahua 1938); José Carlos Chávez, *Peleando en Tomochic* (Juarez 1955); Plácido Chávez Calderón, *La defensa de Tomochic* (Mexico City 1964).

On Pancho Villa by far the best book is Friedrich Katz, *The Life and Times of Pancho Villa* (Stanford 1998), the product of a lifetime's research. Alongside this mountain most other Villa biographies are molehills, but they tend to illustrate Katz's division of the previous lives into hagiography and debunking. John Reed's classic *Insurgent Mexico* (1969) tends to promote the heroic version as do Manuel A. Machado, *Centaur of the North: Francisco Villa, the Mexican Revolution and northern Mexico* (1988); Elías Torres, *Vida y hechos de Francisco Villa* (Mexico City 1975); Federico Cervantes, *Francisco Villa y la revolución* (Mexico City 1960); Ramón Puente, 'Francisco Villa', in *Historia de la Revolución Mexicana* (Mexico City 1936), pp. 239–70. The 'black legend' of Villa appears in Celia Herrera, *Francisco Villa: Ante la Historia* (Mexico City 1981) and Rodrigo Alonso Cortés, *Francisco Villa: el quinto jinete del apocalipsis* (Mexico City 1972). A more nuanced and ambivalent approach is evident in Eugenio Toussant Aragón, *¿ Quién y como fue Pancho Villa* (Mexico City 1979), a psychobiography linking Villa's teetotalism and sexual excess with childhood trauma; Haldeen Braddy, *The Paradox of Pancho Villa* (El Paso 1978) and Enrique Beltrán, 'Fantasía y realidad de Pancho Villa', *Historia Mexicana* 16 (1966), pp. 71–84.

Fundamental to any research into Villa is Martín Luis Guzmán, *Memorias de Pancho Villa* (Mexico City 1964). An English translation of this by Virginia H. Taylor has appeared as *Memoirs of Pancho Villa* (Austin 1966). Katz's monumental biography makes use of no less than three texts of the Guzmán original, of which only one was published. Of the many accounts of Villa's early life (mostly apocryphal) to have appeared, the most curious is surely Percy N. Furber, *I took Chances: From Windjammers to Jets* (Leicester 1954). More valuable is the memoir by Luis Aguirre Benavides, *De Franciso I. Madero a Francisco Villa: Memorias de un revolucionario* (Mexico City 1966).

Of the personalities Villa met before the Revolution broke out in 1910 the two most significant were Silvestre Terrazas and Abraham González. Terrazas's reflections are contained in 'El verdadero Pancho Villa', *Boletín de la Sociedad Chihuahuense de Estudios Históricos* (Chihuahua) 6 No. 10 (September 1949), pp. 290–95; 6 No. 11 (October–November 1949), pp. 307–10; and 7 No. 6 (November 1950), pp. 453–55; also in Silvestre Terrazas, *El Verdadero Pancho Villa* (Mexico City 1985). For Abraham González see William H. Beezley, *Insurgent Governor: Abraham González and the Mexican Revolution in Chihuahua* (Lincoln 1973) and Francisco R. Almada, *Vida, proceso y muerte de Abraham González* (Mexico City 1967). See also the Instituto Nacional de Estudios Históricos de la Revolución Mexicana publication *Abraham González* (1985); Joaquín Márquez Montiel, *Hombres célebres de Chihuahua* (Mexico City 1953); Francisco R. Almada, *Gobernadores del estado de Chihuahua* (Mexico City 1951).

THE RISE OF MADERO AND THE FALL OF DÍAZ

The rebellion in the north is covered in Miguel Sánchez Lamego, *Historia militar de la revolución en la época maderista*, 2 vols (Mexico City 1977); Gene Z. Hanrahan, *The Madero Revolution: The Origins of the Revolution in Texas, Arizona, New Mexico and California 1910–11* (London 1976); Santiago Portilla, *Una sociedad en armas: insurrección antireeleccionista en México, 1910–1911* (Mexico City 1995); Francisco R. Almada, *La revolución en el estado de Chihuahua*, 2 vols (Mexico City 1965); José C. Valadés, *Historia general de la revolución mexicana*, 5 vols (Mexico City 1976); Alfonso Taracena, *La verdadera revolución Mexicana (1901–11)* (Mexico City 1991); Manuel Gamiz Olivas, *Historia de la Revolución en el estado de Durango* (Mexico City 1973); Benjamin Herrera-Vargas, *La revolución en Chihuahua, 1910–1911* (Mexico City n.d.)

Local studies come into their own at this point. See particularly Mark Wasserman, *Persistent Oligarchs: Elites and Politics in Chihuahua, Mexico, 1910–1940* (Durham, North Carolina 1993); Benjamin Thomas and Mark Wasserman, eds., *Provinces of the Revolution: Essays on Regional Mexican History, 1910–1929* (Albuquerque 1990); Benjamin Thomas and William McNellie, eds., *Other Mexicos: Essays on Regional Mexican History, 1876–1911* (Albuquerque 1984); Oscar J. Martínez, *Border Boom Town: Ciudad Juárez since 1848* (Austin 1978); William H. Beezley, 'State Reform during the Provisional Presidency: Chihuahua 1911', *HAHR* 50

(1970), pp. 524–37; Lowell L. Blaisdell, *The Desert Revolution: Baja California, 1911* (Madison 1962).

The US factor appearas in Edward Haley, *Revolution and Intervention: The Diplomacy of Taft and Wilson with Mexico, 1910–17* (Cambridge, Mass. 1970); Karl M. Schmitt, *Mexico and the United States, 1821–1973; Conflict and Co-existence* (New York 1974); Berta Ulloa, *La revolución intervenida, relaciones diplomáticas entre México y Estados Unidos 1910–14* (Mexico City 1971); Moise S. Alperovich and Boris T. Rudenko, *La revolución mexicana de 1910–17: La política de los Estados Unidos* (Mexico City 1976); Clarence C. Clenenden, *Blood on the Border: The United States and the Mexican Irregulars* (New York 1969); Howard F. Cline, *The United States and Mexico* (1968); Linda B. Hall and Don M. Coever, *Revolution on the Border: The United States and Mexico, 1910–1920* (Albuquerque 1988); Paul V. N. Henderson, *Mexican Exiles on the Borderlands, 1909–1913* (El Paso 1979); Leon C. Metz, *Border: The US – Mexico Line* (El Paso 1989); James A. Sandos, *Rebellion in the Borderlands: Anarchism and the Plan of San Diego, 1904–1923* (Norman, Oklahoma 1992); Paul J. Vanderwood and Frank N. Samponaro, *Border Fury: A Picture Postcard Record of Mexico's Revolution and US War Preparedness, 1910–1917* (Albuquerque 1988).

The secondary (but none the less important) personalities of 1911 are dealt with in the following works: Orozco in Michael C. Meyer, *Mexican Rebel: Pascual Orozco and the Mexican Revolution, 1910–1915* (Lincoln, Nebraska 1967) and Ramón Puente, *Pascual Orozco y la revuelta de Chihuahua* (Mexico City 1912); Garibaldi in Giuseppe Garibaldi, *A Toast to Rebellion* (New York 1937); Limantour in José Yves Limantour, *Apuntes sobre mi vida pública, 1892–1911* (Mexico City 1965) and Kenneth M. Johnson, *José Yves Limantour v. United States* (Los Angeles 1961). Interest in Magón and the Magonistas has become a growth industry. See Colin M. MacLachlan, *Anarchism and the Mexican Revolution: The Political Trials of Ricardo Flores Magón In the United States* (Berkeley 1991); Juan Gómez Quiñones, *Sembradores: Ricardo Flores Magón y el Partido Liberal Mexicano: A Eulogy and Critique* (Los Angeles 1977); Ethel Duffy Turner, *Ricardo Flores Magón y El Partido Liberal Mexicano* (Mexico City 1984).

Further relevant material on Zapata (additional to that cited for the chapter on the rise of Zapata) is as follows: Lola Elizabeth Boyd, ed., *Emiliano Zapata en las letras y el folklore mexicano* (Mexico City 1979); Carlos J. Sierra Brabatta, *Zapata: señor de la tierra, capitán de los labriegos* (Mexico City 1985); John H. McNeely, 'Origins of the Zapata Revolt in Morelos', *HAHR* 46 (1966), pp. 153–69; Arturo Warman, 'The Political

Project of Zapatismo', in Friedrich Katz, ed., *Riot, Rebellion and Revolution: Rural Social Conflict in Mexico* (Princeton 1988), pp. 321–38; François Chevalier, 'Un facteur décisif de la révolution agraire au Mexique: le soulèvement de Zapata, 1911–1919', *Annales*, E.S.C. 16 (1961), pp. 66–82.

The spreading ripples of the Zapata movement through neighbouring states can be traced in a number of works: Ian Jacobs, *Ranchero Revolt: The Mexican Revolution in Guerrero* (Austin 1982); Atenedoro Gómez, *Monografía histórica sobre la génesis de la revolución en el estado de Puebla* (Mexico City 1960); Moisés Ochoa Campos, *Historia del estado de Guerrero* (Mexico City 1968); Jesús Romero Flores, *Historia de la revolución en Michoacán* (Mexico City 1964); Hector R. Olea, *Breve historia de la revolución en Sinaloa* (Mexico City 1964); Romana Falcón, 'Los orígenes populares de la revolución en 1910: El caso de San Luis Potosí', *Historia Mexicana* 29 (1979); Alfonso Francisco Ramírez, *Historia de la revolución en Oaxaca* (Mexico City 1970); Manuel González Calzada, *Historia de la revolución en Tabasco* (Mexico City 1972); Luis Rubluo, *Historia de la revolución mexicana en el estado de Hidalgo*, 2 vols (Mexico City 1983); Jan Bazaut, *Cinco haciendas mexicanas: tres siglos de vida rural en San Luis Potosí* (Mexico City 1975); Ciro de la Garza Treviño, *La revolución en el estado de Tamulipas, 1885–1913* (Mexico City 1973); Antonio Nakayawa, *Sinaloa: el drama y sus actores* (Mexico City 1975); Hector F. Castañedo Jiménez, *Jalisco en la revolución* (Guadalajara 1988); Jose G. Zuno, *Historia de la revolución en el estado de Jalisco* (Mexico City 1971); Octavio Gordillo y Ortiz, *La revolución en el estado de Chiapas* (Mexico City 1986); Cuauhtémoc González Pacheco, *Capital extranjero en la selva de Chiapas, 1863–1962* (Mexico City 1983); Robert Wasserstrom, *Class and Society in Central Chiapas* (Berkeley 1983).

The closing stages of Madero's struggle against Díaz (and Díaz's failure to contain this revolt as he had contained earlier ones) are examined in Paul J. Vanderwood, 'Response to Revolt: The Counter-Guerrilla Strategy of Porfirio Díaz', *HAHR* 56 (1976), pp. 551–79 and Don M. Coerver and Linda B. Hall, *Texas and the Mexican Revolution: A Study in State and National Border Policy, 1910–1920* (San Antonio 1984). A good source for 1910–11 is the work written on the Mormons in Northern Mexico: Karl E. Young, *Ordeal in Mexico: Tales of Danger and Hardship Collected from Mormon Colonists* (Salt Lake City 1968); N. S. Hatch and B. C. Hardy, *Stalwarts South of the Border* (El Paso 1985); and Harold Taylor, *Memories of Militants and Mormon Colonists in Mexico* (California 1992). There is additional material on Pascual Orozco in Roderic A. Camp, *Mexican Political Biographies, 1884–1935* (Austin

1991); Alberto Morales Jiménez, *Hombres de la revolución mexicana* (Mexico City 1960) and Joaquín Márquez Montiel, *Hombres célebres de Chihuahua* (Mexico City 1953).

The growing importance of ideology is highlighted in John D. Rutherford, *Mexican Society during the Revolution: A Literary Approach* (Oxford 1971) and James D. Cockcroft, *Intellectual Precursors of the Mexican Revolution* (Austin 1968). The last days of Díaz are graphically covered in a number of accounts by travellers, journalists and eye-witnesses: Patrick O'Hea, *Reminiscences of the Mexican Revolution* (London 1966); Edward I. Bell, *The Political Shame of Mexico* (London 1914); Anita R. Brenner and George Leighton, *The Wind that Swept Mexico* (New York 1943); Ernest Gruening, *Mexico and its Heritage* (1928); Timothy G. Turner, *Bullets, Bottles and Gardenias* (Dallas 1935); Henry Baerlein, *Mexico: The Land of Unrest* (1914).

As might be expected, academic interest in the women of the Revolution has quickened in recent years. Ana Macías, 'Women and the Mexican Revolution, 1910–1920', *Americas* 37 (1980), pp. 53–82 is a pioneering essay, but since then the following have appeared: Ana Lau and Carmen Ramos, *Mujeres y revolución, 1900–1917* (Mexico City 1993); Elisabeth Salas, *Soldaderas in the Mexican Military: Myth and History* (Austin 1990); María Herrera-Sobek, *The Mexican Corrido: A Feminist Analysis* (Bloomington 1990). Mercenaries get a good airing in Lawrence D. Taylor, 'The Great Adventure: Mercenaries in the Mexican Revolution, 1910–1915', *Americas* 43 (1986), p. 25–45 and, especially, in the two-volume work by the same author *La gran aventura en México: El papel de los voluntarios extranjeros en los ejércitos revolucionarios mexicanos, 1910–1915* (Mexico City 1993). Some roistering adventures are recounted in the memoir literature: Edward S. O'Reilly, *Roving and Fighting: Adventures under Four Flags* (New York 1918) and Ira J. Bush, *Gringo Doctor* (Ohio 1939) are typical examples.

Machine guns are explained and analysed in John Ellis, *The Social History of the Machine Gun* (1975) and G. S. Hutchinson, *Machine Guns: Their History and Technical Employment* (1938).

MADERO AND ZAPATA

The awkward Madero interregnum is covered in all the standard books (such as Ross and Cumberland already cited), but there is additional material in Francisco R. Almada, *El presidente Madero y los problemas populares* (Chihuahua n.d.); Heliodoro Arias Olea, *Apuntes históricos de la revolución de 1910–1911* (Mexico City 1960); Marcelo Caraveo, *Crónica de la revolución (1910–1929)* (Mexico City 1992); Mario Contreras and Jesús Tamayo, *México en el siglo XX: 1900–1913* (Mexico City 1983); William W. Johnson, *Heroic Mexico: The Narrative History of a Twentieth-Century Revolution* (San Diego, 1984) and Luis Lara Pardo, *Madero: Esbozo Político* (Mexico City 1938). Among the important eyewitness accounts are those by Bell, Gruening and Strode (already cited) plus Rosa E. King, *Tempest over Mexico: A Personal Chronicle* (1936) and Rafael Aguilar, *Madero sin Máscara* (Mexico City 1911).

The conflict between Madero and Zapata was fought initially with words, later with swords. For the ideological contest see Arnaldo Cordova, *La ideologia de la revolución mexicana: formación del nuevo régimen* (Mexico City 1973) and Arturo Warman, 'The Political Project of Zapatismo', in Friedrich Katz, ed., *Riot, Rebellion and Revolution: Rural Social Conflict in Mexico* (Princeton 1988), pp. 321–38); Robert A. White, 'Mexico: The Zapata Movement in the Revolution', in Henry A. Landsberger, ed., *Latin American Peasant Movements* (Ithaca, New York 1969). The ideology of Zapatismo, by now taking clearer and clearer shape, is best studied in Chantal López and Omar Cortés, eds., *Manifiestos Emiliano Zapata* (Mexico City 1986). The same authors have edited Zapata's letters, *Cartas Emiliano Zapata* (Mexico City 1987) and his decrees, *Leyes y decretos Emiliano Zapata* (Mexico City 1987). See also Miguel León Portilla, *Los manifiestos en Nahuatl de Emiliano Zapata* (Mexico City 1978). For further insight into the ideology of Zapatismo see Robert P. Millon, *Zapata: Ideología de un campesino mexicano*. The 'black legend' of Zapata and his alleged atrocities gets its classic treatment (if that is the right phrase) in H. H. Dunn, *The Crimson Jester* (1934). See also Armando Ayala Anguiano, *Zapata y las grandes mentiras de la revolución mexicana* (Mexico City 1985) and Antonio Melgarejo, *Los crímenes del Zapatismo* (Mexico City 1979).

Madero's attempt to suppress Zapata's movement by force is dealt with in David G. La France, *The Mexican Revolution in Puebla, 1908–1913: The Maderista Movement and the Failure of Liberal Reform* (Wilmington, Delaware 1969); Arturo Langle Ramírez, *Huerta contra Zapata, una campaña desigual* (Mexico City 1981) and George J. Rausch, 'The Early Career of Victoriano Huerta', *Americas* 21 (1964), pp. 136–45. The Reyes revolt is covered in Gene Z. Hanrahan, *The Election of Madero, the rise of Emiliano Zapata and the Reyes Plot in Texas* (1978) and E. V. Niemeyer, *El general Bernardo Reyes* (Nueva Leon 1966). The Catholic opposition to Madero is highlighted in Jorge Adame Goddard, *El pensamiento político y social de los Católicos Mexicanos, 1867–1914* (Mexico City 1990); Jean Meyer, 'Le Catholicisme social au

Mexique jusqu'en 1913', *Revue Historique* 260 (1978), pp. 143–59; and Antonio Ruis Facius, *La juventud católica y la revolución mexicana, 1910–1925* (Mexico City 1963).

Felipe Ángeles, the great underrated figure of the Revolution, has begun to attract attention. See particularly Odile Guilpain Peuliard, *Felipe Ángeles y los destinos de la revolución mexicana* (Mexico City 1991); Federico Cervantes, *Felipe Ángeles en la revolución: biografía 1869–1919* (Mexico City 1964); Alberto Calzadíaz, *General Felipe Ángeles* (Mexico City 1982); Matthew Slattery, *Felipe Ángeles and the Mexican Revolution* (Ohio n.d.); Bernardino Mena Brito, *Felipe Ángeles, federal* (Mexico City 1936); Abraham Pérez López, *Diccionario biográfico hidalguense* (Mexico City 1979) and the publication by the Instituto Nacional de Estudios Históricos de la Revolución Mexicana, *Felipe Ángeles* (1985).

VILLA AND MADERO

For Villa's career in 1912 Friedrich Katz, *Pancho Villa, op. cit.* is incomparable. The same can be said for Alan Knight, *The Mexican Revolution*, 2 vols (Cambridge 1986), in respect of the Orozco rebellion, for which see especially vol. 1, pp. 289–333. Some further light is thrown by Charles H. Harris, 'The "Underside" of the Mexican Revolution: El Paso', *Americas* 39 (1982), pp. 69–83 and *The Border and the Revolution: Clandestine Activities of the Mexican Revolution, 1910–1920* (New Mexico 1988). See also Pastor Rouaix, *La revolución maderista y constitucional en Durango* (Durango 1932). Villa's private life is explained in Luz Corral, *Panco Villa en la intimidad* (Mexico City 1976). An invaluable source for Villa's time in prison is Gustavo Madero, *Epistolario* (Mexico City 1991).

The year 1912 saw Villa face to face with the monstrous Huerta. For an unconvincing attempt to rehabilitate this villain see William L. Sharman and Richard E. Greenleaf, *Victoriano Huerta: A Reappraisal* (Mexico City 1960). A diametrically opposite viewpoint appears in Nemesio García Naranjo, *Memorias* (n.d.). The most balanced view is Michael Meyer, *Huerta: A Political Portrait* (Lincoln, Nebraska 1972). See also José Fernando Rojas, *De Porfirio Díaz a Victoriano Huerta, 1910–13* (Mexico City 1913). For the concomitant rise of the military during the rise of the Huerta ascendency consult: Arturo Langle Ramírez, *El militarismo de Victoriano Huerta* (Mexico City 1976); Michael C. Meyer, 'The Militarisation of Mexico, 1913–14', *Americas* 27 (1971); Edwin Lieuwens, *Mexican Militarism: The Political Rise and Fall of the Revolutionary Army* (Albuquerque 1968); Jorge Alberto Lozoya, *El ejército mexicano, 1911–65*

(Mexico City 1970); J. Barragán Rodríguez, *Historia del ejército y la revolución constitutionalista* (Mexico City 1966).

For Madero's regime and its errors see, in addition to Ross, Cumberland, etc. previously cited: José Vasconcelos, *Breve historia de México* (Mexico City 1937); Francisco L. Urquizo, *Viva México* (Mexico City 1969); Manuel Bonilla, *El régimen maderista* (Mexico City 1962); Andrés Molina Enríquez, *La revolución agraria de México de 1910 a 1920*, 5 vols (Mexico City 1937); Adrián Aguirre Benavides, *Errores de Madero* (Mexico City 1980); Moisés González Navarro, 'El Maderismo y la revolución agraria', *Historia Mexicana* 37 (1987), pp. 5–27; David G. La France, 'Many Causes, Movements and Failures, 1910–1913: The regional nature of Maderismo', in Thomas Benjamin and Mark Wasserman, *Provinces of the Revolution: Essays on Regional Mexican History, 1910–1929* (Albuquerque 1990); Nikolai M. Lavrov, *La revolución mexicana de 1910–1917* (Mexico City 1978); Manuel González Ramírez, *Fuentes para la historia de la revolución mexicana: la caricatura política* (Mexico City 1955). Félix Díaz is another key figure in the Revolution. He is studied in Luis Liceaga, *Felix Díaz* (Mexico City 1958) and Peter V. N. Henderson, *Félix Díaz, the Porfirians and the Mexican Revolution* (Lincoln, Nebraska 1981).

The downfall of Madero is narrated in a number of eyewitness accounts, notably Bell, Gruening, Moats already cited, and in two volumes by Edith O'Shaughnessy, *A Diplomat's Wife in Mexico* (New York 1916) and *Intimate Pages of Mexican History* (New York 1920). The single most valuable printed source is Manuel Márquez Sterling, *Los últimos días del presidente Madero* (Havana 1917). For the unspeakable role played by the fanatical Henry Lane Wilson see Gene Z. Hanrahan, *The Murder of Madero and the role played by U.S. Ambassador Henry Lane Wilson* (London 1981); John P. Harrison, 'Henry Lane Wilson: el trágico de la Decena', *Historia Mexicana* 6 (1957), pp. 374–405; George J. Rausch, 'Poison-pen Diplomacy: Mexico 1913', *Americas* 24 (1968), pp. 272–80; P. A. R. Calvert, *The Mexican Revolution 1910–1914: the Diplomacy of Anglo-American Conflict* (London 1968). Lane Wilson's own self-serving account is in *Diplomatic Episodes in Mexico, Belgium and Chile* (New York 1923).

THE REVOLT AGAINST HUERTA

Among the general works focusing on the year 1913 the following are particularly valuable: Alfonso Taracena, *La verdadera revolución mexicana (1913–1914)* (Mexico City 1967); W. Dirk Raat, *Revoltosos: Mexico's*

Rebels in the United States, 1903–1923 (Texas 1981); Héctor Aguilar Camín and Lorenzo Meyer, *In the Shadow of the Mexican Revolution: Contemporary Mexican History, 1910–1989* (Austin 1993); Alfredo Breceda, *México revolucionario, 1913–1917* (Madrid 1920); J. L. Becker, *De cómo se vinó Huerta y cómo se fue: Apuntes para la historia de un régimen militar* (Mexico City 1914); Salvador R. Mercado, *Revelaciones históricas, 1913–1914* (New Mexico 1914).

Carranza is the focus of a number of studies: Douglas Richmond, *Venustiano Carranza's Nationalist Struggle, 1893–1920* (Lincoln, Nebraska 1983); Bernardino Mena Bruto, *Carranza, sus amigos y enemigos* (Mexico City 1953); Alfonso Taracena, *Venustiano Carranza* (Mexico City 1963); Jesús Castro Carranza, *Origén, destino y legado de Carranza* (Mexico City 1970); Enrique Krauze, *Venustiano Carranza, puente entre siglos* (Mexico City 1987); Francisco Urquizo, *Venustiano Carranza* (Mexico City 1976); Manuel W. González, *Con Carranza: Episodios de la revolución constitucionalista, 1913–1914* (Mexico City 1933); Luis Cabrera Blas Urrea, *La herencia de Carranza* (Mexico City 1920); Juan Gualberto Amaya, *Venustiano Carranza: caudillo constitucionalista, segunda etapa – febrero de 1913 a mayo de 1920* (Mexico City 1947). See also William Beezley, 'Governor Carranza and the Revolution in Coahuila', *Americas* 33 (1976); José Vasconcelos, *La tormenta* (Mexico City 1983); Georges Wolfskill and Douglas Richmond, eds., *Essays on the Mexican Revolution: Revisionist Views of the Leaders* (Austin 1979); Roderic A. Camp, *Mexican Political Biographies, 1884–1935* (Austin 1991); Antonio Nakayawa, *Sinaloa, el drama y sus actores* (Mexico City 1975); Alberto Morales Jiménez, *Hombres de la revolución mexicana* (Mexico City 1960); Ildefonso Villarello Vélez, *Historia de la revolución mexicana en Coahuila* (Mexico City 1970); Clodoveo Valenzuela and Chaverri Matamoros, *Sonora y Carranza* (Mexico City 1921).

Villa's *annus mirabilis* in 1913 can be followed in a number of works: the Martín Luis Guzmán *Memoirs* and O'Hea *Reminiscences* already cited; Ramón Puente, *Villa en Pie* (Mexico City 1937); Louis Stevens, *Here Comes Pancho Villa* (New York 1930); Roberto Blanco Moheno, *Pancho Villa, que es su padre* (Mexico City 1969); Haldeen Braddy, *Cock of the Walk. Qui-qui-ri-qui! The Legend of Pancho Villa* (Albuquerque 1955); Nellie Campobello, *Apuntes sobre la vida militar de Pancho Villa* (Mexico City 1940); Luis M. Gárfias, *Truth and Legend on Pancho Villa* (Mexico City 1981); Francisco de P. Ontiveros, *Toribio Ortega y la Brigada González Ortega* (El Paso 1914).

Predictably, Obregón has received a lot of attention: Linda B. Hall, *Álvaro Obregón: Power and Revolution in Mexico 1911–1920* (Texas 1981);

E. J. Dillon, *President Obregón: A World Reformer* (1922); *José Rubén Romero, Álvaro Obregón: Aspectos de su vida* (Mexico City 1976); Djed Borquez, *Obregón: Apuntes biográficos* (Mexico City 1929); Jorge Aguilar Mora, *Un día en la vida de General Obregón* (Mexico City 1982); Narciso Bassols Batalla, *El pensamiento político de Álvaro Obregón* (Mexico City 1970); David C. Bailey, 'Obregón: Mexico's Accommodating President', in Georges Wolfskill and Douglas Richmond, eds., *Essays on the Mexican Revolution: Revisionist Views of the Leaders* (Austin 1979): Mario A. Mena, *Álvaro Obregón: historia militar y política, 1912–1919* (Mexico City 1960); Juan de Dios Bojorquez, *Forjadores de la revolución mexicana* (Mexico City 1960); Ramón Puente, *La dictadura, la revolución y sus hombres* (Mexico City 1938); Charles Hall, 'The Miracle School', *HAHR* 75 (1995); Miguel Alessio Robles, *Obregón como militar* (Mexico City 1935); Enrique Krauze, *El vértigo de la victoria: Álvaro Obregón* (Mexico City 1987); Ramón Eduardo Ruíz, *The People of Sonora and Yankee Capitalists* (Tucson 1988).

VILLA AT HIS ZENITH

The O'Hea *Reminiscences* are particularly valuable here, as is John Reed's *Insurgent Mexico* (London 1969). See also Reed's articles in *The Sun*, January 1914, in *Metropolitan Magazine*, February 1914, and in *The World*, March–May 1914. On Reed's relationship with Villa see additionally Jim Tuck, *Pancho Villa and John Reed: Two Faces of Romantic Revolution* (Tucson 1984); Manuel A. Machado, *Centaur of the North: Francisco Villa, the Mexican Revolution, and Northern Mexico* (Austin 1988); James C. Wilson, ed., *John Reed for 'The Masses'* (Jefferson, North Carolina, 1987); Robert Rosenstone, *Romantic Revolutionary: A Biography of John Reed* (New York 1982); Jorge Ruffinelli, *Reed en México* (Mexico City 1983); Tamara Hovey, *John Reed: Witness to Revolution* (New York 1982). For other eyewitness accounts of Villa see Francisco Urquizo, *Recuerdo que . . .* (Mexico City 1985); Jessica Peterson and Thelma Cox Knowles, eds., *Pancho Villa: Intimate Recollections by People who Knew Him* (New York 1977); Juvenal (Enrique Pérez Rul), *¿Quién es Francisco Villa?* (Dallas 1916); Carlos Badillo Soto, *A sus órdenes mi general* (Durango 1993).

For Chihuahua under the Villista hegemony and for Villa as governor of the state one can begin with Frank Tannenbaum's classic *The Mexican Agrarian Revolution* (Washington 1930) and then proceed to the more modern scholarly studies, viz: Friedrich Katz, 'Pancho Villa as Revolutionary Governor of Chihuahua', in Georges Wolfskill and Douglas

Richmond, eds., *Essays on the Mexican Revolution: Revisionist Views of the Leaders* (Austin 1979), pp. 26–31; Friedrich Katz, *Villa: El gobernador revolucionario de Chihuahua* (Chihuahua 1984); Friedrich Katz, 'Pancho Villa's Agrarian Roots and Policies', in D. A. Brading, *Caudillo and Peasant in the Mexican Revolution* (Cambridge 1980); Friedrich Katz, 'Agrarian Changes in Northern Mexico in the Period of Villista Rule', in James W. Wilkie et al., eds., *Contemporary Mexico* (Berkeley 1976); Florence and Robert Lister, *Chihuahua: Storehouse of Storms* (Albuquerque 1966); Oscar Betanzos et al, *Historia de la cuestión agraria mexicana. Campesinos, terratenientes y revolucionarios, 1910–1920* (Mexico City 1988); Enrique González Flores, *Chihuahua de la independencia a la revolución* (Mexico City 1949); Manuel González Ramírez, *La revolución social de México*, 3 vols (Mexico City 1966); William K. Meyers, 'Pancho Villa and the Multinationals: United States Mining Interests in Villista Mexico, 1913–1915', *JLAS* 23 (1991), pp. 339–363; Gral Matías Pazuengo, *Historia de la revolución en Durango* (Cuernavaca 1915); Franciso R. Almada, *La revolución en el estado de Chihuahua*, 2 vols (Mexico City 1965); Graziella Altamirano and Guadalupe Villa, *Chihuahua: Una historia compartida, 1824–1921* (Chihuahua 1988). For the treatment of the Spanish see Josefina MacGregor, *Mexico y España del porfiriato a la revolución* (Mexico City 1992); Clara E. Lida, ed., *Tres aspectos de la presencia española en México durante el porfiriato* (Mexico City 1981).

A good study of Villa's marshals is needed. There are some pointers in the legendary ballads, as examined in Enrique Sánchez, *Corridos de Pancho Villa* (Mexico City 1952) and Antonio Avita Hernández, *Corridos de Durango* (Mexico City 1989). The idea of Villa poised between the angel of light (Felipe Ángeles) and the angel of darkness (Fierro) has been a popular one and is the theme of several studies: Enrique Krauze, *Francisco Villa: Entre el ángel y el fierro* (Mexico City 1987); Bernardino Mena Brito, *El lugarteniente gris de Pancho Villa* (Mexico City 1938); Jorge Mejía Prieto, *Las dos almas de Pancho Villa* (Mexico City 1990). The classic source for Fierro is Martín Luis Guzmán's *The Eagle and the Serpent* (New York 1965). Whether it was Fierro or Villa himself who killed Benton is discussed in Benavides, *De Francisco Madero* already cited, and Clarence C. Clendenen, *The United States and Pancho Villa: A Study in Unconventional Diplomacy* (New York 1972). See also Guzmán, *Memoirs of Pancho Villa*, op. cit., and Reed's *Insurgent Mexico*.

For Villa as movie star see Aurelio de los Reyes, *Con Villa en México: Testimonios de camarógrafos norteamericanos en la revolución* (Mexico City 1985) and for Raoul Walsh's account consult his autobiography *Each*

Man in his Time (New York 1974). For the wider cinematic ramifications of Villa see Aurelio de los Reyes, *Cine y sociedad en México* (Mexico City 1981); Margarita Orellana, *La mirada circular: el cine norteamericano de la revolución mexicana, 1911–1917* (Mexico City 1991); Clifford Irving, *Tom Mix and Pancho Villa* (New York 1982) and Deborah Mistron, 'The Role of Pancho Villa in the Mexican and American Cinema', *Studies in Latin American Popular Culture* 2 (1983), pp. 1–13.

THE END OF HUERTA

Woodrow Wilson dominates the story of Mexico in 1914. There is a huge literature both on him and the gunboat diplomacy in Vera Cruz of which the following are typical. On Wilson's policy in general: Arthur S. Link, *The Papers of Woodrow Wilson*, 69 vols (Princeton 1994), *Wilson: The New Freedom* (Princeton 1956), *Woodrow Wilson and the Progressive Era, 1910–1917* (New York 1963) and *Wilson*, 5 vols (Princeton 1965); J. M. Blum, *Woodrow Wilson and the Politics of Morality* (Boston 1956); Louis M. Teitelbaum, *Woodrow Wilson and the Mexican Revolution, 1913–1916* (New York 1967); Dirk W. Raat, *Mexico and the United States: Ambivalent Vistas* (Athens, Georgia 1992); Mark T. Guilderhus, *Pan-American Visions: Woodrow Wilson in the Western Hemisphere, 1913–1921* (Tucson 1986) and Guilderhus, *Diplomacy and Revolution: US–Mexican Relations under Wilson and Carranza* (Tucson 1977). On the intervention in Vera Cruz see Robert E. Quirk, *An Affair of Honor: Woodrow Wilson and the Occupation of Vera Cruz* (New York 1964); John S. D. Eisenhower, *Intervention! The United States and the Mexican Revolution, 1913–1917* (New York 1993); Berta Ulloa, *La revolución intervenida: relaciónes diplomáticas entre México y los Estados Unidos, 1910–1914* (Mexico City 1971); Charles C. Cumberland, 'Huerta y Carranza ante la ocupación de Veracruz', *Historia Mexicana* 6 (1957), pp. 534–47; Berta Ulloa, 'Carranza y el armamiento norteamericano', *Historia Mexicana* 17 (1967), pp. 253–61; Leonardo Pasquel, *La revolución en el estado de Vera Cruz*, 2 vols (Mexico City 1972).

Works on US agents of various stripe who had contacts with Villa include: Hugh L. Scott, *Some Memories of a Soldier* (New York 1928); Joseph P. Tumulty, *Woodrow Wilson As I Knew Him* (New York 1921); Will B. Davis, *Experiences and Observations of an American Consular Official During the Recent Mexican Revolution* (Chula Vista 1920); Larry D. Hill, *Emissaries to a Revolution: Woodrow Wilson's Executive Agents in Mexico* (Baton Rouge 1973); George M. Stephenson, *John Lind of Minnesota* (Minnesota 1935); Dorothy Pierson Kerig, *Luther T. Ellsworth,*

US Consul on the Border During the Mexican Revolution (El Paso 1975); Gene Z. Hanrahan, *Blood Below the Border. American Eyewitness Accounts of the Mexican Revolution* (1983); see also Hanrahan, *Abajo el gringo . . . Anti-American Sentiment During the Mexican Revolution* (1982).

The disappearing Ambrose Bierce has generated his own industry. Representative titles include: Paul Fatout, *Ambrose Bierce: The Devil's Lexicographer* (Norman, Oklahoma 1951); Carey McWilliams, *The Mysteries of Ambrose Bierce* (New York 1931); Roy Morris, *Ambrose Bierce: Alone in Bad Company* (New York 1995); Richard O'Connor, *Ambrose Bierce: A Biography* (Boston 1967) and, of course, the fictional treatment by Carlos Fuentes, *The Old Gringo* (New York 1985). Other American writers who made significant trips south of the border include Lincoln Steffens, for whom see *The Autobiography of Lincoln Steffens*, 2 vols (New York 1931) and Justin Kaplan, *Lincoln Steffens: A Biography* (New York 1974). Jack London's animadversions can be followed in Philip S. Foner, ed., *The Social Writings of Jack London* (New York 1964); Andrew Sinclair, *Jack* (1978); Robert Barltrop, *Jack London: The Man, the Writer, the Rebel* (1976) and Alex Kershaw, *Jack London: A Life* (1997). On Mother Jones see Philip S. Foner, *Mother Jones Speaks: Collected Writings and Speeches* (New York 1983).

1914 was also the year when the Great Powers became sucked into the Mexican conflict. Of the many volumes devoted to this issue the following are noteworthy: Isidro Fabela, *Historia diplomática de la revolución mexicana*, 2 vols (Mexico City 1985); Carlos Iliades, *México y España durante la revolución mexicana* (Mexico City 1985); Lorenzo Meyer, *Su Majestad Britanica contra la revolución mexicana, 1900–1950: El fin de un imperio informal* (Mexico City 1991); Pierre Py, *Francia y la revolución mexicana, 1910–1920: la desaparición de una potencia mediana* (Mexico City 1991); Esperanza Durán, *Guerra y revolución: las grandes potencias y México, 1914–1918* (Mexico City 1985); William S. Coker, 'Mediación Británica en el conflicto Wilson–Huerta', *Historia Mexicana* 18 (1968), pp. 224–57; Thomas Baecker, *Die Deutsche Mexikopolitik 1913–14* (Berlin 1971).

The shadowy German policy towards Huerta is traced in Michael C. Meyer, 'The Arms of Ypiranga', *HAHR* 50 (1970), pp. 453–56; Thomas Baecker, 'The Arms of the Ypiranga: The German Side', *Americas* 30 (1973), pp. 1–17; Thomas Baecker, 'Los intereses militares del imperio Alemán en México, 1913–14', *Historia Mexicana* 29 (1972); and above all in Friedrich Katz's *The Secret War in Mexico* (Chicago 1981). The increasingly important issue of oil is dealt with in Jonathan C. Brown, *Oil and Revolution in Mexico* (Berkeley 1993); Kenneth J. Grieb, 'Standard

Oil and the Financing of the Mexican Revolution', *California Historical Society Quarterly* 50 (1971), pp. 59–71; Lorenzo Meyer and Isidro Morales, *Petróleo y nación (1900–1987)* (Mexico City 1990); H. Knowlton, *History of Standard Oil Company (New Jersey): The Resurgent Years 1911–27* (New York 1956); Charles W. Hamilton, *Early Oil Tales of Mexico* (Houston 1966).

For Villa's triumphant campaign in 1914 an excellent and often overlooked study is Federico Cervantes, *Francisco Villa y la revolución* (Mexico City 1960). For this campaign see also Sergio Candelas Villalba, *La batalla de Zacatecas* (Zacatecas 1989); Aldo Caserini, *Le battaglie di Pancho Villa: L'eopoea della rivoluzione messicana* (Azzate, Italy 1972) and the publication by Instituto Nacional de Estudios Históricos de la Revolución Mexicana entitled *Toma de Torreón*. Villa's army is examined in Arturo Langle Ramírez, *El ejército villista* (Mexico City 1961); E. Brondo Whitt, *La división del Norte (1914) por un testigo presencial* (Mexico City 1940); Guadalupe Gracia García, *El servicio médico durante la revolución mexicana* and Luis Aguirre Benavides and Afrian Aguirre Benavides, *Las grandes batallas de la División del Norte* (Mexico City 1979).

The last days of Huerta are covered in Berta Ulloa, *La revolución escindida* (Mexico City 1979); Kenneth J. Grieb, *The United States and Huerta* (Lincoln, Nebraska 1969); Paul V. Henderson, 'Woodrow Wilson, Victoriano Huerta, and the Recognition Issue in Mexico', *Americas* 41 (1984), pp. 151–76; Alfonso Taracena, *La verdadera revolución mexicana (1913–1914)* (Mexico City 1967); George Rauch, 'The Exile and Death of Victoriano Huerta,' *HAHR* 42 (1962), pp. 133–51; and in a plethora of eyewitness accounts, especially the already cited Edith O'Shaughnessy, *A Diplomat's Wife in Mexico* and Mrs Alec Tweedie's *Mexico from Díaz to the Kaiser*.

THE CONVENTION OF AGUASCALIENTES

For Carranza's crucial role in the six months after Huerta's overthrow see John Mason Hart, *Revolutionary Mexico: The Coming and Process of the Mexican Revolution* (Berkeley 1987); Adolfo Gilly, *La revolución interrumpida* (Mexico City 1994); Charles C. Cumberland, *Mexican Revolution: The Constitutionalist Years* (Austin 1972); Alfonso Junco, *Carranza y los orígenes de su rebelión* (Mexico City 1955); Ignacio Suárez, *Carranza forjador del México actual* (Mexico City 1965). For Zapata continue with the works by Womack and Brunk and see, additionally, José T. Meléndez, *Historia de la revolución mexicana* (Mexico City 1936);

Armando de María y Campos, *La vida del general Lucio Blanco* (Mexico City 1963); T. V. Buttrey and Adon Gordus, 'The Silver Coinage of Zapata, 1914–1915', *HAHR* 52 (1972), pp. 456–62. H. H. Dunn, *The Crimson Jester: Zapata of Mexico* (New York 1934) is remarkable only because it gives credence to the absurd stories about Zapata's alleged atrocities.

Conditions in Mexico City at this time are the subject of Francisco Ramírez Plancarte, *La ciudad de México durante la revolución constituciona-lista* (Mexico City 1941). The urban proletariat of Mexico City and elsewhere has attracted a lot of attention: Alan Knight, 'The Working Class and the Mexican Revolution, *c.*1900–1920', *JLAS* 16 (1984); Rodney Anderson, *Outcasts in Their Own Land: Mexican Industrial Workers, 1906–1911* (De Kalb, Illinois 1976); Barry Carr, *El Movimiento Obrero y la Política en México, 1910–1929*, 2 vols (Mexico City 1976); Rosendo Salazar, *La casa del obrero mundial* (Mexico City 1962); Ciro F. S. Cardoso et al., *La clase obrera en la historia de México, de la dictadura porfirista a los tiempos libertarios* (Mexico City 1980); John M. Hart, *Anarchism and the Mexican Working Class, 1860–1931* (Austin 1978); Jean Meyer, 'Los batallones rojos de la revolución mexicana', *Historia Mexicana* 21 (1971), pp. 1–37; Jean Meyer, 'Les Ouvriers dans la Révolution Mexicaine: Les Bataillons Rouges', *Annales ESC* 25 (1970), pp. 30–35.

The amazing adventures of Obregón while Villa's 'guest' can be followed in a number of (often contradictory) sources. There is Obregón's own account in the boastful *Ocho mil kilómetros en campaña* (Mexico City 1970) which can be supplemented by Francis C. Kelley, *Blood Drenched Altars* (Milwaukee 1935). Then there are the Villista accounts: by Silvestre Terrazas, *El verdadero Pancho Villa*, op. cit.; by Luz Corral, *Pancho Villa en la intimidad*, op. cit.; by other Villistas, as in Juvenal, *¿Quién es Francisco Villa?*, op. cit.; and Federico Cervantes, *Francisco Villa y la revolución*, op. cit. See also Luis Aguirre Benavides, *De Francisco Madero*, op. cit.; Enrique Krauze, *Plutarco E. Calles: Reformar desde el origen* (Mexico City 1987) and Rubén Osorio Zuñiga, *Pancho Villa, ese desconocido* (Chihuahua 1991). The conflicts between Obregón, Hill and Maytorena are delineated in Héctor Aguilar Camín, *La frontera nómada: Sonora y la revolución mexicana* (Mexico City 1977).

The convention at Aguascalientes has generated a sizeable literature: Robert E. Quirk, *The Mexican Revolution, 1914–1915: The Convention of Aguascalientes* (Bloomington, Indiana 1960); Luis Fernando Amaya, *La soberana convención revolucionaria, 1914–1916* (Mexico City 1966); Vito Alessio Robles, *La convención en Aguascalientes* (Mexico City 1979);

Florencio Barrera Fuentes, *Crónicas y debates de las sesiones de la soberana convención revolucionaria*, 3 vols (Mexico City 1965); José de Jesús Medillin, *Las ideas agrarias en la convención de Aguascalientes* (Mexico City 1986); Richard Roman, *Ideología y clase en la revolución mexicana: La convención y el congreso constituyente* (Mexico City 1976). The great set-piece description of Soto y Gama at Aguascalientes is in Martín Luis Guzmán's *The Eagle and the Serpent* already cited.

THE CONVERGENCE OF THE TWAIN

The entry of the *zapatistas* into Mexico City and subsequent events are described in a number of accounts: Hudson Strode, *Timeless Mexico* (New York 1944); Randolph Welford Smith, *Benighted Mexico* (New York 1916) and Leone B. Moates, *Thunder in their Veins*, op. cit. Surprisingly, neither Womack, *Zapata* nor Katz, *Villa* treat of the Villa-Zapata meeting in any detail, but there is a protracted look, drawing copiously on the reports to the US State Department by American envoy León Cánova, in Enrique Krauze, *Siglo de Caudillos: Biografía política de México 1810–1910* (Mexico City 1994). See also Herlinda Barrientos et al., *Con Zapata y Villa; tres relatos testimoniales* (Mexico City 1991). The pact of Xochimilco is laid out in Manuel González Ramírez, *Fuentes para la historia de la revolución: Planes políticos y otros documentos*, vol I (Mexico City 1974). For Lucio Blanco as the possible bridge between the two see Jorge Aguilar Mora, *Una Muerte sencilla, justa y eterna: Cultura y guerra durante la revolución mexicana* (Mexico City 1990) and José C. Valadés, *Rafael Buelna: Las caballerías de la revolución* (Mexico City 1984). On the lost opportunity of December 1914 see Octavio Paz, *Postdata* (Mexico City 1970).

For the ideology of Zapatismo and its contrasts with Villismo see Knight, *Mexican Revolution*, op. cit. *passim*. Other important studies are Arturo Warman, 'The Political Project of Zapatismo', in Friedrich Katz, ed., *Riot, Rebellion and Revolution: Rural Social Conflict in Mexico* (Princeton 1988); Warman, *Y Venimos a Contradecir*, op. cit.; Robert A. White, 'Mexico: The Zapata Movement and the Revolution', in Henry A. Landsberger, ed., *Latin American Peasant Movements* (Cornell 1969); Robert P. Millon, *Zapata: The Ideology of a Peasant Revolutionary*, op. cit.; Friedrich Katz, 'Peasants in the Mexican Revolution of 1910', in Joseph Spielberg and Scott Whiteford, eds., *Forging Nations: A Comparative View of Rural Ferment and Revolt* (Michigan 1976); Franz J. Schryer, *The Rancheros of Pisaflores: The History of a Peasant Bourgeoisie in Twentieth-Century Mexico* (Toronto 1980); Dudley Ankerson, *Agrarian*

Warlord: Saturnino Cedillo and the Mexican Revolution in San Luis Potosí (De Kalb, Illinois 1984); Jane Dale-Lloyd, 'Rancheros and Rebellion', in Daniel Nugent, ed., *Rural Revolt in Mexico and US Intervention* (San Diego 1988); Laura López de Lara, ed., *El agrarismo en Villa* (Mexico City 1982). The question of 'social banditry' is a huge, complex and much-discussed issue. In a Mexican context one can do no more than scratch the surface. See Eric Hobsbawm, *Primitive Rebels* (1965) and *Bandits* (1969); Richard W. Slatta, ed, *Bandidos: The Variety of Latin American Banditry* (New York 1987) and Eric Wolf, *Peasant Wars of the Twentieth Century* (1973); see also Anton Blok, 'The Peasant and the Brigand: Social Banditry Reconsidered', *Comparative Studies in Society and History* 14 (1972), pp. 494–503.

For events in the south-east and the inroads made by Carranza's proconsuls there see Allan Wells, *Yucatán's Guilded Age: Haciendas, Henequen and International Harvester, 1860–1915* (Albuquerque 1985); Gilbert M. Joseph, *Revolution from Without: Yucatán, Mexico and the United States, 1880–1924* (Durham, North Carolina 1980); Jorge Glores, 'La vida rural en Yucatán en 1914', *Historia Mexicana* 10 (1961); Luz Elena Arroyo Irigoyen and María del Carmen Barreneche, *El cambio social en sureste de México: Dos estudios* (Mexico City 1985); Alicia Hernández Chávez, 'La defensa de los finqueros en Chiapas, 1914–1920', *Historia Mexicana* 28 (1979), pp. 335–69; Gilbert M. Joseph and A. Wells, 'Seasons of Upheaval: The Crisis of Oligarchical Rule in Yucatán, 1901–1915', in Jaime E. Rodríguez, ed., *The Revolutionary Process in Mexico: Essays on Political and Social Change* (Los Angeles 1990), pp. 161–85. A useful contrast can be drawn between the south-east and the other areas of rural Mexico at the time, as described in Raymond Buve, *El movimiento revolucionario de Tlaxcala* (Tlaxcala 1994) and David G. La France, *The Mexican Revolution in Puebla*, op. cit.

The role of Vasconcelos and other intellectuals is described in Roderic A. Camp, et al., *Los intelectuales y el poder en México* (Mexico City 1991). See also Joaquín Cárdenas Noriega, *José Vasconcelos, 1882–1982: Educador, Político y Profeta* (Mexico City 1982) and Vasconcelos's own account in *Memorias: Ulises Criollo La Tormenta* (Mexico City 1983). Villa's womanising is described in a number of accounts, including those by Silvestre Terrazas and Luz Corral already cited, and in Peterson and Knowles, *Pancho Villa: Intimate Reflections*, op. cit. The best source for Zapata's private life in Mario Gill, *Episodios mexicanos: México en la hoguera* (Mexico City 1960).

SOURCES

CIVIL WAR

The civil war of 1915 is covered in a number of detailed volumes: Alfonso Taracena, *La verdadera revolución mexicana 1915–1917* (Mexico City 1992); Miguel A. Sánchez Lamego, *Historia militar de la revolución en la época de la convención* (Mexico City 1983); Berta Ulloa, *La encrucijada de 1915* (Mexico City 1979) and *Veracruz: capital de la nación (1914–1915)* (Mexico City 1986); John W. F. Dulles, *Yesterday in Mexico* (Austin 1961). The battles of Celaya and León-Trinidad are covered in detail in the *villista* literature, e.g., Guzmán, *Memoirs*; Silvestre Terrazas, *El verdadero Pancho Villa* op. cit.; Federico Cervantes, *Francisco Villa*, op. cit.; and in representative books such as Edgcumb Pinchon, *Viva Villa! A Recovery of the Real Pancho Villa* (1933). Obregón's side of things is in his *Ocho mil kilómetros*, op. cit. Another valuable memoir for the battles is Gabriel Gavira, *General de Brigada Gabriel Gavira. Su actuación político-militar revolucionaria* (Mexico City 1933). Carranza's 'take' is in Manuel W. González, *Contra Villa: Relato de la campaña, 1914–1915* (Mexico City 1935). There is a very valuable guide to the campaign in the lengthy introduction to the 1966 edition of Obregón's *Ocho mil* by Francisco J. Grajales. Additionally there is a monograph published by the Instituto Nacional de Estudios Históricos de la Revolución Mexicana entitled *Batalla de Celaya* (Mexico City 1985). For the greater importance of Trinidad than Celaya see Juan Barragán Rodríguez, *Historia del ejército*, 2 vols, op. cit.

For a thorough analysis of the social composition of the armies, a who-fought-who examination, and the fascinating counterfactual of a Villa presidency see Alan Knight, *Mexican Revolution*, op. cit, vol 2. The role of Peláez is set out in Jonathan Brown, *Oil and Revolution in Mexico*, op. cit., and Friedrich Katz, *Secret War*, op. cit. The reasons that led men to side with Carranza and the Constitutionalists rather than Villa (and even the reasons for desertions by *villistas*) are explained in Federico González Garza, *La revolución mexicana* (Mexico City 1982); Beatriz Rojas, *La pequeña guerra: Los Carrera Torres y los Cedillo* (Michoacán 1983); Alberto J. Pani, *Apuntes autobiográficos* (Mexico City 1951); Armando de María y Campos, *Mugica: Crónica biográfica aportación a la historia de la revolución mexicana* (Mexico City 1939) and José Santos Chocana, *Obras completas* (Mexico City 1954).

For Villa immediately after Trinidad see Jorge Aguilar Mora, *Una muerte sencilla, justa y eterna*, op. cit.; Gilberto Álvarez Salinas, *Pancho Villa en Monterrey* (Monterrey 1969); Begoña Hernández y Lazo, *Las batallas de la Plaza de Chihuahua, 1915–1916* (Mexico City 1984). For Villa's tangled relationship with the USA and its souring there are pointers in Juan Ignacio Barragán and Mario Cerutti, *Juan F. Brittingham y la industria en México, 1859–1940 (Monterrey 1993)* and Alden Buell Case, *Thirty Years with the Mexicans: In Peace and Revolution* (New York 1917). Eyewitness accounts are especially valuable for this period and into Carranza's hegemony. Noteworthy are M. Cuzin, *Journal d'un Français au Mexique, Guadalajara: 16 Novembre–6 Juillet 1915* (Paris 1983) and Daisy Cadden Pettus, ed., *The Rosalie Evans Letters from Mexico* (Indianapolis 1926). The almost simultaneous deaths of four of the great villains of the Revolution, Urbina, Fierro, Orozco and Huerta, are dealt with in Juvenal, *¿Quién es Francisco Villa?* op. cit.; Louis Stevens, *Here Comes Pancho Villa*, op. cit.; Ira Jefferson Bush, *Gringo Doctor*, op. cit.; Ernest Otto Schuster, *Pancho Villa's Shadow* (New York 1947); Edith O'Shaughnessy, *Intimate Pages*, op. cit.; and Barbara Tuchman, *The Zimmermann Telegram* (New York 1966).

THE PUNITIVE EXPEDITION

By early 1915 all Zapata's best achievements were behind him, see Edgcumb Pinchon, *Zapata the Unconquerable* (New York 1941). See also Carlos Reyes Avilés, *Cartones Zapatistas* (Mexico City 1928); H. Alonso Reyes, *Emiliano Zapata: Su vida y su Obra* (Mexico City 1963). For the agricultural commissions see Marte R. Gómez, *Las comisiones agrarias del sur* (Mexico City 1961); Antonio Díaz Soto y Gama, *La revolución agraria del Sur y Emiliano Zapata, su caudillo* (Mexico City 1960); Eyler N. Simpson, *The Ejido: Mexico's Way Out* (Chapel Hill, North Carolina 1937). The military operations are covered in Federico Cervantes, *Felipe Ángeles en la Revolución: Biografía (1869–1919)* (Mexico City 1964); José Morales Hesse, *El General Pablo González: Datos para la historia, 1910–1916* (Mexico City 1916); Oscar Lewis, *Pedro Martínez: A Mexican Peasant and his Family* (New York 1964); Estado Mayor del Vicente Segura, *Historia de la Brigada Mixta 'Hidalgo', 1915–1916* (Mexico City 1917) and Rosa King, *Tempest over Mexico*, op. cit.

The growing tensions between Mexico and the United States are examined in: Isidro Fabela, *La política interior y exterior de Carranza* (Mexico City 1979); Charles H. Harris, 'The Plan of San Diego and the Mexican–United States War Crisis of 1916: A Reexamination', *HAHR* 58 (1978), pp. 381–408; Emily S. Rosenberg, *World War One and the Growth of United States Predominance in Latin America* (New York 1987); Robert Freeman Smith, *The United States and Revolutionary Nationalism in Mexico, 1916–1932* (Chicago 1972); David F. Houston, *Eight Years with Wilson's Cabinet, 1913–1920* (New York 1926) Louis G. Kahle, 'Robert Lansing and the recognition of Venustiano Carranza', *HAHR* 38 (1958), pp. 353–72. German intrigues are the subject of Reinhard R. Doerries, *Imperial Challenge: Ambassador Count Bernstorff and German–American Relations, 1908–1917* (Chapel Hill, North Carolina 1918); James A. Sandos, 'German Involvement in Northern Mexico, 1915–1916: A New Look at the Columbus Raid', *HAHR* 50 (1970), pp. 70–89; Holst von der Goltz, *My Adventures as a German Secret Agent* (New York 1917) and Barbara Tuchman, *The Zimmermann Telegram*, op. cit.

Villa's sensational attack on Columbus has predictably prompted a plethora of studies. See Friedrich Katz, *Pancho Villa y el ataque a Columbus, Nuevo México* (Chihuahua 1979); Friedrich Katz, 'Pancho Villa and the Attack on Columbus, New Mexico', *American Historical Review* 83 (1978), pp. 101–30; Larry A. Harris, *Pancho Villa and the Columbus Raid* (El Paso 1949); Charles H. Harris and Louis R. Sadler, 'Pancho Villa and the Columbus Raid: The Missing Documents', *New Mexico Historical Review* 50 (1975), pp. 335–46; Haldeen Braddy, *Pancho Villa at Columbus: The Raid of 1916* (El Paso 1965); Víctor Ceja Reyes, *Yo, Francisco Villa y Columbus* (Chihuahua 1987); Clarence C. Clenenden, *The United States and Pancho Villa*, op. cit.; Tom Hahoney, 'The Columbus Raid', *South-West Review* 17 (1932), pp. 161–71; Francis J. Munch, 'Villa's Columbus Raid: Practical Politics or German Design?', *New Mexico Historical Review* 44 (1969), pp. 189–214; Bill Rakoczy, *Villa Raids Columbus NM* (El Paso 1981); Rafael Trujillo Herrera, *Cuando Villa entró en Columbus* (Mexico City 1973); E. Bruce White, 'The Muddied Waters of Columbus, New Mexico', *Americas* 32 (1975), pp. 72–98; Alberto Calzadíaz Barrera, *Porqué Villa atacó Columbus: Intriga internacional* (Mexico City 1972).

The Punitive Expedition, involving Mexico in a three-way conflict, can be approached from three perspectives. First, the American: Frank Tompkins, *Chasing Villa* (Pennsylvania 1939); Herbert Molloy Mason, *The Great Pursuit: General John J. Pershing's Punitive Expedition Across the Rio Grande to Destroy the Mexican Bandit Pancho Villa* (New York 1970); Michael L. Tate, 'Pershing's Punitive Expedition: Pursuer of Bandits or Presidential Panacea?', *Americas* 32 (1975), pp. 46–72; Haldeen Braddy, *Pershing's Mission in Mexico* (El Paso 1966). Secondly, the Carrancista: Alberto Salinas Carranza, *La expedición punitiva* (Mexico City 1936); Isidro Fabela and J. E. Fabela, *Documentos históricos de la revolución mexicana*, vol. 4 (1968). Finally, the *villista*: Nellie Campobello, *Apuntes sobre la vida militar de Francisco Villa* (Mexico City 1940) and Federico Cervantes, *Francisco Villa y la revolución*, op. cit.

Biography (and autobiography) proves its worth to the historian here. On Pershing there is Richard O'Connor, *Black Jack Pershing* (New York

1961); Donald Smythe, *Guerrilla Warrior: The Early Life of John J. Pershing* (New York 1973) and H. A. Toulmin, *With Pershing in Mexico* (Pennsylvania 1935). Patton yields an even richer seam: Ladislas Farago, *Patton* (1964); I. V. Hogg, *Patton: The Biography of General George S. Patton* (1982); Martin Blumenson, *Patton* (1985); Blumenson, ed., *The Patton Papers*, 2 vols (Boston 1974) and, above all, the outstanding biography by Carlo d'Este, *A Genius for War: A Life of General George S. Patton* (1995).

THE TWILIGHT OF ZAPATISMO

For the increasing chaos in Mexico from the end of 1916 onwards see (for the diseases) Alberto Pani, *La higiene en México* (Mexico 1916); Moises González Navarro, *Población y sociedad en México (1900–1970)*, 2 vols (Mexico City 1974); William H. McNeil, *Plagues and People*; J. C. Cloudesley-Thompson, *Insects: A History* (1976); (for the destruction on the railways) Alberto Pani, *Apuntes autobiográficos* (Mexico City 1951); Fernando González Roa, *El problema ferrocarrilero* (Mexico City 1919); (for the economy) James W. Wilkie, *The Mexican Revolution: Federal Expenditure and Social Change since 1910* (Berkeley 1967); E. J. Kemmerer, *Inflation and Revolution: Mexico's Experience of 1912–17* (Princeton 1940); John Womack, 'The Mexican Economy during the Revolution, 1910–1920: Historiography and Analysis', *Marxist Perspectives* 1 (1978). For the great 'flu pandemic of 1918 see Fred R. van Hartesveldt, *The 1918–1919 Pandemic of Influenza: the Urban Impact in the Western World* (1992) and Richard Collier, *The Plague of the Spanish Lady: The Influenza Pandemic of 1918–19* (1974).

Political events can be followed in Alfonso Taracena, *La verdadera revolución mexicana. Sexta etapa (1918 a 1921)* (Mexico City 1992); Álvaro Matute, *Historia de la revolución mexicana, período 1917–24: La carrera del caudillo* (Mexico City 1980); Jorge Flores Vizcarra and Otto Granados Roldán, *Salvador Alvarado y la revolución mexicana* (Sinaloa 1980); Miguel Alessio Robles, *Historia política de la revolución* (Mexico City 1985); Félix Palavicini, *Mi vida revolucionaria* (Mexico City 1937). Carranza's anti-catholicism and its long-term consequences can be followed in Robert E. Quirk, *The Mexican Revolution and the Catholic Church*, op. cit.; Jean Meyer, *The Cristero Rebellion: The Mexican People between Church and State, 1926–29* (Cambridge 1976); Eduardo J. Correa, *El Partido Católico Nacional y sus directores* (Mexico City 1991). The constitutional conference at Querétaro and the 1917 constitution have spawned many books and monographs, viz: Eberhardt Victor Niemeyer,

Revolution at Querétaro: The Mexican Constitution Convention of 1916–1917 (Austin 1974); Berta Ulloa, *La constitución de 1917* (Mexico City 1983); Pastor Rouaix, *Génesis de los artículos 27 y 123 de la constitución política de 1917* (Mexico City 1959); Félix Palavicini, *Historia de la constitución de 1917*, 2 vols (Mexico City 1980) and Palavicini, *Los diputados* (Mexico City 1976). See also Salvador Cruz, *Vida y obra de Pastor Rouaix* (Mexico City 1980); Manuel Robles Linares, *Pastor Rouaix: Su vida y su obra* (Mexico City 1976).

The revolt of Félix Díaz can be followed in the Díaz biographies already cited, especially Luís Liceaga, *Félix Díaz*, op. cit., and Gene Z. Hanrahan, *The Rebellion of Félix Díaz* (1983). The *felicista* revolt was in many ways *the* classical externally motivated rebellion, and the prize was oil. See Emily S. Rosenberg, *Spreading the American Dream: American Economic and Cultural Expansion, 1895–1945* (New York 1982) and Rosenberg, 'Economic Pressures in Anglo-American Diplomacy in Mexico, 1917–1918', *Journal of Interamerican Studies and World Affairs* 17 (1975), pp. 123–52; Lorenzo Meyer, *México y Estados Unidos en el conflicto petrolero (1917–42)* (Mexico City 1991) and Meyer, 'La revolución mexicana y las potencias anglosajones', *Historia Mexicana* 34 (1984), pp. 300–352; Dennis J. O'Brien, 'Petróleo e intervención: Relaciones entre Estados Unidos y Mexico, 1917–1918', *Journal of Interamerican Studies and World Affairs* 17 (1977), pp. 123–52; Alfred Vagts, *Mexico, Europa und Amerika unter besonderer Berücksichtigung der Petroleumpolitik* (Berlin 1928).

The late period of Zapatismo, its decline in Morelos but spreading influence elsewhere is best followed in Gildardo Magaña, *Emiliano Zapata y el agrarismo en México*, 5 vols (Mexico City 1985). See also Magaña and Carlos Pérez Guerrero, *Zapata y el agrarismo*, 5 vols (Mexico City 1952); Alfredo Breceda, *México revolucionario, 1913–1917*, 2 vols (Madrid 1941); Arturo Warman, *We Come to Object*, op. cit.; Laura Espel, ed., *Emiliano Zapata: Antología* (Mexico City 1988) and Gabriel García Cantu, *Utopias Mexicanas* (Mexico City 1963). For events in neighouring provinces see Thomas Benjamin, *A Rich Land, a Poor People: Politics and Society in Modern Chiapas* (Albuquerque 1989); Thomas Benjamin and William McNellie, eds., *Other Mexicos: Essays on Regional Mexican History, 1910–1929* (Albuquerque 1990); Manuel González Calzada, *Historia de la revolución mexicana en Tabasco* (Mexico City 1972); Raymond Buve, 'Neither Carranza nor Zapata! The Rise and Fall of the Peasant Movement that Tried to Challenge Both, Tlaxcala, 1910–1919', in Friedrich Katz, ed., *Riot, Rebellion and Revolution*, op. cit.; Francisco José Ruíz Cervantes, *La revolución en Oaxaca: El movimiento de la soberanía, 1915–1920* (Mexico City 1986); Luis Espinosa, *Defección del General José Isabel Robles en la Sierra de Ixtlán, Oaxaca* (Mexico City n.d.).

For the loss of Michoacán to Chávez García and others see Verónica Oikion Solano, *El constitucionalismo en Michoacán: El período de los gobiernos militares (1914–1917)* (Mexico City 1992); Fernando Bernitez, *Lázaro Cárdenas y la revolución mexicana* (Mexico City 1977); Jesús Romero Flores, *Historia de la revolución en Michoacán* (Mexico City 1964); José Bravo Ugarte, *Historia sucinta de Michoacán*, 3 vols (Mexico City 1964); Luis González y González, *Pueblo en vilo. Microhistoria de San José de Gracia* (Mexico City 1972); Enrique Krauze, *Caudillos culturales en la revolución mexicana* (Mexico City 1976); C. Bernaldo de Quiros, *El bandolerismo en España y México* (Mexico City 1959). For Zapata's murder see Ettore Pierri, *Vida, pasión y muerte de Emiliano Zapata* (Mexico City 1979); Octavio Paz, *The Labyrinth of Solitude* (New York 1985); Roger Parkinson, *Zapata: A Biography* (1975); Frank Tannenbaum, *Peace by Revolution*, op. cit.; Ernest Gruening, *Mexico and its Heritage* (1928).

THE DECLINE OF VILLISMO

Friedrich Katz, *Pancho Villa* really comes into its own with Villa's later life, presenting a masterly survey of the last eight years. For the late period when Villa was once more a guerrilla, certain primary sources are fundamental: José María Jaurietta, *Seis años con el General Francisco Villa*, 2 vols (Mexico City 1935); Víctor Ceja Reyes, *Cabalgando con Villa* (Chihuahua 1987); A. Pérez Mantecón, *Recuerdos de un villista: mi campaña en la revolución* (Mexico City 1967); Ernest Otto Schuster, *Pancho Villa's Shadow: The True Story of Mexico's Robin Hood as Told by His Interpreter* (Mexico City 1947).

There is also a lot of useful secondary literature devoted wholly or partly to this period: Federico Cervantes, *Francisco Villa y la revolución*, op. cit.; Francisco R. Almada, *La revolución en el estado de Chihuahua*, op. cit.; Alberto Calzadíaz Barrera, *Villa contra todo y contra todos*, 2 vols (Mexico City 1965); and *El general Martín López* (Mexico City 1975); Lucio Quintero Corral, *Pancho Villa derrotado en Tepehuanes, Durango al intentar tomar la ciudad de Durango* (Ciudad Juarez 1990); Carlos H. Canto y Canto, *Los halcones dorados de Villa* (Mexico City 1969); Arturo Langle Ramírcz, *Crónica de la cobija de Pancho Villa* (Mexico City 1973); Oscar W. Ching Veda, *La última cabalgata de Pancho Villa* (Chihuahua 1977); I. Lavretski and Adolfo Gilly, *Pancho Villa: Dos ensayos* (Mexico

City 1978); Manuel Lozoya Cigarroa, *Francisco Villa, el grande* (Durango 1988); Rafael F. Muñoz, *Relatos de la revolución* (Mexico City 1985); Hernán Robleto, *La mascota de Pancho Villa: Episodios de la revolución mexicana* (Mexico City 1960); Elías L. Torres, *20 vibrantes episodios de la vida de Villa* (Mexico City 1934); Torres, *Vida y Hazañas de Francisco Villa* (Mexico City 1975); Juan Bautista Vargas Arreola, *A sangre y fuego con Pancho Villa* (Mexico City 1988).

Since Villa was a constant thorn in the side of the United States in the years 1916–20, not surprisingly many relevant studies involve the American factor. See Martín Luis Guzmán, *The Border and the Revolution* (New Mexico 1990); Charles H. Harris and Louis R. Sadler, *The Border and the Revolution: Clandestine Activities of the Mexican Revolution, 1910–1920* (New Mexico 1988); Gene Z. Hanrahan, *Counter Revolution along the Border* (1983); Thomas H. Naylor, 'Massacre at San Pedro de Cueva: The Significance of Pancho Villa's Disastrous Sonora Campaign', *Western Historical Quarterly* 8 (1977); Daniel Nugent, ed., *Rural Revolt in Mexico and US Intervention* (San Diego 1988); Américo Paredes, *A Texas–Mexican Cancionero: Folksongs of the Lower Border* (Urbana, Illinois 1976); James A. Sandoz, 'Northern Separatism during the Mexican Revolution: An Inquiry into the Role of Drug Trafficking, 1919–1920', *Americas* 41 (1984), pp. 119–214; Noé Palomares, *Propietarios norteamericanos y reforma agraria en Chihuahua, 1917–1942* (Ciudad Juárez 1992); Óscar J. Martínez, *Fragments of the Mexican Revolution: Personal Accounts from the Border* (Albuquerque 1983).

With the death of Felipe Ángeles and Carranza, two more of the giants of the Mexican Revolution had perished while Villa still survived. For Ángeles's end see Adolfo Gilly, 'Felipe Ángeles camina hacia la muerte', in Odile Guilpain, *Felipe Ángeles y los destinos de la revolución mexicana* (Mexico City 1991); Ignacio Solares, *La noche de Ángeles* (Mexico City 1991); Alvaro Matute, ed., *Documentos relativos al general Felipe Ángeles*, op. cit.; Federico Cervantes, *Felipe Ángeles en la revolución*, op. cit.; Matthew Slattery, *Felipe Ángeles and the Mexican Revolution*, op. cit. For the last days of the Carranza's regime and Carranza's assassination see Armando de Maria y Campos, *Mugica: Crónica biografica aportación an la historia de la revolución mexicana*, op. cit.; Luis Prieto Reyes et al., *VII jornadas de historia occidente: Francisco J. Mugica* (Michoacán 1993); Martín Luis Guzmán, *Muertes históricas* (Mexico City 1990); Francisco Serralde, *Los sucesos de Tlaxcalantongo y la muerte del ex-presidente de la república C. Venustiano Carranza* (Mexico City 1921); Miguel Márquez, *El verdadero Tlaxcalantongo* (Mexico City 1941); John W. F. Dulles, *Yesterday in Mexico*, op. cit.; Ramón Beteta, *Camino a Tlaxcalantongo*

(Mexico City 1961); Fernando Beñitez, *El rey viejo* (Mexico City 1959); Francisco L. Urquizo, *Asesinato de Carranza* (Mexico City 1959). For the role of de la Huerta in securing amnesty for Villa see Roberto Guzmán Esparza, *Memorias de don Adolfo de la Huerta* (Mexico City 1957).

EPILOGUE AND CONCLUSION

The most detailed study of Villa's last three years is Eugenia Meyer, *La vida con Villa en la hacienda de Canutillo* (Mexico City 1973). Other useful sources for this late period are Marte R. Gómez, *La reforma agraria en las filas Villistas, años 1913 a 1915 y 1920* (Mexico City 1966) and Marte R. Gómez, *Pancho Villa: Un intento de semblanza* (Mexico City 1972); Jessica Peterson and Thelma Cox Knoles, ed., *Pancho Villa: Intimate Recollections by People Who Knew Him*, op. cit.; Luz Corral de Villa, *Pancho Villa en la intimidad* op. cit.; and Rubén Osorio Zuñiga, *Pancho Villa: ese desconocido*, op. cit. Villa's relationship to the complex politics of Chihuahua in 1920–23 is examined in Mark Wasserman, *Persistent Oligarchs: Elites and Politics in Chihuahua, Mexico, 1910–1940* (Durham, North Carolina 1993); Luis Aboites Aguilar, *La irrigación revolucionaria: Historia del sistema nacional de riego del Río Conchos, Chihuahua, 1927–1938* (Mexico City 1988); Ramón Eduardo Ruíz, *Labor and the Ambivalent Revolutionaries: Mexico, 1911–1923* (Baltimore 1976); Manuel A. Machado, *The North American Cattle Industry, 1910–1975: Ideology, Conflict and Change* (Texas 1981); Mark Wasserman, 'Strategies for Survival of the Porfirian Elite in Revolutionary Mexico: Chihuahua during the 1920s', *HAHR* 67 (1987), pp. 87–107. The ravings of Chihuahua's governor are contained in Ignacio C. Enríquez, *Ni capitalismo ni comunismo: una democracia económica* (Mexico City 1950).

The death of Villa, his funeral and later decapitation are dealt with in a number of books: Antonio Vilanova, *Muerte de Villa* (Mexico City 1966); Víctor Ceja, *Yo maté a Francisco Villa* (Chihuahua 1979); Elías L. Torres, *Como murió Francisco Villa* (Mexico City 1975); Oscar W. Ching Vega, *La última cabalgata de Pancho Villa*, op. cit.; Martín Luis Guzmán, *Muertes históricas*, op. cit.; Guillermo Ramírez, *Melitón Lozoya: único director intelectual en la muerte de Villa* (Durango n.d.); Bill Rakoczy, *How did Villa Live, Love and Die?* (El Paso 1983); Alberto Calzadíaz Barrera, *Muerte del Centauro* (Mexico City 1982); Elias L. Torres, *Hazañas y muerte de Francisco Villa* (Mexico City 1975); Victor Ceja Reyes, *Yo decapité a Pancho Villa* (Mexico City 1971). Obregón's death is described in John W. F. Dulles, *Yesterday in Mexico*, op. cit. and in Martín Luis Guzmán, *Muertes históricas*, op. cit.

General interpretative works on the Mexican Revolution tend to stress that its status as true 'revolution' – involving major socio-economic change – has been overdone. See, for example, Alan Knight, 'The Mexican Revolution: Bourgeois? Nationalist? Or Just a "Great Rebellion"?', *Bulletin of Latin American Research* 4 (1985), pp. 1–37; Ramón Eduardo Ruíz, *The Great Rebellion: Mexico 1905–1929* (New York 1980). The ultimate in scepticism comes in Vicente Blasco Ibáñez's *Mexico in Revolution* (New York 1920). Other interesting assessments are in John Womack, 'The Mexican Revolution', in Leslie Bethell, ed., *Mexico Since Independence* (Cambridge 1991); Carlos Fuentes, *The Buried Mirror: Reflections on Spain and the New World* (Boston 1992); Lorenzo Meyer, *La segunda muerte de la revolución mexicana* (Mexico City 1992); Jean Meyer, 'Periodización e ideología', in James Wilkie et al., eds., *Contemporary Mexico* (Berkeley 1976); Ilene V. O'Malley, *The Myth of the Revolution: Hero Cults and the Institutionalization of the Mexican State, 1920–1940* (New York 1986).

One of the most difficult issues to resolve is the death toll in the Revolution. Two very different estimates emerge in, for example, Lewis F. Richardson, *Statistics of Deadly Quarrels* (Pittsburgh 1960) – 'up to 316,227 deaths' (p. 48) – and J. M. Roberts, *Twentieth Century. A History of the World: 1901 to the Present* (1991) – 'a million deaths' (p. 372). There is no doubt in my mind that the Roberts figure is closer to the truth.

INDEX

Acapulco, 218–19, 317, 361

Agua Prieta, 85, 86, 296, 310

Aguascalientes, 23, 157, 162, 239, 240, 254, 255, 269, 302, 303, 304, 373

aircraft, 100, 116, 234, 317, 326, 397

Anenecuilco, 36, 39, 42, 44, 47, 49, 50, 51, 52, 88, 351, 387

Ángeles, Felipe, 54, 206, 207, 222, 224, 227, 228, 233, 234, 236, 237, 238, 240, 242, 246, 253, 254, 255, 258, 260, 261, 263, 273, 278, 279, 280, 283, 287, 288, 289, 290, 292, 293, 295–96, 297, 299, 301, 302, 303, 304, 306, 358, 359, 399
  account of, 203–04
  campaigns in Morelos, 125, 126, 203
  attitude to Zapata, 125, 203, 259, 358, 379
  escapes death under Huerta, 180
  meets Zapata, 259
  joins Villa, 203–04
  detestation of Carranza, 203, 234, 237, 242, 375
  commanding Villa's armies in 1914, 224–228, 238, 239, 240
  opposes execution of Obregón 253–55
  works for Villa-Zapata alliance, 259, 261, 273, 277, 279
  in 1915 campaign against Obregón, 287–90, 295–96, 297, 299, 301, 302, 303, 304, 306
  returns to Villa in 1918, 375–77
  capture and execution of, 378–79
  as possible president, 203, 228, 233, 258, 278, 375, 378

Apaches, 54–58, 63, 64, 71, 74, 77, 133, 160, 216, 230, 279, 325

Army, role of (and militarism and militarisation), 20, 78, 81, 87, 96, 98, 99, 117, 119, 123, 139, 142, 143, 144, 147–48, 150, 159, 163, 169, 193, 203, 214, 216, 249, 257, 346, 397

atrocities, 76, 93, 94, 105, 122–23, 124, 130, 135–36, 147, 154, 164, 172, 179, 184, 196–97, 199, 218, 222, 239–40, 280–81, 311, 318, 320, 321, 323, 331–32, 335, 337, 338, 368, 369, 371, 376, 397

Baja California, 15, 115, 179, 218, 294

banditry, 59, 62–63, 68, 84, 123,

185, 196, 199, 267, 268–69,
270, 280, 281, 292, 307, 334,
347, 348, 349, 351, 356, 401
barbed wire, 37, 63, 100, 297, 300,
304, 309, 377
battles: Agua Prieta (1), 85–86
   Agua Prieta (2), 309–10, 319, 320,
   323
   Casas Grandes, 82–83
   Ciudad Juárez, 86–87, 92, 95–96,
   98
   Celaya, 298–301, 304, 309, 367,
   370, 381
   Cuautla, 93–94, 99
   Monterrey, 295
   Parral, 135–36
   Rellano (1), 133–34, 138
   Rellano (2), 138–40
   Saltillo, 236
   Tierra Blanca, 173–75, 199, 205,
   273
   Torreón (1), 170–71
   Torreón (2), 224–28, 232, 235,
   291, 307, 308
   Trinidad (Leon), 301–04, 316,
   370
   Zacatecas, 238–40, 241, 291,
   307–08
Benton, William, 200–03, 229, 231,
285, 385
Bierce, Ambrose, 230–31
Blanco, Lucio, 176, 246, 248, 249,
251, 258, 283, 355, 396, 399,
401

Calles, Plutarco Elias, 11, 166, 251,
252, 286, 309–10, 347, 381,
383, 384, 386, 391–92, 393,
394, 395, 396, 399
Carranza, Venustiano, 11, 97, 99,
108, 151, 170, 181, 183, 190,

191, 194, 197, 198, 203, 205,
207, 208, 216, 219, 222, 230,
235, 243, 251, 252, 253, 254,
259, 260, 268, 273, 275, 277,
278, 281, 296, 297, 298, 299,
300, 302, 305, 306, 307, 310,
320, 326, 328, 335, 336, 353,
373, 387, 399, 401, 402, 403, 404
account of, 160–61
and events of 1911, 161–62
and Madero presidency, 162–63
and Orozco rising, 162
attitude to Huerta regime, 163
in Sonora, 179, 180
role of in Benton case, 202
moves HQ from Sonora to
   Ciudad Juárez, 223
loses battle of wills with Villa,
   237
becomes First Chief, 238
enters Mexico City, 244
harsh attitude to Mexico City,
   245, 264–65
fears Villa-Zapata alliance, 246
negotiations with Zapata, 247
breaks off talks with Zapata,
   250–51
defies Convention, 261–62
declared rebel by Convention,
   262–63
negotiates with Convention,
   282–83
absorbs rump of Convention, 283
greater resources in civil war, 287
in Veracruz, 287–88
proconsuls of, 194, 258, 268, 289,
   341, 349, 390
weaknesses and strengths, 291–95
good as propagandist, 292–93
recognised by USA, 309, 317,
   318–19, 320

opens campaign against Zapata,
317
attitude to Punitive Expedition,
325, 329–31
outwits Woodrow Wilson, 382–84
dealings with Pablo González,
337–38
policies of in 1916–17, 338–49
corruption of, 346
beset by revolts, 356–57
worried by Chávez García,
356–57
launches final campaign against
Zapata, 358–59
plans Zapata's murder, 359–60
disastrous policies in
Chihuahua, 363, 366, 367,
374, 375, 376, 379
suffers from arms embargo, 364
sends large army against Villa,
367
courtmartials and executes
Ángeles, 378–79
tries to perpetuate rule, 379–80
opposes Obregón, 380–81
tries to arrest Obregón, 381
flees Mexico City, 381
assassinated, 382–83, 385, 388
PERSONALITY, PSYCHOLOGY
AND ATTITUDES OF:
antiAmericanism, 162–63, 165,
221, 228–29, 241, 258, 290,
294, 319, 329, 344, 345, 372,
381
political ideology of, 163–64, 166,
344, 355
personality of, 164–65, 231, 286,
291, 342–43
relations with Villa, 175–76, 179,
202, 223, 231–33, 241
autocratic tendencies, 180, 237,

241, 246–47, 256, 257–58,
262, 263, 289–90, 340, 345,
374, 380, 386
machiavellianism of, 235–37, 242,
287
as machine politician, 247–48,
256, 340–41
political movement of, 249, 257,
258, 266, 270, 286, 288–89
anticlericalism, 255, 257, 290, 293,
296, 343
cruelty, 172, 369–70
responsible for atrocities, 164
ambitions of, 233
attitude to Obregón, 244, 254,
286–87, 312, 335, 344–45
attitude to Zapata, 355
Catholic Church, role of in Mexican
Revolution, 5, 11–12, 14, 15,
34, 40, 41, 66, 67, 115, 118,
128, 134, 148, 166, 194, 242,
281, 290, 292, 293, 313, 343,
346, 348, 397, 398
Cerro Prieto, 76, 77, 79, 96
Chao, Manuel, 168, 169, 170, 195,
204, 205, 208, 231, 232, 233,
297
Chávez García, Ines, 356–57, 358,
399
Chiapas, 34, 35, 39, 102, 116, 182,
257, 267, 289, 295, 341, 349,
356, 362
Chihuahua (state), 15, 17, 33, 48,
53, 54, 55, 56, 57, 59, 60, 62,
63, 64, 65, 66, 67, 68, 69, 71,
74, 77, 78, 81, 82, 85, 90,
103, 104, 123, 124, 128, 130,
131, 132, 133, 134, 138, 142,
143, 144, 145, 146, 151, 162,
165, 166, 167, 168, 169, 170,
173, 176, 179, 182, 187, 191,

192, 193, 194, 196, 200, 203,
204, 205, 206, 209, 210, 229,
231, 232, 241, 242, 252, 255,
267, 278, 281, 287, 289, 290,
291, 301, 304, 305, 306, 312,
321, 322, 325, 327, 329, 330,
331, 334, 363, 374, 376, 384
Chihuahua City, 75, 76, 80, 133,
138, 139, 169, 172, 173, 175,
200, 204, 208, 210, 224, 251,
253, 254, 255, 310, 311, 320,
331, 334, 365, 366, 368–69,
371, 377, 378
Chinese, 103, 106, 320, 367, 370
científicos, 10–11, 15, 24, 44, 54, 65,
161, 401
Ciudad Juárez (see also battles), 16,
23, 76, 82, 85, 100, 103, 106,
131, 132, 139, 142, 149, 161,
162, 175, 200, 201, 205, 223,
231, 232, 246, 311, 320, 331,
377, 379, 390
Coahuila, 25, 27, 29, 73, 76, 81,
103, 104, 105, 117, 138, 139,
151, 160, 161, 162, 163, 166,
176, 182, 209, 235, 236, 288,
289, 291, 296, 309, 325, 335,
355, 384
constitutional conventions:
  1) Mexico City, 242, 256
  2) Aguascalientes, 256–63, 266,
  273, 280, 286
  3) Querétaro, 345–46, 354, 402
Convention (sovereign body of
  1914–15), 258, 259, 260,
  261–63, 280–86, 313, 314,
  315, 316–17, 335
corridos, 91, 94, 274, 281, 291, 342,
  403
Creel, Enrique, 65–68, 69, 74, 77,
  99, 102, 129, 143, 175, 193,

195, 201, 363, 402
crime and punishment (see also
  banditry), 8, 127, 147, 190,
  193, 244, 403
Cuautla, 46, 51, 90, 93, 107, 112,
  113, 114, 183, 184, 186, 219,
  355, 358, 360, 387
Cuernavaca, 45, 50, 90, 93, 94, 99,
  107, 109, 110, 111, 112, 119,
  121, 122, 123, 124, 137, 154,
  181, 183, 219, 240, 241, 248,
  249, 250, 273, 315, 316, 318,
  337, 338, 352, 358, 359

De la Barra, Francisco, 85, 98, 106,
  110, 111, 112, 113, 114, 117,
  137
De la Huerta, Adolfo, 166, 167,
  381, 383–85, 387, 391–92,
  395, 396–97, 401
De la O, Genovevo, 46, 88, 89, 92,
  108, 111, 121, 122, 123, 124,
  125, 126, 155, 181, 185, 219,
  246, 250, 269, 315, 317, 318,
  352, 358, 359, 375, 399
Díaz, Félix, 126, 145, 147, 152–53,
  160, 181, 214, 215, 272, 338
  rebellion of (1912), 150–51, 377
  imprisoned, 151
  in Decena Trágica, 153–56
  doublecrossed by Huerta, 157–58,
  347
  revolt in Oaxaca, 347–50, 355,
  356, 359, 382
  ends revolt, 387
Díaz, Porfirio, 37, 42, 43, 44, 45,
  47, 50, 51, 53, 54, 55, 57, 63,
  64, 65, 66, 67, 72, 76, 84, 88,
  90, 104, 106, 110, 111, 115,
  116, 117, 131, 132, 134, 137,
  139, 147, 149, 153, 160–61,

164, 168, 177, 206, 213, 231, 241, 280, 291, 305, 313, 340, 343, 344, 345, 346, 347, 373, 379, 381, 397, 401
career of, 5–6
80th birthday celebrations, 1–3
dictatorship of, 6–25
interviewed by James Creelman, 18, 24, 25, 28, 45
challenged by Madero, 25–32
re-elected in 1910, 31–32, 35
attitude to Morelos, 45–46, 88–89, 92, 93
reaction to outbreak of Revolution, 73–74
fails to blunt Revolution, 76–78
rapidly losing ground, 80–81, 83
increasingly desperate, 85
tries to negotiate, 86–87
signs treaty of Ciudad Juárez, 94–95, 98, 99, 377
reluctantly goes into exile, 98
resignation of, 105
departs for exile in Europe, 105
personality of, 18–19
disease, 138, 240, 273, 314, 338, 339, 357–58, 399
División del Norte (Villa's army), 140, 170, 171, 207, 208–09, 228, 232, 236, 237, 240, 241, 242, 254, 277, 287, 291, 300, 304, 306, 308, 311, 368, 372
dorados, 207–08, 306, 310, 312, 321, 364, 365, 368, 371, 372, 374, 386, 392, 394
Durango (state), 58–60, 76, 84–85, 99, 103, 104, 149, 165, 168, 190, 194, 196, 267, 269, 272, 287, 289, 290, 291, 312, 321, 364, 371, 395
Durango city, 103, 169, 171, 196–97, 256, 379
dynamite (see also máquina loca), 86, 95–96, 100, 101–02, 134, 136, 138–39, 199, 217, 226, 229, 339

economy, Mexican, 11, 12, 13–15, 19–20, 21–22, 67, 217, 397
ejidos, 15, 251, 272, 387, 404
El Paso, 16, 23, 73, 81, 86, 95, 100, 139, 146, 167, 210, 324, 377, 378

Fierro, Rodolfo, 174, 204, 206, 208, 213, 254, 255, 280, 281, 296, 297, 303–04, 307, 316, 328, 352, 356, 364, 399, 401
account of, 199–201
expert in máquina loca, 175
death, 308
Figueroa brothers, 92–93, 107, 108, 110, 111, 114, 118, 121, 185, 186, 272
finances, Mexican, 10–11, 18, 22, 30, 76–77, 117, 216, 217–18, 305, 314, 339–40, 384
foreign capital and foreign capitalists, 16–18, 31, 43, 64, 66, 72, 221, 305, 306, 322, 343–44, 345, 347, 367, 374
France, role of and Mexican relations with, 4, 5, 14, 17, 18, 36, 45, 54, 63, 101, 105, 130, 160, 216, 228, 305, 319, 358

Garibaldi, Giuseppe, 83, 99–100
Garza, González Roque de la, 255, 258, 273, 284, 313, 315
Germany, role of, 294, 309, 319, 322, 324, 329, 331, 333, 344, 348, 359, 372, 373

González, Abraham, 62, 68–69, 74,
    84, 127, 129, 130, 131,
    132–33, 136, 139, 142, 143,
    146–47, 166–67, 188, 206
González, Pablo, 138, 162, 180, 226,
    235, 236, 286, 287, 291, 295,
    316, 318, 350, 355, 356, 380,
    382
  account of, 176, 335, 359
  campaigns in Morelos, 318, 335,
    337, 338, 349, 355, 358–59
  contrives Zapata's murder, 360–62
  exiled, 387
Great Britain, role of and Mexican
    relations with, 5, 10, 17, 73,
    142, 155, 200–203, 213,
    215–16, 228, 256–57, 319,
    347, 385
Guadalajara, 13, 16, 234, 235, 296
Guerrero, 33, 89, 92, 114, 117, 121,
    124, 137, 182, 185, 186, 218,
    267, 269, 270, 315, 317, 318,
    336, 356, 358, 361, 381
Guevara, Che, 63, 404
Gutiérrez, Eulalio, 258, 262, 265,
    277, 278, 280, 282–83, 296,
    311, 313
Guzmán, Martin, 188, 199, 309

haciendas, 12, 13–14, 22, 24, 35–36,
    37, 39, 40, 44, 47, 50, 77, 88,
    90, 91, 99, 102, 107, 116, 126,
    129, 148, 168, 192, 197, 198,
    201, 206, 214, 267, 268, 271,
    289, 296, 314, 341, 342, 349,
    350, 390, 401
Hermosillo, 16, 146, 165, 279, 309
Herrera family, 62, 376
Herrera, Castulo, 74, 75, 76, 95

Hidalgo, 8, 34, 103, 113, 203, 267,
    317, 336, 355
Hill, Benjamín, 166, 179, 251, 252,
    253, 286, 303, 355, 384, 388,
    399, 401
Huerta, Victoriano, 10, 87, 94, 98,
    105, 117, 125, 130, 148, 153,
    160, 168, 169, 170, 174, 178,
    185, 190, 191, 192, 193, 194,
    195, 197, 201, 202, 203, 208,
    209, 223, 226, 228, 232, 238,
    247, 255, 258, 292, 305, 317,
    318, 335, 340, 343, 347, 348,
    370, 373, 381, 399, 401
  account of, 136–37, 213
  commanding in Morelos, 111–14,
    136, 165
  clash with Villa, 137–38, 140–41
  defeats Orozco, 138–39
  strained relations with Madero,
    139, 141, 142, 145, 147
  ambitions of, 139
  hatred for Madero, 137, 138, 143,
    145, 217
  hatred for Villa, 140, 143
  tries to execute Villa, 140–41
  tries to assassinate Villa, 141–42
  tries to convict Villa of desertion,
    143–46
  dismissed by Madero, 145
  drunkenness of, 144, 149–50, 151,
    153, 158, 167, 181, 220, 228,
    242, 309
  threatens alliance with Orozco,
    150
  treason of, against Madero, 152,
    153–54, 155–57
  conspiracy revealed by Gustavo
    Madero, 156
  arrests Madero, 156
  arrests and executes Gustavo

Madero, 156
doublecrosses Félix Díaz, 157–58
assassinates Madero, 158–59, 163,
 165
regime of, 163–64, 213–18
attitude to Catholic Church, 245
has Abraham González murdered,
 166–67
brutality and atrocities of, 172,
 184, 215
faces up to threat from Villa, 172
and campaign against Sonora, 179
declares martial law in Morelos,
 181–82
under pressure in northern
 Mexico, 186
disliked by Woodrow Wilson,
 214–16, 219–20
makes overtures to Zapata,
 221–22
attempts divide and rule, 222
underrates Villa, 224
defeated at Zacatecas, 240
desperately seeks peace terms,
 240–41
final exit, 241–42
goes into exile, 242
death of, 308–09

Indians (see also Apaches, Yaquis,
 Mayas), 14–15, 19, 32, 33–35,
 40, 41, 63, 89, 99, 103, 109,
 136, 147, 166, 176, 180, 194,
 206, 227, 260, 292, 293, 349,
 377

Jalisco, 43, 104, 166, 190, 269, 271,
 296, 306, 397
Jojutla, 89, 90, 91, 92, 107, 110,
 114, 118, 123, 124, 125, 218,
 219, 318, 338, 358, 359

Jonacatepec, 93, 110, 123, 125, 183,
 219, 338, 355, 358, 359, 360
Jones, Mary, 230
Juárez, Benito, 4–5, 18, 27, 28, 35,
 65, 89, 160, 162, 163, 164,
 165, 172, 176, 204, 228, 244,
 266, 305, 340, 345, 361, 380

Katz, Friedrich, 61
King, Rosa, 51, 90, 137
Knight, Alan, 84, 103, 133, 150,
 165, 192, 203, 270, 272, 290,
 292, 402

land (real estate) and land reform,
 15, 32, 63–64, 65, 66, 71, 77,
 102, 107, 109, 111, 116, 117,
 120, 123, 134, 147, 148, 163,
 166, 192, 204, 206, 208, 222,
 232, 234, 242, 246, 247, 262,
 267, 268, 271, 272, 276, 277,
 281, 290, 293, 313, 314, 315,
 340, 343, 344, 350, 374, 387,
 389, 404
León, 16, 103
Limantour, José Yves, 11, 15, 22,
 24, 29, 30, 76–77, 85, 87, 98
London, Jack, 230

machine guns, 82–83, 93, 94, 95–96,
 100–01, 105, 117, 135, 153,
 154, 156, 171, 174, 175, 183,
 297, 300, 303, 304, 309, 322,
 331, 368
Madero family, 25–26, 29, 73, 85,
 132, 138, 161, 257, 283, 306
Madero, Emilio, 196, 283, 287, 295,
 306
Madero, Evaristo, 27–28
Madero, Francisco, 51, 52, 54, 62,
 67, 68, 71, 76, 78, 103, 104,

124, 131, 134, 135, 161, 166,
168, 172, 179, 180, 188, 198,
203, 204, 216, 217, 219, 222,
223, 224, 232, 242, 244, 245,
247, 248, 257, 259, 266, 272,
278, 280, 281, 282, 290, 291,
328, 340, 343, 344, 347, 348,
354, 375, 399, 401, 403
personality of, 25, 115–16, 156
early career, 25–29
spiritualism of, 26–28, 115–16,
134
challenges Díaz for presidency,
28–29
interview with Díaz, 29–30
imprisoned, 31–32
escapes to USA, 32, 51, 52, 73
issues Plan of San Luis Potosí,
32, 72
rebels against Díaz, 32
and outbreak of Revolution,
72–74
crosses into Mexico, 81
in alliance with Orozco and Villa,
81
early actions in the Revolution,
81–82
relations with Orozco, 82, 83,
94–95, 96–98
relations with Villa, 69, 83, 84,
94–95, 96–98, 99–100, 130,
133, 136, 140–41, 142, 145,
146–47
wounded in battle, 83
gaining ground, 83
and battle of Ciudad Juárez, 86
negotiates with Díaz, 86–87, 93
relations with Zapata, 89, 92, 99,
106–113, 117–18, 119–22
attitude to land reform, 89
signs treaty of Ciudad Juárez, 94,
377

weakness and vacillation of,
96–97, 119
a reformist not a revolutionary,
98, 102, 104, 106–07, 116–17
triumphal entry into Mexico City,
105–06
campaigning in 1911 election, 113
elected president, 115
style in Cabinet, 115–16, 124
policies of, 117, 129
attempts military solution of
Morelos problem, 122–26
attitude to Chihuahua, 129
attitude to Orozco rising, 138,
139
strained relations with Huerta,
139, 141, 142, 143, 145, 147
sends stay of execution for Villa,
140–41
inadequacy as president, 147–51
actions during *Decena Trágica*,
153–56
reappoints Huerta, 154
arrested by Huerta, 156
assassinated by Huerta, 158–59,
163, 165, 166, 167, 178
Madero, Gustavo, 85, 100, 117, 132,
143, 145, 152, 153, 156–57,
188, 255
Madero, Raul, 73, 111, 112, 114,
140–41, 205, 253, 254, 255,
283, 295, 306, 385, 392
Magaña, Giraldo, 144, 145, 246,
353, 355, 356, 358, 387
Magón brothers, 24, 66, 74, 82, 83,
84, 115, 230, 260
máquina loca, 134, 138, 175
Martínez, Paulino, 260, 273, 280
Mayas, 9–10, 33, 34, 53, 99, 137

Maytorena, José Maria, 166, 167,
    180, 234, 251, 252, 257, 286,
    293, 306, 307, 309, 310, 375,
    401, 403
Mazatlán, 16, 146, 234, 312
mercenaries, 95, 135, 136, 200,
    206–07
Mérida, 22, 34, 182
Mexican Revolution, nature of,
    79–80, 84, 100, 102–04,
    131–32, 151, 154, 197, 204,
    221, 261, 263, 266, 267, 268,
    269–70, 284, 286, 288–90,
    292, 299, 335, 385, 399–404
Mexico, geography of, 12–13, 33,
    53, 138, 139, 165, 224, 308,
    310, 384
Mexico City, 2–3, 13, 14, 15, 16,
    33, 38, 42, 43, 51, 53, 54, 55,
    65, 71, 73, 81, 90, 102, 103,
    104, 105, 106, 108, 112, 115,
    119, 121, 124, 129, 130, 133,
    134, 135, 138, 139, 140–41,
    142, 144, 148, 150, 152,
    153–59, 162, 163, 166, 170,
    177, 181, 182, 183, 214, 218,
    221, 222, 226, 228, 233, 235,
    236, 238, 241, 243–46, 249,
    250, 251, 254, 255, 261,
    264–65, 271, 272, 277, 279,
    280, 282, 283, 285, 286, 287,
    291, 292, 297, 298, 306,
    313–14, 316, 318, 319, 329,
    330, 333, 335, 337, 338, 339,
    341, 348, 350, 363, 368, 373,
    378, 379, 381–82, 383, 398
Mexico, Federal District of, 33, 115,
    124, 182, 186, 315, 316, 336,
    337
Mexico State, 92, 104, 114, 121,
    124, 125, 182, 186, 219, 315,
    316, 317, 336, 343

Michoacán, 33, 43, 92, 121, 182,
    186, 219, 269, 271, 273, 296,
    306, 336, 353, 356–57, 397
mining, 13, 20–21, 22, 29, 35, 63,
    66, 67, 103–04, 217, 241, 269,
    366, 387
Montaño, Otilio, 43, 120, 183, 274,
    336, 351–52, 353, 357, 399
Monterrey, 16, 31, 176, 240, 295,
    305
Morelos, 33, 36, 38, 40, 42, 44–47,
    49, 51, 53, 71, 87, 88, 89, 90,
    92, 99, 103, 104, 107, 108,
    110, 111, 113, 114, 118, 119,
    120, 121, 123, 124, 125, 128,
    130, 133, 181–82, 183, 185,
    186, 192, 194, 218, 219, 246,
    247, 249, 259, 260, 263, 265,
    267, 268, 269, 270, 271, 272,
    273, 276, 279, 284, 288, 313,
    314, 315, 316, 317, 318, 320,
    335, 336, 337, 338, 349, 350,
    351, 355, 356, 357, 358, 360,
    361, 362, 373, 387
  sugar planters of, 37–38, 43, 44,
    45, 107, 111, 114, 122, 126,
    149, 182, 184, 264, 315, 387
Mormons, 66, 198

Neri, Felipe, 93, 94, 185, 352
Nogales, 16, 146, 178
Nuevo Laredo, 16, 176, 235, 240,
    296
Nuevo León, 13, 16, 24, 27, 29,
    104, 121, 161, 246, 248, 283,
    325, 356, 387

Oaxaca, 4, 5, 7, 11, 12, 19, 34, 102,
    114, 117, 123, 150, 182, 257,
    267, 268, 289, 317, 336, 338,
    341, 347, 350, 356

Obregón, Alvaro, 139, 160, 165, 166, 189, 194, 203, 231, 242–43, 246, 247, 250, 258, 283, 289, 306, 308, 310, 311, 319, 320, 329, 337, 341, 359, 368, 370, 399, 401, 402, 403, 404
early life, 176–77
marriages, 177
late entrant to Revolution, 177–78
rebels against Huerta, 178
as chief military figure in Sonora, 178–79
manipulation of Yaquis, 179–80
wins victories in Sonora, 179
becomes Commander-in-Chief, North-West, 179
campaign in 1914, 233–35
races to Mexico City, 234–35
enters Mexico City, 243
harsh attitude to Mexico City, 244–45, 264–65, 287, 313–14
tortuous negotiations with Villa, 251–56
threatened with death by Villa, 253–55
attends Aguascalientes conference, 259, 261, 262–63, 280
chooses Carranza over Villa, 263
as capitalist, 270
occupies Puebla, 284
key figure in civil war, 286
occupies Mexico City, 287
outthinks Villa in civil war, 297
moves up to Celaya, 297
digs in at Celaya, 297–98
defeats Villa at Celaya, 298–301
executes prisoners, 300
defeats Villa at Trinidad, 301–04, 316

attempts suicide, 303
career under Carranza, 354–55
opposes Carranza, 379–80
contests presidency, 380–81
rebels against Carranza, 381–82
wins struggle against Carranza, 382–83
uncertain how to deal with Villa, 384–85
wins 1920 election, 386–87
presidential policies of, 387–88, 402
correspondence with Villa, 385, 388, 389, 391
and 1924 election, 391–92
plans Villa's assassination, 392–96
as hidden hand behind Calles, 397
seeks re-election as president, 397
assassinated, 398
PERSONALITY, ATTRIBUTES AND ATTITUDES OF:
psychology of, 177, 181, 235, 245, 253, 255–56, 259, 297, 300–01, 303, 378, 380, 381, 396
love of jokes, 177, 180–81, 380, 392
attitude to Carranza, 180, 234–35, 244–45, 282–83, 286–87, 312, 335, 344–45, 355, 367
attitude to Catholic Church, 245, 254, 292, 313, 343, 388, 397
as military commander, 233, 234–35, 287, 291, 297
ambition of, 286
ambivalence, 287–88
political talents, 292, 341
attitude to Yaquis, 347
dislike of Villa, 354

hostility towards Pablo González, 368–69
links with Zapata, 354–55, 356
legend of, 304–05
O'Hea, Patrick, 198, 199, 200, 370, 385
oil, 16, 17, 23, 64, 73–74, 220, 289, 290, 294, 295, 296, 320, 345, 347, 348–49, 387, 396
Ojinaga, 76, 77, 223, 231, 321, 322, 372
Orozco, Pascual, 77, 78, 104, 115, 120, 129, 142, 143, 147, 149, 152, 167, 168, 169, 172, 173, 174, 175, 181, 185, 194, 195, 196, 198, 238, 247, 255, 259, 272, 280, 305, 365, 381, 399
in alliance with Villa, 76
losing ground to Villa, 79–80
in alliance with Madero and Villa, 81
relations with Madero, 82, 83, 94–95, 96–98
military supremacy in Durango, 84–85
in battle of Ciudad Juárez, 86, 95–96
social movement of, 102–03, 104, 131–32, 133, 134–35, 150
rebellion of, 121, 123, 124, 130–36, 138–40, 165, 178, 198
defeat at Rellano, 138–40
manifesto of, 134
personality of, 134
death, 309
legend of, 131

Palafox, Manuel, 188, 219, 248–50, 260, 276, 283–84, 313, 315, 316–17, 351, 352, 353, 357
account of, 182–83, 357

Parral, 60, 79, 128, 130, 134, 135, 142, 144, 168, 208, 329, 367, 368, 370–71, 375, 376, 392, 393, 394, 395
pastoral economy, 13, 15, 17, 44, 60, 192, 193, 195, 294, 305, 339, 404
Patton, General George, 330
Peláez, Manuel, 289, 347, 348, 350, 356, 359
Pershing, General John Joseph 'Blackjack', 323, 324–32, 338, 339, 346, 350, 363, 365, 368, 372, 377
Piño Suarez, 30, 115, 129, 134, 158–59, 180, 204
Plan of Ayala, 120, 121, 130, 144, 181, 183, 185, 222, 243, 246, 247, 248, 249, 250, 251, 254, 259–60, 261, 266, 276, 279, 350, 351, 355, 357
Plan of Guadalupe, 163, 230
Plan of San Luis Potosí, 32, 72, 89, 96, 107, 132, 163
proletariat (Mexican working class), 19–22, 67, 103, 105, 148–49, 242, 249, 292, 300, 344–45
Puebla, 19, 23, 30, 33, 42, 43, 73, 89, 90, 92, 93, 110, 114, 117, 119, 120, 121, 123, 124, 125, 182, 185, 186, 218, 219, 235, 258, 267, 269, 270, 272, 284, 297, 288, 315, 316, 317, 336, 338, 349, 350, 351, 353, 356, 358
Punitive Expedition, 325–34, 339, 363, 365, 372, 374, 377

Querétaro (see also Constitutional Conventions), 6, 15, 23, 297, 314

Quintana Roo, 45, 54, 89, 104, 120, 267

railways (see also *máquina loca*), 3, 15–16, 38, 44, 63, 65, 66, 75, 82, 83, 85, 100, 123, 124, 125, 134, 138, 166, 168, 170, 181, 183, 186, 190, 199, 200, 209, 214, 224, 225, 233, 238, 241, 254, 265, 269, 288, 295, 298, 303, 320, 329, 336, 337, 339, 340, 371, 379, 382

Reed, John, 62, 68, 106, 160, 188, 191, 194, 196, 197, 198, 199–200, 204, 209, 211, 227, 230, 243, 275, 342

Rentería, Austreberta, 390–91, 393, 396

Reyes, Bernardo, 24, 25, 27, 30, 46, 99, 111, 112, 113, 115, 118, 131, 137, 145, 147, 151, 152–53, 158, 161, 347

Robles, Juvencio, 125, 126, 247, 318, 335

campaigns in Morelos, 122–24, 182, 183–86, 218

rurales, 8, 19, 22, 23, 34, 39, 56, 103, 115, 130, 159, 201

Saltillo, 16, 160, 165, 226, 228, 235, 236, 295, 305, 330, 339

San Luis Potosí, 16, 31, 32, 141, 151, 162, 236, 248, 267, 283, 297, 356

Santa Anna, Antonio López de, 4–5, 18, 54, 150, 160, 305

Seáñez, Soledad, 128, 390, 396

Sinaloa, 43, 84, 102, 144, 149, 165, 166, 179, 257, 306, 309

Sonora, 9, 17, 20, 21, 25, 33, 43, 48, 53, 54, 55, 71, 85, 103, 104, 130, 137, 139, 151, 163, 165, 166, 167, 175, 177, 178, 179, 182, 194, 203, 216, 223, 229, 231, 232, 233, 234, 242, 243, 251, 252, 262, 286, 289, 291, 296, 306, 307, 309, 310, 321, 322, 325, 347, 379, 381, 383, 403

Soto y Gama, Díaz, 121, 250, 267, 283–84, 313, 315, 351, 352, 353

account of, 248–49

at Aguascalientes conference, 260–61

Spain and Spaniards, Mexico's relations with, 5, 17, 36, 38, 91, 103, 191, 194, 216, 227, 293, 320, 340, 348, 367

Steffens, Lincoln, 230

Steinbeck, John, 63

Tabasco, 23, 72, 116, 182, 341, 348, 349

Taft, William, 23, 74, 85, 133, 134, 149, 152, 155

Tamaulipas, 17, 104, 161, 297, 325, 356, 374

Tampico, 16, 17, 217, 220, 232, 235, 240, 241, 289, 290, 294, 295, 296, 297, 305, 347, 349, 356

Tepic, 16, 43, 81, 136, 166, 234, 235, 257, 306, 307

Terrazas family, 15, 54–55, 57, 58, 60, 61, 62, 65, 67, 69, 74, 77, 84, 99, 102, 129, 131, 132, 143, 145, 168, 169, 170, 175, 193, 196, 201, 223, 363, 389, 402

Terrazas, Luis, 53, 54, 57, 63, 65, 74, 143, 195, 230

Terrazas, Silvestre, 67, 68, 69, 79, 192, 193, 195, 200, 204–05, 232, 236, 237, 289, 311

Texas, 16, 32, 56, 66, 72, 115, 146–47, 161, 216, 333, 347, 372, 390

Tlaxcala, 23, 92, 121, 186, 267, 336, 355, 356

Torreón (see also battles), 16, 103, 106, 133, 136, 138, 141, 142, 165, 169, 170, 171, 173, 200, 209, 210, 224, 237, 239, 241, 251, 255, 256, 287, 301, 304, 368–69, 370, 376, 392

Torres, Juana, 210–11

Tweedie, Mrs Alex, 39

United States (see also Punitive Expedition; Veracruz occupation), role of in Revolution and Mexican relations with, 4, 5, 12, 15–17, 20–21, 22, 23, 25, 29, 31, 53, 55–58, 66, 67, 71, 72, 73–74, 81, 85–86, 95, 98, 100, 115, 124, 129, 133, 134–35, 139, 140, 149, 151–52, 155, 161, 166, 168, 169, 173, 174, 178, 186, 193, 195, 201–02, 207, 208–09, 213–14, 215, 216, 217, 219–20, 221, 223, 227–31, 232, 240–41, 245, 247, 251, 254, 259, 274, 279, 282, 284, 287, 289, 290–91, 293–95, 305, 307, 309, 311, 317, 318–19, 324–25, 328–33, 337, 340, 342, 344, 345, 347, 348–49, 355, 358, 359, 360, 372, 375, 378, 379, 384–85, 387, 396, 402, 403

Urbina, Tomás, 68, 76, 84, 140, 147, 167, 168, 169, 170, 172, 190, 194, 205, 206, 208, 210, 213, 224, 254, 255, 258, 269, 272, 280, 282, 283, 289, 297, 399
account of, 196–97
downfall and death, 307–08

Vasconcelos, José, 29, 30, 156, 162, 188, 203, 259, 262, 281–82, 293, 381, 388, 397

Veracruz, 8, 15, 16, 19, 30, 34, 35, 38, 42, 43, 72, 73, 102, 105, 113, 126, 137, 150, 151, 158, 182, 214, 215, 241, 246, 257, 262, 264, 273, 286, 287, 294, 295, 298, 302, 303, 304, 330, 339, 342, 344, 347, 348, 349, 355, 356, 377, 381, 382, 396
occupation of by US forces, 220–21, 228, 238, 240, 241, 264, 294, 320

villages, 12, 13–14, 32, 34–35, 37, 38–39, 40–41, 44, 64, 65, 66, 67, 71, 88, 89, 90, 102, 125, 147, 183, 184, 201, 266, 292, 315, 316, 337, 349, 350, 351, 356, 372, 373, 374, 376, 379, 401, 402

Villa, Antonio, 127, 142, 167

Villa, Francisco ('Pancho'), 74, 149, 151, 160, 165, 166, 176, 186, 219, 230, 243, 244, 265, 269, 313, 316, 337, 339, 341, 344, 346, 347, 348, 349, 350, 356, 357, 359, 381, 399, 401
childhood and youth, 58–61, 68
family of, 58, 391
pursues trade of butcher, 60, 127, 142
as guerrilla leader, 68, 71, 75–76

enters Revolution, 71, 75
second-in-command to Herrera,
    75–76
unseats Herrera, 76
in alliance with Orozco, 76, 78
early battles of, 76, 79
second-in-command to Orozco,
    79–80
attains military equality with
    Orozco, 80
in battle of Ciudad Juárez, 86
marries Luz Corral, 127–28
attitude to Orozco rising, 130–33
in battle for Parral against
    Orozco, 135–36
clashes with Huerta, 136–38,
    140–41
in campaign against Orozco, 139
founds Division del Norte, 140
attempted execution by Huerta,
    140–41, 187
attempted assassination by Huerta,
    141–42
in jail in Mexico City, 142–46
planning jailbreak, 145
breaks out of jail, 146
in Texas, 146–47, 167
wants revenge on Huerta, 167
treats with Maytorena, 167
treats with de la Huerta, 167
crosses Río Grande, 167–68, 178
guerrilla war against Huerta,
    168–70
fights pitched battles against
    Huerta, 170–72
wins battle of Torreón, 170–71
executes prisoners, 172, 190,
    239–40, 283
attacks Chihuahua City, 172
takes Ciudad Juárez by ruse,
    172–73

fights battle of Tierra Blanca,
    173–75
master of Chihuahua, 175
as governor of Chihuahua, 190,
    191–95
and Benton case, 200–203
and Mutual Film Company,
    211–12
opens 1914 campaign against
    Huerta, 223–24
wins battle of Torreón, 224–27
hoodwinked by Carranza, 235–37
wins battle of wills against
    Carranza, 237
recognises Carranza as First
    Chief, 238
supreme command of Division del
    Norte, 238
wins battle of Zacatecas, 238–40
contacts with Zapata, 186,
    222–23, 242, 245–46, 249–50,
    258, 259, 260, 261, 271,
    272–73, 284, 288, 373
correspondence with Zapata, 246,
    247, 263, 294, 306, 320
tortuous negotiations with
    Obregón, 251–56
threatens to shoot Obregón, 253
plans to assassinate Obregón,
    254–55
denounces Carranza, 254–55
open breach with Carranza, 256
stays away from Convention of
    Aguascalientes 259, 262
appointed General-in-Chief of
    Convention, 262
meeting with Zapata, 273–79,
    284, 288, 387
provides little help for Zapata,
    279
reign of terror in Mexico City,
    280–81, 283, 313

contempt for Convention, 282–83

fights civil war against Carranza and Obregón, 286–311

throws away chances in civil war, 287–88

political weaknesses, 290–92

thought likely to win civil war, 290–91

in Monterrey, 296

rejects Ángeles's advice about Celaya, 298

defeated in two battles of Celaya, 298–301

loses battle of Trinidad, 301–04

reasons for losing civil war, 304

legend of invincibility destroyed, 305–07

orders Urbina executed, 307–08

retreats to Sonora, 308

attacks Agua Prieta, 309–10

attacks Hermosillo, 310

crosses Sierra Madre to Chihuahua, 310

switches to guerilla warfare, 311–12

wages war on gringos, 319–21

attacks USA, 321–22

raid on Columbus, 322–24, 373, 385, 390

threatened by Punitive Expedition, 326–32

wounded at Guerrero, 327, 363

holed up in cave, 327, 363

assassination attempts against, 332–333

wins kudos for defying Punitive Expedition, 334

revival of fortunes, 363–64

raids throughout Chihuahua, 364–72

attacks Chihuahua City, 365

barbarism of, 369–70

battles against federal armies, 369–72

losing ground, 372–73

declared 'beyond amnesty', 373

blocked by militias, 374

influenced by Ángeles, 375–76

disagrees with Ángeles, 376–77

attacks Ciudad Juárez, 377

attacks Durango, 379

petitions for negotiated peace, 383–84

marches to Coahuila, 384

signs peace treaty with Obregón, 385, 390

correspondence with Obregón, 385, 388, 389, 391

lays down arms, 385

in retirement at Canutillo, 386–89

assassinated, 393–94

PERSONALITY, ATTRIBUTES AND ATTITUDES:

family of, 58, 391

physical description of, 69–70

psychology of, 88, 97, 141, 181, 187–88, 189–90, 208, 258, 291, 297, 312, 326, 404

as social bandit, 59, 62–63, 68, 84, 270

skill as gunfighter, 68, 70, 80, 170, 188

skill as horseman, 70, 209, 212, 277, 405

teetotalism, 70, 189, 405

as womaniser, 70–71, 128, 168–69, 209–11, 213, 278, 285, 370, 404–05

'wives' and girlfriends of, 70, 127–28, 145, 209–11, 390–91, 392

literacy of, 144, 189, 196
audacity of, 79, 80
taste in food and drink, 68, 167
leadership qualities of, 80
as military commander, 172, 175,
 189, 195–96, 206–09, 228,
 233, 297, 299
emotionality of, 108, 128, 211,
 371, 405
lack of financial acumen, 189,
 191, 193, 207, 218, 294, 305
attitude to and relations with
 Madero, 69, 83, 84, 94–95,
 96–98, 99–100, 127, 130, 133,
 136, 140–41, 142, 145,
 146–47, 167, 188, 204, 223,
 281, 283, 354, 377
attitude to USA, 60, 61, 169,
 171, 191, 193, 194, 206, 207,
 221–22, 228–30, 241, 290,
 293–94, 310, 319–20, 326,
 330–31, 364, 366–67, 373,
 374, 376, 377, 378, 389
attitude to intellectuals, 204–06,
 306–07
attitude to education, 190, 206,
 266
attitude to Fierro, 199–200
dealings with Carranza, 175–76,
 179, 202, 223, 231–33, 241
detestation of Carranza, 236–37,
 254, 275, 342
attitude to Obregón, 354, 388
inadequacy of as national leader,
 278–79
mood swings, paranoia and self-
 destructive behaviour in late
 period, 285, 306, 311, 372
legend of, 61–63, 83, 84, 127,
 133, 168, 187, 208, 212, 228,
 363

contrasted with Zapata, 70–71, 88,
 102–03, 128, 143, 189, 194,
 219, 260, 270, 274–75, 279,
 281, 284–85, 291, 318, 341,
 373, 403–05
Villa, Hipólito, 70, 127, 142, 167,
 205, 210, 258, 293, 311,
 389–90, 391, 394, 396
Villa, Luz Corral de, 127–28, 133,
 198, 203, 210–11, 253, 257,
 390, 391, 396
villismo, 71, 104, 190, 191–92,
 193–94, 196, 204–05, 206,
 208, 255, 257, 258–59,
 271–72, 288–89, 312, 363,
 372–73, 375–76, 401

Walsh, Raoul, 212
Wilson, Henry Lane, 140, 149, 162,
 181, 203, 214, 219, 228
personality of, 151–52
hatred for Madero, 142, 152, 158
hatred for Villa, 142
role of in downfall of Madero,
 152–53
role of in Decena Trágica, 155–56
evil genius of Madero
 assassination, 158–59
Wilson, Woodrow, 152, 159, 177,
 201, 213, 214, 215, 219, 232,
 234, 247, 255, 259, 290, 294,
 306, 307, 309, 310, 314, 317,
 318–20, 364, 372, 373
dislike of Huerta, 214–16, 219–20,
 221, 228, 241
and US occupation of Vera
 Cruz, 220–21
backs Villa against Carranza,
 228–29
aspirations for Mexico, 241
attitude to Villa, 322, 324–25

cooperates with Carranza, 325

orders Punitive Expedition, 325

and the diplomacy of Punitive
Expedition, 328–33

Womack, John, 47, 184, 260, 263,
313, 355–56

women, role of in Mexican society,
118–19, 128, 168–69, 194,
209, 265, 308, 314, 369, 398

women soldiers (*soldaderas*), 90, 184,
209, 317

Yaquis, 9–10, 29, 33, 53–54, 99,
104, 116, 130, 137, 179, 206,
234, 243, 251, 257, 306, 310,
321, 347, 397

Yucatán, 9, 22, 25, 34, 35, 39, 53,
54, 71, 104, 113, 114, 120,
129, 137, 182, 186, 267, 268,
289, 295, 318, 341, 390

Zacatecas, 16, 81, 235, 236, 237,
239, 240, 254, 256, 371

Zapata, Emiliano, 74, 87, 98, 102,
104, 116, 130, 131, 133, 137,
138, 147, 150, 165, 197, 198,
205, 213, 216, 230, 244, 305,
306, 339, 346, 347, 348, 375,
381, 387, 399, 401, 402

origins, 33–34

childhood and youth, 36–42

family of, 36–39, 41–42, 122, 125,
274, 284, 387

elected village chief of
Anenecuilco, 47

military service, 48–49, 50

visits Mexico City, 49

moves against Hospital hacienda,
51–52

joins Revolution, 88

attitude to Madero's revolution,
89–92

emerges as Supreme Chief of
Revolution in the south, 91

as guerrilla leader, 92

negotiates with the Figueroa
brothers, 92–93

musters out his men, 109

and Morelos politics, 107–14

marriage of, 118–19

issues Plan of Ayala, 120

revolts against Madero, 121–23

spring offensive of 1912, 123–25

raids Puebla, 125

fortunes revive in Morelos, 149

defies Huerta, 160

rebels against Huerta, 181–82

goes onto offensive against
Huerta, 183

forms Revolutionary junta, 185

entourage of, 182–83, 248, 260,
266

controls much of southern
Mexico, 186

as military commander, 195

opens 1914 campaign, 218–19

rejects overtures from Huerta,
221–22, 241

contacts with Villa, 186, 222–23,
242, 245–46, 249–50, 258,
259, 260, 261, 271, 272–73,
284, 288, 357, 373

fights way into Mexico City, 243

negotiates with Carranza, 247

negotiates with Americans, 247–48

evasive with Carranza's envoys,
249

hawkish posture, 250

ends talks with Carranza, 250

correspondence with Villa, 246,
247, 263, 294, 306, 320

stays away from Convention, 259,
263, 280
sends delegation to Convention,
259
enters Mexico City, 264–65
and banditry, 268–69
in Mexico City, 273–78
meeting with Villa, 273–79, 284,
288, 357, 387
inadequacy of as national leader,
278–79
disillusionment with Villa,
279–81, 283–84, 288, 316
leaves Mexico City, 284
apathy towards Carranza/Villa
struggle, 284
declining importance in national
politics, 286
takes no part in civil war, 287–88,
297, 298, 302
takes to guerrilla warfare again,
318
strikes back at Pablo González,
335–38
on defensive in 1917, 350–55
links with Obregón, 354–55, 356
tries to build popular front
opposition to Carranza, 356
losing ground in Puebla, Guerrero
and Michoacán, 356
hit by flu epidemic, 357–58
attacked by González in 1918,
358–59
declared 'beyond amnesty', 373
assassinated, 360–62, 378, 385
PERSONALITY, ATTRIBUTES
AND ATTITUDE OF:
psychology, 47–8, 265, 277, 291,
342, 357, 404, 405
as dandy, 38, 42, 47, 49, 128,
265–66, 274
obsession with title deeds, 38, 50,
219
skill as horseman, 48–49, 91, 277
love of bullfighting, 48, 52
as military commander, 195
womanising of, 47, 118, 284–85,
353, 357, 404–05
political thought and ideology of,
42, 43, 90, 134, 266–67,
269–71, 290, 315, 341
failings as politician, 313, 316,
317
attitude to and relations with
Madero, 89, 92, 106–113,
117–18, 119–22, 259, 354
attitude to Orozco, 130–31, 134,
143, 181, 185, 259
attitude to USA, 219, 221, 314,
316, 319, 320, 355, 358
attitude to Félix Díaz's revolt,
349–50, 351, 354
contempt for Carranza, 251, 275,
277
attitude to Ángeles, 259, 358
as 'second-stage' revolutionary,
251
late paranoia of, 352, 353
impact of on Mexican Revolution,
261, 404
legend of, 51, 91, 109, 115, 222,
243
contrasted with Villa, 70–71, 88,
102–03, 128, 143, 182, 189,
194, 219, 260, 270, 274–75,
279, 281, 284–85, 291, 318
Zapata, Eufemio, 39, 41, 42, 70,
110, 113, 128, 185, 205, 219,
265, 284, 352–53, 355, 389,
399
Zapata, Josefa Espejo de, 118–19,
128, 284

zapatismo and *zapatistas*, 90, 93–94, 102–03, 104, 107, 108, 109, 110, 111, 113, 114, 116, 121, 122, 123, 125, 126, 130, 131, 133, 144, 151, 155, 169, 182, 183, 184, 185, 218, 219, 243, 247, 248–49, 251, 256–57, 260–61, 262, 264, 265–69, 271–72, 279, 280–81, 288, 297, 304, 313–14, 316, 317, 318, 338, 350–52, 387, 401